Blacks in American Films
and Television

GARLAND REFERENCE LIBRARY
OF THE HUMANITIES
(VOL. 604)

BLACKS IN AMERICAN FILMS AND TELEVISION

An Encyclopedia

Donald Bogle

GARLAND PUBLISHING, INC.
New York & London   1988

The photographs in this book come from the author's collection and from Paramount Pictures, Warners Bros., Columbia Pictures, and United Artists.

Library of Congress Cataloging-in-Publication Data

Bogle, Donald.
  Blacks in American films and television.

  (Garland reference library of the humanities;
vol. 604)
  Bibliography: p.
  Includes index.
  1. Afro-Americans in motion pictures.
2. Afro-American entertainers—Biography—Dictionaries.
3. Afro-Americans in the motion picture industry—
United States. 4. Afro-Americans in the television
industry—United States. I. Title. II. Series.
PN1995.9.N4B58   1988   791.43'08996073   87-29241
ISBN 0-8240-8715-1 (alk. paper)

Printed on acid-free, 250-year-life paper
Manufactured in the United States of America

*It is with pleasure that
I dedicate this book to a
number of people who have
been very encouraging during
the long period it took to
complete this work:*

To my mother

to John Bogle and Robert Bogle

*and to seven fast and fearless friends:
Jeanne Moutoussamy-Ashe
Zeffie Fowler
Sarah Orrick
Douglas Rossini
Barbara Reynolds
Bruce Goldstein
and, last but not least,
Joerg Klebe*

Contents

Introduction

As a kid sitting in movie theaters transfixed by the giant figures I saw on the big screen or sitting glued to the television set intrigued by its tiny, flickering images, I was always, from the very beginning, fascinated by the black faces I saw come and go. Black performers in movies and television cast a beguiling spell over me that has been hard to shake.

For a black viewer like myself, however, watching American movies and television can never be a casual affair. Too much of what we see seems too poorly defined. Too much of what we watch elicits from us a set of mixed emotions. On the one hand, we can be dismayed, shocked, or angered by the black images Hollywood has hoped we'll believe to be true, images, more often than not, which are little other than formulas and stereotypes. Yet on the other hand, we find ourselves invigorated, excited, and moved by the undeniable power of individual black performances. Sidney Poitier in *A Raisin in the Sun*. Dorothy Dandridge in *Carmen Jones*. Diana Sands and Lou Gossett in *The Landlord*. Ethel Waters in *The Member of the Wedding*. Such performances can send us off into private reveries that linger on and on and on. Yet one day, we know, we have to rouse ourselves from our private dreams and deal with some basic facts in order to better understand what we've enjoyed, and why, what has enraged us, and why.

Even during those early years of my moviegoing and TV-watching experience, I think I was struggling to sort out the incongruities of what I viewed, to clear up the disparities. Always my curiosity and thirst for information led me to the library in search of some comment on a particular film, character, or personality. Usually, I returned home empty-handed, without any answers to some basic questions. For instance, I wondered, as I watched on television a broadcast of the original 1934 version of *Imitation of Life*, what effect this movie had had on the black community when first released. Moreover, what had happened to the actress Fredi Washington, who had touched a national nerve when she had played Peola—a light-skinned black girl who passes for white? Why, too, had Paul Robeson appeared in so many films made abroad? What were his British films like? Had there really been a black director named Oscar Micheaux, who had started producing/directing/writing motion pictures in the silent period and continued working—on his own, outside Hollywood—into the late 1940s, making films geared especially for black audiences? Why was it that Dorothy Dandridge, after her great success in *Carmen Jones*, did not appear in another film for almost three years? Why had the "Amos 'n' Andy" series been taken off television? Had Spencer Williams, whom I had seen as Andy Brown on reruns of that series, actually once directed all-black movies? Why were television series like "I Spy" and "Julia" considered such groundbreakers in the 1960s? The questions kept coming. And they still keep coming today. The subject of blacks in American films and television was, for the most part, undocumented when I was growing up, and sadly, there is still not enough information on the subject today.

Fortunately, I've been able to answer some of my own questions, mainly by researching and writing on the subject myself. With my first book *Toms, Coons, Mulattoes, Mammies, & Bucks: An Interpretive History of Blacks in American Films*, I was able to deal with black images in American films from the days of *Uncle Tom's Cabin* and *The Birth of a Nation* to the era of the black-oriented films of the 1970s. Later with my book *Brown Sugar: Eighty Years of America's Black Female Superstars*, I focused on black women in the world of American popular culture: their contributions, their public images, sometimes their troubled private lives. The completion of both books satisfied definite personal curiosities and questions. I had been free to examine issues, personalities, trends that had alternately puzzled, irritated, intrigued or touched me in one form or another. Yet I still felt there was more in the area I wanted to cover.

Oddly enough, my chance to further explore the subject came about at the least likely of times. Not long after *Brown Sugar*'s publication, I began work with German Educational Television on an adaptation of that book as a four-part documentary series for PBS. During the pre-production stages of the series, I was excited to have the opportunity to gather old and new film footage. As I screened the material, I became fascinated all over again with films I had seen in the past and invigorated by those I had not previously viewed. During this time, I began making detailed notes for myself, listing the credits for the films and TV shows I saw but most importantly, jotting down comments, ideas, impressions of certain key sequences or themes. I kept my notes, which grew in length, in a little folder on my desk. Soon I had a whole stack of folders sitting in a file cabinet.

I was not sure how I would ever use those notes and lists of film/TV credits. Then the unexpected happened. One afternoon I had lunch with an old friend, Jeff Conrad of Garland Publishing, and he asked if I would be interested in writing a book—an encyclopedia—about blacks in American films and television. It would be a collection of synopses of important black-oriented films and television programs with credits for each production and with some type of critical commentary. That day, I felt as if the gods were looking down on me rather favorably, for a change.

Once I began the formal work on this book, I frequently wondered if I'd gotten more than I'd originally bargained for. I had not realized exactly how much material had to be covered, how much work I had in store for me. There were still many other films I had to screen. Some I saw at The Library of Congress, others at odd hours on television or at revival theaters in New York, many, many more which I had a chance to see, thanks to video cassette rentals. At first, I planned to deal with every black-oriented film released. But I narrowed my focus. For the most part, I've concentrated here on what might be called mainstream

American movies: those films that have been widely distributed, reaching the big cities and the small communities and towns throughout the country. These are movies, which, for better or worse, have become a part of our national shared experience. Yet they are films which have affected white America in one way and black America in an entirely different manner. Included in this book are comments and credits on such films as *The Birth of a Nation, Gone with the Wind, Imitation of Life* (the 1934 version and the 1959 remake), *Cabin in the Sky, Stormy Weather, Pinky, Home of the Brave, Carmen Jones, The Defiant Ones, A Raisin in the Sun, Sweet Sweetback's Baadasssss Song, Shaft, Lady Sings the Blues, Richard Pryor Live in Concert, Beverly Hills Cop, Jumpin' Jack Flash,* and many, many more well-known popular titles. But I have also felt compelled to deal with some features not so familiar to the mass audience but which have been important nonetheless in black film history: such features as *Nothing but a Man; The Cool World; Cry, The Beloved Country; Georgia, Georgia;* and a number of black-oriented films of the 1970s such as *The Legend of Nigger Charley, Trick Baby,* and *Mandingo.* These last three features, often labeled blaxploitation movies, have almost disappeared, wiped from the public record. And I believed it important to provide some comment and information on them in order that a later generation will have an idea of what the films (good and bad; many indeed were terrible) were like, why they succeeded or failed.

At the same time, I wanted to provide information on some of the race movies of the past, those all-black films made (between 1919 and 1949) for black audiences and produced outside the Hollywood system. With the race movies, I thought of focusing on what might be called total black cinema: black films by blacks for blacks. But contrary to what many assume, the race movies were not always made by blacks. In fact, by the late 1930s and 1940s white filmmakers had just about taken over the race movie market. Although more progressive, "positive" black images turn up in these films, sometimes so, too, do stereotypes. Regardless, I've included here entries on such race movies as *Boy! What a Girl, Juke Joint, God's Step Children, Broken Strings,* and of course, on such important independent black filmmakers of the past as Oscar Micheaux and Spencer Williams. Included also are entries on the work of more recent black independents such as Melvin Van Peebles, Spike Lee, and Billy Woodberry. This book does not deal, however, with documentary films and such significant black documentary filmmakers as Bill Miles and William Greaves. Documentaries are indeed a category unto themselves. Nor are there entries either on European or African films about the black experience. Thus I have not had a chance to examine some films of great interest to me such as Sembene's haunting *Black Girl* and *Ceddo,* Euzhan Palcy's powerful *Sugar Cane Alley,* Marcel Camus's glorious reworking of the Orpheus myth, *Black Orpheus,* Jean-Jacques Beineix's stirring dazzler of the 1980s, *Diva,* and Bertrand Travernier's mournful *'Round Midnight.*

During the period when I was researching television history, I found myself traversing rocky ground. So much of television history remains unexplored, not only as it pertains to black America but to the medium itself. I viewed some of the old television programs at the Museum of Broadcasting, others at The Library of Congress (which had quite a number of episodes of the "Amos 'n' Andy" series), still more on cable stations that specialize in reruns, and others on video cassette rentals. Here I've included entries with general credits for the major black-oriented series, from the days of "Beulah" and "Amos 'n' Andy" to those of the "The Cosby Show." Also included are comments/credits on major mini-series such as "Roots" and "Backstairs at the White House" and such important TV movies as "The Autobiography of Miss Jane Pittman." I have also listed certain programs in which important black characters appeared such as the series "Barney Miller" with Ron Glass. The reader should note, however, that in the introductory essay on television, I've discussed the appearances of such performers as Eddie "Rochester" Anderson on "The Jack Benny Show," Nichelle Nichols on "Star Trek," and Gail Fisher on "Manix"; consequently, there are no individual entries for these particular general interest series. For the reader who might be in search of a certain TV (or film) title for which there is no entry, I suggest that the index immediately be consulted. For instance, Gary Coleman's appearances in the TV movie "The Kid with the Broken Halo" and the feature film *On the Right Track* are referred to in the profile on the actor.

As for the series of biographical profiles included in this book, they are clearly selective, not comprehensive.

There are also a series of biographical profiles. Early on, I set limits on what type of performers I would include in this section. Not included are such figures as Louis Armstrong and Claudia McNeil, who have appeared in American films and television, but each of whom is best known for work in another medium, in Armstrong's case, in music, in McNeil's, theater. Consequently, the profiles provide commentary and information on major film/TV personalities such as Sidney Poitier, Stepin Fetchit, Hattie McDaniel, Richard Pryor, Dorothy Dandridge, Paul Robeson, Diana Ross, Cicely Tyson, Bill Cosby, Redd Foxx, and Eddie Murphy. At the same time, there are biographical entries on some lesser-known figures who have long interested me and about whom I felt something should be said: such performers as Juano Hernandez, Ivan Dixon, Rosalind Cash, Minnie Gentry. The filmographies I have provided for each performer do not list everything that performer has appeared in; instead I've sought to provide listings which would give a general indication of the scope of the performer's work and career. The profiles concentrate primarily on actors and actresses. Because there have been so few black directors, writers, producers within the film-TV industry, the black actor/actress has found himself/ herself in a tight, tough position where on certain occasions, he or she has had to just about direct himself/herself, becoming his/her own auteur. Consequently, the work of black performers remains crucial in fully coming to grips with the history of blacks in movies and television. There are some entries, however, on such black directors as Gordon Parks, Sr., Gordon Parks, Jr., and Michael Schultz.

Mainly what I've sought to provide here is the type of reference guide I've always wanted: a book that would list credits for black films and television programs, that would also look at the body of work of certain key performers, and that would place this material and information in some kind of historical context, letting a reader know why, say, a movie like *Sweet Sweetback's Baadasssss Song*, which may look dated to contemporary audiences, once had such a great impact on young black moviegoers of the 1970s, who were anxious/starved for a defiant black movie hero. But most importantly, I've sought to make this a reference guide that also provides some kind of voice, a point of view, a commentary on films that have affected so many of us for so long.

All in all, the three years it has taken to put this book together have been a stirring, trying, lopsidedly invigorating period. I'm still under the spell of certain performances. And I still value the reveries those performances bring me. But I think I see some things a bit more clearly.

No book is ever written without the help (or hindrance) of others. Therefore I would like to offer my appreciation to a number of people who were of great assistance to me. Foremost I would like to thank my cousin Bettina Glasgow Batchleor, with whom it has always been good to hash out ideas. The same has been true of my dear friend Marian Etoile Watson of Fox Television, with whom I saw a number of the more recent films. Whenever I was stuck on locating information on a particular film or television program, I could usually rely on Bruce Goldstein of New York's Film Forum, who has a remarkable knowledge of film and television history. At a time when I found myself seated at New York's Schomburg Research Center, sifting through years of old copies of the black weekly magazine *Jet* to find television credits for black actors and actresses, Robert Katz was of immense help in enabling me to locate information I sought. I would also like to thank Barbara Humphries of the Motion Picture Division of The Library of Congress, Cheryll Greene of *Essence*, Barbara Reynolds of *USA Today*, the staff in the theater collection at The Library of Performing Arts at Lincoln Center, the staff at the Museum of Broadcasting, and of course, the staff at the Schomburg Center for Research in Black Culture, notably James Murray, the Schomburg's director Howard Dodson, and especially, Deborah Willis-Thomas, the center's very knowledgeable photographic curator, who was of great help in tracking down certain stills of black performers. Naturally, I would also like to thank for his help and encouragement Joerg Klebe of the German Educational Television Network. Mariskia Bogle has also provided some wonderful suggestions and insights. And then, of course, special mention must go to a special group of friends and colleagues: Doug Rossini, Nels Johnson, Carol Leonard, Harry Ford, Marie Dutton-Brown, Alice Richardson, Anna Deavere Smith, Linda Tarrant-Reid, Susan Peterson, and Martin Radburd. For their assistance, I would like to also thank several people at Garland Publishing: Phyllis Korper, Paula Ladenburg, and Rita Quintas. And last and perhaps most of all, my thanks go to my very patient editor, Jeff Conrad.

Throughout the release date for each film appears in parentheses following the film title. The same applies for TV movies and miniseries. The year or years in which a TV series ran on prime time also appear in parentheses following the series title. I have also indicated the period in which an actor or actress worked in a series or guest-starred in an episode of a series by again listing the date in parentheses after the series title.

List of Abbreviations

AIP: American International Pictures

B: Born

D: Director

d: Died

Ex. P. Executive Producer

MGM: Metro-Goldwyn-Mayer

P: Producer

R: The company that released or distributed the film

S: Scriptwriter

UA: United Artists Pictures

Selected Bibliography

Baldwin, James. *The Devil Finds Work*. New York: The Dial Press, 1976.

Barnouw, Erik. *Tube of Plenty: The Evolution of American Television*. New York: Oxford University Press, 1975.

Bedell, Sally. *Up the Tube: Prime-Time TV and the Silverman Years*. New York: The Viking Press, 1981.

Buckley, Gail Lumet. *The Hornes: An American Family*. New York: Alfred A. Knopf, 1986.

Bogle, Donald. "'B'. . . for Black." *Film Comment*, October 1985.

Bogle, Donald. *Brown Sugar: Eighty Years of America's Black Female Superstars*. New York: Harmony Books, 1980.

Bogle, Donald. "The Dorothy Dandridge Story." *Essence*, October 1984.

Bogle, Donald. *Toms, Coons, Mulattoes, Mammies, & Bucks: An Interpretive History of Blacks in American Films*. New York: The Viking Press, 1973.

Carroll, Diahann, with Ross Firestone. *Diahann!* Boston: Little, Brown and Company, 1986.

Dandridge, Dorothy, and Earl Conrad. *Everything and Nothing: The Dorothy Dandridge Tragedy*. New York: Abelard-Schuman, 1970.

Davis, Sammy, Jr., and Jane and Burt Boyar. *Yes, I Can: The Story of Sammy Davis, Jr.* New York: Farrar, Straus and Giroux, 1965.

Ellison, Ralph. *Shadow and Act*. New York: Signet Books, 1966.

Evers, Carolyn. *Sidney Poitier: The Long Journey*. New York: Signet Books, 1969.

Fadiman, Regina K. *Faulkner's Intruder in the Dust: Novel into Film*. Knoxville: The University of Tennessee Press, 1978.

Fiedler, Leslie A. *The Inadvertent Epic: From Uncle Tom's Cabin to Roots*. New York: A Touchstone Book, 1979.

Fiedler, Leslie A. *What Was Literature: Class Culture and Mass Society*. New York: Simon and Schuster, 1982.

Greenfield, Jeff. *Television: The First Fifty Years*. New York: Crescent Books, 1981.

Gussow, Mel. *Don't Say Yes Until I Finish Talking: A Biography of Darryl F. Zanuck*. New York: Doubleday & Company, Inc., 1971.

Horne, Lena, and Richard Schickel. *Lena*. New York: Doubleday & Company, Inc., 1965.

Kael, Pauline. *Reeling*. Boston: Little, Brown and Company, 1976.

Kael, Pauline. *Taking It All In*. New York: Holt, Rinehart and Winston, 1984.

Kael, Pauline. *When the Lights Go Down*. New York: Holt, Rinehart and Winston, 1980.

Kanfer, Stefan. *A Journal of the Plague Years: A Devastating Chronicle of the Era of the Blacklist*. New York: Atheneum, 1973.

Keyser, Lester J., and Andre H. Ruszkowski. *The Cinema of Sidney Poitier*. New York: A.S. Barnes and Company, 1980.

Klotman, Phyllis Rauch. *Frame by Frame: A Black Filmography*. Bloomington: Indiana University Press, 1979.

MacDonald, J. Fred. *Blacks and White TV: Afro-Americans in Television Since 1948*. Chicago: Nelson-Hall Publishers, 1983.

McNeil, Alex. *Total Television: A Comprehensive Guild to Programming from 1948 to 1980*. New York: Penguin Books, 1980.

Mapp, Edward. *Directory of Blacks in the Performing Arts*. Metuchen, N.J.: The Scarecrow Press, 1978.

Marill, Alvin H. *The Films of Sidney Poitier*. Secaucus, N.J.: The Citadel Press, 1978.

Meeker, David. *Jazz in the Movies*. New York: The Da Capo Press, 1981.

Parish, James Robert. *Actors' Television Credits 1950-1972*. Metuchen, N.J.: The Scarecrow Press, 1973.

Poitier, Sidney. *This Life*. New York: Alfred A. Knopf, 1980.

Robbins, Fred, and David Ragan. *Richard Pryor: This Cat's Got Nine Lives*. New York: Delilah Books, 1982.

Robeson, Paul. *Here I Stand*. Boston: Beacon Press, 1958.

Robin, Jeff. *Richard Pryor: Black and Blue*. New York: Bantam Books, 1984.

Sampson, Henry T. *Blacks in Black and White: A Source Book on Black Films*. Metuchen, N.J.: The Scarecrow Press, 1977.

Sklar, Robert. *Movie-Made America: A Cultural History of American Movies*. New York: Vintage Books, 1975.

Toback, James. *Jim: The Author's Self-centered Memoir on the Great Jim Brown*. New York: Doubleday & Company, 1971.

Van Peebles, Melvin. *Sweet Sweetback's Baadasssss Song*. New York: Lancer Books, 1971.

Vidor, King. *A Tree Is a Tree*. New York: Harcourt, Brace and Company, 1953.

Waters, Ethel, with Charles Samuels. *His Eye Is on the Sparrow*. Garden City, N.Y.: Doubleday & Company, 1951.

Wertheim, Arthur Frank. *Radio Comedy*. New York: Oxford University Press, 1979.

Wiley, Mason, and Damien Bona. *The Oscars*. New York: Ballantine Books, 1986.

Wolper, David, with Quincy Troupe. *The Inside Story of TV's "Roots."* New York: Warner Books, 1978.

Wood, Robin. *America in the Movies or "Santa Maria, It Had Slipped My Mind!"* New York: Basic Books, 1975.

The Encyclopedia

Movies

Movie memories are often short. In the 1980s as audiences casually slipped into theaters to watch Eddie Murphy in *Beverly Hills Cop* (1984) or *Golden Child* (1986) or Richard Pryor in *The Toy* (1982), a new generation of moviegoers assumed black film history had begun with such films and such stars, right there and then in a maladjusted age of punk and New Wave, political conservatism, and Third World paranoia. For some, with a bit more hindsight, the history appeared to have started with the then-recently departed black-oriented movies of the 1970s such as *Shaft* (1971) or *Super Fly* (1972). Actually, black film history in this country is far older than most members of its 1980s audience. And it is a history that is resolutely diverse, complex, and contradictory, a full-bodied saga of sound and fury, full of twists and turns yet always rich in detail and unexpected achievements.

In its initial stages during the period of silent films, from the early 1900s to the late 1920s, from the days of *Uncle Tom's Cabin* (1903) through *The Birth of a Nation* (1915) and afterwards, black film history looks simply like a study in stereotypes; a crew of gentle Toms, doomed mulattoes, comic coons, overstuffed mammies, and mean, menacing, violent black bucks. Because the important black roles were usually played by white actors in blackface (and also because the films themselves were written, produced, and directed by whites), the characterizations in these early years were stiff, embarrassing, crude. Occasionally, a director like the great Erich Von Stroheim cast real black performers for brief appearances—as in the famous brothel sequence of his *Wedding March* (1928)—as *exotics*: overheated sensual "sex slaves" who served as a colorful backdrop in his elaborate panoramic view of a decadent European culture stumbling about on its last legs. On another occasion, as in *Queen Kelly* (1928), Von Stroheim also cast blacks in defiance of the censors in a deathbed sequence—set in an African brothel—in which a black priest administered the last rites to a dying white woman. Here Von Stroheim's characters looked as if they might evolve into people rather than being treated simply as "darky jokes," which was clearly the case in so many other Hollywood films (including those of such masters as Harold Lloyd and Buster Keaton). But still the black characters were pawns used for unusual atmospheric effects to further illuminate the themes of depravity and decadence; the Negro character still had not emerged as a subject fit for full cinematic exploration.

Much of that changed, however, with the advent of the sound motion picture. The Hollywood studios realized talking films needed sound, movement, rhythm. And, of course, who could be more rhythmic than the American Negro? Consequently, in 1929 there appeared two all-talking, all-singing, all-colored major studio productions, *Hearts in Dixie* and King Vidor's moody and often moving *Hallelujah*. Here such performers as Stepin Fetchit, Nina Mae McKinney, Daniel Haynes, Victoria Spivey, and Clarence Muse sang, danced, rocked and reeled, enlivening the then-evolving American movie musical with their distinctive energy level—and their sheer delight at finally working in films.

Afterward, during the troubled, turbulent years of America's Great Depression, audiences saw black performers regularly on screen. At first glance, this era, too, seems like little more than the familiar lineup of stumbling, shuffling, eye-popping, teeth-clacking, grinning, giddy black servants. The Depression era, however, was a peculiar and complexly ambiguous Golden Age for certain black actors, who introduced to American films a new timing and rhythmic thrust and a comic assertiveness. Usually fast-talking, imaginative, idiosyncratic, and well-schooled in the art of scene-stealing, the actors of the 1930s attacked their roles with confidence and a crisp control.

Thus the screen was bombarded with an array of wildly exuberant personalities: the controversial, nihilistic, and gifted Stepin Fetchit, slow-moving and slow-talking, repeatedly trying to maneuver his way out of his servant chores; the optimistic, enduringly enthusiastic Bill "Bojangles" Robinson, teaching little Shirley Temple to tap dance up the magic staircase in *The Little Colonel* (1934); the haughty, rowdy, no-nonsense Hattie McDaniel, speaking her mind and just about driving everybody up the wall with her high-flung sense of superiority; the fragile, uniquely comic and pathetic Butterfly McQueen, presenting hysteria in a way never before witnessed on an American movie screen; the baffling, bewildering Willie Best and Mantan Moreland, exhibiting their coon antics with no sense of shame but with a rousing, energetic display of comic ingenuity; the clever, witty, resourceful, manipulative Eddie "Rochester" Anderson, waiting on and consistently outwitting his boss Jack Benny; the defiantly proud Paul Robeson, speaking out against discrimination on screen and off; and the iridescently melancholic Fredi Washington. The individual and collective styles of these performers grew out of their personal experiences in the black community and out of their professional experiences in the rough-and-tumble worlds of black theater and black vaudeville. Their high sense of style elevated them, and through style the black actors turned their cheap, trashy, demeaning stereotyped roles inside out, refining, transforming, and transcending them. The great black performers did not simply play characters. Rather they played *against* their roles.

During this period, one Hollywood film, more than any other, *Imitation of Life* (1934), had an uncanny effect on the black community. The movie's subplot told the tale of a light-skinned black girl, Peola (Fredi Washington), who rejects the submissiveness of her mother (Louise Beavers) to cross the color line. Melodramatic, corny, and hokey as this tearjerker might now appear, it hit a nerve cord in black America and aroused diverse and heated reactions. On the one hand, the mulatto daughter was viewed as heartless for having deserted her mother and for having denied her racial heritage, yet, on the other hand, many knew, at least intuitively, that the movie had not fully explained the daughter's position. Black America fully understood what the mad search for personal freedom was all about, and in this respect, there was identification with Peola. Here, too, audiences saw American racism crashing in on the black family itself. In the long run, the subtext of *Imitation of Life*, the messages creeping through the main plotline, let audiences know there was indeed something called a race problem in America. And two fine black actresses—Beavers and Washington—had been able to hint at the complex set of emotional and psychological dynamics of black lives in a white nation.

Imitation of Life was a box-office bonanza, luring whites and blacks into theaters across the nation. Two years later Warner Bros. released the all-black *Green Pastures*. Based on the hit Broadway play, this comic fantasy about an all-colored heaven (featuring the splendid actor Rex Ingram as de Lawd) was a commercial success, which, like *Imitation of Life*, indicated there was a black movie audience in need of films touching in some way or another on its experiences. Yet for many years following *Imitation of Life* and *Green Pastures*, the film industry steadfastly ignored the black audience and the race theme.

At the same time, though, independent filmmakers working outside Hollywood released a different kind of product: "race movies," all-black features made especially to please a black audience. Race movies had first appeared during the silent era in the aftermath of D. W. Griffith's *Birth of a Nation*. More than any other movie in history, Griffith's Civil War epic, with its images of marauding Negro troops, power-mad mulattoes, and lusty black bucks, sent shock waves through black America, galvanizing its leaders into an uproar of protest and action. The NAACP launched a formal protest movement against the film, setting up boycotts and picket lines. And soon there appeared a group of independent black filmmakers—Emmett J. Scott, the brothers George and Noble Johnson, and the legendary Oscar Micheaux—who scrambled for money (from the black bourgeoisie or white backers) and quickly formed production companies, determined to make all-black films that stressed black America's achievements. Their first films—*The Realization of a Negro's Ambition* (1916), *Trooper K of Troop K* (1916), *The Birth of a Race* (1918), and *The Homesteader* (1919), all initially serious tributes to black endurance and ambition—were important mainly because they proved that black cinema could exist.

Afterward scores of other film companies (Reol Productions, The Unique Film Company, The Norman Film Manufacturing Company, The Frederick Douglass Film Company), some black owned, others white controlled, sprang up in places as diverse as Jacksonville, St. Louis, Philadelphia, Chicago, and New York, often using the abandoned studios of mainstream film companies that had moved to California.

Their low-budget films, frequently technically crude and misshapen, were shown at segregated theaters in the South, at big-city ghetto movie houses in the North, and on occasion, at black churches, schools, and social gatherings—almost anyplace where it was possible to reach a black audience. Before this movement of independents ended, approximately 150 such companies had come into existence and hundreds of films had been produced.

Sometimes plodding, sometimes didactic, sometimes deliriously disjointed, many of the race movies were, quite frankly, terrible. They were not always free of stereotypes, either. Then, too, as time went on, more whites took over the race movie market—producing, directing, distributing the films—so this was hardly a case of total black cinema. Still the race movies presented black audiences with an alternative cinema: here in the all-black westerns, musicals, melodramas, romances, and mysteries, the characters were no longer simply maids, butlers, or bootblacks but black doctors, lawyers, teachers, detectives—bourgeois figures who were the bold embodiment of the racial philosophy of the period that emphasized that one should never do anything to hinder the race only to further it. In such films as *The Bull Dogger* (1923, featuring black rodeo star Bill Pickett, performing feats of heroism), *The Flaming Crisis* (1924, the story of a tough black newspaperman falsely accused of murder, fighting to prove his innocence), and *The Flying Ace* (1926, spotlighting a black aviator who, in midair, rescues a fair black damsel in distress), black America also saw itself incorporated into the national popular mythology, and a new set of archetypes emerged: heroic black men of action, who were walking representatives of black assertion and aggression, who, of course, gave the lie to America's notions of the Negro's place. Some race movies, such as the 1927 *Scar of Shame* or Oscar Micheaux's 1937 *God's Step Children*, were "highminded" statements on the nature of black life in America or on the racial dynamics—divisions and tensions—within the black community itself. Of the black filmmakers directing the race movies, Micheaux and Spencer Williams had careers that stretched over several decades. Race movies, however, repeatedly plagued by financial and distribution problems, just about vanished by the end of the 1940s. (The black-oriented films of the 1970s and also later a movie like Spike Lee's 1986 *She's Gotta Have It* might very well be viewed as a continuation of the old race movie, for these later films were also geared to reach the mass black audience.)

During World War II, though, mainstream commercial filmmakers returned to the Negro theme with two big all-black musicals, *Stormy Weather* and *Cabin in the Sky* (both released in 1943). The talents of such legendary stars as Ethel Waters, Lena Horne, Bill "Bojangles" Robinson, Eddie "Rochester" Anderson, Cab Calloway, Louis Armstrong, and Katherine Dunham were on brilliant display, and both films remain classics in the history of the Negro as entertainer.

But a real change of image in Hollywood films came about at the end of the decade. The Second World War had altered the national consciousness. An outspoken NAACP had called for an image change in American films. Black G.I.s, having fought abroad for the rights and freedom of others and having returned home and discovered their own rights were still being denied, became more vocal about the nation's injustices and inequities. The film industry soon picked up on the new postwar attitudes with the release of the problem pictures—films such as *Home of the Brave*, *Pinky*, *Lost Boundaries*, and *Intruder in the Dust* (all released in 1949), which touched on the racial issues then confronting the nation. And here at last were motion pictures in which the black character was the protagonist and the black problem was the central theme. Although the films were not without compromises, they managed nonetheless, as Ralph Ellison has writen in his essay "The Shadow and the Act," to get at deep centers of American emotion. "Dealing with matters which, over the years, have been slowly charging up with guilt," Ellison wrote, "they all display a vitality which escapes their slickest devices."

These films led the way to the phenomenal emergence of Sidney Poitier in the 1950s. In such features as *Edge of the City* (1957) and *The Defiant Ones* (1958), Poitier's characters appeared to be radical departures from the past. No singing, no dancing, no clowning for them. They were intelligent, upright, dignified figures. But in time, the fundamental distortions and confusions underlying the Poitier films showed through. Often Poitier's Noble Negro heroes sacrificed their freedom or their lives in order to aid, in some form or another, the dominant white culture. Still Sidney Poitier himself was always bigger and better than the roles he played. Along with such performers as James Edwards, Ruby Dee, Juano Hernandez, Ossie Davis, and later Claudia McNeil, Diana Sands, and Louis Gossett, Jr., he presented a new type of black film acting technique: intense, urban, introspective. Almost single-handedly, Poitier also proved that a dramatic black actor could and should work consistently in American films. He remains one of the great film actors, black or white, of the Eisenhower era.

In the 1950s, there was also the extraordinary beauty, Dorothy Dandridge, a remarkable screen actress whose characters are perhaps the movies' archetypal tragic mulatto figures. Her significance cannot be underestimated. The star of such films as *Carmen Jones* (1954) and *Porgy and Bess* (1959), Dandridge left behind a personal story and legend (the kind always important to the mythology of American cinema), a distressing tale of a gifted woman whose career was cut short by an industry not yet ready, as Poitier has said, for all she had to offer. Unable to find the right movie roles consistently, Dandridge ended her life tragically, dying of a pill overdose in the mid-1960s. Today her film roles are all the more affecting (like those of Marilyn Monroe) because of the personal vitality as well as the vulnerability that distinguishes her work.

By the 1960s, black audiences hungered for a new type of black film and black film hero: something that would touch on the new national mood of black militancy and cultural nationalism. Curiously, perhaps even perversely enough, only Jim Brown's woodenly rough-and-tough action characters seemed to suggest any sort of aggressiveness or anger at this time. But the one-dimensional Brown heroes were not enough. Finally, in the early 1970s, Melvin Van Peebles's now classic, independently produced *Sweet Sweetback's Baadasssss Song* (1971), as well as Gordon Parks, Sr.'s *Shaft* (1971) and Gordon Parks, Jr.'s *Super Fly* (1972)—each controversial and sometimes contradictory, presented black audiences with a seemingly radicalized black hero: a black man fundamentally at odds with the system, out to assert himself and to triumph over a culture that had always denied him his basic freedoms.

Following the phenomenal success of those three films, the movie industry picked up on the films' theme and turned it into a formula: a strong aggressive black man bests Whitey and waltzes off into the sunset—with a cache of money and his old lady, too. Soon there emerged what was called the *blaxploitation film*, a movie that played on the needs of the black audience for heroic figures but a film that did not answer those needs in realistic terms. *Black Caesar* (1973), *Black Jesus* (1971), *Black Samson* (1974), *Hell Up in Harlem* (1974), *Truck Turner* (1974), *The Legend of Nigger Charley* (1972), *The Soul of Nigger Charley* (1973), *Boss Nigger* (1975)—the list goes on and on. The heroes of these films lived in the world of the ghetto and knew their turf inside out. Contemporary audiences sometimes laugh at these figures, unable to understand their uncanny historical significance. Yet as shoddy as so many of those features were, the heroes of the films were predecessors of the high-stepping character of John Travolta in *Saturday Night Fever* (1977), of the oppressed, lower-class, gritty style of the protagonist portrayed by Sylvester Stallone in his first *Rocky* movie, even of the genially slick, tough cookie quality of Henry Winkler's Fonzie on the television series "Happy Days." The black-oriented films of the early 1970s injected into American cinema a new intensity of spirit and a harsh new urban landscape as well as a rampant, fierce sexuality that sometimes strikes the moviegoer as an act of aggression against the system. The convoluted vision of the early 1970s' black heroes was echoed in later films, such as *Mean Streets* (1973), *Taxi Driver* (1976), *Dog Day Afternoon* (1975), *Blue Collar* (1978), and *Fingers* (1978). Sadly, though, the white directors and writers of many of the black movies were rarely able to see their heroes in anything but one-dimensional terms. Urban warfare films that could have soared fell flat. And with a terrifying thud. None of these films had the artistically worked-out political power and resonance of something like the Australian film *The Chant of Jimmie Blacksmith* (1978) or of African filmmaker Ousmane Sembene's *Black Girl* (1969). Then, too, if ever a period needed a young, vibrant Poitier, who could communicate the complexity of all human motivation, be it political, social, or personal, it was surely the early 1970s.

Occasionally, more sensitive black-oriented films appeared: *Buck and the Preacher* (1972), *Lady Sings The Blues* (1972), *Sounder* (1972), *Claudine* (1974), *Sparkle* (1976), in which performers such as Cicely Tyson, Paul Winfield, Lonette McKee, and, yes, even Diana Ross and Diahann Carroll gave vibrant, dramatic, and moving portrayals. In these films, too, women had strong, vital characters to play. And within the established film industry more black directors came to the fore: Sidney Poitier, Ossie Davis, Michael Schultz, Stan Lathan. For a brief spell, it looked indeed as if a vital new black Hollywood had emerged. But by the end of the 1970s the black audience had turned away from the proliferation of shabby black action films. Soon these movies themselves faded away. Unfortunately, the film industry did not search for other types of black films: more perceptive, realistic, and diverse products with which the black audience could connect or identify in a personal way. Such independent filmmakers as William Greaves, St. Claire Bourne, Haile Gerima, Warrington Hudlin, and later Katheleen Collins, Julie Dash, Charles Burnett, and Billy Woodberry sought to make films which would give black audiences a choice of image. For one can see clearly that a constant problem of black cinema in this country has been not simply a lack of images but a lack of choice among images as well.

Curiously, the 1980s sparked several unusual developments. Foremost, black performers once again were moved to the background of major American films. Pam Grier, a genuine star of energetic, perversely enjoyable B-movies in the 1970s, played supporting roles in *Fort Apache: The Bronx* (1981) and *Something Wicked This Way Comes* (1983). And Billy Dee Williams, black America's Prince Charming in the 1970s films *Lady Sings the Blues* (1972) and *Mahogany* (1975), found himself supporting the likes of Sylvester Stallone in *Nighthawks* (1981) and the Star Wars kids in *The Empire Strikes Back* (1980) and *The Return of the Jedi* (1983). Commercial American cinema seemed to be turning its back on the black theme and the black hero.

Yet, movie history is seldom without its paradoxical jolts, and so, surprisingly, in the mid-1980s, two unexpected commercial hits examined black themes, characters, situations: Steven Spielberg's *The Color Purple* (1985) and Spike Lee's *She's Gotta Have It* (1986). When Spielberg, one of the most successful of all Hollywood directors, decided to adapt for the screen black writer Alice Walker's novel *The Color Purple*, there was concern within the industry that such a picture would never sell. Of course, Spielberg proved the cynics wrong. The film, however, unleashed a wave of controversy within the black community. Some loved the film because it was a rare attempt to explore the lives and tensions of black women. (Of all screen characters, the black woman had consistently been the one most ignored. On the rare occasions when black women were prominently featured, they were often cast as rather scary, highflung exotics. Clearly that was the case with the great Tina Turner in *Mad Max: Beyond Thunderdome* [1985] and Grace Jones in *A View to a Kill* [1985] and *Vamp* [1986].) Others, however, were in an uproar because of the depiction of its black male characters, who seemed little more than overcharged caricatures. Once again the issue of screen control arose. What would *The Color Purple* have been like had a black director been able to film it? At the same time, though, away from the big studios, shooting in the streets of Brooklyn, was independent black filmmaker Spike Lee, whose low-budget, offbeat *She's Gotta Have It* introduced a new type of black movie comedy. Lee touched a nerve within black America. And his ingenious work was rewarded with long lines of movie patrons that stretched around the blocks in anticipation of seeing Nola Darling and her three suitors. Once again, much as Van Peebles had done in the 1970s, a black filmmaker had proven that black audiences were waiting for movies with images they could relate to and identify with. In the hands of Lee, the black independent movement of the 1980s found commercial viability.

Yet the industry executives still refused to focus on the work of the independents, choosing instead to spotlight a new phenomenon in movie history: the rise in the 1980s—for the first time—of genuine black box-office movie superstars, Richard Pryor and Eddie Murphy. Interestingly enough, huge stars as both Murphy and Pryor were, both found themselves, in such films as *Stir Crazy* (1980), *48 Hrs.* (1982), *Trading Places* (1983), and *Superman III* (1983), cast as sidekicks to such white stars as Gene Wilder, Nick Nolte, Dan Aykroyd, and Christopher Reeve. Often their roles reminded us of Eddie "Rochester" Anderson's brilliant characterization as Jack Benny's right-hand man in movies of the 1930s. One wondered, however, just how far black film history had progressed. Much too often their films failed to uncover the tensions or conflicts of black men in pursuit of some goal or personal aspiration. Instead the films were tributes to the theme of interracial male bonding. That theme was also at the heart of such television series as "Miami Vice" and "The Insiders"; it also was the basis for such features as *White Nights* (1985, with Gregory Hines and Mikhail Baryshnikov), *Running Scared* (1986, with Gregory Hines and Billy Crystal), *Enemy Mine* (1985, with Louis Gossett, Jr., and Dennis Quaid), *Iron Eagle* (1986, with Gossett and Jason Gedrick), *Firewalker* (1986, with Gossett and Chuck Norris), and of course, the Billy Dee Williams and Sylvester Stallone 1981 vehicle *Nighthawks*. (This theme, probably best described as the *Huck Finn fixation*—the tough, assertive white man learns about emotion and the spirit from his good black friend—stretches back to movies like *Casablanca* in 1942 with Humphrey Bogart and Dooley Wilson as Sam and *The Defiant Ones* with Sidney Poitier and Tony Curtis.) But it was distressing, almost tragic, to watch stars of the caliber of Murphy and Pryor struggling in pictures like *48 Hrs.* and *The Toy* to help some anxious or troubled white male character overcome some physical adversity or emotional trauma. Rarely were Murphy or Pryor seen in romantic situations with black women, causing the stars sometimes to look, for all their modernity, like asexual pods of the past. Pryor and Murphy were much too big as personalities and had too attractive personas for this type of treatment.

Yet perhaps one of the era's greatest perversities was the simple fact that Pryor in his three fascinating concert films—*Richard Pryor Live in Concert* (1979), *Richard Pryor Live on the Sunset Strip* (1982), and *Richard Pryor Here and Now* (1983)—not only showcased his comic genius at its absolute best but also indicated the skill and artistry that can come to the screen when a black artist has a chance to create his own image, to mold and shape his own characters, to express his point of view. These concert films, along with Pryor's noble failure *Jo Jo Dancer, Your Life Is Calling* (1986) and Lee's successful *She's Gotta Have It*, were among the most optimistic signs in black movie history in many a year. They made us aware that black film artists, if given the opportunity, can come up with the same kind of dazzling achievements black music stars have had when they controlled their material.

In retrospect, the history of black films in this country has certainly not yet reached its high point. But already, amid the stereotypes, the misconceptions, and the myths, some special accomplishments have reached out to us and fired our imaginations. Our only mad hope now is that these achievements mark neither an end nor a middle but rather a mighty beginning.

She's at it again! Carol Speed as a demoni-cally possessed young woman in Abby; *skilled actor William Marshall in the background, looking as if he wished he could levitate his way out of this film.*

Abby (1974)

D. William Girdler. *S.* G. Cornell Layne; from a story by Layne and William Girdler. *P.* Girdler, Layne, and Mike Henry. *R.* AIP. Cast includes: Terry Carter (later of TV's "Battlestar Galactica"); Juanita Moore; and Nathan Cook.

While digging for ancient religious artifacts in Nigeria, a dignified, erudite black minister/archaeologist (William Marshall) inadvertently unleashes evil spirits. Later these devilish forces make their way to Louisville, Kentucky, where they rapidly invade the rather nubile body of the minister's pretty daughter-in-law (Carol Speed). In no time, the once-sweet lass is kicking up her heels, dressing up like a hooker, and speaking in tongues. (The minister may not understand what she's saying, but those of us familiar with four-letter words certainly do!) More follows: the girl foams at the mouth, objects levitate, doors slam, furniture flies. The minister must find a way to rid the girl of these evil forces. Sound familiar?

Released not long after *The Exorcist*, this was clearly a cheapie take-off (or should we just say rip-off) of that very popular film. (At one point, apparently this was even to be called *The Blackorcist*.) Throughout poor William Marshall, a talented actor who must know he's too good for this trash, looks as if he's aching to do some levitating of his own: up, up, and away from this thing.

Unfortunately, the movie's done without a shred of humor. Rarely has evil been used so effectively as a metaphor for tedium.

Adios Amigo (1975)

D. Fred Williamson. *S.* Fred Williamson. *P.* Fred Williamson. Executive Producer, Lee W. Winkler. *R.* Atlas Films release of a Po' Boy Production. Cast includes: James Brown, Thalmus Rasulala, Robert Phillips, and Lynne Jackson.

In this episodic, slapdash comic Western, Richard Pryor's a crafty con man, forever using tall, tough Fred Williamson as his foil. Actually, Williamson, who not only stars but also produced, wrote, and directed, is the real con artist because somehow he persuaded Pryor to appear in this disjointed effort. The whole thing is little more than a series of skits, better suited for television. Yet because most of the skits feature a performer as skilled as Richard Pryor, you can't go entirely wrong.

Pryor breezes through with an engaging wild gleam in his eyes. Actor Williamson provides a nice, relaxed touch. He and Pryor play well together: Pryor always plays well with co-stars because even when they don't work up to par, he always does. It's quite amusing to watch him relate to the white characters here, most of whom are cast as empty-headed bigots. Like Eddie "Rochester" Anderson in some of his films with Jack Benny, Pryor simply looks *through* the whites who give him commands, so confident, buoyant, and superior that the whites are little more than jokes that unfortunately he must sometimes tolerate. Pauline Kael once wrote: "Pryor's comedy isn't based on suspiciousness about whites, or on anger, either; he's gone way past that. Whites are *unbelievable* to him." Seldom has that been more apparent than in this sloppy, technically poor film that has a spicey mad zip whenever Pryor shows up.

A brief appearance that turned into a classic: Hattie McDaniel (c.) as the scene-stealing, gum-chewing maid in the dinner episode of Alice Adams *(with, l. to r., Ann Shoemaker, Fred MacMurray, Katharine Hepburn, and Fred Stone).*

Alice Adams (1935)

D. George Stevens. *S.* Dorothy Yost and Mortimer Offner; adaptation by Jane Murfin, from a novel by Booth Tarkington. *P.* Pandro S. Berman. *R.* MGM. Cast includes: Evelyn Venable; Frank Albertson; Fred Stone; and Anne Shoemaker.

Here Hattie McDaniel's brief appearance is a classic example of a talented black performer who, under the guidance of a perceptive director, comes on the screen for a few key scenes and unleashes her high-falutin' style to just about walk away with the picture.

The movie centers on Katharine Hepburn as Alice Adams, a small-town social climber—a poor girl who wants desperately to fit in—who meets and sets out to impress a handsome rich boy (Fred MacMurray). He is invited to dinner with the girl's family. To ensure the evening's success, the Adamses hire a Negro cook to prepare and serve the meal. No one, however, seems more aware of the low status of the Adams family than the cook, who seems to feel she's lowering herself by serving the dinner.

The cook, of course, is played by McDaniel—in her formidable and unorthodox fashion. From her entrance, she makes her remarks—while rambunctiously chewing gum—in a manner that no other movie maid had ever dared. Instructed by the mistress of the house to serve soup, McDaniel asks, "But don't you think it's getting pretty hot for soup?" Naturally, the weather *does* prove too warm for soup, and later when asked airily by Alice to "Please take this dreadful soup away," McDaniel just about stops dead in her tracks and stares at the girl imperially, indeed almost contemptuously, as if to say, *I done tol you so.*

Repeatedly, McDaniel's character makes fun of the family's attempts to put on airs. Her lethargic dining-room entrances and exits, the offhand manner in which she carries her tray—all cue us in to the fact that she could not care less about trying to please these no 'count white folks! When Alice haughtily speaks in French, McDaniel is ready to undercut the woman's airs by giving a monosyllabic grunt.

After *Alice Adams*'s opening, one newspaper critic wrote: "The recital would be incomplete if it neglected to applaud Hattie McDaniel for her hilarious bit as hired maid during the classic dinner scene."

This film helped firmly fix the nature of Hattie McDaniel's relations with her white employers for the rest of her film career. Through her attitude—her tone of voice, her body movements, her facial expressions—she puts them in *their* place without overtly offending them. If anything, she looks down on them and is even rather openly condescending, while pretending to be the model servant.

Added note: In this film, as in others early in her career, McDaniel was billed as Hattie McDaniel*s*.

All The Fine Young Cannibals (1960)

D. Michael Anderson. *S.* Robert Thom; suggested from the novel *The Bixby Girls* by Rosamond Marshall. *P.* Pandro S. Berman. *R.* MGM. Cast includes: Louise Beavers.

A troubled-young-kids-in-love film starring Natalie Wood, Robert Wagner, George Hamilton, and Susan Kohner. Lush production values. A romantic melodramatic script. Drifting about in search of happiness, what the characters really need (what the script could use, too) is a good dose of commonsense or perhaps just some simple maturity.

Nevertheless, the movie is endurable, particularly when Pearl Bailey shows up as a self-destructive, boozed-out, dying Billie-Holiday-type blues singer. Well, folks, Pearlie Mae's about the healthiest-looking dying person we'll ever see on screen, but she holds our attention. At one point, Wagner (as a confused jazz musician) and Bailey (as the trusted friend on whom he depends) become *very* chummy. But in the strict movie code of the time, they are seemingly just platonic friends. Of course, our own ideas about the two—what must be transpiring when the camera is not around—is what gives the film a rather amusing kick. By the end though, a heartbroken Pearl has tragically died. Poor Pearl. Poor movie.

All the Young Men (1960)

D. Hall Bartlett. *S.* Hall Bartlett. *P.* Hall Bartlett; a Hall Bartlett/
Jaguar Production. *R.* Columbia Pictures. Cast includes: prize-
fighter champion Ingemar Johansson; teen idol of the day, James
Darren; Paul Richards; Glenn Corbett; and comedian Mort Sahl.

A fairly bland and cliched war movie (the Korean conflict), featuring
Sidney Poitier as a stalwart troop commander contending not only with
enemy gunfire but also the prejudices of the white soldiers in his unit.
Previous films such as *Home of the Brave*, *The Steel Helmet*, and even
Poitier's low-budget *Red Ball Express* had already handled this subject and
done better with it at that. One sequence is memorable: Alan Ladd,
injured, is in need of a blood transfusion, which eventually comes from
Poitier. Following the transfusion, both Ladd and Poitier seem to cautiously eye one another, no doubt wondering just what effect this
infusion of *negra blood* will have on this fair-haired white officer! Unintentionally amusing and certainly a small point, but it's one of the
better moments in this static action picture.

Time wrote: "Sidney Poitier [is] an accomplished actor so discrimi-
nated against because of his color that he will probably never be allowed to play a character who is not strong, sensitive and noble."
Poitier himself once said: "I was unable to work in that movie, even on
an elementary level, with any degree of imagination." It shows.

Amazing Grace (1974)

D. Stan Lathan. *S.* black writer Matt Robinson. *P.* Matt Robinson.
R. United Artists. Cast includes such oldtimers (in cameo appear-
ances) as Stepin Fetchit (dismal); Butterfly McQueen; and Slappy
White; also such then up-and-comers as Moses Gunn and lovely
Rosalind Cash as a testy high-yaller lady called Creola.

An awkwardly and often clumsily executed movie that seems to suffer
from tired blood—as does its leading lady, Moms Mabley. (While making this movie, Mabley suffered a heart attack and had to wear a
pacemaker for the duration of the filming.) Often this reminds one of
the race movies of the 1940s: it focuses on a seemingly wise little old
lady, who, out to rid the city of Baltimore of its political corruption, is
determined to do something that will "further the race, not hinder it."
Throughout one senses the young black director Stan Lathan (his first
big studio production) struggling to keep this thing moving—and to
inject the slack script with vigor and intelligence. Because this is one of
Mabley's few screen appearances, she's the main reason for seeing
Amazing Grace. Despite her age (she was in her 70s) and poor health, she
occasionally manages to sparkle and shine with a pleasantly devilish and
girlish glow in her eyes. She's a legend long past her prime but a legend
captured on celluloid nonetheless. Earlier in her career, Mabley appeared in the independently produced films *Boarding House Blues* (1948)
and *Killer Diller* (1948).

The Angel Levine (1970)

D. Jan Kadar. *S.* Bill Gunn and Ronald Ribman. *P.* Chiz Shultz (this
was a Belafonte Enterprises Production). *R.* UA. Cast includes: Ida
Kaminska; Milo O'Shea.

Harry Belafonte plays the guardian angel of Zero Mostel in the movie adaptation of Bernard Malamud's novel Angel Levine.

One has high hopes for this allegorical tale about a black angel (Harry Belafonte) coming to comfort an elderly orthodox Jewish tailor (Zero Mostel) who, saddled with an invalid wife, has just about given up on everything. Directed by Czechoslovakian Jan Kadar, who had previously filmed the award-winning *Shop on Main Street*, the picture strives hard for a realistic gritty quality with characters, settings, and city streets that look used and decaying. But nothing jells emotionally, especially the developing relationship between Belafonte and Mostel, who give credible performances (although Mostel is still a ham), yet who, even at the end of the film, seem as if they've just been introduced. Belafonte himself (with a pencil-thin mustache and often dressed in a black leather jacket and a dark sweatshirt) looks street-handsome (far different from his polished good-boy appearance in *Carmen Jones*) and is clearly primed for action. When Gloria Foster shows up (as Belafonte's girlfriend—she doesn't know he's died and now become an angel on probation), we think the juices might start flowing. But Foster—sullen, withdrawn, cold—gives the same performance she's executed too many times before. And in this long drawn-out film, all anybody does is talk, talk, talk. The liveliest moments belong to Barbara Ann Teer as a welfare clerk who gives Mostel a hard time—and who also endows *The Angel Levine* with some much needed humor—and *attitude*.

Anna Lucasta (1958)

D. Arnold Lavan. S. Philip Yordan, from his play of the same title. P. Sidney Harmon. R. UA (a Longridge Enterprise, Inc. Production). Cast includes a number of very talented black performers, many of whom found themselves up against a brick wall in the Hollywood of the 1950s: Frederick O'Neal; Isabelle Cooley; Rosetta Le Noire; Alvin Childress (who played Amos on the "Amos 'n Andy" TV series); Henry Scott; and Georgia Burke. Saddest to see, however, is

James Edwards, the former star of *Home of the Brave* (the great black hope in the Hollywood of the late 1940s), playing a throwaway role.

One of the few all-black *dramatic* films to come out of the Hollywood factories before the 1970s. (Even during the 1970s black movie boom, such attempts at "serious" all-black dramatic films had been rare, the disappointing 1976 *River Niger* being one of the few that comes to mind.) Usually, Hollywood preferred all-black movie musicals such as *Hallelujah*, *Stormy Weather*, or *Porgy and Bess*. Past films centering on "the Negro problem" such as *Pinky* and *Intruder in the Dust* focused on relations between the races. Here, though, is a black family drama (a precursor to *A Raisin in the Sun*) as well as the tale of a fallen woman. Originally, the play *Anna Lucasta* had been performed with a white cast. (The 1949 movie version starred Paulette Goddard.) But in the late 1940s, an all-black stage version in New York had met with success, briefly propelling its leading lady, Hilda Simms, into the limelight.

In the 1950s, however, Eartha Kitt was in her giddy heyday as a media sensation, and in hopes that she might have some box-office clout, United Artists brought her to the West Coast to star as Anna, the prostitute who's forever at odds with her family and herself. Anna's father (Rex Ingram) wants to marry her off to a well-to-do young man. But Anna's taken up with a raunchy sailor (Sammy Davis, Jr.). And so, like most American family dramas, there is constant bickering and quarrelling. And like most fallen women dramas, there is also much carousing and carryings-on. Kitt and Davis seem to enjoy their rowdy scenes best although they are not quite anyone's idea of a dynamic sexy couple.

Despite its unusual look at black life, *Anna Lucasta* falls very flat, unable to decide what it's really about. The film can never get itself together enough to tell us individual family stories as well as a collective one as do dramas like *Cat On A Hot Tin Roof* and *A Raisin in the Sun*. The cast, too, apparently unsure what the point of view should be, seems to be stumbling about. It's no wonder the film failed at the box-office.

A point of interest: Rex Ingram, as the father with an incestuous eye for his daughter Anna, looks like a wreck, and it's rather disheartening to see the once vital star of *Green Pastures* and *Moonrise* so weathered and defeated-looking. Having been through his share of professional and personal tensions, his face and his body reveal the pressure and perhaps the disillusionment, too. All of this adds something to his characterization, which, whether you think it's one of his better or one of his least convincing performances, keeps us watching him nonetheless. *Variety* praised him: "Ingram as old Joe Lucasta is excellent from start to finish. As the story develops, it is made clear that under his pretense of detesting a daughter who has become a streetwalker, he is also fighting off his own temptations, for Joe is in love with his own daughter. Fogged by age and alcohol, stubborn and stern, Ingram creates a vivid portrait of the old man, and to a large extent he steals the show."

This was Rex Ingram's last important movie role. (He shows up later in a bit as Diahann Carroll's father in *Hurry Sundown*.) Perhaps *Variety*'s comments serve as a final fitting tribute to a very gifted, distinctive screen performer.

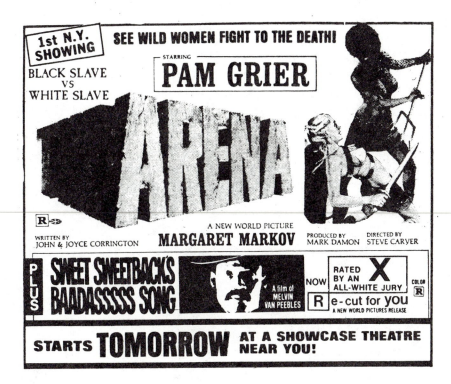

The Arena (1974)

D. Steve Carver. S. John and Joyce Corrington. P. A Roger Corman Production. R. New World. Cast includes: Lucretia Love and Paul Muller.

Pure exploitation. Ancient Rome. Female gladiators. Plenty of violence plus sex plus, shall we say, *provocative* glimpses of Pam Grier—playing a Nubian princess, Mamawi, who, along with Margaret Markov as a Druid priestess named Bodicia, is captured by centurians, taken to Rome, and sold into slavery. It's fairly easy to figure out the rest of the movie. Like Grier's other successful sexploitation film of this period *Black Mama*, *White Mama* (in which Markov was also her co-star), this might have been a riotous pop fantasy/parody. But the filmmakers are far too dimwitted for true invention. So the viewer must here satisfy himself with unintentional self-parody; thus you can make it through a viewing of this thing without completely losing your senses.

The Bedford Incident (1965)

D. James B. Harris. S. James Poe; based on the novel by Mark Rascovich. P. James B. Harris and Richard Widmark. R. Columbia Pictures. Cast includes: Eric Portman; James MacArthur; Donald Sutherland; Martin Balsam; and Wally Cox.

Tensions mount as a U.S. Naval vessel stalks a Soviet submarine in the North Sea.

Following in the wake of *Fail Safe* (1964) and *Dr. Strangelove* (1964) this flat Cold War drama—touching on American political fears and paranoia—is redeemed occasionally by the likably hammy performance of Richard Widmark as the psychotic captain of the American sub. Sidney Poitier turns up as a journalist: intelligent, straitlaced, a bit cocky, and almost unbelievably earnest.

No reference whatsoever was made to Poitier's color in this film, which, within the film industry, was viewed as a positive move: it indicated that a skilled black actor could play any type of role. In *The Hollywood Reporter*, James Powers wrote, "He simply plays a man." (I suppose this means that a *black man* is not simply a *man*. What then is he?) Ironically, black audiences of the 1960s *wanted* Poitier to play roles in which his color was an issue. The denial of this important actor's blackness appeared to be a suppression of the race issue itself as well as a tactic for making the most popular black film star in the world even more acceptable to white audiences.

Poitier thus found himself in the middle of a complex situation and debate. He himself may not have known what to do. He seemed damned if he did and damned if he didn't. Only a black star in America could have been faced with this type of dilemma. Aside from all the flap about the role, Poitier's performance is tentative and aimless. In *The New Yorker*, Brendan Gill described Poitier's work as "distressingly inept."

Best Defense (1984)

D. Wiliard Huyck. *S.* Gloria Katz and Williard Huyck; based on the novel *Easy and Hard Ways Out* by Robert Grossbach. *P.* Gloria Katz. *R.* Paramount Pictures. Cast includes: Kate Capshaw and David Rasche.

A fairly wretched film starring two popular comics of the 1980s, Eddie Murphy and Dudley Moore. The picture cuts back and forth between Moore as a hapless defense plant engineer working in 1982 to find a crucial component in a supertank's missile system and Murphy as the soldier commanding the tank in 1984 in Kuwait. Nothing ever comes together here, including the two stars who have no scenes with one another. (Moore's sequences were shot in Hollywood; Murphy's in Israel.) "Further exasperating proof that we are now up to our eyeballs in summer trash," wrote Rex Reed, who ranked the film among the Ten Worst of 1984. This was one of Murphy's rare flops.

Beverly Hills Cop (1984)

D. Martin Brest. *S.* Daniel Petrie, Jr.; story by Petrie and Danilo Bach. *P.* Don Simpson and Jerry Bruckheimer. *R.* Paramount Pictures. Cast includes: Judge Reinhold and John Ashton (as two LA cops who come to befriend Murphy); Steven Berkoff (as the suave villain Victor Maitland); the real Detroit homicide detective Gilbert Hill (as police supervisor Gilbert Todd); and the riotous Bronson Pinchot (as the art gallery assistant Serge, who, as Janet Maslin wrote, "even steals scenes from Mr. Murphy, which can't have been easy.")

Eddie Murphy's fourth movie and the first in which he has a real starring role. Cast as a Detroit cop, Axel Foley, roaming through Beverly Hills in pursuit of the killers of his best friend, Murphy is at the center of the action rather than a backup support as he was in *48 Hrs.* and *Trading Places*. The action itself, however, is the stuff of which TV dreams are made: car chases, gun battles, corny jokes. Murphy's color is of no great consequence here although at times the film exploits it. In one sequence, Murphy, being told that he cannot get a room at a posh Beverly Hills hotel, goes into a loud-mouth-uncouth-uncontrollable-

The box-office hit that made Eddie Murphy a superstar: Beverly Hills Cop, *in which Murphy teamed with Judge Reinhold (c.) and John Ashton.*

nigger routine that is neither particularly funny nor well-played. (The scene lacks the bite and menace and that true crazed quality that Richard Pryor brings to this kind of situation.) Yet audiences of the 1980s howled at this scene and others, rejoicing every time Murphy used a four-letter word or told somebody off. For white audiences, Murphy's both a working-class underdog (he wears his sneakers and sweatshirt in the most elegant of settings) and something of a likable smartass kid who's amusing because he's got such unbridled confidence and such a big mouth—the kind that almost always lands him in trouble.

It is rather sad, however, to see the way in which Murphy's character has been sexually neutralized here. Cast opposite him as a childhood friend who now runs a fancy Beverly Hills art gallery is white actress Lisa Eilbacher. Theirs is a strictly platonic relationship. Had *Beverly Hills Cop* starred Sylvester Stallone (as had been originally planned), surely the film would have paired Stallone and Eilbacher romantically. Why, one wonders, have the producers denied Murphy the true status of a leading man: a little romance? If they feared that Murphy's large white following might have been offended at seeing him woo a white actress on screen, couldn't the filmmakers have cast a black actress as the former childhood friend? Would that not have been more credible anyway? The murdered buddy of Murphy is also played by a white actor. Coming from the streets of Detroit (the very city whose ghettoes had gone up in flames during the race riots of the 60s), the character's friends logically would have been black. But Eddie Murphy is plopped into a white environment in order that the mass white audience can better identify with him and connect with the picture itself. It's an unrealistic plot maneuver that reveals Hollywood's cynicism about this major black star and his audience.

Murphy himself, appealing, skilled, and slick, lacks depth and complexity yet keeps the action moving and has an astounding audience rapport. His talent can't be denied.

Generally, Murphy and the film were well received. *The New York Times* critic Janet Maslin wrote that Murphy "wins at every turn." *People* called him "the funniest screen cop since the Keystones." And Rex Reed wrote: "They're writing specially tailored vehicles for him the way they used to order up scripts for Gable, Bogart, and the Marx Brothers. Eddie Murphy is the star of the minute, if not the day. . . . *Beverly Hills Cop* fits the cool, fresh-mouthed, jiveass hipness of Murphy's screen persona like a crash helmet."

Beverly Hills Cop II, released in 1987, is hardly a sequel; it's a clanky remake of the first feature.

The Big Doll House (1971)

D. Jack Hill. P. Roger Cormon/New World Production. Cast includes: Judy Brown and Roberta Collins.

Shot in the Philippines, this low-budget, trashy women's-prison-film helped launch the career of a black starlet named Pam Grier. Here amid all the prison shenanigans—plenty of sadism, kinky sex, and the requisite violence—Pam's cast as a zonked-out sexy inmate. Although she doesn't have the leading role, she's the only real star in the film. That hardly means Grier's a Duse of the cheapies. But she does exhibit that strange mixture of passivity and aggressiveness that frequently lay at the core of her later enjoyably campy screen heroines. The movie's too cheap and coarse to be of interest to any except aficionados of Grier—and the women's-prison-movie genre.

A follow-up to *The Big Doll House* titled *The Big Bird Cage*—another Pam Grier women's prison drama—appeared in 1972.

The Bingo Long Traveling All-Stars and Motor Kings (1976)

D. John Badham. S. Hal Barwood and Matthew Robbins; based on a novel by William Brashler. P. Rob Cohen. R. Universal. Cast includes: James Earl Jones; De Wayne Jessie; Tony Burton (who later played Apollo Creed's right hand man in *Rocky*); Mabel King; and that polished old pro Joel Fluellen.

A slick and sometimes engaging story of an all-black baseball team traveling through the country in 1939.

New York Times critic Vincent Canby thought this a "genial, slapdash, high-spirited, and occasionally moving comedy." Indeed it is all these things, and the picture has some solid performances. Billy Dee Williams cuts a dashing figure (so much so that *New York*'s John Simon said Williams "happily blends the virtues of the dedicated actor and the matinee idol"). Richard Pryor also has some good moments. (Here you sense a man just biding his time until true movie stardom comes his way.) And newcomer Stan Shaw (as the black player who's going to go off and play for the major leagues) almost walks away with the last part of the film. Throughout director Badham (who later did *Saturday Night Fever*) carries the action along with a decent rhythmic flow.

Yet despite the assets, there is something weak-livered and pallid about this whole enterprise and something bland, too. In its examination of the type of experiences that a Satchel Paige may have endured, no real insight surfaces about the duality of black lives. Imaginatively, the movie toys with the idea that the whites of the time will not accept the Negro athletes simply as men; the black baseball stars also have to be jokesters or clowns. (They are a bit like The Harlem Globetrotters of the late 1940s and 1950s.) Seeing the movie, we understand that in the past in order to survive in a society that judges only the external *role*, all blacks had to be actors in a sense. But too much of this interesting subject is left unexamined and undramatized. And although the ending is poignant and rather memorable, the picture is without a spine: no tight forward thrust, no compelling character to bring sense to the various loose-jointed episodes.

Finally, one tends to agree with critic Frank Rich's assessment at the time: "In recent years, no Hollywood film about black America has attempted, as this movie does, to combine ambitious thematic intentions with high-spirited comedy . . . but you admire it more for what it attempts than what it actually delivers; out of extraordinary materials, this film's creators have fashioned a singularly ordinary movie."

The Birth of a Nation (1915)

D. D. W. Griffith. *S.* D. W. Griffith and Frank E. Woods, from Rev. Rhomas Dixon's *The Clansman* and *The Leopard's Spots*. Director of photography: G. W. "Billy" Bitzer. *P.* D. W. Griffith. *R.* Cast includes: Henry B. Walthall (as Ben Cameron); Mae Marsh (as Flora); Miriam Cooper (as Margaret); Josephine Crowell (as Mrs. Cameron); Spottiswoode Aitken (as Dr. Cameron); Jennie Lee (as Mammy); Lillian Gish (as Elsie Stoneman); Mary Alden (as Lydia Brown); George Siegmann (as Silas Lynch); Walter Long (as Gus); Ralph Lewis (as Senator Stoneman); and Tom Wilson (as Stoneman's Negro servant).

A legendary classic, a racist masterpiece. Technically innovative and sweeping. Director Griffith made brilliant use of the close-up, cross-cutting, rapid-fire editing, the iris, the split screen shot, and realistic and impressionistic lighting. His once-record-breaking $100,000 spectacle ran over three hours and eventually altered the entire course and concept of the feature film. But the treatment of its black characters has also made this possibly the most controversial American film ever released.

An Old South/Civil War/Reconstruction Era drama, *The Birth of a Nation* focuses on the family of kindly Dr. Cameron. On the Cameron plantation in Piedmont, South Carolina, masters and slaves are friendly. In the fields, the darkies contentedly pick cotton. Lively pickaninnies dance and perform for their white masters outside the slave quarters. Mammy joyously runs the big house. All is calm, at peace, in order during these glory days of the Old South.

Then the War breaks out. The old world of gentility collapses. A troop of Negro raiders terrorizes the Cameron family. And all the South undergoes "ruin, devastation, rapine, and pillage." Afterward during the Reconstruction period, carpetbaggers (led by the corrupt white Senator Stoneman) and uppity niggers from the North move into Piedmont, exploiting and corrupting the former slaves, unleashing the sadism and bestiality *innate* in the Negro, turning the once-congenial darkies into renegades, and using them to "crush the white South under the heel of the black South." "Lawlessness runs riot!" reads a title card. The old slaves quit work to dance. They roam the streets, shoving whites aside. They take over the political polls, disenfranchising the white citizens. A black political victory culminates in an orgiastic street celebration. Blacks dance, sing, drink, rejoice. Later they conduct a black Congressional session, itself a mockery of Old South ideals, in which the freed Negro legislators are depicted as lustful, arrogant, idiotic. They gnaw on chicken legs and drink whiskey from bottles while sprawling with bare feet upon their desks. During the Congressional meeting, the stench created by the barefoot Congressmen becomes so great that they pass as their first act a ruling that every member must keep his shoes on during legislative meetings.

Matters reach a heady climax when the lusty renegade black buck Gus hotly pursues the delicate young Cameron daughter. Rather than submit, the poor thing—the Pet Sister as she's called—flees and throws herself from a cliff into the "opal gates of death." (Interestingly enough, during a 1970s showing of *The Birth of a Nation* to an all-black audience at Howard University in Washington, D.C., when the poor Pet Sister jumped to her death, the black audience stood up and cheered. *The Birth of a Nation* can still rouse tension and hostilities.) Later the mulatto Silas Lynch attempts to force the fair white Elsie Stoneman (played by Lillian Gish) into marrying him. Finally, when all looks lost, a group of stalwart, upright white males, wearing sheets and hoods, no less, soon have a victorious confrontation with the blacks. Defenders of white womanhood, white honor and white glory, they restore to the South everything it has lost, including white supremacy. Thus we have the birth of a nation. And the birth of the Ku Klux Klan, too!

Absurd as some of the plot of *The Birth of a Nation* might sound today, the film had enormous power and extraordinary effects. The final ride of the Klan was an impressive piece of movie propaganda, superbly filmed and brilliantly edited. Indeed it was so stirring that audiences screamed in terror and delight, cheering the white heroes and booing, hissing, and cursing the black baddies.

Griffith also "introduced" the mass movie audience to the black film stereotypes that were to linger in American films for the next 70-some years—the noble, loyal manageable Toms, the clownish coons, the stoic hefty mammy, the troubled "tragic" mulatto (she's Senator Stoneman's mistress), and the brutal black buck. All had appeared in previous short films; indeed they were carryovers from popular fiction, poetry, and

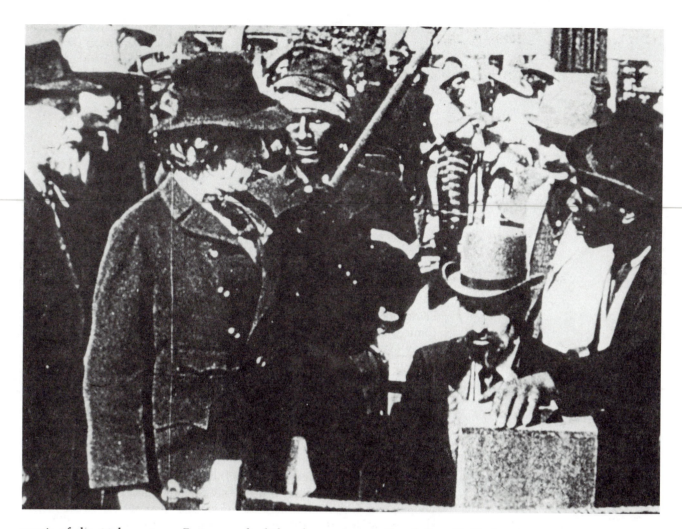

music of the 19th century. But never had they been given such a full-blown dramatic treatment—and in a film seen the world over. Of course, the stereotypes in *The Birth of a Nation* were all the more disturbing and grotesque because the major black roles were played by white actors in blackface. (Real blacks had only minor parts.)

The Birth of a Nation became one of the biggest moneymakers in movie history. At a private White House screening, President Woodrow Wilson exclaimed, "It's like writing history in lightning." Like *The Clansman*, the Thomas Dixon novel on which it was based, the movie appealed to the nation partly because of its mythic view of the Old South and particularly because of its exploration of the great white American nightmares: interracial sex and the strong sexual black man. A scary black/white fantasy, the film's ending wiped away white America's sexual fears about the Negro and temporarily at least permitted the national psyche to relax.

Controversy, however, followed *The Birth of a Nation*. The NAACP launched a formal protest movement against it. (In later years when the film was re-released, there were new protests.) Afterwards the film industry, fearing controversy more than anything else, assiduously avoided any depiction of strong, aggressive, defiant sexual black men. Most of the black males audiences were to see in later films of the late 1920s and 1930s were comic, non-threatening figures such as the

D. W. Griffith's classic, racist masterpiece The Birth of a Nation, *in which a group of black males take over a small Southern town.*

21

characters played by Stepin Fetchit and Bill "Bojangles" Robinson. The buck figure actually does not return in full force in American films until some 55 years later with such pictures as *Shaft* and *Sweet Sweetback's Baadasssss Song*. At the same time, some black leaders, determined to counteract the shocking black images of *The Birth of a Nation*, set out to make black films with positive characters, and eventually there was a whole new wave of independent black filmmakers such as Oscar Micheaux.

Black and Tan (1929)

D. Dudley Murphy. *S.* Dudley Murphy. *P.* Dick Currier. *R.* RKO Radio.

A gilded, artsy fantasy, with much soft focus and a memorable sequence of multiple images dancing across the screen. The same year that *Black and Tan* was released, its director, Dudley Murphy, filmed the great Bessie Smith in the all-black musical short *St. Louis Blues*. This, too, is an all-black musical short (17 minutes), featuring another great black artist, Duke Ellington. There isn't much of a plot here. Early in the film two dimwitted comic coon characters show up, spouting dialogue so stereotyped that many may feel uncomfortable hearing it. But mostly the focus is on the relationship between Ellington and the lovely Fredi Washington, who plays a fatally ill dancer. In the big climactic sequence, Washington performs a flamboyantly exotic dance number, which proves perhaps too flamboyant, and she collapses in the middle of the performance. Afterwards this gorgeous creature lies near death and has but one request, which no film fan has ever forgotten: will the Duke perform the Black and Tan Fantasy. Could Ellington refuse? Thus the Ellington Orchestra hovers near this goddess's deathbed. It's corny and sentimental and, of course, totally implausible. But nobody cares because the whole thing is whipped up with such a dreamy insouciance and such a sweet melancholic moodiness that the film never fails to please.

Black Belt Jones (1974)

D. Robert Clouse. *S.* Oscar Williams. *P.* Fred Weintraub and Paul Heller. *R.* Warner Bros. Cast includes: Gloria Hendry; Alan Weeks; Esther Sutherland; and Eric Laneuville (who later appeared on the TV series "St. Elsewhere."

Fighting the mob to save a black self-defense school in Watts!? Well, yes, that's the plot of this West Coast cheapie released during the height of Hollywood's blaxploitation era and starring black-belt champ Jim Kelly, who had previously appeared in the very popular Bruce Lee movie *Enter the Dragon*.

Sometimes technically inept, sometimes embarrassingly written, sometimes just plain foolish, *Black Belt Jones* is also sometimes surprising fun: it's popcorn, comic-strip entertainment that moves swiftly and has a good kick now and then. Kelly, stolid and wooden as ever, lacks the grace and fluidity of the great Bruce Lee. And he repeatedly relies on his two stock facial expressions when he feels called upon to emote: a boyish smile (to let us know he's a good guy) and a mean hard tough guy scowl (to let us know he *don't* take *no* stuff from nobody). Neither's convincing. Yet both add to the exaggerated nature of the material, endowing him with comic-book-hero status.

Also around: Scatman Crothers, who's often enough dapper and funny, giving one of his most pleasurable, least stylized performances.

Black Caesar (1973)

D. Larry Cohen. *S.* Larry Cohen. *P.* Larry Cohen and Peter Sabiston. *R.* American International Pictures. Cast includes: Gloria Hendry; Julius Harris; D'Urville Martin; and Art Lund.

Fred Williamson stars as the smooth, tough dude determined to rise to the top. A gangster melodrama turned black. Cheap, tawdry, technically shabby, dramatically uneven. Noteworthy mainly because it marks the rise of the then new type of 1970s black movie hero: street-smart, sexy, powerful, aggressive, and a self-anointed vigilante of sorts, who is morally ambivalent if not reprehensible. In 1974, a sequel *Hell Up in Harlem* appeared.

Black Girl (1972)

D. Ossie Davis. *S.* Black woman playwright J. E. Franklin, based on her play. *P.* Lee Savin. *R.* Cinerama Releasing Corporation. Cast includes: Brock Peters; Leslie Uggams (as the wholesome bourgeois black girl); Ruby Dee; and the vituperative Gloria Edwards and Lorette Greene, as one of the screen's bitchiest pair of wicked sisters.

Sometimes you watch a film aware its structure is all wrong or that technically someone has failed to do his homework or that the idea buried at the heart of the picture hasn't been worked out in dramatic or cinematic terms. Yet you still can't dislike the picture; and, in fact, if it's ever shown later on television, you find yourself seeing it again, the second time around filtering out the many flaws and focusing on what it was you did like about the movie: the deeply felt emotion at its center.

That's the case with Ossie Davis's *Black Girl*, the story of three generations of black women: the youngest (Peggy Pettitt), a dancer struggling to find out who she is; the girl's mother (Louise Stubbs); who remains blind to her past mistakes, justifying them to herself on the grounds that she only wanted the best for her family; and the grandmother (Claudia McNeil) who sees her own history repeating itself. Seldom has this type of drama about the problems and predicaments peculiar to black women (yet of interest to all of us) reached American films or television. (Maya Angelou's "Sister, Sister", *Claudine*, *Mahogany*, and *A Raisin in the Sun* are some of the rare works touching on the same theme.) Director Davis doesn't seem to have any film technique under control. But he connects splendidly to his actresses, giving each her *moment* and permitting them all to push all the way for effects.

At the time of *Black Girl*'s release, *Variety* praised it as the best Negro family life drama since *A Raisin in the Sun*. The paper also wrote that Louise Stubbs "makes an auspicious bow as an actress who could carve an important niche for herself as a character actress in films." That didn't happen. Nor was *Black Girl* a commercial success, partly because as *Variety* pointed out, the studio did not know how to handle it, promoting the film as a work exploding with rage and booking it into movie houses that catered to the action film crowd of the period. Such bookings, *Variety* added, could "only disappoint those ticketbuyers who want to see a bit of blood-letting and may well keep away serious filmgoers who would have been rewarded by the fine directing and acting."

A very uneven period piece. But worth seeing.

Black Eye (1974)

D. Jack Arnold. *S.* Mark Haggard and Jim Martin; based on Jack Jeff's novel *Murder on the Wild Side. P.* Pat Rooney Production. *R.* Warner Bros. Cast includes: Richard Anderson; Rosemary Forsyth; Floy Dean; and Larry Mann.

In this fascinating, tawdry little B-picture, black cinema's perennial tough guy (and King of the B's) Fred Williamson plays a post-Watergate detective who, while investigating a dope ring, becomes caught up in a pervasively corrupt and disorienting system. Everything has been turned topsyturvy, the old verities have gone haywire, and he has got to understand the mess before he can do anything about it. Even his girlfriend (Teresa Graves) has fled him, not to rush into the arms of another man but to those of another woman. The moment when Williamson realizes what his lady is really up to is handled with a surprising degree of sophistication. Caught in a bind, the Fred Williamson hero nonetheless sails through this movie with ease, dexterity, and a modicum of humor.

Within its limitations, *Black Eye* is not bad to eye at all.

The Black Godfather (1974)

D. John Evans. *S.* John Evans. *P.* John Evans. *R.* Cinemation Industries. Cast includes: Rod Perry; Jimmy Witherspoon; Diane Sommerfield; and Damu King.

A charter member of the let's-get-Whitey school of black movies of the early 1970s.

A black crime syndicate, led by its resilient and right-on black godfather (a baadd brother, with whom nobody messes, not even the Man), wins control of the organized crime territory in its neighborhood. But these are unusual hoods. The dear boys also have do-gooder instincts. They are determined to wipe out their community's heroin trade (that exploits their brothers and sisters, you see!)—and the white Mafiosi who run it. The movie climaxes with a bloody shoot-out. And in between there's some steamy sex and also much sloganizing by the hoods: "The essence of our struggle is independence"; "Money buys dignity. Power is a crime"; and, of course, "Power to the people."

If the people really had power, they would have made certain this movie was never filmed!

Variety called it a "fast but overly-long black gangster film which carries good exploitation values for the action market." And Archer Winston of *The New York Post* added that "in its juvenile, action-packed way it's not as bad as some."

But, ooohhh, it *is* as bad as some—and worse. That it trivializes basic political sentiments of the period may not bother anyone today. Nor is anybody likely to be disturbed by a simple fact the movie completely ignores and overlooks: all crime syndicates, black or white, exploit the people. But *The Black Godfather*'s shoddy technical quality and its clear lack of direction and focus, however, fairly much will limit its appeal.

A good example of the type of black action movie that killed off the black movie market. Black audiences had just *had it* with this kind of slovenly, poorly scripted and directed mess.

Black Gunn (1972)

D. Robert Hartford Davis. *S.* Franklin Coen. *P.* John Heyman and Norman Priggen. *R.* Columbia (a Champion Production). Cast includes: Martin Landau; Brenda Sykes; and a striking lineup of black athletes: Vida Blue; Timmy Brown; Bernie Casey; Tommy Davis; Gene Washington; and Deacon Jones.

A group of black Vietnam vets, led by young Scott Gunn (Herbert Jefferson, Jr.), robs the syndicate in order to finance the people's revolutionary movement. In so many black action films of the early 1970s, the black hoods and crooks seldom rob or kill just to benefit themselves; we're always told of their political commitment, their compulsion to help the cause. Helping the cause, it turns out, simply means making some money quickly through a low-budget film that fills the pockets of Hollywood's white producers.

Naturally, the mob catches up with Scott Gunn and promptly blows him away. Then onto the scene struts Scott's big brother, known simply as Gunn and played by Jim Brown, who sets out to find his brother's killers. What follows are car chases, bloody fist-fights, gun battles, and a climactic warehouse explosion. Along the way, we're to believe Brown's Gunn has become politicized. Of course, some people will believe anything.

Tacky, shallow, exploitative, this film was made by Britishers in the United States and was shot during the period of Brown's movie heyday. "Jim Brown still sports a Herculean physique," wrote *Variety*, "but his voice remains strangely expressionless and almost feminine. Still he does know how to glower and throw a mean punch." That may be the most this film has to recommend it.

Black Like Me (1964)

D. Carl Lerner. *S.* Carl and Gerda Lerner; based on John Howard Griffin's book *Black Like Me*. *P.* Julius Tannenbaum. *R.* Continental Distribution Company. Cast includes: Al Freeman, Jr.; Roscoe Lee Browne; Billy Allen; Eva Jessye; Clifton James; Will Geer; Thelma Oliver; Richard Ward; Sorrell Booke; Matt Clark; and David Huddleston.

This low-budget movie reversed Hollywood's standard crossing-the-color-line theme. It's based on the best-selling book by white author John Howard Griffin, who had performed an unusual social experiment. Griffin had undergone a special chemical treatment to darken his skin. Then "passing" as a Negro, he hitchhiked across the South to see firsthand a black man's America. Actor James Whitmore plays Griffin, who, during his travels, is shoved on buses, chased by white hoodlums, mistreated by employers, refused employment, and questioned about his sex life. Repeatedly subjected to such humiliations, he witnesses the cruelty and hatred that infest the land.

Today *Black Like Me* looks wearily dated, without the freshness and imaginative quality of even earlier films such as *Pinky* and *Intruder in the*

Dust. Some also tend to view this film as but another example of a white man slumming on holiday. (Many people feel the same way about the 1986 *Soul Man*, which treats similar material comically.) In some respects, *Black Like Me* is a continuation of the tragic mulatto theme: the film's thesis, in the long run, was that here was a white man being treated so shamelessly simply because his skin's been darkened a shade. Still this crude and naive B-movie was an earnest attempt to confront and expose racism in America, and on that very basic level, the film still says something to us about racial attitudes of the 1960s (if not later).

Black Mama, White Mama (1973)

D. Eddie Romero. *S.* H. R. Christian; from an original story by Joseph Viola and Jonathan Demme. *P.* John Ashley and Eddie Romero. *R.* AIP. Cast includes: Eddie Garcia; Laurie Burton; and Lynn Borden.

Two female convicts, one a black prostitute arrested on trumped-up charges (Pam Grier), the other a white revolutionary (Margaret Markov), escape from an island prison together. But they cannot escape one another, thanks to a chain that links them. On the run from the authorities, they fight it out, at one point toppling over and rolling about in the mud. Eventually, a lopsided kind of affection develops between the two. Heard anything like this before? Well, probably so, because this is a female version of the Sidney Poitier/Tony Curtis film of 1959, *The Defiant Ones.*

Filmed in the Philippines, this isn't *that* bad although the idea of parody unfortunately doesn't seem to have entered the filmmakers' minds. Consequently, they've lost out on a golden opportunity. But because we know more than the director and writer, I think the audience sometimes is amused. Funniest sequence: when Pam and her white friend attack two nuns, strip them, then don their habits, which they wear while hitchhiking! They are picked up by a grungy, lusty driver who soon learns these sisters of action, not the cloth, cannot be messed with.

Bearable, mildly diverting, providing a glimpse of the Pam Grier screen persona that would soon become an important force in commercial black cinema of the mid-1970s. A woman's-prison-picture with the expected sexiness, sadism, lesbianism.

Black Samson (1974)

D. Charles Bail. *S.* Warren Hamilton, Jr.; story by Daniel B. Cady. *P.* Daniel B. Cady. *R.* Warner Bros.; an Omini Picture. Cast includes: Carol Speed; Mike Payne; William Smith; and veteran black actor Napoleon Whiting as Old Henry.

First there had been *Black Jesus*, then *Black Caesar*, and finally this one, *Black Samson*, another tale of a powerful contemporary urban black hero with near-legendary strength. A self-styled vigilante determined to keep the pushers and mobsters out of his neighborhood, nitery owner Samson (Rockne Tarkington) patrols the streets and pummels his enemies with the greatest of speed and ease. After a white hood tries moving in on Samson's turf, the film climaxes with the black community itself standing united against its exploiters. It's an adolescent fantasy, not very well served up.

The Black Six (1974)

D. Matt Cimber. S. George Theakos. P. Matt Cimber. R. Cinemation. Cast includes: Rosalind Miles and Maury Wills.

What a crackerjack action fantasy this might have been! Its plot is great pop fun: after a black biker discovers his brother has been murdered by a troop of white Hell's Angels types, he sets out with five black motorcycle buddies to get the white biker baddies. Picture climaxes with a flamboyant motorcycle battle. The one memorable thing is the cast of black bikers, all of whom were then major pro football players: Gene Washington, Lem Barney, Willie Lanier, Carl Eller, Mercury Morris, and "Mean" Joe Greene (in the days before he did his famous Coca-Cola commercial). In 1974 to see these powerful black he-men stomp down the white macho villains must have pleased many a black schoolkid. But the picture never has any real spirit or zip to it.

Blackboard Jungle (1955)

D. Richard Brooks. S. Richard Brooks; based on the novel by Evan Hunter. P. Pandro S. Berman. R. MGM. Cast includes: Vic Morrow; Anne Francis; Louis Calhern; Margaret Hayes; Rafael Campos; Paul Mazursky; and Jameel Farh (Jamie Farr).

Released in the Eisenhower 1950s, *Blackboard Jungle* was considered a wrenching expose of the American high school. It was also a favorite. for teenagers of the period. Much of its power then and now rests in the vibrant performance of the young Sidney Poitier, who plays Gregory Miller, an intelligent, complex student who fears that in the outside world he will be a second-class citizen without a chance to do much of anything. He snarls, agitates, acts tough, and displays his virility more effectively here than in almost any other film. "Come on! Go ahead! Hit me!" he yells to the white teacher (played by Glenn Ford), who he believes represents the oppressive system. Here the disaffected young of the 1950s saw a young man of action who refused to take any crap from anybody. Yet Poitier's Miller was also a bruised, sensitive student forced to live outside society, as much a classic loner as those other 1950s heroes, Marlon Brando, James Dean, and Montgomery Clift. Some of Poitier's earlier impact is lessened at the movie's conclusion when he aids teacher Ford against a student with a switchblade. But Poitier's screen code of decency and honor is reaffirmed.

Today *Blackboard Jungle*, like Brando's *The Wild One*, creaks along and reveals itself as a not particularly well-done movie. But young audiences still respond with excitement, feeling no doubt the same identification with its confused and troubled teens as did audiences of the past.

Blacula (1972)

D. William Crain. S. Raymond Koenig and Joan Torres. P. Joseph T. Naar. R. AIP. Cast includes: Denise Nicholas; Thalmus Rasulala; the pretty Emily Yancy; Jitu Cumbuka; and Ketty Lester (who years earlier had recorded the hit record "Love Letters").

Popping up at the height of the blaxploitation film's popularity, this standard Hollywood formula picture had a nifty twist: it's Dracula in blackface. An African prince (William Marshall), haughty, dignified, and erudite (typical characteristics for a William Marshall character), is

Dracula in blackface? William Marshall as the blood-sucking (blood-curdling, too) Blacula.

bitten by Count Dracula. He's also separated from his queen (Vonetta McGee). Two hundred years later, he appears on the streets of LA, and he's out for blood!

Some campy moments turn up. This is perhaps passable TV-type entertainment. But a clever satiric tone, clearly what's needed, is also clearly what's missing.

Blazing Saddles (1974)

D. Mel Brooks. *S.* Mel Brooks, Richard Pryor, Norman Steinberg, Andrew Bergman, and Alan Uger. *P.* Michael Hertzberg. *R.* Warner Bros. Cast includes: Alex Karras; Mel Brooks; Slim Pickens; John Hillerman; and David Huddleston.

Richard Pryor had a hand in the script for this spoof of old movie Westerns, and sometimes his delirious manic touch shows. He was also to have starred but dropped out at the last minute, which is too bad, for while Cleavon Little, as a black sheriff in a white town, isn't unsuitable, he lacks the highstrung imagination, indeed the craziness, of Pryor. Little can't reverse the racial stereotypes the way Pryor can; he's unable to bring out the absurdities of whites and turn them into coons. Often he just seems along for the ride, and occasionally, he doesn't seem to be in on the movie's jokes. Consequently, part of the point of *Blazing Saddles* is lost: we're supposed to see that this black sheriff succeeds with this racist white community simply because he's clever and resourceful enough to know he must play the role of the town's dumb nigger. Playing the dumb nigger (with a 1970s-style double consciousness), he's able not only to survive but to triumph. That, however, is a subject the picture both spotlights and evades at the same time.

Essentially a series of TV skits and routines, *Blazing Saddles* is embarrassingly uneven. Brooks' familiar anti-gay jokes point up a fact some moviegoers ignore: a few decades earlier, this type of movie might have had similar anti-black jokes.

Still Madeline Kahn (in a wicked parody of Marlene Dietrich) and

Harvey Korman (as a character called Hedley Lamarr) have goofy moments. And has anyone ever forgotten the sequence of Kahn flirting with Cleavon Little while she dangles a huge sausage roll before him? Best sequence: the cowboys of the Old West sit around eating beans. Immediately, the childhood rhyme comes to mind: "Beans, beans, good for your heart. The more you eat them, the more you—oops!" Well, Brooks completes the rhyme for us.

Bless Their Little Hearts (1984)

D. Billy Woodberry. Edited by: Billy Woodberry. Cinematography by: Charles Burnett. S. Charles Burnett. P. Billy Woodberry. Cast includes: Nate Hardman; Kaycee Moore; and Angela, Ronald, and Kimberly Burnett.

Like *A Raisin in the Sun*, Billy Woodberry's *Bless Their Little Hearts* is a glimpse of a black family in a period of crisis. An unemployed father, a tense mother, and puzzled, anxious children are pawns in a morality play without a moral. One always senses hovering about them a larger social framework—a disinterested society—that has no place or time for these lives. There are two virtuoso sequences, each stretched almost to the point where we fear they'll be overblown. One sequence focuses on the father as he cuts his young son's fingernails. "You want to be a sissy?" the father roughly says to his son. "Go get the nail clippers." As the father challenges the boy's virility, the child silently seems terrified. It's a tough, even brutal scene that somehow miraculously takes us into the heads of both father and son. The other sequence focuses on an argument that explodes between husband and wife after she has learned of his affair with another woman. The quarrel goes on and on, the actors so much into their characters that it's almost too real (almost too personal), much like Ingmar Bergman's *Scenes from a Marriage*. Director Woodberry stops the scene at precisely the right moment, just at the point where it's arrived at an emotional truth that we cannot back away from. Blistering, disturbing, deeply felt—yet at times almost clinically detached—*Bless Their Little Hearts* is the work of an independent black filmmaker who should have a wider audience.

In *The New York Times*, Vincent Canby called it "a small, self-assured, independent American film that, though severely even-tempered, never disguises its own anger or that of its characters."

A graduate of UCLA's film school, Woodberry completed his film with grants from the Film Fund, the American Film Institute, the National Black Programming Consortium, and the Institute of American Cultures at UCLA. Previously, he had made a short called *The Pocketbook*. His collaborator on *Bless Their Little Hearts* was Charles Burnett, director of the highly praised *Killer of Sheep* (1977).

Blue Collar (1978)

D. Paul Schrader. S. Paul and Leonard Schrader. P. Don Guest. R. Universal (a T.A.T. Communications Company Production). Cast includes: Ed Begley, Jr., and Cliff de Young.

High on some critics' lists as a powerful, socially significant black-oriented film.

One can respect some of the skill that's gone into this film (and one can sit fascinated by the slow accumulation of pain and despair the movie records). But it's hard to warm to *Blue Collar* or see it as anything more than a studious, rather uninspired exercise in social determinism.

Here's the story: hard-pressed for cash and fed up with the quality of their lives and jobs, three automobile factory workers rob their union's headquarters, only to discover in the process the union's loan-sharking activities. Afterwards they set out to blackmail the union, and predictably, the union—the system itself—closes in on the men, destroying their friendship and wiping out the life of one of them.

Theodore Dreiser's influence is easy to spot here but the film lacks Dreiser's depth and his power of articulating the mixed drives and dreams, the fundamental dualities, of human beings who seem to invite the fate awaiting them. Dark, brooding, and despairing throughout, a heavy monotony hangs over the film, and the lives of the central characters are treated without much insight. There is some condescension here. For these men, as humdrum and dreary as their day-to-day existence at the automobile plant may be, seem to have so little capacity for enjoyment. One feels it is not so much the conditions that strap them in as the personalities of the men themselves. Then, too, the film never suggests an alternative for them. Couldn't they quit the plant or seek new jobs?

What goes disastrously wrong, too, is the depiction of the friendship itself of two black men and one white who bring to their relationship no history of race or discord. We cannot see or understand the bridges they've had to construct to connect to one another or the barriers they've had to break down. Had that been dramatized, then the audience might have really seen the forces that can unite oppressed people of all colors—and the forces that could also draw them apart. The relationship seems contrived, and thus the film itself seems fitted together without any organic flow, rhythm, or perceptiveness.

The actors themselves—each giving a fine performance, and in the case of Yaphet Kotto an excellent one—are not granted, however, much breathing space. They're director Schrader's pawns. Several critics have praised Pryor here for his serious work. In *The New York Times*, Vincent Canby wrote: "The center of the film, however, is Mr. Pryor who, in *Blue Collar*, has a role that for the first time makes use of the wit and fury that distinguish his straight comedy routines. It's a sneakily funny performance right up to the film's angry . . . ending." Canby may have something of a point but the truth of the matter is that Pryor, for the most part, shows he's capable of *doing* dramatic characters, that he's indeed an *actor*. Yet his performance lacks the inspired quality of his looney work in such movies as *Silver Streak* and even *Which Way Is Up?*

All in all, this is a textbook primer of a pseudo-Marxist film that can be appreciated as such although not much more.

Added note: this first directing assignment for Paul Schrader has some of the same urban intensity as his screenplays for *Taxi Driver* (1976) and *Hardcore* (1979).

The Blues Brothers (1980)

D. John Landis. *S.* Dan Aykroyd and John Landis. *P.* Robert K. Weiss. *R.* Universal. Cast includes: John Lee Hooker (glimpsed briefly); Matt "Guitar" Murphy; Carrie Fisher; Henry Gibson; and Twiggy.

"If Universal had made it 35 years ago, *The Blues Brothers* might have been called Abbott and Costello in Soul Town"—so wrote *Variety* of this $30,000,000 debacle.

Here those perpetual adolescents John Belushi and Dan Aykroyd play the Blues Brothers, Jake and Elwood, characters they developed for the television comedy series "Saturday Night Live" and for a series of concert performances as well. With their black suits, dark glasses, narrow ties, and floppy hats, the two are parodies not so much of traditional black blues singers as of the white beatnik jazz musicians of the 1950s. Even at that, the parodies are shaky and without enough definition to be sustained for more than 6 or 10 minutes, the length of a TV skit. Unfortunately, here the Blues Brothers are on screen for over two hours as they set out to raise $5,000 for their childhood parish by regrouping their old band and staging a huge concert. In the process of bringing the group back together again, the pair lay waste to the city of Chicago and other parts of the Midwest: there are car chases, crashes, bombings, and mayhem galore (not much of which is very funny) as well as cops, Nazis, and the Army, all hot on the trail of Belushi and Aykroyd. Along the way, too, the ersatz blues stars meet some authentic black artists: James Brown, Cab Calloway, Ray Charles, and Aretha Franklin, all used callously and rather cruelly as exotic backup supports for the antics of the "white boys." Herein lies the movie's essential tastelessness and insensitivity.

Once again the urban ghetto is depicted as little more than a playful jungle: the black stars, the streets, the churches, the record shops are alive with action. But all are there simply for the tourists to peruse and marvel over or to mock, too. At the grand finale, Cab Calloway, dressed resplendently in white tie and tails, cannot even perform his big number "Minnie the Moocher" without the camera repeatedly cutting away from him to concentrate on the shenanigans of Belushi and Aykroyd. The cutaways reveal a basic indifference if not unconscious disregard for this great black performer's talent. Calloway's used simply as filler material.

In many respects, *The Blues Brothers* is really an ugly film, reverberating on supposedly chic 1980s-style white hipness (the same kind of hip humor that was at the core of the *Saturday Night Live* skits and also was present in a movie like *48 Hrs.*) that wants its audience to think it's all right and even cool to laugh at the old racial jokes and stereotypes (we're all supposedly adult enough now not to take that kind of thing seriously—or as an insult to anyone) but which, at heart, believes the stereotypes and jokes to be the real thing. The old jokes about black America have become the white idea of soul.

But perhaps there always is a silver lining somewhere, and thus, as in movies of the past, the black performers rise above their roles and infuse *Blues Brothers* with a dizzyingly high energy level and some supremely entertaining moments. In the case of Aretha Franklin, here's a star who, like Robeson in *Show Boat*, transcends the film itself. At first, it's a bit disconcerting to see the great Aretha as a tacky-looking waitress, who's trying to hold onto a man with itchy feet. But then she sings "Think," and her delivery is powerful, deeply felt, and very funny, too. In *New York*, critic David Denby wrote: "Hectic, exhausting, often gross and stupid, *The Blues Brothers* nonetheless makes a tiny purchase on immortality when Aretha Franklin opens her mouth to sing." She brings light and movement to the screen but then disappears.

And Pauline Kael wrote:

> It has taken all these years for Aretha Franklin to reach the screen—and then she's on for only one number! Getting her into *The Blues Brothers* was the smartest thing that the director John Landis did; letting her get away after that number was the dumbest. When she sings "Think," . . . she smashes the movie to smithereens. Her presence is so strong she seems to be looking at us while we're looking at her. She's so completely there . . . that you can't come down enough to respond to what follows. . . . When *The Blues Brothers* . . . leaves Aretha behind, you know that the moviemakers don't know what they're doing.

Aretha Franklin's performance will no doubt become a classic sequence. And simply because, like *Cabin in the Sky, Stormy Weather,* and *Carmen Jones, The Blues Brothers* features legendary black performers, it will be of some interest in years to come. But it's a mean spirited, messy, petty picture that makes light of its greatest assets.

Body and Soul (1924)

D. Oscar Micheaux. P. Oscar Micheaux. R. The Micheaux Film Corporation. Cast includes: Julia Theresa Russell and Mercedes Gilbert.

Some audiences take one quick look at this silent film by black director Oscar Micheaux and cry out, "Awful!" Actually, disjointed and raggedy as *Body and Soul* frequently is, the movie is not without its pleasures or insights. Chief among the pleasures is the appearance of Paul Robeson, here making his movie debut in dual roles. As a good guy (a staple of the black bourgeoisie) and also as a shifty preacher out to fleece his black followers and to take advantage of the demure young heroine, Robeson is a pretty powerful presence: virile, confident, and intolerably charismatic, he seems completely at ease on screen without those lapses of stiffness that he sometimes fell into during his later films. (He may also seem more like a movie actor here because we don't hear his magnificent voice, which in his sound films never lost its beautifully stagey theatricality.)

It's fun to watch the movie steamroll along, with director Micheaux rarely pulling back from his condemnation of shady black ministers, whom he believed an exploitative and divisive element in the black community. Because of censors, however, (the New York censors' board objected to the portrait of the preacher), Micheaux re-cut his film, cleaning it up (and making it all the more confusing), turning the sad spectacle of a corrupt religious figure into the dream of the young heroine. Once her "nightmare" is over, we're given a conventional rosy ending. Throughout there are cultural signposts that sometimes surprise contemporary viewers: most notably on the wall of the heroine's home is a portrait of Booker T. Washington, the patron saint of a certain segment of the black community at that time.

Clearly a work of historical value.

Body and Soul (1947)

D. Robert Rossen. S. Abraham Polansky. P. Bob Roberts (associate producer); an Enterprise Production. R. United Artists. Cast includes: Lilli Palmer.

A moody, brooding drama centering on a troubled young prizefighter (John Garfield). Featured is the highly skilled Canada Lee, who plays a boxing champion, first defeated by Garfield, then signed on as his former opponent's trainer, and ultimately revealed as the new champ's only friend. *The New York Times* wrote of Lee:

> It is Canada Lee who brings to focus the horrible pathos of the cruelly exploited prize-fighter. As a Negro ex-champion who is meanly shoved aside, until one night he finally dies slugging in a deserted ring, he shows through great dignity and reticence the full measure of his inarticulate scorn for the greed of shrewder men who have enslaved him, sapped his strength, and then tossed him out to die. The inclusion of this portrait is one of the finer things in the film.

Lee gets at his character's insides slowly but steadily, gradually drawing the viewer in, so subtly weaving his spell that you're surprised by the effect his character's death ultimately has on you. It's a classic example of a black performer taking a supporting part and beefing it up with his talent and also his mad conviction and desire to make a statement, to create. This is also a prime example of the gradual change in the depiction of Negro characters in Hollywood films of the post–World War II era. No longer simply comic characters, the black figures are treated more sensitively, used occasionally as statements on the effects of a tight, restrictive capitalistic system.

Body and Soul (1981)

D. George Bowers. S. Leon Isaac Kennedy. P. Menahem Golan and Yoram Globus in association with Kennedy Productions. R. Cannon

Films. Cast includes: Muhammad Ali (in a cameo appearance); Kim Hamilton; Peter Lawford; Perry Lang; and Mike Gazzo.

A loose remake of the John Garfield classic of the 1940s, now turned into the story of a black boxer (Leon Isaac Kennedy) trying to earn money to pay for his kid sister's operation. Hokey and hackneyed, the real aim of this movie is star-making. Cast as lovers, Leon Isaac Kennedy and Jayne Kennedy (at one time a real-life husband-and-wife team) are the would-be stars, who pout, pet, bicker, and quarrel, straining hard to imbue the movie with a romantic larger-than-life movie-star luster, reminiscent of Hollywood's great romantic era of the 1930s and 1940s. The two are attractive but hollow and weak, pallid as lovers and no-wins as personalities, striking us more as bratty, inexperienced teenagers than as a mature screen couple.

Disappointing on all rounds.

Book of Numbers (1973)

D. Raymond St. Jacques. *S.* Larry Spiegel; from the novel by black writer Robert Deane Pharr. *P.* Raymond St. Jacques. *R.* Avco Embassy; a Brut Presentation. Cast includes: Sterling St. Jacques and Reginald Dorsey.

Two urban dudes—an older man (Raymond St. Jacques) and his handsome young protege (Philip Thomas)—set up a numbers racket in a small Southern town during the Depression. The expected naturally happens: run-ins with the local crime establishment; a romance for the young man with a pretty young woman (Freda Payne); the appearance of some colorful supporting characters (namely Hope Clarke and D'Urville Martin); and a climactic shootout in which the older man is killed. Few of the elements really jell or blend, and the movie never becomes the piece of slick entertainment it strives to be. At times it strikes one as a cleaned-up version of something like *Trick Baby* with none of the latter's perverse pleasures.

Added note: Billed here as Philip Thomas, he later added his middle name Michael when co-starred in the TV series "Miami Vice."

Boy! What a Girl (1947)

D. Arthur Leonard. *S.* Vincent Valentini. *P.* Jack Goldberg. *R.* Herald Pictures. Cast includes: Big Sid Catlett and his band; The Slam Stewart Trio; The International Jitterbugs; The Harlemaniacs; Deek Watson and The Brown Dots; Ann Cornell; Milton Woods; and a guest appearance by Gene Krupa.

When many people think of race movies, this is the type that fondly comes to mind: a high-spirited, fast-moving romp with a decent plotline, relatively smooth (or at least unobtrusive) technical transitions, and offbeat "ethnic" performers. (Unfortunately, most race movies are not as good as this one.) *Boy! What a Girl* revolves around two young black showbiz entrepreneurs (Elwood Smith and Duke Williams), who are trying to raise money for a new production. Through a series of likably unlikely plot maneuvers, they persuade a feisty female impersonator to pose as a grande dame called Madame Deborah—in order to enlist money from a hot-and-horny, would-be backer (Al Jackson). The

The Book of Numbers *with Raymond St. Jacques, Freda Payne, Philip Thomas, and in the background Hope Clarke and Sterling St. Jacques.*

backer also just happens to be the father of the two pretty young women (Betti Mays and Sheila Guyse) whom the young men are smitten with. Throughout the proceedings, there is also a huffy landlord (Warren Patterson), who repeatedly yells to the two young men that he has not been paid and wants his room rent. Also on hand: a rent party with plenty of song and dance. And then there is the real Madame Deborah (played by the wonderfully proper Sybil Lewis), who shows up unannounced and decides to have some fun—by not revealing her identity.

The characters are never pushed to the logical extremes we want. And the young male leads are such lousy actors we sometimes feel we're at a high school production. (Worst: they seem to think they're cute.) But as the female impersonator, Tim Moore (later Kingfish of TV's "Amos 'n' Andy") is an enjoyably, hideously unattractive fake Madame Deborah, full of fun and spark. Most importantly, though, there is a communal spirit here: the language, the doubletakes, the movements and postures, the gestures and mannerisms, and the attitudes of the characters are a world unto themselves, all comments on a certain segment of black urban life during the post-World War II era. A pleasurable viewing experience.

Brewster's Millions (1985)

D. Walter Hill. *S.* Herschel Weingrod and Timothy Harris; based on the novel by George Barr McCutcheon. *P.* Lawrence Gordon and Joel Silver. *R.* Universal Pictures. Cast includes: Jerry Orbach; Tovah Feldshuh; Pat Hingle; and Hume Cronin.

His white uncle's will stipulates that black Monty Brewster will inherit $300 million—only if he first spends $30 million within 30 days. It's meant to teach Monty the value of money. That's the premise of this attempt at screwball comedy starring Richard Pryor. *Brewster's Millions* had already been filmed several times: in 1921 with Fatty Arbuckle; in a 1935 British version with Jack Buchanan; in 1945 with Dennis O'Keefe (and a lively Eddie "Rochester" Anderson as O'Keefe's sidekick of sorts). Indicative of the colorless/raceless tone of the 1980s is the fact that almost no effort is made to turn it into a story expressly about a black character. At least in the 1970s, Pryor's film *Which Way Is Up?*, a remake of the Italian film *The Seduction of Mimi* (1974), was grounded in the black community. But now in tune with the 1980s crossover fixation, the black star is dumped into an acceptable, essentially white, racially neutral environment/situation that a large white audience can readily respond to. Even when the lightskinned beauty Lonette McKee, as an accountant assigned to add up all of Brewster's bills, is cast romantically opposite the white blond actor Stephen Collins, no reference to race nor any acknowledgment that theirs is an interracial affair is mentioned. In one sense, this may be good for McKee, the actress. But why are the producers doing all they can to remove the question of race? Once Pryor and McKee start eyeing one another, their romance is kept carefully under wraps: not once is there a passionate embrace between the two. Monty Brewster also has a white sidekick (John Candy) but there is neither much chemistry nor any fireworks between the two. At least when previously directing *48 Hrs.*, Walter Hill had used the interracial dynamics between Eddie Murphy and Nick Nolte to give the film its drive, also some of its edgy stylishness. *Brewster's Millions*, however, just about negates or neutralizes the very thing it hopes ensures box-office success: the great ethnic juices and creativity—and images—of the Crazy Nigger, Richard Pryor.

Watchable and occasionally entertaining but mostly without much pep. The best moments are the last five.

In *The New York Times*, Janet Maslin wrote: "The film does nothing to accommodate Mr. Pryor's singular comic talents . . . a screwball comedy minus the screws."

Bright Road (1953)

D. Gerald Mayer. S. Emmet Lavery; based on the story "See How They Run" by Mary Elizabeth Vroman. P. A Sol Baer Fielding Production. R. MGM. Cast includes: Vivian Dandridge (seen briefly in a teachers' meeting); Barbara Ann Sanders (as Tanya); Maidie Norman; Robert Horton (the only white in the cast); and Renee Beard.

This low-budget "little" movie followed in the wake and the tradition of the big studio problem pictures of 1949: *Pinky, Home of the Brave, Lost Boundaries,* and *Intruder in the Dust,* all of which dealt, in a new and then-daring way with the race problem in America. Here the focus is on the relationship between a black schoolteacher and the wayward black student she tries reaching. The teacher is the young Dorothy Dandridge: pert, pretty, and warm. The student is played by Philip Hepburn, who manages to convey youthful alienation without falling into the petulant "cutesiness" that infects the performances of so many child actors. And making his movie debut as the elementary school principal, who has a crush on the pretty teacher, is a handsome, engagingly shy Harry Belafonte. (Today viewers are often puzzled because Dandridge and Belafonte are not permitted a romantic relationship. Does this reveal the studio's fear of black sexuality?)

Bright Road does not have the dramatic tension or range of the problem pictures or of a movie like *No Way Out* with Sidney Poitier. It isn't a particularly *good* movie either. Often it's flat, humdrum, and too low-keyed and leisurely. Yet many viewers fall under its spell and like it nonetheless, mainly because it's so earnest, sweet-tempered, and mellow. All the performers approach their roles with a sensitivity and conviction that makes the movie appealing and rather touching.

The young Dandridge, only a year away from her triumphant performance in *Carmen Jones,* is lovely to look at, refreshing, and clear-eyed. Often today as black audiences watch her, they connect to this legendary star in a very special way, similar perhaps to the manner in which many respond to films with the young, seemingly innocent Marilyn Monroe. Because we're aware of the personal and professional tragedies that eventually overtook these women, their movies take an added significance and aura—and become documentaries and statements on the women themselves. Here, of course, is a Dandridge image different from that which most are familiar with. The soft and pliant nice girl of *Bright Road* later became the fiery, aggressive hedonist of *Carmen Jones*—and still later the jittery, nervous, sad-eyed melancholic of *Porgy and Bess* and *Malaga*.

At heart, despite its obvious limitations, *Bright Road* remains an unusual product: as one of the few films to deal sensitively with troubled black youth, it's just right for children and young adolescents to view. Yet it is seldom shown, on television or in revival theaters.

Broken Strings (1940)

D. Bernard E. Ray. S. Bernard E. Ray, Clarence Muse, and David Arlen. P. L. C. Borden Productions. R. International Roadshow. Cast includes: Stymie Beard (formerly of the "Our Gang" series) as a comic, shifty-eyed adolescent bad boy; Edward Thompson; Sybil Lewis; and William Washington.

Produced and directed outside Hollywood, this melodrama focusing on a concert violinist in conflict with himself and his son (a bright kid who prefers swing music to his father's classics) remains one of the most entertaining of the independently made all-black films of the 1930s and 1940s. It's clearly a bourgeois tale with everything neatly explained and put together (none of those truly fascinating sloppy loose ends and idiosyncrasies one constantly discovers in Oscar Micheaux's convoluted melodramas). But it was definitely an alternative for black movie audiences weary of Hollywood's comic stereotyped depictions of black characters.

Actor Clarence Muse, whose Hollywood servant roles were usually distinguished by the actor's innate sense of self-respect, finally had a chance to play a high-falutin', dignified professional man. And you can almost see him delighting in every highbrow bourgeois moment and piece of dialogue he has on screen. Possibly, it's his best movie role and should be: after all, he helped write the script!

Sometimes hokey and corny but fastmoving and fun.

Bronze Buckaroo (1938)

D. B. C. Kahn. S. Jed Buell. R. Hollywood Productions. Cast includes: Lucius Brooks; Clarence Brooks; Flournoy E. Miller.

As the star of the black western *Bronze Buckaroo*, singer Herb Jeffries (using his real name Herbert Jeffrey) emerged as an authentic hero for ghetto audiences in the late 1930s. He had all the markings of a true cowboy star: dashing good looks, fancy silver spurs and guns, a trusty sidekick named Dusty, a pretty sepia heroine to rescue, plenty of Tex Ritter/Gene Autry-type hairy heroics and as an added bonus, he had a chance to sing, too, becoming black America's first singing cowboy in the movies. Often sending the ladies in black movie houses into a swoon, Jeffries was clearly a black matinee idol.

Filmed on location at a black dude ranch near Victorville, California, *Bronze Buckaroo* (and another Jeffrey western *Harlem on the Prairie*) has an open and sunny look. Interestingly enough, the race movies' color fixation shows up here too. Jeffries and his leading lady (Artie Young)—light, bright, damn near white—are a hero and heroine contrasted with Jeffrey's dark sidekick (Dusty, of course) and a dark villain played by Spencer Williams.

The whole thing is almost fun. Other Herb Jeffrey westerns include the 1938 *Two-Gun Man From Harlem* and the 1939 *Harlem Rides the Range.*

The Brother from Another Planet (1984)

D. John Sayles. Director of photography: Ernest R. Dickerson (who later shot *She's Gotta Have It* in 1986). S. John Sayles. P. Peggy Rajski and Maggie Renzi. R. Cinecom. Cast includes: Minnie Gentry.

This is the story: a black alien from another planet (Joe Morton) comes to earth (and Harlem) in search of freedom. Somber, sensitive, sometimes impish, he's mute but is blessed with a healing power in his hands. Eventually, he sees a little of everything in Harlem: the basketball courts, the barrooms, the drug scene, the power of those with money, and the earthling's way of dealing with sex. The film reaches a climax first when the alien is able to defeat a corrupt white man who exploits the black community, then when he defeats two henchmen from his planet (one of whom is played by director Sayles) who've come to take him back to a life of slavery, we assume.

The title makes this sound like it's going to be pure fun, perhaps a nifty satire on relations within the black community. But the film limps along, failing to make use of its Harlem setting and also its residents, who are admittedly treated respectfully but who are left stripped of ethnic idiosyncrasies and cultural richness.

It's no doubt a mistake that the alien is mute. There could have been a wonderful play on language with the brother from another planet speaking his mind to the brothers on the street, each wondering where the other is really coming from. Black verbal interplay has always been clever, fun, inventive. So, too, has a sense of black personal style. The alien's clothes set him apart from the other residents, but the filmmaker doesn't seem to know what to do with that. Even a movie like *Blacula*, also about an alien from another time and place arriving in modern-day LA, played with the idea of opposing black styles in language, dress, demeanor. The muteness also seems to emasculate the hero, which may explain why the romantic sequence with Dee Dee Bridgewater and Morton stands out all the more: we see the Brother indulging in some manly pursuits.

Bridgewater is a pleasure here: playful, spunky, sweet. She has a flair as do some of the other black actors that the director cannot match in his own style, which points up what the movie really is: a low-budget, pleasant enough film by a white liberal moviemaker, who likes the idea of black style and energy but who hasn't the foggiest notion how to handle it.

Brother John (1971)

D. James Goldstone. *S.* Ernest Kinoy (who originally called the project *Kane*). *P.* Joel Glickman. *R.* Columbia Pictures. Cast also includes: Will Geer; Bradford Dillman; Zara Cully; and Lincoln Kilpatrick.

Sidney Poitier's production company E & R Productions undertook this project, the story of a mysterious man John Kane (Poitier) who, after many years' absence, returns to his Alabama hometown just before the death of his sister (Lynn Hamilton). No one understands how Kane knew of the woman's illness. As it turns out, Kane's a man who's shown up on the grim reaper's doorstep before, arriving at a time when others close to him hovered near death. A man who's seen almost everything as he's travelled the world over, Kane's a mystical figure of almost superhuman physical strength and mental powers. Highly intelligent, he speaks Russian, Chinese, French, Spanish, German, and Swahili. (Is it no wonder Poitier was called SuperSidney during this period in his career?) But what is John Kane? An angel of death? A fighter for the rights of the common man? The embodiment of human goodness?

Nobody knows. It's doubtful if anyone will care either. Eventually, the local sheriff and prosecutor, both assuming Kane's back in town simply to agitate local black factory workers on strike, decide to investigate him and get him out of town. The movie's so sluggish that we wish them luck. But to no avail.

This vague and shapeless film's huge adoring closeups of Poitier, meant to intrigue and move us, instead simply point up that Poitier, sullen and lifeless, possibly gives his most inaccessible performance. Occasionally the other actors relieve the tedium: Richard Ward (as the proud, tough brother-in-law), Paul Winfield (uncharacteristically cast as a loudmouth troublemaker), and Beverly Todd (lovely and convincing as an educated, sensitive, and alert schoolteacher [a modern black woman] who should know better than to get involved with the withdrawn Kane).

Brothers (1977)

D. Arthur Barron. *S.* Edward and Mildred Lewis. *P.* Edward and Mildred Lewis. *R.* Warner Bros. Cast includes: Ron O'Neal, who garnered excellent notices. "Strong in a brief role," wrote *Variety*. *Newsweek* added: "The most memorable performance comes from Ron O'Neal, now subdued and balding, as the helpful, long-suffering cellmate. . . . Black movies, like O'Neal, have developed a whole new sobriety since the days of *Super Fly*."

Even political radicals need romantic heroes, and in the late 1960s/early 1970s, black activist prisoner George Jackson and the brilliant, fiercely attractive activist college professor Angela Davis were precisely that: a gifted, politically committed, handsome black couple, who appealed very much to the young of the period. Jackson (who wrote *Soledad Brother* and was later killed in prison during an alleged escape attempt) and Davis (who popped up in headlines and on magazine covers when arrested for—and later acquitted of—charges of having aided Jackson's younger brother Jonathan in an aborted prison breakout plot) eventually had the tragic components that make certain cultural heroes mythic and larger than life. *Brothers* tries dealing with the romance between the two (a romance conducted while Jackson was behind bars; the two don't even get to kiss in the movie) and also with the brutality of life for a black man in prison. It's a fictionalized dramatization. (Jackson, played by Bernie Casey, is called David Thomas; Davis, portrayed by the cool beauty Vonetta McGee, is called Paula Jones.)

Newsweek's critic Charles Michener wrote: "A thorough, thoughtful film biography might have raised some troubling questions about the thin line separating radical tactics from common criminality, and it might have examined the conditions that made Jackson's brand of politics so compelling during the turbulent climate of the late 1960s. In its determination to look only on the sunny side, *Brothers* robs Jackson of all the idiosyncrasies that helped make him a hero." At the same time, though, Archer Winston of *The New York Post* felt the movie was a "powerful statement, a tragedy with no happy movie ending tacked on for final comfort." He added that Bernie Casey "has strength and dignity, and he is not asked by director Arthur Barron to indulge in theatrical excesses. Similarly, Vonetta McGee, a good looking actress, makes Angela Davis a very believable teacher-activist."

Bubbling Over (1934)

D. Leigh Jason. *S.* Bert Granet and Burnet Hershey. *P.* A Van Beuren Production. *R.* RKO Radio Pictures. Lyrics and music by Johnny Burke and Harold Spina. Cast includes: Frank Wilson; The Southernaires; Hamtree Harrington; and The Rosamond Johnson Choir.

An Ethel Waters short (20 minutes) focusing on a group of residents in a Harlem tenement. Not much of a story and full of stereotypes. At one point, as her lazy, good-for-nothing husband sleeps on a hammock, Waters, in desperation, tries waking the guy by shoving a stick pin into him. When the director ignores the feeble plot and concentrates on the great Waters, the film takes on some stature. She sings "Taking Your Times," "Harlem Express," and the haunting "Darkies Never Cry," which she turns into a stoic lament and sometimes a bitter, ironic comment on broken dreams, lost hopes. Often when singing, Waters seems inappropriately to flash her wide emblematic Broadway smile, negating some of the pessimistic power of her music. Yet one assumes she uses it as a restraint on herself. If she dropped the smile and warm relaxed manner, her rendition of "Darkies Never Cry" might have been too upsetting for her white audience—and for her.

Buck and the Preacher (1972)

D. Sidney Poitier. *S.* Ernest Kinoy (who later also wrote *Leadbelly* and parts of "Roots"); based on an idea by black writer Drake Walker. Filmed in Durango, Mexico. *P.* Joel Glickman. *R.* Columbia Pictures; an E & R Productions/Belafonte Enterprises Film. Cast includes: Cameron Mitchell; Lynn Hamilton; Errol John; Julie Robinson; James McEachin; Clarence Muse; Nita Talbot; Doug Johnson; Pamela Jones; Dennis Hines; Drake Walker; and Jose Carlos Ruiz.

An action-packed black comedy Western that arrived amidst the flood of blaxploitation films of the period. It came as a total surprise and today ranks as one of the few of its kind—and one of the most entertaining, too.

Set in the years immediately following the Civil War, it features Sidney Poitier as a wagonmaster leading a group of freed slaves to homesteads—and to safety. Joining Poitier is Harry Belafonte as a feisty, funky comic conman of a preacher. Ruby Dee's around, too, as Sidney's faithful woman. (What else???) All are pursued by a band of bounty hunters (led by Cameron Mitchell) determined to take the former slaves back into servitude.

This movie marks Poitier's directorial debut. Originally, John Sargent was set to direct but was replaced after a few days of shooting (reportedly because of friction with Belafonte). Poitier himself then stepped in, and this remains his best and most deeply committed directorial effort. After having starred for years as the liberal fantasy model integrationist hero (always conciliatory and "reasonable"), Poitier re-established his roots with the black community with this item, the first of his movies pitched directly at the black market. This movie's also been enjoyed by white audiences—as have Poitier's other crossover films *Uptown Saturday Night* and *Let's Do It Again*. As a director, Poitier's generous almost to a fault: he turns the picture over to Belafonte, who gives his most robust and idiosyncratic performance. Gone is the passive stoicism of the Mr. Beautiful Black America of *Bright Road* and

Carmen Jones, replaced here by a true eccentric with astounding reserves of personality and character. The picture is Belafonte's.

Poitier himself sleepwalks through most of the action, somber and heroic but lifeless. In future films, director Poitier often remained this way, using each picture to spotlight the talents of a co-star. His second directed feature, *A Warm December*, showcased the lovely Esther Anderson; later he gave such movies as *Uptown Saturday Night* and *A Piece of the Action* to Bill Cosby. It's lamentable because at this point in his career, Poitier was still ripe for challenging dramatic roles, and the movies he directed wasted him as an actor. But you can't have everything. In the case of *Buck and the Preacher*, Poitier's readily forgiven because this is a rousing entertainment with a certain degree of historical significance and political thought, too. The blacks of *Buck and the Preacher* unite with American Indians at one point to battle the white man, their mutual oppressor. Could politically conscious audiences have hoped for more from commercial cinema?

A highpoint is the sequence of Poitier, Belafonte, and tiny Ruby Dee triumphantly riding across the plains. Theaters came alive with patrons openly cheering the trio on. The ride, as well as the picture itself, represented a homecoming of sorts, three talented black stars re-connecting with the black audience in a direct, personal way. An ideal movie for children and adolescents.

Buck Benny Rides Again (1940)

D. Mark Sandrich. S. William Morrow and Edmund Beloin; based on an adaptation by Zion Meyrs of a story by Arthur Stringer. P. Mark Sandrich. R. Paramount Pictures. Cast includes: Phil Harris; Andy Devine; Ellen Drew; Dennis Day; and Ward Bond.

Any Jack Benny movie in which Eddie "Rochester" Anderson appeared is bound to have dazzling bursts of energy and wit. That's certainly the case with *Buck Benny Rides Again*. "Eddie Anderson," wrote *Variety*, "as in *Man About Town*, has a particularly meaty portion of lines and crossfire to deliver a highlighted performance." This marks the period when Rochester/Anderson's career was on the rise, a time when he surprised and delighted audiences not only with his rapidfire delivery but also his dancing. Jack Benny had great control over his films and was thankfully wise and secure enough to let the scriptwriter provide Rochester with moments to showcase his best talents. Benny and Rochester were also almost as much of a team as Bob Hope and Bing Crosby in their road pictures, but no one's ever wanted to admit that.

Most of the fun in watching Rochester was seeing the very clever and resourceful manner in which he outwitted Mr. Benny. In one scene in *Buck Benny Rides Again*, Rochester uses every excuse in the book to get out of Benny's apartment so he can meet his girlfriend. Finally, he says that the stork has presented his aunt with twins this very afternoon, and he must visit. "If I remember correctly," says Benny, "the stork visited your aunt two months ago." "He sure gets around," replies Rochester. Finally the servant wins out. Benny is going to a party and plans to wear his full-dress suit. Rochester tells him the suit is inappropriate and advises him to wear something else. Benny finally complies, wears another suit of clothing and then takes off. The film then very cleverly cuts to the next sequence and who do we see driving up to his girlfriend's apartment in the boss's car wearing the boss's top hat and the boss's dress suit but crafty old Rochester! This kind of thing happens time and again in the Rochester/Benny films.

Throughout *Buck Benny Rides Again*, Anderson's demeanor and clear perspective are those of a man who plays at being a servant yet knows that there's nothing inferior or truly servile about himself. He feels he can operate with the best of them and within the confines of the script, he does just that. He's a thoroughly free, uninhibited spirit.

Rochester is also granted a privilege usually denied black actors, namely some cinematic love life. Theresa Harris, the beautiful brown-skinned actress who was to lose a chance at leading roles because of Hollywood's color fixation, appeared here and in another Rochester/Benny film *Love Thy Neighbor* as Rochester's girlfriend Josephine.

Bucktown (1975)

D. Arthur Marks. S. Bob Ellison. P. Bernard Schwartz. R. AIP. Cast includes some skilled performers, some of whom later went on to better things: Tony King; Bernie Hamilton (previously of the 1964 movie *One Potato, Two Potato*, later of the 70s series "Starsky and Hutch"); Tierre Turner; Thalmus Rasulala; and Carl Weathers (before his days as Apollo Creed in the *Rocky* movies).

"Sin City" should be the name of this small Southern town in which graft and depravity are pervasive. Not only are the whites villainous, hateful, and corrupt; so, too, are many of the blacks. Hero Fred Williamson is the stalwart fellow out to clean up the muck. He's avenging the death of his brother, who's been killed by the town's corrupt white police force. He's also the lucky son-of-a-gun who's making sure his brother's widow, luscious Pam Grier, is well taken care of, in bed and out of it.

Fights, blood, and gore abound but mostly tedium is the call of the day. *Variety* called it "violent garbage" and also commented that Grier's role "could set back femme lib at least a decade." The United States Catholic Conference also gave the movie a "condemned" rating, describing it as a "vicious, mindless" product, "produced as usual by whites, a little paradox that brings to mind the Communist maxim about the greedy capitalist eager to sell the rope that will be used to hang him." Perhaps *Bucktown* is a prime example of what came to be known as the blaxploitation film. But, frankly, it lacks even the kick and kink that have made some features of this genre (namely such Pam Grier sado-masochistic epics as *Coffy* and *Foxy Brown*) sometimes fun and funny. This one's just dreadful.

Bustin' Loose (1981)

D. Oz Scott. S. Roger L. Simon; based on a story idea by Richard Pryor and Lonne Elder III. P. Richard Pryor and Michael S. Glick; Executive Producer, William Greaves. R. Universal. Cast includes: Robert Christian (as the prissy boyfriend Cicely Tyson eventually gives up for Pryor); Alphonso Alexander; Kia Cooper; Edwin DeLeon; Jimmy Hughes; Tami Luchow; Angel Ramirez; Janet Wong; Bill Quinn; and Roy Jenson.

Originally titled *Family Dreams*, this movie had been completed before the accident in which Richard Pryor was so severely burned. But because studio executives were unsatisfied with it, *Bustin' Loose* sat on the shelf for almost two years. After Pryor's accident, however, and the smash box-office appeal of *Stir Crazy*, Universal dusted the movie off, adding some new scenes plus four songs by Roberta Flack, and then released it to commercial success. Critically, *Bustin' Loose* was not well received. But I think most would agree with the assessment of *New York* critic David Denby who wrote: "No one could mistake *Bustin' Loose* for a good movie, but it's friendly and good-hearted in a way that's hard to resist."

At heart, it's a family picture: a flimsy ex-con (Richard Pryor) and a prim schoolteacher (Cicely Tyson) marshall a group of emotionally disturbed children across country (from Philadelphia to a new home in Seattle) aboard a very shaky old schoolbus. The movie has one serious flaw: the rough, often foul language (Pryor's familiar barrage of profanity) is far more appropriate for a nightclub audience than for the Saturday matinee kiddie crowd. Yet even at that, the movie has some special moments, due mainly to Pryor's high-spirited highjinks. His encounter with the Ku Klux Klan is riotously funny and perfectly executed. It's one of the rare sequences in the film directed with a good sense of timing. The oddball romantic pairing of Pryor and Tyson reminds one occasionally of Hepburn and Bogart in *The African Queen*. Although neither has much of a character to work with, they still exude a warm glow when together. Tyson doesn't have any heavy dramatics here (the role really wastes her great talents), but rarely has she been more charming.

Although he receives no billing, Michael Schultz has usually been credited with directing part of this film.

Cabin in the Sky (1943)

D. Vincente Minnelli. *S.* Joseph Shrank; based on the musical play by Lynn Root; lyrics, John Latouche; music, Vernon Duke; additional songs by Harold Arlen and E. Y. Harburg. *P.* Arthur Freed. *R.* MGM.

This was Hollywood's first black musical since *Hearts in Dixie* and King Vidor's classic *Hallelujah* of 1929. Despite its critics, *Cabin in the Sky* remains one of the most entertaining and best-made musicals in the history of American movies.

Based on the very successful Broadway musical, the movie is a fantasy: an all-Negro Heaven and an all-Negro Hell are fighting for the soul of a Common Man, Little Joe Jackson (played to gentle comic perfection by Eddie "Rochester" Anderson). Hell's forces, through the aid of a slinky seductress called Georgia Brown (Lena Horne), almost grab hold of him. But eventually Little Joe's wife Petunia (Ethel Waters) saves the day *and* her man through some *powerful prayin.*

The criticism of *Cabin in the Sky*? Well, once again the image of the American Negro was the singing, dancing, crap-shooting, clowning creature set off in an all-black world of fun and frivolity, removed from the social and political realities of the period. Reviewing the film, *PM* wrote that it ". . . was the same old, unchanging Darktown-strutter business, with special zoot suits and old-time religion added." *Time* added: "The Negroes are apparently regarded less as artists (despite their very high potential of artistry) than as picturesque, Sambo-style entertainers."

During the restless 1960s, politically oriented, younger black audi-

Cabin in the Sky's *star power: Lena Horne (as Georgia Brown), Eddie "Rochester" Anderson (as Little Joe Jackson), and Ethel Waters (as the patient, long-suffering Petunia).*

ences felt the same as *Time*'s reviewer. But by the 1970s and 1980s, the film was looked at in a far different light. Granted *Cabin in the Sky* is neither a serious nor accurate depiction of black life in America. Nor is it authentic black folk culture as the moviemakers would have us believe. But what is authentic, beyond denial, are the vast talents of the extraordinary performers, all of whom bring a high energy level, humor, and a dazzling sense of style to the material. In fact, at any given moment almost everyone looks ready to steal the show. The cast includes some of the most famous black performers of the twentieth century: not only Waters, Anderson, and Horne but also Rex Ingram (as Lucifer, Jr.), Butterfly McQueen, Duke Ellington, Louis Armstrong, Mantan Moreland, Willie Best, Ernest Whitman, Nick Stewart, Ruby Dandridge (the mother of Dorothy), Oscar Polk, Kenneth Spencer, Ford Lee "Buck" Washington, and John "Bubbles" Sublett (of Buck and Bubbles), and the Hall Johnson Choir. Waters performs a lovely rendition of "Happiness Is Just a Thing Called Joe" and scores equally well on "Taking a Chance on Love" with Rochester. Horne and Rochester also have a great duet with a number called "Consequences." The highpoint comes during the big nightclub finale: here Ellington plays, Horne and Waters fight it out over Rochester, and John "Bubbles" Sublett—cool, slick, dapper, and debonair—does a deliriously exciting staircase tap dance to "Shine." All of this is capped with Waters's exuberant (she's part jitterbug, part oldtime chorus girl doing high kicks) dance with John "Bubbles" Sublett. It's an unforgettable sequence.

Among Waters' other fine moments is a very funny scene in which she teaches two scam artists (Ernest Whitman and Nick Stewart) how to play with their own loaded dice. Naturally, she wins!

Funny, charming, and warm, this movie is shown consistently at black film festivals. As in *Stormy Weather* (another all-star, all-black musical released the same year), the black performers transcend their stereotyped roles brilliantly and show themselves off at their very best. Shot in sepia-tone.

California Suite (1978)

D. Herbert Ross. S. Neil Simon; based on his play. P. Ray Stark. R. Columbia Pictures (a Ray Stark Production).

Neil Simon's comic rendition of *Grand Hotel*.

A group of glittering, sophisticated travelers take up temporary residence in the shimmering Beverly Hills Hotel. There they wrestle with their problems and their partners. Included on the guest list are Jane Fonda, Alan Alda, Maggie Smith, Michael Caine, Walter Matthau, and Elaine May, and also as vacationing hotel guests Richard Pryor and Bill Cosby with Gloria Gifford and Shelia Frazier as their respective wives. Unfortunately, while the white stars are provided an opportunity to express some intelligence and ingenuity through their half-baked, pseudo-sophisticated dialogue, the black couples are culturally deprived: at heart, they have no dialogue. Instead they bear the weight of comic slapstick as we watch everything go wrong with their vacation: cars are beyond their control; their hotel room suddenly floods, sending them into a panic; and even on a tennis court, these supposedly "natural-born athletes" are coony clutzes.

Cosby and Pryor portray successful black professionals (they're doctors) but their childish pranks and "primitive" low humor (Cosby bites Pryor's nose at one point) marks them as being out of place in this swanky, privileged hotel. The idea: you can take the coloreds out of the country but, Lord, you can't possibly take the country out of the coloreds. What makes it all worst is that the black slapstick episodes are so much at variance with the relatively cultivated behavior of the rest of the cast.

A redeeming factor might have been inspired performances by Cosby and Pryor. But the best either could have done with this dreary material would have been to have stayed away from it.

Added note: in the original Neil Simon Broadway play on which the film's based, the vacationing doctors and their wives were played by whites.

When *New Yorker* critic Pauline Kael suggested that the Cosby/Pryor sequence smacked of racism, Cosby responded angrily, defending his role in the film.

Car Wash (1976)

D. Michael Schultz. S. Joel Schumacher. P. Art Linson and Gary Stromberg. R. Universal. Cast includes: The Pointer Sisters; George Carlin; Arthur French; Lauren Jones; De Wayne Jessie; Melanie Mayron; Clarence Muse; and Ren Woods.

Did anyone leave *Car Wash* thinking about the solid performance turned in by Ivan Dixon? Did any of the younger audience members of the 1970s who flocked to see this disjointed, effervescent effort even know who Ivan Dixon was? Or the exact place he holds in black film history? Ironically, in this peppy, light-headed glimpse at a day in the life of a car wash in which a number of talented performers with high levels of energy and enthusiasm bounced in and out, it was Dixon's disturbingly quiet and understated performance that anchored the movie in the kind of sturdy reflective realism it seemed hellbent on avoiding.

Car Wash is a loose, free-wheeling and episodic picture that resembles, in structure if not theme, Robert Altman's *Nashville* and parts of *American Graffiti* and even its director Michael Schultz's earlier hit *Cooley High*. Here, as we are introduced to a group of characters frenetically making their way through life's daily joys and dilemmas, the camera seems to ramble about as much as the carefree cast, falling on this sight or scene, casually picking up bits and pieces of dialogue or comic pathos. But the highjinks don't lead anywhere, not even to the kind of thematically unrealistic but dramatically effective climax that gave *Cooley High* a certain shape, if not vision. The emotional zinger (such as the assassination in *Nashville*) that could suddenly shake off the lethargy which the movie has steadily created never comes. Nor are any of the episodes aesthetic entities unto themselves. Nothing is fully thought out in this picture. And instead of some comic truth that would unify the episodes, *Car Wash* settles for leaning back, lying low, and meandering over familiar terrain that's populated by a bundle of loose notions and a troupe of engaging types: the mild-mannered, decent young dude pining over his dream girl, a haughty waitress in a nearby restaurant; the homely, chunky but likable white girl; the nutty mutt of a Maoist, son of the car wash's steamy proprietor; the big, fat jolly brother out for nothing more than a fresh piece of ass; the sensitive, tormented young militant; the prissily confident queen; the gleaming, beaming conman preacher. All these types are worth further examination but the picture passes over them almost as impersonally as it does over the cars being washed and concentrates instead on a series of tired, worn gags and pranks. Hot sauce is poured onto someone's sandwich, and the audience is supposed to howl. Someone else, equipped with Mousketeer ears, peeps at a girl on the toilet. Here *Car Wash*'s sense of humor is stunted without emotional fiber or resilience, the pranks themselves on a par with the fantasies of a twelve-year-old who's been seeing too many TV re-runs of "The Little Rascals" or "The Dead End Kids." Basically, *Car Wash* tells us life is a lark without any serious issues or crises.

So what keeps us watching? At heart, I think it's the feeling that beneath all the merriment and tomfoolery that certain characters— such as the revolutionary and the waitress—are driven by unexplained yearnings and personal fears. The revolutionary (Bill Duke) is the only figure with some type of political philosophy, but, more often than not, he is put into an embarrassing situation. He does not seem hip to what life is really all about. And because the movie so often celebrates the *hip*, he looks as if he's a loser unable to enjoy and simply take things in stride the way the other car washers do. Clearly, this character has not been worked out by writer Joel Schumacher (who also did the script for *Sparkle*), and it is hard to tell whether he is meant as some serious statement on political activism or as an object of satire. Actually, some might feel it would make more sense if the character were both. Duke, however, who plays the part with an uncertain reserve and intensity that are far too ambiguous, looks almost as if he was forced to do the scriptwriter's job, to figure out just who or what the revolutionary stands for.

At the same time, Tracy Reed's waitress might have been able to affect audiences in a far deeper way had not her character been so poorly sketched by the writer. Reed plays the hincty (vernacular for *haughty*), somewhat brittle woman on whom Franklyn Ajaye's character has a heavy crush. But he can't get to first base with her. Reed is a very attractive young actress who might have been dismissed as nothing more than a pretty face had she not infused the script's lackluster creation with her own authority and sense of pride. She is the kind of female all of us have seen any number of times, a cynical, ambitious young woman who no doubt has *had* it with the jive turkeys coming in and out of the restaurant, filling her ears with a lot of sweet-sounding crap. She's looking for something else out of life, and she is one of the few characters in the picture whose dissatisfaction with the daily scheme of things—with life's shortchanges and subtle shoddy tricks—is most obvious.

At the climax when Ajaye warns that she is foolish to wait for someone else to come along when here he is, her black prince, Reed is

High spirits and a loose episodic structure: Michael Schultz's highly successful Car Wash *with (l. to r). veteran actor Clarence Muse, Franklyn Ajaye, two of the Pointer Sisters, and Richard Pryor.*

made to settle for him. Even if the script is unaware of the basic issues here, surely the audience knows intuitively that, of course, she should wait or look for more. Why not? Reed does the scene convincingly. We almost believe she does care for the likable lout. But here the female character's ambition is put down by the male scriptwriter's own lack of insight, and although her consent to date Ajaye provides a fitting romantic denouement, it is hollow, untrue, and basically, a cheap trick.

Structurally and dramatically, *Car Wash* is a washout. Yet audiences continue to *like* it. The film has had important network showings, and it turns up in black film festivals. And what makes the darn thing, shallow as it is, an interesting viewing experience is, naturally, the actors, almost all of whom are good. Such performers as Antonio Fargas (who has been quite good in a string of movies, everything from *Putney Swope* to *Foxy Brown* to *Conrack*), Garrett Morris (from *Cooley High* and TV's "Saturday Night Live") and the indefatigable Richard Pryor appear more at home with their material than do Reed and Duke because, no doubt aware that their figures are caricatures, they play them as such and are intermittently sparkling and entertaining. Sometimes the cast of *Car Wash* appears to be scrimmaging madly for laughs. But more often than not, the actors invigorate the movie with a fresh and wholly original, improvisatory, razzle-dazzle, jivey style that keeps it from being just another TV sitcom. Here being black is the best thing this movie has going for it. Imagine *Car Wash* as a white movie? Would anybody think twice about it?

Amidst all the comic mayhem, though, there is Ivan Dixon, striding through with cool sober assurance. It is hard to believe this is the same actor who played Duff Anderson, the troubled southern black man refusing to kowtow in the highly acclaimed black-oriented "art" film of the 1960s, *Nothing but a Man*. In that earlier film, Dixon was thinner and perhaps more intense. And he had given a first-rate, deeply felt performance that should have brought him stardom. But no significant role followed. The years between that movie and *Car Wash* could not have been easy ones. And Dixon seems to carry his personal history with him.

In *Car Wash*, he looks older, heavier, and wearier, reminiscent at times of that mighty fortress Juano Hernandez in *Intruder in the Dust*. He's a man who knows himself and life's perilous intricacies. He is without either the desire or energy to stoop to prove anything to anyone. As the ex-con not earning enough money to make ends meet, Dixon has a cliched part. When his two children visit him at the car wash, he finds himself caught in a sentimentally hokey scene. Yet he gives in to neither the sentimentality nor falsity of the sequence. He plays it straight and comes across as being a profoundly decent man. The integrity and burning sincerity Dixon communicates are seldom in the script. Instead they are there in the way he speaks to the other characters, in the calm way he looks over and through them, and finally, in the manner in which he persuades a would-be-thief to turn the gun away.

Watching Ivan Dixon in *Car Wash*, we see a man who somehow seems to have kept his dignity intact. He's able to hypnotize even the camera because there remains about him something we cannot fully understand. Throughout much of *Car Wash*, I repeatedly had the feeling that Dixon saw something else going on. It was almost as if he knew what the picture *could be*. He also knew what it was. Something irreducible in him escapes, puzzles, and momentarily transcends *Car Wash*, occasionally sweeping the picture up to reveal the likable hollowness that pervades it and the significant comic social commentary it somehow has lost.

Carbon Copy (1981)

D. Michael Schultz. S. Stanley Shapiro. P. Carter De Haven; Executive Producer, John Daly. R. Avco Embassy. Cast includes: Susan St. James; Jack Warden; and Dick Martin.

Carbon Copy's plot is simple and direct: a middle-aged white executive (George Segal) arrives in his executive suite one fine morning to find a young black man (Denzel Washington) who promptly calls him Dad. The young man is the executive's son, the product of a romance that Segal had had years earlier with a young black woman, now conveniently dead. *Carbon Copy* then proceeds to show the effect of this kid on the executive's lifestyle. Once the secret is out, Segal soon loses wife, job, position, Rolls-Royce, and his own sense of self. Yet all is not lost. After various scrapes and escapades, father and son are blissfully reunited at the fadeout, driving off together in a battered car, heading for the sunset, we assume, aware that they're going to make the best of life no matter what. *Carbon Copy* has a few diverting moments. But, essentially, it's a white movie dressed up like a black one.

Carbon Copy has an appropriate hero for the Reagan 1980s: Mr. average middle-class white American. The movie wants the audience to believe in the myth of the tragic, middle-class, middle-aged white man. That we can handle. We just ignore the jibberish. But what's most distressing about this film is the way in which it disposes of the black actor and the black director.

As the son, Denzel Washington is likable but miscast. He seems well scrubbed and untouched by experience; he belongs on the old "Good Times" TV series, perhaps as one of those endearing, earnest, patently false boyfriends perfect for poor Thelma. There is no indication whatsoever here that this actor would be capable ever of giving a strong, virile performance. But that's precisely what Washington later did on stage in *A Soldier's Play* and then in the film *A Soldier's Story*. One wonders here though how the heck black director Michael Schultz could have committed such a casting flub. Washington hardly looks mulatto. A kid close to the white ideal (like perhaps Brian Mitchell of TV's "Trapper John, M.D."), who's not accepted simply because of the *thought* of black blood, might have made white audiences realize how foolish their whole color syndrome is.

But with all that aside, the black actor of real concern here is the great Paul Winfield, who as a lawyer advising Segal is reduced to a mere walk-on. To see him with nothing to do (not even a solid supporting role) is terribly sad. Is this the best that commercial American movies have to offer one of the finest dramatic actors, black or white, around?

At the same time, director Schultz cannot do anything to beef up the Winfield character or the movie itself, just letting it drag along like a saggy TV sitcom. The choice of Schultz as director, as opposed to the choice of a more idiosyncratic and no doubt less "manageable" black talent, say, like Melvin Van Peebles, points up the movie industry's decision to play it safe with even quasi-black material. There's no director to speak of here, only some kind of floor manager.

In the final analysis, *Carbon Copy* may well be the type of black-oriented movie the industry felt most comfortable with in the early 1980s—not one that dealt with black tensions or joys but one that focused, in a very coy way, on the problems white America believed it had to contend with in black America. (The same is true of the 1986 comedy *Soul Man*.) As such, *Carbon Copy* ends by being bad copy. It's a white movie done in blackface. Even at that, the makeup job's not a very convincing one.

Carmen Jones (1954)

D. Otto Preminger. *S.* Harry Kleiner, from the stage version by Oscar Hammerstein II. *P.* Otto Preminger. *R.* 20th Century-Fox.

A big, lavish, sometimes gaudy, sometimes vulgar, but always energetic and entertaining all-black musical (the first Hollywood had filmed in 11 years). Bizet's hot opera *Carmen* has been transformed into the tale of a fiery parachute factory worker in Florida named Carmen Jones (Dorothy Dandridge), who lures a good clean-cut colored boy (Harry Belafonte) into deserting the army and following after her. Later when she deserts him for a prizefighter named Husky Miller (Joe Adams), the jilted good boy turns bad, finally catching up with Carmen, then strangling her to death. But, of course, because *Carmen Jones* is a musical, while he kills the thing he loves, the poor fellow sings to her at the same time!

Despite the in-built corniness, this black musical, like those few others in Hollywood's history such as *Cabin in the Sky*, *Stormy Weather*, *Porgy and Bess*, and *The Wiz*, spotlights some dazzling black talents: a tame but likably handsome Belafonte; a young Diahann Carroll, long before her emergence as a glamor puss, looking rather like a country girl; a surly, snarling Brock Peters as a villainous army officer (a precursor to his role as Crown in *Porgy and Bess*); a sweet Olga James as Cindy Lou (the good girl); and Pearl Bailey, an absolute marvel of cantankerous vitality and pizzazz. When Bailey belts "Beat Out That Rhythm on a Drum," she does for her sequence what Paul Robeson did for his when he sang "Ol' Man River" in *Show Boat*: she takes the whole high-falutin' nonsense to another level, in this instance one of transcendent fun and high spirits. Roy Glenn and Nick Stewart are also on hand. And glimpsed briefly are jazz drummer Max Roach and the dancer Carmen de Lavallade.

But striding above them all is Dandridge, who was lauded by almost all the critics. *Time* wrote that she "holds the eye—like a match burning steadily in a tornado. Actress Dandridge employs to perfection the method of the coquette: by never giving more than she has to, she hints that she has more than she has given." *Variety* heralded her as "a sultry Carmen, whose performance maintains the right hedonistic note throughout." And *Life* added: "Of all the divas of grand opera—from Emma Calve of the 1900s to Rise Stevens—none was ever so decorative or will reach nationwide fame so quickly as the sultry young lady . . . on *Life*'s cover this week." Dandridge became one of the first black women to appear on the cover of this national publication. Her charismatic star performance won her an Oscar nomination as Best Actress,

Dorothy Dandridge and Harry Belafonte in Otto Preminger's lavish, all-black musical Carmen Jones.

the first black performer ever nominated for an Academy Award in the leading actress category.

Carmen Jones has held up well. Although frequently holding to the familiar Hollywood idea of a "high time in Darky Town"—all the performers seem to be "natural born entertainers"—the film's director Preminger keeps the action moving, and the performers transform the comic book ideas and antics through the high artistic caliber of their work and their determination to give the picture as much energy and style as possible.

"Energy, in fact," wrote *Time*, "is the essence of this picture; the audience is not merely stimulated, it is all but electrocuted. Even the huge CinemaScope screen seems hardly big enough to carry the mass scenes." *Time* added: "It also seems likely that the picture will fling somewhat wider the gates of opportunity for Negro entertainers in Hollywood. For in this picture the actors present themselves not merely as racial phenomena but as individuals, and they put across a *Carmen* that may blister the rear walls of many a movie house."

Although not a blockbuster hit, *Carmen Jones* did turn a profit for its studio.

An added note: despite the fact that both Dandridge and Belafonte were singers, their voices were not considered suitable for the operatic score; therefore their arias were dubbed respectively by Marilyn Horne and LeVern Hutcherson.

Chained Heat (1983)

D. Paul Nicolas. S. Vincent Mongol and Paul Nicolas. P. Billy Fine. R. Jensen Farley Pictures. Cast includes: Stella Stevens; Linda Blair; Sybil Danning; Edy Williams; Nita Talbot; and Henry Silva.

In the mid-1970s, Pam Grier and Tamara Dobson were rivals of sorts, each playing tough, macho super-mamas in such movies as *Coffy* and

Cleopatra Jones. Ironically, Grier had started her career in the early 1970s in such women's-prison-movies as *The Big Doll House* and *Black Mama, White Mama.* Unfortunately, by early 1980s, it almost looked as if Tamara Dobson were about to *end* her career in the same kind of vehicle. *Chained Heat*'s the film in point, a tawdry tale of women behind bars, female inmates fighting it out in a world of violence, drugs, and corruption. The prison officials, as should be expected in this kind of thing, can't be trusted and exploit the inmates while the inmates, in turn, exploit one another. There's steamy sex, lesbianism, and some strong language. Then there's Dobson, long-legged and looking mildly drawn. She knows she's better than this trash, but she gives her famous leg kicks when confronted with some tough opponents and sometimes flashes her sweet smile. Oddly enough, in this potboiler, her screen personality is stronger than in her earlier films. The actress herself has obviously been through *something*, and although the movie has no intention of telling us what that *something* is, it makes her an interesting screen presence nonetheless.

The movie itself is for diehard women's-prison-movie addicts. Surprisingly, there are many such creatures around; it's just unfortunate that most movies dealing with women in chains can't delve into the subject with any sense of style or insight. This kind of exploitative trash *could* be fun but that's not the case here.

A Change of Mind (1969)

D. Robert Stevens. S. Seeleg Lester and Richard Weston. P. Seeleg Lester and Richard Weston. R. Cinerama. Cast includes: Janet Mac-Lachlan, Clarise Taylor, Leslie Nielsen, and Hope Clarke.

A white man's brain is successfully transplanted into the skull of a black man. Science fiction? A civics lesson in biological race relations? A race-relations fantasy? It's a little of all three, although mostly *A Change of Mind* is a serviceable exploitation picture touching on the then-new hot genre for Hollywood: tough, gritty *issue* pictures dealing with black America. The old problem pictures of the 1940s were now thought to have presented black problems in too sanitized a manner (but certainly with more intelligence and conviction). Now a call was going out for dramas telling-it-like-it-is. This film precedes the blaxploitation era, which arrived within the next three years.

Raymond St. Jacques, briefly a leading man in the then-emerging new black Hollywood, plays the black man walking around with a white man's mind. He's a district attorney who's lived a cozy, comfortable, mildly privileged existence, never having had to question social or racial issues that now smack him right in the face. Susan Oliver is well cast as the white man's wife, who simply cannot cope with her husband's new black body!

Variety wrote that "Raymond St. Jacques does a superior acting job in the lead role." It also called *A Change of Mind* "a gimmick picture with enough shock value and imaginative speculation to make this . . . an exploitable entry for the market where racial themes have been well received," but added that "the gimmick overpowers credulity."

Actually, the movie can be endured. Sometimes unintentionally funny, other times straining too hard, it's a B-movie with a bit of a brain but not a great one.

Added note: the music is by Duke Ellington.

China Seas (1935)

D. Tay Garnett. S. Jules Furthman and James K. McGuinness. P. Albert Lewin; an Irving Thalberg Production. R. MGM. Cast includes: C. Aubrey Smith and Dudley Diggs.

A high-seas adventure on a passenger ship that sails from Shanghai to Singapore. On board are a roster of vintage MGM stars of the 1930s: Clark Gable, Jean Harlow, Wallace Beery, Lewis Stone, Rosalind Russell, and Robert Benchley. Quite entertaining and lots of fun. Late in the picture there's a perky surprise: unbilled, Hattie McDaniel shows up. Throughout the picture, we've already seen Gable and Harlow talking fast and tough to one another. He's the only one who can match the Harlow temperament, so we think, until Hattie's arrival. She hasn't much to do but she's just as quick and wittily entertaining as the two principal stars. In one sequence, Harlow asks Hattie, "Would you say I look like a lady?" Reading while reclining on a divan of sorts, McDaniel replies, "Nosum, Miss. I been with you all too long to insult you that way." Harlow then asks, "Say, what's the difference? What's that snotty English dame got that I ain't." McDaniel then says, "She's more refined like. She would never wear that dress with all them shiney beads you got. That dress is more *my* type." She then gives Harlow a devilishly wicked smile. "You been hinting for that dress for a month," Harlow says, "go on and take it." Immediately, McDaniel springs up and goes to get the dress, telling Harlow, "You sure got the right feeling though, honey." McDaniel takes the scene in her hands and is a wonder to behold, showing everyone how she could use her talent to walk away with a scene. She's also supremely confident, relaxed, no-nonsense. Was there ever any other black movie maid who spoke to her mistress while reclining on a divan!

Perfect for movie buffs. Also a perfect example of the black movie servant period at—no doubt unfortunately—its absolute best.

Cinderella Liberty (1973)

D. Mark Rydell. S. Darryl Ponicson; based on Ponicson's novel. P. Mark Rydell. R. 20th Century-Fox. Cast includes: Eli Wallach and Burt Young.

Promoted as an "unexpected love story," this is the drama of a sailor (James Caan), on leave, who meets and falls in love with a beautiful prostitute (Marsha Mason). The real "romance" though is between the sailor and the prostitute's young half-black son, played with smooth precision by Kirk Calloway. Because the boy's mother has had no time for him, the sailor reaches out to the kid, aware that this brash, streetwise, assertive, and intensely likable boy has always had to fend for himself and has rarely looked to anybody for support. Caan and Calloway work quite well together. Vulnerable, bright, funny, Calloway presents a rare screen portrait (one vaguely reminiscent of the boy in the 1940s film *The Quiet One*): a black kid who we know has the will to survive on those mean streets of the city but who, if he doesn't connect to somebody along the way, will lose his fundamental warmth—and his heart, too.

Sentimental, hokey, old-fashioned, tear-jerky yet worth seeing for Calloway's performance and for one of the subjects—a black boy coming of age—the movie struggles to get a grip on.

Claudine (1974)

D. John Berry. *S.* Tina and Lester Pine. *P.* Hannah Weinstein. *R.* 20th Century-Fox release of a Third World Cinema Production, in association with Joyce Selznick and Tina Pine. Cast includes: Adam Wade; David Kruger; Yvette Curtis; Eric Jones; and Socorro Stephens.

A 1970s new-style black romantic comedy/drama that is occasionally too calculating, often synthetic and rather hokey, but mostly entertaining and diverting. It examines the peculiar nature of the type of black male/female relationship first picked at in *Lady Sings the Blues*. It's a domestic comedy/drama that black audiences of the 1970s could respond to without feeling guilty, embarrassed, or cheated. That was a rarity because in the early-to-mid 1970s, no product proved psychologically more difficult for black movie audiences to accept than black comedies. Maybe audiences were reluctant to trust comedy because they knew that in movies of the 1930s and 1940s comedy was the format through which blacks were repeatedly demeaned. Who could ever forget the giggling maids or stammering butlers?

The best comedies grow out of well-developed characters. Black audiences have always found themselves responding not to the fake characters and their unrealistic situations but to the ingenuity of individual black actors who turned their roles and the plots of their movies inside out. Because of past performers like Hattie McDaniel, Eddie "Rochester" Anderson, and Mantan Moreland, past audiences had had a good time. But they had felt guilty about their laughter because at heart it was connected to something fraudulent. The only funny black people, American movies seemed to say, are the dumb-ass niggers. Worse still, the movies wanted us to believe all blacks were great, natural-born comedians because all were childlike figures who never had their wits about them.

What a black audience has always wanted from comedy is fully defined characters who can first be respected, then laughed at. Can a black character be intelligent and funny at the same time? Most movies still don't think so. But *Claudine* proved otherwise. Later so, too, did *She's Gotta Have It*.

At first, it looks as if it's a TV sitcom. The plot mechanics are not very original. A Harlem domestic (Diahann Carroll), living partly on welfare with six kids to support and no husband in sight, meets up with a black sanitation worker (James Earl Jones)—a grubby, smelly garbage man, as her kids are quick to point out. Throughout the movie, the two make love, quarrel, hurt each other, and finally, make up and marry.

Along the way, the woman's children provide dramatic and comic interludes. A daughter gets drunk and traumatically vomits out all her confusion about life as mama looks on. The oldest son turns "militant" and disappears for a time, only to resurface and let us know he's undergone a vasectomy because he doesn't want to be givin' no gal a kid so she has to live on welfare as his family does. At the movie's implausible climax, the same son, running from the cops, breaks in on his mother's wedding and sets the place humming with mayhem. Often with all the embellishments from the children's (as well as the lovers') problems and hassles, the movie turns not too heavily dramatic but too slapsticky and contrived. What saves the movie time and again and makes it special is its sense of character.

Diahann Carroll (with Lawrence-Hilton Jacobs, l., and James Earl Jones) as a Harlem domestic worker living on welfare in Claudine, *one of the few films of the 1970s to focus on the tensions and inner conflicts of a contemporary black woman.*

The children in *Claudine*, like the adults, are sane people trying to survive in an insane world, in this case New York City. At times the way the children talk back to their mother strikes us more like the behavior of middle-class white brats than hard-core ghetto children. Black children seldom battle it out this fiercely with their mothers, mainly because working ghetto mothers, after having toughed it out in the white world every day, are not willing to come home nightly and put up with further hassles in their own homes. In a way, *Claudine* seems part of the same white, liberal fantasy that a movie like *Conrack* is. But whether this film be tinged with white liberalism or not, something else is going on here, too. The children are all astonishingly hip and sophisticated in a way many ghetto children are. We realize the streets turn the young old quickly.

Claudine's children are cynical idealists. They act as if they expect little from life, and their raucous, rowdy cynicism is revealed in their non-stop wisecracks. The kids are equipped with commonsense and wit. They use both as shields from real heartaches and involvement. The oldest son and daughter act as if they do not believe in life or love or any sort of structure. But when the son (Lawrence Hilton-Jacobs) turns to militancy and when the daughter embarks on her first love relationship, we know that all along they've really wanted to believe in these things. Their mother has been the center of their lives. When the strange garbage man with the bloated face enters her life, the entire family fears for Claudine. Claudine's children, rebellious as they appear, love their mother desperately and unequivocally, and they don't want to see her hurt. They like her boyfriend, but they are not about to trust him until he proves himself. In almost all inner-city situations, everybody learns early not to trust just anybody. At times, the young actors seem to know more than scriptwriters Tina and Lester Pine are telling, and they perform with great skill.

Where *Claudine* succeeds best is in its exploration of the relationship between this "ordinary" black man and woman. Here we have two responsible black people caught up in one another, in themselves, and in a system that's closing in on them. They act the way most people in love do: they shout at each other and end up doing all the stupid, silly things they'd probably promised themselves never again to do to anybody else. But love, the movie tells us, works in crazy, imbecilic ways, not in the way movies have traditionally made us think it should.

Claudine does not just want us to know what's happening with a man and woman but wants us to understand how contemporary urban society can wreck a relationship unless the two work like jugglers and acrobats to keep it going. The villain in *Claudine* is an insensitive bureaucratic welfare system. The hero and heroine finally realize they are more important than this system that encourages deceit and dishonesty, and they will fight it out to keep their relationship going.

Much of *Claudine*'s appeal is due to its actors' relish for their roles. The young performers playing the children seem to be enjoying every second they're on screen and they're all very good. As the garbage man turned romeo, James Earl Jones, however, is miscast. Often we're too aware that he is *acting*, that here stands the great black Broadway performer doing a light turn in a movie. In his first sequence, seen lifting garbage pails, his grin is too emphatic, and the enthusiasm and interest he displays in *Claudine* are too stagey. Worst is he doesn't seem to feel this character has any fundamental dignity. Jones makes him something of a clown. Eventually, we accept him. Never really *liking* him, we get *used* to him just as the kids in the picture do.

Often Jones is overshadowed by his co-star Diahann Carroll, who is better suited for the movies than he is. When the camera moves in for a closeup, it latches onto her, and in no time, she wins us with her relaxed charm and intelligence. Moreover in *Claudine*, Diahann Carroll has been able to reconnect herself to the black community. In the 1960s she had been viewed as something of a bourgeois ice maiden; here she is freer and more open. She's not always keeping her guard up, and frequently she connects so well that audiences still cheer her on. Her best scenes are with other actors. She's able to feed off the work of her fellow players to add depth to her own characterization. In one striking sequence when she quarrels wiht her daughter, played by the devastatingly intense young black actress Tamu, Carroll is almost out-acted because Tamu seems to know what it is all about to scream and cry and let loose on all holds. Carroll at first still seems locked in until finally she just lets go and uses Tamu's anguish to create some of her own. She displays a shrewdness here—at times she appears vulnerable and a bit scared, as if wondering how the black audience will respond to her— and she works well. Carroll was nominated for the Oscar as Best Actress of 1974.

Claudine was the first feature produced by Third World Cinema, a three-year-old company dedicated to getting more blacks into the production end of movie-making. During the making of *Claudine*, 28 of the 37 production jobs were held by blacks or Hispanics. The behind-the-scenes story, however, would mean little if what had gone on in front of the cameras had not been so deftly handled. *Claudine* remains an engaging winner, one of the best black commercial films of its period.

Added note: Curtis Mayfield's energetic score is sung in high style by Gladys Knight and the Pips.

Cleopatra Jones (1973)

D. Jack Starrett. *S.* Max Julien and Sheldon Keller; from a story by Max Julien. *P.* William Tennant; co-produced by Max Julien. *R.* Warner Bros. Cast includes: Brenda Sykes; Antonio Fargas; Mike Warren; Esther Rolle; and Theodore Wilson.

Midway in the cycle of black action films, many of which centered on vigilante efforts by the black community against the drug pushers and dealers, came *Cleopatra Jones.* Unexpectedly, it was a hit and spawned a sequel *Cleopatra Jones and the Casino of Gold*, both starring former model Tamara Dobson as the undercover narc agent Cleo. Glamorous, statuesque, sophisticated, and surprisingly sweet-tempered and unassuming, Dobson is a delectable comic-strip heroine come true. It's mighty hard not to like her. What with the picture's sexy role reversals (Dobson is the aggressive defender of the right; Bernie Casey is her mild-mannered, rather passive boyfriend), its campy villainess (Shelly Winters giving a notoriously overblown performance), its fast-moving action sequences, and its self-righteous black-do-goodism theme (the violence is committed all in the name of keeping the ghetto clean and the kids safe), this is, for many, a slick and ready-made piece of entertainment.

Cleopatra Jones and the Casino of Gold (1975)

D. Chuck Bail. *S.* William Tennant. *P.* William Tennant. *R.* Warner Bros. Cast includes: Norman Fell and Caro Kenyatta.

A gaudy sequel to the 1973 *Cleopatra Jones*, once again starring the statuesque Tamara Dobson as an American narcotics agent. This time around she's trying to stomp out the drug trade in Hong Kong that is headed by a villainous creature called the Dragon Lady (played amusingly by Stella Stevens). Helping Tamara do battle is a pretty, spunky Asian sidekick, played by Tanny. Both women are martial arts experts, and it's their kung-fu derring-do that forms the backbone of this action picture. The movie's not as slick or stylish as it should be in order to work, even as a juicily endearing piece of camp entertainment. Instead it unmerrily plods along, dragging us with it.

Dobson, a gorgeous woman, is treated as little more than an asexual pawn, pushed here and there to keep the action going. *New York Times* critic Vincent Canby, however, could not help rhapsodizing over her. "No one in his right mind," he wrote, "would attempt to criticize a mountain peak, a sunset or hurricane. Miss Dobson is a large, beautiful, overwhelming presence whose sexuality is denied by her movie role . . . and by costumes that seem to have been designed for a female impersonator . . . (but she) forestalls all criticism by coming on like one of nature's androgynous wonders."

There's little more to recommend this one, except perhaps as an example of the kind of black macho mama movie that proved popular with audiences of the mid-1970s.

Coffy (1973)

D. Jack Hill. *S.* Jack Hill. *P.* Robert A. Papagian. *R.* AIP. Cast includes: Booker Bradshaw; Allan Arbus; Robert DoQui; and William Elliot.

An avenging angel named Coffy (Pam Grier) sets out to strike down the hoods, the pushers, and the top dope dealer who are responsible for the drug addiction of her hospitalized kid sister.

Simple-minded, violent, bloody, and a technical mess, this is the film nonetheless that made Pam Grier a B-movie star. She attacks, pounds, beats, stomps, and slashes her way through all the mayhem with true grit, gumption, and well—we might as well admit it—a giddy though misguided sense of conviction.

When first released, *Coffy* was justifiably criticized by black intellectuals because of its violence and, shall we say, its less than positive images (the familiar round of dope heads, thugs, and pimp types). Grier was completely dismissed as an actress and as a screen personality. Around the same time, though, some feminists, among them the editors at *Ms.* magazine (which put Grier on its cover), saw Grier's heroines as tough, assertive, non-traditional somewhat liberated movie characters. Today the violence of *Coffy* is still ugly and senseless. But the movie can be enjoyed as a cartoon of a liberated woman. (For the most part, black women have been unable to identify strongly with Grier's heroines of the 1970s, whose exploits are too far removed from the everyday realities of black women's lives.) Grier's high-voltage personality, however, holds up surprisingly well. Often she's so fixated on her task of cleaning out the baddies that she's a one-dimensional howl: funny, campy, engaging.

The Color Purple (1985)

D. Steven Spielberg. *S.* Menno Meyjes. *P.* Steven Spielberg, Kathleen Kennedy, Frank Marshall, and Quincy Jones. Executive producers: Jon Peters and Peter Guber. *R.* Warner Bros. Cast includes: Rae Dawn Chong and Dana Ivey.

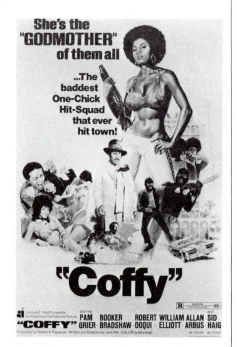

Poster for the film Coffy, *which firmly established Pam Grier as the undisputed queen of B-movies of the 1970s.*

Whoopi Goldberg as Celie in Steven Spiel-berg's adaptation of Alice Walker's The Color Purple, *which set off an unexpected wave of controversy within the black community.*

Whoever would have thought that this film, based on black author Alice Walker's bestselling, Pulitzer Prize-winning novel, would have unleashed such heated debate and controversy? In *The Village Voice*, black feminist writer Michele Wallace called the picture "the Amos 'n' Andy of the 80s." In *New York*, critic David Denby called it a "hate letter to black men." In *The New York Times*, Vincent Canby labelled it "a combination of *Tobacco Road*, *The Wizard of Oz*, and *Imitation of Life*. It makes you laugh, it makes you cry and it makes you feel a little bit of a fool for having been taken in by its calculated, often phony effects." The NAACP and other black groups protested against the picture. Newspapers carried articles with opposing points of view on it, and talk shows, from "Today" to "Donahue" to New York's black-oriented "Like It Is", devoted attention to the uproar. Yet despite the controversy, many critics liked the film and millions of moviegoers, many of whom were black, *loved* it, seeing the picture as the first full-scale screen examination of the experiences and tensions of black women.

Essentially, *The Color Purple* traces almost 40 years (from the early years of the century into the 1940s) in the life of a poor rural Southern woman, Celie. As a girl, she is raped and twice impregnated by her stepfather, who sells her children to a barren black couple. Then he passes her on to another black man, a widower, cruel and demanding, who's just called Mr. He, in turn, pursues Celie's pretty sister Nettie, then banishes her from his home and Celie's life. In the years to come, he steals and hides the letters Nettie writes Celie. Celie's life undergoes a great change when she is befriended by the mistress of her husband, blues singer Shug Avery. The movie climaxes with Celie's growth and maturity and her great assertive moment of rebellion against her husband. Finally, she is reunited, too, with her long-lost sister.

At the center of *The Color Purple* debate was the director's depiction of his black male characters. As Mr., Danny Glover gave a tightly drawn, highly charged performance of a man who's both brute and simp. Unfortunately, the script, by Dutch-born writer Menno Meyjes never takes time to tell anyone who Mr. is. Instead he's used simply as a Victorian-style villain without the shading or development to cue us in on the cultural forces that have shaped and hardened him. One simply has to compare Mr. with the hero of a film like *Nothing but a Man* to see what the film lacks. Here another black man, living in the South, refuses to kowtow to the whites around him and consequently is made to go from one job to another, ultimately unleashing his anger and frustration on his wife. *Nothing but a Man* placed its hero within a very definite cultural context: we understand the society in which he must function and how it erodes his spirit. None of that happens in *The Color Purple*. In fact, the film seems to lack a sense of the black community itself. Moreover it ignores a very definite point of Walker's novel. Her character Mr. also was a tough sadist. But shrewdly and sensitively Walker revealed changes within Mr. and his relationship with Celie, so much so that by the novel's last sections, the two have come to know and love one another. Celie announces the only one who understands her is Mr. It's a powerful moving moment, uncovering for us a view of a black man and black woman who have been able to step outside their culture and American history to discover one another and live a life together with some meaning. The skimpy changes of Mr. in the film are unfathomable, nothing more than a plot device, without explanation, for bringing about the "happy ending" reunion of Celie and Nettie. At the same time, Mr.'s father, played stiffly by Adolph Caesar, is little more than a grumpy, cantankerous walk-on, and Harpo (Willard Pugh), the husband of Sofia, is reduced to a slapstick joke. In the long run, the protesters were right about the film's male characters: they are simply unexamined props put there to make trouble for the women.

But what's most disturbing about the film is its failure to give the viewer the very thing that made the novel so powerful: namely, the voice of Celie. This uneducated black woman, speaking in broken English with a new urgency and rhythm, was a character American fiction had long ignored or overlooked. Walker's gift had been to make us see this woman and also see the way the woman viewed the world. Celie's voice is missing from the movie *The Color Purple* and is replaced by Steven Spielberg's very mundane vision. For all his talent and commitment to the story, he turns Walker's distinctive novel into a formula picture: an old-fashioned melodrama with a mean heavy and a sweet heroine.

Spielberg's characters exist in some never-never land where everything is touched by movie magic. The cinematography is far too bright and pretty: large luminous cottony clouds, brilliantly clear blue skies. Celie takes over Mr.'s large, roomy house, cleans it spotless, even sets up a contraption to hold the pots and pans (it's too cute for words). Except for the scenes recounting the character Sofia's fate at the hands of a disturbed white woman, the script steers clear of issues of race and racism. One never has an idea that these people live through the Depression. And the movie steadfastly avoids the subject its makers no doubt feared would upset viewers most, that of the lesbian relationship between Celie and Shug. It is sexual fulfillment with Shug that helps awaken Walker's Celie to life's possibilities. But here Shug and Celie have an ambiguous touching/smiling scene that is devoid of passion. (The scene is, however, well played.) The lesbian matter is also completely dropped afterwards. This compromise destroys whatever hopes Spielberg had of being true to the novel or the experiences of the women in it. Of course, in all truthfulness, had he examined the lesbian theme, he might well have lost his family audience and also might have enraged some members of the black community. There had been some blacks who had objected to the novel's exploration of the lesbian motif, overlooking the fact that as an artist Walker had the right to explore whatever subject she chose.

But *The Color Purple* story does not end here. As the controversy dragged on and on for months, it was distressing to see so much energy and attention expended on this one movie. For with all its flaws, the film was not the most racist since *The Birth of a Nation*. Nor was *liking it* an indication of a lack of black consciousness. The uproar, more often than not, ignored the basic appeal and power of the film and the reasons why so many, black women, in particular, were affected by it. For many, *The Color Purple* worked because of its women: frayed, jarred, restless, struggling. Whoopi Goldberg's performance might be coy and cutesy, never building until her dinner scene when her long-suppressed strength surfaces, leading her to lash out heroically—with a knife pointed at her husband. Yet regardless, Goldberg's face, as well as the faces of Desreta Jackson, Akosua Busia, Oprah Winfrey, and Margaret Avery, are unlike those we've previously seen in American films. In the past, these women would have played maids, comic servants never to be thought about twice. But when Spielberg's camera moves in for loving close-ups—the camera treats the women with respect and concern—the visual statement itself moves and affects us, even while we may feel cheated by much else that goes on. For the black viewer, there is an unnerving split tension: no matter how much certain elements are rejected, we feel we know something about these women and long to understand them better.

And the actresses themselves are often impressive. Almost completely overlooked by the critics, Desreta Jackson, as the young Celie, gives a glowing portrait of a girl struggling to hold her feelings inside, to keep a cap on her emotions. Jackson doesn't play to an audience as Goldberg does in her early scenes. (Of course, in her big moment—with that darn knife in her hand—the fact that Goldberg is aware of playing to an audience helps her; everyone cheers her on to *kill the nigger*.) Akosua Busia also creates a touching and resilient Nettie. As Shug, Margaret Avery is not as charismatic and sexy as we might want (the part really calls for a high-voltage personality like Tina Turner, who turned the role down, saying she didn't want to play a part she had already *lived*). But Avery does have a weathered, battered air, is slightly wistful, slightly used, slightly sad, yet forcefully durable. And, of course, as Sofia, Oprah Winfrey, large and dowdy, physically falls in line with past strong black women of the screen. We're not supposed to see anything sexually alluring about her. But Winfrey's got grit and some humor inside her.

In the final estimate, it is the women of *The Color Purple* and the traces of Walker's story that propel the movie along. The director really doesn't seem to understand the subtleties and nuances. And, yes, if ever a story cried out for a black writer and director, this is it. But no matter how much some of us might reject the picture intellectually, I don't think it does us much good to ignore the feelings of those moved by it. With those closeups and performances, the picture does touch on the mythic even while it fails to understand what's right there before its eyes. This is the case with so much of black movie history: dazzling black actors or actresses telling us something between the lines, affecting us even as we squirm or resist being touched.

Ironically, the controversy turned the movie into something of an instant classic. Whether loved or hated, *The Color Purple* will be shown for years to come and has found a place in the history of blacks in American films.

Nominated for 11 Academy Awards—including Best Picture, Best Actress (Goldberg), Best Supporting Actress (both Avery and Winfrey were nominated in this category)—the movie won none.

Come Back Charleston Blue (1972)

D. Mark Warren. *S.* Bontche Schweig and Peggy Elliott; based on the Chester Himes novel *The Heat's On*. *P.* Samuel Goldwyn, Jr. *R.* Warner Bros.; a Samuel Goldwyn, Jr. Production. Cast includes: Peter De Anda; Minnie Gentry; Percy Rodrigues; Jonelle Allen; and Maxwell Granville.

A sequel to *Cotton Comes to Harlem*, again featuring those daring, darling Negro detectives Grave Digger Jones (Godfrey Cambridge) and Coffin Ed Johnson (Raymond St. Jacques). Part of the fun of *Cotton Comes to Harlem* had been that some fresh talent had gotten caught up in the joy of making a movie, no doubt never dreaming their end results would be such a box-office success. But by the time of this sequel the whorey Hollywood profit-making machinery had moved in, the exuberant spontaneity was knocked out, and the result: a tepid, jaded, sluggish picture. The actors are anxious to please, but nobody seems to know what to do with them or the story.

Conrack (1974)

D. Martin Ritt. *S.* Irving Ravetch and Harriet Frank, Jr.; based on Pat Conroy's book *The Water Is Wide* about his actual teaching experiences in the South. (Because Pat Conroy's students were unable to pronounce his last name, they called him Conrack; hence the film's title.) *P.* Martin Ritt (who had previously directed *Sounder*) and Harriet Frank, Jr. *R.* 20th Century-Fox. Cast includes: Tina Andrews; veteran Ruth Attaway; and Antonio Fargas and Paul Winfield, both of whom in supporting character parts, give highly idiosyncratic and enjoyable performances.

A liberal young white man (Jon Voigt) takes a teaching job at one of the islands off the South Carolina mainland. His students are a motley group of black kids labeled "slow," who seem to know nothing of events outside their island home. In the world of public education they are the forgotten, the discarded. But the young teacher realizes no one has ever worked with these kids, no one's tried teaching them or inspiring them to learn. In the classroom, he becomes an actor, a clown, and a true teacher, using every imaginative trick he can conjure up, every bit of creative fire and enthusiasm as well as a lot of gumption and showmanship to uncover to the kids the glory of learning about the world around them. He's opposed, however, by the system itself, represented by the condescending school superintendent (Hume Cronyn) as well as the school's principal, a black woman (Madge Sinclair), who's contemptuous of the children, believing them to be so ignorant that they have no chance of ever learning anything. Eventually, having won the battle by actually reaching the students, the young teacher loses the war. He's fired from his job.

At first glance, one tends to agree with *Variety*'s comment that *Conrack* displays an "inadvertent white liberal condescension." Here we find the Great White Father Syndrome wherein (as also seen on the TV series "The White Shadow") it is the good white man who reaches the troubled backward black kids, bringing out the best in them. How much more interesting this might have been had we had a chance to watch a black teacher struggling to connect to the students. (A few years later with Madge Sinclair in the TV movie "I Know Why the Caged Bird Sings" and Cicely Tyson in "The Marva Collins Story," we did get to see such inspired black teachers. But neither TV film was as well directed as *Conrack*. Or as well written.)

In spite of all its flaws, though, *Conrack* is infused with a daffy old-fashioned kind of optimism (the idea that one individual can make some difference) that carries us along. It's funny and frequently affecting because Voight and the young actors respond so well to each other. Madge Sinclair also gives a startling performance that is played, as Pauline Kael has said, with "magnificent physical authority" yet a performance which was completely overlooked at the time when awards were being handed out. "She's so strong and unyielding," wrote Kael, "that she's like an obstinate force of nature." Full of self-hate, Sinclair's character is something of a monster but it's the type I think many of us have seen in schools everywhere: the frustrated, repressed, testy teacher (white or black), embittered by years of work at a job she or he basically hates, who simply pushes the charges through the ranks and doesn't have much pride or enthusiasm in the work he or she is supposed to be doing.

Worth seeing and far more realistic than something like *To Sir with Love*.

The Cool World (1963)

D. Shirley Clarke. S. Shirley Clarke and Carl Lee; based on the novel by Warren Miller. P. Fred Wiseman. R. Wiseman Film Productions. Cast includes: Clarence Williams; Yolanda Rodriguez; Bostic Felton; Gary Bolling; Georgia Burke; and Carl Lee (son of noted stage actor Canada Lee), who later played Eddie in *Super Fly* (1972).

Rarely seen today and unfortunately considered by some a period piece, Shirley Clarke's *Cool World* still retains its sharp edge and disturbing insights. As an early cinematic look at ghetto life, *The Cool World* focuses on a teenage gang leader Duke (Hampton Clanton), whose driving aspiration, so it appears, is to get a gun, a symbol obviously of power and control. But as Clarke's camera follows Duke from his disheveled home life (with a mother, played by Gloria Foster, who is almost too worn out to care about anything) through the mean streets of Harlem, we see Duke's search is for something other than the gun, for something far more disturbing and affecting. He's Richard Wright's native son, a brooding young black man wading his way through a cultural/

social mess, restlessly struggling to discover his *raison d'etre*. Watching this film today, viewers may quickly realize that in so many crucial respects the 1986 remake of Wright's *Native Son* should have been handled in precisely the manner of *The Cool World*: with a sharp eye for detail and a fierce identification with a young hero's howl in the night.

Blistering, unsettling, ironic, *The Cool World*'s semi-documentary approach to ghetto life and ghetto inhabitants was, in the 1960s, totally new to American cinema. *Variety* hailed the film as "a telling look at Harlem and probably one of the least patronising films ever made on Negro life." Although it might seem dated to some today, *The Cool World*'s effects linger with the viewer long after the film has ended.

As Duke, 14-year-old actor Hampton Clanton gives an impressive performance. Later using the name Rony Clanton, he appeared in another ghetto drama *The Education of Sonny Carson* (1974).

Previously, filmmaker Shirley Clarke had directed the controversial *Connection* (1960). Afterwards she directed the fascinating *Portrait of Jason* (1967), a study of a black male prostitute.

Cooley High (1975)

D. Michael Schultz. *S*. Eric Monte. *P*. Steve Krantz; Executive Producer, Samuel Z. Arkoff. *R*. AIP. Cast includes: Cynthia Davis; Christine Jones; Corin Rogers; Sheram Smith; Norman Gibson; Maurice Leon Havis; Joseph Carter Wilson; and Lynn Caridine.

Coming of age in the 1960s: Cooley High *with Glynn Turman, Lawrence Hilton Jacobs, and Corin Rogers.*

Critically well-received and popular with audiences of its day, *Cooley High* is still highly regarded and fondly remembered. At heart, it's a coming-of-age action-comedy, following the adventures of two young high school buddies (Glynn Turman and Lawrence Hilton-Jacobs) in Chicago in the early 1960s: they cut class, sometimes drink cheap wine, throw 25¢ parties, fight and horse around, experience the pangs of first love, and even endure a hair-raising chase in a stolen car.

The Village Voice's James Woolcott called it "the best American comedy so far this year." *The Black American*'s critic said it was "done with humor and love, one can't help but sit back and enjoy every minute. A fun-loving warm and tender film that should be seen by everyone." Lawrence Van Gelder of *The New York Times* added: "*Cooley High* is a black *American Graffiti*, a clear-eyed funny, loving and deeply touching recreation of adolescent life . . . and in its own right it is a superior film. Written and directed with an almost unwavering sense of pace, *Cooley High* pulsates with the careless exuberance of youth and captivates with characterizations and incidents presented."

Seeing the picture today, one often feels it is the energetic soundtrack of 1960s Motown music (rather than the drama on screen) that sets our senses reeling. As it attempts capturing tensions, aspirations, and the bizarre contradictions peculiar to the black experience, *Cooley High* is occasionally a joyful entertainment. But too often the seams show. Written by Eric Monte, the creator of the black sitcom "Good Times," the film often comes across like a series of TV skits and gags that are skillfully stitched together but that ultimately lack real insight, even cohesion. No doubt that's why there has to be a mock-tragic ending with the death of the character Cochise. Otherwise the experiences would seem inconsequential and pointless. The women are simply background fillers. Of course, the dreamgirl is the tight-skinned actress. And in the long run, the picture's a halfbaked tribute to male camaraderie just as *The Bingo Long Travelling All-Stars and Motor Kings*, *Uptown Saturday Night* and *Let's Do It Again* were. Even if enjoyed on *that* level, it still lacks resonance and true dramatic/emotional power. Garrett Morris—later a star on TV's "Saturday Night Live"—and Lawrence Hilton-Jacobs, however, give well-shaded performances.

Coonskin (1975)

D. Ralph Baksi. *S.* Ralph Bakshi. *P.* Albert S. Ruddy. *R.* Bryanston. Cast includes: singer Barry White; Philip Thomas; Scatman Crothers; and black playwright Charles Gordone, author of the play *No Place To Be Somebody*.

In the mid-1970s, this part-animated, part-live action cartoon of a film became something of a *cause célèbre*. Before *Coonskin*'s release, following a special screening at New York's Museum of Modern Art, the Congress of Racial Equality (CORE) denounced *Coonskin* as being racist, nothing more than the familiar collection of demeaning movie stereotypes that black audiences had had to contend with since the days of *The Birth of a Nation*. "It depicts blacks as slaves, hustlers, and whores. It is . . . very insulting," said Elaine Parker, the chairperson of CORE's Harlem headquarters. The civil rights organization then mounted a campaign to halt the movie's distribution. Stung by the pre-release criticism, Paramount Pictures dropped the movie, which was eventually distributed by an independent company, Bryanston. Interestingly enough, the movie's director, Ralph Bakshi, had grown up in the Bedford-Stuyvesant section of Brooklyn and his first two films, *Fritz the Cat* (1972) and *Heavy Traffic* (1973), were early, strikingly unromanticized visions of a harsh urban ghetto scene. Neither was free of distortions though.

When *Coonskin* finally opened, the press turned it into a true media event. The Sunday *New York Times* ran a lengthy piece on it. And pickets lined the streets outside the New York theaters where it played—for a while, that is. For once the reviewers got to it—and after word of mouth from those blacks who did see it spread into the black community—the tempest in the teapot came to an abrupt end. *Cooskin* quite frankly just was not strong enough to elicit vehement reactions of any kind, good or bad.

The movie's an update of the old Uncle Remus tales. It's Br'er Rabbit and the Tar Baby gone urban and "dirty": a sleazy, porny action fantasy that's the complete antithesis of the wholesome, family-oriented Disney type of animated feature. It focuses on three blacks (Brother Rabbit, Brother Bear, and Preacher) who migrate from the hills to Harlem where they are appalled by the big city horrors they encounter. They determine to wipe out the ghetto's rackets empire. Ironically, once they've demolished the white Mafioso and the thuggy cops who are his lieutenants, the three animated "brothers" end up controlling the dope/prostitution/gambling trade themselves. The message is scary.

Yet *Coonskin*'s plot is actually not too different from those countless black action films of this period starring the likes of a Jim Brown or Fred Williamson. And perhaps for that reason, the black audience (much of which was lured into seeing the film simply because of the controversy) did not view it with either shock or outrage. The uproar really simmered down because of the undeniable fact that the film, while dazzling in its animated sequences, had a hack script, a weak lineup of lifeless characters, and a poor mix of its animated and live sections. And, finally, it must be stated that while *Coonskin*'s blacks are indeed embarrassing stereotypes, a strain of truly foul ugliness—about all people—runs rampant here. "The most likely candidates to be offended by *Coonskin* are actually white women and gays," wrote *The New York Post*'s Frank Rich. "These characters, more than the film's blacks, seem to take us to the bottom of Bakshi's personal obsessions."

"*Coonskin* swaggered into town yesterday on the heels of controversy that is liable to keep alive a film that might otherwise perish of its own insubstantiality," wrote Jerry Oster in *The New York Daily News*.

Cornbread, Earl and Me (1975)

D. Joe Manduke. S. Leonard Lamensdorf (who also served as Executive Producer); based on the novel *Hog Butcher* by Ronald Fair. P. Joe Manduke. R. AIP. Cast also includes: Tierre Turner; Larry Fishburne 3rd; Moses Gunn (as stylized and glum as ever); Antonio Fargas (as a lively numbers runner); and Thalmus Rasulala.

A well-intentioned drama about a gifted young black basketball player, the idol of the kids on his block and the great black hope of his community. Good-natured and conscientious, he's the ghetto kid who's going to get out and make something of himself. Suddenly, unexpectedly, however, he's accidentally shot and killed by a white policeman. The community as well as the basketball player's family and the families of the kids who looked up to him as a big brother are all thrown into turmoil.

The film strains hard at treating its material sensitively, honestly, impartially. The white cop is really not a bad cop. It was simply a mistake. Of course, it might have made for a stronger movie if the cop didn't care whether he'd made a mistake or not. But the film wants very much to show us basically decent people caught up in a situation over which no one has real control. Unfortunately, the cop's trial sequences turn soapy and didactic. And the movie's not textured or perceptive enough to be really good.

Rosalind Cash and Madge Sinclair turn in solid performances, while Bernie Casey, former football player, proves he's an actor in the role of a troubled black policeman. The part of the basketball star is played by Keith Wilkes, former UCLA All-American and a one-time player with the NBA's Golden State Warriors.

The Cotton Club (1984)

D. Francis Coppola. S. William Kennedy and Francis Coppola; story by Kennedy, Coppola, and Mario Puzo. P. Robert Evans. R. Orion Pictures. Cast includes: Novella Nelson (a very sly, ingenious performance); Charles Honi Coles (the legendary tap dancer); Gwen Verdon; Fred Gwynne; Julian Beck; James Remar; Larry Fishburne; Bob Hoskins; Joe Dallesandro; and briefly Woody Strode.

Francis Coppola's grandiose look back at an earlier era of jazz babies, gangsters and their molls, giddy socialites, and legendary black entertainers on their way to their first brush with success and fame. It's all centered in the very popular Cotton Club, which from 1923 to 1936 was located at 142nd Street and Lenox Avenue and was advertised as a "window on the jungle . . . a cabin in the cotton" with a lineup of "tall, tan and terrific" black chorus girls, who strutted, stomped, and stormed the stage to the delight of their white patrons.

Coppola focuses on two parallel stories, two sets of brothers, one white, the other black, caught up in the stormy heat and conflicts of the Jazz Age. The white brothers are Richard Gere, a cornet player who falls in love with gangster Dutch Schultz's girlfriend (Diane Lane) and later finds himself a movie star, and Nicholas Cage, a dim-witted lad who falls victim to his own life of crime. The black brothers are played by real-life brothers, Maurice and Gregory Hines, cast as dancers at the Cotton Club. When Gregory Hines's character, Sandman, decides to pursue a career as a solo performer, the brothers part bitterly, only to be reunited at the film's rigged climax. Lonette McKee plays the pretty high-yaller singer who falls for Gregory Hines but who, in pursuit of success, crosses the color line, passing for white while appearing at a fancy downtown white club.

The film brims over with characters, incidents, encounters, and conflicts, a sheer overkill of stories that are mere outlines without any sense of drama or the kind of concrete details that would make all of this come alive. McKee's decision to pass for white suddenly pops up out of nowhere; it really doesn't go anywhere either. When the Hines brothers suddenly battle and dissovle their act, the audience can't muster up much interest because we've had no real indication of any tension between the two. A disastrous mistake also has been made in the handling of the musical numbers: Coppola repeatedly cuts away from the performers, never letting us enjoy the entertainment itself. McKee is permitted to complete "Ill Wind," and we're almost moved by it but the film promptly turns away from her and never uses the song to comment on the character or her situation *or* to give us a true dramatic moment. When Diane Lane sings Ethel Waters's great hit "Am I Blue?" we know there's not much hope here. (Waters was probably turning over in her grave.) This could have been a great movie musical. But the musical numbers are not really selected or developed in terms of character, plot, or even in terms of what the musical material itself has to say.

And finally, most sadly, for many of us *The Cotton Club* becomes most distressing because the black entertainers are shoved into the background. As Pauline Kael has said, "If there's something more upsetting about this movie than there is about other failed epics, it's that a great time in the history of black people has been screwed over." We want this to be the black entertainers' story—at long last. We want to know the way the great stars like Duke Ellington or Ethel Waters or Lena Horne functioned while climbing to success at this black club (black in the respect that all the entertainers were black) that was owned by whites and had only white patrons (except for rare occasions when a black celebrity like a Jack Johnson might show up).

Moreover the film even fails to tell us what the Cotton Club—with its blend of the exotic, the sexual, the forbidden, and the highly imaginative—meant to its white clientele. When the Fred Astaires, the Tallulah Bankheads, the Orson Welleses, and the innumerable socialites showed up—or when listeners around the country heard on radio the weekly Cotton Club broadcasts—what were they responding to? One never gets the sense that this was a groundbreaking period for the black entertainer or that white America was for the first time coming face to face with exuberant high black style.

Great to look at and visually richly textured, *The Cotton Club*'s production values are first rate. Yet the whole concoction is so empty and enervating that we even lose interest in the beauty of its images.

Reviews were mixed. *Newsweek*'s Jack Kroll called it "one of the few original films of the year." David Denby in *New York* wrote, however, that it was "a little stale and movie-ish . . . touches on everything and nothing."

Costing over $50 million, the movie was rife with tension and discord throughout the filming. Coppola came in on the picture late and struggled to get a decent script. The manic madness to rush it into production and complete it as well as the pressure to make something that would *overwhelm* the viewer shows, in ways the moviemakers did not originally intend.

Cotton Comes to Harlem (1970)

D. Ossie Davis. *S.* Arnold Perl and Ossie Davis; based on the novel by Chester Himes. *P.* Samuel Goldwyn, Jr. *R.* UA; a Samuel Goldwyn, Jr. Production. Cast includes a number of black faces, then unknown, now rather familiar: Redd Foxx; Calvin Lockhart (as the crafty minister); Cleavon Little; pretty Emily Yancy (as the widow of Lockhart's partner); Frederick O'Neal; Helen Martin; Theodore Wilson; Vinette (sic) Carroll, and Marion Etoile Watson. Music by Galt MacDermot.

A rambunctious joyride through Harlem with many a bump and pothole along the way, but no one seemed to mind when this feature was first released. It was a tremendous success with the black movie audience, helping to launch the black movie boom of the 1970s. A comedy action film, *Cotton Comes to Harlem* brought to the screen black writer Chester Himes' popular black fictional detectives Grave Digger Jones (Godfrey Cambridge) and Coffin Ed Johnson (Raymond St. Jacques), who are here trying to recover a missing $87,000. Making his directorial debut, Ossie Davis struggles with "technique" but relates well to

*Raymond St. Jacques and Godfrey Cambridge
as Coffin Ed Johnson and Grave Digger Jones
in* Cotton Comes to Harlem.

his actors. Perhaps the funniest scene is Judy Pace outsmarting a
corrupt white cop, who ends up being caught with his pants down.
Black audiences howled with delight over this sequence, loving the idea
of finally seeing a white man made the butt of a black joke.

Excited by the prospect of a new black commercial cinema, *Variety*
wrote: "Urbanwise, a heavy box-office is in view. With a heavy enough
take in the North, even Southern exhibitors will want a piece of the
action. Black audiences there will love it; the whites will go away with
their opinions unchanged."

Contemporary black audiences may wonder what the fuss was once
all about and may frown also at the profusion of stereotypes. But they
may also respond to the energy and zesty excitement of all those
involved in the project.

Countdown at Kusini (1976)

D. Ossie Davis. S. Ossie Davis, Ladi Ladebo, and Al Freeman, Jr.;
original story and screen treatment by John Storm Roberts. P. Ladi
Ladebo. R. Columbia Pictures. Cast includes: Greg Morris (as an
Afro-American jazz pianist, who becomes caught up in revolution-
ary politics); Ruby Dee; Tom Aldredge; Michael Ebert; and Thomas
Baptiste.

This film has one interesting historical footnote: it was financed by the
nation's largest black sorority (85,000 members), Delta Sigma Theta,
under its banner, DST Telecommunications. The sorority's trademark
colors are red and white. And the sorority probably saw lots of red once
this movie was completed. Filmed on location in Lagos, Nigeria, this tale
about the fight for liberation in a fictional African nation is clearly an
attempt to give black audiences a different kind of movie: one that's got
high political ideals and high entertainment values. Amid this clash of
capitalistic greed and revolutionary struggle, the picture strives hard
for old-fashioned adventure, romance, and melodrama with a Ga-

blesque leading man of action. Unfortunately, almost everyone in the film is seriously miscast, although director Davis, who also plays an African patriot, has unexpected grandeur and presence in some shots. But the action is slow and so unworked out that the picture collapses before ever taking off.

Cry, The Beloved Country (1952)

D. Zoltań Korda. S. Alan Paton from his novel. P. Zoltań Korda. R. London Films. Cast includes: Charles Carson; Albertina Temba; Edric Connor; Charles McCrae; Lionel Ngakane; Shayiwa Riba; Ribbon Dhlamini; and Tsepo Gugushe.

Based on Alan Paton's South African novel, *Cry, The Beloved Country* featured veteran actor Canada Lee as an old village priest journeying to Johannesburg in search of a son gone astray. In the city, where he is aided in his search by a young priest (Sidney Poitier), Lee is saddened by the poverty and filth, bewildered by the outright racism, and troubled by the disintegration of his family. His sister has turned to prostitution. His brother is eaten up with resentment and bitterness over the political situation. And his son has murdered a young white man, who was the son of Lee's white neighbor. When the two fathers meet, you may feel you're being set up. But there's a genuine poignancy here. To say that *Cry, The Beloved Country* makes a plea for racial harmony and conciliation does not say enough. Sometimes slow and seemingly adrift, the movie handles its theme with great sensitivity and insight.

This was Poitier's second feature, and it's a bit of a marvel to see him so fresh, so boyish, and so far more relaxed than in some of his later films. As for Canada Lee: the movie came after he'd had a run of political problems and hassles (this was the era of the blacklists and witch-hunts within the entertainment industry). He looks weary and a bit defeated yet gives his strongest and most deeply felt film performance, a fine piece of work that haunts the viewer long after the movie has ended. Later there appeared a musical version of *Cry, The Beloved Country* called *Lost in the Stars*, which was adapted for the screen in 1974 and included Brock Peters and Melba Moore.

D.C. Cab (1983)

D. Joel Schumacher. S. Joel Schumacher; taken from a story by Schumacher and Topper Carew. P. Topper Carew. R. RKO-Universal. Cast includes: Irene Cara (as herself); Anne DeSalvo, and Whitman Mayo (formerly of TV's "Grady" and "Sanford and Son").

One hesitates but can this weak-livered attempt at comedy—with a 1940s bomber crew cast of characters—be called anything other than a coon show for the 1980s? Directed by Joel Schumacher, previously the writer for *Car Wash*, *D.C. Cab* is, in a sense, a remake of that earlier film. *Car Wash* dealt with the plight of the common man, represented by workers in a Los Angeles car wash, and *D.C. Cab* focuses on the same subject, spotlighting this time a motley lineup of hacks at a cab company in Washington, D.C.

Episodic, urban, and straining to pulsate to Giorgio Moroder's lively soundtrack, the film assumes we'll be amused and touched by its comic characters' exploits. There is Xavier, an Hispanic who can't stop making jokes about Hispanics. Then there is Bongo Lennie (the very skilled

DeWayne Jessie), who bounces around with his dreadlocks and is described as a perfect Rastafarian except that he comes from Cleveland. The types go on and on. But with the exception of the black female driver (Gloria Gifford), no character is even of marginal interest or originality. Perhaps most disappointing is the character Tyrone (Charlie Barnett), a pouty, nutty would-be militant (in another era) who dons a wig (complete with hair curlers no less) while he clowns like mad. During Tyrone's big "revelatory" moment, he informs the young white hero (Adam Baldwin as something of a country boy come to the city) that he's not the fool he pretends to be: he's simply a black man playing a simpleton role while trying to survive in the white man's world. The sequence has a grain of truth but no wisdom or insight, and later when the character Tyrone undergoes no further develoment, we know his comments are no more than a cheap device thrown in to make us think the film has a certain consciousness or even a conscience. It's the worst type of "relevant" rhetoric.

Unlike *Car Wash*, which despite its shortcomings and superficiality, was at least directed by a man (Michael Schultz) with an affectionate (albeit sometimes condescending) regard for his characters, *D.C. Cab* simply uses its hack drivers as props in a hack comedy. Failing to capture urban rhythms and fundamentally unconcerned with the lives or feelings of its lower-middle class protagonists, the movie has an almost cruel casualness.

That might explain why a bright spot is Mr. T., as a good-hearted driver determined that the local drug pushers won't corrupt his young niece. He's restrained here, but Mr. T. still recites his lines as if he's just learned to read. But he has some spunk and is, in his own way, committed to his material, no matter how shallow we might think that material is. He's also surprisingly an amusing visual creation, never looking real, always seeming more like a Mr. T. animated doll.

In a generous mood (*why* is anyone's guess), *New York Times* critic Janet Maslin wrote: "*D.C. Cab* is a musical mob scene, a raucous, crowded movie that's fun as long as it stays wildly busy, and a lot less interesting when it wastes time on plot or conversation." In *The New York Daily News*, writer Harry Haun felt the movie fought hard to hide the fact that it "moves in ever-widening circles, toward no place in particular . . . meaningless motion . . . [which] could stand a less literal tuneup."

Actually, *D.C. Cab* was cruel and unusual punishment for a 1980s black audience anxious for black movie comedy.

The Decks Ran Red (1958)

D. Andrew Stone. *S.* Andrew Stone. *P.* Andrew and Virginia Stone. *R.* MGM. Cast includes: James Mason; Broderick Crawford; Stuart Whitman; and Joel Fluellen.

This ineptly written and directed drama about mutiny on the high seas has nothing to recommend it except for the sensational presence of Dorothy Dandridge. Having already won an Oscar nomination for *Carmen Jones*, Dandridge was considered a bonafide star. But her role here is best suited for a rising starlet, not an established leading lady. At this point in her career though, it was apparent to both Dandridge and the studios that they didn't know what to do with her. The great dramatic or musical roles of the 1950s were not going to a colored star.

Yet, paradoxically, she was too extraordinary a beauty and a commodity to be completely ignored. Consequently, her role in *The Decks Ran Red* is an unusual one for a black actress (as unusual today as then; in the 1950s no other black woman ever got a chance at playing this type of role, no matter how shallow it now looks). Simply stated, she plays the only woman aboard a shipload of hearty, lusty, red blooded males. And director Andrew Stone, who had previously directed Lena Horne in *Stormy Weather*, seems far more interested in Dandridge than in the basic action of the film: he treats her as a true movie goddess. Indeed her entrance, when every man on deck seems ready to go into a panting rage, is nicely handled and she's well showcased. Still without a true role to draw on, Dandridge is left floundering and resorts to a Hollywood style of acting familiar in certain films of this period: it's glossy, overheated, jittery, and unreal. Her earnest struggle to play *something* exposes her vulnerabilities and in a way endears her to us. At the same time, she's so unearthly beautiful and desirable that today most viewers still gasp upon first seeing her. The reactions to Dandridge's looks are not too different from the responses of audiences of the 1950s when seeing Elizabeth Taylor in such movies as *Ivanhoe* and *Rhapsody*. These are faces that come but once or twice in a century. *The Decks Ran Red* really runs nowhere except into tedium. But the few scenes where Dandridge shows up will give audiences an idea of the type of special star she could have been.

The Defiant Ones (1958)

D. Stanley Kramer. S. Harold Jacob Smith and Nathan E. Douglas. P. Stanley Kramer. R. Stanley Kramer/UA. Cast includes: Cara Williams; Theodore Bikel; Carl "Alfalfa" Switzer; and Lon Chaney, Jr.

Stanley Kramer's once-celebrated treatise on the theme of interracial brotherhood (actually interracial male bonding). Two convicts, one black (Sidney Poitier), the other white (Tony Curtis), escape from a prison van, shackled together by a two-foot chain. As they flee across country, on the run from the law, the two find they can't run from one another. The white, bigoted and bullyish, and the black, sensitive but burning with resentment because of a lifetime spent reacting to bigotry, fight, argue, and pick at one another. When the two cross a river, the heavy rapids almost take the black man under until the white brings him to safety. "Thanks for pulling me out," says Poitier's character Noah Cullen. "Man," replies Curtis, "I didn't pull you out. I stopped you from pulling me in." By the time the men have been unchained and are free to go their separate ways, a bond of brotherhood unites them. Afterward each at a moment of crisis comes to the rescue of the other, most notably the Poitier character, who, having boarded a freight train that will take him to freedom, leaps off to aid his white friend who is not strong enough to jump up. Aware that the law will now surely close in on him, Poitier sits, cradling a weakened and injured Curtis in his arms, singing "Long Gone" as the sheriff arrives to arrest him.

The Defiant Ones was highly praised. In *The New York Times*, Bosley Crowther found it "a remarkably apt dramatic visualization of a social idea" while Paul V. Beckley in *The New York Herald Tribune* lauded it as "one of the finest dramatic films of our time." *Variety* wrote that the "performances are virtually flawless. Poitier, always a capable actor,

Two cons, chained together, and on the run: Tony Curtis and Sidney Poitier in The Defiant Ones.

here turns in probably the best work of his career . . . a cunning, totally intelligent portrayal that rings powerfully true." The New York Film Critics voted *The Defiant Ones* Best Picture of the Year and Stanley Kramer, Best Director.

Today the movie still works as suspenseful melodrama with hard-hitting and dramatically effective dialogue. And the performances of the two principal actors hold up exceedingly well, Curtis eradicating his image as simply a pretty boy of the 50s and Poitier fulfilling his early promise as a commanding dramatic screen actor. Both men were nominated for Oscars. Poitier later won the Best Actor award at the Berlin Film Festival. In fact, *The Defiant Ones* and *A Raisin in the Sun* contain two of Poitier's most felt performances. Audiences are still jolted from their seats as they witness his anger and his explosions. Curiously enough, Poitier's more sexual here, too, and as a lonely farm woman's eyes linger on Curtis, we wonder why the movie doesn't have courage enough to let us see those same eyes linger on Sidney as well. Some critics have commented on the sexual undercurrents in the relationship between the two men. Pauline Kael has gone so far as to comment that some moviegoers consider it *"The Thirty-nine Steps,* in drag."

Where *The Defiant Ones* does not hold up is in its rigged brotherhood theme. The symbolism—the chain, the business of black and white—is often stilted and downright hokey at times. James Baldwin has commented that black audiences, not at all pleased when the Poitier character jumped from the train to save his white friend, openly jeered him. And it's hard for contemporary audiences, of any color, to listen to Poitier, as he stoically awaits his re-imprisonment, sing "Long Gone." Most difficult to imagine is the fact that the film appeared during a period of protests, sit-ins, and other political demonstrations within the black community. While passive resistance may have then been the acceptable political philosophy, *this* does seem to be pushing things.

But *The Defiant Ones* definitely broke new ground and it firmly established Poitier as a major American film star. In 1985, it was remade as an ABC TV-movie starring Carl Weathers and Robert Urich.

Detroit 9000 (1973)

D. Arthur Marks. S. Orville Hampton. P. Charles Stroud. R. General Film Corporation. Cast includes: Vonetta McGee; Ella Edwards; and Scatman Crothers (as Rev. Markham).

In the Motor City, a black cop (Hari Rhodes) and a white cop (Alec Rocco) battle the forces of urban corruption. Filmed in Detroit. Inept and rather embarrassing to watch.

Dr. Black, Mr. Hyde (1976)

D. William Crain. S. Larry LeBron. P. Charles Walker and Manfred Bernhard. R. Dimension Pictures. Cast includes: Ji-Tu Cumbuka; Stu Gilliam; and Marie O'Henry.

In 1972, under the direction of William Crain, Dracula went blackface, emerging in his new do in a movie called *Blacula*. Four years later director Crain was at it again, this time transforming Robert Louis Stevenson's *Dr. Jekyll and Mr. Hyde* into the story of an affluent black physician (Dr. Henry Pride is his name; he's played by Bernie Casey) who becomes a victim of his own research experiments, turning himself into—you guessed it—a hideous monster. Mr. Hyde, a puritanical prude, is soon out to kill the prostitutes in the area.

This is a typical formula picture: the idea, of course, was that black audiences would buy the same old corn white audiences had previously bought if that corn were cooked up with contemporary racial trappings. Like *Blacula*, the movie works on a very low level, simply because we enjoy seeing the sepia tint lent to a familiar classic. On another level, this film, like *Green Pastures*, is based on a cruel assumption: that it's funny watching lowly Negroes dressed up, playing upper-class characters in the canons of Western literature. Perhaps that's quibbling a bit. Actually, the movie's too good-natured and dull to be vicious.

Bernie Casey has some good moments. And can any movie with Rosalind Cash casting off her usual warm glow be all bad?

Drum (1976)

D. Steve Carter. S. Norman Wexler; based on the novel by Kyle Onstott. P. Ralph B. Serpe. R. UA. Cast also includes: Yaphet Kotto; Paula Kelly; Brenda Sykes; Warren Oates; and Fiona Lewis.

A follow-up to the very successful *Mandingo*. Like its seedy predecessor, *Drum* is an Old South melodrama with a point of view as mangled and misconceived as its characters. Unlike such past Old South dramas as *The Birth of a Nation*, *Gone with the Wind*, *The Foxes of Harrow* (1947), or *Band of Angels* (1957), in which the darkies quietly toiled in the cotton fields, this movie opens the door of the bordello and the bedroom of the Big House, not once flinching from an opportunity for some kinky sex or sadism. In fact, the picture appears to bask in its own frenetic coarseness.

Ken Norton and Pam Grier are cast as slaves who answer to their massa's various needs. He's to be a slave breeder, which means he'll spend most of his days not breaking his back but humping it. Grier's duties are to be in the bedroom when the massa shows up, although, on occasion, she's confident enough to push him away from her bed and into that of the lady of the house. Everyone in *Drum* seems to be living off the fat of the land. Eat. Drink. Carouse. Then fight some.

Because the white master and mistress are depicted as basically two non-threatening daffy dunces, the audience is manipulated into the most dangerously romantic assumption of all, that these "engaging" comic grotesques, who are outside the mainstream of polite American society, are actually another form of society's rejects. They, too, are *niggers*, down-home types to be identified with. The world of *Drum* and *Mandingo* is one big, elaborate, historically distorted de Sade orgy about as pleasant as a whiplash. But strangely enough, audiences of the mid-1970s appeared to eat this movie up, turning it into a box-office smash, and apparently not questioning its shoddy logic.

Many of its sequences remain almost comically disturbing because they are so illogical. During the climactic slave rebellion, the slaves, about to overtake the Big House, decide to kill the house niggers. Of course, we can understand the field hand's resentment of his tomming black brother. But despite what white America may want most of us to believe, the house servant was never the real enemy. If this movie had even a modicum of sense, the decision obviously would have been to kill *first* the slave master—and then if the house servants protested, they, too, would have to go. But *Drum* doesn't have time for any worked-out political thought. At the end of the movie, the slave master is still *quite* alive. And so in one sequence when Pam Grier and her white mistress are seen running from the Big House, a rebel slave spots them, points his gun, and who does he shoot? Why, Grier, his black sister. Then he drops his gun and hustles over to the white mistress for a quick toss in the hay. Curiously, some audiences at the time of the release of *Drum* never questioned the politically indefensible killing of Grier and instead cheered the slave in his pursuit of the white woman. The audience wanted the fireworks, the explosions, the sex. But few seemed to care to think through some of the muddled-headed politics. Past audience reactions to this film were almost as distressing as the picture itself.

As for the actors, none comes off particularly well. Usually, Norton looks anxious to shed his shirt and flex his muscles. To cash in on his box-office appeal (and his fame as a boxer), there are fight scenes for him, probably his best moments on screen, although to his credit, Ken Norton projects a certain intelligence that is way out of place here. Trying for a more subdued—a softer, low-keyed, less gaudy—image, Grier is just about hopeless. She's the type of performer who needs action or a tightly structured sense of character in the script (as was later the case with *Fort Apache: The Bronx*).

Oddly enough, like its predecessor *Mandingo*, *Drum* retains a gaudy s-and-m appeal that fascinates some audiences.

Duel at Diablo (1966)

D. Ralph Nelson. S. Marvin H. Albert and Michel M. Grilikhes. P. Ralph Nelson and Fred Engel. R. UA. Cast includes: Bibi Anderson; Dennis Weaver; and Bill Travers.

A routine Western with two surprises. First, Sidney Poitier shows up, decked out in fancy duds, playing a dandified cowboy, a horse dealer. Second, Poitier's color and his situation (a black man in the Old West) have nothing to do with the movie's plotline. There is a theme of miscegenation here, but this time it's not between white and black. Instead it's white and red (the American Indian). In the novel *Apache Rising* by Marvin H. Albert, on which this movie was based, the Poitier character was not black. At the time of the movie's release, some viewers balked at the idea of a black cowboy, believing such a figure was totally out of place and historically inaccurate. But Poitier proudly pointed to the then recently published, well-documented book *The Negro Cowboy* to prove his film was not playing history wrong. Ironically, today viewers accept Poitier in a Western but balk at the idea of him fighting those Injuns! All of us long for the black man to take up their cause, to see his historical links to the Indians. Poitier's character also seems isolated, completely cut off from any cultural roots of his own.

No doubt because he had long wanted to play a cowboy, Poitier accepted what is basically a secondary role in this film. James Garner is the real star. *Duel at Diablo* may not have turned out the way he wanted (I'm convinced he hoped for a black hero of the West that young black children could identify with), but the next time around when he directed and cast himself as another cowboy in *Buck and The Preacher*, he couldn't have asked for more agreeable results.

Point of interest: Ralph Nelson had previously directed Poitier in his Oscar-winning performance in *Lilies of the Field*.

The Duke Is Tops (1938)

D. Leo Popkin. P. Harry M. Popkin. R. Toddy Pictures and Million Dollar Studios. Cast includes: Lawrence Criner; Edward Thompson; The Basin Street Boys; Monte Hawley; and Everett Brown.

Four years before she was signed by MGM Studios, Lena Horne made her movie debut in the independently produced black film *The Duke Is Tops*. A backstage love story, the picture was soon forgotten, although Lena, as a wide-eyed and rather pepped-up young singer, displayed a natural, fresh quality rarely seen in many of her later Hollywood films when she often came across as an overly controlled ice maiden. After her Hollywood success, however, in the 1943 musicals *Cabin in the Sky* and *Stormy Weather*, Toddy Pictures retitled Horne's debut movie, calling it *Bronze Venus*, and sent it into re-release, hoping to cash in on Lena's new fame.

Lena's co-star is former bandleader Ralph Cooper, who was also one of the founders of Million Dollar Productions, a company that made all-black films in the 1930s and early 1940s.

Dutchman (1967)

D. Anthony Harvey. S. filmed from LeRoi Jones' stage play. P. Gene Persson Enterprises Production.

Hardly a box-office bonanza when released and sadly rarely shown today, this screen adaptation of LeRoi Jones' one-act play *Dutchman* remains a disturbing, sometimes harrowing experience. Filmed in England, it's a grim little parable, beginning with a subway ride and ending with a nightmarish dance of death.

On a New York subway train, a psychotic white woman, Lula (Shirley Knight), meets a studious, mild-mannered young black man, Clay (Al Freeman, Jr.). For the first three-fourths of the picture, he is something of a meek, educated tom, a civilized Negro, who quietly turns the other cheek while Lula taunts him. In the last quarter, Clay suddenly explodes, unleashing his anger as he protests the injustices and atrocities black Americans must live with daily. By the time the subway ride has ended, Lula, having brought Clay's rage to the fore, stabs him to death before a trainload of passive passengers and is well on her way to doing in a second black victim. By its conclusion, too, *Dutchman*, perhaps better than any other piece of dramatic writing of the 1960s, articulates what many then felt were the only options left open to a black man in white America: either he can survive by joining the ranks of the black bourgeoisie (those apers of white manners who are doomed, so Jones felt, to lives without their manhood) or he can lash out at the dominant culture and run the risk of being chopped down. Jones' thesis was not particularly pleasant. Nor was the film. But both worked dazzlingly.

Visually, the movie sometimes stands still, its director unsure what to do with his camera. Reportedly, the movie was shot on a six-day schedule, using three cameras. With the principals taking deferred percentage cuts, the picture cost some $65,000. Nonetheless, Jones' highly-charged theatrical dialogue and the exciting, kinetic performances of Al Freeman, Jr., and Shirley Knight make the movie work.

Edge of the City (1957)

D. Martin Ritt. S. Robert Alan Aurthur, who had also written the teleplay on which the film was based, "A Man Is Ten Feet Tall" that had starred Poitier in the same role on the home screen in 1955. P. David Susskind. R. MGM. Cast includes: Estelle Hemsley (as Dee's mother) and Ruth White.

With this taut, well-crafted, although misleading drama (a true liberal fantasy, if ever there was one), Sidney Poitier finally emerged as a star with one of his strongest yet oversimplified roles. He plays Tommy Tyler, a freightcar loader who befriends a troubled young white man (John Cassavetes). Along with his pert middle-class wife (Ruby Dee), Poitier takes the young man under his wing, showing him the ropes on the job and even introducing him to a pretty young white schoolteacher. The scenes between the black and white couples are done in a relaxed manner without much fanfare: it seems the most natural thing in the world for a group of people, despite their different racial backgrounds, to have a good time together. Yet while this idea seems progressive and positive, the movie steadfastly ignores the more serious cultural differences such friends would either be exposed to or would have to ignore or overcome in order to remain friends. The Poitier character is the essence of goodness: he's bright, fun-loving, generous, sweet-tempered, loyal, without one calculating or mean bone in his body. At the movie's climax, when Cassavetes is taunted on the job by a vicious white bigot, Poitier comes to his white friend's defense. The white man rips into Poitier with racial epithets. A fight ensues, violent and bloody. When Poitier has a chance to injure the bigoted white (played well by Jack Warden), his heart is simply too pure to carry through with such an act. He walks away, then is brutally stabbed in the back with a baling hook by the other man. It's a chilling, emotionally charged sequence. Dying, Poitier's character lies in the arms of Cassavetes, content, in a sense, that he's been true to his white friend. Much later in the film, Cassavetes, having attained a new level of maturity because of his friendship with Poitier, takes on the bigot.

"With this performance," wrote William K. Zinsser of *The New York Herald Tribune*, "Sidney Poitier matures into an actor of stature. His Negro is a man of deceptive simplicity. With his quick smile and exhilarating talk, he can cajole [Cassavetes] out of deep gloom. . . . But underneath he is a man of serious faith and deep strength, and when it's time for him to listen sympathetically or to say something important, he is the finest kind of friend in need."

Time, however, had a different view: "Surprisingly enough, in a Hollywood movie, the Negro is not only the white man's boss, but becomes his best friend and is at all times his superior, possessing greater intelligence, courage, understanding, warmth, and adaptability. The mystery is why so engaging a Negro would waste time on so boringly primitive a white man."

Time had its point, one with which many now may concur. Although Poitier himself defended his character and considered it one of his best, contemporary black audiences find the climax of *Edge of the City* hard to take (the noble black man selflessly sacrificing himself for a white buddy; the same thing happens in another important Poitier film, *The Defiant Ones*). Yet this movie was a clear breakthrough for Hollywood. *Variety* called it "a courageous, thought-provoking and exacting film," adding that it marked "a milestone in the history of the screen in its presentation of an American Negro."

Today *Edge of the City* still has a sharp edge.

Perhaps most gripping and moving is Ruby Dee's big scene. Having learned of her husband's death and spotting the cowardice of Cassavetes, she unleashes a fury of emotions in a sequence in which she is in total control of every line, every move. "He was supposed to be your friend," she cries out, with a startling ring of truth. It is a virtuoso sequence, one of her finest on screen.

Added note: This was the first picture directed by Martin Ritt, who later directed *Sounder*, *Conrack*, and *The Great White Hope*.

The Education of Sonny Carson (1974)

D. Michael Campus. S. Fred Hudson. Based on the book of the same title by Sonny Carson. Music by Coleridge-Taylor Perkinson. P. Irwin Yablons. R. Paramount Pictures. Cast includes: Paul Benjamin (giving one of his now-standard pained father performances); Mary Alice; Don Gordon; Linda Hopkins; Thomas Hicks; and Jerry Bell.

During the black movie boom of the early and mid-1970s, intellectuals, black and white, yearned for a serious, more realistic treatment of the black urban experience. The intellectual community considered such films as *Shaft* (1971) and *Super Fly* (1972) as mere ripoffs. For some, *Sounder* (1972), set in rural black America of the 1930s, seemed too removed from the harsher, more contemporary issues of black life. Thus, when *The Education of Sonny Carson* appeared, based on a true story of a one-time honor student who later becomes a street gang war lord, then a hold-up man, and is eventually thrown into jail where he is brutalized by a sadistic white police force, the critics were anxious to hail it. In *The New York Times,* Lawrence Van Gelder wrote that it "is a howling brute of a film. Riddled with flaws, inexpressive as art, it shakes off its shortcomings with a primal energy that imbues it with terrifying eloquence. . . . This film possesses a very real beauty and power." *Variety* had its say, too: "When the historical dust settles on the first wave of black-oriented films, *The Education of Sonny Carson* should stand up as one of the most outstanding in the genre. Paramount . . . has come up with a rugged, uncompromising, yet thoughtful and sensitive film . . . in the great tradition of 30s Warner Brothers social melodramas." When this movie failed to ignite fires at the box office, many pointed to it with pride, as a perceptive social/political document that was simply ahead of its time and too good for its audiences.

The intellectuals of that period were both right and wrong. Certainly far better than most black-oriented movies of that day, *The Education of Sonny Carson* retains its hard, raw edge, and Rony Clanton, in the title role, uses his exciting drive to keep much of the picture in motion and to provide it with tension and weight. But, in all truthfulness, the film really is not fully developed dramatically. It's a series of tough street scenes with no linking thread, no actual point of view. Everything is simply thrown out at us, sometimes with a disregard for plausibility. The sequence when Sonny's girlfriend, played by former model Joyce Walker, is revealed hooked on drugs comes without any forethought or preparation, and the audience is jolted, not by the horror of the sequence but because it's so out of line with what has already been shown us of the character. The violence, too, while true to that of the urban scene, is really not an organic part of the picture; sometimes, it seems to be there merely for shock value. In the movie's depiction of Sonny, too, there is a curious, subtle strain of masochism running throughout. In the long run, this film certainly keeps us riveted to the screen but is far from satisfying.

Filmed on location in Brooklyn.

Babes in Gangland: Rony Clanton, Joyce Walker, and Jerry Bell in The Education of Sonny Carson.

The Emperor Jones (1933)

D. Dudley Murphy. S. DuBose Heyward, who also wrote *Porgy* (on which *Porgy and Bess* was based) and the novel *Mamba's Daughters* (which was adapted into a hit Broadway play for Ethel Waters and Fredi Washington in 1939). P. John Krimsky and Gifford Cochran. R. UA. Cast includes: Dudley Diggs; Ruby Elzy; Rex Ingram; Jackie "Moms" Mabley; Frank Wilson, and—as Ondine, Robeson's high-yaller, hot-tempered girlfriend—Fredi Washington, whose scenes had to be reshot after the movie executives viewed the daily rushes and became frightened that audiences would think Robeson was holding a white woman in his arms. Second time around, Washington did her scenes, wearing a thick, dark pancake makeup.

The Emperor Jones: *Fredi Washington, darkened in heavy pancake makeup because the producers feared white audiences might think co-star Paul Robeson was playing romantic scenes with a white actress.*

An adaptation of Eugene O'Neill's play and independently produced outside Hollywood (in New York), *The Emperor Jones* traces the rise of a black man, Brutus Jones (Paul Robeson), from pullman car porter and shifty ladies' man to autocrat of an island to a man stripped of his powers and confidence.

An arrogant and strong-willed braggart, Robeson's Brutus is a man who refuses to kowtow to anyone. In one particularly interesting scene on a railroad car, Robeson goes through the stock "yes sirs" and "no sirs" to his white employer but is so full of energy and self-mockery that his behavior is never self-demeaning. Later when he attempts to blackmail his employer (and afterward when he mocks the employer for the benefit of his black woman), he is a black man consciously asserting himself, consciously cutting the Man down to size.

When he argues with a friend in a crap game, Robeson kills him, is sent to a chain gang, where he kills a sadistic white guard and escapes, setting off for a nearby island. Later he usurps the throne of the island's black king. For the next two and a half years, he struts through the palace in his high leather boots. He gazes at himself in his corridor of mirrors. "King Brutus," he proclaims. "Somehow that don't make enough noise." He pauses. "The Emperor Jones!"

In many scenes, Robeson's dazzling to watch, proud and haughty, entirely different from such then-typical black male figures in films as the comic servants of Stepin Fetchit and Willie Best. Indeed *The Emperor Jones* gave Robeson his finest role, yet he thought it tainted because here the Negro was presented as a murderer and a rogue. And contemporary audiences seem to prefer him in a movie like *Song of Freedom*, in which he seems more relaxed. In the long run, because so many people have raved over this film, you're tempted to feel guilty about not really liking it. But the truth of the matter is that, aside from Robeson's performance and its virile image of a black man, the film's a poorly paced, stagey and stagnant rendering of a once-provocative stage play.

The Final Comedown (1972)

D. Oscar Williams. S. Oscar Williams. P. Oscar Williams. R. New World Pictures. Cast includes: Raymond St. Jacques; Maidie Norman; D'Urville Martin; and Celia Kaye.

A coming-of-age film set in the late 1960s/1970s. Told in flashbacks, it details the radicalization of young Johnny Johnson (Billy Dee Williams) from a handsome bright fellow to fiery militant political leader. Partly financed by The American Film Institute, the movie is very much a part of its period, frequently heated and rhetorical, sometimes mopey and dopey (particularly in Johnny's generational differences with his parents), and often enough reflective of the spirit of cultural nationalism and activism that spurred students of this era on. The film remains of interest because it's a signature piece by a black director and also because it marks an early star performance by Billy Dee Williams who, *Variety* wrote, "handles the role skillfully, imbuing the figure with sensitivity and strength" (both of which were to be hallmarks of the Williams screen persona). Here he's both realistically and dreamily rebellious, his performance owing something perhaps to Sidney Poitier's high school rebel in *Blackboard Jungle* and perhaps a little to James Dean's *Rebel Without a Cause*.

The film met with mixed reviews. *The New York Times* wrote that it had "a plot full of personal relations that never avoid the cliches of urban soap opera." But Frances Herridge in *The New York Post* called it "a sizzling confrontation between black rebels and police. You may find it relentlessly singleminded in its theme but it is acted and directed with such fire that you aren't likely to be bored." And *Variety* added: "Black militants. Strong stuff. . . . Solid performances and production values. Looks like big box office, especially on race appeal. Not for conservative communities."

Variety's box-office predictions proved false. But after Williams' success in *Lady Sings the Blues* and *The Bingo Long Travelling All-Stars and Motor Kings*, *The Final Comedown* was re-released in 1977 with a new title *The Blast*. The script, the direction, and the producer credit all went to Frank Arthur Wilson, a pseudonym for Oscar Williams.

Fingers (1978)

D. James Toback. S. James Toback. P. George Barrie. R. Brut Productions. Cast includes: Michael Grazzo; Tisa Farrow; and Marian Seldes.

An existential jaunt into the underworld, starring Harvey Kietel as a man clearly divided by the past and his own view of himself. A concert pianist who works for his tough gangster father as a "collector" of debts, Kietel wearily wanders about, unable to deal with his own sexual drives and his violent fantasies. The one character he looks up to with awe (and fear) and the one character, in turn, who seems to see right through Kietel, into the dark heart of his sexual hangups—is the black Dreems, a former boxing champion, now owner of a small restaurant. Dreems, a sexual grandmaster, lives in moderate high style with two blond "love slaves." And he doesn't seem to have a single fear or inhibition. Sexually, he's totally free and totally daring. Also totally insane.

Dreems is played by Jim Brown. Decked out in a tight pink shirt and tighter white pants, Brown seems more secure in this movie than in previous ones but physically he looks as if he's about to burst at the seams, reminding us a bit of an oldtime whore out to prove he's still got what it takes. For those who enjoyed Brown's knuckleheaded derring-do movies of the late 1960s and early 1970s, *Fingers* no doubt will be a disappointment. Brown doesn't come on screen until the picture is just about over, although when he does appear he is brilliantly showcased by writer/director James Toback. But Brown has also been shamelessly exposed here: his great gaudy mythic movie persona is both apotheosized and disemboweled.

Brown's Dreems lives by his instincts and physical strength, not content unless he's surrounded by his stable of lush young beauties. On one level, he's a violently ribald fantasy figure that may appeal to the pre-pubescent eleven-year-old in all of us. But on another more serious level, Brown once again personifies the white world's view of *black cool*, black sexual hipness. Brown may be better here than in most of his other films, but he has little more to do than rub his lady's buttocks or to smash together the heads of his two white girlfriends. (This later sequence is chilling, shocking, disturbing. It catches the viewer totally off-guard, coming so fast that you don't have time to turn away from the screen.)

In 1971, *Fingers* director Toback had written a book on Jim Brown, who was seen then as a Nietzschean superman, implacable in his (sexual) power, an embodiment of the white American male's terrifying fear and fascination with the black male. Most black athletes have been viewed by the white world in this way. But as you watch the manipulation of Brown at work, you may not be able to stop from howling because it's all so obvious and dated. The picture freezes Brown. His blatant pimp/stud/buck hero has been pinned down. Cheapened and vulgarized here, Brown is not viewed as anything but, again, a walking phallus, one led by Toback, a Harvard-educated, middle-class bright white boy in search of God in Harlem. That's part of Toback's dream. And on some basic level, he succeeds in articulating his vision. But it's not the vision of black moviegoers. For all his skill, Toback does not understand what the black viewer knows to be true or untrue about himself and his world.

A very literary film that often falls apart but which never fails to fascinate and puzzle. For all its distortions, a movie still worth seeing.

Five on the Black Hand Side (1973)

D. Oscar Williams. *S.* Charlie L. Russell, based on his play. *P.* Brock Peters and Michael Tolan. *R.* UA. Cast includes: Ja'net DuBois (looking terrific in the period just before she was to co-star on the TV series "Good Times"); Virginia Capers; Sonny Jim; Frankie Crocker; Bonnie Banfield; and Godfrey Cambridge.

One of the 1970s early new-style black comedies, spotlighting the era's black consciousness. Its theme: liberation. Leonard Jackson plays the rigid, middle-class robot of a patriarch, Mr. Brooks, who's blind to the changes overcoming his children and his wife—a meek, timid creature, called Mrs. Brooks, even by her husband, and played endearingly by the very talented Clarice Taylor. Glynn Turman is the rebellious younger son, spouting the then-popular "militant" rhetoric. D'Urville Martin is cast as the older conventional son.

The movie's best moments come when Mrs. Brooks decides she can no longer take her husband's fussy demands and undergoes a transformation: she sports a new Afro hairdo and promptly presents her husband with a list of her demands. It's *her* liberation that amuses and engages us. The film also climaxes with an African-style wedding that no doubt struck 1970s audiences as hip and very much "with it." Today it looks sweetly sentimental and dated.

Often stagey and technically sloppy, it's a bit like a black sitcom but is blessed with the moviemakers' warmth and affection for the material and the characters.

For Love of Ivy (1968)

D. Daniel Mann. *S.* Robert Alan Aurthur; based on an original story by Sidney Poitier. *P.* Edgar J. Scherick and Jay Weston. *R.* Palomar Pictures International/Cinerama Releasing Corporation. Cast includes: Carroll O'Connor; Nan Martin; Lauri Peters; Leon Bibb; Stanley Greene; Lon Satton; and Hugh Hird.

Based on a story idea by Sidney Poitier, *For Love of Ivy* supposedly tells the tale of a black housemaid, Ivy (Abbey Lincoln), who, weary of the tedium of her life, plans to leave her Long Island job to move to the big city—and to find herself. The white family for whom Ivy works is determined not to lose her, the son of the family (Beau Bridges) going so far as to match her up with a black businessman (Poitier). Once Ivy has a man in her life, she'll no longer have problems or an itch to take off. That's what the young man believes. Unfortunately, the movie believes the same thing.

When first released, the gentle tone and fantasy-laden atmosphere of *For Love of Ivy* (it's like a standard, well-made movie romance of the 1950s with all loose ends neatly tied up at the end) did not sit well with an audience anxious for grittier and more realistic black films. Even the reviewer at *Newsweek* wrote: "Poitier's idea was to present the first inside look at the life and love of a young Negro couple. Fine in theory, but why did he have to do it in a story that not even the most gullible honky would buy?"

Curiously enough, today the picture plays quite well on television and is rather diverting although throughout, despite the clever and sometimes engaging situations and the talents of the cast, Robert Alan Aurthur's script treats Ivy condescendingly and does not have the faintest idea what a black woman's quest for self-identity might really be all about.

Poitier is a rather stiff romantic lead. But the movie does afford him some of his rare love scenes. "I'm not interested in having a romantic interlude on the screen with a white girl," he said at the time, shortly after having starred opposite white actress Katharine Houghton in *Guess Who's Coming to Dinner?* "I'd much rather have romantic interludes with Negro girls." Thus he began work on this feature. Frequently, Beau Bridges threatens to steal the show. But gliding throughout is Abbey Lincoln: poised, tender, touching, and warm, with layers of vigor and intelligence that the movie unfortunately fails to fully tap.

Fort Apache: The Bronx (1981)

D. Daniel Petrie. *S.* Heywood Gould. *P.* Martin Richards and Tom Fiorello. *R.* 20th Century-Fox. Cast includes: Ed Asner; Miguel Pinero (author of the play *Short Eyes*); Danny Aiello; Kathleen Beller; Tito Goyo; Jaime Tirelli; Clifford David; and Rony Clanton.

A controversial, tough-minded urban cop drama centered in the 41st police precinct of the South Bronx. It's also a grisly, bloody nightmarish tourist's view of the ghetto: little is seen of ghetto life here other than the drug-trafficking, the vandals, the junkies, the petty thieves, the killings, the street crowds, an overall mayhem. Even the Bronx's one bright, promising aspect, an antiseptically pretty Puerto Rican nurse (Rachel Ticotin) is ultimately viewed as "blemished": late in the film it is revealed she's a heroin junkie. The nurse's sudden addiction is implausible, and she, the lone positive image the film offers of the community, is the most distressing character. Her dope habit and death wreck any chance of symbolic hope. And it's no wonder community groups of the South Bronx, as well as clerics and politicians, protested against this film, in some cases before the film was even completed. Even New York City's Mayor Ed Koch was quoted in *The New York Times* as saying: "I saw it as a fascinating film in terms of excitement, but a racist film in the following way: there was not one Puerto Rican personality that was without some major character defect."

The film's noble, fair-minded heroes are two white cops, expertly portrayed by Paul Newman and Ken Wahl. But one asks: couldn't the filmmakers have had a Puerto Rican or black cop working hard within his own community to bring about a change? Instead it's the Great Good White Father come to help the savages all over again.

Making a dubiously spectacular appearance is Pam Grier, the former B-movie queen of the 1970s, now cast as a drugged-out, sinister blond-wigged prostitute. As she opens the film by pulling out a gun and blasting to bits two unsuspecting, innocent cops and later killing off whoever even casually crosses her path, she is a terrifying presence, a sexy, lewd killing machine, the film's most lethal and effective figure. Grier approaches her work with honesty and a sure intuitive grasp of her character. Sometimes we wonder as we watch Grier eyeing her victims, ready to knock them off, if she's not thinking of the producers of her tawdry movies of the past. That might help explain why this may be her most accomplished screen performance.

48 Hrs. (1982)

D. Walter Hill. *S.* Roger Spottiswoode and Walter Hill, Larry Gross, and Steven E. de Souza. *P.* Lawrence Gordon and Joel Silver. *R.* Paramount. Cast includes: Annette O'Toole; Frank McRae; James Remar; Sonny Landlam; and Olivia Brown (who later appeared as Trudy Joblin on TV's "Miami Vice."

48 Hrs. with Eddie Murphy (l.) and Nick Nolte as the adversaries-turned-friends in yet another homage to interracial male bonding.

Funny and tense action comedy that was hugely successful and firmly established television comic Eddie Murphy as a viable box-office movie star. Its theme is a familar one, dating back to the days of the movie versions of *The Adventures of Huckleberry Finn* as well as the Stepin Fetchit/ Will Rogers or Eddie "Rochester" Anderson/Jack Benny movies and several of Poitier's big hits in the 1950s—interracial male bonding, done in a pure 1980s style.

Nick Nolte is the San Francisco detective tracking down two killers. Eddie Murphy is the petty thief sprung from jail by Nolte in hopes that he can lead Nolte to the murderers. Like the heroes of *The Defiant Ones,* Nolte and Murphy don't want to be bothered with one another and are (figuratively) chained together in their pursuit of the hoods. The two curse, shout, bicker, battle, and physically pound one another out. By the movie's end, we're to believe they've learned something new about each other and have become true friends.

Rigged from the word go, the film's dialogue is peppered with racial epithets, delivered with full gusto by both performers. This is the type of racist dialogue no moviemaker would have dared in the 1950s. The language would have caused an uproar from the black community had it been used in films of the 1960s or 1970s. But by the 1980s, it's thought to be hip, flip, realistic talk. We're not supposed to feel outraged or shocked; we're supposed to laugh and not be so uptight. Often enough we do laugh but at our own expense. Murphy is so cool and together that we know, too, that no matter what Nolte might say to him, the black comic's going to come back strong and deliver a real zinger. Yet one of Murphy's funniest scenes is also one of the film's most patently fake. He's in a country and western bar. Surrounded by rednecks who look as if they're straight from the pines of Georgia, he

tells the crackers, "I'm your worst fucking nightmare, man. I'm a nigger with a badge." We're led to believe that line says something. It doesn't.

When the men first meet, we know that to Nolte Murphy's just a nigger. And to Murphy, Nolte's just a honky. When the picture ends, we feel the two men still regard each other as nigger and honky but they're now buddies. Perhaps the film inadvertently reveals the most cynical of racial attitudes, that not only do black and white never view each other simply as people but that even when friends they still see each other as racial stereotypes: the nigger, the honky. At least in the Poitier films of the 1950s, one sensed some kind of friendship and trust evolving between the races, even if only because the black man's attempts at accommodation supposedly revealed his larger-than-life humanity.

Murphy—at age 21—is, however, already a consummate screen comic. He doesn't play a character (he's not yet enough of an actor to do that) but he is able to create a brazen star persona: With his perfect timing, he's nervy, aggressive, audacious, completely at home in front of the camera.

Foxy Brown (1974)

D. Jack Hill. *S.* Jack Hill. *P.* Buzz Feitshans. *R.* AIP. Cast includes: Terry Carter; Peter Brown; and Juanita Brown.

Pam Grier's "important" 1970s movies were rowdy action pictures, garish revenge dramas with Pam as a gun-totin', bad-talking, funky, foul, aggressive Florence Nightingale of the ghetto, there to administer to the needs of her oppressed brothers and sisters. She's a dream goddess of the slums who often disrobes and bares her breasts (and more) as she floats through a sado-masochistic comic strip world of blood, guts, and gunfire. Of this type of Pam Grier movie, *Foxy Brown* is without a doubt the best, trashy, lurid, and exploitative as all get out, poorly stitched together, perverse, sometimes degrading its star, and perhaps even pointless and certainly frequently infuriating yet highly enjoyable.

Foxy Brown contains what can only be described as a classic Pam Grier movie situation: out to clean up the ghetto and to get the drug dealers who have brought about her brother's (Antonio Fargas) death, Pam as Foxy catches up with the white villain, has her boys unzip his pants, then has him castrated. Pam carries his organs in a jar (with a liquid, which, we may assume, is formaldehyde) to the man's girlfriend, a treacherous white woman (Kathryn Loder). The jar falls on the floor and breaks, with the contents apparently rolling across the floor. (We view the action not by what we see of the organs but by the white woman's reactions.) Suddenly, the white woman recognizes this material and cries out that it is—her fellow, Steve! Audiences whooped this sequence up, hooted, hollered, cheered, and screamed and shouted as their gal Pam strutted her way to vengeful gory glory.

Throughout *Foxy Brown* there are similar (although less extreme) violent sequences. But Pam always comes out victorious. She infuses this cheap pulp project with her own highly charged, misdirected energy. And it is her perverse straightforwardness, her cockeyed determination to carry through on her do-goodism (despite the inherent violence in her brand of do-goodism), and her supreme single-mindedness as well as her bizarre belief in her material (she actually seems to think these movies mean something) that make her pictures pleasurable to some audiences today.

Friday Foster (1975)

D. Arthur Marks. S. Orville Hampton; story by Arthur Marks. P. Arthur Marks. R. AIP. Cast includes: Godfrey Cambridge (in an embarrassing performance as a swishy designer); Tierre Turner; Thalmus Rasulala; Ted Lange; Jim Backus; Scatman Crothers; Paul Benjamin; and Carl Weathers (cast as a villain; this was way before his days as Apollo Creed in the *Rocky* movies).

By the mid-1970s, black audiences had tired of the black buck films (starring the likes of Jim Brown and Fred Williamson) and of the black supermama pictures as well. Pam Grier, who had starred in the latter, consequently underwent an image change, a softening process in which her studio tried cleaning up her act. The softened Grier turned up here as a fashion photographer, Friday Foster, who uncovers and destroys a white group out to assassinate the black leaders of the land. Some violence erupts but it's not excessive.

Grier looks great and has flashes of humor, although many may prefer the raunchier, rowdier Grier of *Coffy* and *Foxy Brown*. Cast as Grier's right-hand buddy is Yaphet Kotto, who turns in a casual and enjoyable performance. Eartha Kitt (looking a bit weathered) shows up as an eccentric designer, and she struggles hard to invest her sequences with some much-needed flair and at least a sense of campy fun. But Kitt gets no help from the script or the director. In fact, no one else in the cast gets any help either. If director Marks had some wit and a tighter sense of construction, *Friday Foster* might have been diverting. It's on the order of an average made-for-TV movie and probably plays better on TV today than it did originally in theatres.

As it turned out, a cleaned-up Pam Grier wasn't a very commercial item. She could have been though—with the right projects. *Variety* wrote: "One can't blame shoddy plot elements on her, since she so far transcends the silliness of her vehicles. Far more active than any other femme star in the last few years, she just needs a breakthrough major role to come into her own." That didn't quite happen. Soon after *Friday Foster* and *Sheba, Baby*, Grier's days as box-office queen of the B-flicks came to an end.

Ganja and Hess (1973)

D. Bill Gunn. S. Bill Gunn. P. Quentin Kelly and Jack Jordan; a Chiz Schultz Production. R. Kelly-Jordan Enterprises. Cast includes: Leonard Jackson; Sam Waymon; Mabel King; Betsy Thurman; and Bill Gunn.

In the early 1970s, some black intellectuals rallied around this film by black screenwriter and director Bill Gunn. Exhibitors had shown little interest in it. The white critical establishment had ignored it. And because the picture was so different from the standard run of black movies, it looked as if an important work of black art was about to die a quick, unheralded death. Actually, *Ganja and Hess*—sometimes portentous (sometimes, pretentious, too), often murky and moody, and more often than not, doggedly artsy—may not be all its supporters had

An early black cult film and a favorite of the intelligentsia: Bill Gunn's Ganja & Hess, *with Duane Jones (as Dr. Hess Green) and Marlene Clark (as Ganja Meda).*

hoped, but it remains strong on atmosphere and clearly the personal work of an intriguing black filmmaker.

In synopsis, the story might sound like an intellectual's vampire story. Maybe it sounds laughable too. But basically here it is. A handsome black professor, Dr. Hess Green (Duane Jones), stabbed with an ancient dagger, finds himself infected, but neither disease nor death follows. Instead he's now got a yen for blood. He's just gotta have it. In a clever sequence that well updates the old vampire saga, the professor robs a blood bank to quench his thirst. Then, of course, he searches for some good old-fashioned human victims. He's joined on this bloody trail by a beautiful young woman, Ganja (Marlene Clark), the wife of the professor's dead assistant. Once she's been injected, she and the professor are about the classiest set of vampires you've ever seen. Jones and Clark make a stunning pair. And therein curiously lies some of the strange effectiveness of this uneven picture. With their cultivated manners and haughty sophistication, they come to represent, for many, the decadent, Europeanized black bourgeoisie, which, slowly dying, can survive only by feeding on others. The black church is also brought into this symbolic arena. While actor Jones remains subdued, Clark attacks her role with spicy relish: she's a high-flung, high-liver of a bourgeois bitch, and the director seems more enchanted with and admiring of her style than we might want. No doubt she's also meant to represent man's fears of a forceful domineering woman. She's the survivor here.

The movie is also hot for nudity: there's more of it than you might be prepared for. (*Variety* said it was like "a sex film with blood.") Yet occasionally the nudity as well as James Hinton's moody cinematography adds to the film's dark smokey unreal quality. So much is left unexplained and undeveloped that is it any wonder some people *love* this film? It's an intellectual's dream: an open vessel into which one can pour his or her own point of view or over which one can superimpose individual interpretations. Analyzing the film, you may congratulate yourself on your own daffy cleverness. Writer and director Gunn, in this work and others, is always interesting and unexpectedly provocative. *Ganja and Hess* becomes challenging for some because of what it suggests and intimates rather than what it actually delivers.

Georgia, Georgia (1972)

D. Stig Bjorkman. *S.* Maya Angelou. *P.* Quentin Kelly and Jack Jordan. *R.* Cinerama Releasing Corporation. Cast includes: Terry Whitmore; Randolph Henry; Diana Kjaer; and Lars Eric Berenett.

Startling but uneven and rather frustrating drama focusing on a black American pop star adrift while on tour in Stockholm. Moviegoers have a chance to see Diane Sands in one of her rare starring film roles as the tense, confused singer Georgia, fighting to keep herself together as she deals with fans and followers—and also with the people who "take care" of her, one of whom is her gay manager (Roger Furman), the other a mysterious maternal figure called Mrs. Anderson (Minnie Gentry). All three are fascinating objects (they're almost abstractions) but not a one is a wholly believable character, and the relationships among the three—surely the most interesting aspect of the movie, indeed its soul—are left floundering and underdeveloped.

With a script by Maya Angelou, the movie touches on ground ripe for exploration: the black star who is expected not only to be an entertainer but also a spokeswoman for the problems and demands of the black community. Angelou wants us to sense the high-pressured grip of fame, the hysteria and mania that surround the famous, the weariness of the star, who moves from one arena to another, from one gig to the next only to discover herself a commodity and a vehicle for the convoluted dreams or needs of others. She wants us to experience the star's alienation, emotional dislocation, and search for connections. What she wants us to see is indeed unusual material—and it's Angelou's intentions that keep us watching. But nothing is fully worked out here.

The movie looks as if shot on a low budget and thus during Sands' opening press conference and her performance sequence (both sequences which should bristle with vitality), everything seems so sparsely populated that the viewer is distanced from the star's point of view, which is that the crowds, the press, the screams, the cheers are all closing in on her. Nor is the source of Georgia's weariness clear. And

In one of her rare star roles, Diana Sands plays the driven American entertainer Georgia Martin in Maya Angelou's Georgia, Georgia.

the reason for her eventual involvement with a young white photographer (Dirk Benedict), which is the catalyst for the film's dramatic and political climax, is neither dramatized nor spelled out in any telling detail. Sands and Benedict do have a good scene together when their sexual roles are reversed: he's nervous and fearful; she takes the sexual lead; and then the two are fine. But this sequence doesn't fit into the whole of the movie. The white character is simply a prop, used to bring about Georgia's demise.

But a major weakness is the depiction of the character Mrs. Anderson. As played by Minnie Gentry, the character's a bit of a prig, something of a hollow and campy earth mother, too: she wears a proper middle-class lady's wig, speaks in clipped tones, is always carefully made-up, even wears dainty white gloves and appears far more colonized than the earthy Georgia (who at least removes *her* wig, letting us glimpse the black woman underneath). Yet Mrs. Anderson spouts rhetoric about black America and becomes enraged when she learns Sands has taken on a white lover. As writer Angelou shies away from the complex character she's almost created, actress Gentry seems to be winging it, playing a part that's not fully written and bringing to it her own sense of political commitment and maternity. Often audiences have burst into laughter at some of Mrs. Anderson's comments, both because of the delivery and the lines themselves. (Oddly enough, Gentry almost gives a bravura performance.) Yet at the conclusion when Mrs. Anderson declares that Georgia, who's just returned from a day of lovemaking with the white photographer, will not do it again, the audience applauds Mrs. Anderson as she strangles the black star who, we are to believe, has sold out and betrayed her black roots.

The audience reaction is disturbing. In the love/hate relationship that any audience has with a performer, the hate has here won out, and the audience judges that Georgia deserves death. Yet the script is unfair to Georgia, having simplified her. Georgia's sexual/racial defection strikes us as a mild digression, not a way of life. And often we wonder why the lesbian as well as the mother/daughter undertones (between Georgia and Mrs. Anderson) are touched on but never explored. Ultimately the tone of *Georgia, Georgia* becomes moralistic and pseudo-political without a moral center or a political ideology that's been fully delved into. The audience ends up by filling in the holes.

As for Angelou, she's a true puzzle of a writer. In her memoirs, *I Know Why the Caged Bird Sings* and *Gather Together in My Name*, she's a master dramatist, lyrical and poetic yet blessed with down-to-earth commonsense and insights—and with dialogue that's literary but also realistic. Her characters and sequences are always of a piece; she's able to bring all the elements together and to build to a moving climax. One would assume she'd be a marvel with scripts. But in *Georgia, Georgia*, as in her teleplay "Sister, Sister," she doesn't seem in full control of her material or the medium. In the latter, she tells us far too much, narrating rather than dramatizing and revealing high point after high point much too early rather than slowly, dramatically building to an inevitable climax. In *Georgia, Georgia* she tells us too little. Yet as a gifted black female writer, she touches on areas few others have ever approached on film (or TV), and thus her work remains intriguing and often fascinating. Perhaps a stronger director might be able to suggest to Angelou ways to deal with her complex characters and situations in a film.

In the long run, the shallow direction is *Georgia, Georgia*'s greatest flaw. The incidents involving the black American draft resisters living abroad go nowhere—and are, frankly, an embarrassment. This is all the sadder because of the exciting work of Diana Sands, who, from the very opening, at her press conference, is revved up, ready for action, anxious to give a fullblown star/actress performance. Often funny and keenly intelligent, she's sympathetic and mature. As we sit watching Sands, aware that this was one of her last films before her early death, her valiant attempts at characterization and performance are all the more moving.

Definitely worth seeing.

Go, Man, Go! (1954)

D. James Wong Howe. S. Arnold Becker. P. Anton M. Leader. R. UA. Cast includes the real Harlem Globetrotters as themselves; also Ruby Dee; Patricia Breslin; and Slim Gailland (as Slim; he also sings the title song).

An unpretentious precursor of *The Bingo Long Traveling All-Stars and Motor Kings* but without any attempts at "social significance." This low-budget movie (shot on a shoestring budget of $130,000) traces the rise of the Harlem Globetrotters, that razzle-dazzle all-colored basketball team, known as much for its comic shenanigans as its athletic skills. True to the movie traditions of the day, the troupe is led to success—and its triumph past the color barriers of the period—through the efforts of a rather noble, amiable young white promoter, Abe Saperstein (played well by Dane Clark). Movies such as this usually spotlight some white coach or manager with whom the mass white audience can identify. Even in the late 1970s, television's "White Shadow" program still used such a figure. No matter how likable such movie coaches are, Hollywood's use of them is still patronizing condescension: the black boys couldn't have done anything without their good Great White Father figures, who shepherd them through life's difficulties.

Another film about the Globetrotters, *The Harlem Globetrotters*, had appeared in 1951, featuring Dorothy Dandridge. This one's distinguished partly because of its director, James Wong Howe, one of the movie industry's most celebrated cinematographers. After this film, though, Howe never directed another. Another point of interest: turning up as Inman Jackson, a player on the team, is a young, trim Sidney Poitier, looking green and sweetly naive.

The movie's predictable script is a hack job but the interspersed footage of the actual Globetrotters lends a good documentary air. Perhaps this isn't bad for a Saturday afternoon. (But be warned: that's about the only time this should be seen.) Bosley Crowthers in *The New York Times* called it "a lively little independent picture . . . spiced with a lot of colorful action."

God's Step Children (1937)

D. Oscar Micheaux. S. Oscar Micheaux. P. Oscar Micheaux. R. Micheaux Pictures Corporation. Cast includes: Jacqueline Lewis as the adult Naomi; Ethel Moses (the black Harlow); Carmen Newsome; and Gloria Press.

Black director Oscar Micheaux's deliriously enjoyable sepia soap opera. It's all about a sweet-faced, little high-yaller girl, Naomi, deserted by her mother, then cared for by a kindly Negro woman (Alice B. Russell, the wife of director Micheaux). Naomi's got problems, though, and they are readily apparent when she's sent to an all-colored school. This little mulatto is weary of her race and anxious to cross the color line. When she sets the school into a tizzy because of a scandalous rumor she spreads about a teacher, Naomi's promptly packed off to a convent, only to return home some twelve years later. She marries a dark-skinned black man, has a child whom she dumps, falls for her step-brother, and finally gets her wish when, indeed, she temporarily is able to pass for white. But, alas, for poor Naomi, her sins catch up with her, and she finally does everybody a favor by throwing herself into the river. And like a nasty stain on her race, she's washed away.

Sound complicated? Absurd? Trite? Knuckleheaded? Well, yes, *God's Step Children* is all those things. Shot on a shoestring budget, the movie looks tacky and amateurish. So, too, does much of the acting and direction. Yet realities creep through. Without a big studio set-up at his command, independent black director/producer Micheaux shot on locations and sometimes filmed sections of his movies at the homes of friends. Consequently, this movie occasionally has a *real* look to it which the artificial, enclosed world of Hollywood films lacked. The performers, too, are without major studio guile or glamor (although they try hard for the glamor bit) and because they aren't protected by proper lighting and camera angles or even by an opportunity for a second or third take after the first one's gone badly, they, too, have a directness, and in their awkwardness and in their intense attempts at *acting* for the camera, they are sometimes funny and often appealing. Alice B. Russell comes across as something of a downhome dragon lady as she suspiciously eyes little Naomi, wondering what this child will be up to next.

Some critics have written about the undertones in this film, its secret messages and truths. One supposes they are there. But the best way to get at what Micheaux wants us to respond to is simply to sit and enjoy this frequently daffy mess.

Added note: the color syndrome which Micheaux was often criticized for—lights in leading roles, darker blacks in subordinate or clownish parts—pops up here, most notably in the role played by Alex Lovejoy as Naomi's somewhat coonish dark husband.

The Golden Child (1986)

D. Michael Ritchie. S. Dennis Feldman. P. Edward S. Feldman and Robert D. Wachs. R. Paramount Pictures. Cast includes: Charles Dance; Victor Wong; Randall Cobb; and J. L. Reate (as the Golden Child).

An Eddie Murphy comedy that proved highly popular although future generations may be hard pressed to understand why. Murphy plays a freelance Los Angeles social worker, who specializes in finding lost children. When he is enlisted by a beautiful young Tibetan woman (Charlotte Lewis) to help her find a wise, angelic little Tibetan boy (the Golden Child, who is destined to save the world but who has been kidnapped by an agent of the Devil), Murphy (now called the Chosen One) is soon off to Tibet. Much of the film—with its emphasis on special effects, its overblown mix of good and evil forces, and its

Eddie Murphy (r.) with one of the rather exotic creatures he encounters in the supernatural comedy/adventure film The Golden Child.

attempt at fast-moving action sequences in an exotic locale—is watered-down *Raiders of the Lost Ark.* The script is almost nonexistent, and the movie relies on the force and charm of Murphy's personality to carry the action along. Yet Murphy, who's effective in tough urban settings, seems out of place. "Mr. Murphy's comic skepticism in the face of all this is the film's greatest asset," wrote Janet Maslin in *The New York Times.* "But it is worn thin by the awareness that not even he seems able to take the adventure seriously, and by the preposterousness and inconsistency of what surrounds him." Although he is permitted a love interest here (with Lewis), the movie still keeps his sexuality neutralized. There are no explicit love scenes. Moreover, some may wonder why Murphy's not permitted a black leading lady. Because of the filmmakers's desire to reach a large young audience (the picture has a PG rating), Murphy's been stripped of his trademark profanity. Mighty tame here, he remains, however, an assertive, working class-type of black hero, not ready to follow anyone's rules other than his own; oddly enough, a fact as basic as *that* explains part of his appeal.

Gone with the Wind (1939)

D. Victor Fleming. S. Sidney Howard; based on the novel by Margaret Mitchell. P. David O. Selznick. R. MGM. Cast includes: Everett Brown as Big Sam; Oscar Polk as Pork; and Eddie "Rochester" Anderson, barely recognizable under layers of makeup, as Uncle Peter.

Scarlett, Rhett, Ashley, Melanie, Mammy, Prissy, Aunt Pittypat, and a cast of thousands in David O. Selznick's classic Civil War epic. Actually, if *GWTW* is ever viewed as some kind of serious Civil War drama, it fails shockingly. But as a glorious, technicolor pop myth with the Old South, the Civil War, and the Reconstruction periods, all as backdrops, it works. And as a larger-than-life romance—the ups and downs of Scarlett and Rhett—*GWTW* is a triumph, possibly the greatest romantic film ever made in Hollywood.

In *The Inadvertent Epic*, critic Leslie Fiedler has rightly pointed out that *GWTW* and such other popular epics as *Uncle Tom's Cabin, The Birth of a Nation,* and *Roots* all reveal various shifts in the mass imagination. *Uncle Tom's Cabin* presented the good Negro hero, self-sacrificing and accommodating, the essence of Christian stoicism. (Fiedler believes Uncle Tom is really a white mother in blackface and drag.) *The Birth of a Nation* presented the flip side of the coin: the renegade Negro (the baaddd nigger) and also the noble wronged white man, who finally reasserts himself, slips into white sheets and hoods, and restores order to his world. *GWTW* provided the good-nigger-in-chief, Mammy, the great black mother of us all. And later *Roots* finally presented the slave's point of view, marking his transition from rebel to bourgeois colored hero, very much a part of the American way of life. All these popular works (popular as literature and later as stage, film or TV presentations) attest to the fact that the race issue (and America's struggle to come to terms with it) is the one subject that yet fascinates the mass audience, the single social/political historical topic (no matter how superficially it may be treated) that for decades has drawn our nation's attention.

The reactions to *GWTW* over the years (like those to the other three epics) are an index to changes in the public's consciousness and attitudes. When first released, *GWTW*, the movie, was unanimously praised by the critical establishment. Only some left-oriented audiences viewed it as so much tommyrot. Generally, black audiences accepted the film, ever-hungry for some drama that acknowledged the black presence in this country's history and no doubt grateful that the black characters were handled with some degree of sympathy and dignity.

Much later in the restless 1960s, a younger militant black audience rejected the movie as sheer propagandistic fantasy. By the 1980s, however, the movie elicited a different response: starting with the premise that *GWTW* was full of historical and racial distortions, black audiences tended to accept it as a romance and responded to the richly detailed performances, particularly of the gifted black actors. The black performers flipped their stereotyped characters inside out, distinguishing

Scarlett O'Hara and her mother-surrogate, Mammy: Vivien Leigh and Hattie McDaniel in Gone with the Wind.

them through their personal styles, their energy, wit, sometimes their hostility, too. The black women shone brightest.

Often dismissed as simply a scatterbrained simpleton darky, Butterfly McQueen's Prissy is an example of carefully controlled and modulated mayhem. Has anyone ever forgotten the spacey Prissy announcing, upon learning of Miz Melanie's pregnancy, that she'll be there to help with the delivery cause she knows all about birthin' babies, only to scream out in terror on the day of the actual delivery that she don't know nothin' bout birthin' babies? There, as during the siege of Atlanta, McQueen's Prissy displays inspired insanity. While Rhett and Scarlett are behaving heroically during their flight from Atlanta and as Melanie lies with her newborn son in a semi-conscious state in the back of the wagon, McQueen's Prissy periodically screams at the top of her lungs, cuing us in to the fact that the Yankees is comin, the Yankees is comin. Her maddening hysteria anchors the film in a ditsy kind of reality, that of genuine nightmarish fear turned comic, so it can be better handled. And the audience identifies with her fears perhaps more than it has ever wanted to admit.

As Mammy, Hattie McDaniel is a true powerhouse, physically, emotionally, dramatically. Although she supports the values and virtues of the dominant white culture, McDaniel's character, because of the push and power of the actress's own personality, is free of the greatest burden slavery had imposed on black Americans on screen and off: she has absolutely no feelings whatsoever of being inferior. Resilient, independent, feisty, and perceptive, she is the one character who knows Scarlett O'Hara's basic moves and maneuvers—and she never hesitates to speak up. Confident enough to always look all the white characters right in the eye and never shy about expressing her annoyance or anger, McDaniel is tough and at times downright hostile, a woman aware that she's been born, not to take orders, but to give them.

Interestingly enough, the novel *GWTW* ends with Scarlett planning to return home to Tara and feeling secure because "Mammy would be there. Suddenly she wanted Mammy desperately, as she wanted her when she was a little girl, wanted the broad bosom in which to lie her head, the gnarled black hand on her hair. Mammy, the last link with the old days." The movie concludes, however, with no reference to Mammy at all. Too much seems to have passed between the women for this sentiment to hold up. Vivien Leigh's Scarlett and McDaniel's Mammy match one another in temperament throughout, neither ever quite giving in to the other; the same was often true of McDaniel's work with the quick-tempered Jean Harlow in the movies they made together in the 1930s. In her pre-1940s films, McDaniel was often enough at odds with her leading ladies, and her better films are those in which she appeared with actresses who could fight back.

For her performance in *GWTW*, Hattie McDaniel was awarded the Oscar as Best Supporting Actress of 1939, the first black performer ever to win the Academy Award. And it is her performance which gives this romantic film classic some of its backbone and bite.

Gordon's War (1973)

D. Ossie Davis. S. Howard Friedlander and Ed Spielman. P. Robert L. Shaffel. R. 20th Century-Fox. Cast includes: Carl Lee; Tony King; David Downing; and Gilbert Lewis as Spanish Harry.

It's always a pleaure to see Paul Winfield, even in this action film that calls on none of his vast resources as an actor. He portrays a Vietnam veteran returning home to New York to a dead wife, the victim of a drug overdose. Enlisting the aid of three other Viet vets, he becomes a vigilante, determined to rub out the dope dealers.

Plenty of action but not enough story or characterization. In *The New York Times*, Howard Thompson wrote: "This is a worthy film, whose format and substance—a black theme dramatized for practical, constructive purposes—remain exceeded by its goal."

The Grasshopper (1970)

D. Jerry Paris. *S.* Jerry Belson and Garry Marshall; based on the novel *The Passing of Evil* by Mark McShane. *P.* Jerry Belson and Garry Marshall. *R.* National General Pictures. Cast includes: Joseph Cotton; Ed Flanders; and Corbett Monica.

"Well-made, if immoral, look at life among the fleshpots of Vegas," wrote *Variety* of this tale of a young woman's slow, sad decline. Jacqueline Bisset is the striking drifter from Canada, who roams from job to job, man to man, first in Los Angeles, later in Vegas, where she marries a black former pro football player (Jim Brown). Now working at a Vegas hotel as "vice-president in charge of shaking hands," he seems awkward at times, somewhat uncomfortable, aware no doubt he's cashing in on his former fame. Of course, the same could be said of Brown, the actor, who, *Variety* wrote, was "stiff but there is a half-truth about the role that creates a mystique of reality, the ex pro-football star frustrated by being treated like a piece of meat."

After a white man has viciously beaten Bisset, Brown has a chance for heroic moments as he unleashes all his locked-up anger on the man in a brutal fight sequence. As should be expected perhaps, the Brown hero is soon done away with.

In a strange way, though, this is one of Jim Brown's most effective roles. He understands the plight of a black man ill-at-ease in a high-powered world that sees him as a symbol of former glory—sadly, a symbol that can be bought.

Greased Lightning (1977)

D. Michael Schultz. *S.* Kenneth Vose, Lawrence Du Kore, Melvin Van Peebles, and Leon Capetanos. The fact that the film went through so many writers may explain its disjointedness. *P.* Hannah Weinstein. *R.* A Warner Bros. release of a Third World Production. Cast includes: Cleavon Little; Richie Havens; Julian Bond; Minnie Gentry; and Vincent Gardenia.

A formula movie biography featuring Richard Pryor as Wendell Scott, America's first black racing car champion. The social and political milieu (the American South) in which the real Scott functioned, struggled, and triumphed is reduced, of course, to a simplified glimpse of a bright, snappy colored upstart versus some good-ole-Southern-boy rednecks. Director Schultz's most interesting gift (in such movies as *Car Wash*, 1976, and *Cooley High*, 1975)—his depiction of congenial, free-wheeling, breezy souls, bouncing through life as if it were one big groovy lark—is something of a drawback here: everything's too likable, too harmless, too TV-ish. Even the villains are depicted without tension or menace. Then, too, because this is indeed a standard formula picture, not too different from movie biographies of the 1940s and 1950s about singing stars or sports figures, *Greased Lightning* throws in familiar (but light-weight and trivial) obstacles for Pryor's Scott to overcome, plus a long-suffering wife (played by a very subdued Pam Grier, who's never at her best when she's without raunch), and a series of car races, none of which is very excitingly done.

But the real tipoff as to what *Greased Lightning*'s about emerges with the presence of Beau Bridges as a one-time bigoted enemy of Pryor who soon becomes his best buddy. Hollywood always wants us to believe that tensions between whites and blacks are no big deal, and that naturally, when both races have a chance to really *see* one another, they become the warmest of friends. But such films as *Imitation of Life* (both versions in 1934 and 1959), *Edge of the City* (1957), *Virgin Island* (1958), and *Blue Collar* (1978), all of which focus on such interracial buddy systems, never delve into the complexities of such relationships or the individual styles of the particular friends involved. At heart, such films, by refusing to see the true cultural differences of the races, tend to suppress the race issue altogether, almost always at the black charac-ter's expense. And the movies permit white liberal audiences to pat themselves on the back at a "tolerance" theme they can readily accept. They can accept it because it's a pure fantasy.

Throughout *Greased Lightning*, a genial and warm Pryor is pleasant to watch but at his least effective, often giving in to the kind of sentimen-tality that seems the very antithesis of what we think Richard Pryor (the original Crazy Nigger) is all about.

In *Time*, Richard Schickel wrote: "There is not a more likable movie currently on view." But I think most viewers would agree with *News-week*'s David Ansen's assessment: "Once Pryor breaks the color barrier, the story has nowhere to go and lurches awkwardly from decade to decade in search of a properly uplifting finale. The result is like a cheap retread of *The Jackie Robinson Story*."

A sluggish picture without a director or scriptwriter in the driver's seat.

The Great White Hope (1970)

D. Martin Ritt. S. Howard Sackler, based on his play. P. Lawrence Turman. R. 20th Century-Fox. Cast includes a gallery of interesting black actors: Beah Richards; Moses Gunn; Roy Glenn, Sr.; Joel Fluellen; and William Walker.

The highly successful Broadway play based on the life of first black heavyweight champion Jack Johnson (called Jack Jefferson here) was brought to the screen at the start of the 1970s. Repeating the role that made him a star, James Earl Jones played the larger-than-life, self-destructive boxer, who bows to no man *or* woman. Jane Alexander is the tragic Etta, who can't deal with the man she loves or his manic national fame.

Wherever Jack Jefferson goes, the film carefully records the crowds: an affectionate black following and an increasingly hostile white Amer-ica, which sets out to cut him down to size.

Unfortunately, despite the attention paid to detail and some exciting but uneven performances, *The Great White Hope* proves a static dead-weight of a movie, never able to get to our guts or to set us flying emotionally. At the time of this film's release, Muhammad Ali was very much in the headlines, and there are obvious parallels between Johnson and Ali, which perhaps explains why the script is so talky and literal-minded, without poetry or fire. The filmmakers want to *teach* us something about the past and the present. Here was indeed the perfect vehicle for exploring the complex and contradictory effects of fame on black Americans, who find not only that two separate roles are expected of them by white and black America, but also that their talent carries them into a whole new arena with unfamiliar rituals, privileges, and restraints that only the toughest can endure and survive. But too much is set up for us (i.e., Jefferson's meeting with his family, then his black wife). Too little is dramatized.

As for Jones, he gives one of his better screen performances (he was nominated for an Oscar as Best Actor), far better here than he usually is in films, perhaps because he's playing a broad showoff of a character from whom we don't expect nuances or delicate shadings. Anyway, he can be endured and at times even enjoyed. And if anything keeps us interested in the film, he does. Added note: Marlene Warfield plays the black woman Jefferson dumps for the white Etta; you no doubt will wonder why.

The Greatest (1977)

D. Tom Gries. *S.* Ring Lardner, Jr.; based on the book *The Greatest* by Ali, Herbert Muhammad, and Richard Durham. *P.* John Marshall. *R.* Columbia Pictures. The excellent cast (which seldom is called on to do anything special) includes: Paul Winfield; Lloyd Haynes; Ernest Borgnine; Annazette Chase; Robert Duvall; John Marley; Roger E. Mosley (as Sonny Liston); Phillip MacAlister (as the young Cassius Clay); Dina Merrill; Lucille Benson; and James Earl Jones, who regrettably attempts to play Malcolm X.

Another film biography of a sports star, in this case Muhammad Ali. Like such other movie boxer bios as *Spirit of Youth* and *The Joe Louis Story*, both of which are intent on telling a story about a good man who overcomes adversity to triumph, *The Greatest* is simply made and simplistic (perhaps simple-minded, too) with (like *Greased Lightning*) the look and feel of the old low-budget race movies of the 1930s and 1940s. Clumsy and awkwardly written and directed, without attention to detail or any subtle or reflective moments, yet earnest to the core, the film assumes it can get by on its earnestness—and on the extraordinary charisma of Ali, who plays himself. In the latter respect, the moviemakers were right. One rejects the superficial treatment of Ali's life, yet it's hard to turn away because he's so powerfully magnetic. Confident, handsome, and headstrong, he bulldozes his way through: whenever faced with a dramatically challenging sequence, he just gets loud and playfully rowdy, perhaps aware that the camera feels he can do no wrong and is as infatuated and dazzled by him as were Ali's legion of fans. But even at that, no one can excuse the overall shoddiness. A chance for a significant statement on a really remarkable social/political sports figure—an authentic American hero—was passed over in favor of typically trite melodramatics. One never understands the period in which Ali came to prominence nor the courage of his stand against the war in Vietnam. Nor are we asked to confront the complexity and enormity of his religious conversion.

The Greatest Story Ever Told (1965)

D. George Stevens. *S.* James Lee Barrett and George Stevens. *P.* George Stevens. *R.* United Artists. Cast includes: Dorothy McGuire; Carroll Baker; Claude Rains; Sal Mineo; and Jamie Farr.

George Stevens' lengthy (222 minutes), all-star epic on the life of Jesus Christ (played by Max Von Sydow). Such luminous names as Charlton Heston, John Wayne, Angela Lansbury, Telly Savalas, and Shelley Winters play cameos, which often enough distract viewers from the story on screen; it's far more fun to say, "Oh, there goes Shelley!" The only important black in the film, Sidney Poitier, portrays Simon of Cyrene, the man who helps Jesus carry the cross up Calvary. Poitier's not on screen long, and this is clearly not one of his great roles.

Some critics felt he was gratuitously cast, being used in a cheapshot way to point up a theme of interracial unity, then important to audiences of the 1960s. John Simon wrote:

> Here and there the scenarists and director surpass themselves. Simon of Cyrene . . . is played by Sidney Poitier. His attire is blindingly white, and his face—could it be makeup?—appears blacker than it ever was before. Besides setting race relations immeasurably ahead, this reminds us that the values of the film are, underneath all that orgiastic color, plain black and white.

And Bosley Crowther of *The New York Times* added that "Sidney Poitier's Simon of Cyrene . . . is the only Negro conspicuous in the picture and seems a last-minute symbolization of racial brotherhood."

Today Poitier's casting just seems nutty. No one any longer seems perturbed by any racial dynamics (although indeed they are there). And it's kookily pleasurable seeing him up there with all the other big-time white stars of the era. Despite John Simon's comments, Poitier also does have an extraordinary look: handsome, fresh, virile, and, well, genuinely noble.

The Green Pastures (1936)

D. Marc Connelly and William Keighley. *S.* Marc Connelly and Sheridan Gibney, based on Marc Connelly's play, which was suggested by Roark Bradford's stories "Ol' Man Adam an' His Chillun." *R.* Warner Bros. Cast includes: Abraham Gleaves; Al Stokes; George Randol; Ida Forsyne (as Noah's wife); Ray Martin; Charles Andrews; Dudley Dickerson; Jimmy Burress; William Cumby; Ivory Williams; David Bethea; Slim Thompson; and Clinton Rosemond.

An adaptation of Marc Connelly's enormously successful all-colored Broadway play and also the first major studio all-black spectacle since 1929, *Green Pastures* became a hit movie and was for many years the most successful Negro film Hollywood had ever released. It also presents the then very "acceptable" portrait of black life as quaint and charming. The movie wants to pass itself off as genuine black folk culture, but in that respect, it's a fraud. What distinguishes the picture today though and makes it still rather entertaining is its great cast.

It tells a simple story. At a Sunday school class in Louisiana, the kindly Negro teacher Mr. Deshee (George Reed) visualizes the wonders of the Good Book so that his young pupils might better understand their meaning. Thus the biblical characters of old are transformed into contemporary Louisiana Negroes—in vernacular, in customs, and in attitude. Adam (Rex Ingram) and Eve (Myrtle Anderson) are presented as a muscular bronze man and his vain coquettish mate. Cain the Sixth (James Fuller) is a tough no-account and his high-yaller lady friend, Zeba (played with great elan by Edna Mae Harris), a high-strung strumpet. Moses (Frank Wilson) becomes a clever conjurer. And Noah, played splendidly by Eddie "Rochester" Anderson, is a gregarious tom, complete with high hat and raincoat.

In heaven the angels, seraphim, and cherubim are also contemporary Negroes, strutting about with straw hats or uttering quaint Negro colloquisms. "Gangway! Gangway! For de Lawd God Jehovah!" cries archangel Gabriel (Oscar Polk). "Being de Lawd ain't no bed of roses," moans the heavenly host (Rex Ingram). The heaven of *The Green Pastures* ultimately becomes a perpetual Negro holiday, a church picnic, one everlasting weekend fish fry. Harmony and good spirits reign supreme as the Hall Johnson Choir's resonant rendition of spirituals reminds everyone that there is no heaven like a black one.

The Green Pastures opened to unanimous praise from the white press and much of the black. *The New York World Telegram* called it "a beautiful film—the screen version of the tender, gently pathetic, curiously touching Negro miracle play."

The perceptive reviewer for the *Afro-American*, however, wrote that the movie's characterization of the religion of the Negro was only caricature with nothing to it except childlike faith. "Let *The Green Pastures* go for what it is: an interesting and entertaining spectacle with a cast of underpaid colored actors portraying Connelly's conception of . . . unlearned earlier day beliefs of heaven and the *Bible*. Any other viewpoint is outrageous."

At heart, *The Green Pastures* also rests on a cruel assumption: that nothing could be more ludicrous than transporting the lowly language and folkways of the early twentieth-century Negro back to the high stately world before the Flood. The movie plays on the idea of inherent Negro inferiority. It exploits the incongruity of angels with "dirty" faces.

The actors, however, transcend the trash. Playing three different roles, Rex Ingram is a stately Lawd; he elevates the entire picture, giving it substance, weight, and durability. That fine old character actor Ernest Whitman, who later played Bill Jackson on TV's "Beulah," does a nice bit as the Pharoah. Just about everyone else seems caught up in the excitement of making a big movie that touches on the black experience. (Most people in the 1930s did not seriously question the images/characters.)

Marc Connelly's play continued to be popular for many decades. Three television broadcasts of the play appeared in 1951, 1957, and 1959. The BBC also ran a new version of the comedy in 1958.

Guess Who's Coming to Dinner? (1967)

D. Stanley Kramer. *S*. William Rose. *P*. Stanley Kramer. *R*. Stanley Kramer/Columbia Pictures. Cast includes: Isabel Sanford (later Louise on "The Jeffersons") as the Tracy/Hepburn family maid and Virginia Christie.

The movie that made a mint but jolted Sidney Poitier from his throne as America's most popular black actor. Poitier's career has never been quite the same since.

At heart an innocuous film, *Guess Who's Coming to Dinner?* tackled the touchy subject of interracial marriage. A young white woman (Katharine Houghton) returns home to mom and dad (Katharine Hepburn and Spencer Tracy) in the suburbs with a dashing young black man whom she plans to marry. Everybody, upon hearing the news, goes into a tizzy, of course, but in the end, after a major summit meeting of both the bride's and groom's parents, everything is smoothly worked out.

All of this was old-fashioned claptrap done up in a slick glossy style. By concentrating on appealing decent people entangled in personal heartaches, director Kramer diverted the audience from any real issues. In fact, there were no issues here. Poitier's character is close to being a dream prince: good-looking, educated, mannerly, and downright brilliant, a doctor to boot, and even a possible candidate for the Nobel Prize. How could anyone refuse him for a son-in-law?

Actually, therein lies much of the rub. To prove his worth, the black man has met all of white America's standards. The young woman, however, to prove herself worthy of marrying him really has to do nothing, other than to be white and rather ordinary at that. The film also runs away from its theme: a real interracial romantic relationship. Never is the couple seen in a sexy, passionate embrace. About the most we get is a glimpse of them kissing briefly (and oh so politely), seen through the rear-view mirror of a taxi cab. The film just cannot confront this couple's sexuality directly. It's a desexed relationship, sterile and lifeless. There are no real characters in this movie either, just talky objects bouncing about, delivering supposedly bright and clever lines, espousing liberal sentiments without honestly dramatizing them. Then, too, it cannot be forgotten that the film ends with the couple—finally blessed by their families—immediately leaving the country; so the "problem" has clearly been *removed*. (We don't even see them marry.) The picture's most interesting character may well be Poitier's mother, performed in a highly idiosyncratic manner by Beah Richards.

Occasionally likable, also occasionally dull, Poitier is too in tune with the role and sticks to the tired script, which apparently he believes in. Gone is that exciting tension between black actor and his character.

The most difficult scene to accept: Poitier's private talk with his father in which he says he sees himself as a *man*, not a *colored man*. The screenplay doesn't permit any real warmth or a *connection* between the two as we see when Louise Beavers and Fredi Washington work together in the 1934 *Imitation of Life*. Instead with Poitier and Roy Glenn, one feels a definite hostility between father and son that is not explained to our satisfaction. The father is also treated unfairly and condescendingly by the script, which has not the vaguest notion what this type of black man has endured nor what *truths* he might try to impart to his son. The scene is almost painful to watch.

Large audiences, however, seduced by the picture's clever advertising campaign and its star packaging, turned *Guess Who's Coming to Dinner?* into a tremendous commercial success. For the most part critically well-received, the picture was nominated for ten Academy Awards, one of which went to Beah Richards as Best Supporting Actress of the Year. (The only winners, however, were Hepburn for Best Actress and William Rose for Best Screenplay.) But this movie proved the last of the 1960s explicitly integrationist message pictures. And Poitier and director Kramer found themselves often attacked in newspaper and magazine articles by blacks and whites. *The New York Times* ran a now-famous 1967 article titled "Why Does White America Love Sidney Poitier So?," in which Poitier's screen characters were denounced as being too limited and unrealistic to continue having much force. Not long afterwards, Poitier underwent a significant image change as he struggled to keep up with new audience tastes.

Hallelujah (1929)

D. King Vidor. S. Wanda Tuchock, based on a story by King Vidor. R. MGM. Cast includes: Fannie Belle DeKnight (as Mammy); Everett McGarrity (as the poignant kid brother Spunk); and Harry Gray (a 90-year-old employee of *The Amsterdam News* and a former slave, as Pappy).

One of Hollywood's most important all-black films—and also one of the first to be made within the established film community, although white director King Vidor, in order to persuade MGM to let him make the film, invested some of his own money into it.

Having grown up exposed to black culture in Galveston, Texas, Vidor felt that the new medium of sound motion pictures was an ideal way to explore "real Negro folk culture" in America—through black America's music, its internal and external rhythms, its rituals and religion.

He chose a simple story: a good, decent God-fearing young man (Daniel Haynes) falls for the charms of a sexy sepia temptress (Nina Mae McKinney), eventually deserting home and church, family and sweetheart (blues singer Victoria Spivey). The sepia temptress naturally toys with his affections, then dumps him for another man called Hot Shot (William Fountaine), only later to die for her sins in the good man's arms. Redemption and salvation are what we're supposed to think this film's about. But actually it's about mood, rhythm, energy, and sex. *Hallelujah* is sometimes so sexually pent-up that it's unintentionally funny. During the mass baptismal sequence, Nina Mae McKinney's been such a hot little number that we know she's being dunked in the water not so much to purify her as to cool her down.

Shot partly on location in the swamps and forests of Tennessee and Arkansas, the film has long stretches of beauty and power: the lines of white-robed black supplicants awaiting baptism form an image that never leaves you. The energetic and moving music (the spirituals are sung by Dixie Jubilee Choir), the dancing, the language itself are indeed expressions of black folk culture coming to the big screen, creeping up through the apparent text, presenting us with a powerful subtext that throws to waste the chintzy but ditsily enjoyable love theme and some of the grossly accepted stereotypes of this period (the crap-shooters, the carousers, etc.).

In a part originally intended for Paul Robeson, Daniel Haynes, a bit stolid, moves us nonetheless, performing the memorable "Going Home."

Here Nina Mae McKinney plays talking pictures' first tragic mulatto character: she's straight-haired, keen featured, light-skinned—and a very, very troubled girl. The subliminal message: this high-yaller strumpet's problem is that her blood's been mixed somewhere along the line and that mixed blood is always bubblin' and boilin' over, causing havoc for everyone! McKinney, the actress, is energy incarnate and delirious fun to watch: a footloose fancy-free kewpie doll of a star whose fearlessly kinetic Swanee Shuffle is a predecessor to the break dance maneuvers of the 1980s. Her sexiness is also always endearingly girlish and innocent. When Vidor becomes too high-falutingly moody and serious, McKinney shows up and lets us see how black energy can send a picture into a heady tailspin.

The reviews of the period said more about the reviewers than the film. *The New York Times'* Mordaunt Hall wrote that the movie succeeded in presenting the "peculiarly typical religious hysteria of the darkies and their gullibility . . . their hankering after salvation, the dread of water in the baptism." *Variety* commented: "Apparently in the massed ensemble groups, Vidor had a mighty tough job holding that bunch down, yet he held them under remarkable restraint and still brought out the effects desired."

In New York City when *Hallelujah* had simultaneous premieres at the Lafayette Theatre in Harlem and the Embassy in the downtown white area, the black press denounced the racism inherent in the dual opening. Black patrons viewed it as a tactical move by MGM to spare the feelings of "swanky whites," who might not object to watching a screenful of darkies but who most certainly did not want to sit next to any in a theater.

In due time, *Hallelujah* set the tone for the treatment of Negro casts and themes in films by presenting them in idealized, isolated worlds—and the film also became an authentic American classic.

Halls of Anger (1970)

D. Paul Bogart. S. John Shaner and Al Ramrus. P. Herbert Hirschman. R. UA; a Mirisch Production. Cast includes: Ed Asner; Jeff Bridges; Janet MacLachlan; De Wayne Jessie (as the kid whose remedial reading problems are overcome once he starts reading *Lady Chatterly's Lover*); Bob (later Rob) Reiner.

White students are bussed into a ghetto high school in Los Angeles. An insensitive white principal (John McLiam), who acts as if he's running a reform school, doesn't fret much about the racial tension that ensues between black and white. After all he simply wants to keep the kids in line until he goes on to his next big appointment as a school board

Janet MacLachlan and Calvin Lockhart as teachers at a troubled high school in Halls of Anger.

member. Into the fracas steps a handsome, slick black teacher (hand-some, slick Calvin Lockhart), a former basketball champ who has of late been teaching at a white high school. He struggles to reach the kids and eventually earns their respect.

Sound a little familiar? Well, it should because it's a retread of past high school/juvenile delinquent films such as *Blackboard Jungle* and *To Sir with Love*. Of course, this time around we get the subject of reverse discrimination: the filmmakers are anxious for us to know that it's the black kids who are hounding and harassing a "minority" of white students. The gratuitous attempt to place this reverse discrimination theme into a larger historical/social context doesn't add up to much. And, sadly, the black students are depicted more often than not as "unreasonable" militants.

Not much new here, other than the bussing issue, then a hot topic in the news. Actor Lockhart, looking as if he's just strutted off a yacht to spend a few days in the inner city, is curiously enough convincing and pleasant. James A. Watson, however, stirs up some real fire as a restless rebel.

Real racial tensions exploded among cast members during the making of this picture. Later *Variety* predicted: "It should be one of the bigger box-office draws of the season." But the movie was not a big hit.

Hearts in Dixie (1929)

D. Paul Sloane. S. Walter Weems. Dances staged by Fanchon and Marco. P. William Fox. R. Fox Pictures. Cast includes: Clarence Muse (as Uncle Nappus); Eugene Jackson; Mildred Washington; Gertrude Howard; Clifford Ingram.

Sound movies in the late 1920s demanded a new realism *and* a new rhythm, which eventually opened the door in Hollywood for the arrival of black performers. Blessed with a distinct sound all their own, blacks temporarily came into vogue with two major studios releasing in 1929 two all-black, all-talking, all-singing, all-colored musicals, of which *Hearts in Dixie* was the first. (*Halleiujah* followed soon afterward.)

Today the film looks slow-pokish, as if suffering from tired blood. Originally, it had been conceived as a short film to showcase blacks performing spirituals and romping through some minstrel-like shenanigans. But the studio decided to expand it. Plotwise not much happens. Mainly the viewer is treated to the sight of pickaninnies on an old Southern plantation as well as docile black workers, who toil in the fields during the day, then play at night. Almost always, everyone's heart is full of song: as the steamboat *Nellie Bly* floats down the river, slaves contentedly sing. A mournful collection of darkies also croons "massa's in the cold, cold ground." Throughout the black characters are almost mindlessly placid, so much so that the whole film looks like a parody. Here are characters living in shacks and working from sunrise to sunset, and always, instead of real misery or anger or any thoughts of rebellion, they seem to glide through life on some euphoric high brought on, we might assume, by cotton fields and spirituals.

"The spirit of the Southern Negro a year or so after the Civil War is cleverly captured," wrote the critic for *The New York Times*. "It is some-thing restful, a talking and song picture that is gentle in mood and truthful in its reflection of black men of those days down yonder in the

cornfields." One would like to say *The Times* reviewer wrote with tongue in cheek. But that doesn't appear to be the case.

Is there anything here an audience today might enjoy? Well, maybe yes. For amid all the moonlight and magnolia bit appears a screen newcomer, Stepin Fetchit as Gummy, who enlivens the proceedings with his perfect timing and his shiftiness, too. The picture was expanded actually because of Fetchit: the producers realized they had a hot new star on their hands. The fact that this lazy critter is something of an outcast in this world, preferring to play and flirt rather than work, makes him seem almost admirable. He has a scene that yet pleases some black audiences: encountering a young black woman, he tries talking some trash to her.

Then, too, the dancing sequences are exciting (seemingly derivative of actual African tribal dances). The black performers here help introduce much of the carefree exuberance and high energy level that came to be associated with the American movie musical.

And whether we like it today or not, it's still good to see some kind of early attempt at dealing with Negro life.

Hell Up in Harlem (1973)

D. Larry Cohen. S. Larry Cohen. P. Larry Cohen and Janell Cohen. R. American International Pictures. Cast includes: Gloria Hendry; Margaret Avery; Julius Harris; and D'Urville Martin.

A sequel to Cohen's successful *Black Caesar*. Once again Fred Williamson stars as a tough, sexy dude, confident, bold, morally ambivalent. Cheaply made, far too violent, even sentimental at times, this film gives Harlem a bad name.

A Hero Ain't Nothin' but a Sandwich (1977)

D. Ralph Nelson. S. Alice Childress, based on her novel. P. Robert Radnitz. R. New World Pictures. Cast includes: Helen Martin; Glynn Turman (another mannered performance from him); Kevin Hooks; David Groh; Arnold Johnson; Arthur French; Erin Blunt; Harold Sylvester; and Kenneth Green.

In this wholesome family picture from the producer of *Sounder* (Robert Radnitz) and the director of *Lilies of the Field* (Ralph Nelson), a black teenager (Larry B. Scott) becomes hooked on heroin, must endure a painful rehabilitation period, then struggles to put the pieces of his life back together. Larry Scott is a credible, likable young lead but there's not much to his character. Eveyone connected with this production strives hard to say *something*, to give us a picture with *meaning*. Some school children may find something to relate to here, but the whole enterprise is pat and predictable.

Lost in a role that draws nothing out of her, Cicely Tyson seems almost as shockingly misplaced here as she later was in yet another drama about confused youth: the TV movie "Playing with Fire." Tyson does have one near inspired moment. In a bathroom sequence, she scrubs down her wayward son, determined to wash away his sins and his confusions. Her anger becomes almost comically real and high flung. (It's that of an actress grasping for something to work with.) But when the script calls for her to jump (fully clothed) into the tub, apparently trying to wash away her own confusion, the scene is completely wrecked. Although the script sometimes mangles Paul Winfield's character, too, he is in top form. In the sequence in which he speaks of cuff links given to him by a favorite uncle, Winfield handles his line readings so skillfully that young black actors should be made to view him. His rhythms and intonations tell us he comes from the ghetto. But this is not the overdone, overstylized kind of reading that someone like Dick Anthony Williams frequently renders. Nor does he become buffoonish as James Earl Jones often is in *Claudine*. Winfield is perfectly modulated and thought-out, investing his working class hero with a poignant dignity and grace.

Hit (1973)

D. Sidney J. Furie. S. Alan R. Trustman and David S. Wolf. P. Harry Korshak. R. Paramount Pictures. Cast includes: Gwen Welles and Paul Hampton.

A year after the smash success of *Lady Sings the Blues*, Paramount Pictures hoped for another winner with this feature which again teamed

Lady's director with two stars of that film: Billy Dee Williams and Richard Pryor. Williams was cast in the lead as a U.S. drug agent, out to find the drug traffickers (from Marseilles) whose wheelings and dealings, he believes, were responsible for his young daughter's death (she OD'ed). Pryor plays a buddy of Williams. Unfortunately, this movie failed to hit the mark with audiences, who, no doubt, were disappointed to see Williams, a dashing romantic hero (conceivably America's first black matinee idol), playing a humdrum character in a very naturalistic, anemic style, without the florid flourishes that made his character in *Lady* so exciting.

A tepid adventure yarn without much adventure.

Hit Man (1972)

D. George Armitage. *S.* George Armitage; based on the novel *Jack's Return Home* by Ted Lewis. *P.* Gene Corman. *R.* MGM. Cast includes: Bhetty Waldron; Sam Laws; Roger E. Mosley; and Candy All (as the niece Rochelle).

When a director has lavish closeups of his leading lady's face, it's always said he's in love with her. But what are we to make of this film in which the director lavishes closeups on his hero's buttocks? Ah, well. In this revenge tale, Bernie Casey journeys from Oakland to Los Angeles for his murdered brother's funeral. He decides not to leave town until he finds the killer. A remake of the British film *Get Carter*, *Hit Man* moves along at a decent pace, and though cheap and shoddy, envelops the viewer in its sleazeball world of porn movies, swanky brothels, double-crossing friends, and hardened tarty women who are treated as little more than sex slaves. Unable to trust almost anyone other than an overripe motel keeper, hero Casey operates in a pervasively corrupt, dehumanizing atmosphere, which very much reflects some of the social/political nihilism that set in during this period of Vietnam and later Watergate. It's not merely a get-Whitey-movie as were many of the black-oriented films of the time.

With his gun out ready for action: Bernie Casey in Hit Man.

Carrying himself with surprising assurance, Casey's rhythms—his speech, his walk, his attitude, his manner of dress, too—are distinctly early 1970s urban black, direct cultural statements rarely viewed in so authentic a form in American films.

Disturbing, however, is the film's treatment/depiction of black women. When Pam Grier—as a good-natured, good-time gal desiring nothing more in life than to be a top porn star—is punished, for having inadvertently betrayed the hero, by being dumped on an animal ranch and then mauled and (we assume) devoured by a lion, audiences now shudder. So contemptuous is the film of its black women that most are continually kicked around and abused and seldom blessed with any "redeeming" qualities that might engender audience identification or sympathy. The most appealing woman—the motel keeper—is even viewed by the filmmakers as little more than a whore, an easy quick lay. "I know how you like your men. Proud and erect," Bernie Casey tells her. "You ain't the only one who fits that description," she answers. "I'm the only one here," he says. "Give me a dime for a phone call," she tells him, "and I'll fill the room."

Hollywood Shuffle (1987)

D. Robert Townsend. S. Robert Townsend and Keenen Ivory Wayans. P. Robert Townsend. R. The Samuel Goldwyn Company. Cast includes: Craigus R. Johnson; Domenick Irrera; Paul Mooney; Lisa Mende; John Witherspoon; Ludie Washington; Steven Fertig; Brad Sanders; and Keenen Ivory Wayans (as Donald).

Not long after the success of *She's Gotta Have It* (1986) indicated the commercial viability of independently produced black films, Robert Townsend's *Hollywood Shuffle* appeared and emerged as another independent success. As an actor, Robert Townsend had previously given clever, informed performances in such features as *Streets of Fire* (1983), *A Soldier's Story* (1984), *American Flyers* (1985), and *Ratboy* (1986). Yet the right role had eluded him—until he decided to make his own movie with himself as star. *Hollywood Shuffle* was the film, which, incredibly enough, he financed partly with cash advances from his credit cards, shooting the picture on a budget of approximately $100,000. Later he shrewdly pursued distributors and managed to get the Samuel Goldwyn Company to handle the film.

Hollywood Shuffle is a relatively clear-eyed and rather likable look at the life of a Hollywood black actor. The ambitious hero, Bobby Taylor (played by Townsend), yearns to land a plum role but is repeatedly frustrated by his own awareness that the only parts open to black performers in Hollywood are the stereotyped pimps, whores, and gang members. Townsend satirizes those roles as well as the attitudes of the whites controlling the movie industry, who demand that black actors (even those classically trained) play ghetto dudes and toughs speaking such contorted lines as "Why you be gotta pull a knife on me?"

In one hilarious sendup, Townsend focuses on a black acting school "where you can learn Jive Talk 101. Learn to play epic slaves." He also parodies the movie reviewers Siskel and Ebert in an episode called "Sneakin' in the Movies," in which two street brothers give the finger to those films that don't make the mark. In this episode, Townsend walks a fine line: it sometimes looks as if he's further propagating the very stereotypes he otherwise appears to abhor. The same might be said of his later television appearances on "The Tonight Show" and Joan Rivers's "Late Show." On one such program Townsend, then promoting *Hollywood Shuffle*, did a parody of a black actor performing Shakespeare; it was almost painful to watch because the idea behind it was that a black actor would naturally *jive Shakespeare up*.

At the same time, the female characters of *Hollywood Shuffle* are also open to criticism. In *The New York Post*, movie critic Jami Bernard wrote: "The women here are whores or helpmates (Bobby's mother irons his shirt, Bobby's girlfriend murmurs sympathetically)." What weakens the portrait of the women is that as a director Townsend doesn't seem yet to know how to work with his performers. As the hero's girlfriend Lydia, Ann Marie Johnson acts according to the script, which means she plays a vapid role vapidly. Nor can actress Starletta Dupois—often effective in stage productions—do much with her character. Only veteran Helen Martin, after years of having played stereotyped roles on television, seems able to inject some warmth and wisdom into her role as the grandmother.

Lively but uneven, sometimes self-indulgent and sentimental, and frequently striking us as a series of skits that do not always mesh, *Hollywood Shuffle* nonetheless succeeds in some important respects because of the performance of Townsend. When he has to turn serious at the film's climax, he is admittedly weak and unconvincing. But otherwise, whether doing a brilliant impersonation of Stepin Fetchit (and it may well be the best impersonation ever done of this great comic) or delivering a first-rate parody of a British movie butler, Townsend's timing and rhythms are frequently inspired and rather amazing. At the very opening when we hear him announcing "You done messed with the wrong dude, baby," then realize he is simply rehearsing for an audition, we know this is indeed an actor who does not miss a beat—and that this is a movie with an unexpected point of view.

What's most important about *Hollywood Shuffle* is that it springs directly from its black director/writer's consciousness. No one but a black artist could have done this piece of work. Here Townsend—articulating what many of us have felt about the Hollywood system and its rigid stereotyping of black performers—is telling us a story from an insider's vantage point in terms that just about anyone, black or white, in show business or out of it, can understand and (let us hope) identify with.

Townsend later directed the Eddie Murphy concert film *Raw* (1987).

Home of the Brave (1949)

D. Mark Robson. S. Carl Foreman. P. Stanley Kramer. R. UA release of a Screen Plays production. Cast includes: Lloyd Bridges.

Independently produced by 35-year-old fledgling moviemaker Stanley Kramer, *Home of the Brave* launched Hollywood's cycle of problem pictures in the late 1940s. The picture also went against all the then-acceptable theories of Hollywood moviemaking. It was shot on a shoestring budget without big name stars and with an offbeat subject matter. In the successful Broadway play by Arthur Laurents on which the film was based, the hero had been a young Jewish soldier, the victim of anti-Semitism within the military. In the film producer Kramer shrewdly substituted a Negro character for the Jewish protagonist.

Through a series of flashbacks, *Home of the Brave* described the emotional breakdown of a young Negro private, Peter Moss. As he under-

goes examination by a sympathetic medical captain, Moss unravels his tale, revealing a number of racial incidents he endured while on a special five-man mission to a Japanese-held island (during the Second World War). Repeatedly excluded and harassed by his fellow soldiers, Moss had cracked up under the pressure. The viewer learns, however, it was not the island experience alone that led to the black soldier's breakdown. It was the American way of life—and racism—that always forced the Mosses of the world "outside the human race."

Often strong and moving, *Home of the Brave* ended on a conciliatory note that heightened its impact in 1949 but lessens it today. Having recovered, Moss is about to leave the military hospital when he is approached by an easy-going white soldier (Frank Lovejoy), who, with the war now over, plans to open a bar. He wants Moss as his partner. Genuinely touched, the black accepts, equipped now with a new philosophy for the future. "I am different," he says. "We all are. But underneath we're the same."

Home of the Brave's concluding optimism now strikes many as rigged and fake. The white soldier's "noble" gesture is believable only in the movies, and even so there is a tinge of patronage because it is the white man offering his hand to the black man. Yet there is still something decent about the film's sincerity and its optimism.

Today this remains a film of historical importance and interest—and it's a movie that still has a certain wallop, affecting audiences, black and white, in an emotional way. In his essay "The Shadow and the Act," Ralph Ellison wrote that *Home of the Brave* and the other three problem pictures (*Pinky*, *Lost Boundaries*, and *Intruder in the Dust*) all touched on a "deep center of American emotion." These movies got at something American films of the past had never approached (or perhaps feared): a look at the ties between the races and also the deep-seated nests of American racism itself. Despite their flaws or compromises, today they still work because they take a dare and set up a confrontation. One is forced to deal with racial issues.

Finally, much of the power of *Home of the Brave* can be attributed to the startling performance of James Edwards as Moss. His tension, restlessness, sensitivity, and admirable attempt to connect to or at least understand a white world that has continually rejected him make this a fascinating movie character.

The film's release caught the movie industry and the critics offguard. It was a commercial and critical success, proving that audiences then were ready for a new type of black film and black character.

Added note: shooting the film in secrecy, Stanley Kramer called it *High Noon*, a title he used later for one of his other films.

Honeybaby, Honeybaby (1974)

D. Michael Schultz. *S.* Brian Phelan. *P.* Jack Jordan and Quentin Kelly. *R.* Kelly/Jordan. Cast includes: Eric Bell; Mr. Sunshine; and scriptwriter Brian Phelan.

Few remember it but Michael Schultz, before the release of his commercial hit *Cooley High*, directed this half-baked, haphazard would-be thriller about an American interpreter (Diana Sands) who wins a trip to the troubled Middle East and becomes embroiled in Third World politics—and also finds herself in the arms of a dashing adventurer played by Calvin Lockhart. Neither director Schultz nor his cast is at his best. *Variety* called Lockhart's performance "embarrassingly wooden" yet found Sands a "vibrant presence" who unfortunately was "haplessly undermined by an inane and highly confusing script." All the sadder because this marked Diana Sands's last movie performance before her death in 1974. The film also marks a rare screen appearance by the great legendary saloonkeeper (as she called herself), Bricktop, who in the 1920s and 1930s mixed with the rich and famous in her European clubs and cabarets. Technically abominable. Seldom seen.

Honky (1971)

D. William A. Graham. *S.* Will Chaney, based on the novel *Sheila* by Gunard Selberg. *P.* Will Chaney and Ron Roth. *R.* A Jack H. Harris Enterprises release of a Getty-Fromkess & Stonehenge Production. Cast includes: Brenda Sykes; John Nielson; and William Marshall.

Black girl. White boy. A romance. What trash.

Made in the era when black college students sometimes marched and protested to the chant of "Down with the Honky" or "Get Whitey," this is an exploitation film (too innocently dumb and forthright to be called a blaxploitation picture) out to tap the youth market of its day. Now suitable only for those aficionados of the B-movie.

Added note: the pop romantic score is by Quincy Jones.

I Passed for White (1960)

D. Fred Wilcox. *S.* Fred M. Wilcox. *P.* Fred Wilcox. *R.* Allied Artists. Cast includes: James Franciscus and Isabelle Cooley.

Following on the heels of the immensely successful 1959 version of *Imitation of Life* came this low-budget item, which, like its predecessor, told the tale of a light-skinned black girl determined to cross the color line.

Black audiences have howled over this one, particularly during a nightclub sequence in which the high-yaller heroine (Sonya Wilde) dances so rhythmically (so ferociously is more like it) that the other patrons stare at her—and we know she's almost given herself away! The girl is a shrewd cookie though and marries into a hoity-toity proper white family (much like the heroine of another tragic mulatto cheapie *Night of the Quarter Moon*). Alas, what really does her in is her conscience. She becomes pregnant and fears the baby will be black! Poor thing!

Cheap, tawdry, trashy, implausible. But also, dare it be said, sometimes funny and inadvertently entertaining. Recommended for those daredevils with time on their hands and also with a mad desire to spend an hour and a half watching something that hasn't one ounce of redeeming social comment whatsoever.

If He Hollers, Let Him Go (1968)

D. Charles Martin. *S.* Charles Martin. *P.* Charles Martin. *R.* Forward Films Production. Cast includes: Kevin McCarthy; Dana Wynter; and Arthur O'Connell.

A black man, wrongly convicted for the rape/murder of a white woman, escapes from prison, hoping to prove his innocence. Many plot twists and complications here as well as an overall confusion. Writer/director Martin cannot keep all the disparate elements from flying off in different directions. There is a subplot involving a white man who hopes to do away with his wife and who wants the black man to do the job for him.

Variety wrote that the film was "overloaded with racial bigotry, violence, and gunplay angles," which not only is true but, curiously enough, explains the mild commercial success of the picture. *If He Hollers, Let Him Go* arrived at a time when an emerging black movie audience searched for a new type of movie hero, more assertive, more sexual, and more militant than the "good Negro characters" of the 1950s, as represented by Sidney Poitier and Harry Belafonte. Raymond St. Jacques, like Jim Brown, had the required toughness *and* the open, almost defiant sexuality, which is spotlighted here in a very "hot" sex scene with singer Barbara McNair.

The movie, however, did not go as far as black audiences wanted. Not until Melvin Van Peebles' *Sweet Sweetback's Baadasssss Song* and Gordon Parks' *Shaft* did a resolutely sexual black film hero emerge.

Today the film looks like a cheapo (it was), tawdry and sloppily put together.

Imitation of Life (1934)

D. John Stahl. *S.* William Hurlburt; based on the bestselling novel by Fannie Hurst. *P. R.* Universal. Cast includes: Rochelle Hudson; Warren William; Ned Sparks; and Madame Sul Te Wan. Peola at age four is played by Sebie Hendricks. Peola at age ten is played by Dorothy Black, who gives a good intelligent performance.

Two widows—one white, the other Negro—meet. Each has a young daughter to rear. In order to make ends meet, the two women decide to cast their lots together. The white woman, Miss Bea (Claudette Colbert), will work every day at her career, while the black woman, Aunt Delilah (Louise Beavers), will tend to the house. One morning as the black woman serves breakfast, the white woman, taken with the pancakes being served, asks what the recipe is. The black woman confides it's a secret, having been passed down in her family generation after generation. Eventually, with her black friend's help, the white woman markets a pancake mix based on the secret recipe. That mix brings wealth and success. Yet the black woman seems to care for neither. At one point, after Miss Bea has offered Delilah a 20% interest in the budding pancake business, Delilah turns it down. She wants neither money nor a home of her own. Instead she prefers simply to remain by the side of her white friend. In time the black woman endures heartache and tragedy when her young light-skinned daughter, Peola (Fredi Washington), having grown up in Miss Bea's home with whites the same color as herself yet for whom there will always be a world of opportunity and privilege, decides to cross the color line and pass for white. Rejected by her daughter, Delilah's heart breaks and she dies a sad, lonely woman. At Delilah's lavish funeral, the sobbing mulatto daughter returns, aware she has killed her mother.

Shamelessly melodramatic and corny, *Imitation of Life* was a tremendous hit during the Depression era. White and black Americans both responded to its subplot: an unconscious study of America's racial system crushing the black family. Years later Ralph Ellison wrote that Hollywood's problem pictures of 1949, while compromised, touched on a deep center of American emotion. Actually, the same could be said of *Imitation of Life* some fifteen years earlier. The only Hollywood movie of its era that even suggested the existence of such a thing as a race problem in America, the film set off sparks within the black community. Black ministers preached sermons about it while black intellectuals wrote about the film as well. And the movie acquired a legend of its own that still lives today.

Initially, black audiences, viewing Delilah's touching submissiveness as endearing and positive, believed the daughter an ingrate, inconsiderate of her mother and ashamed of her own race. Yet some also felt the movie played the character Peola cheap, failing to get at the heart of her dilemma: here is a black woman who does not seek so much to be white as to have a chance at *white* opportunities and advantages in a fiercely competitive capitalistic society. Intuitively, one senses Peola knows her life is a dead end, that she'll wind up, like her mother, as a servant and little more. Peola becomes a figure of curious rebellion with a daring thirst for freedom. Contemporary audiences, openly conscious of the subtext of *Imitation of Life*, often connect more to the daughter.

The film's two black actresses, forced to play out melodramatic creations, invest their roles with sensitivity and insight. It might appear that Beavers, because her character was considered so sympathetic, has

Louise Beavers and Claudette Colbert as the two widowed mothers who become lifelong friends in the 1934 Imitation of Life, *one of the few Hollywood films of the Depression era to indicate there was such a thing as a race problem in America.*

Louise Beavers as Aunt Delilah, the pancake queen, in the 1934 Imitation of Life.

an easier job. For audiences of the economically troubled 1930s, she communicated an optimism they could latch onto; she was also the essence of Christian stoicism and passivity, particularly in her scenes with the white characters. When working opposite Washington, though, Beavers's acting rhythm changes. One feels a direct bond between the two. In one sequence, after the daughter tells her mother she is leaving home and that should they ever meet again they must act as strangers, Beavers breaks through the bounds of melodrama with an emotional cry that she can't do that, *that she's no white mother.* It's one of her best moments on screen. Equally convincing is a sequence in which she goes to the restaurant where her daughter works as a "white" cashier. She pleads with the girl to come home. She's a woman torn in two, as much by the cheerful role she must play around whites as by what has transpired between her daughter and herself. In the later scenes, the Beavers character, fighting to remain sunny while talking to Miss Bea, is indeed a woman faking it: beneath the lines, we see a heart that's been broken—and also a shift in consciousness. *Variety* wrote at the time: "Picture is stolen by the Negress, Louise Beavers, whose performance is masterly. This lady can troupe. She took the whole scale of human emotions from joy to anguish and never sounded a false note. It is one of the most unprecedented personal triumphs for an obscure performer in the annals of a crazy business."

As Peola, Fredi Washington is lovely, haunted, driven, her eyes liquid, fearful, full of yearning. As a creature trying to break loose to find herself, she has a rhythm and internal torment no white actress could bring to this type of role. Susan Kohner, in the remake of *Imitation of Life*, is the one white actress to get closest to what Washington communicates; someone like Jeanne Crain in *Pinky*, however, can get nowhere near it.

Perhaps the most chilling, truly unsettling sequence: after a late evening talk, Miss Bea and Aunt Delilah, lifelong "friends," retire to their respective bedrooms. Slowly, we see Miss Bea silently go upstairs.

At the same time, we watch Delilah descend to her basement room. Even among the best of interracial friends, the film inadvertently informs us, the racial lines are still tightly drawn.

Today *Imitation of Life* frequently just creeps along, creaking *until* Washington and Beavers show up. It's their movie. And this is a dazzling example of two black performers who transform Hollywood trash into something unique and often powerful.

Imitation of Life (1959)

D. Douglas Sirk. *S.* Eleanore Griffin and Allan Scott. *P.* Ross Hunter. *R.* Universal. Cast includes: John Gavin; Sandra Dee; and Robert Alda.

Douglas Sirk's gilded and glitzy remake of the 1934 classic. Here Lana Turner is cast as the impoverished young widow who eventually becomes successful not as a businesswoman but as a stage star. Juanita Moore portrays her trusty black friend. In the original *Imitation of Life*, some might feel Claudette Colbert's treatment of Louise Beavers is condescending but warm. In this remake, though, Lana Turner doesn't even seem aware that Juanita Moore exists! Turner, the eternal narcissist, is so caught up in her own affairs that she doesn't seem to know *anybody's* around! Her performance, fake and superficial as it is, works in an offbeat way, no doubt because her character is basically selfish and shallow, a woman so hellbent on stardom that nothing else matters or commands her attention.

This remake also attempts "cleaning up" its black subplot. No longer is the black woman called Aunt Delilah. Now she's Annie, which no doubt was thought a more dignified name. Gone, too, is the black woman's pancake recipe, which had carried both women out of the slums. Perhaps the filmmakers thought audiences would question the fact that the white woman grew wealthy off the black woman's endeavors. And the previous image of Beavers wearing a chef's cap as she stood before the grill with a bowl of pancake batter by her side (and a smile on her face) embodied too outdated a stereotype. But, ironically, by stripping away the pancake business, the filmmakers have also stripped away the black woman's basic individuality and her personal tragedy. In the earlier version, we assumed the two women remained together partly because they were in a business together. Here the black woman simply seems to be *hanging around.* She's an understanding maid but little more. Nor do we now sense the tragic waste of the black woman's life because the movie now wants us to believe (*sans* the pancake recipe) she really doesn't have any particular skills or gifts. She has almost nothing going for her.

Here the light-skinned daughter, called Sarah Jane (Susan Kohner) instead of Peola, gets more of the director's attention. She's even permitted a white boyfriend because in this version a white actress is playing the mulatto role, and white audiences were not apt to be offended as they would have been had there been a real interracial couple up there on screen. (Fredi Washington had been left romantically stranded.) Yet even at that, the boyfriend (Troy Donahue), upon learning the girl's true racial identity, promptly beats her up.

Moreover, there is no sense whatsoever of a black community here. Don't this black mother and daughter have black friends with whom they mix? Consequently, at the climactic funeral, which is attended by every black extra Central Casting was able to scrounge up, we're a bit startled. Suddenly, it hits us that the entire film has been told to us from the white woman's point of view.

Yet, with all its shortcomings, *Imitation of Life* worked as entertaining corn, and the racial theme, still not the dominant story, is again the true point of interest. As Annie, Juanita Moore frequently finds herself up against a brick wall. The scriptwriters haven't so much given her a character to play as a joke to turn serious. But she does the nearly impossible: she delivers a touching and effective performance, without the drive, the charm, or the mythic quality of Beavers's work but convincing all the same, so much so that Moore walked off with an Oscar nomination as Best Supporting Actress of 1959 for her performance. As Sarah Jane, Susan Kohner also lacks the intense, mythic quality of Fredi Washington. But Kohner's looks help her out (she has the dark brooding quality the filmmakers wanted) and within the melodramatic framework, she's moving. The funeral sequence is grossly overdone here but fun all the same. We get to hear the great Mahalia Jackson sing. And as Sarah Jane returned, crying out for her dead mother, tears came to the eyes of moviegoers once again, just as they had with the original.

Cliched and fake but engrossing nonetheless, a perfect example of dazzling Hollywood junk food served on a platter with undeniable truths and seasoned with the kind of hokey mythic condiments that few of us can turn away from.

In the Heat of the Night (1967)

D. Norman Jewison. *S.* Stirling Silliphant, based on a novel by John Ball. *P.* Walter Mirisch. *R.* UA. Cast includes Beah Richards; Lee Grant; Scott Wilson; and Warren Oates.

What might have been a routine murder mystery takes a new twist because of a set of racial dynamics and a shrewd piece of casting. Sidney Poitier and Rod Steiger, then two of America's most praised dramatic actors, are out to solve a murder in a small Mississippi town. Steiger, the gum-chewing, typically bigoted local sheriff, doesn't care one bit for Poitier, one of those uppity northern Negro detectives who, while visiting his mother in the South, stumbles onto the crime and decides to stay in town in order to help solve it. What follows, of course, is a civics class lesson in human understanding. Each man learns something about the other and comes to have at least a grudging respect for him.

Although once again almost superhumanly clever and intelligent, Poitier has a solid character to play, and he does so with intensity, flair, true skill, and, at the appropriate points, with restraint, too: during those moments when he has to hold himself in, one sees Poitier bristling with anger and rage. The audience identification with him becomes total and all-enveloping. There is one sequence that has lived on in the memory of black moviegoers for years: a bigoted wealthy white man (Larry Gates), enraged by this assured, arrogant Negro detective, slaps Poitier. Poitier promptly slaps him back! Past black audiences cheered deliriously. Today the reaction is the same.

During a period of unrest in the streets and ghettoes of America, some critics thought this film might do much in the way of promoting racial harmony. Hah! Actually, what the picture did was provide Poitier with one of his most heroic (if not complex) characters, and at a time in history when a young black audience yearned for a new type of black movie hero—one which picked up on the then-new militant spirit— Poitier was temporarily *it*.

In The Heat of the Night was awarded an Oscar as Best Picture of 1967. Steiger walked off with an Oscar as Best Actor of the Year. Poitier, however, fine as his performance was, did not receive an Oscar nomination, a fact that did not sit too well with many black Americans.

Racial fireworks in a small Southern town: In the Heat of the Night *with Sidney Poitier (as Northern detective Virgil Tubbs), Warren Oates (c.), and Rod Steiger.*

In This Our Life (1942)

D. John Huston. *S.* Howard Koch; based on the novel by Ellen Glasgow. *P.* David Lewis. *R.* Warner Bros. Cast includes: Dennis Morgan; Charles Coburn; George Brent; and Billie Burke.

During the early and mid-1940s, black characters in American films underwent a significant image change. Gone were the outlandishly charismatic and eccentric servants—those comic jesters, those lazy bootblacks and butlers, those giggling maids and mammies—who had proliferated in movies of the Depression. Now during the years of the Second World War more dignified New Negro characters slowly turned up (in such features as *The Ox-Bow Incident*, 1943, with Leigh Whipper and even earlier in 1939 with Whipper in *Of Mice and Men*) as the movie industry attempted handling black issues more seriously. *In This Our Life*, starring Bette Davis and Olivia de Havilland, was an early film that presented such a new treatment. Here Davis is a spoiled rich girl, who accidentally kills a child during a wild car ride, then drives away from the scene. The hit-and-run accident is blamed on a young black man, played by Ernest Anderson, the son of Davis's family's maid, played by Hattie McDaniel. Bright, dignified, and composed, the young man studies law at night in order, naturally, to improve his lot in life. Eventually, he's proven innocent of the crime. His story is merely a subplot in this fast-paced melodrama, but director Huston makes it compelling nonetheless. "Ernest Anderson," wrote *Variety*, "stands out in brief appearances as the wrongly-accused colored lad." Audiences today generally agree.

Intruder in the Dust (1949)

D. Clarence Brown. *S.* Ben Maddow. The cinematography is by Robert Surtees. *P.* Clarence Brown *R.* MGM. Cast includes: Elizabeth Patterson (giving a fine performance as Mrs. Habersham); David Brian; Porter Hall; Claude Jarman, Jr. (as Chick); and Elzie Emanuel (as Aleck).

Often considered the best of the Problem Pictures of 1949.

Based on William Faulkner's novel and actually filmed in Oxford, Mississippi (using residents of the town in crowd scenes and in some minor roles), this movie has a non-studio, realistic look and tone (similar to and no doubt influenced by the Italian neo-realists of this post-War period). And the acting is without gloss or glamor; it's a direct and immediate, rather naturalistic (although with the right dramatic flourishes) style new to American studio films.

But the story itself is what still engrosses and affects viewers. A black man, Lucas Beauchamp (Juano Hernandez), having been accused of killing a white southern neighbor, is imprisoned. The whites of the town are soon ready to lynch him, not so much, we soon learn, because they believe he's committed the crime but because he is a black man who has refused to play the part of their town *nigger*. Lucas knows who he is, has faith and confidence in his own worth, bows to no man, and carries himself with the greatest of dignity, so much so that he is indeed superior. In fact, he is so strong that he doesn't believe he has to prove anything to anybody, not even his innocence. He turns, however, to a young white boy, Chick. Sometime earlier Lucas had rescued Chick from drowning. Afterwards he had taken the child home with him so that the boy's clothes might dry. When Chick had then offered the black man money, Lucas had promptly rejected it. His had been an act of hospitality—and fundamental humanity—which cannot be paid for. But because of the South's rigid racial/social codes, Chick doesn't want to "owe" a black man for anything, and his later ambivalence—his hostility and his fascination with Lucas—is the same of that of many of the white townspeople, who feel, "We got to make him a nigger first. He's got to admit he's a nigger. Then maybe we will accept him as he seems to intend to be accepted." Thus begrudgingly feeling he still must somehow repay the nigger for the debt, Chick sets out to find the real murderer.

Intruder in the Dust is a complex film, presented often as a murder mystery. And it succeeds on many levels, as a piece of entertainment and as an artistic statement. "If this movie had been produced in Europe," Pauline Kael wrote, "it would probably be widely acclaimed among American students of the film as a subtle, sensitive, neo-realist work."

Writing of the problem pictures in his essay "The Shadow and the Act," Ralph Ellison said that

> the temptation toward self-congratulation which comes from seeing these films and sharing in their emotional release is apt to blind us to the true nature of what is unfolding—or failing to unfold—before our eyes. As an antidote to the sentimentality of these films, I suggest that they be seen in predominantly Negro audiences. For here, when the action goes phony, one will hear derisive laughter, not sobs. . . . *Intruder in the Dust* is the only film that could be shown in Harlem without arousing unintended laughter. For it is the only one of the four in which Negroes can make complete identification with their screen image. Interestingly, the factors that make this identification possible lie in its depiction not of racial but of human quality.

Intruder in the Dust is not without flaws. The self-congratulatory tone Ellison speaks of is most apparent (as is the one "false note" of the film Pauline Kael has spoken of) at the conclusion when Chick's uncle, a white lawyer, tells the boy, "It will be all right as long as some of us are willing to fight—even one of us," adding, "Lucas wasn't in trouble—we were." That lame line's a bit hard to take.

Finally, though, one leaves *Intruder in the Dust* having seen something else quite startling and new to American movies: it presents us with Hollywood's first black separatist movie hero. As Juano Hernandez plays Lucas, he is a truly towering figure: independent, proud, testy, outspoken, resilient, often impossible, even downright insufferable. It is an impressive performance, one of the strongest in the history of blacks in American films. Hernandez won two European awards for his work. But in the United States, his performance, while appreciated by many critics, generally went unnoticed and was forgotten soon afterward. The same was true of this vastly underrated film.

Island in the Sun (1957)

D. Robert Rossen. *S.* Alfred Hayes. *P.* Darryl F. Zanuck. *R.* 20th Century-Fox. Cast includes: Joan Collins (as a socially prominent woman, who is revealed to have "Negro blood"); James Mason;

Passion and politics in the tropics: (l. to r.) Dorothy Dandridge, Stephen Boyd, and Joan Collins in Island in the Sun.

Michael Rennie; John Williams; Diana Wynyard; Stephen Boyd; Patricia Owens; Hartley Power; and Basil Sydney.

Based on Alec Waugh's best-selling novel about politics and interracial love in the British West Indies, this Darryl F. Zanuck production set out to tackle the theme of miscegenation in a way earlier films like *Pinky* had never dared. It was the first Hollywood film to cast black performers (Dorothy Dandridge, Harry Belafonte) opposite white stars (John Justin, Joan Fontaine) in romantic roles. As such, *Island in the Sun* garnered a great deal of press attention and controversy. Almost immediately, the film was threatened with boycotts by Southern theatres. The South Carolina legislature even considered passing a bill that would fine any theatre showing the movie $5000. According to Zanuck's biographer Mel Gussow, Zanuck himself announced he would personally pay such fines. But the bill was never passed.

Perhaps fears of such an impending controversy inhibited the filmmakers while the movie was being shot. Throughout Alfred Hayes's script is meandering and timid, repeatedly pulling back as if frightened of its subject. Belafonte plays David Boyer, a restless labor leader on the imaginary island Santa Marta. When a wealthy white woman, Joan Fontaine, becomes attracted to him, Belafonte's character cannot seem to make a move toward or away from her. Although the picture titillates the audience with the idea of a passionate romance between the two, no such thing ever occurs. Belafonte's barely permitted to touch her. And, of course, he ends the relationship. He's almost desexed by the script and has none of the fire he displayed in his concert appearances during this time. It's no wonder that movie audiences found him lacking as a leading man.

Dandridge as Margot Seaton, the young island woman involved with John Justin, the aide to the island's governor, fares better for unexpected reasons. In this, her first film since her Oscar-nominated triumph as Carmen Jones, Dandridge has little to do and is without a role to play. But she's beautiful to watch, a fragile goddess whom the audience cannot help being drawn to. Her personal tensions and inner conflicts, as well as her vulnerability, surface here at odd moments. We're not watching an actress playing a character. Instead we're seeing a woman trying very hard to please and to come to grips with a film that really has no place for her. Dandridge herself said that she and Justin had to fight with the studio to permit his character to say he *loved* her.

Almost everyone else in *Island in the Sun* wanders about as if sleepwalking. Director Robert Rossen doesn't seem able to rouse any passion out of his cast or himself. And passion was clearly needed to make the film a success. Throughout audiences long to see Dandridge and Belafonte dump their white co-stars and reach out for one another. Had that happened, this might have been provocative. Instead a movie that should have been sexy and trashily enjoyable is tepid and dull. According to Mel Gussow, in 1963 Zanuck himself said, "I never liked *Island in the Sun.* I didn't like it because they made me compromise the book." The topic of miscegenation, however, surprisingly worked at the box office. The studio's fears proved unfounded. The picture cost $2,250,000 and grossed $8 million.

The film was shot in CinemaScope on the islands of Grenada and Barbados.

J.D.'s Revenge (1976)

D. Arthur Marks. *S.* Jaison Starkes. *P.* Arthur Marks. *R.* AIP. Cast includes: Lou Gossett; Joan Pringle; Carl Crudup; James Louis Watkins; Alice Jubert; Stephanie Faulkner; Fred Pinkard; and David McKnight.

A young law student (Glynn Turman) is possessed by the spirit of a long-dead murdered gangster, who now wants some revenge.

Turman works hard at making us shiver, although as usual he's too studied. And the film plays hard on the interest in the occult and demonic possession then in vogue (à la *The Exorcist*). But the movie is so poorly shot and so jumbled that the best moment of *J.D.'s Revenge* comes when it is finally over.

Jivin' in Be-Bop (1947)

D. Leonard Anderson (black director Spencer Williams has sometimes been credited as co-director). *S.* Powell Lindsay. *P.* William Alexander. Cast includes: Ray Snead; Johnny Taylor; Freddie Carter; Ralph Brown; Dan Durley; Phil and Audrey; Daisy Richardson; and Panch and Dolores.

No plot. No characters. A musical revue interspersed with some dull-witted comic routines. There are only two redeeming factors here: namely Dizzy Gillespie and vocalist Helen Humes. Otherwise the proceedings are pretty dreary.

Jo Jo Dancer, Your Life is Calling (1986)

D. Richard Pryor. S. Pryor with Rocco Urbisci and Paul Mooney. P. Richard Pryor. R. Columbia Pictures. The interesting cast includes: Carmen McRae (as the grandmother); Paula Kelly (as the kindhearted stripper Satin Doll); Billy Eckstine; Diahanne Abbott and Scoey Mitchell as Jo Jo's parents; E'lon Cox (rather good as the young Jo Jo); Fay Hauser (as the first wife Grace); Debbie Allen (as Michelle); and Barbara Williams (as Dawn).

Richard Pryor's semi-autobiographical look at his troubled life. A little of everything we know about Richard Pryor is in this story of a talented comedian named Jo Jo Dancer: the childhood years spent in his grandmother's bordello; the tensions that erupted between an overbearing father and an insecure son; the tender relationship of the young Jo Jo with his mother, a prostitute whom he watches with her customers; the early showbiz experiences in seedy clubs and dives as he builds a reputation; the star years of booze, dope, and temper tantrums; the misunderstandings and quarrels with a string of wives who come and go with regularity. Although much is piled on, almost nothing is dramatically sorted out. So sweetly tempered and lovingly depicted are the early whorehouse sequences that young Jo Jo looks as if he's attending an enlightened day care center for bright children.

Gallantly, Pryor refuses to lash out at any of the women. But that doesn't matter because they're all little more than melodramatic props there to showcase, if anything, Jo Jo's sensitivity. (Pryor's former wife Jennifer Lee criticized the film as a dishonest portrait.) An alter ego figure (played by Pryor) appears early, displaying some signs of vitality. Nothing comes of that either though. Yet disappointing and undeveloped as the picture is, it's of some interest to see the headline stories we've all read about now so broadly etched out from Pryor's point of view. And *Jo Jo* does occasionally give a glimpse of a black community that's sorely missing from other American films of this period. It's a valiant effort and may look better in years to come.

The Joe Louis Story (1953)

D. Robert Gordon. S. Robert Sylvester. P. Sterling Silliphant. R. United Artists. Cast includes: Hilda Simms (who had been the spectacular heroine of the successful black stage presentation *Anna Lucasta*); Paul Stewart; John Marley; and in the role of Joe's trainer Chappie Blackburn, James Edwards.

Almost twenty years earlier, Joe Louis's life had been recorded in *Spirit of Youth*, in which Joe played himself. Neither that film nor this one will turn up on anybody's all-time top ten movie lists. But both were well-remembered special events in the black community, in part because Louis himself was so loved and also because the movies don't set out to tarnish (nor explain in any depth or complexity) his life and image.

Variety wrote:

> Many things might have gone wrong in making a picture like this but fortunately, none of them did. The film . . . rates high on sincerity, is alternately touching, understanding, and heart-poundingly exciting. That's a lot of merits. . . . There is no question that *The Joe Louis Story* . . . is headed for b.o. [box office] wallops among all kinds of audiences. But

even more important is the fact that it shows the Negro on a level which Hollywood too often neglects. It doesn't strain for effects. It doesn't have to.

What all that means is that at heart this is a pleasant B-movie, telling the story of a simple, good-natured young black man, who could box, who wanted to box, and who, in doing so, became, almost without his own awareness, a great national folk hero. With his fame came pressures he had never anticipated. Coley Wallace plays Joe, not with any impressive acting technique but with feeling and reserve and a cautious, gentle strength. Actual fight sequences (from Joe's bouts with Schmeling and Marciano) invest the movie with a Hollywood kind of authenticity: it's real (the fights) and fake (the story) at the same time.

Judge Priest (1934)

D. John Ford. S. Dudley Nichols and Lamar Trotti. P. Sol Wurtzel. R. 20th Century-Fox. Cast includes: Tom Brown and Anita Louise.

Will Rogers stars as the warm, perceptive, perpetually folksy Judge Priest, the hero of a series of stories written by Irvin S. Cobb. The plot is negligible (it focuses mainly on the love of the judge's nephew for a pretty local girl whose father is unknown; the discovery of the father's identity is the story device the picture eventually turns on). The interesting elements are director Ford's *atmospheric touches*, which include the presence of Stepin Fetchit and Hattie McDaniel as servants in the town.

Portraying Rogers's righthand man and best buddy Jeff Poindexter, Fetchit is something of a shock to see: lanky, bald, dimwitted, inarticulate, asexual. But he's a scene stealer and the camera simply cannot take its eye off him. Fetchit seems to operate in a world all his own. When given orders or fussed with, he seems oblivious, reacting and moving instead to the beat of some internal rhythm. The only time he seems jolted into the here-and-now occurs when that walking powerhouse Hattie McDaniel speaks her mind to him. He plays the harmonica at one point, and she tells him to cut the monkeyshine! When she shouts, he listens! A true odd couple, their appearance is indicative of the servant tradition of early 1930s movies, when eccentric black maids and butlers were, for the most part, still hemmed in by their director and by the fundamental racism of their scripts. Yet Ford, who usually treats his black characters with appalling condescension, can't really control these two. He seems genuinely amazed by Fetchit, who is permitted to do his schtick without too much interference. With McDaniel, Ford backs off a bit, but he has been able, in some sequences, to let a sweetness flow from her that other directors missed out on.

A poetic, romanticized piece of Americana, with two charismatic black performers surfacing from the background to grab attention whenever/wherever they can.

Juke Joint (1947)

D. Spencer Williams. S. Generally credited to Spencer Williams. P. Bert Goldberg. R. Alfred Sack Amusement Enterprises.

This race movie is much like oldtime black ethnic theater, a series of skits and routines connected here by a plot which gives each actor a chance to showcase his/her particular talent or attitude. Two men (Spencer Williams and July Jones) arrive in a Texas town, low on cash and in need of a place to stay. They wind up at the home of Mama Lou Holiday (Inez Newell), a hefty number who's forever bawling out her lazy, good-for-nothing husband. Both Mama Lou and hubby are the crudest of stereotypes. Like a child, the husband is given money by Mama Lou and sent to the store to buy meat for supper. He ends up at the local pool hall where he loses the money in a blackjack game. Mama Lou's only joy in life seems to be her daughter Honey Dew, a demure lass (who unfortunately delivers her lines as if she were a first-grade student reading a fifth-grade primer; she's unbelievably bad). When we first meet Honey Dew, she's about to enter a local beauty contest and is being fitted for her dress by Mama Lou. The two get to yakking about the other daughter in the Holiday household—whom Mama Lou has no patience with whatsoever. "Florida is just like her old no good daddy," Mama Lou belts out. Then in very high-minded tones, she adds, "Florida doesn't care for beauty contests and lectures and debates of the higher things in life like you do. All she ever thinks about is men and more men." Mama Lou badmouths this other daughter so much that, well, frankly, we can't wait for Florida to show up. She sounds like quite a gal. When she does appear, we see an actress who's got plenty of attitude but, let us say, not the greatest of acting skills. Her attitude, however, and that of the rest of the cast keep this movie popping and bouncing along. There are also some lines straight out of the ethnic theater of the past. When Spencer Williams is annoyed by his sidekick July Jones, he warns him, "I get to thinking real hard I get sort of ugly in the face." To which Jones replies, "Well, anybody can see you're a hard thinker."

By most standards, this might be considered an atrocity of a picture but *Juke Joint*'s got spirit and some kick and punch. The technical crudities and ineptitude somehow add to the giddy flavor and the vitality: as the actors flub lines and keep going on, we sometimes feel we're watching live theater. Although Williams is a real pro, just about everyone else is consistently poor, and we never know what to expect. This is the kind of film to see with a large audience (preferably black) primed for a night of oldtime fun.

Jumpin' Jack Flash (1986)

> *D.* Penny Marshall. *S.* David H. Franzoni, J. W. Melville, Patricia Irving, and Christopher Thompson; story by David H. Franzoni. *P.* Lawrence Gordon and Joel Silver. *R.* 20th Century-Fox. Cast includes: Annie Potts; Carol Kane; John Wood; and Jim Belushi.

Whoopi Goldberg's first comic movie role; also one of the first all-out Hollywood comedies ever to star a black woman. With the entire wobbly plot wrapped around her, Goldberg tries her darndest to pull the movie off. She plays a New York City computer programmer working in the foreign exchange department of a Wall Street banking firm. When she starts picking up computer messages from a British spy trapped behind the Iron Curtain (he calls himself Jumping Jack Flash), she not only becomes smitten with the guy (via her computer) but also embroiled in an espionage caper as she sets out to help him. She's shot at, drugged, shoved into the East River, mistaken for a terrorist, and dragged by a pickup truck through the streets of New York while trapped in a telephone booth.

Dressed in floppy, oversized, mismatched coats, pants, and sneakers, Goldberg looks, frankly, like a hip bag lady, or perhaps simply like a clown. Even her trademark dreadlocks seem to add to the clown nature of her screen persona; the same might be said of her very name. Part of the mean-spirited humor is to see how this lowly Negress misfit will function in such "cultivated" places as the British Consulate or Elizabeth Arden's posh beauty salon.

Goldberg's quite funny, though, whether screaming out in fear while being abducted by a villainous cab driver (she knocks him over the head with, what else?, a frying pan; in the process, she does sound like past black movie servants who went into conniptions whenever they thought they had seen a ghost) or twisting like crazy to free herself from a paper shredder that threatens not only to eat up her dress but Goldberg as well. A high comic moment also occurs when she crashes a British Consulate party dressed in a gown and shoulder-length blond wig, pretending to be one of the Supremes while lip-syncing to one of their records.

In the scenes of her alone in her apartment, Goldberg is something of a wistful dreamy loner. But the movie doesn't explore that quality. Other times she's just funkily energetic or profane. This is not an acting job; it's a personal onslaught that succeeds rather well. It's just sad that the film itself cannot match her talents.

The film tries very hard to make its audience forget its heroine is a black woman from the black community. The character's name, Terry Doolittle, is not a name we'd associate with a black woman. (It sounds silly and waspy.) Her apartment, with its posters and toys, has few of the cultural trappings or signposts we'd associate with a black woman. At least on "The Cosby Show," the kids' rooms display posters of Whitney Houston or Wynton Marsalis. Then, too, at her job—and throughout her adventures—she's usually surrounded by whites. When she does meet up with black actor Roscoe Lee Browne, cool and elegant, we hope the two are going to have scenes together in which they jam and play off each another's internal rhythms. But none of that here. Instead Goldberg develops a sweet platonic rapport with handsome white actor Stephen Collins. Were Goldberg a white star, their rapport would naturally lead to romance. The worst—and truly unforgivable—moments of the film come at the end when, having saved the British spy she's so enamoured of, Goldberg finally meets him (Jonathan Pryce). The two kind of hold each other for a fast minute or two but are not permitted a real screen kiss. What's the big deal, we wonder. If the interracial romantic theme scares the filmmakers so much, why the heck didn't they just give Goldberg a black leading man? She's sadly as much desexed here as Eddie Murphy had been in *Beverly Hills Cop*. This final neutralized sequence of *Jumpin' Jack Flash* is one of Hollywood's most compromised, possibly one of its ugliest, too.

Generally, the critics praised Goldberg but panned the movie. Rex Reed called it "a Jerry Lewis movie in blackface."

The Klansman (1974)

D. Terence Young. *S.* Sam Fuller and Millard Kaufman. *P.* Black producer William Alexander. *R.* Paramount. Cast includes: Spence Wil-Dee; Luciana Paluzzi; and Cameron Mitchell.

An action-packed dog of a movie with a little of everything.

Plenty of robust characters: a bigoted Southern sheriff who's also a die-

A box-office dud and a critical disaster: The
Klansman *with Lola Falana, O. J. Simpson, and a rather weary Richard Burton.*

hard Ku Klux Klansman; an aristocratic landowner fond of his *negras*; an
educated, uppity black girl, who, having lived in the North, has now
returned to the South to see her dying grandmother—and who decides
to stick around a bit to change the political situation; and a charged-up,
radicalized young black man (a buck!), not about to take any crap from
the honkies!

Plenty of incidents: a rape; a black voter registration drive; a vengeful
KKK out to calm down these rebellious colored townies.

And plenty of big name stars: Richard Burton, Lee Marvin, Linda Evans,
Lola Falana, and screen newcomer O. J. Simpson.

Unfortunately, about the only things missing are some commonsense and a story that's fully worked out and well dramatized. In
essence, despite all the goings-on, nothing of any consequence happens.
Cheap and simple-minded, it's also old-fashioned, failing to put a new
slant on material covered years earlier in such movies as *Pinky, Intruder in
the Dust*, and even Otto Preminger's pop serenade to the New Negra in
the New South, *Hurry Sundown*.

"The whole thing's a blistering incitement to apathy," wrote Judith
Crist in *New York*. "There's not a shred of quality, dignity, relevance or
impact in this yahoo-oriented bunk," wrote *Variety*, adding, "The only
social impact . . . is likely to occur in those situations where audiences
make known their displeasure to management. Bookers are hereby
alerted to the possibility of racially-integrated displays of unanimous
disapproval."

Today this may have a limited camp appeal but not much else.

Lady Sings the Blues (1972)

D. Sidney J. Furie. *S.* Terence McCloy, Chris Clark, and Suzanne de
Passe; from the book by Billie Holiday and William Dufty. Camera:
John Alonzo. *P.* Berry Gordy, Jr.; also Jay Weston and James S.
White. *R.* Paramount Pictures. Cast includes: Isabel Sanford; Vir-
ginia Capers (as Holiday's mother); Paul Hampton; Sid Melton; Scat-
man Crothers; Yvonne Fair; Robert L. Gordy; Pauline Myers; Tracee
Lyles.

Nobody was quite prepared for this screen version of jazz singer Billie
Holiday's life. In fact, a number of people were ready to dismiss the film
right off the bat as simply a fraud and a travesty. From the moment it
had been announced that pop singer Diana Ross would portray Holiday, most thought her all wrong for the role. Where Lady Day had been
all stillness and quiet fire (*the essence of cool*, as Duke Ellington had

described her), Ross was a razzledazzle extrovert, a skinny, highstrung live wire who never seemed to stop moving. Then, too, it was feared the movie would whitewash Holiday's drug experiences and her series of love affairs and marriages.

Well, frankly, the critics of *Lady Sings the Blues* had their points: the finished picture no doubt proved to them that their fears were justified. Watching this movie, one would never guess what an international star Holiday had been: it looks as if she's always hanging out in the same clubs. And one would never understand how Holiday's rough romances left her emotionally depleted. Here there's only one fellow in her life, the black Prince Charming of Billy Dee Williams. Nor can one come to grips fully with the set of pressures Holiday lived with. Although there is a melodramatically jolting Southern sequence with the Klan, there are few of the nondramatic everyday humiliations and tensions that gnawed at and eroded Holiday's spirit: the times when she was told not to mix or mingle with the whites who came to hear her perform; the occasions when she had to use the back entrances of the clubs or take freight elevators so not to offend white patrons; the times club managers and owners complained that her singing style was too slow and moody, not fast or peppy enough. The film simplifies the complex, irons out the complications to give a straightforward, conventional narrative and characters everyone can easily understand.

Yet with all that said and done, *Lady Sings the Blues* succeeded on

Billy Dee Williams and Diana Ross in Lady Sings the Blues: *a simplified version of jazz performer Billie Holiday's troubled life, but one of Hollywood's few black romantic films.*

127

another level, one that might well have pleased Lady Day herself: as lush, romantic reverie. There had never been (still has not been) a black movie like it. There is a dizzy sweep and cockeyed grandeur to this film which follows the young Billie/Diana from her early years in Baltimore to her years of struggle in New York to her periods of acclaim and decline. And Ross performs with such a surprising mixture of confidence, vulnerability, and open-faced charm that you can't help liking and rooting for her. Her sheer indefatigable star power has never been on more dazzling or moving display. She has a restlessness and pushiness, too, not explained by the script. But we know her Billie, like Diana Ross herself, is a ghetto girl who understands that the only thing that can get her out of the ghetto and a world without possibilities or opportunities is precisely this kind of energetic drive. (It's the same kind of drive that propelled other classic black stars like Josephine Baker and Ethel Waters, also ghetto girls. Better than any other black screen actress, Ross has captured this indefinable ghetto-girl thrust for attention and a place in the scheme of things. She understands it. And in a sense, parts of *Lady Sings the Blues* [and *Mahogany*] are movies within movies: snippets of documentary about the struggles and tenacity of Diana Ross herself.)

But what adds yet another dimension to Ross's push is her great chemistry with co-star Williams. As soon as the two meet in the film, almost everything else disappears. And something new comes to American cinema, something only flirted with in the past with a movie like *Bright Road*. There black audiences anxiously watched as Harry Belafonte's hungry eyes gave Dorothy Dandridge a tentative once-over. He wanted her. Badly. And she seemed to want him. Or so we assume from their brief hot *platonic* scenes together. But the script could not be bothered with something as basic as black romance and sex. So these beautiful people never got together. When Dandridge and Belafonte did meet again, the next year in *Carmen Jones*, they were more like overheated sexy adversaries than starstruck lovers. But *Lady Sings the Blues* takes black romance the full, larger-than-life distance: for the first time in a major movie, we see a black couple who meet, court, fight, make up, fight again, are more often than not cautious about commitment (no doubt fearing the kind of emotional entrapment such commitment can bring). In the most famous sequence, the two sit until the early hours of the morning in a nightclub, talking, exploring, trying to outfox one another. It is quite conceivably the most real, romantic moment between a black man and black woman we have seen in a Hollywood film. Is it any wonder that black audiences swooned over and embraced this melodrama, turning it into a great hit?

Also along for the ride, of course, is the young Richard Pryor: loose, jivey, vulnerable, full of fun. He works splendidly with Ross, too. Both he and Williams treat her gently, no doubt aware of the actress's own personal concerns about her very first movie performance. "Individual opinion about *Lady Sings the Blues* may vary markedly," *Variety* wrote, "depending on a person's age, knowledge of jazz tradition and feeling for it, and how one wishes to regard Billie Holiday as both a force and victim of her times. However for the bulk of today's general audiences, the film serves as a very good screen debut vehicle for Diana Ross."

Ross was nominated for an Academy Award as Best Actress of 1972. The picture received four other Oscar nominations. And Motown, which had brought together all the elements of the picture, looked as if its future in the movie business was assured. That was not to be the case.

The Landlord (1970)

D. Hal Ashby. *S.* William Gunn (who later directed the black cult film *Ganja and Hess*); based on the novel by black writer Kristin Hunter. The cinematography is by Gordon Willis. *P.* Norman Jewison. *R.* United Artists. Cast includes: Pearl Bailey; Lee Grant; Robert Klein; Marki Bey (in a surprising intelligent update and elaboration of the tragic mulatto character); Mel Stewart; and Susan Anspach.

A little known, satiric comedy/drama, marking the directorial debut of Hal Ashby, who later directed *Shampoo* (1975) and *Being There* (1979). The unusual, perceptive screenplay is by black writer Bill Gunn.

Mistily realistic and gritty for its time, *The Landlord* focused on a wealthy young white lad (Beau Bridges), who buys a tenement building in the ghetto. He plans to redo the place, turning it into his own private paradise. But while in the ghetto, he starts fraternizing with some of the natives, the local black residents. And they come to change his way of looking at life—and himself. One of the residents is a lovely, jittery young black woman (Diana Sands), with whom the young man becomes romantically involved, although she's already married. She has a child by him. When the woman's black husband learns of this relationship, his entire world seems to collapse right before him—and right before our eyes, too. All the pent-up rage, all the undefined anger, all the restlessness and buried hostilities this black man has had to live with for years, surface in a dramatic explosion that's both startling and delicately etched.

Usually, movie militants (and this was precisely what this character was) are portrayed (by scripts and actors alike) as little more than rhetorical pinheads, men with chips on their shoulders who, so Hollywood would like us to believe, without rhyme or reason to their madness or anger, are just itching for a fight, any fight. In *The Landlord*, however, Gunn's script endowed the husband with a poignant dignity and a keen intelligence, and the explosion was so corrosively logical, yet so unexpected in its intensity, that it indeed inspired awe, pity, and fear. The actor playing the husband was Louis Gossett, Jr. His was one of the most exciting performances of that time.

The same was true of Diana Sands' fine, sensitive work. These two were highlighting a new style of black acting in American films: intense, realistic, urban, politically alert. (Actually, the first ones to bring this style to movies were Sidney Poitier, Ruby Dee, Juano Hernandez, and James Edwards.) Yet the performances of Sands and Gossett went unnoticed. Sands never got as good a movie again, and Gossett had to wait some seven years before he came up with another solid role as Fiddler in "Roots".

It has been said that the movie's distributors—and perhaps the public, too—may have felt uneasiness with the tense, interracial dynamics. The movie was a commercial failure and is now seldom seen.

But *The Landlord* still works exceedingly well as a comment on certain social and political attitudes of the late 1960s/early 1970s and as a true Hollywood rarity—a film that deals neither exclusively with the black or white experience in America but with both.

Leadbelly (1976)

D. Gordon Parks, Sr. *S.* Ernest Kinoy. *P.* Mark Merson; executive producer, David Frost. *R.* Paramount. Cast includes: Art Evans (as Blind Lemon Jefferson); Paul Benjamin; Loretta Green, Lynn Hamilton; and Albert Hall (who later gave an impressive performance in *Apocalypse Now*).

Movie biography of folk singer Huddie Ledbetter's troubled life.

Pleasurable viewing experience that *Leadbelly* often is, you may wonder upon leaving the theatre if you really know anything about Leadbelly, the man, or the period in which he lived. Photographs reveal this singer who became something of a folk hero in the Depression era to have been a hard, tough, mean-looking critter who took nothing from anyone. But actor Roger Mosley, who plays the title role, has an inexpressive round face that is without poetic tension or toughness, that is without experience. This piece of casting is one of the film's greatest weaknesses. This movie needed a Paul Winfield, who could suggest power and sensitivity.

Moreover Leadbelly's various scrapes with the law and the violence that were so much a part of his existence have been softened and left unexplained. That same softening is true of the other characters and incidents in the film, which contains one of the schmaltziest (and perhaps perversely most likable) scenes in the history of black films of the 1970s. Returning to a town that was once thriving and bustling with activity and vitality when he was young, Leadbelly (now gray) finds it a ghost town, dusty and almost deserted except for a lone figure making her way down the trash-littered street. He looks closely and discovers it is a former love (Madge Sinclair). Briefly, they are united again. But, of course, it only happens at the movies. Life seldom has such grand designs.

The lush, bright cinematography of Bruce Surtees simply adds to the inappropriate lush romanticism of *Leadbelly*. Curiously enough, the dark, brooding, smoky, and highly effective look of *Sparkle*, which Surtees was also responsible for, would have served *Leadbelly* well.

The film met with mixed reviews. *Variety* wrote that it was "a fine film . . . compelling in its tragic melodrama" while Archer Winston in *The New York Post* said he had found it "deeply moving." *The New York Times'* Vincent Canby, however, said: "*Leadbelly* is less a failure in execution than a mistake in conception, for if you accept this conception, you must go along with its more or less immaculate vision of triumph over degradation."

Upon its release, *Leadbelly* did become a bit of a *cause célèbre* when director Parks complained that the distributing studio Paramount had mishandled the picture, refusing to provide the big New York opening essential to the movie's success and also devising a misleading ad campaign. Parks felt that ads depicting a muscular, bare-chested man flanked by a full-hipped woman on one side and a fight scene on the other made *Leadbelly* look like a blaxploitation item rather than a "serious" film. He was right.

Off-camera Hi Tide Harris performed the vocals heard on the soundtrack, including Leadbelly's classic "Good Night Irene."

The Legend of Nigger Charley (1972)

D. Martin Goldman. *S.* Martin Goldman and Larry Spangler. *P.* Larry Spangler. *R.* Paramount Pictures. Cast includes: Gertrude Jeannette (as Theo).

Early on, we see an old white plantation owner on his deathbed, attended to by his dear black servant Theo. "I want you to be free when I die," he tells her. Her reply sends contemporary black audiences into a fit of laughter. "I ain't never asked you nothin about no freedom," she says. "I got my obligations right here in my house. If I'd been so worried about freedom, I could have walked off here any time I wanted to and I don't think you'd have sent nobody looking for me. Now you just turn over there and try to get yourself some rest." A few minutes later, almost as an afterthought, she says, "Master Carter, if you want to free somebody, you can free my boy Charley." The credits soon inform us that this film is based on the "historical research" of C. Eric Lincoln. That's a real laugh, too. It's based on Hollywood's desire to make some bucks. Anyway, Charley (Fred Williamson), given his freedom papers, gets into a nasty brawl with the corrupt plantation overseer, whom he kills. The film follows Charley's flight for freedom with two other slaves (D'Urville Martin and Don Pedro Colley) as they are trailed by a bounty hunter. A truly astonishing scene occurs when the trio arrives in another white town. They simply ride in on horseback down the town's main street while the white residents stand by in a state of shock. Where on earth, the whites seem to be asking themselves, did these bold negras come from? We ask the same question. Because no slave in his right mind would ever have behaved like these three: they are 1970s-style slick black dudes, looking more as if they were out for a stroll through Times Square. Later at the local tavern, the trio fight it out with the town whites, who obviously have had enough of these uppity coloreds. The whole enterprise is implausible. Yet it's still fairly easy to spot what black audiences of the 1970s liked: Williamson *is* a strong black man of action. He gives a rather ingratiating performance. What with all the gunfights and warring parties, the picture's made for a black male audience that loved westerns but had almost never seen a black one. The film has its obligatory sweaty sex scene between Williamson and his plantation sweetheart Marcia McBroom. A half-breed

Indian woman also has the hots for Williamson. But the script and director discreetly keep the two apart. Of course, the picture ends with the hero's triumph over all his adversities—and naturally leads way to the sequel *The Soul of Nigger Charley* (1973).

Let the Good Times Roll (1973)

D. Sid Levin and Robert Abel. *P.* Gerald I. Isenberg. *R.* Columbia Pictures; A Metromedia Producers Corporation Production.

Sheer rock-and-roll heaven for anyone interested in such rambunctiously energetic and innovative 1950s music stars as: Fats Domino, Chubby Checker, The Five Satins, The Shirelles, Bo Diddley, The Coasters, Chuck Berry, Bill Haley and The Comets, and the not-to-be believed Little Richard. Filmed during two revival concerts (one at Long Island's Nassau Coliseum; the other at Detroit's Cobo Hall with some additional Fats Domino footage from the Las Vegas Flamingo Hotel), there are also behind-the-scenes gems: a serious, thoughtful Chuck Berry reminiscing about the road years on his old bus; a snappish, quarrelsome, paranoid Little Richard having a "scene" in his dressing room. The music is great fun. The standouts: Chuck Berry doing his duck-squat-walk; Berry performing "Maybelline" and teaming with Bo Diddley for "Johnny B. Goode"; and Little Richard—pompadour, mascara, and drag queen persona intact—as he lets out his gospel wail on such classic numbers as "Lucille," "Good Golly Miss Molly," and "Rip It Up."

An engrossing look at some legendary black rock-and-roll artists.

Let's Do It Again (1975)

D. Sidney Poitier. *S.* Richard Wesley (who also scripted *Uptown Saturday Night*); story by Timothy March. *P.* Melville Tucker. *R.* First Artists/Warner Bros. Cast includes: Calvin Lockhart; John Amos; Denise Nicholas; Lee Chamberlain; Mel Stewart; Julius Harris; Ossie Davis; Billy Eckstine; Jayne Kennedy; and Hilda Haynes.

A followup to the immensely successful crossover movie *Uptown Saturday Night*, again starring Sidney Poitier and Bill Cosby as two working-class/middle-class buddies. Here they're trying to raise money for a new meeting place for their lodge, The Sons and Daughters of Shaka. Their solution: hypnotizing a weakling dumb bumpkin of a boxer (Jimmie Walker) into becoming a ferocious lion in the ring—and thereby winning matches they've placed bets on.

Endurably popular (it's still shown at black film festivals and on television and has already achieved something of a classic status, much like that of *Stormy Weather*), the film's basically for the young of heart—and the young of mind. Richard Wesley's script has nice ethnic touches. But the movie's view of comedy and domestic life is a boy's notion of grownups having fun.

Most disheartening is watching Poitier force himself to do the kind of antics one associates with comic black performers of the 1930s, who had no control over their material—whereas Poitier in the 1970s had almost total control. Pauline Kael got to the core of the matter when she wrote: "It is apparent Sidney Poitier set this project in motion and directed it: he's making films for black audiences that aren't exploitation films. Poitier is trying to make it possible for ordinary, lower

A return of oldstyle ethnic humor but with a new slant: Let's Do It Again *with Bill Cosby, Denise Nicholas, Sidney Poitier, and Lee Chamberlain.*

middle-class black people to see themselves on the screen and have a good time. The only thing that makes the film remarkable is that Poitier gives an embarrassing, inhibited performance. As casual, light-hearted straightman to Bill Cosby he is trying to be something alien to his nature. He has too much pride, and too much reserve, for low comedy [and] for an actor of Poitier's intensity and grace to provide this kind of entertainment is the sacrifice of a major screen artist."

Lialeh (1973)

D. Barron Bercovichy. S. Kenneth Elliot Written. P. Kenneth Elliot Written. Cast includes: the rather nubile newcomer Jennifer Leigh as Lialeh; Larry Pertillar; Darryl Speer; Amy Mathieu; John D. Montgomery; and very briefly Bernard "Pretty" Purdie, who also did the musical score for the picture.

The ads read: "He's slick. He's hard. He's bad . . . And that's good for LIALEH."

He's also black as is his lady friend of the title, Lialeh. And that's what sets this apart from the standard porn movie that became fashionable for some middle-class urban audiences after the mid-70s success of *Deep Throat* and *The Devil in Miss Jones*. *Variety* reported: "Though blacks have never constituted much of a market for hardcore pix, this feature effort . . . is an attempt to lure blacks with soul plus skin, and if it works, it will be of more interest to sociologists than porno buffs."

Like most pornographic films, *Lialeh* obviously exploits its female characters and is often too graphic for its own good. But as one of the few black porn movies to reach a sizeable enough audience, *Lialeh* also, perversely and strangely enough, is rather funny at times, refusing to take itself or its pornography too seriously. Consequently, the sexy scenes are often *sexy* with some occasional ingenious sexual acrobatics. Arthur Bell of *The Village Voice* wrote that it was "sophisticated, sensual, fast-moving, and entertaining. A blaksploitation [sic] sexploitation treat."

133

Lola Falana as a wayward housewife whose affair with a white policeman (Anthony Zerbe) leads to tragedy in The Liberation of L.B. Jones.

The Liberation of L. B. Jones (1970)

D. William Wyler. S. Stirling Silliphant and Jesse Hill Ford; based on Ford's novel *The Liberation of Lord Byron Jones*. P. Ronald Lubin. R. Columbia Pictures. Cast includes: Fayard Nicholas (of the dancing Nicholas Brothers); Zara Cully (later George Jefferson's cantankerous mother on TV's "The Jeffersons"); Lauren Jones; Joe Attles; and Brenda Sykes.

Somber and solemn Roscoe Lee Browne plays the honorable, up-to-date tom hero, a black funeral director living in a small Southern town. He's an accommodationist whose kinky, sexy wife (Lola Falana) has lost all interest in him (how they ever got together in the first place is a true mystery), throwing herself into the arms of a beefy bigoted white cop (Anthony Zerbe). Yaphet Kotto, strong and quiet, plays the then-contemporary "militant" character, coming back to the tiny town to exact vengeance on another of its racist white police officers (Arch Johnson). Lee Majors and Barbara Hersey are the newlyweds visiting the town's reputable, seemingly fair-minded judge. Lee J. Cobb plays that judge, who tries keeping a lid on the town's potboiler passions and reveals himself as not being so fair-minded or reputable after all. Adultery, rape, murder, and castration abound in this steamy, trashy melodrama that's hardly as interesting or as much fun as it may sound.

"Not much more than an interracial sexploitation film," wrote *Variety*. Right.

Lilies of the Field (1963)

D. Ralph Nelson. S. James Poe; based on the novel by William E. Barrett. P. Ralph Nelson. R. UA. Cast includes: Lilia Skala.

Under Ralph Nelson's very slick direction, Sidney Poitier starred as the easy-going Homer Smith, an ex-G.I. who stumbles across a group of refugee nuns in the Arizona desert. Hoping to build a chapel, they see him as their savior. Before Homer knows it, he has begun work on the chapel and is devoting all his time to it and has even taken on a parttime job to earn money to buy additional materials. Charming but light (and offensive to some), *Lilies of the Field* offered Sidney Poitier an opportunity to flex his muscles and be the ingratiating and dependable character he was so good at portraying. For his performance, he won the Academy Award as Best Actor of the Year, becoming the first black actor in history to win the coveted Oscar.

But if Academy Awards mean anything, Poitier should have won his Oscar for his performance in *A Raisin in the Sun*, in which his work was vivid, moving, and disturbing. There was also the pleasure of seeing him operate within the black community itself in a highly realistic setting. For the mass white audience, however, *Lilies of the Field* was a politically more acceptable film. Once again Poitier's character functioned within a liberal white world, and in essence, he was cast as a good-hearted servant. *Lilies of the Field* robbed Poitier of the toughness he had exhibited in other likable roles in *Edge of the City* and *Blackboard Jungle*. And his career afterward was affected in a way from which he has yet to recover. With the exception of *In the Heat of the Night*, the later Poitier was hard-pressed to find strong, convincing, challenging dramatic screen parts. Rarely, too, was he able to get back the aggressive shove and heat of some of his pre-*Lilies* performances. This film marked a major image change for him: Poitier was on his way to becoming Saint Sidney or Super Sidney—the ever-accommodating, squeaky clean hero of such movies as *Guess Who's Coming to Dinner?* and *To Sir, with Love* who would enrage black audiences of the late 1960s.

A sequel to *Lilies of the Field* was later filmed as a TV movie, *Christmas Lilies of the Field*, with Billy Dee Williams in the old Poitier role.

Sidney Poitier, with Lilia Skala, in the film that won him an Oscar, Lilies of the Field.

The Little Colonel (1935)

D. David Butler. S. William Conselman; story by Anne Fellows Johnston. P. B. G. DeSylva. R. Fox Pictures. Cast includes: John Lodge; Geneva Williams; and Nyanza Potts as Henry Clay.

A comedy/drama, set in the post–Civil War era, that might as well be an Old South vehicle. Shirley Temple is the curly-topped lass, out to patch up a feud between her southern grandfather (Lionel Barrymore) and his daughter (Shirley's mom in the film, played by Evelyn Venable) who has married a Yankee. Everything reeks of magnolia and gentility and the supposedly sweet way of life of the South of the past. As is the case with another Temple film, *The Littlest Rebel*, one would never have any idea what the Civil War had been all about, particularly when the screen is flooded with cheery darky servants flocking around their dear little Shirley.

But aside from all that, what's most famous about *The Little Colonel* is the dance number in which the great Bill "Bojangles" Robinson teaches Shirley how to tapdance up the staircase. No matter how many times it's seen and no matter how much one may reject it politically, the sequence still moves and dazzles. Robinson's role is shamelessly stereo-typed. The scenes in which Lionel Barrymore fusses and fumes with him—and in which Robinson almost grinningly "takes it"—are hard on the stomach, not to say the mind. But when Robinson stops the mug-ging to move to the beat of the tap, he communicates an enthusiasm and *joie de vivre* that transcends the shallow mechanics of the movie. One can readily understand why Depression audiences were so enamoured of him. He really does make it look as if, no matter how tough times might be, life could still be breezed through with flair and finesse. *Variety* wrote of his performance:

> Bill Robinson, veteran colored hoofer from vaudeville, grabs standout attention here. Voice is excellent, he reads lines with the best of 'em, and his hoofing stair dance is inge-niously woven into the yarn.

Well, one may not agree with *Variety*'s assessment of Robinson's line renderings. Actually, he sometimes sounds as if reading from a black-board! But one can overlook the paper's giddy enthusiasm because Robinson was a great presence.

Also in the cast is a somewhat subdued Hattie McDaniel. One of the movie's most intriguing sequences occurs when Hattie and Bill take Shirley on a leisurely afternoon stroll: Lord, lo and behold, what does the trio stumble onto but a real, live, downhome style colored revival meeting! What this sequence is doing in this movie is anybody's guess, but like the quasi-revival session in Mae West's *Belle of the Nineties*, it commands the viewer's attention.

The Littlest Rebel (1935)

D. David Butler. S. Edwin Burke, based on a play by Edward Peple. P. B. G. DeSylva. R. 20th Century-Fox. Cast includes: Bessie Lyle (as Mammy); Hannah Washington (as Sally Ann); John Boles; Jack Holt; and Karen Morley.

Sheer, dopey entertainment for those who can enjoy a film while refusing to seriously think about it.

This is a Shirley Temple vehicle, the story of a pint-sized Southern belle during the days of the Civil War. When Shirley's father (a Confed-erate officer) is captured and taken to a Yankee prison camp and her mother dies, little Miss MopTop finds herself adrift on the family's big plantation. Of course, who comes to her rescue but the faithful servant, Uncle Bill, played by Bill "Bojangles" Robinson. He's around to comfort little Shirley, to play and dance with her. And during one sequence when Yankees show up at the Temple mansion, Uncle Bill and the corps of slaves help hide the girl, who goes in blackface, hoping to pass for one of the darkies. The scene has to be seen to believed. The film reaches a heady climax when Robinson and Temple work their way up North where Shirley eventually meets President Lincoln. He's so charmed by the girl that he pardons her father—and the audience can breathe a sigh of relief, knowing little Shirley and Uncle Billy are now free to go off into the sunset together.

This is ersatz Americana steeped in the romantic mythology of the Old South then (and perhaps even now) so popular with audiences. You never know there is really a Civil War going on. And as the critic for *Variety* wrote:

> All bitterness and cruelty has been righteously cut out and the Civil War emerges as a misunderstanding among kindly gentlemen with eminently happy slaves and a cute little girl who sings and dances through the story.

Strangely enough, Temple and Robinson *are* an ideal couple: her grit and spunk are well matched by his high spirits, his calm, and common sense. One knows, however, that no matter how convincingly Robinson plays his role, his character couldn't possibly have but so much common sense because, after all, he remains on the plantation once the Yankees have come presumably to free him. When the two dance together, they are a (psychologically dislocating) marvel: it's all still corny but retains a zip and an effervescent breeziness. In *The New York Herald Tribune*, Richard Watts, Jr., wrote: "The child star is as good a partner for the great Bill Robinson as Miss Rogers is for Mr. Astaire."

Also appearing in the cast is Willie Best as a lazy, dim-witted coon servant, who oddly enough, to contemporary audiences, is a welcome contrast to Robinson's perpetual sobriety.

Lost Boundaries (1949)

D. Alfred L. Werker. S. Virginia Shaler, Eugene Ling; adaptation by Charles A. Palmer; additional dialogue by Furland de Kay; based on W.L. White's story for *The Reader's Digest*. P. Louis de Rochemont. R. Film Classics. Cast includes: Canada Lee; Leigh Whipper; also Susan Douglas and Robert Hylton (as the children whose lives are thrown out of kilter when they discover their "true racial heritage"); and in a bit role, the young black filmmaker William Greaves, who handles himself quite well, giving a characterization that's a total departure—he's bright, charming, articulate, sure of himself—from the type of black male figures audiences had come to expect in American films.

A young light-skinned Negro doctor (Mel Ferrer) and his pretty Negro bride (Beatrice Pearson) plan to live in the South where he will work at a local Negro hospital. But their plans go astray because the Negroes in the area cannot "relate" to so high-yaller a pair. Eventually, the couple moves to a bright, cheery white New England town. There they live and *pass* as whites for some twenty years. He sets up a successful medical practice, tending to white patients. They rear a son and a daughter as whites. They become upstanding integral parts of their

Lost Boundaries featured white actors in the black roles: Susan Douglas, Mel Ferrer, Robert Hylton, and Beatrice Pearson.

white community. And at heart, the two are having a very good *white* life of it—until, naturally, one day their *deep dark* secret is revealed. Why they are Negras! In no time, their world falls apart, as they are shunned by their white neighbors. The film, however, ends on a note of fake racial reconciliation when the town's white minister preaches a sermon to his white townspeople. Afterwards the guilt-ridden townies gingerly approach their former friends, extending their hands, and leading us cynics to believe they've decided to *forgive* these good people for having those nasty teensy-weensy drops of Negra blood.

One can easily make light of *Lost Boundaries* today. Despite the fact that it was based on a true story, much about the film is dated and hokey. It actually insists that we believe the unacceptable: the two are rejected by their black community because they look too white. This, of course, is absurd. In the late 1940s and 1950s, light skin, straight hair, and keen features were valued in the black community, and these people would have had no real problems. But it is intended that we believe the couple has been driven away from the Negro South. There is also a Harlem sequence (the son of the couple, upon learning he is Negro, goes in search of his people)—quite striking in its day—that now may be of dubious value.

Most unacceptable is the casting of white performers in the black roles for purposes of audience identification. In such films as *Pinky*, *Lost Boundaries*, and the various versions of *Show Boat*, all made to please large white audiences, not black ones, whites could better identify and sympathize with the struggles and torments of *real* whites on screen, who were being treated as if they were *colored*.

With the various compromises and cop-outs aside, *Lost Boundaries*, however, is still affecting. And it was well received upon its initial release. In *The New York Times*, Bosley Crowther said it was done with "extraordinary courage, understanding, and dramatic power . . . its statement of the anguish and the ironies of racial taboo is clear, eloquent, and moving." *Time* hailed it as "not only a first-class social document but also a profoundly moving film." And *Variety* wrote:

The Johnston family, whose experiences were dramatized in the film Lost Boundaries: *Anne Johnston, Dr. and Mrs. Albert Johnston, Paul Johnston, Albert Johnston, Jr., and Donald Johnston at a reception in their honor at Harlem's Theresa Hotel in 1949.*

This is a document lit up by an urgent message and expressed in eloquently simple cinematic phrases . . . a personal tragedy that will impinge on all filmgoers irrespective of color. The emotion of this story is so irresistable that it continually breaks through the restraint of the film's subdued and even flat documentary tone. . . . It also shows that the U.S. film industry, having once decided to tackle the most explosive issue in the U.S., is capable of extraordinary courage, intelligence, and human sympathy.

Today *Lost Boundaries*'s semi-documentary style (it was shot in New England on a budget under $600,000 and, as was the case with *Intruder in the Dust*, real townspeople of the area appear in bit roles) and the low-key, often naturalistic performances give it a weight, a poignancy, and a *new* feel not present in Hollywood's studio products of the time. And also as was true of the other problem pictures of 1949, its basic determination to confront the racial question in America puts it in a special class and category all its own. The earnestness of the movie endures.

An important film in the history of black cinema in America.

The Lost Man (1969)

D. Robert Alan Aurthur. S. Robert Alan Aurthur (who previously had written the screenplays for two other Poitier films: *Edge of the City* and *For Love of Ivy*). P. Edward Muhl and Melville Tucker. R. Universal. Cast includes: Beverly Todd; Paul Winfield; Vonetta McGee; Leon Bibb; Virginia Capers; Bernie Hamilton; Richard Anthony Williams; and Lincoln Kilpatrick.

A remake of Carol Reed's classic film about Irish revolutionaries *Odd Man Out* (based on Graham Greene's novel), *The Lost Man* transplants the action to Philadelphia. A group of black militants, led by Sidney Poitier (valiantly seeking to look menacing and hostile what with his dark glasses and mean scowl), out to commit a big payroll heist in order to get money for the family of a group of imprisoned "brothers."

Unfortunately, except for the convincing performance of Al Freeman, Jr., and a few well-staged protest scenes, this movie is without any real tension. And certainly as a political drama it falls flat.

No doubt the film's artistic and commercial failure was a disappointment for Poitier, who, after the criticism of his bourgeois heroes in *To Sir with Love* and *Guess Who's Coming to Dinner?*, had attempted an image change, one more in keeping with the social temper of the time. But he's hard to accept as the lead and is fundamentally miscast. Poitier has always been best at depicting men in complete control of themselves, despite the situation or their own emotional intensity. This part, however, screams out for an actor ready to drop all controls, to do away with any notion of restraint.

Yet aside from the miscasting and the laboriously slack direction of Aurthur, what really wrecks the film (and was considered politically reprehensible by many real activists of the day) is the interracial love affair between Poitier's committed hero and a young white social worker (played by Joanna Shimkus, whom Poitier later married in 1976). For years, black audiences had yearned to see Poitier cast as a healthy, sexual man. Here he has steamy scenes but with a white woman—in a movie supposedly spotlighting black pride, unity, and political conviction—and a movie also pitched at the black audience. Did anybody think this project through?

The music is by Quincy Jones.

Lydia Bailey (1952)

D. Jean Negulesco. *S.* Michael Blankfort and Philip Dunne. *P.* Jules Schermer. *R.* 20th Century-Fox. Cast includes: Juanita Moore (as the slave girl Marie; later Moore appeared as the submissive mother in the 1959 remake of *Imitation of Life*); Charles Korvin; Carmen de Lavallade (as the specialty dancer); William Walker (as the turncoat black General LaPlume); and Ken Renard (giving a *very* tame, rather passive and unimaginative performance as Toussaint L'Ouverture).

The setting is Haiti. The year, 1802. Haitian revolutionary Toussaint L'Ouverture has already led his revolt, abolished slavery, and named himself governor of his island. But Napoleon sends his brother-in-law, General Charles LeClerc, to reclaim this French colonial mainstay. The island itself—with its sudden unexpected killings and attacks, its raging fires, and its hostile jungle (one that no white dare enter alone, unless he's darkened his skin)—is something of an armed camp.

Into this arena comes a white lawyer from Baltimore (Dale Robertson), who searches for a white woman named Lydia Bailey (Anne Francis), hoping simply to get her signature on some papers so he can settle her father's estate. But immediately he's embroiled in the island's warring factions and its steamy political intrigues. He is befriended—and taught some lessons about Haiti's political dynamics—by the towering, deep-voiced leader of the Negro Republicans, a Haitian called King Dick, played splendidly by William Marshall. On one level, King Dick is the 1950s notion of a black buck. As we see him joyously showing off his lineup of eight wives, all of whom he keeps *quite* satisfied, the moviemakers want us to know precisely how this robust man got his name. Not much subtlety here.

Although *Lydia Bailey* focuses on its white hero and heroine, Marshall's King Dick is such a strong, charismatic, and daring character that he completely steals the picture. The movie even ends with a shot of him standing triumphantly at the harbor. We are impressed by his strength and cultivated air and manner. He dresses impeccably in white suits and not only understands the law of the "jungle" but also quotes Plato. He has a perfect command of the English language as well. Partly because of Marshall's bearing and his shrewd colorful performance and partly because of the film's relatively forthright screenplay, this movie is more than simply a rousing adventure tale: it really touches on, albeit in a simplified, movie-like fashion, the Haitian revolution. With the exception of the white-hating black General Mirabeau (overdone by actor Roy Glenn), the black islanders—odd for an American film—are treated with some dignity and sympathy. The general mass audience is led to root for the blacks' victory, and the French are depicted as greedy, materialistic dilettantes. Of course, Hollywood felt relaxed about this black revolution, no doubt because it's in another country and the villains are European, not white American slaveholders.

Still, as with Pontecorvo's *Burn* (1970), island politics creep up amid the action and the fast-moving adventure.

The Mack (1973)

D. Michael Campus. *S.* Robert J. Poole. *P.* Harvey Bernhard. *R.* Cinerama. Cast includes: Carol Speed; Roger E. Mosley; Dick Williams; William C. Watson; Juanita Moore; and Don Gordon.

Of interest mainly because of its surprising popularity in the 1970s. Perhaps its subject matter accounts for its success: a porny pop study of a California pimp.

In the black community of past decades, the old-style pimp had sometimes been viewed as a folk hero of sorts: a smooth-talking, sexy, hip, moneyed man in control of his destiny. At a time when most black men realized a fundamental freedom and power over their lives was denied them at every turn, the pimp, for better or worse, was equated with self-assertion. He also was the embodiment of a capitalistic success story, Horatio Alger running a bordello.

By the 1970s, one might have assumed the pimp would be seen for other things he represented, primarily as an exploiter of women. Instead, young black moviegoers seemed to delight in hero Max Julien's pretty looks, his firm control over his women, his striking array of material comforts (fabulous clothes, cars, and a knockout pad), and his tenacious grip on survival.

Technically a mess without much of a script, the movie's visually unattractive, its gaudy, cheap look and hero going almost hand in hand.

The film was re-released in the 1980s, mainly because by then one of its supporting players had become a genuine box-office star: Richard Pryor, who is resolutely funny and clever.

Mahogany (1975)

D. Berry Gordy. *S.* John Byrum. Diana Ross' costumes by (unfortunately) Diana Ross. *P.* Rob Cohen. *R.* Paramount. Cast includes: Beah Richards; Nina Foch; and Jean-Pierre Aumont.

Mahogany traces the rise of Tracy (Diana Ross), a poor southside Chicago ghetto girl, who hankers to design clothes and be a success. One evening, she not only skips her politico boyfriend's (Billy Dee Williams)

Diana Ross as the ghetto-girl-turned-international-fashion-star in a quintessential black film of the 1970s, Mahogany.

social function but skips town, too. Off she flies to Rome where, under the guidance of a possessive photographer (Tony Perkins), she becomes, almost overnight, an international sensation as a model rechristened Mahogany!

Soon Tracy/Mahogany has everything America has told us to value: fame, money, beauty, success. But much like Priest in *Super Fly T.N.T.*, the poor thing is unhappy. Even her fling at some heated European decadence doesn't look like much fun. The most wickedly adventurous thing she can bring herself to do is to drop some hot candle wax onto herself. If this is all Miss Ross and her director, Motown's chief Berry Gordy, know about decadence, then our hearts go out to them. By the time the picture ends, Tracy has forsaken everything to return to the ghetto (dressed to the nines no less!) and her man Williams (who's looking pretty clean himself). The two are going to live happily ever after.

Badly written and dramatically botched, *Mahogany*'s often disreputable and dishonest, seemingly little more than an old-style rags-to-riches story done in tan. Yet the film still exerts a certain fascination on viewers, and it was a huge commercial success when first released. One reason for its appeal (then and now) may be that, surprisingly enough, along with such films as *Lady Sings the Blues, Claudine, Georgia, Georgia, The Landlord,* and *Sparkle,* it remains one of the few American features that has ever attempted telling a story about a black woman, her dreams, her hopes, her fears. In essence, though, as in *Lady Sings the Blues,* it looks at the successful black woman as little more than woebegone-doomed-glamour-girl.

Here again Diana Ross gives a "terrific" performance as, basically, Diana Ross. Here again, too, as in *Lady Sings the Blues,* Ross is teamed with black matinee idol, Billy Dee Williams, a casting tactic that not only accounted for the smashing success of *Mahogany* but also indicated a shift in the taste and expectations of the mass black film audience. It should be noted that the picture was successful with white audiences as well.

Indeed in some respects, *Mahogany* is a homage of sorts both to the American notion of success and the star magnetism of Ross and Williams. In a past movie like *Carmen Jones,* audiences had gravitated to a striking pair like Dorothy Dandridge and Harry Belafonte. But an actor like Belafonte sometimes seemed too embarrassed by his looks and good fortune to ever fully capitalize on his assets. With Ross and Williams, though, both of whom were born to be black movie stars, high-powered gloss and glow are on proud display. Because the script, lacking the wit and cohesiveness of *Lady Sings the Blues,* failed to provide them with characters to play, the two rely on their images instead—as the archetypal narcissistic dream queen and king from whom nothing is demanded except their extraordinary presence. To their credit, they are charming enough to pull the picture off. But more importantly, in its celebration of stardom, *Mahogany* clearly touched on the mood of the period and now stands as a quintessential film of the mid-1970s.

By this point in American social/entertainment history, no longer did audiences have a great interest in the political celebrity, the Eldridge Cleavers, the Angela Davises, the Mark Rudds, or Abby Hoffmans of a few years earlier. Now, too, no longer was the system, the establishment, viewed as suspiciously as it had been in the restless late 1960s and early 1970s. Thus, at the movie house, gone were the rebellious, defiant buck heroes of such films as *Shaft* and *Slaughter*. Instead movie-goers, in a more relaxed frame of mind, searched for pure escapism and some oldstyle glamour. Once again the movie star (or rock or sports star) who had dramatically made it, on screen and off, into the main-stream of American society was regarded as a hero or heroine. In the case of *Mahogany*, the star who's *made it* is Diana Ross. Yet, interestingly enough, no doubt because Americans have always felt uneasy about their own materialism and thirst for success, movie characters are often ritualistically punished for self-assertion and ambition. Conse-quently, while the audience enjoys watching Diana Ross savor the naughty good life, that same audience feels relieved of guilt feelings (about its own enjoyment of the action) when, after Diana's cinematic trials and tribulations, she gives it all up to return to what the movie says are her roots. No one leaving the film had to feel badly about being star-struck because the star here has been punished by the scriptwriter for tasting/enjoying the good life. Thus audiences could have their cake and eat it, too.

The critics almost consistently panned *Mahogany*. The *New York Post* critic called it "a joke" while Vincent Canby, in *The New York Times*, labelled it "a silly fiction." And Jay Cocks in *Time* added: "Movies as frantically bad as *Mahogany* can be enjoyed on at least one level: the spectacle of a lot of people making fools of themselves." Yet while criticizing the film, many critics, such as the *Village Voice*'s Molly Has-kell, noted the trend it marked in black movie history. Haskell wrote: "*Mahogany* . . . confirms a notion I have expressed before: that the black cinema is taking up where the white cinema left off, and that black movies, drawing on a new black middle class with its attendant values, can render with conviction those boy-girl stories that have been re-placed, in our supposedly adult white movies, with buddy-buddy ro-mances and sex-sated couples. . . . What *Mahogany* does so fascinatingly and sometimes hilariously is to pilfer certain stock cliches of '50s Holly-wood and adapt them to a black milieu. . . . And if you think Ross and Williams don't have audiences eating out of their hands, then you saw the movie with the wrong audience."

Mahogany continues to turn up on television, and even while audi-ences may laugh at it or hate it, they keep watching nonetheless.

Malaga (1960)

D. Laslo Benedek. *S.* David Osborn and Donald Ogden Stewart; from a novel by Donald MacKenzie. *P.* Cavalcade Films. *R.* Warner-Pathe.

Part crime story/part character study, this movie starred Dorothy Dan-dridge as Gianna, a woman living in Europe with a handsome young jewel thief (Edmund Purdom). When he drops her and also double-crosses his partner (Trevor Howard) to flee with stolen gems, both Dandridge and Howard set out to catch up with him. As the two travel through Spain, they find themselves falling in love, although the film does not have the courage to fully examine their relationship. Dorothy Dandridge's manager Earl Mills once said that the making of this movie was one of the actress's most distressing experiences. As had happened with *Island in the Sun*, the producers, fearful of controversy over the interracial love match, were not sure how to handle Dandridge's char-acter. Should Dandridge play an American woman? Should she be cast as some type of "foreigner"? The idea that a white man could fall in love with a black American woman apparently seemed too "daring" for them. So compromises were made with the end result that the entire production sank. Dandridge's race is denied by the scriptwriter throughout.

"Film falls down," wrote *Variety*'s reviewer, "mainly because it cannot make up its mind whether it's a study of the relationship between two interesting people or a straightforward crime chase yarn." Throughout Dandridge is lovely but looks lost, at times strained and disoriented, and unfocused. Strangely enough, this may well be her most vulnerable performance. As with some other films featuring black actresses such as *Mahogany* with Diana Ross, *Porgy and Bess* with Dandridge again, even parts of *Gone with the Wind* with Hattie McDaniel, there is an unconscious documentary taking place within the movie: we become caught up in the personal tensions or drives of the actress herself rather than those of the character she is playing. Thus we discover something apart from what the film originally intended. Here as she drifts about in Europe, almost as alienated as an Antonioni heroine, there is something haunting about Dandridge. Consequently, *Malaga* remains an interesting feature in the study of black women in motion pictures.

The film's original title was *Moment of Danger*.

The Man (1972)

D. Joseph Sargent. S. Rod Serling; based on the novel by Irving Wallace. P. Lee Rich. R. Paramount. Cast includes: Janet MacLachlan; Barbara Bush; Burgess Meredith; Lew Ayres; and William Windom.

When the vice-president of the United States suffers a stroke, a black senator (James Earl Jones) becomes president pro tem of the Senate. Later after the president and the speaker of the House are accidentally killed while attending a summit conference in Germany, the black senator naturally becomes the first black president of the United States.

One only wishes it could be said that *then* the fun really begins. This might have been a slyly clever and satirically nasty political drama. But the picture strives too hard for seriousness without realizing that the first step towards making a serious statement is to do away with the clichés. Moreover it's all weighed down by the ponderous performance of James Earl Jones. Added to all this is a subplot: an attempted assassination of the president of South Africa by a black American student (Georg Stanford Brown).

On the one hand, the movie is determined to confront then-contemporary racial dilemmas and issues. On the other hand, it steadily backs off from them.

Man About Town (1939)

D. Mark Sandrich. S. Morris Ryskind; based on a story by Morris Ryskind, Allan Scott, and Z. Myers. P. Arthur Hornblow, Jr. R. Paramount. Cast includes: Dorothy Lamour; Edward Arnold; Binnie Barnes; and Betty Grable.

A deft and deliriously clever performance by Eddie "Rochester" Anderson sets this Jack Benny movie in motion. Prior to this film, Anderson had already turned up on Benny's radio program. As the wittiest of

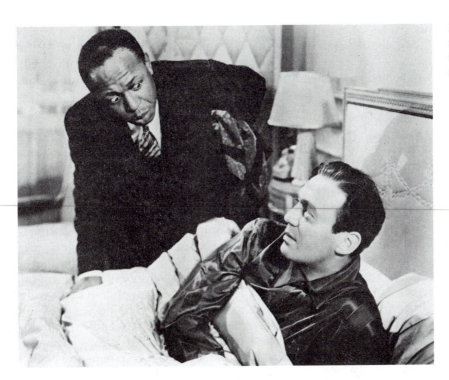

gentlemen's gentlemen, he was a master of timing and always knew how to turn dialogue to his advantage. *Man About Town*, however, was the first film in which Benny and Rochester appeared, and now Rochester proved he was even better on film than radio.

He has a terrific physical presence: round open face, intelligent eyes, a short but beefy body (he looks solid and partly because of his height and mainly because of his demeanor, he has a Chaplinesque universal Little Man quality), and a smile that lets you know he knows more than he's telling you. He's ten steps ahead of everybody else. Like the other great black actors of the 1930s who played servant roles, he seems to operate in a world of his own. Consequently, one feels Rochester never serves anybody other than himself. He and Benny also have an extraordinary rapport. These men talk to one another like friends rather than master and servant.

The story line here is negligible. Benny woos two wealthy socialites and gets himself into various scrapes, the climactic one being disentangled through the bright machinations of Rochester.

When Rochester first appears, he sleeps comfortably in the boss's chair, unaware that Benny has entered the apartment. Once on his feet, he's the clever, manipulative servant always outfoxing the boss. Later when we see him with his feet propped casually on top of the table as he uses Benny's telephone, smokes Benny's cigars, and takes over Benny's apartment, there is no doubt that here is a servant who considers himself more a weekend guest than a subservient domestic.

Throughout the film, Rochester breezes in and out of the action with confidence, savoir faire, and a highly distinctive comic spark. He also shows himself to be just as skillful with his feet as with his dialogue: in short, Rochester can dance! In fact, his dance numbers here steal the show and are enough to make an audience want to rise to its feet and applaud.

"If Hollywood's other comedians are on their toes," wrote *The New York Times*, "the West Coast's domestic employment agencies may expect to be swamped any day now with requests for valets, preferably saddle-colored and answering to the name Rochester. For in Paramount's *Man About Town*, a sly little gentleman's gentleman—or comedian's comedian—called Rochester has restored Jack Benny to the comic map and cleared a sizeable place there for himself."

Man and Boy (1972)

D. E.W. Swackhamer. S. Harry Essex and Oscar Saul. Music supervision by Quincy Jones. P. Marvin Miller; Executive Producer, Bill Cosby. R. Levitt-Pickman release. Cast includes: Henry Silva; John Anderson; and Leif Erickson.

A formula western turned contemporary for its 1970s audience simply by the fact that its protagonists are black. Bill Cosby plays the quiet man of integrity (he's a Civil War veteran), off on an odyssey with his son (George Spell) to recover a stolen horse. But before father and son can return home, they must fight the requisite baddies and, of course, the father must often prove his manhood through physical might and power.

One supposes black westerns have a certain social role, providing young black children with the same sort of mythic structure and heroic struggles that white children have found in movies starring the likes of a John Wayne, Gene Autry, or Randolph Scott. (Black westerns also help set the historical record straight: there really were black cowboys of the Old West.) But in the 1970s and afterwards if a black western couldn't go beyond the dynamics (and the built-in failures) of the familiar formula white western of past film history, then there doesn't seem to be much point in making one. Who wants a black child to grow up with the same distorted macho and territorial values many white children have had foisted on them (values that contributed to bigotry and racism).

Man and Boy sometimes succumbs to the old, outdated values. But it offers something fresh: a black father/son relationship that is intelligent and warm. One might want to compare it to the father/son relationship between Sidney Poitier and George Spell in *They Call Me MISTER Tibbs*. But here the relationship is looser and more mature. Spell is a very skilled young performer. As the mother, Gloria Foster doesn't have much to do, but she provides the third side of the type of black family unit American films have seldom explored.

Thus in a sense *Man and Boy*, although often slow, has a warmly decent feel to it, and the movie's also blessed with the hammily enjoyable performance of Douglas Turner Ward and the very solid one of Yaphet Kotto.

A Man Called Adam (1966)

D. Leo Penn. P. Ike Jones and Jim Waters. S. Les Pine and Tina Rome. R. Embassy. Cast includes: Louis Armstrong; Ossie Davis; Peter Lawford; Lola Falana; Jeanette Du Bois; George Rhodes; Mel Torme; and comedian Johnny Brown.

A humdrum melodrama about a troubled and disaffected jazz musician (Sammy Davis, Jr).

Sometimes moody, the film has a certain effective, albeit unintentional, oppressive quality. This may be because it was so inexpensively produced; it looks as if shot in real darkly-lit bars and clubs.

Sometimes interesting, it has glimmers of funk and fiber, capturing the seediness and sleaze of a life of too many one-night stands. Sometimes the film is lighted with a special glow: that's whenever Cicely Tyson (as the hero's girlfriend) shows up. But it's far too often banal and poorly conceived. It entirely wastes a subject in need of examination: the jazz hero caught up in an exploitative system that yearly drains him of his emotional resources, his talent, and his thirst for living. Years later the French film *Round Midnight* would touch on some of the themes *A Man Called Adam* misses out on. Davis is unfortunately miscast in the lead role.

Mandingo (1975)

D. Richard Fleischer. S. Norman Wexler; based on the bestselling novel by Kyle Onstott and the play by Jack Kirkland. P. Dino De Laurentiis. R. Paramount Pictures. Cast includes: Richard Ward; Ben Masters; Ji-Tu Cumbuka; and Lillian Hayman.

A pulpy, lurid antebellum potboiler that turns the fantasy world of a romanticized film like *Gone with the Wind* inside out. No longer presented as an Eden before the fall, the Old South here is a nightmarish s-and-m turn-on, in which everybody seems sex-starved, slightly mad or depraved, or sometimes just knuckleheaded. James Mason is the campily eccentric white massa, a slave breeder determined that his handsome randy young son (Perry King) settle down and provide the family with a new heir. King's got other things on his mind though, mainly a pretty slave wench (Brenda Sykes), his one true love. But he must contend with his daddy's wishes and soon courts and weds southern belle Susan George, who is not all she seems, having very early on been deflowered by, of all people, her brother. When King turns a cold eye to his new bride, the lady seeks vengeance (and another kind of satisfaction) by leading to her bed a good, faithful Mandingo slave (Ken Norton), who in fact has been so good and so faithful that he is now rewarded with the Old South's most prized possession: this blonde, light-eyed white woman! During the seduction scene, director Fleischer works hard at heating up the audience, which, frankly, often seems to enjoy the encounter more than Norton, who looks as if he can't make heads or tails of what's going on. Later the bride bears Norton's child, who is promptly done away with. Then Norton, young master King's favorite (on the plantation, Norton's a fighter of uncommon strength, a winner of all the matches the master sets up), receives yet another reward for his handiwork once his paternity is revealed: he's thrown into a huge cauldron of boiling water, then has a pitchfork shoved into him! These are but a few of the horrors in this gaudy terror of a film.

"*Mandingo*," wrote Vincent Canby in *The New York Times*, "purports to tell what life on the old plantation was really like, though its serious intentions are constantly denied by the camera's erotic interest in the technique of humiliation, mostly with sex and violence."

The Village Voice added: "Overly fastidious critics have thrown around the word 'trash' so carelessly over the years that the word is no longer credible when real low-down trash like *Mandingo* comes along. This monstrous cross-breeding of *Uncle Tom's Cabin* and *Mondo Cane* in a 50s best-seller style is utterly beyond any redeeming value . . . just schlock to a disgusting degree."

Mandingo with Ken Norton and Susan George: an Old South potboiler, a sexy sado-masochistic turn-on.

And in *New York*, Judith Crist wrote: "An actor like James Mason, a director like Richard Fleischer, and a screenwriter like Norman Wexler may find working [in *Mandingo*] . . . preferable to cleaning latrines; one cannot imagine anyone faced with other alternatives making the choice."

Although roundly dismissed critically, *Mandingo* was a box-office champion, luring in a certain segment of the black audience in large numbers and eventually spawning a sequel, *Drum*, also an Old South drama starring Ken Norton. Wretched as the movie is, strangely enough it also has a sleazy push and pull and a pornographic thrust that keep the action flying—and unfortunately keeps many a viewer glued to the screen. Dare it be said that this atrocity is sometimes rather hard to resist?

Only for the strong of stomach or those fascinated by just how far and engrossingly excessive highflung cheap trash can go.

Maurie (1973)

D. Daniel Mann. S. Douglas Morrow. P. Frank Ross and Douglas Morrow. R. National General Pictures. Cast includes: Stephanie Edwards; Maidie Norman; William Walker; Pauline Myers; and Jitu Cumbuka.

A lukewarm retread of the popular TV movie "Brian's Song." Here again is a tale of the interracial friendship of two athletes. There is again the trauma of a terminal illness. And still again is a drama based on a true story: the case of Cincinnati basketball player Maurice Stokes, mysteriously stricken by a paralyzing illness. For some ten years his teammate, Jack Twyman, fought to raise funds to help his friend's rehabilitation.

Bernie Casey plays the low-key Stokes and Janet MacLachlan is the loyal wife. Bo Svenson is the stalwart teammate. Hard as everyone works to keep this from being just a weepy soap opera, it's no more than that; in fact, it lacks the grip even of daytime TV serials. Everything about this is weak and too good-intentioned.

Although he looks mighty healthy, Bernie Casey (with Janet MacLachlan) plays a doomed, dying athlete in Maurie.

Melinda (1972)

D. Hugh Robertson. *S.* Lonne Elder III, the author of the play *Ceremonies in Dark Old Men* and later the screenplay for *Sounder*. *P.* Purvis Atkins. *R.* MGM. Cast includes: writer Lonne Elder III (as Lt. Daniels); Judyann Elder; and Jim Kelly.

An offbeat murder mystery, often violent and bloody, that nonetheless could have been worse and certainly could have been better had its director Robertson not been so quick to go for the jugular. What happens is simply this: a gilded, conceited pretty boy disc jockey (Calvin Lockhart) meets up with a mysterious, beautiful young woman named Melinda (Vonetta McGee). The two are soon lovers. Then she is murdered. He sets out to find the killer and along the way is aided by an old girlfriend (Rosalind Cash), who still loves him even though he's mistreated her. She also knows he's still obsessed with her rival Melinda. It's a triangle movie with a dead woman as the third party.

The three central performers—Lockhart, McGee, and notably Rosalind Cash—actually make *Melinda* work. Lockhart's shameless narcissism (his character was said to be based on New York's popular black dj Frankie Crocker) verges on self-parody, yet because we think he just might be playing the part cold straight after all, his performance is all the more enjoyable and intriguing. McGee, proclaimed by the *Village Voice* as the most beautiful woman then on the screen, is indeed lovely.

But it is Cash's defiantly intense heroine who endows the movie with its subtext. At the time of *Melinda*'s release, black coeds identified strongly with the Cash character: she represented the modern young black woman misunderstood by her black man because she is, in the long run, too serious. Consequently, he ignores her, gravitating to the more glamorous, more manageable, less demanding Melinda. What with her shaggy Afro and her refusal to play her part in a pretty fashion (indeed she risks looking unattractive to get at the roots of her character's discontent), Cash displays a distinctly politicized early 1970s persona. Hers is a battle of *true* sexual politics, and she's not certain she'll ever win. Nor are we.

Cash has one *tour de force* sequence: in a bank where a persnickety white female clerk and a stodgy white bank officer question her identity, about to refuse her withdrawal of money from an account, she finally unleashes her anger and rage. "Now look I'm getting sick and tired of this," she says. "Now I walk in here and you treat me like I'm some damn crook." "Miss Miller, what's wrong?" the officer asks her, to which Cash replies, "What's wrong! What's wrong, my ass. You know what's wrong. If I were a white woman and walked in here and wanted to get into my bank deposit box, I wouldn't have to go through half this shit." At this point, the clerk tells Cash to *shush*, whereupon Cash announces, "Shush, my ass, bitch! Now look, I want my fucking property or I'm going to burn this bank down!" The language here and the rhythmic thrust in which Cash delivers her lines have an urgent authenticity. This woman sounds like countless enraged city people we've all heard on subways or in the streets. The sequence is both funny and dramatically powerful.

Rosalind Cash herself was such a new presence that one longed to see more of her—in this film and others. Although she worked steadily from the 1970s into the 1980s, she often was forced to grapple with material that went nowhere. Yet she earned a special reputation for herself: audiences knew whenever they saw her that an unusual interpretation of character and dialogue was about to take place.

The Member of the Wedding (1952)

D. Fred Zinneman. *S.* Edna and Edward Anhalt; based on the novel and play by Carson McCullers. *P.* Stanley Kramer. *R.* Columbia Pictures. Cast includes: Arthur Franz and Nancy Gates.

Southern writers like Lillian Hellman and Carson McCullers have sometimes focused on the complex relationship between southern white women and the black women around them. At times while reading such writers, we sometimes feel almost as if we've caught sight of protected white women just as the precise moment when they've suddenly stopped dead cold in their tracks and taken notice of the world around them: near the center of this world is a strong black woman who has cooked or cleaned, nurtured or reprimanded, soothed or berated the white females she has had to work for. Such is the case in this screen adaptation of McCullers's famous novel and play in which the great Ethel Waters had her finest screen role, repeating the part she had originated on Broadway as the one-eyed cook Berenice.

Her hair white, her weight well over 200 pounds, and with a black eye patch in some scenes, Waters looks like a magnificent monument that moves us, whether we like it or not, simply because of its durability and its presence. Today some viewers may be put off by the fact that her character Berenice expends most of her energies and wisdom on two white children—the teenage girl Frankie (Julie Harris) and her little cousin John Henry (Brandon de Wilde)—stoically helping the girl on the rough road to maturity. At one point, she tells Frankie, "Child. Child. Berenice knows. Berenice understands. And now Berenice wants you to sit on her lap so she can quiet you down." No matter how much it might grate us that Waters is not permitted to deliver lines to a troubled black child, the actress herself speaks with a conviction that we know is genuine.

But the Waters characterization—and McCullers's script—go farther. For here is a rare attempt to provide some glimpse of a black woman's life independent of the white world for which she works. In what is very nearly a soliloquy, Waters' Berenice speaks of her experiences and the man she loved more than any other, Ludi, who has died. In closeup, the camera stays on her lustrous face as she gives a perfect reading. It is moving and effective, a great performance by a great actress in one of cinema's true mythic moments. Yet it's a sequence that acting teachers and film historians seem to have forgotten altogether. In another scene when Berenice tells the young Frankie, "We go around trying first one thing, then another. Yet we're still caught. Just the same," she brings in something outside the script, no doubt her own troubled personal experiences, deepening the lines with her knowing stoic readings. She gets far closer to the truth of her black character's experiences than do all the actresses in *The Color Purple*, save perhaps young Desreta Jackson.

Then, too, there are Waters's brief scenes with the young actor James Edwards, as her foster brother, Honey, a troubled young man happiest when away from the white world's dictates and simply playing his horn. Edwards understands jazz musicians and how their art saved their lives. He understands restraints and repressions. "Times like this," he says in a moment of torment, "I feel I gotta bust loose or die." Sometimes stern or impatient with Edwards, Waters turns and faces him at crucial peak moments, and the screen lights up with two splendid black performers, the old guard one-time vaudevillian with the new guard intense method-style actor, each bringing the best out of one another and distinguishing dialogue that in other hands might seem rigged. Of course, one wishes that the movie had been more about these two. Because it isn't is a reason why some black audiences might reject this picture altogether. But there is more here of black lives in disarray and in control than in most other films of the period: it's hard to think of any other movie of that time in which black actors had a chance to relate so tenderly and sensitively with one another. Clearly worth seeing for Waters's big performance and Edwards's brief one as well as those of Harris and de Wilde. Well worth seeing also for what it suggests rather than flat out states.

Later versions of McCullers's play were done for television, with Claudia McNeil playing Berenice in 1958, then Pearl Bailey performing the part in 1982.

Miracle in Harlem (1948)

D. Jack Kemp. *S.* Vincent Valentini; story by Vincent Valentini. *P.* Jack Goldberg. *R.* Herald Pictures Inc. Cast includes: Hilda Offley; Savannah Churchill; Jack Carter; Lawrence Criner; and the Juanita Hall Choir.

Generally considered a technical landmark in the history of race movies, *Miracle in Harlem* appeared towards the end of the early black independent film movement. Ostensibly the movie's a murder mystery centering on a candy-store swindle. But beneath its glossy veneer lies an interesting subtext: it's a look at post-World War II Black America's vision of its new tomorrow of promise and prosperity. Its lead characters—serious, noble, educated, bourgeois, less ethnic—stand as embodiments of the new social/economic philosophy: they are attractive, optimistic, capitalistic go-getters, who believe in the American system of free enterprise and are determined to make the system work for them. These characters are primed for the integrationist movement that will arise in the 1950s. Turning up in *Miracle in Harlem* are some interesting faces: Sheila Guyse (one of the post-War new-style black leading ladies—well-mannered, clean-scrubbed, a bit pampered; she also appeared in *Sepia Cinderella*, 1947, and the underground favorite *Boy! What a Girl*, 1946; William Greaves (a skilled and relaxed young leading man, who later left acting to become the independent producer/director of such documentaries as the 1974 *From These Roots* and also the executive producer of the 1981 Richard Pryor film *Bustin' Loose*); and Stepin Fetchit, clearly a throwback to the past. Yet black audiences did not seem to object to Fetchit's dimwitted character here; he was but one comic figure in a film offering an array of black images.

Aside from the subtext though, *Miracle in Harlem* is a fairly pedestrian movie.

Monkey Hustle (1976)

D. Arthur Marks. *S.* Charles Johnson; story by Odie Hawkins. *P.* Arthur Marks. *R.* AIP. Cast includes: Ruby Ray Moore.

Not even the combined talents of such gifted screen performers as Yaphet Kotto and Rosalind Cash can save this meandering, almost feeble-minded con-game comedy. Released at the time when black-oriented movies were dying out, this now has a historical look to it (that doesn't mean it's a good look; instead students of film simply see what the last sad days of the Hollywood black movies had descended to). Is it no wonder black audiences turned away from such poorly scripted and shoddily thrown-together vehicles?

One bright spot: the engaging work of young Kirk Calloway, who played the mulatto son in *Cinderella Liberty*.

Mother, Jugs, and Speed (1976)

D. Peter Yates. *S.* Tom Mankiewicz, based on a story by Mankiewicz and Stephen Manes. *P.* Mankiewicz and Peter Yates. *R.* 20th Century-Fox. Cast includes: Harvey Kietel; Raquel Welch; Allen Garfield; Bruce Davison; and Larry Hagman.

The adventures of a corps of workers for a private ambulance service in Los Angeles.

Also a joyless attempt at biting satirical comedy in the vein of *M.A.S.H.* but without the latter's bite, satire, and humor.

When Bill Cosby shows up as one of the drivers, one hopes to see a performance that will give the movie some distinction. But that's not the case: Cosby is congenial, familiar, sometimes pleasant, often boring. Occasionally, a certain smugness and self-satisfaction creep into his work, and he's far less appealing and attractive than he thinks. The same could be said of the film.

For what it's worth, it should be stated that this is a film in which a black actor's color is not used as part of the plotline.

Native Son (1951)

D. Pierre Chenal. *S.* Richard Wright and Pierre Chenal. *P.* Jaime Prades. *R.* Argentina Sono Films. Cast includes: Willa Pearl Curtiss (as Hannah Thomas) and Don Dean as Lawyer Max.

For years Richard Wright had hoped to see a screen version of his novel *Native Son*. But the major studios would not touch this tale of a Chicago ghetto youth, Bigger Thomas, who commits two violent crimes. Finally, in 1951, eleven years after the book's publication, a film version was independently produced in Argentina. Wright co-wrote the screenplay with director Pierre Chenal. Released by the small Classic Pictures, the movie was a fiasco, technically ill-conceived and most importantly, lacking the sense of place essential to the story. Footage of Chicago's southside was intercut with sequences shot in Argentina. Audiences felt neither the oppression of the city nor the system. But the movie's greatest liability was its star: 43-year-old Wright played the 20-year-old protagonist Bigger. Then, too, its subject matter was no doubt ahead of its time. Following in the wake of the 1949 problem pictures *Pinky* and *Home of the Brave*, both "gentle" pleas for racial tolerance, here was a story that said America destroyed lives and bred violence. Interestingly, *Native Son* was an attempt to take independent black cinema in a new direction: rather than focusing on an insulated all-black community, it exposed tensions between black and white. But some saw it as an anti-American statement. *Variety*'s reviewer wrote: "With a certain modicum of subtlety, the picture seems to have been made with intent to create an anti-U.S. feeling. It is rather sad that a number of British and U.S.

residents in Argentina should have been enticed into collaborating in this underhand stab at the U.S." The picture failed. A remake (also unsuccessful) appeared in 1986.

New Orleans (1947)

D. Arthur Lubin. S. Elliot Paul and Dick Irving. P. Jules Levey. R. United Artists. Cast includes: "Kid" Ory; Meade Lux Lewis; Zutty Singleton; and Lucky Thompson.

A mediocre 1940s melodrama distinguished only by the presence of Louis Armstrong and Billie Holiday. Armstrong, energetic and assured, seems at ease. (He'd already tommed and cooned his way through several movies, and, sadly, film audiences often thought of him as a ditzy, enjoyable clown rather than as a rare American artist of genius.) *New Orleans*, however, knew no more what to do with Holiday (she's cast as a maid) than *The Blues Brothers*, some 33 years later, knew what to do with the great Aretha Franklin (also cast as a maid of sorts; she's a waitress). Yet Holiday has so much more grace, poise, and style than the white woman for whom she works in the picture that she lays to waste the movie's fundamental tastelessness. Both she and Aretha elevate their movies, conferring on them an artistic stature/dignity otherwise sorely lacking. Performing such numbers as "The Blues Are Brewing," "Goodbye to Storyville," and "Do You Know What It Means To Miss New Orleans," Holiday provides us with a rare opportunity to see her at her radiant, vibrant, creative best.

Suggestion: Watch the musical segments and skip the rest of the movie.

Night of the Living Dead (1969)

D. George Romero. S. John A. Russo. P. Russell Streiner. An Image Ten Production. R. Continental. Cast includes: Judith O'Den and Karl Hurdman.

A low-budget cult horror classic filmed in Pittsburgh with a cast of unknowns. The storyline? Well, the dead arise to attack the living, whose flesh they must eat in order to stay alive themselves. Gory, grisly, graphic, this film sent shivers up the spines of many, injecting a new kind of visceral violent realism into American cinema. For the student population of the period (particularly a bit later in the early 1970s), the film also had political undertones: the zombies were said to represent conformist figures of the 1960s (much as the pod people of *Invasion of the Body Snatchers* had represented conformists of the 1950s), who, having lost all feeling, could do little except feed off others. Most importantly, the hero of *Night of the Living Dead* was a new type for a general interest white film: a tall, upright, intelligent young black man, presented to cool perfection by Duane Jones. He's the voice of reason here, also a man of action, a born survivor, so it seems, until the final moments when he's shot and killed by the police (the fuzz, of course), who mistake him for one of the living dead. Actor Jones has said he doesn't believe the director set out to make any political statement, that the film was intended simply as entertainment. He is probably right.

But it's delirious fun to watch this movie and then to project political theories onto it.

Later there were sequels: *Dawn of the Day* (1979) and *Day of the Dead* (1985).

Night of the Quarter Moon (1959)

D. Hugo Haas. *S.* Frank Davis and Franklin Coen. *P.* Albert Zugsmith Productions. *R.* MGM. Cast includes: Nat "King" Cole, who briefly plays a dramatic role and also sings the picture's theme song; Dean Jones.

A B-movie that hoped to cash in on the racial headlines of its era. A wealthy young Korean War vet (John Drew Barrymore), on vacation in Mexico, meets and falls in love with a pretty "dark" girl (Julie London), whom he marries and carries home to San Francisco. His socialite mother (Agnes Moorehead) couldn't be more pleased until she makes a shocking discovery: the girl's a quarter Negro! "Social Leader's Bride Revealed as a Quadroon" reads the front-page newspaper headline soon afterward. Neighbors throw rocks through the windows of the couple's home. And rarely has an American city been depicted as being in such a tizzy over an interracial couple. When the vet takes ill, his mother virtually imprisons him in her home, then sets out to have his marriage annulled. A courtcase ensues. The picture has something of a happy ending when the couple is reunited, although we in the audience know their real problems may just be beginning.

The whole thing is silly and unreal. Singer Julie London had had a number of black record fans after she had recorded "Cry Me A River." But here in dark pancake makeup, she neither looks nor behaves like a black woman. The movie is filled with howlers. "Where did he propose to you?" the socialite asks her daughter-in-law. "On a beach or a cotton-field?" "Do you have the courage to present them with a bride whose mother was the daughter of a Portuguese Angolan?" London's father (Barry Fitzgerald) asks his prospective son-in-law. Explaining what it means to be black, Anna Kashfi as a light-skinned black nightclub singer proclaims, "We call it the black curtain. There are some people who sneak behind it, some who sneak back away from it, and some others who try to make believe it doesn't exist." And London herself says defensively, "I'm not Negro. I'm white. Mostly white." (Lucky girl!) It's doubtful, too, if anyone's forgotten the courtroom sequence during which London must disrobe. When the mother-in-law fights for an annulment on the grounds that her son had married London unaware of her racial identity, London reveals to the court that at the time of their courtship the young man had seen her nude on the beach. *Therefore* he *had* to know she had no tan and was indeed colored all over. *Therefore* London undresses so everyone can see she's brown all over!

Preposterous, of course. But for black audiences of the period, because the film dealt with the race problem on some level, the movie had a kind of dull-witted, dopey appeal. As much as you might laugh, you keep watching the darn thing.

Also what matters most here is that amid all the fake emotions and the cliched situations, suddenly there appears James Edwards—poised, shrewd, composed—as a lawyer for the bride. During the pointless, inane courtroom scenes, Edwards is so real and astute, his performance so measured and limned, that one takes great pride in seeing what a good black actor can do with junk material even as we feel saddened and disappointed that this was the kind of thing Edwards was often stuck with. Still it's a kind of lopsidedly triumphant appearance for him.

Nighthawks (1981)

D. Bruce Malmuth. S. David Shaber; story by David Shaber and Paul Sylbert. P. Martin Poll. R. Universal. Cast includes: Lindsay Wagner and Persis Khambatta.

After the big black movie boom of the 1970s, a number of stars of that earlier period found themselves playing supporting roles in the 1980s, serving as background for white stars. At times early 1980s movies looked as if they wanted to forget the entire black movie phenomenon of the 1970s. In a manner of speaking, 1980s films seemed anxious to put the black performer back in his place. Sometimes, too, by casting black actors in nondescript roles without mention of race, the films seemed to suppress the race issue altogether. No one is saying here that whenever a black actor appears, there has to be a to-do about race. *But* the fact of a performer's color should not be unrealistically ignored.

One sees some of these new 1980s attitudes in *Nighthawks*, a relatively fast-moving action picture that stars Sylvester Stallone and Billy Dee Williams as two undercover, good-guy New York City cops, out to track down an international terrorist (played marvelously by Dutch actor Rutger Hauer) who shows up in the Big Apple. Stallone is clearly the hero; Williams is reduced to sidekick status without much to do, no more treated like a star here than Paul Winfield was treated as a powerful dramatic actor in the movie *The Terminator* (1986). The moviemakers also make a terrible mistake, in terms of understanding the Williams mystique and star appeal: stranded without a leading lady, he never has a chance to show off his flair for romantic dash. But no one seemed to care about that. The idea is simply that Williams has a marketable name that can now be exploited in a new context. Lifted out of the black movie genre, he's used to make us believe we're seeing a true contemporary drama, one realistic enough to give us an ethnic mix yet at the same time one that does all it can to make us forget that Williams is indeed a black man coming from another culture from that of either the film's hero or villain. (The same is true of Whoopi Goldberg in *Jumpin' Jack Flash*.) He's odd man out, deluxe window dressing yet, distressingly enough, still a pleasure to watch.

No Way Out (1951)

D. Joseph L. Mankiewicz. S. Joseph L. Mankiewicz and Lester Samuels. P. Darryl F. Zanuck. R. 20th Century-Fox. Cast includes: Linda Darnell; Richard Widmark (wonderful as the hood); Ossie Davis; a very young Ruby Dee; Amanda Randolph; Maude Simmons; Dots Johnson; and Stephen McNally.

The movie that launched Sidney Poitier's career in the 1950s.

No Way Out spotlighted the race riots that had broken out after World War II; it also presented a sensitive portrait of the post-War "educated Negro." The plot centers on a young Negro doctor, Luther

Brooks, at a big city hospital. When two white hoodlums are wounded during an attempted robbery, Brooks tends the pair. One of the men dies. The other then accuses Brooks of murder. Thereafter the young doctor fights to prove his innocence. When the remaining white hoodlum organizes a group of racist friends to attack the ghetto area, the city verges on a major race riot. Through an autopsy and a lucky stroke of Hollywood imagination, Brooks proves his innocence and equilibrium returns to the city.

Sophisticated and literate, with crisp and quick-witted dialogue, *No Way Out*, to some degree, touched on some of post-War America's repressed racial hostilities. Likewise its Negro characters were walking exponents of the postwar black doctrines of racial integration and *overprove*. "You got 'em. All A's," the doctor's wife (Mildred Joanne Smith) tells him. "No wonder you're tired. Even I'm a little tired. . . . We've been a long time getting here. We're tired but we're here, honey. We can be happy. We've got a right to be." Negro characters didn't seem entitled to all America had to offer if they were simply ordinary; they always had to be smarter and more ambitious than most mere mortals.

The New York Times called *No Way Out* "a harsh, outspoken picture with implications that will keep you thinking about it long after leaving the theatre." The movie yet retains a certain glossy power although the climax—when Poitier's character dutifully saves the life of the bigot who's previously accused him falsely of murder—is rather hard to take or believe. Sometimes contemporary college audiences shout back to Poitier's character on screen, "Let the creep die, will ya!" Even then, Poitier's noble Negro heroes were a bit hard to believe.

Critic Andrew Sarris has called *No Way Out* "one of the first screen manifestations of Black Power fantasies fabricated by white liberals."

Norman, Is That You? (1976)

D. George Schlatter. S. Ron Clark, Sam Bobrick, and George Schlatter; based on the play by Clark and Bobrick. P. George Schlatter. R. MGM film released by United Artists. Cast includes: Vernee Watson (of "Welcome Back Kotter" on TV) and Jayne Meadows.

Redd Foxx is in a "comic" dilemma. First, his wife (Pearl Bailey) runs off with his brother *and* the family car. Then on a surprise visit to his son Norman (Michael Warren) in Los Angeles, he discovers him living with a white buddy (Dennis Dugan), who's *more* than a buddy. He's baby Norman's gay lover! Afterward, Mother Bailey arrives on the scene, trying to straighten matters out. Father Foxx also enlists the help of a statuesque prostitute (Tamara Dobson) to bring Norman to his senses. But to no avail.

Based on an unsuccessful Broadway play (whose characters were originally Jewish), *Norman, Is That You?* distinguishes itself only because it presents its black family simply as a family, with no drumbeating about color. It was also one of the few films of the period to deal explicitly with a gay theme, although the theme is trivialized, turned into the pablum of weekly sitcoms. Finally, the picture was shot on videotape, then transferred to film. The tape method was cheap and quick and it shows. *Norman, Is That You?* looks terrible: lousy color, undefined images, and poor compositions. The script's just as bad.

The cast gives it their best, but the whole thing is forced and fake. Curiously, bright spots are provided by Dobson, who reveals a sweet vulnerability and a lovely, tender smile that are sometimes touching, all the more so because she brings *heart* to a film that's crass and vulgar.

Nothing but a Man (1965)

D. Michael Roemer. *S.* Michael Roemer and Robert Young. *P.* Michael Roemer, Robert Young, and Robert Rubin. *R.* Du Art Film Labs. Cast includes: a young Yaphet Kotto; Mel Stewart; Leonard Parker; and Stanley Greene.

One of the best black-oriented films of its era: a subtle, quietly intense study of a black man living in the South, refusing to kowtow and suffering the consequences of that refusal. Ivan Dixon is Duff, the railroad worker who leaves the road to marry Abbey Lincoln, a quiet schoolteacher and the daughter of a minister. Hoping for a good, solid life together, the two find the mounting social and racial pressures of their environment closing in on them. Dixon's Duff finally takes out his frustrations and tensions on the woman he loves. The film reaches a moving climax when Dixon, leaving Lincoln, sets off on an odyssey of sorts, visiting his alcoholic, self-destructive father (Julius Harris). When the father dies, Duff finds himself examining not only the older man's life but his own. Eventually, Duff returns to his wife, carrying with him his son by a previous relationship. He's determined now to give his life—and himself—another chance.

Shot in 12 weeks on a budget of $230,000 by two young independent filmmakers (Michael Roemer and Robert Young), *Nothing but a Man* was highly lauded when shown at the Venice, London, and New York Film Festivals (at the latter, as the film ended, an audience of 2,000 burst into spontaneous applause). But distributors stayed away from it, convinced the film had no chance of being a commercial success. When finally released, the film was critically praised and was endorsed by the black intelligentsia.

The years have not lessened its power although, frankly, one now wonders what a black director might have done with the same material. For good as *Nothing but a Man* is, there is an ambience here more European than black American. Sometimes the characters all seem *too* oppressed and weary, without giving us indications of the rich humor and surprising optimism that enabled generations of black Americans to survive during the worst of times. During one sequence when a group of Duff's buddies from his bachelor days visit their newly married friend for dinner, we are presented with the most somber dinner gathering imaginable. These are black men who've worked together, travelled together, had fun together. Surely there would be some reminiscing, some sharing of old high times, some jokes at Duff's expense. When the group leaves Duff's home, they solemnly walk down the street, not one discussing the evening. The sequence rings true to the director's view of his oppressed, saddened black characters. But it doesn't ring true to what we know of black life. Black Americans in social groups always have *spirit*.

Still the performances of Dixon, Harris, and Gloria Foster (as Harris' mistress) are all striking, often remarkable. And in the long run, too, no other American film has yet treated a black male/female relationship with as much sensitivity. Watching Dixon and Lincoln coming to terms with one another and their own lives, we realize, more than ever, how much of the black experience has been ignored or evaded by the American commercial film.

Odds Against Tomorrow (1959)

> *D.* Robert Wise. *S.* John O. Killens; based on a book by William P. McGivern. *P.* Robert Wise. *R.* UA. Cast includes: Mel Stewart; Wayne Rogers; Gloria Grahame; Shelley Winters; and Robert Earl Jones.

Tightly strung bank heist drama. The script (blunt, sensitive, violent) by black novelist John O. Killens manages to capture the tension of the men hoping for the heist (Robert Ryan, Ed Begley, Harry Belafonte) as well as the racial dynamics that eventually undo even the best-laid plans. Killens also provides a rare look at black middle-class life in the 1950s: when Belafonte visits his estranged wife (Kim Hamilton), he finds her in the middle of a PTA meeting. It's a typical New York social scene, a mix of white liberals and bright young black professionals.

Director Wise has brought forth moody *film noir*-ish performances from much of the cast, almost all of whom, notably Ryan, are in fine form. Never a really exciting actor to watch, Harry Belafonte gives nonetheless a felt and convincing portrait of a man whose addiction to horses and nightclubs has ruined his homelife and left him emotionally stranded. This is one of his best film performances. John Brun's black-and-white cinematography reveals a New York of alienation: airless apartments, lonely streets, and dark, smoky, seamy clubs. At times, even Belafonte's smoothly handsome face looks like a striking abstraction. The film's ending has been criticized as trite: the white and black characters most at odds with one another are killed, their bodies burned to the point where the white men cannot be distinguished from the black.

A couple of surprises: dancer Carmen de Lavallade makes a very sleek appearance as a Belafonte girlfriend. And Cicely Tyson, long before stardom, turns up in a club sequence, young, cute, and (for Tyson) a tad raunchy.

An Officer and a Gentleman (1982)

> *D.* Taylor Hackford. *S.* Douglas Day Stewart. *P.* Martin Elfand. *R.* Paramount. Cast includes: Debra Winger and David Keith.

A young-man-in-the-military-comes-of-age story, reminiscent of such movies made in the 1940s. One only wishes the point of view had been updated with shrewd comments and insights on such a figure in the 1980s. Alas, that's not the case here, although audiences did not seem to mind at all; this was a huge box-office hit. According to *Variety* it was the third top-grossing film of 1983, pulling in some $127 million. The one updated matter turns out, pleasantly, to be the casting of Louis Gossett, Jr., as the tough drill sergeant, whose high standards and relentless drive instill in the young man (Richard Gere) a new set of values. The Gossett role itself is old hat. But the fact that a black man is in complete control of the situation is something new and rather refreshing. The idea of a black man passing on a "spiritual" value system to a young white had been done in movies before, such as the various versions of *The Adventures of Huckleberry Finn* and also with Rex Ingram's character in *Moonrise* (1948). But the black characters in those films always stood outside society without real status within the culture.

Originally, the Gossett character was written with a white actor in mind. Hearing of the role, Gossett fought to get an audition, and he had

to go against the long-established grain of thought within the film industry: unless a character is expressly written as being black, a black actor does not have a chance for it. Consequently, black performers cannot just play any role and usually when we see black characters in a basically white film they are symbols planted for specific reasons. That was not the case with Gossett in *An Officer and a Gentleman*, although, luckily, one never forgets he's black, and we may end up reading symbols into the movie, like it or not.

Gossett's work here? Terrific! This is not one of his subtle, brilliant characterizations like that of the axe-wielding husband in *The Landlord* or the clear-eyed, perceptive Fiddler in "Roots". The role is conventionally written in a superficial B-movie style. But Gossett digs deeply to come up with a harsh man but likable, both stubborn and admirable, too. The script doesn't tell us where Gossett's Sgt. Foley comes from or where he's headed, but Gossett's unyielding rigid posture and his unflinching eye-to-eye contact with all those he encounters hint at a man who understands that discipline and structure are the only means by which he can truly live; without them, he might be lost. His actorish embellishments are a pleasure to watch.

Seeing *An Officer and a Gentleman*, we do wonder, much as we do when seeing Hattie McDaniel in *Gone with the Wind*, what goes on in this character's life when he's away from the film's hero. We want the movie—the camera—to give us the other side of his life because the actor's work intrigues us so much we know there must be more than we're permitted to see. So strong is the subtext of Gossett's performance that there was talk of a TV series based on the character Foley in which viewers would learn that, away from the military structure, he was a lonely, driven alcoholic.

For his performance, Lou Gossett won an Academy Award as Best Supporting Actor of 1982, becoming the third black performer ever to win an Oscar and the first to win in the supporting actor category. (The other two winners were Hattie McDaniel and Sidney Poitier.)

Louis Gossett, Jr. (with, l., Richard Gere) as the demanding drill sergeant in An Officer and a Gentleman, *for which he won the Oscar as Best Supporting Actor of 1983.*

The Omega Man (1971)

D. Boris Sagal. *S.* John William and Joyce H. Corrington; based on the novel by Richard Matheson. *P.* Walter Seltzer. *R.* Warner Brothers. Cast includes: Lincoln Kilpatrick and Eric Laneuville.

A sci-fi drama set in Los Angeles after a worldwide bacteriological war has killed off just about everyone. Among the survivors though are Charlton Heston (naturally, the man who once played Moses, then Ben Hur, and later Michelangelo, is the healthiest specimen in the picture, immune to the germ warfare that's affected just about everyone else) and a band of mutants led by actor Anthony Zerbe. Unable to see during the day, the mutants don't come out until nightfall. And on one evening just when they're about to lay waste to Heston, he's saved by a gorgeous black woman, none other than Rosalind Cash. With a puffed-up Afro, a lovely face, and a voice that speaks with tension and conviction, she's forceful and assertive yet somehow still traditionally feminine. (She reminds one of Angela Davis, then very much in the headlines). The Cash character is one of the few original things this film has going for it. But midway in the picture, almost as if the moviemakers were intimidated by the character, Cash's heroine turns soft and gushily romantic, too meek and submissive to keep our interest. Still in the first part of the film, Cash is exciting to watch and at the time of *Omega Man*'s release it looked as if she was about to take the depiction of black women in American films in an entirely new direction.

One Down, Two to Go (1983)

D. Fred Williamson. *S.* Fred Williamson. *P.* Fred Williamson. *R.* Almi Films. Cast includes: Paula Sills; Laura Loftus; and Tom Signorelli.

An inept and sluggish attempt at resurrecting in the 1980s the type of black action picture that had proven so popular in the early 1970s. It even featured four of the biggest stars of that earlier era: Richard Roundtree, Jim Brown, Jim Kelly, and Fred Williamson. As usual, Brown is stiff but resolutely tough, and Williamson displays the light comic touch and relaxed air (with hints of self-parody) that have often made him a rather likable movie hero. Had the script, mediocre hack job that it is, been directed with some flair and verve, the picture might have been a little bit of fun—for 12-year-olds at least. But director Williamson (who produced) just plods along with no attention to detail or to developing his characters or clearly defining his plot mechanics. Consequently, the whole thing ends up as a mess, a boring one at that. Previously, Williamson, Kelly, and Brown had appeared together in two other films, *Three the Hard Way* (1974) and *Take a Hard Ride*. *One Down, Two to Go*, of course, is obviously the wrong title for this one. *Three Down and None to Go* would be more like it.

100 Rifles (1969)

D. Tom Gries. *S.* Clair Huffaker and Tom Gries; based on the novel by Robert MacLeod. *P.* Marvin Schwartz. *R.* 20th Century-Fox. Cast includes: Fernando Lamas and Dan O'Herlihy.

A western 1960s-style. Jim Brown is the lawman hunting in Mexico for Yaqui Joe (Burt Reynolds, the best thing in the movie), a bank robber who, it turns out (true to audience pinings during the period for "relevant" political outlaws), has used his stolen money to buy guns for his people, fellow Yaquis being ruthlessly exterminated by *federales* down below the border. While pursuing Reynolds, Brown meets up with Raquel Welch as, of all things, an Indian revolutionary leader. It stretches plausibility and boggles the mind, to say the least. At the time of its release, the movie's highpoint was the big scene in which Brown beds Welch. Press coverage was intense; so, too, were stories of a Brown/Welch feud. The hype helped out at the box-office. When Brown took Welch in his arms, black audiences (mostly males) were openly jubilant because they felt there was a job to be done and that Jim, the buck, knew just how to do it. In 1969, this act was viewed as having some kind of convoluted political significance. The black hero was bold enough to take the white man's most prized possession, the white woman. Today it all looks more hollow than hot.

100 Rifles, however, did much to establish Brown's stardom and is quite important in the development of his 1960s screen persona as the master of machismo.

Otherwise a very routine action picture, better on late night TV than in theaters.

The Organization (1971)

D. Don Medford. S. James R. Webb. P. Walter Mirisch. R. UA. Cast includes: Barbara McNair (again Poitier's wife); George and Wanda Spell (as Poitier's children); Sheree North; James Watson, Jr.; and some other faces which became very familiar to audiences of the 1970s and 1980s: Bernie Hamilton (formerly the star of *One Potato, Two Potato*, later the police captain in TV's "Starsky and Hutch" series), Raul Julia, Dan Travanty (who later turned up as Daniel J. Travanti on "Hill Street Blues"), Demond Wilson (later Redd Foxx's son on "Sanford and Son"), and Ron O'Neal (who played the title role in *Super Fly*).

The third in the Virgil Tibbs series, in which Poitier again plays the detective he originated in *In the Heat of the Night* and recreated in *They Call Me MISTER Tibbs*. This time around Tibbs, more in tune with the political and militant stirrings of the day, aids a group of radical idealists, out to bust an international drug ring.

Action-full and sometimes fast-moving (with the type of domestic scenes critics complained about in *They Call Me MISTER Tibbs* now toned down), it's still merely a routine item, of interest only because the lead character is black.

Paris Blues (1961)

D. Martin Ritt. S. Jack Sher, Irene Kamp and Walter Bernstein. Based on a novel by Harold Flender. Music by Duke Ellington. P. Sam Shaw. R. UA. Cast includes: Louis Armstrong.

Two ex-patriate jazz musicians, one white (Paul Newman), the other black (Sidney Poitier), each living in Paris, meet two vacationing American women (Joanne Woodward and Diahann Carroll), and of course, romance blossoms. For a brief spell, it looks as if there'll be a nice twist as Newman eyes Carroll. "All white girls look alike to me," he says. But apparently, he changes his mind because soon he's gazing in Woodward's direction, and Carroll falls into the arms of a waiting Poitier. One "pertinent" issue arises: should Poitier's character remain in Paris (where it appears he does not have to contend with racial biases) or return to the States to fight his battles there? Critic Stanley Kaufman felt that *Paris Blues* should have focused more on the story of Poitier's character. But most of the movie, when not providing a sightseer's tour of the city of love, was simply a tepid tale of boy meets girl, loses girl, etc. In this case, the boy and girl are really Paul and Joanne. Poitier and the rather plastic Carroll are kept neatly on the sidelines.

A Patch of Blue (1965)

D. Guy Green. S. Guy Green. Based on the novel Be Ready with Bells and Drums *by Elizabeth Kata. P. Pandro S. Berman. R. MGM. Cast includes: Elizabeth Hartman (as the blind girl); Shelley Winters (who won a Best Supporting Actress Oscar for her portrayal of the girl's vicious, bigoted mother); and Ivan Dixon (as Poitier's brother, who is hotly opposed to this relationship between blind and black).*

A seemingly innocuous film (about a lower-class, blind white girl who is befriended by a kindly Negro, played by Sidney Poitier) that enraged both white liberals and militant blacks during the 1960s. *Time* wrote that the picture was a clear case of "the black leading the blind." In *The New York Times* black writer Clifford Mason added that white America was certainly enamoured of Poitier because "he's running his private branch of the ASPCA, the Black Society for the Prevention of Cruelty to Blind White Girls, the BSPCBWG." *Newsweek* wrote that Poitier was "part Romeo and part Annie Sullivan," adding that "no other film has managed to simultaneously insult the Negroes and the blind." In *The New York Times*, Bosley Crowthers said: "The acting is too patly formulated and Mr. Poitier . . . has to act too much like a saint." Poitier himself said of his roles of this period: "Either there were no women or there was a woman but she was blind, or the relationship was of a nature that satisfied the taboos. I was at my wit's end when I finished *A Patch of Blue*."

The real problem here was that the script treated Poitier's character so condescendingly. Because the hero has such difficulty telling the girl he is a Negro, he emerges as a man without any pride in his own worth or his racial heritage, and it becomes impossible for black audiences to identify with him. In the novel on which the film was based, the blind girl was herself bigoted, and upon learning of the man's racial identity, she turned against him, bringing about his death. It was a scathing, disturbing portrait. But none of this is in the movie's sanitized script. The girl's the milk of human kindness. Perhaps most appalling is the picture's ending. Clearly a romance has evolved (the girl wants to marry her black friend), but it's never consummated. Poitier sends the lass off to a school, concluding the action on a note of ambiguity and evasion. Not long after *A Patch of Blue*, Poitier starred in *Guess Who's Coming to Dinner?*, which treated the business of an interracial romance more openly and in more detail (but not *much* more and with just as many compromises).

A Patch of Blue, however, was a commercial success in both the North and the South. But it alienated the Poitier movie hero from its basic constituency, the black audience.

The Petrified Forest (1936)

D. Archie L. Mayo. *S.* Charles Kenyon and Delmar Daves; from a Robert E. Sherwood play. *R.* Warner Bros.

At a gas station/barbecue stand in Arizona, passions and some pseudophilosophical mutterings run high and wide. Leslie Howard plays a disillusioned writer trying (oh, so desperately) to find meaning in life. Bette Davis is the bright-eyed, optimistic young girl infatuated with him. And Humphrey Bogart is the tough, foul-mouthed gangster Duke Mantee, who bursts into this quiet setting while on the run from the law. Amidst all the high-flung melodramatics there is a fascinating exchange between two seemingly minor characters: two black men, one a pliant, tommish chauffeur (John Alexander); the other, a slick sexy henchman of the gangster (Slim Johnson), who berates his black brother for living by the rules of white men. Exciting, offbeat, and volatile, the black gangster is a totally surprising figure to see in an American film of this period. He is one of Hollywood's first black militant characters—and an intelligent one at that. And in some respects, Johnson's performance is the most striking one in the picture.

A Piece of the Action (1977)

D. Sidney Poitier. *S.* Charles Blackwell, story by Timothy March. *P.* Melville Tucker. *R.* First Artists/Warner Bros. Cast includes: Sheryl Lee Ralph (later the Deena of Broadway's *Dreamgirls*); Sherri Poitier; Ed Love; Hope Clarke; and the very pretty Tracy Reed.

The third in the series of Sidney Poitier/Bill Cosby crossover comedies. Here the two portray con men who are coerced by a crafty police detective (James Earl Jones) into aiding a local community center (on Chicago's rough Southside) and transforming a group of rowdy black teenagers into civilized ladies and gents. It's a cautious retread of material Poitier covered in *Blackboard Jungle* and *To Sir, with Love*.

Audiences continue to enjoy this picture, perhaps because, like its predecessors *Uptown Saturday Night* and *Let's Do It Again*, it is among the few black family-oriented comedies. Apparently, so anxious was the black audience for wholesome family fare (a change from the black action pictures of the 1970s) that it turned something as innocuous and TV-ish as this into a solid box-office hit.

One wonders why the con man hero still pops up in black comedies. Richard Pryor has often been cast as such a figure. No doubt the con man, like the black pimp of old, has been viewed as a figure asserting himself within a system that repeatedly has denied his existence. But by the late 1970s and early 1980s, couldn't filmmakers have come up with another type of assertive black movie hero?

Among the fringe benefits here are some lively performances. Poitier, as a director, has always been generous in showcasing actors, permitting them to shine in a way white directors seldom do with black stars. Cosby is relaxed, inventive, and shrewdly funny (the complete antithesis of the Pryor kind of hero, who's always hyper, never laid back). Poitier even manages to get a mildly diverting performance from

James Earl Jones. (That's no small feat.) Denise Nicholas provides a bright and sassy spin and is, as usual, a pleasure to watch, an actress whose humor always grows out of her intelligence and common sense.

Pinky (1949)

D. Elia Kazan. *S.* Phillip Dunne and Dudley Nichols. *P.* Darryl F. Zanuck. *R.* 20th Century-Fox. Cast includes such veteran black performers as Frederick O'Neal and Nina Mae McKinney (her first big studio job in almost twenty years) and newcomer Kenny Washington (formerly a football player at UCLA; he was also one of the first black players for the Los Angeles Rams) as well as Basil Ruysdael; Evelyn Varden (bitchy and comic as a Southern bigot); and Griff Barnett.

In "The Shadow and the Act," his now-famous essay on Hollywood's problem pictures of 1949, Ralph Ellison wrote that although such films as *Home of the Brave* and *Lost Boundaries* were laden with absurdities, "they are all worth seeing, and if seen, of involving us emotionally. That they do is testimony to the deep centers of American emotion that they touch. . . . It is as though there were some deep relief to be gained merely from seeing these subjects projected on the screen."

Clearly, that is true of *Pinky,* a compromised film that has moved audiences nonetheless. The story is of a light-skinned black girl, Pinky, who, while studying nursing in the North (Boston), has passed for white. Upon returning home to her grandmother (Ethel Waters), Pinky is forced to face the debilitating plight of being a Negro in the Deep South. Humiliated, abused, and caged in, she plans to return to the North where she can live as a free (white) woman. But eventually Pinky comes to a new maturity and racial awareness, ironically brought about through a terminally ill, crusty, aristocratic white woman (Ethel Barrymore), who, intuitively aware of Pinky's dilemma, dies, leaving her estate to this troubled mulatto. Pinky is forced to go to court to hold onto this inheritance. Against all odds, she wins. When her white fiance from the North comes to take her away, she realizes she's been running from herself. Deciding to remain in the South, she converts the prop-

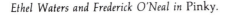

Ethel Waters and Frederick O'Neal in Pinky.

Patrons, black and white, line up for the New York City opening of the 1949 movie Pinky.

erty left to her into a school for young black nurses. The film ends with a saddened Pinky, standing alone, melancholic and misty-eyed, facing a future with a new racial pride but having lost personal happiness with the man she loved. She is, of course, a tragic mulatto.

Whether we like it or not, at every turn, there is something affecting and engrossing about *Pinky*, its undercurrents and its subtext disturbing and intriguing us far beyond our expectations. As the stoic, kindhearted, Christian grandmother, Ethel Waters infuses what could have been no more than an appallingly dated stereotype with genuine warmth, integrity, and an overriding sense of committment. For her work in *Pinky*, Waters was nominated for an Oscar as Best Supporting Actress of 1949.

Still one cannot overlook the film's basic dishonesties. Foremost was the casting of white actress Jeanne Crain as the Negro girl. Because there are interracial romantic sequences between Pinky and her white doctor boyfriend (played by actor William Lundigan), the studio found it then unthinkable to use a real black woman in the part. It was assumed audiences would be in an uproar. Not until Dorothy Dandridge's appearance opposite white actor John Justin in the 1957 movie *Island in the Sun* was the film industry "daring" enough to have a real interracial couple on screen, although, again, the compromises were apparent. One also cannot ignore the basically patronizing attitude inherent in *Pinky*: the black girl finds herself, not through the advice of her black grandmother but through the aid of a white aristocrat. Finally, in *Quality*, the novel by Cid Ricketts Sumner on which the film was based, after the heroine had won her court case to keep the mansion left to her, the place was burned to the ground by the Ku Klux Klan. This unhappy and more realistic ending was entirely scrapped by the studio.

Within the movie industry, many feared the picture would fail commercially because southern exhibitors would refuse to run it. That indeed did happen. In Marshall, Texas, a self-appointed censorship board banned the film. But a feisty exhibitor named L. Gelling showed it anyway, then found himself arrested. He fought the case, which eventually wound up in the Supreme Court. The decision, as reported on June 3, 1952, in *The New York Times*: "The Supreme Court today struck down a motion picture censor ordinance by which the city of Marshall, Texas, disapproved the showing of the film *Pinky*."

So *Pinky* did break ground. *Variety* wrote: "The story may leave questions unanswered and in spots be naive, but the mature treatment of a significant theme in a manner that promises broad public acceptance and b.o. [box office] success truly moves the American film medium a desirable notch forward in stature and importance."

Pipe Dreams (1976)

D. Stephen Verona. *S.* Stephen Verona (who had previously directed *The Lords of Flatbush*). *P.* Stephen Verona and Executive Producer, Barry Hankerson. *R.* Avco Embassy Pictures. Cast includes: Gladys Knight's then-current husband, Barry Hankerson, as her husband in the film; Altovise Davis also shows up.

Variety raved over *Pipe Dream*'s story ("a little gem") and its star Gladys Knight:

> As everyone has been noting for the last few years there is a dearth of bankable femme stars today, and among black women, only Diana Ross is in the first echelon. Pam Grier remains promising but is still stuck in trashy vehicles. That's another reason *Pipe Dreams* is a heartening surprise, for Knight could come into the star ranks at a time when a new face is badly needed. She has charm and grit.

Unfortunately, the paper proved wrong on both counts. The movie—the tale of a woman who journeys to Alaska to win back her husband—failed at the box office and soon disappeared. And, obviously, Knight, despite her immense appeal, did not become a film star.

Today *Pipe Dreams* is a curiosity piece, all the more sluggishly paced when cut up by commercial breaks on TV.

Recommended only for hard-headed Gladys Knight fans.

Porgy and Bess (1959)

D. Otto Preminger. *S.* N. Richard Nash; based on the George Gershwin stage operetta derived from the novel of DuBose Heyward. Libretto by DuBose Heyward; lyrics by Heyward and Ira Gershwin. *P.* Samuel Goldwyn. *R.* Columbia. Cast includes: Ruth Attaway; Clarence Muse; Joel Fluellen; Roy Glenn; William Walker; and Ivan Dixon. Neither Poitier nor Dandridge does his/her own singing. Porgy is sung by Robert McFerrin; Bess by Adele Addison. Choreography by Hermes Pan. Photography by Leon Shamroy. Music direction by Andre Previn. Production design by Oliver Smith.

A Samuel Goldwyn production that's lavish and "tastefully" done, based, of course, on the George Gershwin classic. The story of Porgy, the good-hearted crippled beggar who moves about on a goat cart and falls in love with Bess, a loose woman of a Charleston waterfront slum called Catfish Row, had long fascinated the American public. It had first appeared as the novel *Porgy* by DuBose Heyward in 1925. Two years later Heyward and his wife Dorothy Heyward turned the story into a dramatic play, which ran for 217 performances for the Theatre Guild in New York. Then in 1935 Gershwin transformed it into a folk opera, calling it *Porgy and Bess*. The musical version, however, was not successful and did not find an audience or even great critical acceptance until revivals after Gershwin's death.

Afterwards *Porgy and Bess* played all over the world, becoming an international favorite, many accepting its tale and its music as authentic black folk culture. Of course, nothing could be further from the truth. Haunting, lovely, and memorable as the score is, it is the music of Gershwin, not of a black artist such as a Duke Ellington or even a Fats Waller. And the story itself, while in some productions moving, is at heart condescending.

For black Americans *Porgy and Bess* has always been a mixed blessing. Although one is happy to see black actors get the work, one would prefer a different story, a true black tragedy. *Porgy and Bess* has been accepted by black America only when the director and performers bring something special to it, playing against the characters and the melodramatic plot, rather than with them. Curiously enough, the music, when performed on its own without the framework of the play, always works with a black audience. Indeed "Summertime," which opens the play, is now thought of as a black song, seemingly most effective and felt when performed by a black artist. The same is true of "Ol' Man River" from *Show Boat*.

In the 1950s when it was announced that *Porgy and Bess* would finally come to the screen, there was pressure from some civil rights groups to halt the production. Harry Belafonte, who was originally up for the role of Porgy, refused to do the film, reportedly saying he would not do any role on his knees.

Sidney Poitier was eventually signed. But the subject of *Porgy and Bess* was one Poitier remained reticent about for years. Finally, in his 1980 autobiography *This Life*, he wrote of his feelings in the 1950s, when first approached for the film. "I don't want to do *Porgy and Bess*," he had said. "*Porgy and Bess* is an insult to black people, and I ain't going to play it and that's all there is to it." Poitier went on to explain the subtle ways in which he was pressured into taking the role. There was the possibility he'd lose his part in *The Defiant Ones* if he turned *Porgy and Bess* down. And he also revealed the subtle, political games any Hollywood star learns to play. Producer Samuel Goldwyn was determined to have Poitier in his picture. And one could never afford to openly alienate or offend so powerful a figure in the movie capital.

The making of *Porgy and Bess* proved an ordeal for many of the actors, who constituted a truly all-star cast: Poitier, Dorothy Dandridge, Pearl Bailey, Sammy Davis, Jr., Diahann Carroll, and Brock Peters. Original director Rouben Mamoulian was replaced by Otto Preminger, the temperamental director of the all-black *Carmen Jones*. The set was tense, not only because of a controversy among many blacks about the fact that *Porgy and Bess* was being made but also because of Preminger's autocratic manner. Poitier has written:

> It happened, I think, on the first day I started to work. Otto Preminger jumped on Dorothy Dandridge in a shocking and totally unexpected way. She had done something that wasn't quite the way he wanted it. . . . Dorothy Dandridge, visibly

shaken, started the scene again, hoping to recapture the missing ingredient and save herself from further embarrassment. She hadn't proceeded very far before he exploded again. . . . And on he went. Well, I heard it—watched it—analyzed and categorized it—because one day sure as hell my turn was to come. Nobody went to Dorothy's defense. . . . Totally unable to defend herself, Dorothy Dandridge fell apart. Nowhere in her anguish was there enough venom to dip her dagger into. . . . On that day I learned that the serene look Dorothy Dandridge always wore only served to mask the fears, frustrations, and insecurities that were tumbling around inside her all the time.

Dorothy Dandridge's insecurities and Poitier's tensions (as he predicted, his day with Preminger *did come*; the men had two distinctly different points of view) turned up in the finished project. In the case of Poitier, he seems totally out of place and while often charming, charming is not what's needed. He never sinks his teeth into a role he feels so ill at ease with. Moreover, there he is, the black movie idol of the late 1950s, a time of rising protests, sit-ins, demonstrations, boycotts—the start of a new day in Black America's fight for civil rights—singing, "I got plenty of nothing and nothing's plenty for me." *Porgy and Bess* won him few new fans.

As for Dandridge, she puts her star qualities on brilliant display. As she walks through the theatrical sets of the film, dressed in long, tight skirts and dark wide-brimmed hats, she is a dazzling creation. Even star performers Pearl Bailey and Sammy Davis, Jr., fail to take the screen from her. Again portraying the tragic woman at odds with society, Dandridge's performance is not so much an acting job as it is a star performance. But her open vulnerabilities, nervousness, delicacy, and insecurities enhance her presence and draw an audience to her. For her performance, she won the Foreign Press Award as best actress in a musical.

Far too stagey, the movie never opens up, breathes, or looks like anything other than something shot on a Hollywood soundstage. The exception is the picnic sequence which was filmed—thankfully—out of doors. Preminger and Goldwyn apparently battled over the conception of the picture. The producer wanted to play it safe with a theater-like presentation. Preminger, the rather hedonistic, suave European, wanted some fierce energy with a more contemporary touch. The picnic sequence reveals Preminger, the director, best in this film, although at the moment when Brock Peters as the villainous Crown shows up, attacking Dandridge, the sequence slips into a sleaziness that's energetic but tacky.

As Sportin' Life, Sammy Davis, Jr., is a bit *too* slick but playing to his own rhythm, he's still fresh enough as a performer to be engaging. This role is a great relief as compared to many of his later cutesy or tired, played-out ones. Brock Peters's Crown is something of a buck nightmare while Diahann Carroll's Clara is girlish and sweetly warm. Her "Summertime" aria (which opens the film but uses another singer's voice, that of Loulie Jean Norman) is lyrical and lovely, setting up high expectations that the rest of the film never really delivers. As Maria, Pearl Bailey is unabashed, cantankerous energy, a high-rolling charismatic performer who's not encumbered by the script.

In *The New York Times*, Bosley Crowther called *Porgy and Bess* "a truly magnificent motion picture." *The New York Herald Tribune*'s critic Paul V.

Beckley added: "Deserves respect as one of the most ambitious and, frankly, one of the finest cinematic versions of an opera, and even its flaws ought to be seen in the light of the serious magnitude of the task its makers set themselves." Other critics though found great fault with the film. *Time* wrote that "the worst thing about Goldwyn's *Porgy and Bess*, though, is its cinematic monotony . . . not so much a motion picture as a photographed opera." Generally, audiences tend to agree with this latter reviewer. *Porgy and Bess* often crawls along, and what makes it of interest are the legendary black stars in it.

Pressure Point (1962)

> D. Hubert Cornfield. S. Hubert Cornfield and S. Lee Pogostin; based on "The Fifty Minute Hour" by Dr. Robert Lindner. P. Stanley Kramer. R. Stanley Kramer/UA. Cast includes: Barry Gordon.

Not long after the box-office hit *The Defiant Ones*, producer Stanley Kramer and actor Sidney Poitier teamed again for this airless, cramped melodrama. Poitier plays a prison psychiatrist treating a young patient (Bobby Darin), a vicious paranoid bigot and a Nazi as well. Some hardhitting and dramatic sequences emerge. But there is no heart to this picture. The characters are nameless, referred to simply as "The Doctor," "The Patient," or "The Chief Medical Officer," etc. And this artsy attempt at turning a hot, then still controversial theme into something of an abstract allegorical study prevents direct, sustained emotional and intellectual audience involvement. Darin handles his flashy role well. But Poitier is required mostly to sit, calmly "seething" with anger, we assume, holding back his true feelings while the patient has the freedom to unleash all his racial venom. Towards the end of the film, Poitier does have a chance for an outburst, which, although well delivered by Poitier, is anticlimactic. Following on the heels of the once provocative *The Defiant Ones*, it doesn't say anything *new* either.

The prologue and epilogue of *Pressure Point* are also disturbing compromises. The film opens with a white psychiatrist (Peter Falk) approaching Poitier, asking to be removed from a case in which he must work with a racist young black patient. An older, wiser Poitier then tells the white psychiatrist, through flashbacks, of his previous, similar experience with Darin's character. Essentially, the opening and the ending (which returns to Poitier and the white psychiatrist) are there to soothe and reassure the large white movie audience, to assuage its guilt feelings because, after all, it tells us, everybody is a racist, white as well as black. *Pressure Point* ignores the fundamental roots of racism in America, which are white, not black. Black racism has almost always been a reaction to a system created by white America. But films seldom have realized or elaborated on this point.

Proud Valley (1940)

> D. Pen Tennyson. S. Pen Tennyson, Jack Jones, and Louis Golding, from a story by Herbert Marshall and Alfredda Brilliant. P. Michael Balcon. R. Associated British Films. Cast includes: Edward Chapman and Rachel Thomas.

In this British film (said to have been Paul Robeson's favorite among his movies), Robeson stars as an American seaman working in a Welsh coal mine. One really cannot blame him for liking the film because technically and thematically it holds together better than do most of his others. He also seems relaxed in front of the camera. And no doubt he felt relieved that he wasn't playing the kind of backwoods dolt that he was cast as in *Show Boat* and later the notorious *Tales of Manhattan*. But the movie is infused with a subtle kind of liberal condescension that may well turn off some contemporary audiences. Robeson's character is mighty noble, and what is meant to "endear" and "ennoble" him most is the climactic sequence when he sacrifices himself in the coal mine so that his white friends/brothers might escape in safety. How can one not admire a black man who gives up his life for you? The character really is an undercover servant, in that he is serving members of the Empire, ensuring their welfare. This is the kind of noble Negro hero Sidney Poitier was saddled with in such 1950s films as *Edge of the City* and *No Way Out* when he, too, is something of a sacrificial lamb.

Robeson's impressive, though, dignified and self-contained, and it's worth seeing the movie just to hear him sing his great song "Deep River."

Purple Rain (1984)

D. Albert Magnoli. S. Albert Magnoli and William Blinn. P. Robert Cavallo, Joseph Ruffalo, and Steven Fargnoli. R. Warner Bros. Cast includes: Prince's regular backup troupe: Billy Sparks; Des Dickerson; Brenda Bennett; Jill Jones; and Jerome Benton.

"The New Prince of Hollywood," *Newsweek* wrote. "Smashing feature debut," added *Variety*. And *Rolling Stone* proclaimed, "May be the smartest, most spiritually ambitious rock & roll movie ever made." All were saluting the screen arrival of pop/rock recording star Prince in what, unfortunately, is a sad-eyed, soggy primal fantasy about misunderstood youth.

Semi-autobiographical, *Purple Rain* focuses on the problems, on stage and off, of a young rock musician, simply called The Kid, played by Prince. In his music, he struggles to express what's tearing him apart, to sing the things he cannot say. And what's at the pit of Prince's angst? At home his father berates and beats the Kid's mother. At the steamy clubs where he performs the Kid must contend with a nasty rival (Morris Day of the group Time) and a lovely girl he falls for but mistreats (Apollonia Kotero of the group Apollonia 6). We're to draw connectives between the s-and-m doings of the Kid's parents and the Kid's own tensions with Apollonia. Yet we're never cued in as to what fuels any of these relationships, what draws the parents together and apart. At the basis of the relationships there seems to be little more than the long-suffering masochism of the women. In fact, a glaring weakness of *Purple Rain* is its deplorable treatment of women. In one sequence, a young woman is dumped into a huge trash bin (this is supposed to be funny). In another, Apollonia is made to strip and jump into a freezing lake to prove her love for the Kid, only to learn as she stands naked and shivering that she's jumped into the wrong lake! The *New York Daily News* critic wrote that the film "is painfully ill at ease with its female characters, who are alternately abused and worshipped and whose primary virtue is smiling through pain."

All in all, *Purple Rain* is a distressing, jangly, oldhat backstage musical that, ironically, just might achieve cult film status, mainly because of Prince's androgynous presence and his huge following among record buyers and music video watchers. During the musical segments of *Purple*

Musical star Prince as the Kid in Purple Rain.

Rain, Prince, as in concert, is a striking 1980s pop icon what with his Regency ruffles and his well-tended curly locks: a heady mix of Little Richard, Jimi Hendrix, Sly Stone, and James Dean (Prince owes his brooding pout to Dean), he's fast-moving, funky, playfully naughty and seductive, street-smart, cunning, cynical, also innovative and rather unsavory, too. What goes wrong though is that his is a concert/music video persona, not rounded or shaped or complex enough to sustain a two-hour film plot. Surprisingly, during the *acting* sequences, his video image almost congeals into self-parody for he is all pose and posture, capable of expressing only one mood: the self-indulgent, lost little boy vamp.

Purple Rain does take movie mythology into another direction as it marks the return of the tragic mulatto film. In the old tragic mulatto movies, the mulatto's problems stemmed from the fact that, because of mixed blood, the mulatto was at home in neither white nor black society (*Pinky* and *Lost Boundaries*). In films like the 1934 *Imitation of Life* and *Hallelujah*, the subliminal message seemed to be that the mixed blood led to confusion, heartache, tragedy. Hence Nina Mae McKinney must die in *Hallelujah*, and Fredi Washington in *Imitation of Life* must return repentant, broken-hearted to her mother's funeral. The central characters in *Purple Rain*—The Kid, Morris Day, even Apollonia (who technically is not black)—strike us as keyed-up, confused cursed *light-brighters* (vernacular for light-skinned blacks), flinging themselves every which way, not sure what to do or who they should be. We know next to nothing about the backgrounds of Apollonia and Day. But looking at them we may wonder if we're meant to assume their mixed blood has made them so restless. They are completely unlike the traditional black movie characters of the 1970s, who, we were to assume, were firmly rooted in the black community. As for the Kid, he is the son of a black father (Clarence Williams III) and a white mother (Greek actress Olga Kartalos). The movie doesn't waste time elaborating on black roots or any other kind of roots either. But the idea suggested is that this interracial homelife has unsettled the kid, disrupted his equilibrium.

The fact that *Purple Rain* does not deal with questions of racial identity or heritage indicates a 1980s shift in audience expectations/ consciousness. An audience of the 1940s, 1950s, 1960s would have demanded some kind of analysis or a comment on the "racial" troubles of these characters. Those in the 1980s, however, could not care less. What's important is Prince's look—(he's a crossover god/goddess, part black, part white, part male, part female)—and his stance (sexy and rebellious, but rebellious without an explained cause).

"Probably the flashiest album cover ever to be released as a movie," wrote Vincent Canby in *The New York Times*. "An insidious instance of the MTV-ization of American movies," wrote *People*.

Purple Rain is indeed an elongated music video, at its best during its set performance sequences (Time's numbers are fabulous) and its last 10 minutes when Prince in dazzling concert footage just rolls on and on in glory; at its worst when it believes it's telling us something.

Putney Swope (1969)

D. Robert Downey. S. Robert Downey. P. Herold. R. Cinema V. Cast includes: Arnold Johnson (in the title role); the very skillful Antonio Fargas; Laura Greene (as Mrs. Swope); Buddy Butler; Allen Garfield; and Pepi Hermine (as the President of the United States).

One of the first of the new black films of the late 1960s/early 1970s to take a farcical look at black America. It's part parody, part putdown, part satire: of stereotypes, power manipulations on Madison Avenue, capitalism, and the various hangups infesting the American way of life. Director Downey achieved his end by reversing the racial scales.

The plot is simple. At a New York advertising agency, a black token figure is inadvertently elected chairman of the board. "I'm not going to rock the boat," Putney Swope announces upon his election. "I am going to sink it!" Thereafter in one superbly edited sequence the board of directors is transformed from the lineup of pole-faced white executives, corrupt and hungry for money and power, to a vital new black staff equipped with dashikis and afros, later with guns and munitions. The agency becomes Truth and Soul, Inc. And it sets out to shake up the sensibilities of just about everyone.

By the time the film ends, Putney and company have sunk the boat and at the same time revealed blacks to be just as corrupt and power-hungry as whites. Their black Establishment (best symbolized by Mrs. Swope berating and hounding her scrawny white maid) proves no better than its white predecessor. White has been turned black and black turned white, and everybody is made ugly.

The improvisatory style of the film appears to give the actors a certain freedom, and it captures some of the mood of the period. But at heart the movie is full of distortions, its blacks depicted as natural-born supercharged athletes, high-powered sexy beings, or loud-mouth do-nothings. Instead of examining genuine black cultural follies, the director chooses to satirize the myths, cliches, exaggerations as if indeed they are the true essence of the black experience.

Variety wrote: "Disappointingly, nothing much beyond marginal interest occurs. The comedy is only intermittently funny and the satire is mostly shallow and obvious. However, because of the theme, strong, intelligent exploitation can mean moderate box-office for an art circuit, university town playoff." *Variety* proved both right and wrong about the box-office appeal. *Putney Swope was* a success on campuses but also a commercial dynamo in urban areas throughout the country. For the first time, black audiences were seeing comically assertive black characters. The need for such figures really was not answered (with intelligent comically assertive black characters), but it was being touched on nonetheless.

Today *Putney Swope* has historical significance, but that's about it. Otherwise it's basically a dull-witted, mean-spirited little picture.

Ragtime (1981)

D. Milos Forman. *S.* Michael Weller. *P.* Dino De Laurentiis. *R.* Paramount. Cast includes: James Cagney; Debbie Allen; Mandy Patinkin; Moses Gunn (as Booker T. Washington); Norman Mailer; Mary Steenburgen; Brad Dourif; and Elizabeth McGovern.

Ragtime, E.L. Doctorow's kaleidoscopic, turn-of-the-century "pop epic" novel, a *tour de force* mix of fact and fiction, skillfully plotted and ingeniously balanced, was transformed into a dim and passionless movie melodrama, with one interesting twist: the black ragtime pianist-turned-outlaw, Coalhouse Walker, was now placed by European director Milos Forman at the center of the action. When Walker's Model T is desecrated by bigoted members of a New Rochelle firehouse, he seeks

Howard Rollins, Jr., in his Oscar-nominated role as Coalhouse Walker in Milos Foreman's Ragtime.

legal redress, then, failing that, turns to social activism: he leads a band of "militants" who declare war on all firehouses and eventually take over the Morgan Library, threatening to destroy all its valuables. Walker is the movie's most vivid creation, without whom there would be no reason at all for this film. And it often looks as if director Forman, by choosing to focus on Coalhouse Walker, is telling us that we cannot begin to even approach the American experience of the past without dealing with the racial issue.

In his previous film *Hair*, Forman also had shifted an emphasis: the soundtrack's most emotionally charged song "Easy To Be Hard" (which in the play had been sung by the white character Sheila) was handed over to black performer Cheryl Barnes, who turned this ballad into a compelling battle cry. In both *Hair* and *Ragtime*, Forman seems to approach the emotional core of American life in a way no white American director would have considered: his black characters handle his most intensely felt moments. Without fuss, Forman walks head on into the issue of race and while the political line may not be clear to us, the emotional one is pure, direct, and moving.

As played by newcomer Howard Rollins, Coalhouse, far from the firebrand of the novel, is something of a rebellious moderate, a very polite, polished, controlled man whom we cannot quite believe heads a group of black revolutionaries. (The movie can't quite believe that fact either because the revolutionary movement soon fizzles out.) Rollins, however, uses quiet skills and strength to create a memorable character. *Newsweek* praised the "seething dignified rage of Howard Rollins, a remarkable newcomer." And *Variety* felt the film was "highlighted by Rollins' staggeringly effective portrayal of conscience-wracked pride and an intense screen magnetism that bodes instant stardom." Rollins was nominated for an Academy Award as Best Supporting Actor of 1981 for his performance in *Ragtime*.

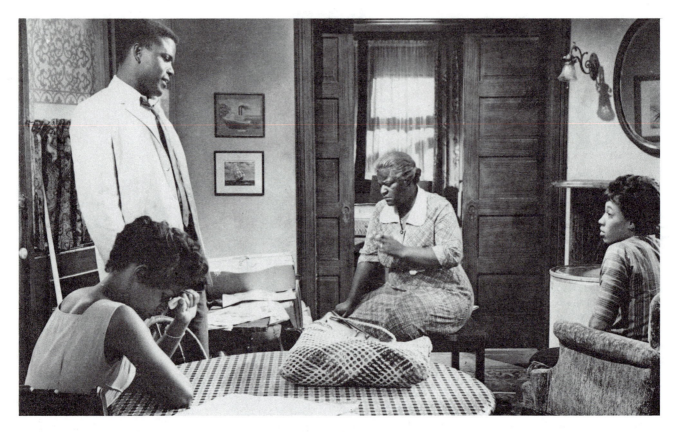

L. to r.: Ruby Dee, Sidney Poitier, Claudia McNeil, and Diana Sands as the troubled Younger family in the screen adaptation of Lorraine Hansberry's play A Raisin in the Sun.

A Raisin in the Sun (1961)

D. Daniel Petrie. *S.* Lorraine Hansberry, based on her play. *P.* David Susskind and Philip Rose. *R.* Columbia. Cast includes: John Fiedler; Joel Fluellen; Stephen Perry (as Travis); and Roy Glenn.

Produced by David Susskind, this screen adaptation of Lorraine Hansberry's prize-winning play remains moving. For one of the rare times in movie history, we have a drama told from a black woman's point of view.

Set in a tiny Southside Chicago apartment, *A Raisin in the Sun* examines the Younger family. For years, matriarch Lena Younger has dreamed of getting out of the flat she shares with her son Walter, his wife Ruth, their child Travis, and her daughter Beneatha. With a ten-thousand dollar insurance policy left to her by her husband, Lena Younger hopes to buy a house in the integrated suburbs. As she makes her plans and dreams her dreams, the personal problems of each member of the household clash with those of the others.

Capturing the tension of blacks enduring lives of unquiet desperation, author Hansberry explored the matriarchal setup in some black homes and examined the emasculation of the black male by a hostile white society. Her work was framed with a gentle humor and much wisdom.

The film's belief in integration may seem a bit dated, and the movie itself is claustrophobic and far from being "cinematic." The sometimes overblown performances, however, remain exciting. Sidney Poitier is at his vibrant, explosive best as Walter. As the kid sister Beneatha, the young Diana Sands, in a highly theatrical performance, bulldozes her way triumphantly through the action. Claudia McNeil's powerhouse portrayal of the mother Lena is the adhesive that thematically holds the picture together. (Has anyone forgotten the sequence in which she slaps Sands and says, "Now repeat after me. In my mother's house, there is God.") Showing up also as Sands' suitors are Ivan Dixon, as the beautifully self-contained African student, and the great Lou Gossett, as the proper young man who's too insufferably middle class for his own good—and for Sands. Finally, there is Ruby Dee, a tiny tower of strength and conviction; her work is splendidly etched and detailed, a consistently special and moving performance.

Red Ball Express (1952)

D. Budd Boetticher. S. J. Michael Hayes. P. Aaron Rosenberg. R. Universal-International. Cast includes: Hugh O'Brien; Alex Nicol; and Bubber Johnson.

Based loosely on the experiences during the Second World War of the actual "red ball express," a mostly black trucking outfit (with white officers leading, naturally) that proved quite heroic. Here the company's been ordered to catch up with General Patton's troops in France and to resupply them with much needed materials. They do so valiantly under very tight and dangerous circumstances, thus helping to prevent the collapse of the Allied offensive.

The real story of these black military heroes could have been daring and gripping—and historically enlightening as well. Instead this trite and often banal film offers mainly a collection of familiar G.I. conflicts and character types. The outfit itself is hardly a black one: it's more of a white company with a scattered black face here and there.

Variety wrote:

> Scripting uses cliched situations and dialog (sic) offering nothing new in the story to bolster the good idea behind the picture. However, it does have the pace of good pulp fiction, a sense of humor most of the time, and is cloaked in enough standard action to play off satisfactorally for less discriminating audiences.

The film also had a young, riveting actor named Sidney Poitier (this was his third film). Poitier's role is a supporting one and his character is as cliched as the others: he's Hollywood's then-standard black soldier with a chip on his shoulder, angry at the world and always seething (rather illogically) with rage at the racial situation. The film wants us to believe he's *looking* for racism.

But Poitier himself, in certain key scenes, bristles with a dazzling intensity, especially when he has a chance to explode emotionally. "Look, *boy*, where I come from you don't give orders. You take 'em," a racist soldier shouts when Poitier asks for a cup of coffee." "I'm not taking any orders from *you*," Poitier lets the white man know. He jumps upon the guy with passion and regains any lost dignity. Young black audiences loved Poitier for it.

Of course, the movie ends with the *acceptable* theme of racial reconciliation. Poitier's character learns to deal with the white world and comes to have a grudging respect for his admirable white lieutenant (Jeff Chandler).

The New York Times wrote: "There is nothing in this film to recommend, with the possible exception of Sidney Poitier and Jeff Chandler." Contemporary audiences no doubt will concur.

Richard Pryor Here and Now (1983)

D. Richard Pryor. S. Richard Pryor. P. Bob Parkinson and Andy Friendly; *Ex. P.* Jim Brown. *R.* Columbia Pictures, an Indigo Production.

The third in the series of Richard Pryor concert movies, all chapters of an ongoing filmic autobiography by this extraordinary comedian. What's most interesting here is Pryor's relationship with his audience. The loud and occasionally rowdy patrons seem to want something from Pryor that he's neither anxious nor willing to deliver. Part of what the audience demands is the old humor, the former high-rolling comic persona, the previous spark, dazzle, and zip that turned his first concert film, *Richard Pryor: Live in Concert*, into a great piece of work. The audience also seems to want "blood" from Pryor and is frequently disrespectful and insensitive. It's a strange sensation sitting in a movie theater with a live audience watching a "live audience" on film at this Pryor concert. Both audiences often shout out to him. They talk back, comment, make requests. So fierce an audience personal rapport has Pryor established, particularly with the black working class, that his followers feel comfortable enough to speak to him as if he were a true member of their family. He's the *brother* who's made it but still remembers, with insight and precision, the old days. In any family situation, though, there are times when all of us want to tell the relatives to buzz off and let us live our own lives. That sometimes happens here. Pryor speaks his mind when the crowd breaks up his rhythm or momentum or when it's not ready for the semi-serious new kind of humor he's working with. (He never, however, really goes off on his audience as he would have in the early years of his career.) But the audience in the concert film misses what the "real" "live" audience in the movie theater sees: when the camera captures Pryor's instant reactions to a call from the audience, Pryor's vulnerability surfaces in living closeup. And it draws the movie audience to him in the most personal of ways. Older now, more experienced, he still barrages us with profanity (which the concert audiences howls over; often just a mention of the word *mother-f - - - - -* is enough to get the crowd going), he's struggling to express in comic and dramatic terms a new mature perspective. He tells us here he's given up on booze and dope.

Unfortunately, though, because much of the material is not fully developed, the film is often disappointing. Pryor himself doesn't seem to feel his oats. When he refers (as he did in his second concert film, *Richard Pryor Live on the Sunset Strip*) to the fire accident that nearly killed him, the audience is initially uneasy. Pryor also has one completely inexcusable joke about a hysterectomy. He cannot make the joke work, it's ugly and tasteless, the kind of material we feel he would have thrown out had he spent more time shaping his act.

Still this remains a frequently fascinating documentary on Richard Pryor. He's far better here, working with his own material, then in other films of this period such as *Superman III* or *The Toy*.

Richard Pryor Live in Concert (1979)

D. Jeff Margolis. S. Richard Pryor. P. Del Jack and J. Mark Travis. *R.* Special Event Entertainment.

Many critics have considered this the best performance concert ever filmed, and there's a good reason why: it is. For audiences of the 1970s who had watched Richard Pryor repeatedly hampered by meaningless and misconceived movie roles, this film came as a surprise and a joy. It was like watching an artist suddenly liberated from a culture's restraints. Here Pryor's gifts for mime and mimicking are brilliantly showcased. So, too, is his uncanny ability to comically dramatize events (some traumatic, others near tragic) from his life. To Richard Pryor there is practically nothing that cannot be made transcendently funny. He brings humor to an account of the first time his grandmother caught him using cocaine; of the occasions when his sons watched as he nearly drowned in a pool; of the time police arrested him for destroying his car; and most triumphantly of the heart attack that he thought would kill him. The latter sequence reveals Pryor's extraordinary talents at their finest. He's able not only to dramatize the pain that ripped through his chest but he also "impersonates" the heart itself as it sends out its piercing terror; Pryor also becomes the hospital medics who tend to him; and at the same time, he stands in the distance as an observer, watching himself—a symbol of puny, vulnerable man—as he struggles to save himself. Pryor attempts to create this same type of objective observer with the alter ego figure in *Jo Jo Dancer, Your Life Is Calling*, but with far less effective results.

Pryor also has priceless, enlightening sequences in which he imitates animals: he becomes a dog sassing his master; a horse relieving himself; and a deer in the woods who suddenly encounters boxer Leon Spinks.

Throughout his language is strong and salty (to put it mildly), and he discusses sex as frankly as ever. He also satirizies sex roles, puncturing the facade of the macho man. If a guy comes at you with a knife, Pryor announces, "Don't try to be macho. You run. And you teach your old lady how to run, too, so you don't have to go back for her." Then, too, he does something that caught white viewers completely offguard but which delighted black audiences because it was a type of satire never before seen in a major film. In popular American culture of the past, white entertainers had often impersonated black dialects, mocking black speech rhythms and intonations as comic abnormalities. Here Pryor satirizes and parodies the speech patterns—and attitudes—of whites. It's a brilliant sendup.

Rich, varied, complex, and hilarious, this concert performance has become rather haunting for recent movie audiences, who have been aware of what followed in Pryor's life after this film—his accident, his later dispiriting movies, and a series of other disappointments which seemed to sap him of some of his comic vitality. One cannot help being moved by the sight of Pryor before those new problems at a time when a great American talent was fully delivering on his early youthful promise.

Richard Pryor Live on the Sunset Strip (1982)

D. Joe Layton. *S.* Richard Pryor. *P.* Rastar and Richard Pryor. *R.* Columbia Pictures.

"When they bury me," Richard Pryor told a *Playboy* interviewer in 1979, "they better dig the hole deep because I may get out of that, too." This film indeed marks Pryor's return from the grave, his first concert feature since his near-fatal fire accident in 1980. The picture lacks the zing and imaginative daring of his first concert movie, for this is a portrait of a man and an artist in transition, coming to terms with a life

Richard Pryor in one of his classic concert films Richard Pryor Live on the Sunset Strip.

he's won back—and also with a huge following of fans whose outpouring of love almost seems to stun him.

Filmed during two separate performances at Hollywood's Palladium, Pryor hops onstage in a snazzy flame-red suit and proceeds to examine some of his favorite topics: race, sex, Africa, free-basing, and the Accident itself. The material's often interesting but not fully worked out. His earlier concert movie, *Richard Pryor Live in Concert*, had been a filmed record of routines, skits, and characters he'd been working with for years in clubs and on records. He had been able to get them down pat without losing any spontaneity or inventiveness. Here not only does he not seem fully at ease with new routines, he's also a bit tense about the audience, too, no doubt aware that for them he's become a legend now, an artist from whom almost nothing less than the extraordinary is expected. Sometimes he is a howl. Who can forget his comment on himself (as being moody and difficult)—"I am no day at the beach"—or his description of his interracial romance with a woman he eventually married, "The first two years we went together she thought her name was White Honky Bitch."

On occasion, the audience gets restless and wants a more worked-out performance, even going so far as to call out for his old Mudbone character routine. Pryor complies. But Mudbone, considered one of his most ingenious characters of the 1970s, seems flat and spiritless here, and one gets ticked off with the impatient audience for not letting Pryor continue on at his own rhythm.

The film climaxes with his description of his accident, which he tries very hard to invest with the same brilliant comic insights and animation he brought to his heart attack experience in the first concert film. But Pryor and the audience both seem uncomfortable, too disturbed by this "serious," "near-tragic" accident. He does get some great mileage out of his dope/free-basing tribulations. Not only does he let us hear his friend Jim Brown cautioning him about using cocaine, he also lets us hear the cocaine pipe itself talking. Two opposing sides are battling for Pryor's psyche, and the cocaine pipe—crafty, sneaky, seductive—wins. Mostly though this accident routine is not funny. Yet it lives on in the memory, as does this very uneven film itself. As a documentary within a "live" performance, this is an absorbing viewing experience: a look at a great American artist reaching out and trying to give new shape and vision to his experiences.

Right On (1970)

D. Herbert Danska. S. Felipe Luciano, Gylan Kain, and David Nelson. P. Woodie King. R. Leacock-Pennebaker.

Street poetry, street theatre, street drama were very much a part of the life (usually the campus life) of the politically motivated and restless young of the late 1960s/early 1970s. For anyone curious about this aspect of our past cultural history, *Right On* may provide some insights. The Original Last Poets (Felipe Luciano, Gylan Kain, and David Nelson) recite their "guerilla poetry" on a New York rooftop. The whole enterprise might look dated, like a series of narcissistic poses by a trio of highly skilled, charismatic young rhetoricians. But they capture the flavor, the spirit, also the high-minded (perhaps self-righteous, too) conviction of the young of that time, determined to change the order of things.

An intense, dramatic dream of the past.

Riot (1969)

D. Buzz Kulik. S. James Poe; based on the novel by Frank Elli. P. William Castle. R. Paramount. Cast includes: Bill Walker; Mike Kellen; and actual warden Frank A. Eyman as the testy warden.

Inmates overtake the Big House, breaking out of their cell blocks and holding guards hostage. A tunnel is secretly being dug under the prison wall for a great escape. Meanwhile riot ringleaders (Jim Brown, Gene Hackman, and Ben Carruthers) try keeping the lid on the rebellious cons but to no avail. Throats are slit. Gunshots rip through chests. A kangaroo court is set up to dispose of prison informers. And on a cell block called Queens Row, homosexual prisoners in drag give a party. Even the mighty macho Brown is approached by a white prisoner who begs to spend the night with him. As Brown's character remains aloof and implausibly untouched, the prisoner's passion merely grows. Brown's low-keyed, understated sadism obviously turns the guy on. The old-fashioned grade-B prison movie will never be the same.

The film closes with order restored, of course. But one character does manage to escape: Jim Brown, the silent black man of action. In terms of movie mythology, this escape is a new development.

Otherwise *Riot* is cheap, gratuitously violent, and undeveloped. "Hot item for action situations," wrote *Variety*.

The River Niger (1976)

D. Krishna Shah. S. playwright Joseph A. Walker. Soundtrack by the rock group War.

Initially, *The River Niger* seemed quite promising. Based on Joseph A. Walker's Tony-Award-winning play, it was, like *A Raisin in the Sun*, a black family drama, taut, tense, and often melodramatically effective. The film version could also boast a stellar cast: Cicely Tyson, Lou Gossett, James Earl Jones, Glynn Turman, Jonelle Allen, and Roger E. Mosley. But the results were dismal: technically poor, stagey and static without dramatic resonance or a sense of direction. It wanders about so much that we can't identify with its characters or have much empathy for them either.

New York Post critic Frank Rich said the film was flooded with incompetence. "Krishna Shah, the East Indian director responsible for the film, has put together an almost completely oblique collage of unfocused family anecdotes, misplaced action shots, unmotivated comings and goings, and gimmicky freeze frames." Rich added: "It's just too bad because *The River Niger*'s inevitable box-office demise is bound to have a chilling effect on future Hollywood projects that share its worthwhile ambitions." Rich was right on all counts.

Rocky III (1982)

D. Sylvester Stallone. S. Sylvester Stallone. P. Irwin Winkler and Robert Chartoff. R. UA. Cast includes: Burgess Meredith; Talia Shire; and Tony Burton.

Once again the Italian Stallion—that noble, goody-two-shoes working class hero Rocky—slugs it out with a black boxer in order to win the championship title. None of the three *Rocky* movies would have worked

Sylvester Stallone is forced to contend with a figure that has traditionally loomed large in the white American psyche—the nightmarish black buck—as played by a menacing Mr. T. in Rocky III.

had fighter Rocky Balboa simply battled another white boxer. Instead what adds tension and makes the stakes even higher is the color conflict, which, of course, feeds on a segment of the audience's fundamental (albeit sometimes unconscious) racism. The same thing has happened obviously in actual boxing history, from the days of Jack Johnson vs. Jim Brady to Larry Holmes vs. Gerry Cooney. The great difference, however, was that by the 1980s, most big-name boxers were all black, fighting it out with one another. Perhaps because there was no true Great White Hope offscreen, Hollywood delighted in giving audiences a fantasy one on screen. Once Rocky ran out of black opponents, he had to tackle a rotten "foreign" one in *Rocky IV* to keep the tension going.

Here director Stallone pulls out all stops. Rocky's opponent, Clubber Lang (played by newcomer Mr. T.), is such an all-out monstrosity, a nightmarish, cartoon version of the legendary troublesome, ornery Nigger—a snarling, harping, foul-mouthed, surly, and barely literate gorilla figure—that audiences (black as well as white) seem to have no choice but to cheer Rocky on. Mr. T.'s Clubber is a subhuman varmint that everyone wants wiped out. *Rocky III* works (terrifyingly so) on this primitive level: the idea is to get rid of this *baad nigger*.

But something more subtle also transpires in this film. Previously, in *Rocky I* and *II*, Carl Weathers, as boxer Apollo Creed, had invested his character with such a shrewd intelligence and confidence that audiences could not help liking him—and respecting him, too. Thus here, as Rocky battles the black buck Clubber, Apollo becomes Rocky's trainer, and although the script confronts and then runs away from the issue, the real story buried here is of Rocky's and Apollo's deep affection for one another. No doubt critic Leslie Fiedler would have had a field day analyzing this relationship for Rocky and Apollo in training (particularly while running on the beach or exercise-dancing in the ring) are a bit like Huck and Nigger Jim on the raft: two perennial boys caught up in one another without necessarily knowing why. The undercurrents give this movie a perverse kick, and no doubt future audiences will howl over certain Rocky/Apollo sequences. Eventually, Rocky wins his bout once he's spiritualized by Apollo: he's made to train at a black gym, surrounded by black fighters, whose offbeat, street-corner-like work-outs endow Rocky with a new rhythm and a new outlook. In one respect, Apollo Creed, the man so perfectly in control of himself in the previous films, has become Rocky's most faithful servant. Apollo gives Rocky heart *and* some *soul*.

Actually, *Rocky III*'s a frenzied, manipulative melodrama that's badly cooked up and sometimes insidiously insulting. (Mr. T.'s performance, indeed his persona, is appalling.) But Weathers, in spite of the implications of his role, still delivers a performance of weight and credibility, of thought and authority.

Rufus Jones For President (1933)

D. Roy Mack. *R.* Warner Bros./Vitaphone.

A short (16 minutes) fantasy/satire on politics, spotlighting two now-legendary performers much earlier in their long careers: Ethel Waters and Sammy Davis, Jr. Around the age of six, pint-sized Davis already had the same face he was to have as an adult, looking like a well-scrubbed, well-rested, cute 50-year-old man with a little boy's body. Singing, dancing, clowning, he is fresh, inventive, clever, a real trouper and charmer, possibly giving his most likable performance. Slim and still a bit slinky, Waters looks far different here than from the huge, earth-mother figure she was to popularize in *Pinky* and *The Member of the Wedding*. She has a chance to sing her big hit "Am I Blue." She also sang that song, along with her tough, chip-on-the-shoulder "Birmingham Bertha," in the 1929 film *On with the Show*, in which, however, she had to wear a headrag and do the backwoods black woman bit. Here though, dressed in a long white gown, she's statuesque with hints of glamor and that old-time Broadway razzmatazz. In one sequence, Waters (now back in her rags and tatters) takes little Sammy on her lap and rocks him to sleep. It's a delirious, sentimentally charged piece of nostalgia, movie heaven for aficionados. It should be noted though that much of the film is *rigidly* stereotyped and offensive.

Sanders of the River (1935)

D. Zoltań Korda. *S.* Jeffrey Dell, Lajos Biro, and Edgar Wallace; based on a novel by Edgar Wallace. *P.* Alexander Korda. *R.* UA. Cast includes: Nina Mae McKinney, looking like a Hollywood star on tour, playing an African princess.

In *The Whole World in his Hands*, a book about her grandfather Paul Robeson, Susan Robeson writes that Robeson accepted the role in *Sanders of the River* because he felt

> if he could portray an African leader with cultural integrity and accuracy he would be making a contribution in helping people—especially black people—to understand the roots of African culture. . . . *Sanders of the River* became a turning point in my grandfather's life . . . and a decision he came to regret deeply.

Seeing *Sanders of the River* today, one can well understand Robeson's regrets, for the picture is a shocking homage to British colonial rule. It centers on Sanders, a British territorial commissioner in Africa, a stalwart, decent chap who keeps the hot-headed warring African chieftains in line. Of course, they are a primitive bunch in need of white control and dominance. During a rebellion who should help Sanders restore order to the dark continent but a loyal African chief (a former convict, no less) named Basambo (Robeson)—the name is almost as disturbing as some of the character's antics. Bosambo, of course, is the colonized, "civilized" black man, on whom the Empire can count.

Now almost laughable, the film remains nonetheless upsetting, in some ways more so than a film like *The Birth of a Nation*, perhaps because the major black characters in the Griffith epic are played by whites in blackface and we tend not to think of them as black but as daffy racist pop creations. Here, however, we find the great Robeson, not playing an African leader but a British puppet. And it's neither easy nor pleasant to watch. He does manage, however, to bring some stature and presence to an otherwise nightmarish stereotype. It is impossible not to like Paul Robeson, the man.

Interspersed is real documentary footage of various religious and war dances, and we are given glimpses (albeit distorted) of African village life. According to Susan Robeson, director Korda sent a 15-man crew into remote areas of Africa where they travelled more than 15,000 miles in four months and shot traditional African ceremonies and gatherings.

Robeson himself was outraged by the film. He felt the movie's editor had changed the whole direction of the picture, cutting out key scenes. It's been said Robeson, to prevent distribution of *Sanders of the River*, tried, unsuccessfully, to buy all rights and prints.

Satchmo the Great (1957)

D. Aram Avakian. Narration by Edward R. Murrow. *P.* Edward R. Murrow/Fred W. Friendly. *R.* UA.

In his early Hollywood films—*Pennies From Heaven* (1936), *Artists and Models* (1937), and *Dr. Rhythm* (1938)—the great Louis Armstrong often had had to tom and coon it up, performing stereotyped comic shenanigans before he had a chance to play his horn. For some black audiences, it was hard to watch him, and many Americans lost sight of his rich talent and skill. Almost twenty years later, Armstrong was the focal point of the documentary *Satchmo the Great*, which sought to set the record straight: on Armstrong, the man, the humanitarian, and the internationally famous artist of the highest stature. An Edward R. Murrow and Fred Friendly production, *Satchmo the Great* grew out of an earlier CBS "See It Now" broadcast, which was expanded from its original half hour to sixty-three minutes. Murrow narrated this documentary, which covered Armstrong on a European tour and was highlighted by his trip to the Gold Coast in Africa. The film ended with his triumphant appearance with Leonard Bernstein and The New York Philharmonic at Lewisohn Stadium. Although far from being a race movie, it had a similar intent: to give an audience an alternative view of a certain aspect of American life and culture.

Save the Children (1973)

D. Stan Lathan. *S.* Matt Robinson. *P.* Matt Robinson, *Ex. P.* Clarence Avant. *R.* Paramount. Cast includes: the Reverend Jesse Jackson; Sammy Davis, Jr.; Brenda Lee Eager; The Chi-Lites.

An uneven concert film featuring some legendary performers: The Jackson Five, Marvin Gaye, Nancy Wilson, Jerry Butler, Cannonball Adderly, The Staple Singers, The Temptations, the Reverend James Cleveland, Gladys Knight and The Pips, Curtis Mayfield, Isaac Hayes, Wilson Pickett, Roberta Flack, and finally, Zulema, who is a dazzling standout, a real surprise star among so many other stars. The occasion: the 1972 Operation PUSH exposition in Chicago.

Interspersed among the entertainment segments is documentary footage of the period. Some of the Vietnam sequences still shock and pain the viewer and give the film a certain bite. Some might feel the director exploits such footage for a cheapshot effect. But that's debatable. What gives the film its pull and thrust, though, is the vitality of youth and enthusiasm, in this case being that of director Lathan (then about 28 years old) and scriptwriter Matt Robinson. Both were black artists finally getting a chance to work within the Hollywood system, and it must have been rather exhilarating for them. Each also had the hopped-up energy of the 1960s inside him, believing that a black film could be a *statement* and a commercial success, too. Robinson's script is sometimes hokey and corny. And Lathan's directorial hand is not always steady. But, frankly, *Save the Children* is a *felt* piece of commercial work, and today it works in part as a period piece, in part as a record of an event, and in part as entertainment. The sum may not live up to the parts. But I don't think anyone minds.

Say Amen, Somebody (1983)

D. George T. Nierenberg. *P.* George T. Nierenberg and Karen Kierenberg. *R.* UA Classics. Cast includes Sallie Martin (in her 80s, she's still a no-nonsense, haughty diva); the twin O'Neal Brothers; Delois Barrett Campbell; Billie Barrett Greenbey; Rhodessa Barrett Porter; Billie Smith; and Zella Jackson Price.

A spirited, unexpectedly rousing documentary about black pioneers of gospel music, headlined by 83-year-old composer Thomas A. Dorsey (who first worked with blues singer Ma Rainey in the 1920s, then began the amazing groundwork for gospel music in America during the Depression) and singer Willie Mae Ford Smith (an uncannily skilled and gifted performer who at age 78 still has great reserves of wit and vigor).

A cast of other fascinating figures turns up (the most interesting are the women) as the movie shows us the performers in action at churches or conferences. We also see some of the women in private life, as they struggle to balance their careers and home lives, often having to contend with families and husbands who do not fully understand why these women are not content simply to sit home and tend to household chores. The women themselves explain that they are charged up with doing the work of the Lord!

Frankly, there is not enough gospel music in the latter part of the film, and one longs to see more of the Barrett Sisters, lead by a true powerhouse. Then, too, it doesn't show us the other side of gospel when the performers can be "overcome" by the abandonment and release the music can inspire. (Many middle-class black churches still shy away from too much of this music perhaps for that reason.)

Still it's an absorbing film, one ironically that shows women far more independent and liberated than either they or anyone else might expect.

Scar of Shame (c. 1927)

D. Frank Peregini. S. David Stackman. P. Sherman Dudley. R. The Colored Players Film Corporation of Philadelphia. Cast includes: Harry Henderson; Norman John Stone; Ann Kennedy; William E. Pettus; Pearl MacCormick; Lawrence Chenault.

Produced outside Hollywood by The Colored Players Film Corporation of Philadelphia, this silent film about the relationship between a black concert pianist and the poor, lower-class young black woman he marries is quite possibly the best independent black film of the silent era. At first the hero is so prim and proper that audiences frequently laugh at him—and also at some of the obvious plot machinations. The film strikes us as having sprung right out of the lap of Victorian melodrama (it did) with a stock set of villains and heroes. But here an old formula acquires new meaning because of its black cast and situation. Gradually, one becomes absorbed (almost entranced) in heroine Lucia Lynn Moses's dreamily corny melancholia and in the film's revelations of social/class distinctions and divisions that existed within the black community. Because the young woman lacks her husband's "breeding," the movie lets us know she can never be a fit mate for him. Ashamed of his wife, the young man even keeps her hidden from his socially prominent mother. Clearly, he's a black man who has sacrificed passion in the name of his own convoluted notions of social progress/success. Inadvertently, the film also touches on black America's color caste system. As was the case with many other race movies, the leads are all light-skinned; the heavies (the girl's father and his racketeer friend) are dark and "uncouth." Is the girl a victim of her "dark" biological background? Although the film does not come right out with such a statement, it is certainly suggested.

Because *Scar of Shame* was filmed with some sensitivity, determined to present its protagonists with sympathy and dignity, too, one might automatically assume it was put together by black filmmakers. But both its director and writer were white.

Melodramatic and manipulative but also oddly touching and surprisingly effective.

Scream, Blacula, Scream (1973)

D. Bo Kelljan. S. Joan Torres, Raymond Koenig, and Maurice Jules. P. Joseph T. Naar. R. AIP. Cast includes: Pam Grier; Don Mitchell; Michael Conrad; Craig Nelson; Lynne Moody; Bernie Hamilton; Barbara Rhoades; Jane Michelle; and Richard Lawson (who later turned up in another horror film, *Poltergeist*, and as one of Diahanne Carroll's suitors on "Dynasty").

This sequel to the successful *Blacula* (1972) should instead be called *Scream, Audience, Scream*—and not in terror but boredom.

That African Prince of Darkness is back on modern city streets, his eyes sad, his voice mournful, and his body thirsting for you-know-what. But there's no hope for Blacula or us here for this movie is, dare we say it, not only anemic but often downright bloodless, too.

Sergeant Rutledge (1960)

D. John Ford. *S.* James Warner Bellah and Willis Goldbeck. *P.* John Ford, Willis Goldbeck, and Patrick Ford. *R.* Warner Bros. Cast includes: Juano Hernandez and Constance Towers.

Whenever John Ford's legions of admirers defend the master against cries of racism, they usually point with pride to *Sergeant Rutledge,* a study of racial prejudice during the post-Civil War period.

A Negro trooper (Woody Strode) is falsely accused of double murder—and of raping a white woman. Told in flashbacks, the film slowly unravels the mystery, revealing the true murderer and, along the way, establishing the trooper's stoic nobility.

The fact that director Ford tackled this subject is, I suppose, admirable. Contemporary audiences are, of course, enraged by his earlier depiction of American Indians and by his treatment of Stepin Fetchit's "lovable" lazy coon characters in such films as *Judge Priest* and *Steamboat Round the Bend* (1935). But *Sergeant Rutledge,* laudable as its intentions may be, is stilted and stillborn, a somber plodding tale that tries too hard to be earnest and stresses the idea of racial tolerance without always *feeling* it.

What's impressive, however, is Woody Strode. "*Sergeant Rutledge* may not add up to Mr. Ford's finest hour," wrote *The New York Times,* "but it certainly is Mr. Strode's." At times Strode seems wooden and far too controlled. But if ever the idea of *presence* meant anything in a movie, this is it: you can't get the image of this monumentally dignified and poised man out of your head. A great cinematic icon.

Shaft (1971)

D. Gordon Parks, Sr. *S.* John D. F. Black; based on the novel by Ernest Tidyman. *P.* Joel Freeman; a Sterling Silliphant/Roger Lewis Production. *R.* MGM. Cast includes: Gwen Mitchell; Christopher St. John; Drew Bundini Brown; Arnold Johnson; and Buddy Butler.

When his daughter (Sherry Brewer) is kidnapped by the mob, a Harlem underworld boss (Moses Gunn) hires a black detective named John Shaft to find the girl. That's the basic plotline of this once immensely popular film, which is not much different from a conventional white detective story. But black audiences loved watching Richard Roundtree's exploits as Shaft: he handles the ladies with proper aplomb, rubs out the baddies with appropriate macho skill, and struts his wares in his leather coat with sheer confidence and glee, all to the bop and sway of Isaac Hayes' pulsating score. Here's a black man who knows who he is and is not about to take anything from anybody.

Parks' direction is neither surprising nor innovative and certainly lacks the pictorial lushness of his earlier film *The Learning Tree.* At times *Shaft* looks downright tacky. Yet it must be admitted that Parks' strong identification with Shaft as a slick, pretty, sexy dude gives the picture unexpected heat and zip; it's doubtful if any white director would have taken as much relish in the hero's derring-do.

Curiously enough, though, no doubt because Shaft is at heart a man-of-the-law-type hero, this film in later years has proven far more acceptable to the large white audience than such features as *Sweet Sweetback's Baadasssss Song* and *Super Fly* (neither of which has ever had a television network showing as did *Shaft*, both of which have true underground, outlaw heroes, free of traditional bourgeois values). Later *Shaft* was even turned into a routine television private eye series.

Added note: at the time of *Shaft*'s release, its studio, the great MGM, was in the midst of financial difficulties. MGM thought *Shaft* might make a little bit of money. Of course, it made a mint and helped keep MGM in business. Also: Isaac Hayes won an Oscar for his score, one of the most famous in movie history.

Shaft in Africa (1973)

D. John Guillerman. S. Stirling Silliphant; based on characters created by Ernest Tidyman. P. Roger Lewis. R. MGM. Cast includes: Frank Finlay; Spiros Focas; Thomas Baptiste; Neda Nrneric; and Debebe Eshetu.

In this glossy, colorful adventure tale, Shaft returned to the big screen for a third time—just before moving on to television land as the star of a short-lived series.

Here detective John Shaft (Richard Roundtree) finds himself infiltrating a neo-slave smuggling ring. Young men of the Ivory Coast are being carried off to France as cheap and illegal labor. Of course, hero Shaft smashes the slave ring and even ends up with a beautiful maiden, the lovely Vonetta McGee. Along the way, he also lets his audience know that "I'm not James Bond, simply Sam Spade."

A mildly diverting but often sluggish action film. The last in the *Shaft* series.

Shaft's Big Score (1972)

D. Gordon Parks, Sr. S. Ernest Tidyman. P. Roger Lewis and Ernest Tidyman. R. MGM, of a Stirling Silliphant/Roger Lewis Production. Cast includes: Drew Bundini Brown; Julius W. Harris; Moses Gunn; Rosalind Miles; Joe Santos; Kathy Imrie; and Joseph Mascolo.

The same team that had put together the box-office smash *Shaft* worked on this sequel: Parks, Sr. directed, Ernest Tidyman wrote the script, Urs Furrer was the director of photography, and Richard Roundtree was back as the star. The results the second time around were lackluster and disappointing.

The story: shortly after he stashes away a quarter of a million dollars in a coffin in Harlem, a man is blown to bits by a bomb, planted, of course, by the movie's villain. Afterward just about everyone's out to find the money, including detective John Shaft, who was not only a buddy of the dead man but is also a "gentleman friend" of the man's sister. Shaft hopes to use the money for child care in the ghetto. Consequently, we're to feel that the noble Shaft's heart (and that of the "socially conscious" moviemakers) is in the right place. What's not in place here, though, is a sense of fun or adventure, which many audiences had found in the first *Shaft* movie.

Still the *Shaft* power at the box-office proved strong enough for MGM to release one more film in the series, *Shaft in Africa*, which came a year later.

Sheba, Baby (1975)

D. William Girdler. S. William Girdler, from a story by Girdler. P. David Sheldon. R. AIP. Cast includes: D'Urville Martin and Austin Stoker.

Pam Grier's last picture on her AIP contract and the one that formally marked the end of her reign as the queen of the heap of B-movies. Here glamorized in typical Hollywood fashion, she's a private detective out to help her father, whose loan company is about to be taken over by the mob.

The problem with Grier's post-*Coffy/Foxy Brown* films is mainly that her characters have no rambuctious grit or energy. She's far too polite here and too middle class. The unimaginative filmmakers haven't been able to come up with a new conception of the Grier persona, one that could be more ladylike but still feisty. Grier's early movies didn't always know what to do with her humor and energy either, but those films were so crude and casual that Grier herself, freed of too much formal structure, came through as a strong personality and kept the pictures alive. Her confidence was amusing and kept us all on edge. But here she's as tentative as everyone else; obviously, she wanted to keep her career alive and realized an image change was crucial because of new audience tastes but wasn't sure in what direction to go.

She's Gotta Have It (1986)

D. Spike Lee. S. Spike Lee. (He also edited the film.) Music by: Bill Lee, the director's father. P. Sheldon J. Lee. R. Island Pictures; a Forty Acres and a Mule Filmworks Presentation.

Once Hollywood's black movie boom of the 1970s had ended, black audiences of the 1980s had little to look forward to from American movies other than an occasional "black" feature like *A Soldier's Story* or the controversial *The Color Purple*. Although there were black independent filmmakers working outside Hollywood, some complained that the independent films were not broad based enough to reach a large black audience in need of "mass" entertainment. In time, a gloom settled over black moviegoers. Would there not appear again a *personal* black filmmaker like an Oscar Micheaux or a Melvin Van Peebles who, despite whatever limitations or shortcomings, would touch base with the black audience, examining or exploring that audience's shared, collective attitudes and outlooks? Most were not very optimistic. Then just when least expected, there arrived *She's Gotta Have It*, the work of a 29-year-old black filmmaker named Spike Lee, who had shot his movie in Brooklyn in 12 days on a budget of $175,000 and soon discovered he had a hit on his hands. Suddenly, for many black movie-goers, the gloom lifted.

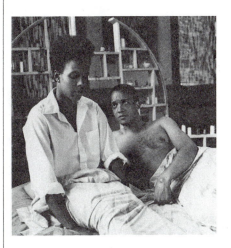

The black independent film goes mainstream: Spike Lee's She's Gotta Have It *with Tracy Camila Johns and Redmond Hicks.*

From the start of *She's Gotta Have It*, the minute the camera of black cinematographer Ernest Dickerson focused on the candy-faced heroine Nola Darling (played by Tracy Camila Johns)—in her bed, rising like a goddess from her slumber—audiences knew they were watching a different kind of black film, in which conventional formal narrative structure, plotline, and characterization have been thrown aside in favor of a loose-limbed, jivey, free-wheeling style. Nola and the other characters are introduced to the audience by titles, then they speak directly to the camera, telling us who they are, what they want, and the common dilemma they're all confronted with: namely, Who Is Nola Darling Going To Sleep with?

Here's the situation: Nola, a graphics artist living in a loft in Brooklyn, has three boyfriends. Hardly the traditional movie heroine (who in the past had to be true to one man or run the risk of being labelled nymph or whore and then be punished for her "looseness"), she's closer to the conventional movie playboy, the kind of fellow who has so much fun with so many lovers that he never wants to decide on any one. Nola likes all the men in her life. It's the guys, though, so entangled in convention and their own male egos, who feel she must make a choice.

The three men are a motley crew: there's Jamie (Tommy Redmond Hicks), a bit straitlaced, quite dependable, seemingly mature and understanding and also rather dull; there's the wildly narcissistic Greer Childs (John Canada Terrell), who focuses on Nola during those rare moments when he takes his eyes off himself; and there's the bespectacled, mildly dufus, insecure smartass Mars Blackmon, who, realizing he lacks Jamie's stability and Greer's good looks, tries wooing and winning Nola through laughter. He's an unabashed cutup who raps out the movie's most memorable line: "Please, baby, please, baby, please, baby, baby, baby, please." As played by director Spike Lee, Mars is the movie's liveliest and most unusual character. He's a spark plug who keeps the action moving.

Things head towards a climax at Nola's Thanksgiving dinner, attended by all three men, who eye each other suspiciously, crack jokes on one another, and hope Nola will come to her senses and realize that *he* is right for her and that the other two are just jerks. Of course, by the movie's end, Nola really hasn't changed. She'll never be a one-man woman. Nor would we ever want her to be.

Some lauded Nola Darling as a feminist heroine, which is probably way off the beam. As director Lee pointed out, the movie's really about men's attitudes about women. The men in *She's Gotta Have It* are really the ones who've got to have it: a woman cast in their birdbrained image of what woman's role should be. In comic competition with one another, they reveal their own vanities and vulnerabilities, their misconceptions and hangups. Who can forget the sight of Nola, poised on her bed for a feast of lovemaking, then forced to wait while her ardent lover, pretty boy Greer (so obsessed with self-love that he thinks he's about to do her a favor) slowly undresses and then meticulously folds each article of his clothing before slipping into bed with her? When Nola lies in bed with Mars, she must listen to his comic chatter and then watch him comically leap about in sneakers and jockey shorts. (What kind of guy is this anyway? He keeps his sneakers on when making love??) And when Jamie becomes enraged because she has not made a choice among the three, Nola finds herself sexually brutalized by him in the film's most disturbing sequence. It's disturbing because we are never quite sure of Nola's feelings about what looks like a rape to us. While Nola frequently explains her view of life and men to the audience, we take her at face value, without challenging any of her comments or pushing for further elaborations. Nola's something of a beautiful, intelligent blank backdrop for a study of the follies and foibles of the men.

Yet what pleased women who saw this film was that the director never treated free-as-a-breeze Nola as a whore. Instead he elevates the ordinary black woman to contemporary urban goddess. Actress Tracy Camila Johns looks and behaves like the pretty girls we've all seen in Brooklyn or Philadelphia or Washington, D.C., or wherever. She does not have the you-can-drop-dead-for-all-I-care gloss of beauties like Vonetta McGee or Brenda Sykes. Nor is she as charismatic or mysterious as we might want. But that works to the film's advantage, making it seem more natural and real, with a heroine the mass black audience could identify with because she does not seem weighed down by Hollywood's typical glamorization.

Of course, *She's Gotta Have It*'s basic appeal is that it's a battle of the sexes. And almost nothing pleases an audience more. Yet how often had black audiences had a chance to see a black couple in films intelligently, playfully picking at one another? Most importantly, though, what made the sexual clashes work for the black audience was that here were black characters relaxed about their blackness, not spouting hollow political rhetoric (as had been the case in some of Hollywood's black movies of the 1970s) nor strutting about jivily trying to *outblack* one another. Instead the audience saw ordinary people who accept their color and cultural bearings as matter-of-fact, providing us with a portrait of black characters in everyday personal roles. The performers in *She's Gotta Have It* worked well with one another, expressing romance or anger or joy, under the guidance of a director who, although he knows their weaknesses and foolishness as well as their strengths, does not treat them as aliens as a white director might have done. He endows them with affection and warmth.

It would be a mistake to overpraise this funny and fresh satire of sexual attitudes and role playing by proclaiming it a flawless end-all of black movies. *She's Gotta Have It* does suffer from a pointless color sequence as well as the fact that the characters, while charming, are not developed enough for us to believe we understand them. Nor are such subordinate characters as Nola's former roommate (played by Spike Lee's sister, Joie Lee) and also the lesbian Opal (Raye Dowell), who's after Nola, around long enough to add another texture to the film and perhaps give us more of a woman's point of view.

Following the release of *She's Gotta Have It*, it was announced that director Lee signed a three-movie deal with Island Pictures. Much like Melvin Van Peebles before him, Lee was well covered by the press, appeared on numerous talk shows to plug the picture, and emerged as something of a 1980s-style folk hero for black America. *She's Gotta Have It* became a part of a historical progression: it reaffirmed what Micheaux, Van Peebles, and independents of the 1970s felt confident of, that, if given the chance, offbeat, highly idiosyncratic, independent, *personal* work could reach a large black audience. The film was also successful with a segment of the white audience.

Lee's earlier film was the 1981 *Joe's Bed-Stay Barber Shop: We Cut Heads*. In 1987 he directed *School Daze*.

Show Boat (1936)

D. James Whale. *S.* Oscar Hammerstein II, from the Broadway musical he wrote in 1927 with Jerome Kern. Based on a novel by Edna Ferber. *P.* Carl Laemmle, Jr. *R.* Universal. Cast includes: Eddie "Rochester" Anderson; Clarence Muse; and Charles Winninger.

The second of the motion picture versions of the Jerome Kern/Edna Ferber classic. While the apparent focus is on the innocent heroine Magnolia Hawks (Irene Dunne) and her love for Gaylord Ravenal (Allan Jones), the mind and heart soon drift to a tale of miscegenation and the plight of the misty-eyed Julie, a definitive example, along with Fredi Washington's Peola in *Imitation of Life*, of Hollywood's doomed tragic mulatto figure. Of course, the movie is fraudulent in a very important way: Julie is played by white singer Helen Morgan. Having created the role in the original Ziegfeld stage version, Morgan admittedly comes up with a convincing performance. Clearly, she knows what to do with the songs "My Bill" and "Can't Help Loving That Man of Mine."

Still this film has its moments, many of which are provided by Hattie McDaniel as Queenie and Paul Robeson as Joe, cast as servants, yes, but working with such assurance that the movie serves them (and their talents) instead. When Robeson sings "Ol' Man River," he brings the melodrama alive and even manages to triumph over the images we see as we hear him. When Robeson sings the lyrics about *toting that barge* and *lifting that bale* and *spending another night in jail*, he's seen in the most stereotyped of montage sequences. But one forgets all that. The voice—the power, the resonance, and most importantly, the conviction in it—makes the sequence itself one of the most memorable in American movie musical history. And now the song is repeatedly associated with Robeson.

Added note: There have been three versions of *Show Boat*. The first, in 1929, starred Stepin Fetchit as Joe and Gertrude Howard as Queenie. The later 1951 version featured William Warfield as Joe and Ava Gardner (in the role Lena Horne longed to play) as the mulatto Julie. Dropped altogether were the stereotyped comic interludes of Joe and Queenie.

Silver Streak (1976)

D. Arthur Hiller. *S.* Colin Higgins. *P.* Thomas L. Miller and Edward K. Milkis; *Ex.P.*, Martin Ransohoff and Frank Yablans. *R.* 20th Century-Fox. Cast includes: Patrick McGoohan; Ned Beatty; Clifton James; Ray Walston; and Valerie Curtin. Also featured: Scatman Crothers, performing some comic coon antics that are a pure throwback to films of the 1930s.

A pedestrian comedy that was hugely successful (and remains so when now shown on television), due in great part to the work of Richard Pryor. Unfortunately, the first half of the movie concentrates on a murder mystery aboard the train the Silver Streak, which is traveling from Los Angeles to Chicago. Gene Wilder is the innocent witness of the crime. Jill Clayburg is his romantic interest. Pryor shows up midway in the film and then walks off with it. He and Wilder have a now classic scene together in a train station's men's room where Pryor teaches Wilder how to "act" *black*. Had any other actors done this sequence, it would have smacked of the worst type of blatant racism.

As the sequence now stands, it's funny because Pryor is so brilliantly in control of himself, the action, and the material. Then, too, Wilder is such a likable, pathetic sad sack that it's impossible to feel hostile towards him.

It's too bad the rest of the movie isn't as inventive. Worst though, despite Pryor's exciting work, is the manner in which the filmmakers try domesticating him, turning him into Wilder's true blue buddy, neutralizing the anarchic craziness and menace that are so much a part of Pryor's appeal *and* his comedic genius. This film, as well as *Blue Collar* and the Pryor/Wilder *Stir Crazy*, also promotes a view of interracial friendship as fraudulent as that of the Rochester/Jack Benny movies of the 1930s and 1940s. Without Pryor, this movie would have been a zero. With him, it has some dazzling bright spots.

The Skin Game (1971)

D. Paul Bogart. S. Pierre Marton (Peter Stone). P. Harry Keller. R. Warner Bros. Cast includes: Brenda Sykes; Susan Clark; Edward Asner; and Andrew Duggan.

James Garner is a pre-Civil War con man who comes up with an ingenious con game: he repeatedly sells his black partner (Louis Gossett) in one slave town after another to one simpleton slave owner after another. After each sale, Gossett quickly escapes, teaming up with Garner for yet another sale. No real edge or satiric bite. But the two leads work well together, making this a sometimes likable offbeat comedy.

Master and servant but with a twist: Louis Gossett, Jr., and James Garner in the con-man comedy Skin Game.

Slaughter (1972)

D. Jack Starrett. S. Mark Hanna and Don Williams. P. Monroe Sachson. R. AIP. Cast includes: Marlene Clark; Rip Torn; Stella Stevens; and Don Gordon.

As a former Green Beret whose parents have been killed, Jim Brown is determined to wreak vengeance on the syndicate folks who rubbed them out. Grisly, simpleheaded, action-packed, and often tacky. But audiences of the time (mainly black males) turned it into a commercial success, so much so that *Slaughter* spawned a sequel, *Slaughter's Big Rip-off* (a title that actually suits the first perfectly). Brown was at a high point in his gaudy career, and he struts about rather confidently. It's the confidence, rather than any acting skill, that gets him through. Aside from him, there's not much worth seeing here.

Slaughter's Big Rip-off (1973)

D. Gordon Douglas. S. Charles Johnson. P. Monroe Sachson. R. AIP. Cast includes: Brock Peters and Don Stroud.

Gaudy sequel to the gaudy original, both of which star that 1970s master of macho, Jim Brown. As in the first, Brown's a sepia Superman, again almost single-handedly taking on the mob. An avenging angel, out to get back at Whitey, Brown gives a performance (if it can be called that) which is unduly confident and self-congratulatory. Much action, little logic here.

There was no *Slaughter III*, and Brown's career was about to slip into decline after his heady heyday in Hollywood in the 1960s and early 1970s.

The Slaves (1974)

D. Herbert J. Biberman. S. Herbert J. Biberman, black novelist John O. Killens, and Alida Sherman. P. Philip Largner. R. Continental; a production of Theatre Guild Films in association with the Walter Reade Organization. Cast includes: Robert Kya-Hill; Shepperd Strudwick; Aldine King; Gale Sondergaard; Julius Harris; and veteran performer Eva Jessye.

Ponderous high times in the Old South. A pre-Civil War drama (and an undercover remake of *Uncle Tom's Cabin*) that focuses on a kind-hearted Christian slave (Ossie Davis), who is sold by his kind-hearted liberal Kentucky master to a Mississippi plantation owner (Stephen Boyd). Throughout Davis seems so uncomfortable with his character that it almost looks as if he's squirming up there on screen. But can we blame him? His character's Christian stoicism (actually his Christian masochism) is piled on so heavily that the audience loses connection with him almost altogether and starts gravitating towards the more enjoyable sadistic highjinks of the sexy evil young white massa. Dionne Warwicke turns in an implausible performance as the slave gal who fiddles away her time up dere in dat old big house with dis handsome white massa. Stock scenes and characters abound, whether it be the inhumane slave auctions or the elderly, kindly dumdum faithful servants who seem to relish the idea that they're, well, slaves!

One startling scene: Boyd recounts to his white friends the rich achievements of African history. It's one of the rare occasions in film history in which Africa's past is given its due. But, of course, when we realize that the once-mighty Africans are now enslaved on plantations by these white Americans, that history's power and people are negated.

Most emotional sequence: Barbara Ann Teer saying, "It ain't fair," as she bids farewell to screen husband Davis after he's been sold to the new plantation.

This was an early attempt to reach the then-new evolving black movie audience.

A Slender Thread (1965)

D. Sydney Pollack. *S.* Stirling Silliphant. Based on Shana Alexander's *Life* article "Decision to Die." *P.* Stephen Alexander. *R.* Paramount Pictures. Cast includes: Telly Savalas; Ingus Arthur; and Dabney Coleman.

A distressed white woman (Anne Bancroft), ready to end her life, phones a suicide crisis center. The medical student on the other end who uses all his powers of persuasion to learn her identity and thus to get a rescue team to her is the very noble Sidney Poitier. This marked the screen return of both Bancroft and Poitier since winning their Oscars respectively for *The Miracle Worker* and *Lilies of the Field*. Much to-do was made over this fact and another: there was no mention of Poitier's race here. True it *is* a colorless role he's saddled with. As several critics pointed out, Poitier indeed becomes the invisible man. Any threat whatsoever of his blackness (and this interracial casting) is wiped away as the movie studiously avoids dealing in even the most casual way with the character's racial identity.

A Soldier's Story (1984)

D. Norman Jewison. *S.* Charles Fuller; based on his Pulitzer Prize-winning play, *A Soldier's Play*. *P.* Norman Jewison. *R.* Columbia Pictures. Cast includes: Art Evans; Larry Riley (as the gentle guitar-plucking C.J.); and Patti LaBelle.

One of the 1980s' better black-oriented films: A Soldier's Story, a taut psychological murder mystery with (l.). Adolph Caesar and Denzel Washington.

A well-made, prize-winning play transformed into an enjoyably old-fashioned well-made movie. Also: one of the best black-oriented films of the 1980s.

The year is 1944. The place: A Louisiana army base where a black sergeant has been murdered. A mild-mannered, educated Northern Negro captain, assigned to solve the crime, arrives on the base—to the surprise of everyone, white and black. A colored man so highly ranked in the armed forces has never been seen in these here parts before. The reactions to the captain are amusing because they're so overdone.

Through flashbacks, the film soon emerges not only as a taut murder mystery but also a tidy study in race relations: between black and white and between black and black. As it turns out, the murdered black sergeant has been a riddle of contradictions: on the one hand, tough, critical, even cruel and contemptuous of his black platoon; on the other, proud and haughty, anxious for racial progress. He's torn in two, full of maddening self-hate, split, as the play says, "by the madness of race in America."

Although it lacks the disturbing, cryptic vision and the general menacing air of the stage production, the movie version nonetheless is clever and absorbing. Thanks to talented black writer Charles Fuller (here adapting his play for the screen), the film confronts issues and concerns (within the black community) that the mass audience otherwise might never be exposed to. The film's enlivened by the skilled ensemble acting. Sometimes, perhaps because here several actors are repeating roles they played on stage, the performances strike us as a bit stagey; the actors seem to have their parts down pat without much room for spontaneity or the sudden unexpected new insight. Still there is exciting work here.

In the type of Good Negro role Sidney Poitier played in the 1950s and 1960s, Howard Rollins's intelligence and contained intensity keep the action rolling. As the complex, symbolic Sgt. Waters, Adolph Caesar, although sometimes far too theatrical, snaps us all to attention whenever he appears. Surprisingly, though, Denzel Washington, as the quiet-fire, sensitive, more militant young soldier, gives such a strong and adroit performance that he almost claims the picture as his own.

An added note: the somewhat cheery ending, wherein we get some gentle buddy-buddy interplay between the white captain and the black captain, is unpardonable and third-rate, a cheap, hack attempt by the filmmakers to assuage white audience guilt feelings with the kind of fairytale white/black we're-gonna-make-it-somehow-by-sticking-to-gether-in-the-future sentimentality that was a staple of the problem pictures of the late 1940s and 1950s. It's one of the things that killed the problem pictures off. Also: if this reminds you of *In the Heat of the Night*, that may be because it has the same director and often the same point of view on relations between white and black.

Some Kind of Hero (1982)

D. Michael Pressman. *S.* James Kirkwood and Robert Boris. Based on a novel by James Kirkwood. *P.* Howard W. Koch. *R.* Paramount Pictures. Cast includes: Ray Sharkey (as Pryor's buddy in Vietnam) and Paul Benjamin. Sadly, the skilled Olivia Cole and the disarming Lynne Moody are wasted in nothing parts.

Richard Pryor, as a former POW in a Vietcong camp, returns home to Los Angeles, the city of sunshine and dreams, to discover he has a new

Richard Pryor as a Vietnam vet, with Margot Kidder, Herb Braha (l.), and Peter Jason, in Some Kind of Hero.

nightmarish war to wage: his wife and her new boyfriend have run through his savings; his mother has had a stroke and been placed in a nursing home; the army is withholding all his back pay because of a "confession" document he signed in Vietnam stating that the United States was conducting an illegal war there (he had signed the paper only in hopes of saving the life of a dying military buddy); and to make matters worse, Pryor's teeth are falling out. With few alternatives, Pryor turns first to friendship from a heart-of-gold prostitute (Margot Kidder) and then to a life of crime as a stickup man to bring in a few dollars.

Writing in *The New York Times*, Vincent Canby found *Some Kind of Hero* "very engaging . . . written, directed and acted with amiability. . . . Mr. Pryor . . . (has) material for his most complete, most honest characterization." One could only wish to agree. But in all truthfulness, the movie is a shambles. Clearly, it could have been a blistering statement on the experiences of many Vietnam vets, returning home from an unpopular war to find themselves disoriented and dismissed by the society they had fought for. Instead the movie's as disoriented as its hero and can come to grips with neither the complexity nor pathos of the leading character's situation. From the very start—a long, rambling passage set in Vietnam—the director fumbles about trying to find the right tone, unable to decide whether he wants a surreal touch or a heavy-handed, violent, realistic approach. The fumbling continues in the LA sections; it's part old-fashioned melodrama and part new-style loose and loony Pryor. But none of the material or various styles meshes together.

Like *Richard Pryor Live on Sunset Strip*, *Some Kind of Hero* was released not long after Pryor's accident in which he was severely burned. For Pryor fans at this time, he could do no wrong. The film was a hit. But like so many Pryor movies, it's a poor vehicle for a great style. "It's high time," wrote David Ansen in *Newsweek* "Pryor stopped redeeming badly made movies and surrounded himself with talents equal to his own."

Something of Value (1957)

D. Richard Brooks. S. Richard Brooks, based on the novel by Robert Ruark. P. Pandro S. Berman. R. MGM. Cast includes: Juano Hernandez; William Marshall; Wendy Hiller; Dana Wynter; Tommie Moore; and Juanita Moore.

In 1957, many critics found this a provocative film. It was the first Hollywood movie to deal "seriously" with the Mau Mau uprising in Kenya and with the whole question of colonialism in Africa. Sidney Poitier and Rock Hudson were starred as a black and white raised side by side in Africa. Once they reach manhood, the two go separate ways, Hudson becoming a member of the Establishment and Poitier soon joining the terrorizing Mau Mau movement. The politics—and the history—that gave rise to the Mau Maus is glossed over; this is simply a troupe of violent, plundering, murderous natives. Poitier, however, true to his noble Negro roots of the 1950s, is made repeatedly to question the movement, and at the film's climax, when confronted with his former boyhood friend Hudson, Poitier's character almost seems ready to sacrifice himself, no doubt in remorse for his previous dirty deeds. The once-rebellious Poitier character, of course, *must* die in the film. Generally, the movie seems to agree with a line of dialogue spoken by Hudson: "I want the same thing for us as he [Poitier] does. Only I think there's a different way of getting it." Of course, that different way is the same *old* way of white patronizing the "good" natives.

The simplified politics here may shock and irritate contemporary audiences. Compared to a later film such as *The Chant of Jimmie Blacksmith*, a scathing indictment of colonial powers in Australia with a plot line somewhat similar, *Something of Value* lacks force, conviction, and complexity. It's a prime example of Hollywood turning politics to melodrama and "entertainment."

What propels the movie forward though, what indeed gives it some resonance even today, is Poitier's galvanizing performance. He infuses his character with vigor, intelligence, and defiance. This was a very important role for him, and some critics feel it established him as a star. He won a citation for his work at the Venice Film Festival and was hailed by the American press. *Variety* wrote that he delivered "an outstanding portrayal. He carries the picture and gives it power and strength. . . . The performance has depth and great understanding . . . it is Poitier's film." *Newsweek* added: "If only to watch one startling performance, *Something of Value* is worth a visit. Sidney Poitier has turned into a full-fledged star." And Bosley Crowther added in *The New York Times*: "Sidney Poitier gives a stirring, strong performance as the emotion-torn black friend. It is his display of pounding passions and the frequent burst of shocking savagery that throw shafts of sharp illumination through this notable black-and-white film."

For newer audiences today who don't realize what an exciting actor Poitier was, this film, along with *The Defiant Ones* and *Blackboard Jungle*, shows him about to reach the height of his powers.

Song of Freedom (1936)

D. J. Elder Willis. S. Fenn Sherie and Ingram D'Abbes. R. Hammar-British Lion. Cast includes: Orlando Martins.

One of Paul Robeson's most likable movies (and performances), despite the neo-colonialist theme that pervades.

Robeson plays Zinga, a London dockhand who becomes a concert hall star, then uncovers his ancestral roots. Once he has learned he is a descendant of Queen Zinga, the ruler of a remote African island during the sixteenth century, and that he is now the heir to the throne of

Cazanga, he packs his bags and is off to Africa. There, he brings *culture* and *civilization* to a people ruled for centuries by *primitive* witch doctors.

Filmed in Great Britain (and, of course, influenced by the British notion of the white man's burden, with Robeson in this instance cast as an agent of sorts of the Empire), *Song of Freedom*'s political implications may be too much for some. So, too, may be the coon antics of Robert Adams as Robeson's comic servant. Then there is as well the rather arch domestic life of Robeson and wife Elizabeth Welch, who together are almost too wholesome and bourgeois to be true. Although made far from Hollywood, there is a sweetly enjoyable touch of Hollywood in Welch's glamorized, mildly phony presence. She had formerly been a singer on the New York stage and had introduced Cole Porter's "Love for Sale," and her sophisticated worldliness always shows up in her work.

But for the most part, if you keep your wits about you, *Song of Freedom* is diverting, nicely paced, and rather amusing. Robeson, having had it for the time being with the American movie companies, seems at ease and is a real joy to watch and a better *screen* actor here than in the highly touted *Emperor Jones*. When he sings, he's all the more striking. "His arresting personality, the dignity of his demeanor, and the moving richness of his voice are easily 75% of the production," wrote *Variety*, which also said of the film itself: "Should enjoy popularity in most spots, and sure to do well in popular priced houses." That last statement may not seem of much importance today. But *Song of Freedom* was, unlike a Hollywood production, a movie starring a black man—and thus a movie that could only recoup its investment if audiences paid to see this black star. As it turned out, the film was not a hit in the States. But *Song of Freedom* still pops up at film festivals and occasionally on television.

Song of the South (1946)

> *D.* Harve Foster (live action sequences). Wilfred Jackson (animated sequences). *S.* Dalton Reymond, Morton Grant, and Maurice Rapf. *Associate P.* Perce Pearce. *R.* RKO release of a Walt Disney Production. Cast includes: Luana Patton; Lucille Watson; and the great voices in animation sequences of black actors Johnny Lee and Nicodemus Stewart.

Children seem to enjoy this Disney story of a lonely Southern boy, Johnny (Bobby Driscoll), who, with his parents separated, finds joy and magic in the stories of a gentle old Negro named Uncle Remus (played by James Baskett). What makes the movie special for kids (and adults) is the Disney studio's adroit combination of live action drama mixed with cartoon sequences. Uncle Remus wizzes past our eyes with animated butterflies and bluebirds by his side. It's hard not to be impressed by the technical expertise and professionalism that have gone into this movie.

But the theme itself is old hat. The picture is set on an Atlanta plantation. The black servants, dressed in their gingham and head scarves, are a friendly, co-operative bunch, quietly going about their chores without any signs of unrest or discontent. When the young master has been injured, the servants stoically gather in front of the big house, hoping for the po' chile's recovery. At times, some of this may remind audiences of the 1929 *Hearts in Dixie*. Here again is a pastoral view of the Old South—and this was released in 1946, mind you, after the Second World War had ended.

Uncle Remus himself finds his greatest pleasure in entertaining little Johnny. Life for him is just zip-a-dee-do-dah. Baskett plays Remus as jolly and kindly, a sugary paragon of contentment, domesticity, and servility. Two puzzling sequences stand out. In the first, as Remus pays a visit to the plantation's local mammy, played by Hattie McDaniel (who, unfortunately, is too subdued here), while she prepares a meal, we suddenly wonder if these two are meant to be courting one another. But Remus is so joyously desexed that we immediately dismiss such an idea as preposterous. Clearly, Hattie McDaniel could not waste her time on the likes of him. The second sequence occurs when Remus, instructed by little Johnny's mother (Ruth Warrick) not to tell the boy stories any more, is so disheartened that he packs his duds and sets out to leave the plantation. Where is *he* going? we wonder. Could slaves just pick up and come and go as they pleased? It's then that we realize the period of this movie (whether pre- or post-Civil War) has never been clearly specified. But the sentiments are based on a very tired Old South mythology.

Interestingly, the one virtue of the Joel Chandler Harris tales, on which the movie was based, was that, although they distorted the black plantation experience, at least they revealed the moral insights of Uncle Remus. His gift had been to transliterate the social framework of his own community into animal adventures. In the movie the animated Br'er Rabbit and Br'er Fox are a delight as examples of clever animation. But their escapades are a showcase for the Disney specialty rather than any comment on the old Negro character's philosophical outlook.

Although commercially successful, *Song of the South* was criticized by both black and white reviewers. The Manhattan Council of the National Negro Congress called on the people of Harlem to "run the picture out of the area," then out of New York State. The NAACP joined the criticism, insisting that the movie gave "an impression of an idyllic master/slave relationship which is a distortion of the fact."

Song of the South also signaled the demise of the Negro as fanciful entertainer or comic servant until, that is, the 1970s when similar figures turned up on television's new black sitcoms. Entangled in the script, the actors here are unable to come up with the diversions and perversities that had distinguished the servant figures in Hollywood films of the 1930s.

Yet, perhaps not unsurprisingly, *Song of the South* lived on to be revived periodically by the Disney Studios into the 1980s.

The Soul of Nigger Charley (1973)

D. Larry G. Spangler. S. Harold Stone. P. Larry G. Spangler. R. Paramount Pictures. Cast includes: Denise Nicholas (as the love interest); young actor Kirk Calloway (who later gave a convincingly attractive performance as Marsha Mason's mulatto son in *Cinderella Liberty*); and D'Urville Martin (again cast as Williamson's trusty sidekick).

A sequel to *The Legend of Nigger Charley*, which also starred former football player Fred Williamson in the title role. Here Williamson's Nigger Charley is out to free a group of slaves being held in a Mexican village by former Confederate soldiers. The Confederates don't seem to want to accept the fact that they've lost the war and that slavery has been abolished. The filmmakers don't seem to want to accept the fact that you need a clear head and some mother wit to tell this kind of story. "Essentially," wrote A.H. Weiler in *The New York Times*, "gunfire, not characterization, is the order of the day."

Watch out, the baadd buck is back! Fred Williamson (r.) with D'Urville Martin in The Soul of Nigger Charley.

Soul to Soul (1971)

D. Denis Sanders. P. Richard Bock and Tom Mosk. R. Cinerama. Cast includes: Roberta Flack; Les McCann; Santana; Wilson Pickett; and The Voices of East Harlem.

A return-to-the-motherland kind of documentary, focusing on an all-night 15-hour soul concert performed in Ghana during a weeklong celebration of that nation's independence. Aside from the concert footage, there are sequences heralding black America's discovery of its African connectives/roots: thus we see Americans and Africans talking together as well as Roberta Flack on a tour to a former slave fort.

The performance footage is sometimes rousing but technically far from what it should be. The lighting and editing are frequently poor, to say the least. The movie does convey a late 1960s atmosphere though, the excitement of black America taking a newfound pride in itself and its past. There is also added interest here today: it features Tina Turner—with husband Ike—in the days before their split and her eventual rise to superstardom.

Sounder (1972)

D. Martin Ritt. S. black writer Lonne Elder III, based on a novel by the white writer William H. Armstrong. P. Robert Radnitz. R. 20th Century-Fox. Cast includes: Taj Mahal; Eric Hooks; and Carmen Matthews.

Earlier in his career with *Edge of the City, Paris Blues,* and *The Great White Hope,* director Martin Ritt had worked with black themes, struggling very earnestly to come to grips with his black characters' anxieties and hopes—but never successfully getting to their insides or revealing to us the complexities and intricacies that made them tick. Nor had Ritt fully succeeded in showing us these characters in relation to the white culture surrounding them. There was always something too pat and rigged about those earlier films. With *Sounder,* though, Martin Ritt finally pulled together all the disparate elements and impressions that had previously eluded him. *Sounder* is a triumph of character and action: moving, lyrical, taut, intelligent, and perceptive with performances in which every line rings true and clear.

At heart, it is a black family drama, focusing on a sharecropper family in Louisiana in the 1930s. When the father (Paul Winfield) is arrested for having stolen food to feed his children, he is imprisoned. Behind bars, he struggles to hold his family together—and to hold himself together as well.

The film also follows the experiences of the oldest son, played sensitively by Kevin Hooks, who, through the help of a concerned black schoolteacher (Janet MacLachlan), is exposed to a world outside his small community and is soon on the road to maturity.

And at the same time, the film concentrates on Rebecca (Cicely Tyson), the wife and mother, who must keep things going during her husband's absence, contending also with a hostile white world that demands her silence about much that she sees and experiences. Cicely Tyson's eyes and demeanor, however, tell us at every turn what she's thinking, feeling. There is a great sequence in a local store where the white owner hounds Tyson about paying her bill. When the camera moves in for a closeup, we see that Tyson fights to keep her emotions in check, determined not to explode. We understand her rage but we

Sounder, one of Hollywood's rare, sensitive black family dramas, with Cicely Tyson and Kevin Hooks.

also sense her keen awareness that should she have an outburst, she runs the risk of losing everything and being stomped down. For one of the first times in the history of American cinema, we experience the various tensions American blacks were forced to live with and the necessity, when around whites, of always playing a role. Yet *Sounder* shows us (as did "Roots" later) that, away from the white power structure, the black characters are acutely conscious of who they are and of the roles they make themselves play.

Heroic and majestic, Tyson has a true *tour de force* sequence when her husband returns home from prison. Looking out, seeing a figure in the distance, dismissing it at first, then curiously looking on again, revealing to us then her moment of recognition, she calls out and runs towards him. It is a memorable, great moment in American movies.

It is now assumed that *Sounder* was universally praised by the critics upon its release. Although the film generally was well received, some of the top critical organs in the country found it lacking. *The New York Post's* critic wrote: "In some curious way . . . some of the stiffness that used to be found in interracial movies in the South has crept back. . . . There's something tentative about this plea for justice." And in *The New York Times*, Roger Greenspan added: "It would be comfortable to praise *Sounder* . . . [but it] lacks the excitement that may have come from plumbing greater depths and discerning a few tougher, less accessible insights. . . . *Sounder* was produced by Robert Radnitz, who specializes in children's films, and directed by Martin Ritt . . . who poses something of a problem. An earnest, conscientious director, he seems to strive for classical plainness, but to succeed only in being ordinary." Later, also in *The New York Times*, Vincent Canby found it to be "much less disturbing than soothing," also "sweet and inoffensive," and that it "patronizes the 'littleness' of its characters."

It has to be admitted that *Sounder*'s portrait of black Americans harked back to the past. The characters are safely distanced in the Depression and they are without the outright rebelliousness and rage of the then contemporary urban figures of such films as *Shaft* and *Sweet Sweetback's Baadasssss Song*. Often they seem passive and submissive. They are both—but only within the bounds of survival. *Sounder*'s protagonists do not lie to themselves or their viewers. They don't parade a chic *rhetorical* radicalism. Instead they live by and cope with everyday realities, determined to find in life whatever pleasures and triumphs are available.

The facts of the story in *Sounder* are perhaps open to question but that is almost beside the point when compared to the emotional statements on screen.

Sounder went on to win Academy Awards and its lead performers, Tyson and Winfield, were nominated for Oscars as Best Actress and Best Actor of 1972. The black audience, oblivious to the critics, also discovered *Sounder* on its own and loved it. So, too, did white audiences.

The sequel to this film, *Sounder, Part II*, was released in 1976, but is virtually forgotten.

Sparkle (1976)

D. Sam O'Steen. Cinematography by Bruce Surtees. Music by Curtis Mayfield. *S.* Joel Schumacher; from a story by Schumacher and Howard Rosenman. *P.* Howard Rosenman. Executive producers: Beryl Vertue and Peter Brown. *R.* Warner Bros. release of a Robert Stigwood Organization production. Cast includes: Beatrice Winde and Paul Lambert.

One of black America's first cult films.

The movie follows the rise and fall of three Harlem sisters who, guided by two boyfriends, form a singing group in the late 1950s. Immediately, visions of The Supremes spring to mind, and *Sparkle* might have been more effective had it kept the comparison going. But before *Sparkle*'s group gets its feet off the ground, the lead singer (the oldest sister played by Lonette McKee) gets hooked not only on a sadistic stinker (Tony King) but drugs as well. She aims not so much for the top as for rock bottom. That's where she ends up before the movie is even half over, and this is one of the picture's serious flaws. On the one hand, *Sparkle* sets out to reveal the way in which the entertainment industry can eat up, ravage, then discard a talented young beauty. It wants to tell us the story of someone like Florence Ballard, an original member of The Supremes who left the group, later ended up on welfare, then died at the age of 32. Yet, on the other hand, *Sparkle* veers in a far-too-romantic direction. The sister is done in not by the pressures of show business but by her own romantic folly. Never is there any explanation for McKee's desperate, self-destructive attachment to Tony King. Nor does the movie explain why she, the hippest of the sisters, is, in actuality, the weakest. At the same time, *Sparkle* does not elaborate either on another sister who spouts 1960s rhetoric in a distinctly 1950s milieu, then leaves home to discover, we assume, her own racial/cultural identity. This character sees most clearly the hidden fears and complexities of the group's life. But her tale is dropped before ever being developed.

Sparkle is weakest in its second half when the focus shifts to the youngest sister, Sparkle (Irene Cara), whose boyfriend Stix (Philip

FROM GHETTO TO SUPERSTARS

"Sister & The Sisters."

The brothers who built them up and brought them down.

Featuring the sensational music of
CURTIS MAYFIELD

SPARKLE · Starring PHILIP M. THOMAS · IRENE CARA · LONETTE McKEE · DWAN SMITH
MARY ALICE · DORIAN HAREWOOD And TONY KING as Satin
Produced by HOWARD ROSENMAN · Directed by SAM O'STEEN · Screenplay by JOEL SCHUMACHER
Story by JOEL SCHUMACHER and HOWARD ROSENMAN · Executive Producers BERYL VERTUE and PETER BROWN
Music by CURTIS MAYFIELD · TECHNICOLOR®

Music from the motion picture "Sparkle" sung by Aretha Franklin available on Atlantic Records and Tapes.

Thomas) is able, with money borrowed from a wealthy white man, to get the wheels of her career moving. Sparkle's record not only makes the charts but she soon appears at Carnegie Hall on a bill with Ray Charles, no less! Of course, no movie could give us the heroine's big night unless everything is literally at stake that evening. In this case, while Sparkle sings, Stix stands with a gun pointed at his head. The wealthy white man's henchmen demand that he let them "buy" part of Sparkle's contract. But, young and idealistic, Stix holds out—and eventually is released by the henchmen (who no doubt admire his spunk). And Stix then makes it back to Carnegie Hall in time to stand by the side of Sparkle's mother as his gal sings her way to glory.

Sparkle's preposterously unrealistic ending indicates the movie's steadfast refusal to consciously disturb its audience. Sparkle and Stix are the most naive characters, yet they are the ones who become successful. American audiences often still cherish their notions that innocence and virtue are always rewarded. There has to be that happy ending. And *that*, in effect, is what does disturb us. Why could they not have had Stix sell the contract, then show up at the concert hall, and smile at the singing Sparkle? We would have had a happy ending of sorts. But we would better understand just what kind of compromise and corruption success in this country often entails.

But *Sparkle* has much else going for it. The film moodily reverberates with its actors and the director's feel for them. Like *Cooley High*, *Sparkle* traces young black lives, capturing tensions, aspirations, and bizarre contradictions. But it pushes farther than *Cooley High* and has more scope and vision. If handled differently, it could have been genuinely epic.

The solid cast not only includes Irene Cara but also Dorian Harewood, Mary Alice, Dwan Smith, and Armelia McQueen (who later turned up in the Broadway show *Ain't Misbehavin'*). All these performers stand back, however, when Lonette McKee comes along. McKee teases, flirts, chews gum, shakes her ass, pouts, and gets haughty, consistently holding the screen. In closeups that were almost mythically endearing, she is a magnetic, compelling figure. Pauline Kael wrote of McKee and the film:

> [McKee] puts the dirty fun of sex into her songs, with the raw charge of a rebellious, nose-thumbing girl making her way. . . . The subject that's passed over—why the thug [Tony King] wants to possess and destroy [McKee's character], who so obviously has everything it takes to become a star, and why she's drawn to him—is a true modern subject, and not just for the rock world. Lonette McKee is the actress to drive this theme into one's consciousness because she has the sexual brazenness that screen stars such as Susan Hayward and Ava Gardner had in their youth. You look at the sheer taunting sexual avidity of these women and you think "What man would dare?" and the answer may be: only a man with the strength to meet the challenge or a man so threatened by it that he's got to wipe the floor with the girl. . . . Movies now seem to be almost begging for this theme to come out.

Sparkle, with its flaws and faults, remains nonetheless a fascinating movie. It was also a precursor to Broadway's big hit of the 1980s: *Dreamgirls*, also the tale of three black ghetto girls encountering heartache and tragedy on the bumpy road to stardom as singing stars.

Initially, *Sparkle* was a disappointment at the box office. Yet somehow word of mouth spread on it, the film survived and had become by the late 1970s and early 1980s a cult film for black high school kids around the country. Added note: Aretha Franklin recorded an album of songs (called *Sparkle*) from the film.

The Split (1968)

D. Gordon Flemyng. S. Robert Sabaroff; based on the novel *The Seventh* by Richard Starks. P. Irwin Winkler and Robert Chartoff. R. MGM. Cast also includes: Donald Sutherland; Jack Klugman; and Warren Oates.

An unformed and meandering melodrama about a bank heist at a football stadium, led by former real-life football player turned movie actor, Jim Brown. In a role originally slated for Lee Marvin, Brown had one of his first important leading parts. For an emerging black film audience, anxious for an aggressive black hero, Brown certainly seemed *tuff enough*, even though he's also rather dull.

Diahann Carroll appeared in a completely undeveloped supporting role, that of Brown's ex-wife. It really stretches credulity to think these two could ever have been married. She's far too sophisticated and ambitious for the likes of this jock. Carroll's character is killed off much too early, but considering the way *The Split* turns out (and also considering Carroll's performance—unfelt and stiff), she may have felt relieved to be out of it quickly.

"The Metro release," wrote *Variety*, "drowns in its own gratuitous violence, lacks any genuinely sympathetic characters, and cops out amateurishly at fade-out. Fast exploitation playoff in action situations should produce some good b.o. [box-office] response, mainly in urban areas."

Technically, *The Split* was not considered a black film because so many "name" white performers were featured, such as Ernest Borgnine, Julie Harris, and Gene Hackman. But a segment of the black audience supported the film nonetheless.

St. Louis Blues (1929)

D. Dudley Murphy. Musical arrangements by: W. C. Handy and J. Rosamond Johnson.

It runs only 17 minutes, is technically static, and not particularly well paced, but *St. Louis Blues* is the only film the legendary blues singer Bessie Smith ever appeared in, and for that reason alone, it has to be seen. Bessie's in love with a *mean papa* named Jimmy (played by Jimmy Mordecai). The classic black female blues performers like Bessie often enough sang of men who were rotten to the core, lowdown two-timers and no-accounts who couldn't be trusted. Jimmy takes up with a high-yaller gal (Isabel Washington), sending Bessie into a passionate tizzy. When the Empress of the Blues delivers her lovesick lines to him ("Jimmy, don't leave me. *Please* don't leave me."), she sounds as if she's reading from a Dick and Jane primer and is a surprisingly poor actress. Maybe she just can't handle the submissive, lovelorn bit; it's perhaps too alien to her character. Throughout though she's wonderful, in other ways; you like her spirit and her look. When Bessie speaks her mind to Isabel and rips into the lass, literally throwing her to the floor, she's got heat, fire, and conviction. She's also perfect when letting off steam with a janitor who's dared to tell her to quiet down. But most importantly, who could ever forget her deeply felt rendition of the title song? Haughty, husky, hungry, earthy, confident, and supremely committed to her music, Bessie Smith is magnificently larger than life here, a true dark diva, who lives up to her legend as one of America's great original artists.

St. Louis Blues (1958)

D. Allen Reisner. *S.* Robert Smith and Ted Sherdeman. *P.* Robert Smith. *R.* Paramount Pictures.

The life of black composer W. C. Handy, Hollywood style.

When this movie turned up, it appeared as if all-star black movie musicals might be coming back into vogue. *Carmen Jones* had already been released in 1954, and *Porgy and Bess* arrived in 1959. But *St. Louis Blues* transformed the incidents in Handy's life (his difficulties with his father, his blindness, the return of his vision) into a routine B-picture, which included a familiar triangle: the cleancut young black man torn between the good black gal back home (Ruby Dee) and the wicked city woman (Eartha Kitt). During one sequence when the two women meet, goody-two-shoes Dee is decked out in light colors (to signify her innocence and purity; white's always the color of angels) and naughty Eartha's in black (the color of evil). Perhaps the movie's real handicap was the miscasting of singer Nat "King" Cole in the leading role. Debonair, suave, and very skillful in nightclubs, he proved weak and uncharismatic as an actor. Today the reason for seeing *St. Louis Blues* is because of the all-star cast surrounding Cole, some of whom very rarely turned up in films and almost all of whom were wasted here: Mahalia Jackson, Ella Fitzgerald, Pearl Bailey, Cab Calloway, Juano Hernandez, and—portraying Handy as a child—little Billy Preston, who later grew up to be a fiercely energetic rock star.

Stir Crazy (1980)

D. Sidney Poitier. *S.* Bruce Jay Friedman. *P.* Hannah Weinstein. *R.* Columbia. Cast includes: Jobeth Williams; Craig T. Nelson; and Georg Stanford Brown in a rigidly stereotyped role as a prison queen. *Variety* commented that Brown was "particularly offensive in a major role as a lisping, limp-wristed gay inmate." Unfortunately, in American films black performers sometimes go from playing one stereotype to another.

Two out-of-work New Yorkers (Richard Pryor and Gene Wilder), en-route to greener pastures in another part of the country, find themselves locked up in an Arizona jail for a bank robbery they didn't commit. That's when the fun is supposed to start as we watch their prison antics. Instead the picture simply plods along, occasionally showcasing the stars' talents but more often than not burying them in a pedestrian, witless mess.

Consistently panned by the critics. *Newsweek*'s David Ansen wrote that it was "only intermittently funny. . . . Director Sidney Poitier serves his leading men well, but he hasn't begun to merge the bits and pieces into a unified whole." *New York*'s David Denby added: "It's a slovenly, loose-jointed movie, with anecdotes that lead nowhere and minor performances that don't come off." And *The New York Times'* Vincent Canby said it was "a prison comedy of quite stunning humorlessness."

But no matter. Audiences ignored the critics altogether, turning this mediocrity into a box-office bonanza. Because Pryor and Wilder had been a hit as a comedy team in *Silver Streak*, the reteaming certainly contributed to this movie's success as did the fact that it was the first film released after Pryor had been severely burned in an accident in California. Pryor had made headlines around the country, and he was bigger box office than ever. Many rushed to see this great self-destructive comic genius out of curiosity; others were hoping Pryor's manic quality would shine through, turning this into a daring new-style comedy. But Pryor doesn't have enough to do. Wilder's the true hero, and Pryor, shockingly in the year 1980, is something of a black sidekick/servant figure. Poitier's direction is almost shamelessly sluggish. Why he insists upon doing comedies, clearly a genre he's ill suited for as an actor or director, is anybody's guess.

There is one classic sequence; in a reprise of a scene in *Silver Streak* when he teaches Wilder how to be black, here Pryor, as he and Wilder walk down the corridor to their prison cell, tells his white buddy that they *gotta be badd*—in order to survive behind bars. Pryor's got a giddy bop. And this is the movie's funniest moment, its best executed sequence.

Stormy Weather (1943)

D. Andrew Stone. *S.* Frederick Jackson and Ted Koehler. Songs by: Andy Razaf, Fats Waller, Harry Brooks; Dorothy Fields, Jimmy McHugh; Ted Koehler, Harold Arlen; Koehler, James P. Johnson, Irving Mills; Cab Calloway. Cast includes: Dooley Wilson (formerly Sam in *Casablanca*) as Gabe; Nicodemus Stewart (later Lightnin' of TV's "Amos 'n' Andy") as the chauffeur; Babe Wallace as the insufferable Chick Bailey; that fine character actor Ernest Whitman (later he played Bill on TV's "Beulah") as Jim Europe; and the very funny Mae E. Johnson as Mae.

A musical extravaganza, featuring an all-star black cast. There's not much plot here, mostly just some mumblings about a backstage romance between two entertainers who fall in and out of love and then, of course, back in love again. The two entertainers are played by Lena Horne and Bill "Bojangles" Robinson—who looks old enough to be her

An unlikely piece of casting: Bill "Bojangles" Robinson and Lena Horne as the romantic leads in the all-black Hollywood musical Stormy Weather.

father. (He was—she was about 26; he'd turned 65.) Horne's daughter Gail Lumet Buckley has said, "Lena loathed Bill Robinson and nearly everything connected with *Stormy Weather*" and thought that he was "the biggest Uncle Tom in show business." Some of Lena's attitude creeps through. The two have almost no chemistry together. But apart, they're fine. Although far from his prime (and a fairly terrible actor), Robinson performs a lively Riverboat tap number that displays his cool "copacetic" style. Horne—not necessarily the warmest of actresses—nevertheless is so goddessy cute that you don't want to stop looking at her. She gets to sing "I Can't Give You Anything but Love"—and also her signature song "Stormy Weather." Almost 40 years later in her Broadway show *Lena Horne: The Lady and Her Music*, Horne said that in her early years she had not sung "Stormy Weather" quite right. Yet the sequence of her standing by a window singing the Harold Arlen lyrics lives on in our movie memories.

But there are many other top acts and performers here. The Katherine Dunham Dance Troupe does a moody misty ballet to the title song. Ada Brown has a chance to belt out some bluesy numbers. Cab Calloway comes on strong—in an oversized white zoot suit. Flournoy E. Miller (of Miller and Lyles) with Johnny Lee does a classic black comedy skit, performing "indefinite talk," in which the two men speak to one other, with each never letting the other complete a sentence; yet they understand one another perfectly. And then there is Fats Waller. Once he's seated at the piano performing his famous "Ain't Misbehavin'," you're in a state of sheer bliss, aware that the movie is building to a high you had not anticipated. We all assume, though, that no one act can then top everything we've already seen. But then the impossible happens: there is an act that just about tops everything, the fabulous Nicholas Brothers. Dressed elegantly in tuxedos, their faces lighted up with enthusiasm for their work, the two—Harold and Fayard—perform a staircase/split number that is, in intricate technical terms, a marvel. Audiences actually sit straight up in their seats to watch the number, amazed and incredulous: this highly demanding performance is so perfectly executed—

splendidly stylized yet seemingly spontaneous, too, without any sign of strain or sweat—that it truly commands our respect and inspires awe. There's another ingredient here that makes the dance buoy up our spirits: it's the spirit of the brothers themselves, who communicate a joy in pleasing *us*, the audience. Their work frames the movie, bringing it to an almost intolerably pleasurable peak.

This movie has been shown at countless black film festivals. Sometimes a skeptical audience sits, ready to reject the film, assuming there will be nothing but stereotyped images. (Actually, the black characters are here evolving into the middle-class figures we've seen in films of the 1950s.) But five minutes into *Stormy Weather*, you're hooked and never have second thoughts about the remarkable talents of these first-rate black entertainers.

The film was said to have been loosely based on the careers of black entertainers Jim Europe, Noble Sissle, and Adelaide Hall.

Clarence Robinson and Nick Castle did the choreography.

The Story of a 3 Day Pass (1968)

D. Melvin Van Peebles. *S*. Melvin Van Peebles; story by Melvin Van Peebles. *P*. Guy Belfond. *R*. Sigma III—A Filmways Company.

Erroneously touted as "the first feature film ever directed by a Negro" (at the time, no one seemed to know anything about the films of Oscar Micheaux and Spencer Williams), this first feature of Melvin Van Peebles—shot in France in six weeks on a budget of $200,000—told the story of an affair between a black American soldier (Harry Baird), who's stationed in France, and a young white French woman (Nicole Berger). The interracial pairing of black man/white woman (as opposed to the black woman/white man taboo which had been broken with Dorothy Dandridge's later films) was considered daring and in some quarters, yes, downright shocking. Van Peebles himself seemed audaciously amused by the reactions to such a pairing. In the film while on vacation with his lady friend in Brittany, the black soldier is suddenly visited by some of his white buddies from the military base. Their racism soon rises to the fore in a sequence that is almost hysterically comic (*their* hysteria makes it funny). Promptly they report this "incident" to their commanding officer, a rabid racist. Later back on the base, the soldier is confined to his quarters. His behavior has been almost too much for the military brass to bear!

At the time of its release, the idea that a black man could direct a motion picture was one thing; the idea that his style might be experimental and playful (the editing is jerky, the white characters are frequently burlesque-type caricatures, the hero has an alter ego appearing throughout to cue us in to the state of schizophrenia a black man can be forced to live in) was all the more surprising for some critics.

For contemporary audiences though, much of the film seems tame and self-conscious, not fully worked out in terms of plot or style. A bizarre but intriguing sequence of a group of travelling black clubwomen is left dangling. And Van Peebles's attitude toward women remains disturbing. So unattractively presented is the white actress that it's hard to figure out what the hero sees in her. Is he merely flattered by the notion that a white woman finds him sexually attractive? Does he ever regard her as a "person," something other than a *white woman* to be laid? Because she's used in the movie merely as a plot device, an integral one no less, as well as an undeveloped comment on racial dynamics (namely those of the white military figures), we can't come to any terms with her or the relationship. In the long run because Van Peebles considers her (and later many of the women in *Sweet Sweetback's Baadasssss Song*) as disposable items, he weakens his work and deprives us of any new insight.

In *The Village Voice*, critic Andrew Sarris, writing that Van Peebles "hardly qualifies as a pioneer in any significant sociological context," believed the film "more French oblique than Hollywood direct in its stylistic orientation." (One has to agree with the latter comment.) In *The New York Times*, Renata Adler considered it "a flawed, talented little movie . . . attractive, shaky, and awkward," while in *The Saturday Review*, Hollis Alpert wrote enthusiastically that the film was "pleasantly and sincerely made, so filled with delightful touches of humor and for a first effort, so surprisingly adept technically." Regardless of their opinions, the critics took the arrival of this movie and its black director seriously. There was to be a similar critical response almost twenty years later with another black director's breakthrough work, Spike Lee's *She's Gotta Have It*. Although it should have long been self-evident, the idea now emerged that the best qualified person to deal on screen with the black experience was a black director. Another evolutionary step had been taken in black film history.

Sugar Hill (1974)

D. Paul Maslanksy. S. Tim Kelly. P. Elliott Schick. R. AIP. Cast includes: Richard Lawson and Robert Quarry.

If her brother's been killed by a gangster and his henchman, what's a poor girl to do? Well, this one (the pretty Marki Bey) summons up the potent forces of Voodoo to help exact vengeance. She's aided by an old Voodoo priestess (Zara Culley, before she became George Jefferson's mother on the TV series "The Jeffersons")—and an ornery troop of the "undead" led by part-sinister, part-comic Baron Samdei (Don Pedro Colley). The influence of *Night of the Living Dead* shows.

Offbeat and dumb.

Super Fly (1972)

D. Gordon Parks, Jr. S. Phillip Fenty. P. Sig Shore. R. Warner Bros. Cast includes: Sheila Frazier (as Priest's girlfriend); Julius Harris; Carl Lee; and Charles McGregor.

A very successful, controversial film centering on a Harlem cocaine dealer, Priest (Ron O'Neal), who wants out of the drug business. But first he must defeat the corrupt white syndicate bosses who control him. He does precisely that at the film's heady climax. Afterwards we know he's going to waltz off into the sunset with his cache of money and his old lady, too. The basic plot of *Super Fly* was to be repeated in scores of other blaxploitation films.

Super Fly's real structural problem (and the root of its controversy) was that it was so real and so fake at the same time. The Harlem settings— the streets, the clubs, the back alleys—are authentic. A new kind of black social realism comes to the screen. Authentic, too, was the drug scene the picture dramatized. Yet the hero himself, mysteriously and seductively played by O'Neal, is romanticized to the hilt, and he sells his dope to

Meet SUGAR HILL and her ZOMBIE HIT MEN!

The Devil Woman— Her Voodoo Powers Raised The Dead, She's Super-Natural!

SUGAR HILL

SAMUEL Z. ARKOFF Presents
"SUGAR HILL"
an American International Picture Starring
MARKI BEY · ROBERT QUARRY · DON PEDRO COLLEY
Produced by ELLIOT SCHICK Directed by PAUL MASLANSKY Color by Movielab
Original Music Composed by NICK ZESSES and DINO FEKARIS
"SUPERNATURAL VOODOO WOMAN" Sung by "THE ORIGINALS" Available on Motown Records

whites. Some black parents were openly disturbed when their children adopted the Priest look: the long hair, the insolent pout, the wide brim hats, and the long, sweeping coats. (The same thing was to happen in the 1980s with the great success of Prince's film *Purple Rain*, only then parents had to contend with the fact that their sons were now wearing mascara and eye liner.) Eventually, *Super Fly* was criticized for glorifying its dope dealer protagonist. Moreover its fantasy ending (Priest, who as the ads said has a "plan to stick it to the Man," stomps down the white syndicate boss) was also thought *morally* unsuitable and obviously dishonest (*nobody ever walks away from the mob*); because black films with black heroes were still new, younger audiences tended to take the pictures far more literally. The film, which was made for under a half million dollars, eventually grossed over $12 million and spawned a sequel, *Super Fly T.N.T.*, and also acquired a legend for itself.

Today one responds still to Curtis Mayfield's dreamy score—and like it or not, Ron O'Neal's Priest still cuts a very dashing figure. The movie itself is still part real, still part trashy fantasy, and possibly still more interesting and seductive than we'd like. It should be noted that women here are frequently treated as excess baggage.

Super Fly T.N.T. (1973)

D. Ron O'Neal. S. Alex Haley, from a story by Ron O'Neal and Sig Shore. P. Sig Shore. R. Paramount Pictures. Cast includes: Shelia Frazier; Robert Guillaume; and Jacques Sernas.

A plodding, lackluster sequel to the controversial blockbuster *Super Fly*.

In the old days, Hollywood wanted us to know its black characters solved all their problems once they got religion. In the early 1970s, they got political instead. Here Priest, the handsome, dashing drug dealer of the first *Super Fly* film has left New York and taken his loot and his old lady to Rome, where he lives the luxuriant high life: a fabulous pad, sporty clothes (a bit on the campy side), and, of course, a *baaddd* car. But poor Priest is tormented, suffering a testy identity crisis, the likes of which have seldom been seen in an American movie. He sulks, broods, whines, and *attitudinizes* like mad. The solution? Well, Priest feels like his old self once he's become politically involved. Thus, soon we see him zip off to Africa to smuggle guns into an oppressed diamond-rich nation, which is controlled by greedy French imperialists.

The idea for this movie must have sounded great in story conferences. *Political involvement* was a way to clean up the Super Fly image, to make him do penance for his past indiscretions, to turn this popular hero "relevant" and make him more acceptable not only to a middle-class audience but also to what the moviemakers considered to be "the black militant" segment of moviegoers at the time. But seldom has the film industry been able to handle a political theme with any kind of sense or insight, and *Super Fly T.N.T.* is a badly mangled film without a clearly drawn or executed plotline—and without a true political thought in its empty head. The performers, perhaps with the exception of Roscoe Lee Browne, simply drift about on screen. "It's nice to know that Priest is out of drugs and into nationalism," wrote Judith Crist in *New York*, "but it would be nicer if [Ron] O'Neal bothered to act—or direct." So self-indulgent is O'Neal's direction here (his acting, too) that occasionally the film becomes rather fascinating to watch, not so much as a statement on the Super Fly character as on the actor's own heady narcissism. In the end, one tends to agree with *The New York Times* critic, who complained the movie was long on talk, short on action, and at heart "a wet firecracker."

Originally, this movie was to have been released by Warner Bros. But, according to *Variety*, that distributor backed out at the last minute, presumably in fear of further controversy within the black community. Paramount then stepped in to distribute the picture, only to discover it had a dull mess on its hands. T.N.T., by the way, means (in black vernacular) *taint nothin to it*. Truer words were never spoken.

Superman III (1983)

D. Richard Lester. S. David and Leslie Newman. P. Pierre Spengler. An Alexander and Ilya Salkind production. R. Warner Bros. Cast includes: Annette O'Toole; Margot Kidder; Jackie Cooper; Robert Vaughn; Annie Ross.

That man of steel again performs aerial feats of surprise and wonder, yet this movie itself fails to take off; the same is true of the performance of Richard Pryor. Cast as a villain—a computer whiz who aids a group of meanies out to clip Superman's wings via some ersatz kryptonite that Pryor's concocted—Pryor's meant to be the star of the movie. (It's said he received $4 million for appearing in it.) But, in actuality, he's an old-style comic servant, meek and submissive, bug-eyed and often scared out of his wits, performing antics that are frequently crude and embrrassing. The penthouse ski slope sequence is one of the worst. And a terrified-Pryor-flying-through-the-air-in-the-arms-of-a-confident-Superman isn't any better. One episode (not directly involving Pryor) does stand out: Superman (temporarily transformed into a bad guy because of that ersatz kryptonite) battles his alter ego, Clark Kent, the evil and good sides of man in a classic struggle for control. This struggle might also well serve as a metaphor for Pryor's plight in the picture: Richard Pryor, the gifted artist, in a duel with Richard Pryor, the commercial entertainer, who sometimes accepts a shabby role without thinking what it means or how it might degrade him. Unfortunately, unlike the Superman/Clark Kent duel in the film, Pryor's better half does not win.

Sweet Sweetback's Baadasssss Song (1971)

D. Melvin Van Peebles. S. Melvin Van Peebles; also scored by Van Peebles. P. Melvin Van Peebles and Jerry Gross. R. Cinemation Industries. Cast includes: Rhetta Hughes; Mario Van Peebles; John Amos (briefly); Megan Van Peebles.

"All the films about black people up to now," director Melvin Van Peebles told *Newsweek* in 1971, "have been told through the eyes of the Anglo-Saxon majority—in their rhythms and speech and pace. They've been diluted to suit the white majority, just like Chinese restaurants tone down the spices to suit American tastes. I want white people to approach *Sweetback* the way they do an Italian or Japanese film. They have to understand *our* culture." Van Peebles added, "In my film, the black audience finally gets a chance to see some of their own fantasies acted out—about rising out of the mud and kicking ass."

It may be difficult for a contemporary audience to understand the

On the road with Sweetback—and a friend he's met along the way: Melvin Van Peebles as the star and director of Sweet Sweetback's Baadasssss Song.

extreme impact of this historic, legendary movie, let alone to actually enjoy the film. But before its appearance, black characters, in sentimental films that sought to promote the idea that things could work out between white and black, were always tame and manageable without any sexual or political defiance. *Sweetback*, however, not only took the wraps off a black man's sexuality (it plays on the myth of black male sexual omnipotence) but also was an open declaration of war on White America. Until he sees two white cops savagely beat a young black revolutionary, a black pimp/stud called Sweetback has pursued a life of pleasure without much thought about anything. Now he's suddenly radicalized and compelled to act: he hacks up the two corrupt white cops, then sets out to escape, to cross the border, and of course, to triumph. He does escape, makes it to the border, then lets us know he's coming back to collect some dues.

Many found this movie (particularly the sex-and-violence sequences) shocking and an outrage. In *The New York Times*, Vincent Canby wrote, "Instead of dramatizing injustice, Van Peebles merchandizes it." And in *Ebony*, Lerone Bennett denounced the film and its stereotypes as "trivial" and "tasteless."

But, as they flocked in huge numbers to see it, black audiences of the time saw something else: the movies' first black man of action. The cinematic techniques, too—the unusual camera angles, the rapid editing, the superimpositions, the stop action, the shifts in focus, the episodic dreamlike (or nightmarish) script—were also new to black films. And Van Peebles—who had shot the movie in 19 days on a budget of $500,000 using cheap nonunion personnel (this enabled him to employ more blacks behind the scenes) by pretending he was making a porn film—emerged as a folk hero of black cinema. Not only did he direct but he also produced, wrote, scored, and edited the picture. His comments to the press also struck the right black political/artistic note.

Viewed today, *Sweetback* still has some charge and compels our attention, although many will be disturbed and angered by its treatment of women. Many were outraged when it was first released. Others will feel—justifiably—that it's a heady male fantasy, true to only one view

211

of the black experience and not a statement on a larger, more realistic portrait of black life in America. But the movie changed the whole conception of what a black film character should be, and its startling, unprecedented success with black audiences proved there was a place for a new kind of black movie. Black Panther leader Huey Newton called this "a great revolutionary document."

Take a Hard Ride (1975)

D. Anthony M. Dawson. S. Eric Bercovici and Jerry Ludwig. P. Harry Bernsen. R. 20th Century-Fox.

Macho stars Jim Brown, Fred Williamson, and Jim Kelly are reunited here, after having appeared together successfully in *Three the Hard Way*. At first this seems like an offbeat Western, simply because of its hearty black protagonists. One is geared up for some of the verve and zing of a black Western like *Buck and the Preacher*. But, unfortunately, this one's little more than dumdum goodies versus dumdum baddies. Technically shoddy and a B-picture through and through, this type of poor product eventually turned the black film audience against the black action movie in the 1970s. *New York Post* critic Archer Winston wrote that, despite a fine supporting cast (which includes Dana Andrews, Catherine Spaak, Barry Sullivan, and the enjoyably villainous Lee Van Cleef as a bounty hunter), nothing could bring *Take a Hard Ride* "out of its proper resting place, down there at the bottom of the barrel with all the other big but utterly routine Westerns."

Tales of Manhattan (1942)

D. Julien Duvivier. S. and original stories: Ben Hecht, Ferenc Molnar, Donald Ogden Stewart, Samuel Hoffenstein, Alan Campbell, Ladislas Fodor, L. Vadnal, L. Gorog, Lamar Trotti, and Henry Blankfort. P. Boris Morros and S. P. Eagle. R. 20th Century-Fox. Cast includes: Ethel Waters; Eddie "Rochester" Anderson; Clarence Muse; George Reed; The Hall Johnson Choir; Rita Hayworth; Charles Boyer; Ginger Rogers; Henry Fonda; Caesar Romero; Charles Laughton; Edward G. Robinson; Elsa Lanchester; and Thomas Mitchell.

"In cast and writing credits, this is probably the most ambitious picture ever to come out of Hollywood. Several million dollars worth of stars and featured players," wrote *Variety*, "stumble or waltz through the episodic story." But what a waste—especially regarding the black performers who turn up in the all-black final segment of this story about a tail-coat which is passed from one owner to another. When the coat, which has $50,000 stuffed into it, is dropped from an airplane onto a backwoods southern cotton field, the darkies in the field praise de lawd for sendin' dem dis here money. And soon we are treated to the spectacle of watching them decide how to disperse the funds. The entire black segment is patronizing and rigidly stereotyped, a true effront to the great talents involved, including Paul Robeson, who later denounced the film and never made another movie appearance.

Tamango (1958)

D. John Berry. S. Lee Gold and Tamara Hovey. R. Hal Roach Studios. Cast includes: Jean Servais; Alex Cressan (as the rather pouty rebel slave Tamango); and Clement Harari.

On board a slave ship, the natives are growing restless with talk of rebellion. But the ship's captain (German actor Curt Jurgens) is too busy eyeing a fetching slave girl (Dorothy Dandridge) to notice much else. The girl, of course, is torn between *concerns* for the captain and anguish over the state of her people.

Much to-do was made over the pairing of Dandridge and Jurgens. The ads for the movie read: "Love As Bold and Daring As the Casting" and "The story they said could never be filmed!" *Variety* had high hopes for the picture. "This could shape as a potent box-office contender," its reviewer wrote, "because of its rugged subject matter. . . . There are some torrid clinches between white star Curt Jurgens and American Negro actress Dorothy Dandridge. But this is not cheapened, and film stacks up as an actioner, with plus hypo factors that could make for a general play-off in the U.S., with perhaps the South excluded." Still, the movie proved controversial. Two versions of *Tamango* went out: one with more explicit love scenes for European audiences; another sanitized version for American theaters. Even at that, no major American distributor was interested in touching it, for fear of controversy over the interracial love theme.

The movie is frequently laughably melodramatic and implausible but occasionally enjoyable too. Much as audiences like her, Dandridge is so heavily made-up and speaks in such "polished" finishing-girl-school tones that she seems more as if she's a deb about to take a stroll along Hollywood Boulevard than as a woman being held captive on a slave ship. Towards the end of her career, Dorothy Dandridge didn't seem to be *in* her movies: that glazed look on her face indicated she was somewhere else. This is one of those later films.

Based on a novel, by, of all people, Prosper Merimee!

Slaveship glamour girl: Dorothy Dandridge in Tamango, *a misconceived tale of a mutinous slave revolt.*

That Certain Feeling (1956)

D. Norman Panama and Melvin Frank. S. Norman Panama and Melvin Frank. P. Norman Panama and Melvin Frank. R. Paramount. Cast includes: Jerry Mathers (the Beaver of television's "Leave It to Beaver") and "Li'l Abner" cartoonist Al Capp.

The comic black servant tradition in American films flowered in Depression era movies, reaching a peak with the performances of Eddie "Rochester" Anderson, Hattie McDaniel, and Butterfly McQueen. Here the black servants were, because of the individual performers, true eccentrics, crazy larger-than-life, unmanageable oddities. In the 1940s, the servant tradition continued but without great distinction. Following the Second World War and a healthy change in national attitudes, the servant figures were replaced by the New Negro characters—often the problem people—of Sidney Poitier, Dorothy Dandridge, and Harry Belafonte. But, strangely enough, in the mid-1950s after Pearl Bailey had become such a popular comic nightclub star, Paramount Pictures attempted to exploit Bailey's box-office potential and also to revive the old comic servant format by casting her as the funny maid Gussie in the big Bob Hope movie *That Certain Feeling*.

This is a triangle picture: Hope and George Sanders are both after Eva Marie Saint. Previously married to Saint, Bob Hope's character tries to win her back. But nobody knows that, except, of course, Gussie.

True to the wise meddlesome servants of the past, Gussie, at a crucial moment confronts Saint with certain realities the white woman has been running from. "Do you mind if I say something?" Gussie asks, then tells Saint, "If you ask me, you ain't got that man completely washed out of your hair." "Well, nobody asked you, Gussie," Saint replies. "Well, somebody had better before it's too late." The maid then lets Saint know, "Honey, when it comes to the male animal, I ain't equipped. I'm over-equipped. I been married now and then myself and I know the problem." Saint still doesn't get the message, so Gussie turns outright manipulator. One evening, she gets Hope and Saint alone together, makes sure they have the right food and atmosphere, even plies them with alcohol, and when things still aren't heated enough, sings a ditty to loosen things up: "Zing Went the Strings of My Heart." By the movie's end, Hope and Saint are reunited. And Gussie's right there by their side.

In the late 1930s, *That Certain Feeling* might have worked better. But in the mid-1950s, its concept of the happy-go-lucky-all-for-the-boss black maid was stale and patronizing. In just three years Broadway's *A Raisin in the Sun* with Ruby Dee and Claudia McNeil would show the other side of the black domestic, who returns home to contend with troubles of her own. Bailey, however, immensely likable and in control of herself, somehow manages to stand apart from the material and not be demeaned by it. Her fundamental aloofness points up the script's inadequacies.

Today it's also interesting to watch Bailey in her scenes with Saint. Here in glorious technicolor, audiences see a striking visual contrast: the pale, almost albino white of Saint next to the vibrant chocolate of Bailey, who looks sensational despite the fact that neither lighting nor camera angles showcase her at her best.

Bailey also sings the title song.

That Man Bolt (1973)

D. Henry Levin and David Lowell Rich. *S.* Quentin Werty and Charles Johnson; based on a story by Johnson. *P.* Bernard Schwartz. *R.* Universal. Cast includes: Teresa Graves; Miko Mayama; and Byron Webster.

He is a currency courier (hopping from one colorful locale to another), a kung-fu expert (why naturally), and (it should go without saying) a wiz with ladies of all colors and persuasions. He's also battling an international crime syndicate. At the same time, the audience must battle the boredom of this sloppy, less-than-routine action picture. Its star? Why who else in this era of the blaxploitation film but Fred Williamson, the king of the black B-flicks.

They Call Me MISTER Tibbs (1970)

D. Gordon Douglas. *S.* Alan R. Trustman and James R. Webb. *P.* Herbert Hirschman. *R.* UA. Cast includes the great Juano Hernandez (in a throwaway role); Beverly Todd; Anthony Zerbe; Edward Asner; and Martin Landau.

A sequel to *In the Heat of the Night*, in which Sidney Poitier once again plays detective Virgil Tibbs. Now living in San Francisco with his wife (Barbara McNair) and family, Poitier's Tibbs sets out to solve another murder mystery.

Some critics complained that too much attention in the film was focused on Tibbs's family life. True the domestic scenes have little to do with the plotline and simply slow down an already pedestrian script but Poitier himself seems anxious here to show another side of black life: the black middle-class experience, black citizens with values and aspirations no different from those of white America. Perhaps the movie's best-executed scene occurs when Poitier, having caught his young son sneaking cigarettes, takes him off, sits him down, hands the boy a cigar, then demands that he start puffing away. He wants his son to learn early on what cigarette smoking is really all about. Perhaps inconsequential but the scene is well played by both Poitier and the engaging George Spell and remains one of the few sequences ever filmed of a black man relating in a special, concerned, and affectionate way to his son. To some that may not mean much but for black audiences, it answers a certain need, one often overlooked by American films. (This movie appeared, of course, before "The Cosby Show.")

Otherwise this picture is hokum. In *The New York Times*, Vincent Canby wrote: "With *They Call Me MISTER Tibbs*, Poitier establishes another inalienable right, that of the black movie star to make the sort of ordinary, ramshackly entertaining, very close to pointless movie that a white movie star . . . has been allowed to get away with for most of his career. Actually, this may be one of the most important rights of all, for eventually it should allow Poitier to behave less like a solemn abstraction and more like a real, vulnerable man."

Thomasine & Bushrod (1974)

D. Gordon Parks, Jr. S. Max Julien. P. Harvey Bernhard and Max Julien. R. Columbia Pictures. Cast includes: Joel Fluellen; Jason Bernard; George Murdock; Jackson D. Cane; and Kip Allen.

During the mid-1970s, Vonetta McGee and Max Julien, glittering stars of the *new* Black Hollywood, were something of a junior-league Taylor and Burton for the black community. Such publications as *Ebony*, *Jet*, and *Black Stars* reported the comings and goings of this attractive, well-matched "modern" couple, who seemed to have the right mix—for the times—of glamor and the then-requisite social/political consciousness. When McGee and Julien teamed for *Thomasine & Bushrod*, they worked hard at playing on their public image. The ads for the film read: "Thomasine & Bushrod. Driven by Love . . . And Bank Robbing . . . Known to Have Many Friends Among Indians, Mexicans, Poor Whites, and Other Colored People." What they came up with, however, was a bit like a tepid, sepia *Bonnie and Clyde*: a meandering tale of a sexy pair of bank robbers in the days of old. Part Western, part feisty romantic comedy, the movie has some mildly entertaining segments but is far too fragmented and sluggishly directed. Midway in the film, the appearance (at different times) of characters played by Juanita Moore and Glynn Turman seems strikingly out of place (so much so that one spends much of the remainder of the film trying to figure out exactly what the scriptwriter and director have in mind) yet, strangely enough, their arrival lends the movie a certain cornball atmosphere and zip that it

In love and on the lam: Vonetta McGee and Max Julien as the doomed bank-robbing couple in Thomasind and Bushrod.

desperately needs and that reminds one a bit of Andy Warhol's *Lonesome Cowboys*. As with the Warhol film, it becomes mildly intoxicating to watch the inept craziness up there on the screen. Unfortunately, that's not enough though.

An added word on Glynn Turman. Often praised (and vastly over-rated) for his dramatic performances, he has had varying degrees of success in films and TV; sometimes he's effective; sometimes he's terrible. This appearance falls into the latter category.

Shot in New Mexico.

Three Tough Guys (1974)

D. Duccio Tessari. S. Luciano Vincenzoni and Nicola Badalucco. Executive in charge of production: Stanley Neufeld. R. Paramount Pictures. Cast includes: Fred Williamson and Paula Kelly.

Perhaps not bad viewing for late-night-TV addicts who want a fast moving, violent story but not much else. A good example, too, of the 1970s blaxploitation film as it was trying to move into another direction. This was an Italian and U.S. co-production, starring Lino Venturi (as a hardened priest) and Isaac Hayes (as a former cop), out to get a troupe of bank robbers. Shades of *The French Connection* are apparent, and by casting the white Italian Venturi with the black American Hayes, the producers hoped for a broad audience appeal, bringing in not only male customers who like action tales but also the very large black film audience of the period.

Actually, perhaps the real reason the producers cast Hayes was that they may have thought that was the only way to get him also to do the movie's score. Hayes is likable but without real menace or macho conviction.

tick . . . tick . . . tick (1970)

D. Ralph Nelson. *S.* James Lee Barrett. *P.* Ralph Nelson and James Lee Barrett. *R.* MGM. Cast includes: Fredric March (as the town's crafty old mayor); Janet MacLachlan (as Brown's wife); Richard Elkins (as the quiet black deputy); Bernie Casey (as a "militant" black); and Lynn Carlin.

Steamy southern town action picture with an attempt at social consciousness.

County Sheriff George Kennedy loses his re-election bid to a black upstart, Jim Brown, who must now prove himself to the townspeople.

A very predictable melodrama with shades of *In the Heat of the Night.* White and black must learn at least to have a grudging respect for one another.

Film marks the Jim Brown movie hero's full ascension into the ranks of the American establishment. In his first big film *The Dirty Dozen,* Brown was a renegade trying to go right. Now he's the right arm of the law itself. Not long after this film, when his followers tired of seeing him supporting the system, Jim Brown turned renegade and raunchy again in such pictures as *Slaughter* and *Black Gunn,* although for the record his heroes have never been outright, rebellious outlaws.

T.N.T. Jackson (1975)

D. Cirio Santiago. *S.* Dick Miller and Ken Metcalf. *P.* Cirio Santiago. *R.* New World Pictures. Cast includes: Stan Shaw; Pat Anderson.

A Kung Fu Mama Movie.

The ads read: "She's a One Mama Massacre Squad." She's a pretty American lass (Jeanne Bell) who, arriving in Hong Kong in search of her brother, becomes embroiled in wiping out a nasty heroin ring (led by Stan Shaw). Predictable chopsocky picture with plenty of leg kicks by Bell, here hoping to follow in the footsteps of Pam Grier and Tamara Dobson, whose tough mama movies had proven there was yet another segment of the black movie market for the industry to exploit.

"Routine fodder for the grind house circuit" wrote *Variety.*

To Sir, with Love (1967)

D. James Clavell. *S.* James Clavell (who later wrote *Shogun*); based on a novel by E. R. Braithwaite, British Guiana's former ambassador to the UN. *P.* James Clavell. *R.* Columbia Pictures. Cast includes: Suzy Kendall and Christian Roberts.

Years earlier in *Blackboard Jungle* Sidney Poitier had played a restless, hopped-up student against the establishment, represented mainly by his high school teacher (Glenn Ford). By 1967, though, Poitier himself had become, in the minds of moviegoers, so much an establishment figure that now he was cast as the stalwart, dedicated teacher, trying to calm down a batch of rebellious high school students, mostly white, and in London, no less.

At first Columbia Pictures held up the release of *To Sir, with Love*, fearing there was no audience for it. When finally distributed, it was pitched as a youth-oriented movie with advertisements publicizing the presence of such rock/pop favorites as The Mindbenders and Lulu (who sang the title song). But, strangely enough, in an era of political unrest among the young of America, this tame, lightweight apolitical fantasy seemed to enchant audiences of all ages—and colors—and soon it was evident as well that the most popular star in America was Sidney Poitier. In other films, Poitier had proven himself as an actor. Now he was proven *box office*.

To Sir, with Love indeed entertains but it's shallow and disheartening. For all his skill as an actor and for all his charm, too, Poitier seems wasted and misused as the antiseptically wholesome teacher. In *The New Yorker*, Penelope Gilliatt wrote that Poitier "is a firm actor, and must be a right-minded man, but one hankers for the character he played in *Blackboard Jungle* instead of the point-making prigs he takes on now. . . .

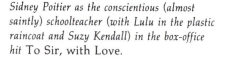

Sidney Poitier as the conscientious (almost saintly) schoolteacher (with Lulu in the plastic raincoat and Suzy Kendall) in the box-office hit To Sir, with Love.

If the hero of this Pollyanna story were white, the pieties would have been whisked off the screen and his pupils blamed for cringing. The fact that he is colored draws on resources of seriousness in audiences which the film does nothing to earn."

In the more realistic book on which the film was based, the black hero had a romance with a white teacher. But none of that occurs here. The character is bland, without flaws or idiosyncracies. Writing in *The Saturday Review*, Hollis Alpert pointed out: "Poitier isn't allowed to get the girl (or even *a* girl) in the end, and all the handsome masculinity he represents must wait for the day when mores and attitudes change sufficiently to allow him to respond to the love signals sent his way by white females who aren't particularly concerned about color barriers." This type of denial of Poitier's sexuality turned many of his movie characters into *respectable* but sterile figures whom black audiences had trouble relating to.

Poitier himself was satisfied with the film and took great delight in the letters from all over the world that poured in praising his work. Today adolescents still take a certain delight in what Bosley Crowther of *The New York Times* called "a cozy, good-humored, and unbelievable little tale." It remains disappointing, however, to see one of America's most gifted dramatic talents so shallowly used in what amounts to as little more than a dopey teen dream picture.

Together Brothers (1974)

> *D.* William A. Graham. *S.* Jack De Witt and Joe Greene; from a story by De Witt. *P.* Robert L. Rosen. *R.* 20th Century-Fox. Cast includes: Glynn Turman; Ahmad Nurradin; and Lincoln Kilpatrick.

The need for black movie heroes was so strong in the early 1970s that moviemakers gave us such heroes in all shapes and sizes. Strong, too, was the need for justice, the righting of past wrongs. Cops and officials were usually viewed as having betrayed the black public trust. And the best way to get things done was to do them yourself. Thus the vigilante movies, of which films like *Gordon's War* and *Together Brothers* head the list. Here the vigilantes are ghetto gang members out to find the man who has killed a friend of theirs, a black cop (Ed Bernard). The crime has been witnessed by the younger brother (Anthony Wilson) of a gang member. Thus the gang must save the kid, too.

Cheaply made, technically poor, notable only as an example of the kind of upbeat action movie black audiences of the time were interested in.

The Toy (1982)

> *D.* Richard Donner. *S.* Carol Sobieski; based on a French film by Francis Veber. *P.* Phil Feldman. *R.* Columbia Pictures; a Rastar Film.

Based on a 1979 French film of the same title by Francis Veber, this plodding, feeble-minded, slack/hack comedy is possibly Richard Pryor's worst film. The movie's basic premise is enough to discourage even the hardiest of Pryor fans: a wealthy white man (Jackie Gleason), anxious to please his spoiled (obnoxious) nine-year-old son (Scott Schwartz), hires/buys a black man to be the child's toy, to answer and cater to the boy's every whim, caprice, and tantrum. Unfortunately, the man who

One of Richard Pryor's least liked films: The Toy, *co-starring Jackie Gleason.*

becomes the toy (he's an unemployed journalist with mortgage payments to meet) is Richard Pryor. By the time the movie ends, we are to believe that the black man and white boy have touched one another's lives and become true friends. But the whole thing is patently false and almost shockingly condescending. Pryor gives into the kind of *tom* sentimentality that only a Bill "Bojangles" Robinson (in his films with Shirley Temple) could have mastered. He's done in by the material, and it's both sad and embarrassing to see this great, daring, fiendishly aggressive comic reduced to crude plantation parlor games. *The New York Times* wrote that "Everyone is wasted." That includes such supporting players as Virginia Capers, Ned Beatty, Tony King, and Annazette Chase. An appallingly rotten movie.

Trading Places (1983)

D. John Landis. *S.* Timothy Harris and Herschel Weingrod. *P.* Aaron Russo. *R.* Paramount. Cast includes Denholm Elliott.

A smidgin of *Putney Swope* and a dab of *The Prince and The Pauper* form the backbone of this sad sack comedy, starring Dan Aykroyd and Eddie Murphy, both former stars (at different times) of television's "Saturday Night Live." Here we see them cast as, respectively, a snotty upper-class white boy and as a poor black flimflam creature of the streets. Through the dimwitted machinations of two wealthy old white buzzards (Ralph Bellamy and Don Ameche) who make a bet as to which is more important to man's fate, his heredity or his environment, Aykroyd and Murphy are made to shift places. Will Aykroyd, divested of his assets and the benefits of his upbringing (he loses his job, his pretty, affluent girlfriend, even his apartment and highly efficient butler), turn to a life of crime? Will Murphy, picked up off the streets and dropped into Aykroyd's former comfortable shoes, destroy the company the white man once worked for? If it doesn't sound like much fun, that's because the picture isn't. At the beginning, Murphy has a few bright moments but he doesn't have a character to work with, and at this stage in his career, he isn't enough of an actor to manufacture one out of the slim pickings left to him.

There is a particularly grating episode when Murphy brings some of his former rowdy low-life friends to his new surroundings. When the group parties like mad, turning the plush pad inside out, the moviemakers unintentionally show which side of the bet they are really on: these dancing, prancing colored heathens definitely prove that their heredity has spoiled their chances of ever appreciating the finer things in life. It's an ugly and insidious sequence.

Equally insidious is the tired theme running throughout this comedy, again it's that of interracial male bonding. As was the case with Richard Pryor opposite Gene Wilder in *Silver Streak*, Murphy imparts to his new white friend Aykroyd some spirit, a looser way of looking at life. As was again the case in *Silver Streak* and *Stir Crazy*, while this movie prides itself on the idea of presenting racial equality, the inequities still abound: Aykroyd is the script's real star. He is granted the reward of every leading man: a pretty leading lady (the lovely Jamie Lee Curtis, who, unfortunately, is as badly used here as Murphy). Murphy, the prototypical isolated black buddy who comes out of nowhere, doesn't have a chance for a romantic relationship. Such black buddies are usually without women; thus the scripts strip these characters of sexual threat.

Anemic and unimaginative piece of work.

A romantic triangle? Hardly. Dan Aykroyd (r.) is paired with Jamie Lee Curtis (c.), while Eddie Murphy appears to be sexually stranded in Trading Places.

Trick Baby (1973)

D. Larry Yust. S. T. Raewyn, A. Neuberg, and Larry Yust; based on the novel by Iceberg Slim (a pseudonym for Robert Beck, a one-time black pimp turned writer). P. Marshal Backlar. R. Universal. Cast includes: Vernee Watson; Ted Lange (who later played the bartender Isaac on the TV series "Love Boat"); Clebert Ford (as a rambunctious ghetto minister); and Charles Weldon.

A con-game movie with an offbeat duo of con artists; an older black man called Blue (Mel Stewart) and his young cohort/protege, White Folks (Kiel Martin), a lightskinned black man (son of a black prostitute and her white "trick") who could easily pass for white but who, unlike most movie mulattoes, prefers to be black. (The difference in this mulatto's attitude can be attributed to the simple fact that he's been created by a black man, writer Iceberg Slim; there is no difference, however, in the white moviemakers' minds as how best to cast the role—he's played by a white actor.)

The film follows the adventures and exploits of the two, touching on their father/son relationship without much to-do. Part of the pleasure here is watching White Folks outsmart the white folks, often because, mistaking him for being white, they don't expect to be tricked by a man of their own color. We all laugh, too, when a young white woman, with whom White Folks has just made love, seems stunned by his sexual prowess; she hadn't expected so much from a white dude. There's also pleasure to be seen in Mel Stewart's adroit performance as a Grand Old Man of the ghetto. Eventually, the action and characters disintegrate, though, as the movie loses steam in the second half. Not great. Not too bad either. Mostly endurable and occasionally perversely pleasurable.

The beauty and the buck: Paula Kelly and Robert Hooks in Ivan Dixon's Trouble Man.

Trouble Man (1972)

D. Ivan Dixon. *S.* John D.F. Black. *P.* Joel D. Freeman. *R.* 20th Century-Fox. Cast includes: Paul Winfield; Julius Harris; and Ralph Waite (of "The Waltons," no less).

The story's about a black detective named Mr. T. (Robert Hooks), who is entangled in a nasty gang war. When he's not out pumping bullets or talking baad, Mr. T's in his lush apartment (the camera lingers over his lineup of shoes, shirts, expensive suits)—or with his lush girlfriend (Paula Kelly), a nightclub singer so dazzled by Mr. T. that she refuses to accept engagements out of town, preferring to lie in wait—and in heat—for her man. "No matter that her hair is cut Afro, nor that the *objets d'art* surrounding her are African," wrote Vincent Canby in *The New York Times*. "She's still a house slave."

The subtext creeping through this film is that it doesn't matter what one does to make it in the system or to acquire all the materialistic goodies the system says we should value as long as one does indeed get his share of the pie. Everything here, including Mr. T.'s girlfriend, is reduced to an expensive item. At the climax when the hero is about to rub out a white gangster, he first eyes the man's overdecorated apartment, then exclaims, "That honky sonofabitch sure knows how to live."

Ironically, this movie arrived at a time when the values of American capitalism were being openly questioned and often denounced by a large student population as insensitive and overbearing. Yet *Trouble Man* salutes rather than questions those values. Never does it take issue with the established order. Its hero is as much the American capitalist as the corporate man at ITT or IBM (and during this period in American political/social history, one would have assumed he would have been scorned just as much). Surprisingly, the movie was directed by Ivan Dixon, one of the screen's most sensitive directors.

Trouble Man zips along, however, on a fast, crazed energy level, which may partly account for its commercial success.

Added note: Marvin Gaye's soundtrack adds to the film's lopsided vigor and sexiness.

Truck Turner (1974)

D. Jonathan Kaplan. *S.* Leigh Chapman, Oscar Williams, and Michael Allin. *P.* Paul M. Heller and Fred Weintraub. *R.* AIP. Cast includes: Annazette Chase; Alan Weeks; Paul Harris; Sam Laws; and sadly, Nichelle Nichols (formerly of TV's "Star Trek", who is appallingly misused).

The man who once sang about Shaft *decides he wants to be* Shaft: *Isaac Hayes as the tough hero of* Truck Turner.

A bit earlier in his career, Isaac Hayes had sung about *Shaft*, winning an Oscar for his highly effective movie score. In time, though, Hayes decided he wanted *to be Shaft*. And therein his problems may have begun. This, along with *Three Tough Guys*, is one of his *Shaft*-like pictures. He plays a detective tracking down convicts who have jumped bail.

Hayes looks the part: muscular, sturdy, macho. But he really cannot *act* the part, and curiously enough, his deep resonant voice has a gentle quality—indeed a certain sensitivity—that doesn't work in the violent comic-book world of this movie.

The film is obviously negligible and lays waste of almost all its performers, including the very talented Yaphet Kotto.

Under the Cherry Moon (1986)

D. Prince. *S.* Becky Johnson. *P.* Bob Cavallo, Joe Ruffalo and Steve Fargnoli. *R.* Warner Bros. Cast includes: Steven Berkoff; Francesca Annis; Alexandra Stewart; and as Prince's frisky roommate Tricky, none other than Jerome Benton.

Prince's second film, a hymn of praise to the wonders, glories, beauty, midriff, and pout of, well, of course, Prince. Strikingly shot in black and white (by Michael Ballhaus), self-indulgent, and both over- and under-done, it's another Princean tragic mulatto entry, 1980s-style, with the diminutive star playing Christopher Tracy, a gigolo on the French Riveria in pursuit of a pretty spoiled heiress (Kristin Scott-Thomas). Perhaps future generations will find this dreamily boring high camp. For now, though, *The New York Times* assessment will do: "For all those out there who can't get enough of Prince, *Under the Cherry Moon* may be just the antidote."

Music by Prince and the Revolution.

Uptight (1968)

D. Jules Dassin. *S.* Jules Dassin, Ruby Dee, and Julian Mayfield; based on the novel by Liam O'Flaherty. *P.* Jules Dassin. *R.* Paramount. Cast includes: Ruby Dee, Frank Silvera; writer Julian Mayfield (as the turncoat); Max Julien; Roscoe Lee Browne; Janet MacLachlan; Ketty Lester; and Robert DoQui.

The first American film to spotlight black "revolutionaries" and the separatist movement of the 1960s, *Uptight* was set in Cleveland's Hough ghetto area shortly after the assassination of Martin Luther King, Jr. Non-violence died with King in Memphis, declare the dashiki-clad revolutionary protagonists as they arm themselves with guns and slogans. When one of the group's leaders is turned into the police by a fellow member of the organization, the militants track down and assassinate the informant. Little else happens.

Most considered *Uptight* a major disappointment. *Variety* wrote, "Despite its apparent ambitions and pretensions, *Uptight* is really a film, hammered out to capitalize upon, rather than explore, the complex facets of racial problems."

Audiences had waited anxiously for a film that would dramatize the chaos of the streets. On the surface, with its trappings—the ghetto, the beards, the beads, the afros, the armaments—the film looked contemporary but underneath it was compromised and dishonest, preachy and didactic. Based on John Ford's 1935 film *The Informer*, *Uptight*, having substituted black revolutionaries for the Irish rebels of Ford's drama, failed to grasp the complexities that distinguished the new black movement and set it apart from past rebellions. As the protagonists stormed about the streets of Cleveland, they emerged as little more than pent-up black brutes. The biggest cheat: audiences never see a heated black/white confrontation. In fact, if the movie made any statement at all, it was that blacks were effectual mainly at wiping out one of their own.

Uptown Saturday Night (1974)

D. Sidney Poitier. *S.* Richard Wesley. *P.* Melville Tucker. *R.* A Warner Bros. release of a First Artists Production. The cast includes: Rosalind Cash; Lee Chamberlain (as Madame Zenobia); Johnny Sekka; Lincoln Kilpatrick; Ketty Lester; Don Marshall; and Harold Nicholas (as Little Seymour).

This was a great hit with black audiences when first released and has remained an enduring crowd pleaser, which just goes to prove perhaps that the high communal spirits of a talented cast can, more often than not, save an otherwise pedestrian film.

Uptown Saturday Night's script is not without some charm. Two ordinary working fellows (Sidney Poitier and Bill Cosby) take off for an evening of relaxation and fun at a nearby gambling joint, Miss Zenobia's. There they encounter some jazzy nightlife figures, laughing it up and carrying on to music and highflung gaiety. Suddenly, though, Miss Zenobia's is robbed by a group of masked men. The two ordinary fellows lose everything—their wallets, their winnings, their optimism—and worst of all, as they later discover, a lottery ticket worth $50,000. Thereafter, the men set out to recover their belongings. Along the way, they meet up with an array of colorful personalities played by Flip Wilson, Richard Pryor, Harold Nicholas, and Paula Kelly.

By the end of the movie, the ticket is recovered and we can safely assume everybody's going to live happily ever after.

In many respects, *Uptown Saturday Night* is a comedy of chaos without the insane, anarchic chaos that's needed. With the exception of Pryor, Wilson, and occasionally Cosby, nobody has the *outrageousness* of a Tim Moore or a Mantan Moreland screaming, "Feets, do your stuff!" Moreover, the humor all too often is stale. When Roscoe Lee Browne, as a corrupt politician dressed in suit and tie, sitting in his office under a picture of Richard Nixon, rapidly changes the picture to one of Malcolm X and quickly dons a dashiki when he learns his colored constituency is paying him a call, don't we realize we've seen this type of thing on television sitcoms week after week? Do we not laugh because we think it should be funny? In the climactic sequence when Poitier jumps from a bridge and is followed by Cosby who jumps to save his friend because Poitier cannot swim, doesn't anyone recall a similar episode with Paul Newman and Robert Redford in *Butch Cassidy and the Sundance Kid*? Then, too, don't audiences feel cheated by the way in which the film's female characters are shoved into the background? Much of the movie seems like an adolescent romp for two repressed males.

In the long run, the problem with *Uptown Saturday Night* may be that its prime creators—director Poitier and writer Richard Wesley—are not at ease with the material. This was the third film Poitier had directed. His direction here, reveals, as does his performance, that he has little sense of humor and that he has perhaps gotten himself involved with this project mainly to keep up with changing times. His previous films had not been the huge box-office hits he no doubt felt he needed. And it's disquieting and embarrassing to see him performing the type of comic antics (popping his eyes or doing extended double-takes) that his dramatic career had previously seemed so diametrically opposed to. One wonders if writer Richard Wesley can believe in the material either. The lightweight highjinks here are a far cry from Wesley's dramatic plays *Black Terror*, *The Sirens*, and *The Mighty Gents*.

Consequently, what with a director and writer who appear at odds with their material, the film itself has a lopsided sensibility and an ambivalence toward itself and its own perspective. In one respect, *Uptown Saturday Night* wants to be an equalizer of black society. Socially, its characters are all on the same level. One might like to say that the film espouses a kind of Marxian ideal of a new democratic classless culture. But that's hardly the case. The movie simply denies basic class strata within the black community, refusing to differentiate between various black lifestyles and points of view. At the same time, the picture extolls middle-class values *yet* wants to break free of those values and explode with the old-style humor of a *Green Pastures* or *Stormy Weather*. *But* it's also embarrassed by the old humor. The filmmakers seem unsure what the picture should be about or what tone it should have. And if ever a movie seemed pentup or afraid of its own shadow, *Uptown Saturday Night*'s probably it.

Yet *Uptown Saturday Night*'s not a truly bad picture, for it manages to generate good feelings and to engage one's interest. Mainly, audiences continue to respond to the actors, most of whom play cameo parts, providing rich caricatures rather than characters: there is Harry Belafonte's spirited Brando/*Godfather* parody; Calvin Lockhart's wildly narcissistic Silky Slim; Flip Wilson's "loose lips" sermon; and Richard Pryor's frantic detective Sharp Eye. Bits and pieces are inspired. In fact,

Wilson's and Pryor's monologues are so unlike the rest of the film that it almost seems as if they've written their own material and directed it, too. Throughout the mood is so innocently playful and so uncluttered with the violence and gunplay that were so popular at the time of *Uptown Saturday Night*'s release that audiences have enjoyed watching black actors working well with one another in a piece of work that does have very clear cultural bearings and signposts (the church picnic is the perfect setting for the climax) so many other black films past and present have lacked.

Uptown Saturday Night also pleased white audiences, becoming in the mid-1970s a crossover hit and later having important prime-time television airings. And, strangely enough, despite its shortcomings and disappointments for many movie lovers, the film has become something of a black comic classic. Two successful follow-ups to it—starring Poitier and Cosby—appeared: *Let's Do It Again* and *A Piece of the Action*.

Virgin Island (1958)

D. Pat Jackson. *S.* Phillip Rush and Pat Jackson. Based on Rob White's novel *Our Virgin Island*. *P.* Leon Clore and Grahame Tharp. *R.* Film-Around-the-World. Cast includes writer Julian Mayfield.

One of Sidney Poitier's most neglected films—and justifiably so. It's a light comedy romance starring John Cassavetes as an American writer who, while vacationing in the Virgin Islands, woos and weds a pretty English girl (Virginia Maskell) and eventually takes her off to a nearby deserted island. Away from civilization, the two happily set up housekeeping—with the aid of a cool islander played by Poitier. Ruby Dee also turns up as Poitier's love interest.

One year earlier, Cassavetes, Poitier, and Dee had appeared together in Martin Ritt's taut social drama *Edge of the City*, each giving a strong and vivid performance. Consequently, it's a bit embarrassing to see them cast here in an essentially throwaway drama—and it's also disconcerting to see Poitier and Dee function as mere local color material, familiar black backups for the "more serious" action, which, of course, involves the white stars.

A Warm December (1973)

D. Sidney Poitier. *S.* Lawrence Roman. *P.* Melville Tucker. *R.* First Artists/National General Pictures. Cast includes: Johnny Sekka; Yvette Curtis; and the wonderful folk singer Letta Mbulu.

A handsome, widowed American doctor, in London with his young daughter, falls in love with a mysterious African beauty, who, as it turns out, is not only dying of an incurable illness but is also the well-bred aristocratic niece of an African diplomat. Thus is the stuff of black fairy tales made. Thus is the plot of this hokey story starring Sidney Poitier and newcomer Esther Anderson.

Like *For Love of Ivy*, Poitier's other foray into the world of antiseptic, middle-class black romance, *A Warm December* was met with mixed reviews from critics and audiences alike. Part *Love Story* (the woman's fatal illness is sickle cell anemia), part *Roman Holiday* (this beauty also seems on a holiday of sorts), it was too bourgeois for some tastes and often too tame and wholesome for its own good. Yet when shown on television today, it runs more smoothly (the commercials break up some of the tedium and aimlessness) and proves itself rather likable: one of the very few romantic films with black stars.

Poitier's a bit miscast as the dashing doctor. Both *The New York Times'* Roger Greenspun and *The St. Louis Dispatch's* Joe Pollack felt he was a bit old, at age 50, to play this romantic hero (he looks mighty fit though). Anderson, a true beauty but not necessarily a true actress, is nonetheless captivating and thoroughly charming. Seldom has a black woman been permitted to be so relaxed and vulnerable on screen. Usually, the great dark divas had to have push and pull to get any attention But Poitier's camera gently eases in to caress its goddess-like heroine, handling her gently with loving care. Anderson's character, although pure fantasy, is the type any audience could swoon over, and it was a distinctly new depiction of a black woman in American films.

Watermelon Man (1970)

D. Melvin Van Peebles. S. Herman Raucher. P. John B. Bennett. R. Columbia Pictures. Cast includes: D'Urville Martin and veteran comic Mantan Moreland, making, according to the production notes, his 310th movie appearance.

Godfrey Cambridge (with a surprisingly effective makeup job; he appears in whiteface) stars as your typical everyday white suburban racist, who awakens one fine morning to discover his skin has turned black! Now he must live as a Negro! As should be expected, the effect on this insurance agent is devastating: his boss, after checking his contact lenses to make sure he's been seeing straight, reassigns Cambridge to cultivating the black insurance market; his doctor suggests he get himself a new black physician; the office minx, caught up in the idea of hot black male sexuality, pursues him like mad; eventually the poor guy loses his wife (Estelle Parsons) and family.

This is really an updated tragic mulatto story: we're actually supposed to feel sorry for this white man who loses everything because of a color change. It's a bit like the white executive in *Carbon Copy*, whom we're to feel sympathy for because he's losing everything due to the sudden appearance of a son he had years before by a black woman. The pathos is misdirected, the direction itself is uneven, and the laughs rarely come when and where they're supposed to. "Not much of a picture," wrote *Variety*, "but as transient innocuous entertainment it is harmless."

Interesting as a historical piece.

Added note: Melvin Van Peebles also wrote the film's score.

Wattstax (1973)

D. Mel Stuart. P. Larry Shaw and Mel Stuart. R. Columbia. Cast also includes: The Reverend Jesse Jackson; Little Milton; Jimmy Jones; Albert King; Rance Allen Group; and Bar Kays.

A concert film featuring such stellar recording stars as Carla Thomas, Rufus Thomas, Isaac Hayes, Johnnie Taylor, Kim Weston, The Staple Singers, The Emotions, The Dramatics, and Luther Ingram.

Amidst the proceedings, the film cuts to Richard Pryor, whose brief appearance—it's more like an interview in which he discusses his childhood and does various bits and pieces of material—is invigorating, amusing, and often startling, all the more so because he seems to know what he's doing whereas the makers of this music documentary often don't know where to focus or what they want to say.

The filmed concert was part of a seven-hour event sponsored by the Stax Organization (the black record company in Tennessee) and the Schlitz Brewing Company, marking the seventh annual Watts Summer Festival. There doesn't seem to be much idea here as to what the concert represents.

The stars, however, remain stars. And it's still entertaining to see them.

Which Way Is Up? (1977)

D. Michael Schultz. *S.* Carl Gottlieb and Cecil Brown. *P.* Steve Krantz. *R.* Universal. Cast also includes: De Wayne Jessie; Gloria Edwards; Dolph Sweet; Danny Valdez; and Bebe Drake-Hooks.

Which way is *out* might be more to the point—out of this jumbled effort at social/sexual satire. Richard Pryor is cast in three roles: (1) as Mr. Average Guy, a blue-collar worker who picks oranges in Southern California and is perplexed by his job and his wife and his mistress; (2) as the perplexed Mr. Average Guy's father, a lusty old cuss who doesn't seem perplexed by anything; and (3) as a feisty, rather foul minister, rambunctiously seducing a large percentage of the women in his congregation. As a *farceur*, Pryor is a wonder to watch: high-spirited, quick-witted, diverse, consistently inventive. He keeps the movie moving, gives it a freshness, and is the sole reason for its commercial success.

But everything else is just dopey. Based on Italian director Lina Wertmuller's *The Seduction of Mimi*, an energetic treatise on the machismo of the Italian male as well as an examination (halfbaked, however) of the social/sexual forces that tie that male up and make his life a befuddled and unsatisfying battleground, *Which Way Is Up?* can't seem to Americanize the story with clarity and pertinent social comments. When Pryor's average guy hero unwittingly becomes embroiled in the activities of union organizers in the orange groves, he's shifted from one city to another, from one woman to another, too. Later he has to contend with the mob. Gradually, we see him corrupted and deadened by the system. There seems no way out for him. Yet the movie doesn't present us with the character's point of view (therefore his bewilderment only bewilders us more, and we can't get close enough to his feelings to be sympathetic), and the sex and politics do not mix at all.

In its treatment of black women, the movie conforms to an old-line Hollywood tradition, dividing the women into color categories. The dark-skinned Marilyn Coleman is cast as the homely, pathetic, almost gross woman Pryor seduces out of revenge, not desire. At the same time, the brown-skinned attractiveness of Margaret Avery (cast as Pryor's frigid wife) is overlooked and the actress is treated as little more than a tossaway. On the other hand, the lush, soft, romantically enticing dream girl is played by the ravenously beautiful *light-skinned* Lonette McKee. It's disheartening to see Hollywood's color casting system at work in the film of a black director.

Richard Pryor (with Gloria Edwards) in one of his various guises in Which Way Is Up?

Wholly Moses (1980)

D. Gary Weis. *S.* Guy Thomas. *P.* Freddie Fields; *Ex. P.*, David Begelman. *R.* Columbia Pictures. Cast includes: Laraine Newman; James Coco; Dom DeLuise; and Madeline Kahn.

A lumpy Old Testament comedy (sorry, there's no better way to describe it) starring Dudley Moore as an ancient religious hero named Herschel who, overhearing God's instructions to Moses via the Burning Bush, sets out himself to be the first to lead his people out of slavery—into the land of the hopelessly dull. A number of guest stars turn up in bits, notably Richard Pryor as the funny Pharaoh. Otherwise though it's as *Variety* said, "tame, tired, predictable."

Willie Dynamite (1973)

D. Gilbert Moses. *S.* Ron Cutler. *P.* Richard D. Zanuck. *R.* Universal Pictures. Cast includes: Thalmus Rasulala; Roger Robinson; George Murdock; Albert Hall; Norma Donaldson; Juanita Brown; and Royce Wallace.

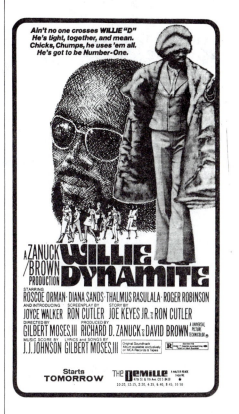

Very stagey without the filmic flow and fluidity it seems to be crying out for, this film nonetheless sets out to tackle a subject most blaxploitation films of its period either ignored or glamorized: the black pimp, his rise and fall. Roscoe Orman, a young stage actor of that time (who later appeared on the children's television series " Sesame Street"), plays the tough, flamboyant hero who's always decked out to the nines in designer Bernard Johnson's rather campy clothes. He picks up a sweet young thing (Joyce Walker), whom he wants to groom for big time on the streets. His plans are foiled, however, by Diana Sands (in one of her last performances) as a former streetwalker determined to save this girl from a life that will lead nowhere. Orman must also contend with a rival pimp. And, of course, amid these conflicts there are the cars, the clothes, the fancy pads, the beatings, etc., etc. Our feelings about the pimp hero are always mixed, mainly because the director often seems in awe of him. The movie's a low-budget job that wants to show us the effects of a decadent capitalistic system that pushes certain black men into lives of crime. But rather than pushing for a tragic grandeur that could have elevated the entire black movie boom of this period (the black pimp could be a quintessential American tragic hero), the picture settles for a wholesome upbeat ending that stretches credulity.

Interesting for what it half-heartedly tries to explore.

The Wiz (1978)

D. Sidney Lumet. *S.* Joel Schumacher, who previously wrote the scripts for *Car Wash* and *Sparkle* and who later directed and co-wrote *D.C. Cab*; based on the play by William F. Brown, produced on stage by Ken Harper; music and lyrics by Charlie Smalls. *P.* Rob Cohen. *R.* Universal. Cast includes: Theresa Merritt (as Auntie Em).

The most expensive American movie musical then ever made (estimated at some $30 million, excluding the huge advertising campaign) and the last important black-oriented Hollywood film of the 1970s, marking an end of a black movie era. A major disappointment, too.

Dorothy with Toto: Diana Ross in The Wiz.

In its pre-production phase, *The Wiz* had to look like a winner. There was an all-star cast, everyone from Diana Ross, Michael Jackson, Richard Pryor, and Nipsey Russell to Lena Horne (whose daughter, Gail, at one time was married to the film's director Sidney Lumet). The movie was also based on a hot Broadway ticket: the long-running *Wiz*, an all-black version of *The Wizard of Oz*, done in a playfully hot, pop/jazzy style with hip dialogue and much mother wit as well as a festive, high-energy atmosphere (enhanced, of course, by Geoffrey Holder's witty costumes). On stage, black choreographer George Faison had cleverly fused new popular black dance routines with a touch of the old Broadway traditional style, serving up his mixture in a distinctive fast-moving manner. As a Broadway show, *The Wiz* reminded theatre audiences of carnival time in Haiti, a time for sheer flamboyant fantasy with some nice little homey lessons to be learned along the way. The show also proved how black talents could invigorate old familiar forms. Initially, the white critical establishment had closed in on the play, some outraged by the idea that an American classic would be redefined in black style. But the public, white as well as black, discovered *The Wiz* on its own, and eventually, the show, which almost died during its first weeks, lived on for years on The Great White Way and even won several Tony Awards. It ushered in a new era of the all-black Broadway show, leading the way for *Eubie,* the black version of *Guys and Dolls, Bubbling Brown Sugar.* The stage version of *The Wiz* had been a brazen triumph of black ingenuity.

But the film version proved a significant setback for blacks in American movies. Had this been a commercial success, the movie studios might well have continued making black-oriented films—and a different type of black film as well. The studios, however, chose only to see the movie's failure, not the reasons for that failure. The movie was a soggy wet blanket that no large audience wanted to be bothered with. What really killed the movie was simply the fact that no longer were black hands in control. Instead the movie's most important creators—the director Sidney Lumet and the writer Joel Schumacher—were white artists, totally out of tune with the material (its built-in folkloric quality) and the style of the performers.

Unable to come up with a black idiom (dialogue *and* plot), writer Schumacher simply plods his action along, unaware of the black speech rhythms, intonations, and humor that are essential for this type of project. His script sets Dorothy (originally the girl from Kansas, the American heartland) in a modern urban setting, taking her from New York's uptown (when we first meet her, she's never been below 125th Street) to downtown and then across the Brooklyn Bridge. Here Schumacher assumes one learns more about life *downtown* while uptown is too much of a protective cocoon. It might have been funnier had Dorothy, a wholesome middle-class lass from the sticks or mid-Manhattan—a student, say, at the Dalton School—journeyed uptown to see what her soul brothers and sisters were up to. She would have learned far more.

At first glance, Tony Walton's sets look sensational, dazzling the eye as we glimpse *five* Chrysler Buildings on the New York skyline as well as a huge red Apple for a kind of sunset. We also delight in seeing one of statues of the lions at the 42nd Street Library suddenly come to life. But the script can never turn these overscaled backdrops into intimate settings. The characters are always removed from their environment and seldom give an indication of being part of urban life. The original Dorothy was firmly grounded in her locale: she was a Kansas girl through and through and that explains why her quest to get back to her roots was all the more endearing and moving. But the Dorothy here doesn't seem to have roots of any kind, and she and the other characters drift through the urban village as if on an elaborate movie set. No real sense of place exists here.

At the same time, director Lumet doesn't connect to his characters. In such past films as *The Pawnbroker* (1965), *Dog Day Afternoon* (1975), and *Serpico* (1973), Lumet understood big-city rhythms and energy, the city's bite and madness, and also the kind of delirious high that can come about amid such flux and diversity. But the city of New York is neutralized here, simply a series of long shots of big colorful exteriors. Even in his elaborate dance sequences, Lumet often keeps his camera away from the action, held back in a standard long shot position, almost as if he were afraid of the high-voltage energy here. On stage, the dancers seemed ready to leap out at you. But on film, partly because there are not enough closeups to reveal to us their joy in dance or their enthusiasm for their material, the dancers are distanced from us. It's almost as if we're not seeing a movie musical at all. Instead we have a series of stills and not very expressive ones at that.

Conceptually, much else goes wrong. When *The Wiz* was released, there were complaints that leading lady Diana Ross (then 34 years old) was too old, also the wrong type for the naive, innocent Dorothy. What with the change in locale, though, Ross might have been able to inject an urban sexiness into her character (who's been turned into a 24-year-old kindergarten teacher). But she's made far too wholesome and timid. In her first films *Lady Sings The Blues* and *Mahogany*, the great thing about Diana Ross was her portrait of the independent, aggressive, assertive, modern urban young black woman, a creature determined to get what she wanted, not always using her head, perhaps, but using her guts anyway. Audiences loved her maddening drive. Her movie persona was

On the road to Oz: Ted Ross (as the Cowardly Lion), Michael Jackson (as the Scarecrow), Diana Ross (as Dorothy), and Nipsey Russell (as the Tin Man) in The Wiz.

similar to the one she had as the lead singer with The Supremes. Here stood a black girl/woman who could do anything. *The Wiz* puts Diana Ross off on a quest for self-identity. But she never makes any kind of aggressive move. Because of the character's age, we should assume that once getting out in the world, she'll like her freedom, her long-delayed liberation. Of course, she'll want to visit home again to see everybody. But she should be returning home with a new maturity and sophistication. The folks back home always love seeing their babies return all grown up, sporting new clothes and some new attitudes that indicate they've learned something. Dorothy doesn't seem to have learned anything new. Stripped of glitter makeup and her glitzy style, Ross herself strives hard for a sweetness, a softening of the previous bold, aggressive image, but she's pallid and hollow. In *Lady Sings the Blues*, her fusion of sweetness and shyness with gutsiness and drive made her rounded and intriguing, almost *real*. Here she does seem far too old to be so sweetly naive. And, curiously, partly because the script denies her a love interest, she's asexual as well.

Although all the actors seem glued to the artificial sets, some fare a bit better than Ross. Nipsey Russell, as the Tin Man, was singled out (justifiably so) by several critics for his performance. In *Time*, John Skow wrote: "Nipsey Russell, whose rusty tinman is easily the best characterization of the film, sings an oozy and oleaginous . . . ballad 'Slide Some Oil to Me.'" *New York*'s David Denby added that Russell was "wonderfully dignified and sad as Tin Man, mourning with abundant feeling his non-existent heart." And Pauline Kael wrote: "The one performer who is able to ride right over the messy carelessness is Nipsey Russell." Kael cited his two numbers "Slide Some Oil to Me" and "What Would I Do If I Could Feel?" as the movie's best, adding that Russell, "understands that the roles are vaudeville-comedian turns. And, though his tap dancing is unexciting, he shows here that all his years of playing the inoffensive black entertainer in front of white audiences haven't softened him as a performer; he has the true pro's integrity of style."

Seeing Russell is a joy. *The Wiz* affords him a rare opportunity to do something special on screen, and he delivers. Weak as the film is, the role's the best of his career.

As the scarecrow, nineteen-year-old Michael Jackson has a sweet-natured delivery and presence that make him boyish and shy, a far cry from the fever-pitch performances on his music videos "Beat It" and "Billie Jean" that were to come in the 1980s. Repeating the role he originated in the Broadway production, Ted Ross isn't as rousing a cowardly lion as we'd like, in part because the camera can't seem to pick up on his bravado. Lumet just keeps pulling back! Another Broadway original, Mabel King, does manage to make her Evillene's sweatshop sequence a real star turn, although her power and range were far more intense and comically frightening on stage.

As The Wiz himself, Richard Pryor just seems out of place. Lodged in the World Trade Center, his Wiz looks as if he'd like to jump from the observation deck. Pryor and Ross had worked splendidly together in *Lady Sings the Blues*, but they can't seem to work up much of a rapport here. Watching Pryor struggle with this nonexistent character, one experiences an eerie sense of waste.

Finally, showing up at the movie's climax as the Good Witch Glinda, the great Lena Horne looks trapped and strapped in her elaborate glitzy costume. Behind her is a dark starry sky, and she seems pinned to these skies much as she was pinned to a pillar when she sang of love and loneliness in her MGM movies of the 1940s. Hollywood didn't know what to do with her then, and they still can't figure out how to handle her in the late 1970s. But Horne herself sings "Believe in Yourself" with the conviction of a polished veteran and a true artist, bringing to it a gospel bravado and some anger—and yes, even a surprising sense of history. Lena's attitude here seems to be that if no one else in this movie knows what he's doing, she does. She personifies the perennial star who's been misused yet has learned how to wring every moment to get the best out of what otherwise might have been the worst. "*The Wiz* does have one immortal," wrote Jack Kroll in *Newsweek*, "Lena Horne, who jolts the movie to an entirely new dimension . . . singing with a fiercely exultant dignity."

Horne is the film's high point.

And now with all this said and done, noting that *The Wiz* is flat and uninspired, mechanical and devoid of great feeling (its early dinner sequence at Auntie Em's, before Dorothy gets lost in the snowstorm, is the movie's most felt moment, although some complained it was too much like a Pepsi commercial), one must add that *The Wiz* may well become a classic, simply because it's one of the few big-budgeted black films the industry turned out in the 1970s (the last big-budgeted black musical had been *Porgy and Bess* in 1959), and its all-star black parade is destined to be of interest to later generations just as *Cabin in the Sky* and *Stormy Weather* are. So audiences are bound to view it, out of curiosity if nothing else, and one also has the nagging feeling that later audiences may well get so hepped up by seeing black legends on screen that they'll overlook the simp direction and script and come away with some kind of half-baked satisfaction anyway.

Such is movie history.

Television

The year was 1950, a time when television sets were rapidly turning up in American homes and gradually transforming our national habits and perspectives. The programs of the day—be it "The Aldrich Family" or "Fireside Theatre" or Ed Sullivan's "Toast of the Town"—were sometimes docile and naive or loud and brash but almost always reassuring, rather soothing, and supremely *safe*. Early, though, in the middle of this predictable often bland television terrain, there appeared an unlikely personage: a black woman starring in a weekly sitcom. Understanding, warm, friendly, hers was hardly an image that rattled or shook up her national viewers. Yet still she had brought about the unexpected: she had introduced color—black in this instance—to American television. The actress was Ethel Waters. The sitcom, "Beulah" (1950–1953). Television has never been the same since.

What "Beulah" and Waters launched was the topsy-turvy, perplexing history of blacks in the primetime network series. From "Beulah's" days in the Truman and early Eisenhower years on through the eras of Kennedy and Johnson, Nixon and Ford, Carter and Reagan, and under the guise of the Kingfish or Andy Brown, Alexander Scott or Julia Baker, Chet Kincaid or Fred Sanford, Florida Evans or George Jefferson, Jane Pittman or Kunta Kinte, Arnold or Webster, or all the Huxtables, black faces, characters, performers, situations, contrivances, and controversies have relentlessly careened across our television sets. Often the blacks we've seen in the primetime network show have been skilled performers using their special styles to trample content. Or sometimes some performers have simply played by the rules of the game. But the history of blacks on the primetime network series, like that of blacks in films, has been fraught with its own peculiar set of contradictions, its own array of internal frictions and frustrations, and its own tiny evolutionary steps.

The character Beulah sets the history in motion (as the first black series star). But hers was not the tube's first black face. Black entertainer Bob Howard had hosted his own 15-minute nightly program "The Bob Howard Show" on CBS from 1948 to 1950. And the dazzling jazz pianist Hazel Scott had been hired by the Dumont Network in early 1950 to star in the 15-minute-three-nights-a-week "Hazel Scott Show." Each had been groundbreakers: a black man and a black woman had hosted their own network programs. Yet neither had grabbed hold of the American imagination. Each was quickly forgotten. Not so with "Beulah."

"Beulah" told the story of a chubby black maid who worked for a white family, the Hendersons. For a nation that would come to cherish programs featuring a tightly knit communal unit with a predictable set of characters, relationships, and situations, this sitcom was ideal. Audiences lapped it up. Every week there was the crazy joy of watching warm-hearted Beulah standing in the same house, working in the same kitchen, and unraveling (or sometimes instigating) the same set of problems for the Hendersons. Unlike Howard or Scott, who vanished from sight after their musical numbers, Beulah was an integral part of a wholesome middle-class setting. A repository of mother wit and common sense, she insured that setting's stability. Plainly, this was an old-fashioned, stale fantasy that, like so many past movies, incorporated blacks into the American dream: like everyone else, Beulah lived in a spotless, comfortable home, but, of course, she had to clean it and never, in anyone's wildest imagination, would she own it. The Negro had made it into the television's cultural mainstream. But only as a maid.

As the black audience watched Beulah, no doubt it accepted her "ideal" working situation with some satisfaction (at least she wasn't lazy) and some skepticism, too. But mostly the audience focused on Beulah's relations with her black friends Oriole and Bill. Here early in television's history, the vast audience was racially split, as would be the case for decades to come, during which a black audience would respond to a "black" series in an entirely different manner from its white counterpart. For black America, "Beulah" was television's only glimpse of a black community where blacks worked, talked, joked, lived together. For white America, however, "Beulah" offered an ideal homogenized community in which the family unit remained secure and so, too, did the racial status quo: "Beulah" had no racial dissensions, only racial harmony and togetherness in an ordered, wonderful world. Beulah and the Hendersons had a breezy camaraderie without any cultural differences and certainly without any conflicts or disputes over such trifles as Beulah's work load, Beulah's hours, or Beulah's pay. Doing her job just because she enjoyed it, Beulah seemed to get a kick out of all them pots and pans. Ironically, no such harmony existed on the "Beulah" set. The series kept losing its leading ladies. After the first year, Ethel Waters became fed up and fled from the show. Hattie McDaniel was set to replace her but took ill and left. Finally, Louise Beavers took over but after two seasons, she packed her bags.

Still because "Beulah" presented an identifiable black personality that audiences could relate to, the series made the Negro seem real to viewers in a way no other type of television did. For the duration of the Eisenhower era, sports shows might showcase black athletes like Jackie Robinson or Ezzard Charles. Or variety shows might feature such entertainers as Eartha Kitt, Pearl Bailey or Sammy Davis, Jr. And eventually, the news programs—which would cover extensively the Civil Rights Movement and later the Black Power Movement—might inject a note of immediacy and urgency about social or political issues, bringing them right into American homes. But for many viewers such programs represented unusual special events, not necessarily the stuff of their everyday lives. But a network primetime series like "Beulah", with its weekly sameness (same set, same characters, same tangle of relationships), had the air of the predictable and the permanent. The situations on the primetime series, especially the sitcoms, were often based in a home and supposedly expressed the attitudes of typical American viewers. In the long run, one might never know what to expect from the news or a sports show. One always knew the basic premise of a series like "Beulah" and the others that followed.

For the black performer, of all series genres, none proved more important than the sitcom, mainly because it was and has continued to be the only type of program to acknowledge or comment on black life, no matter how trivial or superficial that acknowledgment or comment might be. Throughout the history of television, only two dramatic series have focused on blacks: "Palmerstown, U.S.A." and "Harris and Company," each of which had a quick death. The most important of all black dramatic television events, "Roots," was a mini-series, a special, not a weekly occurrence. Repeatedly, the television industry and its viewers (not to mention the sponsors and advertising agencies that control so much of what's seen) shied away from dramatic black series, which might have raised too many doubts or questions about American history, past and present. But with the laughter that ensued from the sitcoms, obviously the idea has always been that no matter what the problems, Negroes remain cheery and content. Consequently, the sitcom black, whether as star or backup support, appeared early and endured, returning strong (as was the case in the 1970s) after periods of long dormancy.

Today what's surprising is that "Beulah" had been on the air only a year when another black sitcom appeared, thus giving audiences two black-oriented shows running concurrently. Such an occurrence would not happen again for more than a decade. That second sitcom, "Amos 'n' Andy" (1951–1953), however, has now proved to be the most controversial of all black television programs. Whereas Beulah functioned in a white world with its carefully drawn parameters, "Amos 'n' Andy" frolicked along almost as if white people were not allowed anywhere near the series, almost as if they did not exist at all. Having already been a hit radio series for over two decades (it first appeared in 1928 with whites playing the black roles; later some black actors were added to the cast), television's "Amos 'n' Andy" recounted the adventures and highjinks of Kingfish, Andy, Lawyer Calhoun, Lightnin', Sapphire and her Mama. It introduced something totally new to the medium: an all-black cast. Only occasionally did whites appear.

The series arrived, however, in the middle of an idealogical hurricane. The NAACP, pepped up with postwar optimism and determined to fashion a new image for black America, denounced the series as an insult to the Negro race. Other groups also complained. Despite the criticism, however, black audiences, in the privacy of their homes, often seemed to enjoy the series, sorting out the distortions and stereotypes to focus on the talents of the remarkable cast. In the hands of the black actors, old-style ethnic theater had come to the tiny tube. While the black audience knew these characters did not realistically represent the black experience—the show was all satire and parody—it could understand the NAACP's concerns and position: because the servile comic black characters of both "Beulah" and "Amos 'n' Andy" were the only black images of note on television, white America might accept them as some real examination or comment on black lives. TV had already failed to provide an alternative image for audiences to select from. Curiously, the character Beulah was not as staunchly criticized, perhaps because, well-mannered and well-spoken, hers was a softer, more bourgeois image (which the NAACP might have found almost acceptable; after all, Beulah heartily embraced the American work ethic) whereas some of those wildly raucous lowlife folks on "Amos 'n' Andy"—who fractured the English language and laid waste to bourgeois attitudes and pretensions—were anything but respectable emblems of black middle-class life. In an era which would see integration as a social ideal, the rebellious community of jokesters, pranksters, and eccentrics of "Amos 'n' Andy" was not the type that could readily fit into the dominant white society.

Here, though, very early in its history, television found itself confronted with controversial issues. Decades earlier, films had also been at the center of outcries over the black image. D. W. Griffith's 1915 *The Birth of a Nation* had been protested against, banned and boycotted in a number of communities yet had gone on to make a mint at the box office. Controversy may have added to the film's commercial appeal; it certainly did not hurt. But *Birth of a Nation* and other controversial movies were outside the home. Television, plopped right into the living room in front of the family, could not live with the controversial. Only years later would controversy enhance the appeal of a series with the appearance of a show like "Soap" (1977–1981), which, when finally aired after much hoopla, proved not so controversial or disrupting after all. So in 1953 after only a two-year run, CBS took "Amos 'n' Andy" off the network primetime schedule, keeping reruns of the series in syndication, however, until 1966.

Once "Amos 'n' Andy" had left primetime, more than a decade passed before another series arrived that starred a black performer ("I Spy" with Bill Cosby). During the Eisenhower era and the early Kennedy years, too, some syndicated non-primetime series, however, used blacks in supporting roles or as background material. Such syndicated "jungle" series as "Ramar of the Jungle" (1952–1953), "Jungle Jim" (1955), and "Sheena Queen of the Jungle" (1955–1956) took place on the dark continent of Africa, employing a sea of dark faces to carry spears and look mean and tough until the white hero or heroine reminded them who was in charge. These shows also frequently ran in the afternoon time slot, appealing to a young audience.

More important, though, were the black performers on the prime-time white sitcoms: Eddie Anderson as Rochester on *The Jack Benny Show* (1950–1965); Willie Best as Charlie, the elevator "boy" on "My Little Margie" (1952–1955). Willie Best again, as Willie, the handyman on "The Stu Erwin Show" (1950–1955); Ruby Dandridge, as housekeeper Delilah, who kept things in order for the Banks family on "Father of the Bride" (1961–1962); Amanda Randolph as Louise, the housekeeper in Danny Thomas's show "Make Room for Daddy" (1953–1964); and Amanda's sister Lillian Randolph as Birdie Lee Coggins (repeating a role she had originated on radio), the housekeeper of the syndicated "The Great Gildersleeve" (1955).

In later years it would become fashionable to put down these performers, dismissing them along with their roles. It is one of the more disturbing, sometimes shocking, aspects of black cultural history that often one quick cursory look at the past elicits simply a denunciation, rarely an insight. Because in the world of entertainment so much of what we see seems steeped in the stereotype—because so much of what we see in performances we assume was controlled completely by whites—few try to sort it all out: to see where a misconceived character ends and an actor's ingenuity begins. What's surprising and intriguing about past white sitcoms with blacks is that the white worlds—so very pretty, so ordered, so antiseptically clean, with characters whose manners and mores are so geared towards pleasing, being cheerful or peppy or all-American healthy—reveal themselves as being patently fake, hollow, artificial through and through, inhabited by plastoids rather than human beings. The white actors and actresses distress us with their pert smiles and unvaried speaking and acting rhythms.

Yet when a black actor or actress suddenly shows up, their very color and attitude inject a contrasting level of reality. Unlike the black performers playing servants in movies of the early 1930s, the TV servants seldom used those rigidly thick dialects. Nor were they dressed in gingham or tatters. Nor were they sentimental loyalists. Instead, like Beulah, most dressed well, spoke a "proper" version of English warmed over with their own rhythmic inflections and intonations. Sometimes the performers do silly things, no doubt about it. But they always strike us as real people. On "The Jack Benny Show," Eddie Anderson's Rochester, without that former gleam in his eyes, admittedly looked a bit frazzled and tired and worn. (He probably was; he had played Benny's manservant on radio and in films for almost twenty years.) But true pro that he was, he still knew how to get mileage from a line of dialogue, was comfortable enough with the professional persona he had done much to create (that of a servant who refused to see himself as one; knowing he was no different from his boss, he actually considered himself smarter) that he sauntered through his scenes with remarkable alacrity and agility. To the very end, Anderson's Rochester knew how to make his entrance in a world in which he was the only black surrounded by whites: with head up and a bounce in his stride, he moved with confidence and a note of condescension as well. His attitude seemed to be that he had to help out these poor white folks who could not feed themselves, could not care for themselves, half the time could not think clearly for themselves either. He, Rochester, however, knew exactly who he was and felt blessed at being so supremely self-sufficient. Likewise the Randolph sisters laughed, smiled, grinned but also could roll their eyes and shake their heads at the antics of the white folks they were stuck with. Although we might despise the fact that blacks were depicted only as comic servants on the sitcoms, we should not ignore the fact that the actors themselves helped make many of these series watchable, pumping up the mundane with their personal idiosyncrasies just as years later Robert Guillaume as Benson on "Soap" and Esther Rolle as Florida on "Maude" (1972–1978) would get the juices flowing, often turning some old stale white bread into fresh wholewheat. Here we see, as in films, the saving grace of some sitcoms, that some performers transcended those stereotypes to create vibrant characters. Ironically, years later those black actors who finally had a chance to play serious roles were themselves frequently bland and indistinguishable from one another, unable to create characters we took an interest in. Did anyone ever care a hoot about Don Mitchell as Ironside's sidekick? Or Don Marshall as one of the earthlings on "Land of the Giants" (1968–1970)?

Yet for a black community in search of a progressive, assertive, also more assimilative image of itself, one that was less ethnic and could be viewed as fitting more comfortably into the cultural mainstream, the TV servants of the early era became anachronistic embarrassments who eventually had to go.

But in the Eisenhower 1950s what else was there of the black experience to see on television? Well, for a brief time, hope loomed on the horizon with the appearance of "The Nat 'King' Cole Show" (1956–1957) on NBC. The music of singer Nat "King" Cole, mainstream pop rather than ethnic rhythm and blues, had already won him a large national following. And Cole himself came across as a model gentleman: smooth, polished, soft-spoken, debonair, easy-going, urbane. The black community could find no fault in Cole, who won great support from the black press when launching his program. But advertisers—and the advertising agencies—feared Cole could never win the southern television market, considered the most conservative area of the country (and, of course, the most racist, although no one put it quite in those terms in those days). In the South and the North, some NBC affiliates did refuse to carry the Cole series, which suffered from poor ratings in general. NBC stuck with it longer than most expected, however, even going so far as to expand it from a 15-minute program to a half-hour one. But after a year, the network dropped it.

Otherwise so rarely were blacks seen that, by watching the tube, one might have assumed that Negroes were not a part of American life or history. No blacks were seen regularly on the family dramas or the westerns or detective stories. Instead the Negro seemed to be handled as something of a Special Event as he/she turned up as a guest on the variety shows or as a participant in the sports shows (be it a baseball game or boxing bout). Sometimes a series like Edward R. Murrow's "Person to Person" (the celebrity interview show that ran from 1953 to 1961) might focus on Eartha Kitt or Louis Armstrong. Or Murrow's documentary series "See It Now" (1952–1955) might feature Armstrong or Marian Anderson. Then, too, there were the special dramatic programs. In 1955, Ossie Davis starred in a production of Eugene O'Neill's *The Emperor Jones*. Struggling young actor Sidney Poitier also made rare television appearances on Ponds Theater's 1955 "Fascinating Stranger" and "The Parole Chief" (1952) as well as The Philco Playhouse 1955 production of "A Man Is Ten Feet Tall," a rare TV attempt to examine racial tensions. The Hallmark Hall of Fame also broadcast two all-black productions of *Green Pastures* (1955, 1957). Of course, this gentle comedy, first done on the stage in the 1930s, depicted an agreeable, naive Negro and plainly did not contribute anything toward a progressive new black image.

During this time, only one dramatic black star appeared on television with a relative degree of regularity: Ethel Waters. She starred in such productions as the 1955 General Electric Theater "Winner by Decision" (with Harry Belafonte), Playwrights' 56's 1955 production of *The Sound and the Fury* (which five years later became a feature film again with Waters playing Faulkner's Dilsey), Matinee Theater's "Sing for Me" in 1957, and later on such programs of the 1960s as Route 66's "Good Night, Sweet Blues" (1961) and Great Adventure's "Go Down Moses" (1963). In these and her other TV dramas, Waters's roles were not as demanding as her earlier ones in theater and movies. But still quite well known to the American public, she had become such a national archetype—the ever-endurable strong black woman—that primetime maintained a special reserved spot for her, which was not the case with any other black performer of that age. Otherwise, dramatic television for the Negro was a blank.

A change in television's view of the Negro came about only with a change in the social/political temper in American society. In the late 1950s and early 1960s, as an increasingly more vocal black America launched its Civil Rights Movement, television found it had no choice but to cover the protests, sit-ins, demonstrations. Nightly, the network news exposed viewers to incredible scenes in which fire hoses were turned on protesters, attack dogs were unleashed, and billy clubs were openly used. Also introduced to the television audience were the new black leaders—Martin Luther King, Jr., with his cool, more "acceptable" style and Malcolm X with his incendiary power—each of whom, aware of the medium's power, used television to get their messages across. Each emerged also a media star. Eventually, a new portrait of the Negro—more educated, articulate, no longer servile—had to make its way into the primetime series schedule.

The subtle image shift started slowly. But as early as 1961, the sitcom "Car 54, Where Are You?" featured among its regular cast two black actors playing cops: Nipsey Russell and Frederick O'Neal. Then dramatic series such as "The Defenders" (1961–1965), "The Nurses" (1962–1965), "The Fugitive" (1963–1967), "The Naked City" (1958–1963), and "Slattery's People" (1964–1965) took the lead in featuring (as guests, not cast regulars) such new-style dramatic black talents as Ruby Dee, Louis Gossett, Jr., Diana Sands, Ivan Dixon, and Ossie Davis. During the Kennedy and Johnson years, as these programs reflected the slow integration of blacks into American life, the Negro protagonists stood as social symbols, emerging as metaphors for social/political inequities or injustices. Whenever a black character appeared, he seemed to have a tag pinned to him, indicating what particular social problem he was meant to represent.

The first dramatic series, however, to include a dramatic black performer as a cast member was the shortlived "East Side, West Side" (1963–1964). In this drama about a New York City social worker (George C. Scott), Cicely Tyson was hired to play the office secretary. Although not prominently featured in each week's episode, Tyson nevertheless, through her presence and her very appearance, introduced a new statement in black womanhood. Neither conventionally pretty nor one of those bland, ever-smiling untroubled women, she came across as resolutely intelligent and committed to a personal set of ideals. Sporting an Afro, she represented for young black America a politically-aware woman who, by refusing to straighten her hair, had abandoned Western beauty standards to connect to her African roots. In 1967, Tyson also made a breakthrough with her appearances on the daytime soap opera "The Guiding Light."

In 1965, other ground was broken with the arrival of the NBC series "I Spy." Today because the program looks so hopelessly innocent, it might be hard to imagine the controversy this series once provoked. But NBC fretted about the southern market's reaction to a program co-starring a white actor (Robert Culp) and a black one (Bill Cosby) in which the two men appeared on equal footing. Actually, when we look at old episodes today, it's obvious that Culp's Kelly was usually in command, just as Don Johnson would be some 20 years later when working on "Miami Vice" (1984) with black actor Philip Michael Thomas. But, in large part because of Cosby's performance and persona, "I Spy" was successful, not shooting to the very top of the ratings but winning support nonetheless, especially from the young. Without any rough ethnic edges, Cosby's was a very modulated, middle-class style and stance, just the type of image both the NAACP and the large viewing audience wanted. To his credit, Cosby also had the air of a man who could not be sold short.

Just as important as the Cosby persona, though, was the theme "I Spy" introduced to television, that of interracial male bonding, which previously had been hinted at but not explored in the Jack Benny/ Rochester relationship. This theme was never fully explored on "I Spy" either, but the subject had been brought out of the closet. Now audiences came face to face with a fantasy almost as alluring to the American consciousness as that of the all-knowing Mammy figure: namely that of a passionate (but safely nonsexual) union between black and white. Seeing Cosby and Culp together at work and play, linking arms and psyches to pull through difficult times and situations, audiences could get lost in a wish-fulfillment dream that assured them that everything remained fine and dandy between the races, that indeed the turbulent history of race relations might not really have happened at all. Without any cultural gaps to overcome, the stars of "I Spy" start off on a common ground. Their soothing, anxiety-free relationship also negates a previous nightmare of the national psyche: that of the brutal black buck, out to tear down the white man and his system—and to take his woman.

Arriving during an era of intense racial turmoil, "I Spy" projected a vision of an ideal time and land where black and white went hand in hand. Interestingly enough, the series took place not in the United States but always in foreign lands. Regardless, its ideal interracial male relationship was to be repeated regularly on such television series as "NYPD" (1967–1969 with Robert Hooks and Jack Warden), "Tenspeed and Brownshoe" (1980 with Ben Vereen and Jeff Goldblum), "Enos" (1980–1981, with Samuel Wright and Sonny Shroyer), "Stir Crazy" (1985 with Larry Riley and Joseph Guzaldo), "The Insiders" (1985–1986) with Stoney Jackson and Nicholas Campbell), and the leading exponent of them all, "Miami Vice," in which Don Johnson and Philip Michael Thomas repeatedly reassure each other of their mutual loyalty and support. The interracial dynamics in "I Spy" are what made this otherwise routine series work and have an impact on American popular culture. And so now the Negro had come into American homes not as a servant but as a trusted, reliable friend.

One year after "I Spy"'s debut, other such Negro friends were seen in network series: Greg Morris as ace mechanic Barney Collier on the popular "Mission: Impossible" (1966–1973); Hari Rhodes was the African conservationist in the African adventure series "Daktari" (1966–1969, once again, of course, a white star was the focal point of the program, assisted naturally by his black buddy); and Nichelle Nichols as Lieutenant Uhura, a member of the starship *Enterprise* crew on "Star Trek" (1966–1969). Black audiences had a special regard and affection for Nichols because part of the fun of watching "Star Trek" was to see if Captain Kirk cast any furtive glances in Uhura's direction. So intolerably sexy was she that one felt somebody on the *Enterprise* must be panting for her. That same game of spotting undercover sexual vibes enhanced the appeal of "Mannix" (1968–1975), which featured Gail Fisher as secretary Peggy Fair to hunk hero Mike Conners. She was pert and pretty; he was tough and strong. Together they were mighty close.

But, of course, any suggestion of sexual interplay between the races was taboo on the tube. Yet interracial sex was never far from anyone's mind, the best example of that being an incident that occurred in 1968 when Harry Belafonte appeared with British pop star Petula Clark on her special "Petula." As the two performed together, Clark had held Belafonte's arm, thus sending the sponsor, the advertising agency, and the network up in arms. It was feared that mere touch might suggest the idea of a sexual attraction between the two that would shock and alienate the vast TV audience. For years to come interracial sex/romance would remain a forbidden subject. In the 1970s when the young white hero of the daytime soap opera "Days of Our Lives" took an interest in an attractive young black girl played by Tina Andrews, so many viewer letters of protest against such a pairing poured in that eventually Andrews was written out of the show. Her character went off to Howard University to study. And that was that. Later in the 1980s when Georg Stanford Brown and white actress Kirstie Alley had hot and steamy love scenes in the mini-series "North and South," letters might have poured in had not Brown's character been conveniently killed off (in punishment, of course, for having dared defile a white woman). Alley's character, an abolitionist, was also depicted as such a driven, neurotic soul that audiences no doubt accepted her interracial marriage to Brown as the ploy of a very disturbed woman. Nevertheless, she, too, ended up dying in the series.

Negro buddies, helpmates, friends, and companions showed up, though, on other series of the 1960s. Some color came to the Old West in the form of Raymond St. Jacques in 1965 as Simon Blake on "Rawhide." In 1965 Ivan Dixon was one of the American soldiers in a Nazi prisoner-of-war camp during World War II on "Hogan's Heroes." On the 1966 "Hawk," police hero Burt Reynolds was assisted by black detective Wayne Grice. Don Mitchell aided—and stood stolidly behind the wheelchair of—Raymond Burr on "Ironside" (1967–1975). A runaway slave named Gabe Cooper, played by Roosevelt Grier, appeared on "Daniel Boone" in 1969. After its long run had begun, "Peyton Place" in 1968 brought on a black family played by Ruby Dee, Percy Rodrigues, and Glynn Turman. And then on "The High Chaparral," light-skinned black actor Frank Silvera, who often played "foreigners," portrayed the father of Linda Cristal (from 1967 to 1970); both presumably were Mexicans. This was a rare instance in which a black actor was free to play a non-black role without any to-do.

But with this new activity and opportunities for dramatic black performers, a Negro still was not cast as a full-fledged series star (Cosby was considered a co-star in "I Spy") until the arrival in 1968 of the much-maligned "Julia". Starring Diahann Carroll as Julia Baker, a widowed nurse rearing her young son, Corey, in California, at first glance the series seemed ideal for the era of President Johnson's Great Society. Unlike "Beulah"'s maid-heroine, "Julia" presented an attractive, educated, self-supporting black woman who was just as capable a wage-earner and do-er as her white counterparts. "Julia"'s covert message was simple: Julia was making it in a forward-looking society that had a place for her.

White audiences applauded the series. Black audiences also—at least initially—delighted in viewing a program with some semblance of black life. But it soon became apparent that "Julia"—tame and timid, romanticized and prettified—had appeared at a surprisingly inopportune time. For by 1968, the days of passive resistance—the student sit-ins—had been replaced by an explosive era during which ghetto riots shot up throughout the nation. The new group of black political leaders such as Stokely Carmichael, H. Rapp Brown, and later Angela Davis spoke of American society's history of racial inequities and violence. The Kerner Commission's report had also stressed that the black unrest that had led to the riots was a direct outgrowth of white racism. "Julia," however, focused on the middle-class heroine's harmonious and cutesy relationships with her white employer, her white neighbors, indeed her white community and white way of life with no more a suggestion of racial conflict than there had been on "Beulah." The program denied the historical events and attitudes of its day, removing itself completely from the social concerns and issues, not to mention the harsh urban realities of black life in America. Viewing the series in political terms, liberals and young more militant blacks criticized and eventually denounced the program as false and distorted. Years later in her autobiography *Diahann*, Diahann Carroll wrote of how her struggles to have a more realistic black point of view injected into the series went nowhere. Here one of the television industry's most glaring problems— the fact that black images were created by white hands—came squarely to the forefront. Carroll also wrote that finally, in part because of the criticism, she decided not to continue in the series after its third season. Once again, as with "Amos 'n' Andy," controversy closed in on a popular black sitcom.

Also debuting in 1968 was "The Mod Squad." Here the television industry shrewdly adapted to changing times by simply reshaping a familiar formula and genre to give them a seemingly fresh and "with it" look: in this instance, the old-style cop show had been updated with counterculture attitudes by the casting of black actor Clarence Williams III with white performers Michael Cole and Peggy Lipton as three near drop-outs brought back into the system to help clean it up. Because it at least paid some lip service to social change and then-current rebellious attitudes among the American young, white and black (with his puffed-up Afro and his distinctive scowl, Williams looked like a militant campus student), "The Mod Squad" met with acceptance and avoided controversy in a way "Julia" could not. Yet militant black heroes never became primetime superstars. A series like "The Outcasts" (which ran one season, 1968-1969) that featured Otis Young as an outspoken, independent black man never caught on with audiences.

Curiously, the last years of the 1960s and the very early 1970s proved a period of transition: audiences, black and white, still were unsure what they wanted from black television characters. Nor were the television executives at all certain how best to handle the black problem and the black experience. Blacks could not be ignored; they were too much in the headlines. So various shows employed various styles to reach the audience. A series like "Room 222" (1969-1974)— about a high school teacher trying to reach students, black and white— dealt with such issues as drugs and adolescent alienation but adopted a gentle tone while doing so and met with some success. The series introduced Lloyd Haynes and Denise Nicholas as late-1960s-style black educators: articulate, sincere, dedicated, yet more inclined toward helping the young accept the system's demands rather than leading them off in revolt.

The same could be said of the hero of "The Bill Cosby Show" (1969-1971), Chet Kincaid (played by Cosby), a high school gym teacher in Los Angeles. The series, however, failed to find an audience. Interestingly enough, Cosby's pliant and middle-class image here proved ineffective. The show, like "Julia," seemed evasive, not problem oriented enough for an era with social conflicts very much on its mind. Yet, ironically, more than a decade later during the new conservatism of the Reagan years, Cosby would return with a similar middle-class image but would meet with extraordinary success the second time around.

Despite its failure, the earlier Cosby series, however, did touch on a trend that became quite successful throughout much of the 1970s. Often Cosby employed friends or oldtimers in show business. On one classic episode, he starred veteran performers Jackie "Moms" Mabley and Mantan Moreland as Chet Kincaid's aunt and uncle, a quarrelsome couple repeatedly berating and bickering with one another. Shrewdly, Cosby contrasted his cool, rather straitlaced style with their looser, funkier hot tirades; it was a glimpse of the newly educated, polite bourgeois versus the old raucous, loud, uninhibited downhome older generation. Their timing perfect, their sense of character splendid, their own personalities meshing together wonderfully, Mabley and Moreland stole the show, showcasing ethnic theatre at its best. Neither would have been out of place on "Amos 'n' Andy." With this particular episode, Cosby paid homage to a form of black entertainment that looked as if it had vanished.

Ironically, during the early Nixon years when educated black characters were the leads in the all-black series "Barefoot in the Park" (1970-1971) or "serious," dramatic supporting characters were important supporting figures in everything from "The Young Rebels" (1970-1971) to "The Young Lawyers" (1970-1971) to "The Interns" (1970-1971) to "The Silent Force" (1970-1971) to "The Mary Tyler Moore Show" (1970-1977), it would not be long before television did a surprising flipflop. Suddenly, the oldstyle ethnic humor—now in new younger hands—made a remarkable comeback; in fact, it came to dominate the influx of black sitcoms of the 1970s.

The first show to indicate the re-emerging popularity of ethnic humor was "The Flip Wilson Show" (1970-1974). With such weekly guests as Richard Pryor, Bill Cosby or Lena Horne, this gifted comedian created a black communal atmosphere, his routines, skits, and character parodies (such as Reverend LeRoy), all having grown out of the black theater and black clubs that had influenced the actors of TV's "Amos 'n' Andy." Yet now a double-consciousness was at work. Aware that his audience was as much white as black, Wilson's humor stressed aggression and an uncanny sense of survival. At the center of his show, his character Geraldine—gregarious, fun-loving, outspoken, sassy—was a loud, raunchy lass equipped with a knowledge of the ways and attitudes of the streets and of men. "Don't touch me. You don't know me," was Geraldine's steady refrain, informing us week after week that here was a black woman able to take care of herself. Frequently criticized precisely because some objected to the Geraldine character as a throwback to Sapphire (she was, but she had a built-in awareness of the effect she had on audiences), the program met with great success anyway, launching Wilson as a major TV star of the early 1970s. At the same time, "All in the Family" (1971-1983) repopularized ethnic humor of another sort. (Some might say it simply repopularized oldstyle comic racism.)

Whoever would have guessed, though, that now when—at long last—black television series would come into vogue (with several running concurrently), most would be comedies featuring families or friends hootin' and hollerin' and carryin' on as much as had old Kingfish and his friends from the Mystic Knights of the Sea? Leading the way of the new-style, old-style black-cast ethnic sitcoms in 1972 was "Sanford and Son"—the story of a Los Angeles junk dealer and his grown son and their rowdy network of buddies—which shot to the top of the ratings and propelled veteran comic Redd Foxx to mainstream stardom. Following its success, viewers could tune in to such series as "That's My Mama" (1974–1975), "Good Times" (1974–1979), "What's Happening!!" (1976–1979), and the immensely successful "The Jeffersons" (1975–1985). Emerging at the same time were attempts at another type of black-oriented series: "Get Christie Love" (1974–1975), "Shaft" (1973–1974), and "Tenafly" (1973–1974), all action detective/cop shows, which failed to win audience support. For the television audience of the Nixon and Ford years, there was a clearly defined interest and enthusiasm in seeing ethnic types but only if these types could provide laughter. Except for "Sanford and Son" and perhaps "The Jeffersons," invigorated by the testy, garrulous performances, respectively, of Foxx and Sherman Hemsley, these shows were mostly 1960s rhetoric/1970s shallowness. Thus so many of the sitcoms were labelled as part of the New Minstrelsy.

On one level, the series succeeded in introducing the television viewer to homes and lives in America different from those presented on such shows as "Father Knows Best" (1954–1963) or "The Brady Bunch" (1969–1974). America now acknowledged its black population. But whereas a show like "Father Knows Best" had displayed an emotional truth in many of its episodes despite the ideal world it presented, many of the new black sitcoms were weak and pallid, their basic situations and family relationships having been created by persons—white writers, directors, producers—from an entirely different cultural experience and perspective. Seldom presenting a sensitive, intimate portrait of black life, the shows were also littered with stereotypes. Most of the mothers—large, overweight, dowdy, dark-skinned—were mammy figures. Some of the husbands or children (like J.J.), simply the old coons.

Throughout the 1970s, though, black sitcoms continued to come—and go: "Grady," (1975–1976), "Sanford Arms" (1977), "Baby, I'm Back" (1978). Primetime dramatic shows about blacks rarely appeared. Yet, ironically, two of the most important television dramatic events of the 1970s focused—in serious and thoughtful terms—on the black experience: first "The Autobiography of Miss Jane Pittman" (1974), which marked a new maturity for the TV movie; and then "Roots" (1977), the mighty mini-series that won unprecedented high ratings and engulfed the imagination of the entire nation during its eight-night run. Epic, sweeping, larger-than-life, empowered with strong, vibrant performances, "Roots" changed television history. Not only did its success elevate the mini-series's stature (indicating audiences would stay home night after night to follow a drama), but it also proved the popularity of family sagas that spanned many generations. Both "Jane Pittman" and "Roots" also indicated that the race question—indeed race dramas—was still very much on the minds of the American public. Yet neither had a lasting effect on black television programming. One might have assumed a flock of similar serious black dramas would have paraded across the airways. But no such thing happened. True some dramatic black specials did appear not long after "Roots"'s success: "Backstairs at the White House" (1979), "Green Eyes," (1976) "King," (1978), "Attica,"

(1980), "Roots: The Next Generations" (1979), and "Palmerstown USA" (1980-1981). But for the duration of the Carter years, television went without a significant racial change in its weekly dramatic fare.

By the politically conservative Reagan 1980s, no one had much hope of seeing a provocative program that treated black America with any sensitive insight. In fact, audiences seemed on such a conservative bent that even the black-cast sitcoms were beginning to look passe. Now whenever important black characters appeared in comedy series, usually they were lifted out of the black community and placed into a white environment—be it a family or work situation—basically a non-ethnic cultural setting which the vast white audience could readily identify with. A good example was the hit "Diff'rent Strokes" (1978-198?) that starred pint-sized Gary Coleman and Todd Bridges as two orphaned ghetto lads who went to live in the home of a white Park Avenue millionaire. Had this been an early 1970s series, the boys would have moved in with black relatives rather than be ensconced in the cultural milieu of a great white father figure. But for the late 1970s/early 1980s audience, the millionaire provides the material comforts (as well as the subliminal emotional ones) that the black community supposedly can never hope to match. Gary Coleman became a major child star because of "Diff'rent Strokes," but like our friend Beulah, only by showing up in a white home. Not long afterward such series as "Webster" (1983) and "Gimme a Break" (1981) also featured black characters at the center of white households/environments. The racially mixed combo comedy of the early 1980s became the most successful type. Later black performers appeared on other essentially white programs: Diahann Carroll on "Dynasty," Philip Michael Thomas on "Miami Vice," Stoney Jackson on "The Insiders," Larry Riley on "Stir Crazy." The fact that again, as of old, no racial tensions erupted between the characters indicated a suppression of the race issue.

Midway in the 1980s, TV history took another twist with the appearance and extraordinary popularity of "The Cosby Show." Here was an unusual black family sitcom that did not easily find a network home. Assuming audiences would never sit week after week to watch the ins and outs of black family life, ABC had rejected the series, despite the fact that Cosby was a major star. NBC thought otherwise. Taking a chance on the show, network executives, along with just about everyone else, were surprised to see the program immediately shoot to the very top of the ratings, staying in the number one spot week after week, even maintaining that number one position during its summer reruns. The series success also helped a troubled NBC re-establish its prestige and become the number one network in the ratings.

Much of the credit for the show's success went to Cosby himself, its creator. Already such black directors as Bill Duke, Stan Lathan, Georg Stanford Brown, Roy Campanella, Jr., and Gilbert Moses had directed episodes of major primetime programs, thus providing a black point of view, even when not necessarily needed, where none had existed in the past. But not until the advent of Cosby's show had there been a program in which the governing sensibility—the absolute first and last word on just about every detail—lay in black hands. Moreover, Cosby had not taken the easy route out. He had refused to fall back on the standard raucous ghetto family that cracks jokes or sounds off on one another. Instead his was a richly humorous depiction of black upper-middle-class life, a study of people, in so many respects, no different from white America, yet in other very specific and subtle ways, quite different. His series had shown the connective tissue between two separate cultural experiences in America. Some critics complained that the series was too soft and idealized, not focused enough on the type of realities most black families had to contend with. Regardless, an important new step had been taken in television.

Afterward, network executives, assuming they had spotted a new trend, brought a few other black-oriented shows to the airways: "Charlie & Company" (1985), "Melba," (1986) and "Amen" (1986). Of the three, only the last met with a degree of success, thanks primarily to the performance and popularity of star Sherman Hemsley. The problem remained the same: unlike "The Cosby Show," these black series lacked the type of black control and input that might have made them refreshing and distinctive. The industry had immediately returned to its old concepts and formulas.

And so, after almost forty years since "Beulah" had made its first appearance, the television executives, the sponsors, the advertising agencies who controlled so much of what America viewed, did not seem to have learned very much. More black faces had turned up on the small screen. But one still had a very rare glimpse of the rhythms and passions, the outlooks and attitudes, the dreams and aches, of black life in America. "The Cosby Show" had revealed what some new blood—and new color—could do for the tube, infusing it with a new perspective and taking it in a new direction that grasped the attention and respect of almost everyone. Now it was simply up to the networks to gather their wits and decide to give others of that new blood and new color a chance to work within the television industry. Only then would we be able to get "Beulah" out of the Hendersons' house and into a pad of her own.

TV Series

"Amen" (premiered 9/17/86)

NBC. *Ex. P.* Ed Weinberger, who had been a co-creator of "Taxi" and "The Cosby Show." The first episode was shot under the direction of black director Stan Lathan. Some of the later episodes were the work of another black director, Bill Duke. Cast includes: That powerhouse of the New York stage Barbara Montgomery.

This show marked the return to series television of Sherman Hemsley, the testy, wisecracking star of the long-running "The Jeffersons." Cast here as a Philadelphia church deacon named Ernest Frye, Hemsley is up to his old tricks, verbally barking and biting at just about anybody in sight, forever anxious to let off some steam. That's much of Hemsley's appeal: never holding anything in, he satisfies our need to *get everybody told.*

In the series' opening episode, the sparks flew. Unhappy with the overweight pastor who has let church attendance fall, Hemsley's Frye cries out, "Either you have to lose some weight or we have to build a bigger church." Later he adds, "People are complaining that you're blocking the view of the choir." And at one point, he informs the poor man, "God gave each of us a temple. You have torn yours down and put up a Pizza Hut." Has the chunky preacher any choice but to resign? Once the church hires a new minister, played by Clifton Davis (marking his return to series television after his "That's My Mama" days), the sitcom focuses on conflicts between the two.

Were it not for Hemsley, this sitcom's true oddity (or audacity)

Clifton Davis (l.) is the handsome new minister; Sherman Hemsley is the irascible deacon in the "church comedy" "Amen."

would be blatantly apparent: this is essentially a comedy about the black church (and by suggestion a comment on the black religious experience). We can't imagine a television comedy about a Waspy Presbyterian or Episcopalian church being made, at least not without a serious uproar.

Anyway. Lively, fast-moving, minstelsy, "Amen" has a great deal of old-style hootin' and hollerin'. And Hemsley himself has not really come up with a character much different from his George Jefferson. His unabashed headstrong energy carries the thing along though. Without him, the series wouldn't have, well, *a prayer*. The series went on to score in the top fifteen in the ratings. And Anna Maria Horsford, as the whiney, man-crazed daughter, acquired a following.

"Amos 'n' Andy" (6/51 to 6/53)

CBS. *D*. most episodes by Charles Barton. The production was supervised by Freeman Gosden and Charles Correll. Cast includes: Johnny Lee (as Lawyer Algonquin J. Calhoun) and Nick Stewart (as Lightnin').

One of the most famous and controversial sitcoms. Also surprisingly one of the best made and acted.

Having originated as a radio series, "Amos 'n' Andy" was the brainchild of two white men, Freeman Gosden and Charles Correll. In 1926 in Chicago, the two first created a radio series called "Sam 'n' Henry," which centered on the comic exploits of two black men who spoke broken English with rigid, heavy dialects. Two years later, "Sam 'n' Henry" became "Amos 'n' Andy," now the story of Amos Jones and Andrew Hogg Brown, two black men who had migrated from the South to Chicago, and later to Harlem, in search of a better way of life.

In 1929, the series was picked up and run nationally by NBC. Its impact was astonishing. During the fifteen minutes that the program aired (it played six times a week, from 7:00 to 7:15 in the evening), much of America seemed to come to a halt. It was said that bars, restaurants, department stores, sometimes even movie theaters just about closed up shop to wheel out radios for their customers to hear the show. On any given night if you walked through the streets of a small town or city, it's been said you could also hear the familiar voices of Amos and Andy coming from open windows everywhere. Presidents such as Coolidge, later Truman and Eisenhower, all boasted of loving the series. In fact, when "Amos 'n' Andy" eventually went to television, both Truman and Eisenhower gave casting suggestions to the producers. From the radio program came new national catch phrases: "I'se regusted," "Check and double check," "Now ain't dat sumptin'," and "Holy Mackerel." The series became a part of Americana (a part of the nation's collective experience); the characters took on a folkloric status.

"Amos 'n' Andy" reached the peak of its popularity during the 1930s. At one point, the series reached an audience of some forty million listeners. No doubt Americans took the show to heart because its characters expressed—in acceptable comic terms—Depression-era concerns and issues. The characters were always looking for work. They always had money problems. So anxious was Andy to get a few dollars in his pocket that he was forever falling prey to elaborate get-rich schemes and deals.

On radio, the whites playing the roles came up with stereotyped and

"Amos 'n' Andy"

American television's most controversial sit-com: "Amos 'n' Andy" with Spencer Williams (as Andy Brown), Tim Moore (as the outlandish George "Kingfish" Stevens), and Alvin Childress (as Amos Jones).

overdone dialects and situations. Originally, the creators Gosden and Correll played all the roles; later a few real black actors were brought into the series. With an inbuilt condescension in its scripts, "Amos 'n' Andy" was able to boost the spirits of its vast white audience by making that audience believe that if these lowly *coloreds* could make it through hard times, then surely anyone else could, too. For most, "Amos 'n' Andy" was enjoyable racist trash.

Yet although "Amos 'n' Andy" was never authentic black humor, what cannot be denied is that for those black Americans who listened to the program, there was an awareness that the show's slick fraudulent comedy was based on real elements of a black folk humor tradition. The show's creators had observed the language, the attitudes, the rhythm of rural black Americans. But they had not *understood* what they had seen. Had black performers at least been permitted to play all the roles on radio, it would have been a far different kind of program. But perhaps what's most important about the series is that during the troubled Depression era, ersatz black humor—in the most distorted of forms—was being used successfully to convey optimism and enthusiasm for life. The same was true of movies of the period, as audiences marvelled over the way such black stars as Hattie McDaniel and Eddie "Rochester" Anderson marched about, using their spontaneity and personal sense of humor to overturn or simply endure life's headaches and problems.

For two decades, "Amos 'n' Andy" remained a popular radio fixture. In 1943, it became a half-hour show. Then in 1948, CBS paid Freeman Gosden and Charles Correll the then-unprecedented sum of $2.5 million for the rights to the series. The future of "Amos 'n' Andy" looked bright.

But neither CBS nor the program's creators were prepared for the change in national temperament after the Second World War. Within black America, a new political consciousness and a new awareness of the importance of image had emerged. And so from the moment CBS announced plans to film "Amos 'n' Andy" as a television series, using real black performers, a controversy sprang up within the black community. At the forefront stood the NAACP, which, at its 1951 convention, denounced the series because "it tends to strengthen the conclusion among uninformed and prejudiced people that Negroes are inferior, lazy, dumb, and dishonest." The organization called for public condemnation and a boycott of the show. The Committee for the Negro in the Arts also said that "hundreds of thousands of dollars have been spent to insult Negroes for 30 minutes a week."

The real problem, of course, was that television viewers were given no choice of black images to select from.

Because the television version of "Amos 'n' Andy" has acquired a negative legend, it's now repeatedly viewed through a distorted lens without its place in history or the power of its performers fairly assessed. Today the series' characters now strike audiences at first glance as being creatures from another time zone. The dialects are frequently (but not always) broad and theatrical. Every piece of dialogue or schtick is pushed to the limit, to a heady, almost delirious point of excess. Once one adjusts to the rhythms the actors create, it's hard not to become caught up in their comic dramas. And it soon also becomes apparent that the performers are all first-rate and often inspired.

Basically, the series deals with members of the black fraternal lodge, The Mystic Knights of the Sea. The most serious character is Amos (Alvin Childress), co-owner of the Fresh Air Taxi-Cab Company. Hardworking, mild-mannered, sensible, gentle, Amos is a family man devoted to his wife and daughter. He's one of the few characters who seems untheatrical, rather natural, and "real." In this cast of extroverts, Amos is also a bit boring.

Then there is Andy Brown (Spencer Williams). Usually dressed in a suit with a derby on his head and a cigar in his mouth, Andy's an engaging dunce, who's always falling in love and forever embarking on some hare-brained scheme to make a quick buck or live the good life. Whenever troubled or in doubt about some matter, Andy rushes off for advice from his friend George "Kingfish" Stevens.

As it turns out, Kingfish, as played by the immensely gifted Tim Moore, is the series' true star. Has there ever been a character as *bodaciously* larger than life as Kingfish? Not even Stepin Fetchit in his flamboyant heyday could match this fiendishly outlandish figure. During this period in American television history—before images had become so safely reassuring and wholesomely middle class—there appeared an array of tube eccentrics: saucy and scarily outrageous heroes and heroines like Lucy, Uncle Miltie, and Sergeant Bilko, not a one of whom was your ordinary, everyday next-door neighbor type. Forever full of ideas for earning some extra money or for getting a job in show business, a character like Lucy, if pushed, pushed back. Despite all the distortions about women, marriage, and male/female relationships, Lucy and some other early television stars still dazzle us because of their magnetic momentum, their non-stop single-mindedness, their positions as figures outside the realm of the ordinary, the expected, the mundane. If anything, they were anti-bourgeois individualists, bucking the established rules to live out their own personal craziness. "Amos 'n' Andy"'s Kingfish, who uses Andy just as Lucy used Ethel in her schemes, is very much a part of this old tradition. Likable but never comforting and a predecessor of sorts to Richard Pryor's Crazy Nigger, Kingfish's rowdy approach to life may have been one of the things that distressed the NAACP at a time when cultural assimilation was thought a viable, positive social goal for the black community. Kingfish was always too loud, too brash, too outspoken, too much of a show-off to ever mix with refined white folks.

Of course, Kingfish was not the only larger-than-life figure on the show. At home, he had to contend with his wife Sapphire, the shrew of all shrews, and his mother-in-law, Mama, neither of whom ever gave him a break. If matters became too sticky, they simply locked Kingfish out of the apartment. Part of what was so funny about high-stepping braggart Kingfish was that he was hopelessly henpecked, able to manipulate everyone except the women at home. His mother-in-law problems turned comic what many American males at the time viewed as a real dilemma. The important women on "Amos 'n' Andy"—Sapphire (Ernestine Wade), Mama (Amanda Randolph), and Madame Queen (Lillian Randolph, who was forever trying to snare Andy)—were all harpy battle-axes, yappin' and yellin' at the drop of a hat. Because of their *loud* explosions, they've never been forgiven. No one can ever deny that the black women on this series were rigidly stereotyped. They were not permitted to be "soft" or traditionally feminine. But it cannot be denied either that the actresses play their roles brilliantly.

Despite the stereotypes (almost everyone seems a bit of a simpleton), the entire cast is an example of an ideal ensemble acting troupe. They bring an inspired sense of the outrageous to their roles. Their timing is perfect. The doubletakes, the sly winks, the rapid interplay among characters are skillfully executed. And in many respects, it's like watching ethnic theater, the type that black audiences saw at the Apollo and other black theaters when Moms Mabley, Slappy White or Dusty Fletcher performed. Many of the television performers, such as Tim Moore, had had years of training and experience in black vaudeville and were accustomed to playing their laughs to a black audience. Moore's stagey timing and his penchant for mugging were geared for the black audience. While the white actors who had originated the Amos and Andy characters on radio had had to approximate a dialect, Moore knew the rhythm and the language, the intonations and inflections inside out. In the original, the white actors also seemed to look down on their characters. But Tim Moore seemed to genuinely love his Kingfish role. It's interesting that much later in television history when Moms Mabley and Redd Foxx finally made it to the mainstream, black audiences were happy to see these ethnic stars of the past get a big break. Their humor and approach to comedy were no different from those of the "Amos 'n' Andy" TV cast. But because of the new social attitudes in the 1970s, Mabley and Foxx were acceptable to audiences.

Sadly, television's "Amos 'n' Andy" was ethnic comedy yanked from its cultural context. Had the series been performed at black theaters for black audiences, no one would have thought twice about it. Because the program was aired on national "white" television—reaching a white audience that saw the characters as true embodiments of the American Negro—it struck many as a distortion that historically *had* to go.

An interesting aspect of the show today is its tame look. The characters live in spotless middle-class settings, without any of the grime of ghetto life that turned up later in a series like "Good Times" or "Sanford and Son." This is also an isolated world with very few whites or any mention of racial problems.

Bowing to pressure from the NAACP and other groups, CBS dropped "Amos 'n' Andy" from its network lineup after only two seasons. (There were 78 episodes.) But the show was kept in syndication until 1966. Ironically, a whole new generation of school kids, black and white, saw the reruns, usually right after arriving home from school, viewing it along with the old "Our Gang" series, another popular show in syndication. Curiously among this audience, which was gradually being introduced to new black images on television and in films, the series seemed almost harmless. Today viewed in its proper historical/cultural framework, "Amos 'n' Andy" often works for a black audience.

"The A-Team" (2/8/83 to 6/14/87)

NBC.

When NBC program chief Brandon Tartikoff breezed into the Larry Holmes/Gerry Cooney title boxing bout in Las Vegas, he spotted Mr. T.—fresh from his success in *Rocky III*—at the center of the large crowd's attention. It didn't take Tartikoff long to come up with an idea for a new show. To producer Stephen Cannell, he wrote the following memo: "*Road Warrior. Magnificent Seven. Dirty Dozen.* 'Mission: Impossible.' All rolled into one. And Mr. T. drives the car."

That's precisely the kind of series Cannell helped create in "The A-Team," which revolves around a small band of Vietnam veterans: John Hannibal Smith (George Peppard), the group's leader and a master of disguises; Templeton "The Face" Peck (Dirk Benedict), a handsome charmer; Howling Mad Murdock (Dwight Schultz), a nutty pilot; Amy Allen (Melinda Culea), a reporter sometimes along for the ride (but not along very long; she was later replaced by Maria Heasley); and B.A. (for Bad Attitude) Baracus, a mechanic and driver, tough and loudmouthed, and played with a comic strip/community theater precision by Mr. T.

Wanted by the authorities, the vets are soldiers of fortune, self-appointed vigilantes, too, who hire themselves out to the unfortunate, determined to right wrongs, to aid, protect, and defend. On the two-hour pilot that launched the series, the group rescued an American newspaperman and an entire Mexican village from shifty bandits who were in league with guerrillas exploiting the poor peasants. Patriotism rang loud and clear on this series, which was an embodiment of the populist notion that rugged individualists grouped together in the name of true law and order were what makes a country strong and great. The show incorporates the Negro (via Mr. T., the real star of the show) into this populist mythology. But he's an action figure of astounding brawn and almost no brain. Admittedly, Mr. T. was not the coon here; that distinction went to Schultz's pilot, whom Mr. T.'s buck seldom failed to growl at. Of course, too, as *People* wrote, here sheer lawlessness was often saluted in the name of maintaining law and order. Violence and Mr. T.'s gaudy huffing and puffing were the chief ingredients for this series' success. At one point, The National Coalition on Television Violence found this the most violent program on the air, citing an average of 34 offensive acts per hour (versus an average of seven on other primetime shows). Parents were concerned because among the program's phenomenal 42 million viewers, some seven million were preteen children, ranging in age from two to eleven (all of whom idolized Mr. T.). The show's producer ignored the report. And "The A-Team" and Mr. T. remained at the top of the ratings, ranking for awhile (before the arrival of "The Cosby Show") as NBC's most successful series. During its fourth season, "The A-Team"'s ratings slipped disastrously. And word of dissension among the cast as well as tales of T.'s temperament and arrogance spread to the press. At one point, George Peppard labelled T. "an embarrassment." The next year NBC revamped the series, adding Robert Vaughn to the cast. But "The A-Team"'s glory days had vanished.

"Baby, I'm Back" (1/30/78 to 8/12/78)

CBS. *Ex. P.* Lila Garrett and Charles Fries.

"MISSING PERSON" read an advertisement for this series. Under those words were two mug shots of a black man (actor Demond Wilson). So who is this missing person? He's America's black father. Wilson played Ray Ellis, a man who walked out on his wife (Denise Nicholas) and two children (Tony Holmes and Kim Fields), but suddenly returns to their lives after seven long years. Moving into his wife's apartment building in Washington, D.C., he struggles to win her back but must contend with the objections of her feisty mother (Helen Martin) and her priggish army officer boyfriend (Ed Hall).

Denise Nicholas had some decent moments on this series, employing her intelligence and confidence to project a far more "modern" image of an educated, go-getter black woman than that of the mammy-like mothers on most of the black sitcoms such as Esther Rolle on "Good Times" or Mabel King on "What's Happening". But the basic premise of this series was a throwback to the past: at heart it's about a black father who's a shiftless but likable fellow, a bit like some of the characters on "Amos 'n' Andy" but without any of that series' outrageous sense of character. At the time of this series, there was a joke making the rounds: "What's the most confusing day in the black community? Father's Day!" The series reflects the sentiments of this joke—unfortunately. Helen Martin's mother-in-law, ever ready to hoot or holler, is also a relic of another era, although she displays a rather enjoyable mean scowl.

A short-lived series, pleasant at times but disheartening. Created by Lila Garrett and Mort Lachman.

"B.A.D. Cats" (1/4/80 to 2/8/80)

ABC.

Jimmie Walker appeared as Rodney Washington.
LaWanda Page played Ma.

"Barefoot in the Park" (9/24/70 to 1/14/71)

ABC.

The Neil Simon Broadway hit *Barefoot in the Park* had already been turned into a successful movie starring Jane Fonda and Robert Redford. Then someone got the very bright idea to turn it into a TV series but to do it in blackface. Scoey Mitchell played Paul Bratter, the young attorney working for Kendrick, Keene, and Klein. Tracy Reed was cast as his pretty bride, Corie. Thelma Carpenter played Corie's busybody mother, Mabel, a domestic for a Park Avenue family. And Nipsey Russell appeared as Honey Robinson, friend to the family and owner of a local pool hall.

Frankly, this was a terrible series. With the exception of Mitchell (who had problems with the producers and was eventually fired), no one here comes off well. That's a pity because the actors are talented yet wasted. In the case of Tracy Reed, she's almost completely bogged under by her ditsy heroine; she doesn't seem able to do anything with the part, and her appearance in this short-lived series may have seriously damaged her career. It wasn't until five years later that she showed what she was capable of—with her fine work in *Car Wash*.

The problem is not, as some would have us think, that the black characters are middle class. During this period, the only realistic black characters were thought to be those firmly entrenched in the ghetto. But what's really haywire is that the characters are *unbelievable* black middle-class figures. All one has to do is compare them with the realistic family on "The Cosby Show" in the 1980s or even Cosby's earlier series "The Bill Cosby Show." No attempt whatsoever has been made to alter the rhythm, the style, the idioms, the situations of the black newlyweds to enable an audience to understand what makes them so different from their white counterparts—and what also makes them so much the same. Everything's so Waspy, hunky-dory that it's almost as if the performers were speaking in a foreign language in a foreign land, almost as if they were performing something as alien to them as Kubuki Theater.

The series folded after four months.

"Baretta" (1/17/75 to 6/1/78)

ABC.

Michael D. Roberts was featured as the street-style informant Rooster, who often enough provided comic relief.

"Barney Miller" (1/23/75 to 9/9/82)

ABC.

Ron Glass was featured as Det. Ron Harris.

"Battlestar Galactica" (9/17/78 to 8/17/80)

ABC.

From 1978 to 1979, Herb Jefferson, Jr., appeared as Lt. Boomer and Terry Carter as Col. Tigh.

"Benson" (9/13/79 to 8/30/86)

ABC. Cast includes: Rene Auberjonois; Didi Cohn; and Billie Bird.

When "Soap" hit the airwaves in 1977, the press, along with various religious and ethnic groups, was up in arms, quick to dissect and debate this new series' controversial themes: adultery, homosexuality, nymphomania, transsexualism, impotence. Once the outcry died down, attention shifted from the themes to the characters, particularly an oddball black butler named Benson, who, played ingeniously by Robert Guillaume, nearly walked away with the show. The most independent and outspoken (also ironically the most Waspish) member of the Tate family's household, Benson, from the start, was finicky, demanding, and sardonic, a servant who, like Rochester, never thought of himself as such. He was known for his sneer, which, as *TV Guide* once pointed out, conveyed "by little more than pursed lips, a sidelong glance and the bare glimmer of a twinkle in a narrowed eye—the bemused disdain" with which he regarded those he worked for. Benson never hesitated to call things as he saw them. Nor did he hesitate to talk back. Should the doorbell ring, he might quickly toss a glance at a family member and ask, "You want me to get *that!*" Or if pushed too far and told to get one thing or another, Benson almost always seemed ready to respond, "Get it yourself." For his performance, Guillaume won an Emmy as Best Supporting Actor in a Comedy Series for 1978/1979, then starred in a spinoff series called, naturally, "Benson."

Here Benson has gone to work for a cousin of the Tate family, the widower Governor Gatling (James Noble), who, having just moved into the executive mansion, is the most befuddled and bewildered of politicians, a dope of a leader if ever there was one, unable to do much of anything without the counsel of the trusty Benson. Benson also must cope with the governor's precocious daughter Katie (Missy Gold) and a Storm Trooper of a housekeeper, the German Gretchen Kraus (Inga Swenson). So smooth and efficient a manservant is Benson that he becomes the budget director in the governor's administration and eventually—yes, anything is possible in the world of TV sitcoms—Lt. Governor.

Immensely successful, "Benson" owed much of its appeal to its star Guillaume, who went to great pains to depict his character as a highly individualized, strong-willed figure, not some lackey dolt. He was roundly praised by the critics, too. In *The New York Times*, John O'Connor wrote:

> Played by Robert Guillaume with a mixture of haughtiness and amiable contempt—the kind of thing that Clifton Webb used to do so well—"Benson" is a cleverly beguiling creation . . . one of the most successful comedy series to be unveiled so far this season. The script is bright, the pacing crisp, and the execution polished.

O'Connor also wisely pointed out that the series ran the risk of "being the equally dangerous equivalent of a fantasy . . . black Benson becomes the figure in charge. The conception feeds on illusions of the power of the 'little people.'"

And, of course, "Benson" was indeed a "little people" wish-fulfillment comedy that also propagated a very old notion: that at heart black servants are happy, content, and despite their griping, able to find great satisfaction in their work while also developing affection for those

darling white folks who employ them. Despite Guillaume's performance, the very nature of the series—the fact that Benson must remain tied to a white household—suggested that Benson, on a deeper level, never really lost sight of his place of service. Had Benson broken all ties with the Governor to live his own life, we would have had a far different story. (Just as we'd have had a far different story had Webster gone to live with his uncle.) But then there would have been no series at all.

As time moved on, the series suffered from tired blood, its wise-cracks losing their comic sting, the whole shebang becoming lamely predictable. And had it not been for Guillaume the series would have been seen early on for what it was: a rather standard sitcom formula relying on one simp gag after gag. Once "The Cosby Show" revealed what could be done on sitcoms in terms of character (black and white) and situation—a seamless fabric of realistic rather than manufactured crises—"Benson" looked all the more dated.

"Beulah" (10/3/50 to 9/22/53)

ABC. Cast includes: William Post, Jr., as Harry Henderson (later David Bruce played the role); Ginger Jones, as Alice Henderson (later June Frazee played the role); and Clifford Sales as Donnie Henderson (later Stuffy Singer played the role).

Although "Julia" is often cited as the first TV sitcom to star a black woman, that distinction actually falls to "Beulah," the story of a friendly black maid working for the white family, the Hendersons. The character Beulah had originated on the "Fibber McGee and Molly" radio program and was first played by a white actor, Marlin Hunt. So popular was the character that in 1945, a series was developed around her. Hunt again played the role, later to be replaced by another white actor, Bob Corley. Then Hattie McDaniel played the part.

When "Beulah" came to television, Ethel Waters was cast in the title role for a season, then was replaced by McDaniel, who fell ill, and in turn was replaced by Louise Beavers. Today it's fascinating to see these three important black character actresses all playing the same dippy maid. The best of the three? *Waters*—so real that she lay waste the shallowness of the series, endowing her Beulah with a warmth and a cunning wisdom that transcend the mammy stereotype. McDaniel, who looks tired and done in, gives a merely perfunctory performance, without any of her characteristic spunk and feistiness. It is rather sad to watch her. She doesn't look well at all. In fact, she died in 1952, soon after having very briefly played the role on TV. (One surviving episode of McDaniel as Beulah is still around, available on video cassette.) Beavers's Beulah is so jolly, wide-eyed, and giggly girlish that at times you just want to tell her to quit the simp act. And often you are just about ready to knock some sense into her. Yet what saves her is, as always, a fundamental sweetness of temper that, like it or not, is frequently endearing.

After its initial run, the show stayed in syndication for a time, but because of black protests against its stereotyped characters, "Beulah" was removed from the airwaves. Contemporary black audiences are seldom enraged by the series, often finding it tame and almost prehistoric: almost none of the situations involving the interactions between black and white is credible. Ironically, the Henderson family is composed of such patently wholesome middle-class types that they're true plastoids and just about impossible to take, with the exception perhaps of the son Donnie Henderson, who's a likable precursor to Beaver of the "Leave It to Beaver" series. The interactions between the black characters—Beulah, her friend Oriole (played at different times by Butterfly McQueen and Ruby Dandridge), and Bill Jackson (the love of Beulah's life, played at various times by Percy "Bud" Harris, Dooley Wilson, and Ernest Whitman)—seem more relaxed and although often silly (and in the case of Ruby Dandridge, sometimes annoyingly fake), the black characters genuinely seem to relate to one another as people, not characters.

As for Beulah herself, except when played by Waters, she's so caught up in her white employers' lives, so busy trying to patch up their problems, that she has very little life of her own. No wonder, we think, she can't get her boyfriend Bill to marry her. When Ernest Whitman played Bill, he shrewdly turned a shiftless handyman into a relatively assured, decent fellow. This character was once viewed as an embarrassment to black America because he wouldn't do the honorable thing and make Beulah his wife. Now, however, as we watch him finagle his way out of marriage, while also on occasion calling Beulah his "passion pigeon," he's representative of any male, giving his lady friend a sweet, jivey line while preserving his freedom. The weekly chats between Beulah and Bill that closed the show are some of the series' best moments.

"The Bill Cosby Show" (9/14/69 to 8/31/71)

NBC. Cast includes: Lillian Randolph (as Chet's mother Rose, 1969–1970); Beah Richards (as Rose, 1970–1971); Lee Weaver (as Chet's brother Brian); De De Young (as Brian's wife Verna, 1969); Olga James (as Verna 1969–1971); Donald Livingston (as Roger, son of Brian and Verna); Joyce Bulifant (as Mrs. Patterson, the school guidance counselor); Sid McCoy (as Mr. Langford); and Joseph Perry as Max.

A half-hour weekly sitcom that starred Bill Cosby as Chet Kincaid, a high school gym teacher in Los Angeles. Unlike the later very successful "The Cosby Show," this earlier series lacked Cosby's controlling sensibility and his remarkable sense of pacing. Sometimes it's slow and anemic. Often Cosby, rather than playing a character, performs as if delivering a monologue in his nightclub act. (No one seems to mind *that* a bit though.) On occasions when social issues pop up, they're dealt with in a relatively intelligent fashion (mainly because of Cosby's attitude; he never strains for a hot and heavy black rage effect; he's a man of cool reason). Although there's no great depth here, at least we're not pounded over the head with rhetoric as was the case with the more successful 1970s sitcoms like "Good Times." This series remains a rarity: a genuine black middle-class comedy, touching on the aspirations and goals of a system-oriented, upwardly mobile segment of the black community. Cosby's an educated professional black man, relaxed and easy-going, true to himself, without pretensions and clearly not trying to be an imitation of a white man. Audiences of the time, however, found the middle-class nature of the series politically tame and out of step. (They were right.) That might explain why it lasted only two seasons. Today it's worth seeing in reruns.

"Carter Country" (9/15/77 to 8/23/79)

ABC.

Actor Kene Holliday was featured as Sgt. Curtis Baker, a city slickster black deputy often in comic conflict with his boss, Chief Roy Mobey (played by Victor French). Vernee Watson appeared as Lucille Banks, who married the character Baker on an episode in 1979.

"Charlie & Company" (9/18/85 to 1/28/86; 4/25/86 to 6/6/86)

CBS.

This half-hour sitcom about a black middle-class Chicago family was often criticized and dismissed as little more than a clone of "The Cosby Show." Flip Wilson played Charlie Richmond, an office worker at the Department of Highways. (Where on earth did the writers ever come up with that one?) Gladys Knight played Wilson's schoolteacher wife, Diana, who often humors him but does little to shake him out of his insecurities. As the oldest son, Junior, Kristoff St. John displayed some charm and glimpses of maturity otherwise sadly lacking in this series. And Fran Robinson as the daughter Fern was, well, all right. But the youngest son Robert, played by Jaleel White, suffered shockingly from TV kid cutesyness. You just want to lock this little pain away somewhere. The problems raised on the series were treated in a half-baked manner, whether it be a tepid attempt at dealing with the daughter's concern about sex and pregnancy or the father's rather bizarre efforts to be a buddy to the oldest son, going so far as to hang out and party with the lad. Flip's Charlie looked as if he were suffering from a case of arrested development. The sequences of Charlie at his office seemed like filler material. And his office cronies were such a bumbling batch of dullards that they gave the typical working man a bad name.

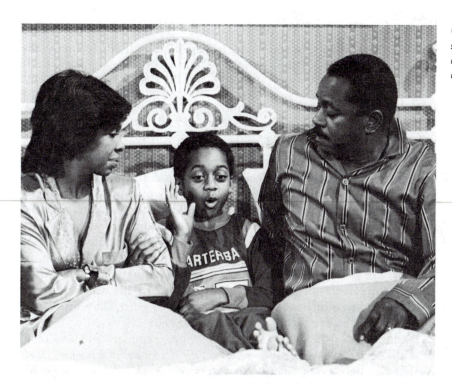

Gladys Knight, Jaleel White, and Flip Wilson on "Charlie & Company," a sitcom often criticized as being little more than a "Cosby" clone.

Della Reese was brought on for some episodes, playing Charlie's testy aunt.

"Flip exudes all the warmth of Claus von Bulow," *Washington Post* critic Tom Shales wrote, adding that the series was a "negligible drag." *The New York Times* called it "a pointless 'Cosby' carbon." And the critic for *USA Today* added, "Charlie lacks Cosby's control. . . . If Cosby is a revelation, Charlie's a bore."

"Checking In" (4/9/81 to 4/30/81)

CBS. Cast includes: Ruth Brown (as floor supervisor Betty); Liz Torres; Patrick Collins; Jordan Gibbs.

By the early 1980s, Marla Gibbs as the character Florence on "The Jeffersons" had become so popular that it was decided to star her in her own spinoff series. Here Gibbs's Florence Johnston has left the Jefferson household to work as executive housekeeper at a posh Manhattan hotel, the St. Frederick. There she supervises a staff (of typical TV-type oddballs) and contends with a stodgy boss, the hotel manager (played by Larry Linville).

Out of her element here, Gibbs's Florence lasted about a month on her own, then checked out of this series and was shuttled back to "The Jeffersons."

"The Cop and the Kid" (12/4/75 to 3/4/76)

NBC.

A tough Irish cop becomes guardian to a young black orphan of the streets named Lucas Adams and played by Tierre Turner.

"The Cosby Show" (premiered 9/20/84)

NBC. Most episodes were directed by Jay Sandrich, formerly the director of "The Mary Tyler Moore Show." In some episodes, Earle Hyman and Clarice Taylor appeared as Cliff Huxtable's parents. Jazz singer Joe Williams and Ethel Ayler also played the parents of Claire Huxtable. Created by Ed Weinberger, Michael Leeson, and William H. Cosby, Jr., Ed.D. Theme music by Stu Gardner and Bill Cosby. *P.* Caryn Sneider Mandabach and Carmen Finestra.

This series took everyone by surprise. Bill Cosby had long been a TV fixture, but when he had decided he wanted to do a black family comedy, many TV executives had thought it wouldn't work, claiming that the sitcom was dead as a popular entertainment form and also that American audiences were no longer interested in shows about black families. In the early 1980s it was assumed that blacks could be successful only on such crossover programs as "Diff'rent Strokes" or "Gimme a Break," in which black characters mixed with whites in what were usually unrealistic (or unpalatable) situations. Earlier Cosby himself had tried to do a different kind of black series with "The Bill Cosby Show." But it had failed to win a large audience.

Well, "The Cosby Show" turned TV programmers upside down. First the series garnered rave reviews. An "irresistibly charming, flawlessly executed sitcom," *Newsweek* wrote, while John O'Connor in *The New York Times* added that the series was "a rare commodity—a truly nice development in a medium that seems increasingly preoccupied with trash. . . . You look at "The Cosby Show" and you feel, most of the time just plain good . . . (it) displays signs of intelligence, insight, and a clever sense of humor." Immediately, "The Cosby Show" shot to the top of the ratings. At one point it was seen by 38.3 million people, roughly one third of the TV audience. Its extraordinary success marked a return of the sitcom and also helped propel NBC from third to first place in the primetime ratings. It also inspired such imitations as "Charlie and Company" with Flip Wilson. Most importantly, though, the series proved audiences would watch a black program weekly—and one that did not rely on the standard, jivey, or bickering antics of comic black characters.

The series centered on a black obstetrician, Cliff Huxtable (Cosby), his attorney wife Claire (Phylicia Ayers-Allen, who later was billed as Phylicia Rashad), and their five children (played by Sabrina LeBeauf as Sondra; Lisa Bonet as Denise; Malcolm-Jamal Warner as Theo; Tempestt Bledsoe as Vanessa; and Keshia Knight Pulliam as Rudy), who live comfortably in a New York brownstone. Huxtable and wife are a modern black couple: attractive, well-informed, witty. The kids are bright, well-brought-up youngsters, with all the emblems of an upper-middle-class black life. Unlike most sitcoms that used gags to move the action along, "The Cosby Show" focused instead on a series of "small moments" in the characters lives, seemingly "little" events that alter their consciousness. Cosby himself explained his hopes for the series: "I said to the writers I don't want sitcom jokes. I don't want jokes about behinds or breasts or pimples or characters saying, 'Oh, my God' every other line. What we want to deal with is human behavior."

Such was the case on the first season's special Thanksgiving episode. Here audiences were introduced to the Huxtable's oldest daughter, a sophomore at Princeton who, having tasted independence for the first time, now returns home for the holiday, full of new ideas and plans—

yet toting four bags of dirty laundry with her. She's half grown up, half still Daddy's little girl. Cosby's character Cliff approached her gingerly, trying to be the regular in-charge father he's always been. Yet he's aware her world and his are changing. There was a delicacy to Cosby's work here that had rarely been seen before. And there was a delicacy to the episode, too, which sensitively recorded the daughter's passage to adulthood.

Not long after that episode, another episode appeared that in the history of black images on American TV proved more important than it might have looked at first.

Here Cliff Huxtable was startled to discover that his son (his only son, mind you) has a pierced ear with an earring stuck in it, done solely to please a girl. This tickles Cliff to no end. When Cliff's parents visit the Huxtable household, he cannot wait to tell his father what the youngest Huxtable male has done. To his surprise, Cliff is reminded by his father of the time he conked his hair to woo a girl—the girl now being the woman Cliff's married to. Then to the surprise of Cliff's father, his wife—Cliff's mother—reminds him of the time he tattoed himself to impress—her. Each Huxtable male is embarrassed by his exploits in the name of love. And each sees that time alters a lover's style but not his great desire to impress or please, even in the corniest way, a loved one. The episode ended with the three Huxtable males sitting together on the sofa, eyeing one another furtively, then affectionately wrapping their arms around each other.

One of the most popular programs in television history, "The Cosby Show," featuring the Huxtable family: (front row) Denise (Lisa Bonet), Cliff (Bill Cosby), Rudy (Keshia Knight-Pulliam), Claire (Phylicia Rashad), (back row) Sondra (Sabrina LeBeauf), Vanessa (Tempestt Bledsoe), and Theo (Malcolm Jamal-Warner).

What appeared perhaps to be a tame episode really was something quite new to TV: a rare glimpse of black fathers and sons relating with warmth and regard for one another.

For too long on television, popular shows had borne out the lopsided notion that there was no such thing as the black father or at least a responsible mature black father who's there in the home. On a series like "The Jeffersons," George Jefferson had snapped, barked, and bopped about so much that usually it looked as if his poor son Lionel spent most of his time simply trying to appease George or to get out of the old man's way. True some affection existed between the two but it was TV-type affection, the kind that's there as a plot device or a means of reassuring the audience that things are really all right with the American family. Then on "Sanford and Son," Fred and Lamont revealed some affection for one another, but they were more like teenaged brothers (Fred sometimes coming across as the kid brother) than adult father and son. On series like "What's Happening!!" or "That's My Mama," audiences saw households headed by black women, who grew impatient with the shenanigans and growing pains of their overgrown sons.

But on "The Cosby Show," Bill Cosby carefully and skillfully established week by week an engaging relationship with his TV son. Sometimes they were playful rivals. Other times we watched Cosby lead his son onto the road to manhood, whether it be an episode where Theo had his first shave or the one in which he must read his father's speech at a big benefit dinner that Cliff cannot attend. In the area of images for black children—white ones, too—this new development was quite important. Moreover, Cosby and Malcolm-Jamal Warner were true ensemble actors, never trying to upstage one another as was the case with the actors on some earlier sitcoms. At the same time, Cosby's character seemed to dote on each of his daughters, too, sometimes appearing to be congratulating himself on having actually brought such bright, attractive females into the world. Occasionally, Cosby was criticized for focusing too much on the son. During the third season, some attention was shifted to the daughters.

Part of the appeal of Cosby's character is that he's so fallible: a knowledgable man who's also sometimes goofy (he seems to relish strutting about showing off his pot belly) and frequently obstinate. Everyone knows he'll always end up by understanding his children, but what makes him special is that he always has to go through a ritual of being "Dad" first: saying no to whatever they request, then testing them, then halfway giving in. Cosby wants to behave like the traditional stern father he himself no doubt had. But the kid in him—which we see in the gleam in his eye or that little-boy way of his as he prances through the house when he thinks he's got the best of a situation—always flips him around so that he comes to grapple with his children's dilemmas and tensions in a very hip 1980s fashion. Able to communicate with the kids on their level, giving us a true meeting of the minds, he is, however, not one of the kids. Nor does he let them forget that as their old man he will always have the last word. One of the best lines ever uttered in the series stated the case: "I am your father. . . . I brought you into this world and I'll take you out."

Likewise Cosby's Cliff Huxtable functioned in a very contemporary way with his wife, a professional, like him, accustomed to doing some things her way. Occasionally at comic loggerheads with wife Claire, Cliff does not always win. Then, too, unlike other TV couples with kids and hectic households, the two, far from being sexless, enjoy the kids but enjoy each other as well and are happy whenever they can steal some time alone together. Audiences even glimpsed the pair in moments of under-the-cover foreplay, certainly a first for domestic life on television.

"The Cosby Show" was not without its critics, some of whom felt it an idealized portrait of an American family, something of a black version of "'Father Knows Best." Such criticism is not without its points. But, whether we like it or not, the series reflects 1980s attitudes, those of a more system-oriented black audience. Cosby himself defended the show by telling the press: "Some people have said our show is about a white family in blackface. What does that mean? Does it mean only white people have a lock on living together in a home where the father is a doctor and the mother a lawyer and the children are constantly being told to study by their parents?" And in the long run, "The Cosby Show" proved a blessed relief from something like "Good Times," which, under the guise of having genuine social concerns, cracked jokes about tenements, rats, ghetto life itself and was frequently more bombast and rhetoric than anything else. "The Cosby Show"'s cultural bearings were more subtly presented, whether through references to such black writers as Richard Wright and Zora Neale Hurston or to the fact that on the walls in the Huxtable home are paintings by black artist Varnette Honeywood. In one startlingly moving episode, the youngest child Rudy sits alone watching a television replay of Martin Luther King, Jr.'s famous "I have a dream" speech. On another episode, when Theo struggles with a class paper about the March on Washington, his parents and both sets of grandparents reminisce movingly about their own experiences more than twenty years earlier when they had attended the March. Episodes also featured the Huxtable family comically lip-synching to the music of Ray Charles and James Brown. In no other sitcoms, would viewers have been exposed to any of this material with its carefully deliberated cultural signposts, indicating to us the varied historical and cultural experiences of black America. Then, too, in one episode (during the second season), there was even a sign in Theo's room that read "Abolish Apartheid." According to *Newsweek*, that sign caused an uproar on the show's soundstage because an NBC censor wanted it removed. Cosby himself said he'd have no such thing. "There may be two sides to apartheid in Archie Bunker's house," Cosby said, "but it's impossible that the Huxtables would be on any side but one. That sign will stay on that door and I've told NBC that if they still want it down, or if they try to edit it out, there will be no show." Of course, the sign stayed. In so many respects, the Huxtables' was a model household for the contemporary black family in America (at least the type that used TV for role models) and apparently for much of the white viewing audience, too. And, of course, after years of having heard from sociologists and psychologists that there was no such thing as a black father in black homes, audiences must have found it ironic that in the mid-1980s the most popular father in America was a black one, Cosby.

With this series, Bill Cosby scored where many other black artists failed: he was able to use a popular medium to express his sensibility, his vision of black middle-class life.

In the fourth season, the character Sondra married Elvin (Geoffrey Owens). There also was a spinoff, "A Different World," in 1987, focusing on the character Denise's college experiences.

"Diff'rent Strokes" (11/3/78 to 8/31/85; 9/27/85 to 8/30/86)

NBC/later moved to ABC. Cast includes: Dana Plato as Kimberly; Shaver Ross as Dudley Ramsey; and, in the days before she became a pop diva, Janet Jackson (1981–1982) as Willis's girlfriend Charlene; also Charlotte Rae Cas as Mrs. Garrett (1978–1979); Nedra Volz as Adelaide Brubaker (1980–1982); Mary Jo Catlett as Pearl Gallagher (1982–1986).

A long-running, popular series. Also an example of the type of crossover sitcom that was popular in the late 1970s/1980s. Around the time of the demise of such black comedy series as "Good Times" and "What's Happening!!," television executives believed white audiences no longer had much interest in watching all-black series. The idea now was to pair black characters/situations with white characters (with whom the large white television audience could identify). That notion led to sheer fantasy in which the interracial setting/situation might not have been objectionable had there been some semblance of everyday reality in the series. That was not always the case with "Diff'rent Strokes."

Two black children, Arnold and Willis Jackson, are adopted by a Park Avenue millionaire, Philip Drummond, who had once promised his housekeeper that, should anything happen to her, he would care for her sons. Other members of the Drummond household include his daughter Kimberly and the new housekeeper, Mrs. Garrett. Early episodes trace the boys' adjustment to the high life. Having been born and reared in Harlem, the older brother, twelve-year-old Willis (Todd Bridges)—streetwise and somewhat sulky—sometimes longs for his old

Photo below left: the irrepressible Gary Coleman and Todd Bridges as two Harlem brothers, who are adopted by a Park Avenue millionaire (photo below right, Conrad Bain, with Coleman on his lap) in "Diff'rent Strokes."

routine and neighborhood. But the younger, spunkier, brighter child, eight-year-old Arnold (Gary Coleman) takes his new lifestyle in stride: he loves the limos, the servants, the posh living quarters.

The series was one of NBC's few new hits in the 1978–1979 season. Its success was attributed to Gary Coleman, whose comic timing was perfect. So, too, was his uncanny precociousness. Top NBC executive Fred Silverman had originally spotted Coleman in a pilot for a remake of the "Our Gang" series; he insisted that a new series be developed around this very bright kid. Was there ever a TV child star quite like this one? A hip, modern, savvy, sepia Little Lord Fauntleroy—brazenly independent and aggressive, a born survivor—he tossed off his barbs with the ease and assurance of a seasoned pro. In the first two seasons of this sitcom, Coleman was at his best, so skilled for his age that he was sometimes hard to believe.

Neither Coleman nor the series, however, was without critics. Some felt Coleman too precocious for his own good. (What was happening to the kids of America that they'd become so outspoken!) Others complained about the premise of the series which, like the later "Webster," wanted its audience to believe the young black children are without relatives or black family friends to care for them. (There is no black community to speak of in this series.) And, of course, much like "The White Shadow," "Diff'rent Strokes" seemed locked into The Great White Father Syndrome: it is the sensitive liberal white man Drummond (played by Conrad Bain) who guides the boys to maturity while offering them a life in which all their material and emotional needs are promptly fulfilled. "Diff'rent Strokes"'s subtext tells its viewers that whiz-kid Coleman, supposedly the best and brightest the black community can hope to come up with, belongs in this type of special (white) environment. And, of course, Coleman also represents the merry black child born to bring sunshine and joy into the lives of his good white friends. "Diff'rent Strokes," however, did focus, in early episodes, on obvious realistic racial differences. Often visitors to the Park Avenue household were startled when Drummond introduced the Jackson brothers as his sons. Nor did Coleman's Arnold ever back off from a racial quip. In this respect, the show was different from "Webster," which at times seemed embarrassed by its own basic plot premise.

Of course, without the interracial family bit here, "Diff'rent Strokes" would have been quite a tired series. Those very aspects of the show that often might have annoyed black audiences also made it a hit—and such a durable curiosity. As Coleman grew older on the series, it was sometimes painful to watch him. Because of his health problems (he'd had a kidney transplant), his growth had been stunted and his face often looked puffy and worn. The scripts tried maturing him. But it never worked. Here reality intruded on the TV fantasy in a startling way.

"Double Dare" (4/10/85 to 5/22/85)

CBS. Devised by Gary Michael White; developed by Leon Tokatyan.

An action series that starred Billy Dee Williams as Billy Diamond, a master burglar, who, arrested by a policewoman, is told he must either work undercover to help the police department or go straight to jail. Naturally, he chooses the former but insists first that his one-time partner, Sisko (Ken Wahl), be sprung from a prison term in order to help him. Much was made over the pairing of Wahl and Williams, a duo of a

An elegant cat burglar turned police operative: Billy Dee Williams in the short-lived series "Double Dare," here with guest star Danny Dayton.

cocky, aging streetwise kid and a worldly sophisticate. True to his glamour image, Williams lives in high style in a San Francisco mansion with a silver Rolls Royce, a sumptuous wardrobe, priceless art objects all around him, and a testy, snobbish butler (Joseph Maher).

Untrue to Williams' image, though, he's not afforded an opportunity for projecting warmth or vulnerability (both certainly out of place in this thing). Instead Williams and Wahl solve hack crimes in what proves to be a predictable cops and robber series. "It is no better or worse than dozens of other detective romps floating around the TV schedule," wrote John O'Connor in *The New York Times*. He added:

> But, as usual in this kind of endeavor, there is a dreadful sense of waste hovering above the general mediocrity. . . . The average weekly series is not likely to be very innovative or challenging, but a little more effort might come up with something better than this for employing established talent.

"Dynasty" (premiered 1/12/81)

ABC. Created by Richard and Esther Shapiro.

Television takes occasional tiny evolutionary steps. One such step: the appearance of Diahann Carroll (and briefly Billy Dee Williams) on the nighttime soap opera "Dynasty" midway in that series' long run. (Carroll arrived in the fourth season; Williams joined during the fifth.) The settings of the nighttime soaps—"Dynasty," "Dallas," "Falcon Crest"—had always been the province of the rich and famous, the powerful and influential, the glamorous and the exciting. The tough-minded, aggressive heroes and heroines, with their fancy cars, fabulous homes, and smashing wardrobes, were often larger-than-life embodiments of a decadent capitalistic system in which the American Dream has become woefully yet enjoyably perverted. It's the land of the survival of the greediest—and the bitchiest. The nighttime soaps had also been lily white. Except for an occasional appearance by someone like Raymond

St. Jacques as a doctor on "Falcon Crest," the nighttime shows never spotlighted an important black character. And the idea crept up that, in these highpowered arenas, only whites were equipped to really wheel and deal.

That changed when Carroll played Dominique Deveraux, a haughty singer who, having lived abroad for years where she's been an extraordinary success (we think of Josephine Baker, of course), returns to Denver to settle a score with "Dynasty"'s paterfamilias Blake Carrington (John Forsythe). It turns out that old Blake and Dominique are brother and sister, both having been sired by the same father. That father had fallen in love with Dominique's black mother, a seamstress who bore his child in secrecy. Dominique's real name, we later learned, was Millie Cox. Now Devereaux announces she's out to cause havoc unless she's fully recognized as a member of the very deluxe Carrington clan.

Promoted as TV's first black bitch, Carroll exuded the appropriate glamour and sophistication. Her character's entrance was TV-spectacular: before the camera showed her face, we saw her expensive luggage and her glitzily clad body. Once she opened her mouth, she started tossing out orders to a hotel clerk, letting us know here was a woman who had to be reckoned with. Carroll's wardrobe and settings (her all-white hotel suite) were elegant and posh, just as much so as those of her white counterpart on the series Alexis Carrington Colby (Joan Collins), with whom Carroll's Dominique has good bitchy run-ins.

Yet with all this aside, Carroll seemed to lack the sting of a true bitch goddess, striking us instead as sweet-tempered and conciliatory. For years Carroll had appeared in nightclubs where, as she sang, she knew

TV takes a tiny evolutionary step: high-style black glamour comes to "Dynasty" in the form of Diahann Carroll (as Dominique Deveraux) and Billy Dee Williams (as Brady Lloyd).

the importance of pleasing and charming an audience, always being careful never to give offense. That desire to ingratiate seemed to carry over on the series, sometimes even during her haughtiest sequences; she didn't seem confident enough *not* to please. Moreover, the scriptwriters proved unsure about how far to go with the character. With racial politics very much the call of the day, the producers seemed unwilling to unsettle their huge white audience, which might have become annoyed and alienated if this black bitch were really too bitchy. Truly powerful, self-assured black characters, male or female, have never been very popular on TV or in the movies. Imagine Eartha Kitt playing the Dominique role? Just one snarl from that Cat Woman and everybody in the cast would have been ready to run for his/her life.

Perhaps the scriptwriters committed the unforgivable after Blake Carrington's dying father admits that Dominique is his daughter and even leaves her a large inheritance: there follows a dinner celebration sequence with Carroll and the Carrington clan—Blake, Krystle, the son Steven, and others. Here Carroll's Dominique announced that this evening was like a fantasy come true: at last she was with her family. We wondered what about the other half of her family, the black side that had reared her? Shouldn't Dominique express some feelings about that side as well? Has the character completely forgotten her black roots? (Later in the series Dominique does make a passing reference to her black relatives.) But clearly the point of "Dynasty"'s Dominique is that the tragic mulatto character now has finally made it to the Big House. But what she is to do there seems beyond the comprehension of all concerned.

Dominique's husband, Brady Boyd, portrayed by Billy Dee Williams, also suffered from the scriptwriters'/producers' indecisiveness. Boyd was a record producer, immensely successful and worldly, reminding us a bit of Berry Gordy, Jr., of Motown. Williams cut a very likable, dashing, romantic figure, almost flawlessly so. But Boyd never developed into a powerful, threatening character. Even Williams grew bored; he left the series after one season.

Yet, curiously, it was often the scenes of Williams and Carroll together that really made their appearance on the show worth seeing, for the two indeed were black stars—glamorous, dreamy concoctions—coming to the tiny homescreen. (Had Midwesterners ever envisioned such black personalities?) More importantly, in the mid-1980s, a time when black America seemed anxious to move into the system and change it (a political philosophy best represented by Jesse Jackson's candidacy for the Presidency in 1984), Carroll's and Williams's "Dynasty" characters indicated that blacks could well make it into the big time. That may explain why the NAACP, which in the early 1980s had been critical of Hollywood's treatment of minorities in front of and behind the camera, lauded "Dynasty"'s inclusion of these two black characters. In the world of pop culture, that was indeed a first.

Later other black characters were brought into the series. Troy Beyer played Jackie, Carroll's daughter by a white lawyer. (Now the series had two tragic mulattoes.) Calvin Lockhart and Richard Lawson were also cast as possible suitors for Carroll. After her second season on the show, Carroll's character—despite some encounters with the head honcho bitch Alexis Carrington—faded into the woodwork, almost of no interest to viewers.

"Enos" (11/5/80 to 9/19/81)

CBS. Cast includes: John Dehner; John Milford; C. Pete Munro; and Leo V. Gordon.

A spinoff of "The Dukes of Hazzard."

Here Deputy Sheriff Enos Strate (Sonny Shroyer) has taken his hide off to Los Angeles where he joins the police force and is assisted in his exploits by a decent West Coast fella named Turk (Samuel E. Wright), who ain't a bad cop at all. Of course, Turk's also black, so the theme of interracial buddyism now has just about run the gamut, showing us that even a dumb old country boy like Enos can get along with—and get a job done with, too—a trusty sidekick of color. Predictable series. Short lived too.

"Facts of Life" (premiered 8/24/79)

Kim Fields played Tootie Ramsey.

"Fame" (1/7/82 to 8/4/83)

NBC.

Based on the movie *Fame*, this dramatic series focused on a group of talented students at New York's High School for the Performing Arts. Its young protagonists not only impatiently pushed themselves toward show business careers but also grappled with personal drives and fears. As a study of competition and ambition among the urban young (as well as a series with weekly coming-of-age tales and highly charged and well-choreographed production numbers), "Fame" was well received by the critics. Among its cast were Gene Anthony Ray (as the ghetto youth Leroy Johnson, who's a skilled dancer), Erica Gimpel (as Coco Hernandez), and Debbie Allen (who repeated the role she had originated in the film as the tough-minded dance teacher Lydia Grant).

Samuel Wright (l.) is a city slickster cop who teams up with a good-ol'-country-boy partner, played by Sonny Shroyer, in "Enos."

Allen also choreographed and directed some episodes. "Fame" ran on NBC for a little over a year. Afterward new episodes were run in syndication. Janet Jackson joined the cast as Cleo in the syndicated episodes.

"The Flip Wilson Show" (9/17/70 to 6/27/75)
NBC.

The first successful black TV series of the 1970s and also the first successful black variety series in the history of American television. Previously, Nat "King" Cole, Sammy Davis, Jr., and Leslie Uggams had all unsuccessfully tried hooking a national television audience into watching their song-and-dance-and-humor variety programs. In the 1970s, however, changing times and attitudes as well as Flip Wilson's great talent enabled this comedian to reach a large audience.

Weekly, Wilson portrayed comic characters who became quite famous: there was Reverend Leroy, the bebopping preacher of the What's Happening Now Church; Sonny, the janitor; Freddie Johnson, the dashing playboy; and most famous of all, the notoriously sassy lady with the "rotary-drive hips" Geraldine, whose retorts—"What you see is what you get" and "The devil made me do it"—almost became national slogans. Geraldine's talk about her boyfriend Killer also made *him* almost as well known as she. Other Geraldine pearls: "Whooo-eee! Watch out, honey! Don't touch me! Don't you ever touch me!" and "When you're hot, you're hot. When you're not, you're not."

But Wilson's show was not without controversy. The irony, of

The devil made him do it: *Flip Wilson, as a dressed-to-the-nines Geraldine, with guest star Phyllis Diller on the hit variety program "The Flip Wilson Show."*

course, was that at a time when a young politically outspoken black student population was demanding that white America look at black America in a new way, television's first groundbreaking black series of this new era should have what many felt were dated or insulting images. Some saw Geraldine as little more than an update of that grand old harpy Sapphire on "Amos 'n' Andy." Generally, the black intellectual community dismissed the series. And white audiences no doubt felt comfortable in both enjoying and condescending to the program at the same time.

Yet the mass black audience seemed to respond to the program in a totally different manner, seeing the series perhaps best for what it was. Comic lowlifers that Wilson's characters were, they were presented nonetheless with genuine affection and insight. Essentially, like the performances of the black actors on "Amos 'n' Andy," Wilson's work was authentic oldstyle ethnic humor which, because it was broadcast on national television, seemed lifted from its proper cultural context. His material flourished best in black theaters and clubs, but it was ethnic humor at its finest.

Weekly, Wilson's show also featured such guest stars as Lena Horne, Bill Cosby, Richard Pryor, Mahalia Jackson, B. B. King, Melba Moore, and Muhammad Ali.

"Fortune Dane" (2/15/86 to 3/22/86)

ABC. *Ex. P.* Barney Rosenzweig (who had also produced "Cagney & Lacey"), Ronald M. Cohen, and Carl Weathers. Cast includes: Joe Dallesandro; Penny Fuller.

His name is Fortune Dane. As a child, he had been orphaned and then adopted by a banker named Charles Dane (portrayed on the first episode by Adolph Caesar). Later he became a football hero, then a police detective, and now works as a trouble-shooter for a tough female mayor of a big city. Weekly, of course, in the hour-long episodes, Dane, as played by Carl Weathers (the flashy muscular Apollo Creed of the *Rocky* movies), solves crimes and endures the expected rigamarole of an action hero: the shoot-outs, killings, chases, betrayals.

Perhaps of historical note is the simple fact that here weekly episodic television did get a black hero of assertion with clear signs of sexuality. In fact, perhaps there was too much emphasis on his physical powers and presence. Dane's biceps and pecs are on prominent display. In the opening credits, not only is our guy Fortune seen going through his daily, sweaty exercise romps but also showering while the camera celebrates his fitness. "Imagine if you will," wrote John O'Connor of *The New York Times*, "a 'Jane Fonda Workout' video expanded into a weekly series." Fortune's such an upfront hunk that women just can't resist throwing themselves at him. In one episode, a pretty white assistant district attorney is so determined to crack a casino murder case that she tells Dane, "If you help me solve this, I'm yours for a night, a weekend, whatever suits, short of matrimony." As O'Connor pointed out, "When it is recalled that even a hint of interracial sex not too many years ago was enough to leave most television executives hyperventilating, 'Fortune Dane' is a sure sign of how lifestyles, or at least attitudes, in the United States have changed." Yet although Dane is never the sexually antiseptic figure that TV's Shaft was, there is unfortunately something cold and almost impersonal about his sexuality.

Otherwise, the series itself, however, was all old-style formula. Weathers, so effective and strong in some of his film adventures, seemed here unable to weather the storms of the trite and the predictable.

"Get Christie Love!" (9/11/74 to 7/18/75)

ABC. Cast includes: Charles Cioffi and later Jack Kelly.

After the box-office success of the karate-kicking-tough-black-mama movies of Tamara Dobson and Pam Grier, television made way for a similar heroine with the appearance of Teresa Graves as Christie Love, an undercover cop for the Los Angeles Police Department. We can only assume she's undercover so that Graves will have a chance to wear some sporty, colorful clothes and to show off her *bod*. An alumna of television's "Laugh-In" series, Graves had a sweet, slightly spaced but perky quality, quite appealing but perhaps not gritty enough for this urban action series. *The New York Times* found her "stunningly sexy" but noted that otherwise "Get Christie Love!" "is just like 638 other action adventure cliches dredged up by the studios and networks in the last few years." The series lasted only one season, and afterwards Graves, who had given us television's first black female cop, just about disappeared from the entertainment scene.

"Gimme a Break" (premiered 10/29/81)

NBC. Cast includes: Kari Michaelson; Lauri Hendler; Lara Jill Miller; John Hoyt; and Howard Morton.

Is there no better way to describe this sitcom (about a black housekeeper working for a white family) than as a supposedly-hip update of the old "Beulah" show? Probably not. As Nell Harper, the chubby, gutsy, sassy but ah-shucks-she's-really-a-sweetie-pie servant to widowed police chief Carl Kanisky and his three daughters, Nell Carter sorts out the kids' problems, tends to cranky Kanisky, and (once Kanisky has died) is determined to hold the family together. During the first seasons the subtext was clear: Nell and Kanisky, played by Dolph Sweet, were really a bickering married interracial couple, squabbling over the children and the household. Just as Beulah had a next-door neighbor Oriole to dish the dirt with, so Nell (in 1984) had Telma Hopkins as her wisecracking friend Addy. Together the two sometimes went at it like Abbott and Costello. As if to loosen the character from the stereotyped mammy mold, the series permitted Carter to dress up and chase after a fellow or two. While always funny, Carter, however, came across, to use the old pre-feminist expression, as man-crazy and a bit pathetic, too. Later Rosetta Le Noire appeared as Nell's mother, apparently to inject some new life into the series and also to further round out Nell's character. But the basic concept remained unaltered: again an all-sacrificing large black woman nurtures a white family, often forsaking her own life to do so. In its sixth season, the show underwent a change in format. Nell moved to New York (with friend Addy) to care for Joey Donovan, a young white child she was devoted to, and his brother Matthew (played by real-life brothers Joey and Matthew Lawrence). By then, the character had become so sentimental and immersed in the welfare of little white charges that viewers no doubt felt embarrassed for her.

An update of the old "Beulah" series? Nell Carter as the lovable housekeeper Nell, with Telma Hopkins as her friend Addy, on "Gimme a Break."

Like other talented black women cast in such a manner, Nell Carter frequently played against the concept, endowing her character with a haughty and healthy self-assurance. But later in the series, Carter's ingenuity and freshness wore thin; her work sometimes became too sappy and slick. She sounded as if she were an old-time entertainer who had been on the Vegas circuit too long. Generally, Carter was best when she let a mean streak show or when her flagrant narcissism (that juicy Nell-like delight in herself) got so far out of hand that one sensed the character and the actress could not have cared less about the family on the show; here was a woman interested most in self and self-aggrandizement.

"Good Times" (2/8/74 to 8/1/79)

CBS. Created by Eric Monte and Michael Evans. Developed by Norman Lear. Cast includes: Johnny Brown as Mr. Bookman (1977–1979, the testy building janitor) and Theodore Wilson (1978–1979, as Sweet Daddy).

This half-hour weekly series about the problems and joys of the Evans family was the 1970s' first black family sitcom and has been considered something of a groundbreaker. Clearly, it can be credited with having introduced to national TV a new point of view on black life: the series offered a portrait of a black family living in the slums (a tenement building on Chicago's Southside that is referred to as "cockroach towers") and confronted daily with a set of harsh urban realities. "Good Times" focused on Florida Evans (who, played by Esther Rolle, first appeared as the maid on "Maude"), her husband James (John Amos), and their three children: J.J. or Junior (Jimmie Walker), Thelma (BernNadette Stanis), and Michael (Ralph Carter). As the father searched for a better job, unemployment was a recurring theme. Discrimination and poverty were also dealt with. Disgruntled and angered by his economic plight, the father James announced on one episode, "The President said he was going to bring us all together but no one told us it would be on a bread line." Weekly, the show's theme song spoke of "temporary layoffs and easy credit ripoffs . . . (and) keeping your head above

"Good Times": the joys and sorrows of the Evans family. Photo below left: Jimmie Walker as the "Dyn-O-Mite" kid, J.J.; Janet Jackson as Penny; BernNadette Stanis as Thelma; and Ja'net DuBois as Willona. Photo below right: Esther Rolle as Florida, with her children Michael (Ralph Carter) and Thelma (BernNadette Stanis).

water." "Good Times" managed to touch on some of the language, the rhythms, and attitudes of ghetto experience. Seen at one point in some 18 million homes, the series seemed to elicit viewer identification from blacks and whites alike who saw the struggle for economic and social survival of the Evans family as being part of their own. Always stressed, however, was the theme of America as a land of opportunity. And in some cases, white viewers were permitted to patronize this likable black family, who managed to keep their humor and their sunny smiles despite so many difficulties.

Viewed today, the series seems very much a period piece with its shortcomings more than apparent. Too much of its political stand—its determination to confront social problems and ills—strikes us as merely rhetorical, the most biting comments usually coming from the youngest (and therefore least threatening) family member, Michael, who studiously keeps himself abreast of black history and achievements and who writes "my favorite person" school essays on Malcolm X and Jesse Jackson. Had the older Evans children been blessed with more serious attitudes or insights, the series might have really attained the "socially committed" goals it wanted us to believe it sought. Instead poor Thelma was used for the most part as a backdrop for jokes or for showcasing the problems of other family members. Worst was the fact that the oldest Evans child, J.J., seemed barely literate.

Repeatedly, the audience was reminded that J.J. was an artist, a supposedly talented young black man trying to find his way. But Walker failed to communicate any type of artistic intensity or perceptivity (let alone something as fundamental as intelligence). What he became best known for was his trademark expression "Dyn-O-Mite" and his coon antics, which were throwbacks to Stepin Fetchit and Willie Best but without any of the former's nihilistic poise or the latter's slyly acute sense of timing. Perhaps the most telling comments on J.J. were made by Esther Rolle to *Ebony*:

> I resent the imagery that says to black kids that you can make it by standing on the corner saying "Dyn-O-Mite!" He's 18 and he doesn't work. He can't read or write. He doesn't think. The show didn't start out to be that. Little by little . . . they have made J.J. more stupid and enlarged the role. Negative images have been quietly slipped in on us through the character of the oldest child.

"Good Times"'s most valuable assets proved its most expendable. As next door neighbor Willona Woods, Ja'net DuBois brought a zesty, sweetly sexy warmth to the series. Had she been cast as the mother, "Good Times" would have moved miles away from the traditional dowdy black mother (code word: Mammy) image that unfortunately weighed Rolle down. At the same time while audiences were happy with John Amos's character James—TV's most serious and arresting black father— Amos, after hassles with the producers, left the show. During the 1976– 77 season, it was explained that James Evans had been killed in a car accident. Never were the series' inadequacies more evident than on the episode dealing with James's death: hollow, synthetic, unable to link its comic characters with a tragic situation, it was an infantile mess.

But the problems for "Good Times" did not end here. During the 1977–1978 season, Esther Rolle, after contract disputes with Norman Lear's company, did not appear, it being explained that Florida and a new gentleman friend Carl Dixon (Moses Gunn) had married, then moved to Arizona for his health. Janet Jackson joined the cast as Penny, a battered child who looked mighty healthy. And Ja'net DuBois's character Willona was beefed up. But the real star was J.J., who turned much of the season into a minstrel show.

By the 1978–79 season, Rolle returned to the series. Ben Powers appeared as Keith Anderson, the husband of poor Thelma, who, in the eyes of the writers, could not have asked for anything better. It's now shocking to see the way this young black female character was handled. But by then, the series had lost any spunk or ingenuity it might once have had. "Good Times" soon left the network airwaves, but it ran in syndication for years.

"Harris and Company" (3/15/79 to 4/5/79)

NBC. Cast includes: David Hubbard (as David Harris); Renee Brown (as Liz Harris); Lia Jackson (as J.P. Harris); Eddie Singleton (as Tommy Harris); Dain Turner (as Richard Allen Harris); James Luisi (as Harry Foreman); Lois Walden (as Louise Foreman); Stu Gilliam (as Charlie Adams); and C. Tillery Banks (as Angie Adams).

After the death of his wife, a black auto worker, Mike Harris (played by Bernie Casey), moves his five children from Detroit to Los Angeles. The father becomes a partner with a white couple in an auto repair business. This dramatic series focused on the problems of the family as well as the father's friendship with his partners. It had the predictable black/white brotherhood theme. In one episode when one of his sons is stricken by a mysterious illness, Harris is in need of money and must decide if he should abandon his partnership to take a higher-paying job as a master mechanic at another company. Naturally, he opts to remain loyal to his friends at the repair shop. Things turn out well though. His son's illness is the result of a virus that is soon treated and cured.

Because "Harris and Company" was one of the few attempts at presenting a weekly black family drama, many hoped to see the series succeed. But it proved too timid in tone and far too pat to grab hold of an audience. In *The New York Post*, critic Mel Ruderman wrote, "The interracial aspect is handled on such a lofty plane one can only applaud the script's intentions while questioning its reality." And in *The New York Times*, John J. O'Connor added, "The widowed father is noble and saintly enough to make Daddy in 'Father Knows Best' look like an insensitive meanie. . . . This is all very comforting, of course, but unfortunately, it is also slightly boring. Transforming everybody into a goody-two-shoes results in a curiously lifeless production."

"Harris and Company" grew out of a 1978 TV-movie titled "Love Is Not Enough," which also starred Bernie Casey and was directed by Ivan Dixon.

The series ran for four weeks.

"He's the Mayor" (1/10/86 to 3/21/86)

ABC. Cast includes: Al Fann (as Hooks's father) and Pat Corley (as the town police chief).

Kevin Hooks, who had previously appeared as one of the students in the series "The White Shadow," returned to series television as the star of "He's the Mayor." Playing a twenty-five-year-old college grad who becomes the mayor of his hometown, Hooks, like the rest of the cast,

Kevin Hooks plays the former athlete who becomes his hometown's mayor in "He's the Mayor."

found himself weighed down by puerile scripts and slovenly direction. "No Vote for This Mayor," was the comment of *The New York Post*'s TV critic in reviewing this sitcom, which folded after only a few weeks.

"Hill Street Blues" (1/15/81 to 8/27/87)

NBC. Cast includes: Michael Warren (as Officer Bobby Hill), Taurean Blacque (as Det. Neal Washington), and J.A. Preston (as Mayor Ozzie Cleveland). Among the guest stars: Alfre Woodard, who won an Emmy in for her appearance in the show.

"Hill Street Blues," a 1960s-style series—focusing on social ills and tensions—which, ironically, was aired (with varying degrees of success) in the Reagan 1980s; with Michael Warren (l.) and Charles Haid.

An updated cop show with a gritty beat and realistic stories focusing on the police officers of the Hill Street Station (located in a large unnamed city). The officers themselves were an assorted ethnic mix, each distinguished by some personal habit or idiosyncrasy. The series—what with its cast, its tough language, its harsh urban look, and its emphasis on such social problems as drugs, prostitution, and departmental corruption at the police headquarters—seemed more like something out of the politically-committed 1960s than of the New Wave 1980s. At first viewers also must have considered it a problem-oriented oddity; the series took some time before finding an audience. But the critics loved the show, praising it highly. In its first season, "Hill Street Blues" was a big Emmy winner. Weekly as regulars or as guest stars, a number of talented black actors and actresses also had a chance for more challenging work here. Tough, gritty, adult.

"I Spy" (9/15/65 to 9/2/68)

NBC. *P.* Sheldon Leonard, Mort Fine, and David Friedkin.

In April 1965, *The New York Morning Telegraph* carried the following item:

> No network television series next season will be watched more closely . . . than NBC-TV's "I Spy," in which a Negro performer is the co-star. Among the things the television industry will watch carefully from week to week are the ratings and the number of affiliate stations that do—or don't—give clearance to the series.

As the first major series to feature a black actor in a leading dramatic role with an integrated cast, "I Spy" caused quite a stir. In this action series about two traveling undercover agents in search of criminals while under the guise of being a tennis champ and his trainer, white actor Robert Culp and Bill Cosby were cast as equals. But just how equal was open to debate. At one point, no one seemed sure if the two men, when seen riding in a car, should both sit together in the front seat. And what about hotel accommodations as the men traveled? Were they to occupy the same room? Would there be any suggestions of racial discrimination, which would prevent Cosby from staying at certain hotels? Some of these problems were circumvented by having the two men operate outside the United States and fight crime in foreign lands. Actually, the country they traveled in was Idealized Homogenized TV Land where real racial conflicts or tensions never emerged. Cosby himself was cleancut without any rough ethnic edges. Years later Cosby told a writer for *Essence* his "I Spy" dilemma:

> I had to dress and talk like "them" or I was considered uneducated. But if I dressed or spoke too well, as in *better than*, then I was threatening and that was no good. With all of this, I still had to live with me in that role, making the character acceptable not just to white America but to me and to blacks everywhere. It was a box I was in.

One other problem: would Cosby have romances or would that make him too much of a sexual threat? Generally, while Culp came across as something of a ladies' man, Cosby struck a more serious, less sexually agile pose. Always though he had a sexual tension about him and was never neutered. And he did appear opposite various black women: Cicely Tyson, Nancy Wilson, and Gloria Foster. The latter once said: "'I

Television's first examination of the theme of interracial male bonding: Robert Culp (l.) and Bill Cosby as the heroes/buddies of "I Spy."

Spy' has been the one program on which you can see an array of Negro women, where you can see a healthy exchange between a black male and a black female." She was right.

To his credit, Cosby played his character Alexander Scott with a piercing cool. On a medium that demanded the agreeable, he exuded charm but always with a suggestion of discontent, a certain serious edge. Hardly "himself" here (as he appeared to be on his later hit series "The Cosby Show"), Cosby did work well with Culp, the two creating a plausible friendship that seemed based on mutual respect and a degree of affection. Theirs was the first of TV's interracial male teams. And, ironically, the interracial pairing—and the subtext growing out of it on various episodes—is the only aspect that distinguishes the series today. Otherwise it's distinctly ordinary. Cosby won three Emmys for his performance on the series.

"The Insiders" (9/25/85 to 6/23/86)

ABC. Cast includes: Gail Strickland as the editor of *Newspoint*. Characters created by Bobby Roth.

After its first disastrous episode, this routine "Miami Vice" clone became intermittently diverting. A weekly hour-long action series, it had a fairly preposterous premise: two undercover investigative reporters disguise themselves in each episode as they infiltrate various crime groups; all of this is done so that they can come up with top-notch inside stories for a publication called *Newspoint*. As in "Miami Vice," we have a racially mixed team. White actor Nicholas Campbell plays the bright, post-1960s flower child Nick, who writes the stories. His partner is a crafty black ex-con Mackey (Stoney Jackson), who three years earlier had been caught by Nick in a scam. But Nick had not turned Mackey in. Ever since, Mackey, considering Nick his best pal, has worked hard to help the guy ensnare other hoods, and also to prove his own undying loyalty to Nick. On the premiere episode, Mackey teaches Nick how to break into a car and drive off with it within a few seconds. As a black dude of the streets, Mackey, so the script insists, *naturally* knows about breaking in and entering. While Nick is cerebral, Mackey represents the black man as a born thief, a natural at *getting over*.

What with his mascara and long curly locks, actor Stoney Jackson looks like Prince and on occasion, is determined to act like Eddie Murphy. Whenever possible, he rushes into a Murphyesque I'll-get-loud-on-you-Whitey routine. One of his favorite undercover disguises is as a Rastafarian with long dread locks and a thick accent; this is almost a direct steal from the West Indian character Philip Michael Thomas adopted while undercover on "Miami Vice." Worse still: Jackson sometimes acts as if he thinks he's pretty hip stuff. "The Insiders" also has plenty of soundtrack music. Some sequences, too, look like music videos. Although this nonsense can be enjoyed, there's not much original here. In *The New York Times*, John O'Connor wrote: "This is the Just-Keep-It-Moving School of television production. . . . On the theory that if you throw enough of this stuff at the television screen, some of it is bound to stick, 'The Insiders' could have a chance." (It didn't; the series folded.) In *The Washington Post*, critic Tom Shales added that the series "takes pains to resemble 'Miami Vice': two pains—Nick Campbell and Stoney Jackson." Enough said.

The theme of interracial male bonding lives on in the "Miami Vice" clone "The Insiders," starring Nicholas Campbell (l.) and Stoney Jackson as a crime-solving journalistic team.

"Ironside" (9/14/67 to 1/16/75)

NBC.

A police drama in which Don Mitchell played Mark Sanger, bodyguard and assistant to the series' central character Robert Ironsides (played by Raymond Burr).

"The Jackson Five" (9/11/71 to 9/1/73)

ABC.

A Saturday morning cartoon series for children with animated characters based on the popular singing group The Jackson Five. Voices for the characters were provided, of course, by the five Jackson brothers themselves: Jackie, Tito, Jermaine, Marlon, and Michael.

"The Jacksons" (6/16/76 to 7/7/76; also 1/26/77 to 3/9/77)

CBS. *Ex. P.* Joe Jackson (father of the Jackson clan) and Richard Arons.

A half-hour summer replacement variety series featuring the singing group once called The Jackson Five, now rechristened The Jacksons—Jackie, Marlon, Tito, Michael, and Randy Jackson—along with their three sisters—Maureen (Rebie), La Toya, and Janet. The group also danced. Wonderfully. Jermaine Jackson, having left the group to perform on his own, did not appear in the series. Originally slated for a three week run in 1976, the series was brought back in 1977.

"The Jeffersons" (1/18/75 to 7/23/85)

CBS. Created by Don Nicholl, Michael Ross, and Bernie West; developed by Norman Lear. Cast includes: Paul Benedict as Harry Bentley; Ned Wertimer as Ralph the doorman; Ernest Harden, Jr., as Marcus Wilson.

A long-running, immensely successful sitcom revolving around the exploits of George Jefferson (Sherman Hemsley) and his wife Louise (Isabel Sanford). Originally, both characters had appeared as neighbors of Archie Bunker on "All in the Family." When the spinoff series was developed, the idea was to spotlight George as a mirror image of Archie, in blackface. On early episodes, George—a brash, loud-mouth, successful, upwardly mobile black man in the dry-cleaning business who is as bigoted as Bunker—bounced around, joyously making fun of *honkies* or putting down his neighbors, The Willises (Roxie Roker and Franklin Cover), an interracial couple (TV's first). Black audiences enjoyed George's mock black/white confrontations. Even in this most simplistic of racial encounters, TV was acknowledging racial tensions and divisions. Always given the upper hand, George never backed off from anyone. Hemsley, short and slightly built, also represented for many a common Little Man up against the big boys. Hemsley's slight stature may well also have enabled white audiences to be amused by his outbursts rather than threatened. What black audiences sometimes could not tolerate was George's hyperactiveness; for all his talent, Sherman Hemsley frequently sprang up and down, talking rapidly and nonstop, like a toy on a string.

A focal point of "The Jeffersons" was George's relationship with his wife, affectionately called Weesie. Theirs was a traditional TV-style marriage, replete with weekly pet peeves and misunderstandings as Louise occasionally struggled to liberate herself from George's clutches *and* his misconceptions while George, naturally, craftily maintained the upper hand. No ground was broken in its depiction of the American marriage, be it black or white. And although Louise's was the voice of reason, Sherman Hemsley's highly skilled way with a line and his almost surreal confidence made his the most distinctive voice on the program.

Also featured was the Jeffersons' son Lionel (Mike Evans in 1975; later by Damon Evans, no relation, 1975–1978), who married Jenny (Berlinda Tolbert), the Willis's daughter. The writers hobbled about trying to invest the Lionel/Jenny/George relationship with some zing but finally ignored it. Lionel himself came and went on the show. Mike Evans returned to the role from 1979 to 1981.

Movin' on up: "The Jeffersons," the highly successful 1970s–1980s' sitcom about an upwardly mobile black couple, George and Louise Jefferson (played by Sherman Hemsley and, r., Isabel Sanford), here with their outspoken maid, Florence (Marla Gibbs).

During the first seasons, some spicy flavor was provided by Zara Cully as Mother Jefferson, George's adoring mother who simply could not abide daughter-in-law Louise. Crotchety and mean as piss, Cully's harridan never hesitated to put Louise in her place. It was frequently fun to watch their encounters because Sanford's Louise was at times such a phony prig.

After Cully's death in 1978, *The Jeffersons* focused more on another comic foe, this time one for George, in the person of Marla Gibbs as the maid Florence. Although few wanted to admit it, Gibbs became the real female star of the series, energizing it with her perfect timing and her skillfully executed line readings. A true ensemble player who never stepped on another performer's lines (as she so easily could have done with Sanford), Gibbs's character fell very much in line with the clever servants of the past, a tradition in films and TV that dated back to Hattie McDaniel and Eddie Anderson, those wise subordinates who readily outwitted and outmanuevered everyone else and whose keen, sly intelligence stood head and shoulders over that of everyone else. The twist here was that Florence answered back not to a white boss but a black one. Had the maid been played by a white actress, the black audience would have been up in arms. But black viewers accepted Florence's retorts because George often seemed too big for his britches and in need of a sensible sister to shoot through his schemes, his pretensions, and his braggadoccio and to remind him of his roots.

Gibbs and Hemsley played together superbly. And the audience's awareness of their testy relationship kept the action spinning. "Are you sure you don't want any lunch?" Louise asks George. "Did Florence cook it?" he asks. "Yes," Louise replies. "Then I'm sure I don't want any lunch," he says. For her part, Florence addressed him, the master of the house, as Shorty. Stating her view of life (and also her position in the Jefferson household), Gibbs's Florence also delivered a classic line: "How come we overcame and nobody told me."

During its ten-year run, "The Jeffersons" underwent many changes and elicited different types of criticism. In the early years, black activists dismissed it as a stereotyped portrait of a bickering, harping comic black couple. (Yes, Louise did fall into the mammy tradition.) By the 1980s, though, a black writer like Mary Helen Washington in a *TV Guide* article criticized the show for having lost its ethnic realities, its juice and spunk, becoming as the years moved on less and less black. Gone was Louise's afro as well as her use of double negatives and the word *aint*. No longer were we reminded that once she had worked as a maid to help George through a tight financial situation. Gone also was some of George's old raunchiness, the type exhibited when he had once spoken of playing "Pin the Tail on the Honky." Because the writers had cleaned up the Jeffersons's act, the program had become bland and racially neutralized. Washington had her point. And conversely, she indicated that the series, despite the comic image, had brought to American TV, much as had "Sanford and Son," a lopsidedly black point of view, albeit one filtered through many white hands (the writers) but then invigorated again through the performance of the cast.

In retrospect, "The Jeffersons" offered no great statement on black America's ideals or goals. Nor did it focus on black social ills or problems (as "Good Times" pretended to do). But it did mark a significant continuation of old-style ethnic theater/humor and brought pleasure to many black audiences who felt communal links with the confidence of George and Florence. The theme of black aggression has long appeared only in the guise of comedy. And here "The Jeffersons," despite whatever other distortions, succeeded.

When the series lost its treasured time slot on Sunday evenings and was pitted against "The A-Team" on Tuesday nights, its ratings dwindled. Some cast members felt that CBS had sabotaged the show, that the series might have lived on in a better time position. They may have been right.

"Julia" (9/17/68 to 5/25/71)

NBC. Cast includes: Lloyd Nolan (as Dr. Morton Chegley); Lurene Tuttle (as Hannah Yarby); Michael Link (as Corey's buddy, Earl J. Waggedorn); Betty Beaird (as Marie Waggedorn); Mary Wickes (as Melba Chegley); and Allison Mills (as Carol Deering).

Much attention was focused on this sitcom, which made a piece of television history: here for the first time since "Beulah" was a series starring a black woman. The woman, Diahann Carroll, was, however, not a cheery domestic; instead she was an educated, independent professional wage-earner. Audiences had not been exposed weekly to this kind of character. And NBC, which years before had carried "The Nat 'King' Cole Show," was taking a chance on this series.

"Julia" itself was modest: the tale of a young widowed black woman (her husband had been killed in Vietnam) named Julia Baker, trying to raise her young son Corey (Marc Copage) while working as a nurse in Los Angeles. The opening episode was promising. Here Julia phones a prospective employer, a Dr. Chegley, inquiring about a job. At one point she says she feels he should know that "I'm colored." "What color are you?" he asks. "I'm a Negro." "Have you always been a Negro, or are you just trying to be fashionable?" He ends up hiring her, of course. Thereafter weekly Julia shuffles her duties between the office and her home. But rarely ever again is the business of Julia's race brought up. For the most part, hers was an antiseptically pure, middle-class world untroubled by social unrest or political issues. One would never imagine this was filmed in an era of student protests and a time when cultural nationalism was on the rise within segments of the black community. "Julia"'s removed from all that. Conveniently, in terms of the way the script treats Julia's life, she's almost colorless. Carroll herself strikes viewers as a pretty Hollywood confection: pert, pleasing, thoroughly inoffensive, almost without a breath of idiosyncrasy. In the long run, the series itself seems ordinary and harmless. It ended up doing well in the ratings.

But "Julia" also suffered a critical backlash. The liberal white press attacked it as did young, politically active black audiences, all complaining that it evaded the political and social realities of the period, presenting a false portrait of black life. Years later in her autobiography *Diahann*, Diahann Carroll wrote of the tensions she experienced while filming "Julia" amid so much controversy. Few realized better than she that "'Julia' was a terribly mild statement about everything—period."

Seeing the series today, some ironic bright spots turn up. Among those are the actors playing Julia's various boyfriends: Paul Winfield and Fred Williamson, each of whom is fun to watch as he courts this stolidly upright and proper diva. These men seem to be on their best behavior, holding back on their sexual urges and impulses. Yet neither is a neutered clod. Virginia Capers appeared in the first season. And in those episodes in which Diana Sands appeared as Julia's cousin, Carroll and Sands have a sweet rapport. When Carroll has worked with other black actresses, a little fire and competitive edge have arisen. Almost always the other actress, be it Sands or later Rosalind Cash (in "Sister, Sister"), seemed to jolt and jab Carroll, determined to get her off her high horse and into the world of real acting. Sometimes it works. Sometimes it doesn't.

Diahann Carroll as the rather plastic young nurse, Julia, with her employer, Dr. Chegley (Lloyd Nolan), in the groundbreaking but controversial sitcom "Julia."

The oldstyle minstrelsy returns: T. K. Carter (standing) as the genie Shabu, who transforms the humdrum life of a bland TV weatherman (Richard Gilliland), here seen levitating, on "Just Our Luck."

"Just Our Luck" (9/20/83 to 12/27/83)

ABC. Cast includes: Ellen Maxted; Rod McCary; Richard Shaal; and Hamilton Camp.

A bland television weather broadcaster (Richard Gilliland) stumbles across a green bottle, which, low and behold, contains a genie inside. "I am Shabu, your genie," the bottle's occupant announces. "I must serve you for 2000 years or until your death, whichever comes first." He adds, "I am ready to serve my master." Thanks to the genie, the weatherman is transformed from plodding, unappealing dud to sexy, charismatic TV star. The genie, it turns out, is a black fellow. And let there be no doubt about it, as Shabu stands by always ready to aid and advise, to encourage and magically alter his new white buddy's life, he's a 1980s-style slave. It should be noted that others in the show's cast cannot see Shabu. Talk about an Invisible Man. As the genie, actor T.K. Carter fails to distinguish himself and is an embarrassing throwback to past eras of movie *coons*. "The only thing Shabu can't do," wrote Kay Gardella in *The New York Daily News*, "is turn the series into an unqualified success. All the highjinks in the world can't pull that off." Agreed.

"The Lazarus Syndrome" (9/4/79 to 10/16/79)

ABC. Cast includes: Peggy Walker and Peggy McKay.

The ads for the premiere episode of this series read: "Sparks Fly when a Brilliant Surgeon Meets a Hot-Tempered Reformer. But the Real Fireworks Begin When They Fight for Something Bigger—A Hospital Run To Save Lives, Not To Make Money. If They Can Stick Together, They Just Might Beat The System."

The key words here are the last: *just might beat the system*. This series appeared at the tailend of the 1970s, not the 1960s, and audiences were not greatly attracted to anti-Establishment stories. Nor were they much interested in the interracial buddy-buddy theme suggested by the casting of Louis Gossett, Jr. (as the "brilliant surgeon," a dedicated cardiologist), and Ronald Hunter (as the "hot-tempered reformer," a former newspaper reporter, now a hospital administrator). The two battle insensitive doctors, the hospital's endless bureaucracy, and the big bucks health care costs in America. They also have tense, demanding personal lives. While Hunter worries about a divorce and a new girlfriend, Gossett struggles to keep his marriage (to Shelia Frazier) together.

The Lazarus Syndrome refers to the belief of patients that doctors can cure any ill. But nothing could cure the ills of this series' ratings. Although "The Lazarus Syndrome" had moments of interest and bite, audiences stayed away from it. The show was taken off after a month to be reshaped but never returned. It's unfortunate because Gossett's character was a much-needed image for network television: a strong, sensitive, educated black man, the tiny tube's most dispensible figure as it turns out.

One of the first dramatic series to star a black actor: the short-lived "The Lazarus Syndrome" with Louis Gossett, Jr.

"Love Thy Neighbor" (6/15/73 to 9/19/73)

ABC.

A young middle-class black couple, Ferguson and Jackie Bruce (played by Harrison Page and Janet MacLachlan), moves into an all-white housing development in Los Angeles. Their next door neighbors? A working-class white couple, Charlie and Peggy Wilson (Ron Masak and Joyce Bulifant). Both husbands are employed by the same company, Turner Electronics. The black man is an efficiency expert; the white, a company steward. Of course, we're to be amused by the racial reversal, the fact that the black Ferguson is refined and cultivated; the white

Charlie's a good ole boy slob. Often the laughs are based on racial differences. At one point when Ferguson has been proudly puttering around in his garden, he tells his friend Charlie "I've got a green thumb" to which Charlie naturally replies, "You could have fooled me." Funny? Or just dumb? "The show blends slices of surburbia," wrote *Newsweek*, "with a few dollops of social consciousness in a watered-down version of the recipe that made a success of "All in the Family.'"

Based on a British sitcom, "Love Thy Neighbor" was a summer replacement which in the fall, like the leaves on the trees, dropped out of sight.

"Magnum, P.I." (premiered 12/10/80)

CBS.

This detective series starring Tom Selleck featured actor Roger E. Mosley as T.C., helicopter pilot and right-hand man to the show's hero.

"Melba" (premiered 1/28/86)

CBS. Cast included: Jamila Perry (as Moore's daughter); Barbara Meek; Lou Jacobi; and Gracie Harrison.

On "Melba" as a recently divorced New York City working woman with a young daughter to rear, singer Melba Moore had the distinction of being the first black woman to have her own network sitcom named after her. But that distinction ended up not meaning much, so plagued

Singer Melba Moore (c.), the star of her own weekly sitcom "Melba," which co-starred (behind Moore) Barbara Meek (l.), Gracie Harrison, and (in front of Moore) Jamila Perry.

by problems and bad luck was this series. Foremost the critics liked Moore but hated the program. Some complained that Moore's working-mother character was depicted as being far too man-hungry. The show was in serious need of strong scripts and crisper direction. Most unfortunately, though, it debuted on the same day that the space shuttle *Challenger* exploded, killing its seven astronauts. Network officials felt audiences were simply too upset to watch a new comedy that evening. The next week the show was pre-empted. And in the long haul, "Melba" ended up disappearing from the airwaves after only one episode! Six months later CBS tried reviving it. But this next episode ran on what turned out to be the lowest-rated night in the history of CBS. There was no hope for the series after that.

"Miami Vice" (premiered 9/16/84)

NBC. Created by Anthony Yerkovich. *Ex. P.* Michael Mann. Cast includes: Edward James Olmos (as the dour Lt. Martin Castillo); Michael Talbott (as Det. Stan Switek); John Diehl (as Det. Zito); Olivia Brown (as Det. Trudy Joblin); and Saundra Santiago (as Det. Gina Navarro).

An action series about two vice detectives in Miami, "Miami Vice" owed much of its appeal to its stars (an interracial combo), its look (a highly polished glittering surface of striking colors: lime green walls; hot pink neon signs; a nighttime skyline of deep blues and purples; bright white suits and sunny beaches; and clothes that were liquid blues or grey, mauve, fushia, or soft pastels, all the slightly surreal colors of fantasies or nightmares), and its sound. Almost any week the soundtrack included music by such stars as Tina Turner, Lionel Richie, The Pointer Sisters, or Glenn Frey. Sometimes when the writers failed to come up with a plot or set of characters that kept the viewers' interest, the music carried the episodes along.

The series also made excellent use of its locale: the seedy underworld of Miami, with its smut dealers, flesh peddlers, drug kingpins, pimps, prostitutes, and hustlers of every sort. Rarely, however, did the camera dwell on areas of urban rot and decay. Instead it highlighted the art deco splendors of the city's South Beach area and spotlighted Miami's various ethnic mixes, presenting a city that was both glamorous and seamy, colorful and tawdry. Never having looked quite so inviting or so good, the city of Miami, in a way, was air-brushed; the gloss and glow that "Miami Vice" endowed on Miami gentrified the place and was far removed from the gritty realism of a series like "Hill Street Blues."

Fitting snugly into this beautiful vista were the stars Don Johnson and Philip Michael Thomas, as the undercover detectives, one white, one black, who strutted about in designer digs. Both blessed with the looks of models, they were basically handsome blank faces into which the audience could read whatever it wanted. Neither was a bad actor. Yet neither was an especially idiosyncratic one either. Johnson's Sonny Crockett pouted and fumed a lot. He lived alone (his wife had left him) and walked about with a look that suggested loneliness and alienation.

About all the audience knew of Thomas's agreeable narcissist Ricardo Tubbs was that he had first come from New York to Miami in search of the Colombian drug dealer responsible for his brother's death. Perhaps because he had nothing better to do—no real roots in the East—he stayed on in Miami. Except for their jobs and bonds to one

Fashion plate, dandified detectives: Don Johnson (l.) and Philip Michael Thomas in "Miami Vice," which not only changed the visual style of the cop show but also may have presented 1980s' audiences with the definitive interracial male couple.

another, there was not much more for the audience to know about either of these enigmatic loners. Nor would anyone have really cared to know more; had more been revealed, the audience might have been jolted into thinking about what it was seeing. Mostly what was seen were two nonchalant, low-key personalities who never disrupted the arty prettiness of the show and were thus able to lull the audience into the realm of Hollywood glamor and make-believe that the series was steeped in. Basically, the creators of "Miami Vice" were so fussy about the details of its look because they did not want the audience to spot what lurked underneath: "Miami Vice" was simply another cop show, which fell in line with the kind of stories about law-enforcement heroes that had been enduringly popular in American folklore and popular culture for as long as anyone could remember, from the days of the cowboy-and-injuns westerns to those of "Dragnet," Clint Eastwood's *Dirty Harry*, and "Starsky and Hutch."

In the politically conservative mid-1980s, when every Yuppie worth a Brooks Brothers outfit wanted to be a part of the system yet *cool* and *with it*, a cop show could not possibly have a fresh contemporary look if its heroes were grubby or ordinary (thus "Miami Vice" had fashion-plate heroes) or, most importantly, too questioning of the social/political order. Thus, despite the streetwise dialogue, "Miami Vice"'s heroes were as untroubled by what they saw and as detached as "Dragnet"'s Joe Friday and partner Frank. True they became angry with the drug pushers or were sometimes so turned off by the violence they saw that it seemed as if they could walk away from it all at any minute. But they didn't. These withdrawn and numbed nihilists were men so much without hope that to walk away would have meant nothing. Where would they have gone? It was a mess everywhere.

Crockett's and Tubbs's lack of passion about anything made them ideal for the Reagan 1980s: they were dapper urbanites, aware of social and political issues but devoid of social or political concerns. They didn't want to change the world; they wanted to clean it up. They represented a flight away from social problems. To spot "Miami Vice"'s unreality, one need simply compare it with "Hill Street Blues," on which the urban problems, the natural look of the stars, the messiness of the police headquarters, the concerns of the protagonists about social issues and tensions all seem to grow out of the 1960s. It, too, glorified its cop heroes, yet it showed their warts.

Basically, "Miami Vice," like most cop shows from "Dragnet" to "Cagney and Lacey," the ill-fated "Lady Blue," and "Spenser: For Hire," trumpeted the endurance of the system and the people who guard it. (Perversely, it also glamorized its criminals.) While the audience is told there are sometimes corrupt bum-apple cops, mainly it's taught, as if in a civics class, that police officers are men and women of honor who deserve respect. Such shows want the viewers to be good citizens and not to make waves. Weekly, as they give a steady dose of violence, they are salutes to law and order, covert forms of an old type of propaganda that urges the viewer not to seriously question the law.

But with "Miami Vice," there was another element: an interracial friendship that assured the audience that everything was just fine and dandy between the races in the country. The race problem has disappeared. Because the white Sonny Crockett has crossed over certain lines (racial, social, style) to have a working and personal relationship with a "spiritual" black buddy, he struck many as being hip, cool, more an individualist, not living in a white man's white bread world. He's like the white beatniks of the 1950s who seemed cooler than cool because they had black jazz artists as friends. Some probably have viewed Sonny as a dude with some soul, which makes him not really white but a guy with a suntan. Yet Crockett could cross over without any qualms because he was always in control, always the fundamental leader of this two-man team, the star of the series. Any time he wanted to get rid of his suntan and return to being all white and leave his black buddy in the dust, we knew—he knew, too—that he could.

Tubbs, almost as detached as Sonny, never seemed to consider himself this white guy's sidekick. (That was to his credit.) He was something of an empty vessel, just sitting there. The only time the audience really thought of Tubbs as being black were the occasions when, while undercover, he had a chance to use a Carribean accent and a street-pimp bounce. Then he seemed to be playfully connecting to "roots" and communal ties, breaking away from the melancholy numbness to reveal vitality and to act like a "brother" on the streets.

Together Crocket and Tubbs were both an ideal visual contrast and a perfect visual team. Of course, whenever one of them fell for a pretty woman on the show, she always had to go; often enough, she was revealed as being corrupt. Nothing could be permitted to break these two guys up. But they don't so much represent a real black and real white as they do a fantasy tan, a very acceptable color/concept for the 80s. They aren't heroes of real life but of teen dreams.

In the long run, "Miami Vice" was tied very much to past TV shows: it was a cop story enlivened by upbeat music and a fresh visual style. And its leading characters were a bit like Tony Curtis and Sidney Poitier in *The Defiant Ones*, chained/handcuffed together by their job, a time-worn racial mythology, and standard TV heroics. The saving grace was perhaps that with Philip Michael Thomas, audiences did see a black man in a major weekly series—functioning not in an all-black comic world but in the kind of integrated working situation many viewers themselves might have had to deal with. Thomas also emerged as television's first black male sex symbol, which was no easy feat.

The Invisible Man? Greg Morris as Barney Collier on "Mission: Impossible," with Barbara Bain and Martin Landau (r.).

"Mission: Impossible" (9/17/66 to 9/8/73)

CBS. Cast includes: Peter Graves (as Jim Phelps; he replaced Steven Hill who had appeared as the group's chief on the first season of the series); Martin Landau, Barbara Bain, Peter Lupus, and at various times later in the run, Lesley Ann Warren, Sam Elliot, Lynda Day George, and Barbara Anderson.

"Your mission, Jim, should you decide to accept it. . . ." Spoken on a miniature tape recorder that immediately afterward self-destructed, these were the words that set the action spinning each week on this long-running popular 60-minute action series about the IMP (Impossible Mission Force), a government agency that sent out its team of intrepid agents on various espionage capers. Featured was Greg Morris as Barney Collier, a top-notch mechanic and electronics expert. Morris's character was one of television's New Negro figures in the 1960s: an intelligent, articulate, professional operating successfully in the white world. (Gail Fisher as the secretary on "Mannix" was another such type.)

Today we see that Morris's Barney is in many respects The Invisible Man of TV: the series makes no big to-do about Morris's color; in fact, it seems to want to forget race altogether. One must remember that this show appeared at the time when ghettoes around the country were shooting up in flames. The black separatist movement was also slowly moving into the cultural vanguard. But the Morris hero is a man without any such "real" cultural context or any ethnic identity. He's something of an isolated figure, a black man coming out of nowhere. It's hard, however, not to like or respect the character. He's totally inoffensive, is often ingratiating, attractive, and in terms of television's tiny evolutionary steps, he is indeed important: a black strong and capable of making decisions although we never forget that he's not the head of IMF; he's one of those who follows orders.

The series itself moves swiftly and remains entertaining. A very serviceable comic-strip style.

"The Mod Squad" (9/24/68 to 8/23/73)

ABC.

Like American films and theater in the late 1960s, television also underwent changes because of the social/political upheaval in the nation at that time. This action series tried touching on new political attitudes and concerns (the youth movement, the black movement) and featured Clarence Williams, III (as Linc Hayes), Michael Cole (as Pete Cochran), and Peggy Lipton (as Julie Barnes)—"one black, one white, one blonde." The three were, of course, The Mod Squad, modern young undercover cops working for the Los Angeles Police Department.

Some viewed the series as schizoid because one week it might explore then "relevant" issues (campus unrest, drug addiction, ghetto tension, draft evasion, slum landlords; there was even a version of the My Lai massacre on one episode) while the next week it would pursue the conventional villains of action series (the hoods, the kidnappers, the killers, the mobsters, the motorcycle gangs). A reason for the schizophrenia was that there were two producers, alternating week to week, with distinctly different attitudes on what the series should be.

Of course, in this period of black separatism (and the rise of black cultural nationalism), the very nature/format of the series assuaged any national fears of blacks fully rebelling against the system: because we see black and white heroes working together to solve their crimes, the series tells its audience that basically white and black are willing to stick together and work things out. Had this series three black protagonists, Middle America would have promptly switched the channel; had there been three white stars, the series would have lacked the extra contemporary touch that gave it some punch. Still the young protagonists gave "The Mod Squad" a very fresh look and beat. And surely no black teenager of the period has ever forgotten Williams: tall, surly, sensitive, strong, with a huge Afro and an intensity that was new for television. In purely pop terms, he was the tiny tube's first black militant hero.

Tige Andrews also appeared as Captain Adam Greer.

A period piece that remains fun to watch.

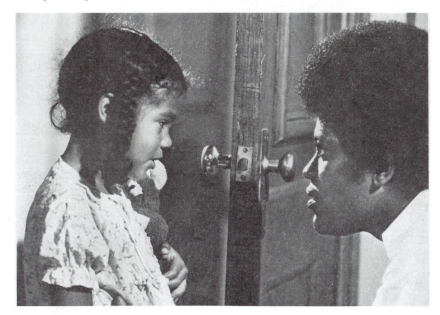

The tube's first militant hero, who appeared during the 1960s, an age in search of "relevancy": Clarence Williams III as Link on "The Mod Squad," here with guest star Mia Fullmore.

Revamping familiar material: Ron Glass (seated) and Demond Wilson in "The New Odd Couple."

"The New Odd Couple" (10/29/82 to 6/16/83)

ABC. Cast includes: Sheila Anderson (as Cecily Pigeon); Ronalda Douglas; Bart Braverman; John Shuck; and Telma Hopkins in a couple of episodes as Felix's former wife Frances.

This Neil Simon material, first a hit Broadway play, then a hit movie, and afterward a successful television series with Tony Randall and Jack Klugman, was given a black slant when Demond Wilson appeared as sportswriter Oscar and Ron Glass as photographer Felix in this short-lived series remake. Although Glass gave the show some professional spit-and-polish, the material itself was never adapted to a black milieu with a new black point of view that might have made the series—and its characters—fresh and appealing. One never senses a black community from which these men have come or in which they now live. Consequently, the old criticism of so many black sitcoms applied: it does strike one as a white show done in blackface. Still it wasn't *that* bad of a series. No doubt though because viewers could still see the real thing with the very popular reruns of the original series, this one never took off.

"One in a Million" (1/8/80 to 6/23/80)

ABC. Cast includes: Mel Stewart (as Raymond); Richard Paul; Keene Curtis; Ralph Wilcox; and Billy Wallace.

As Shirley, the waitress, on the series "What's Happening," Shirley Hemphill had become one of the most popular of the cast members. Some enterprising TV executives believed her a strong enough personality to star in her own series. In "One in a Million," she played a taxi driver, Shirley Simmons, who had been held in so high esteem by one of her passengers that, upon dying, he left her the chairmanship of a

Lady cab driver turned millionairess: Shirley Hemphill on "One in a Million."

multi-million dollar corporation, Grayson Enterprises. Thereafter Shirley does her best to look out for the interests of the common folk.

A knuckleheaded fantasy with none-too-bright performances or scripts. Short lived. Blessedly so.

"The Outcasts" (9/23/68 to 9/15/69)

ABC.

Set during the aftermath of the Civil War, this series about a pair of bounty hunters—one black, the other white—has been considered something of a television breakthrough. Don Murray played Earl Corey, a Virginia aristocrat and former slave owner; Otis Young portrayed Jemal David, a former slave. Weekly as the men were seen traveling together to track down criminals, audiences were exposed to racial tensions and conflicts. Often the characters argued or fought. Young's character David might well be viewed as televison's first angry young black man. He is determined to make his white partner drop certain assumptions and to see life from another vantage point, that of a black man. The series very much reflects the mood of the country in the late 1960s; rather than ignoring racial problems, it seemed to seek them out. "The Outcasts," however, never caught on with viewers. It lasted one season and has rarely been seen in syndication. Otis Young later appeared in the 1973 film *The Last Detail*.

"Ozzie's Girls" (syndicated 1973)

Brenda Sykes played the college co-ed Brenda MacKenzie.

"Palmerstown, USA" (3/20/80 to 6/9/81)

CBS. The early scripts were by Robert Rudin, who had previously handled teenage characters sensitively on the series "James at 15" and "Room 222." *Ex. P.* Norman Lear and Alex Haley. Cast includes: Bill Duke as Luther Freeman (the black father) and Janice St. John and Beeson Carroll (as the parents of the white child); also Michael J. Fox. "Palmerstown, USA" had an initial seven-week run in 1980, then later briefly returned in 1981 with a shorter title "Palmerstown."

In explaining what this series was all about, author Alex Haley (who conceived the idea for this program) spoke of his childhood—and a childhood friend—in Henning, Tennessee:

> What happened to me and my little white friend Kermit was an experience shared in practically every town in the South. We ate in each other's homes, slept on pallets on the floor, got spanked by our respective mothers from time to time. But when we were about 12, Kermit said to me, 'You know, Alex, pretty soon, you're gonna have to call me Mister.' I froze at the remark and began to withdraw. Our friendship ended a few weeks later. Puberty ended our innocence.

"Palmerstown, USA" is a look back at Haley's boyhood days, focusing on the friendship of a black boy, Booker T. Freeman (played by Jermain Hodge Johnson) and a white boy, David Hall (played by Brian

Godfrey Wilson), both living in the same southern town during the Depression. They are like boys anywhere at anytime with the same pranks, secrets, and rituals. But each becomes embroiled in the racial tensions of the grownups around them. On the premiere episode, the black boy's father, a blacksmith, has a bitter disagreement with the white boy's father, the local grocery store owner, over a grocery bill of $3.20. The black man says he's been overcharged. The disagreement, of course, escalates. While the proud, honorable but stubborn menfolk are at odds, the wives of the men manage to maintain a friendship, and the children still play together, although the tension filters down to the point where they call one another "nigger" and "white trash." The real culprits in this case are the town's local lowlifers—bigoted and stupid—who have nothing better to do than to push this disagreement almost to the explosive point. The real enemy, the series itself often seemed to say, was a class system; "unenlightened" rednecks are the true trouble-makers.

On each week's episode there was a familiar town crisis and soon a too-familiar form of resolution as well as a too-familiar pat view of black and white women, and black and white children who work things out. The relationship between the black and white mothers seemed hollow because it was so idealized without true emotional reverbera-tions and complexity. The depiction of the white woman—in every-thing from the way she stood and spoke—(indeed the language she used) when with her black friend—ignored the realities of the South's racial codes. Regardless of the interracial friendships/relationships that existed, no one ever forgot race. The desire to transcend racial lines is what infused such relationships with such intensity.

So much of the atmosphere of "Palmerstown, U.S.A." was so dream-like and nostalgia-laden with simple, decent bourgeois black characters whose value system and lifestyle are no different from those of their white friends that we lose track of what this series should be all about: that some people can overcome class/cultural/racial differences. Of course, what Haley wants to present here is another view of black life, the middle-class experience, the black southern family steeped in tradi-tion and self-pride. That, however, came across far better in "Roots: The Next Generations." Here everything's too pasteurized and Walton-ish. The series ignores the basic fact that no matter how close in lifestyle southern black Americans might have been to their white neighbors, there was a difference between them brought about because of the past history of slavery—and also because of a rich African cultural heritage that lived on in the black family. Black Southerners would never have dreamed of giving up those differences.

Yet with all this said and done, black audiences of the early 1980s were happy to see this short-lived, well-intentioned series, perhaps mainly because its black protagonists were not cracking jokes or shout-ing *Dyn-O-Mite*. Nor were they in the thick of a false jovial urban exis-tence. Not only was this one of the rare dramatic black television series but also an earnest attempt to bring recent past history close to us.

Almost everyone in the cast was rather nondescript without much dramatic spark. The two little boys playing the leads had been selected from over 4,000 candidates in twelve states. Jermain Hodge Johnson was a third-grader from Houston, Texas; Brian Godfrey Wilson was a fifth-grader from Mobile, Alabama. Neither had ever acted before. It showed, too, for neither could build a character. But Jonelle Allen as the mother of Booker worked hard to come to terms with her character and

the situation in which that character found herself. Sometimes she was way off base and too dramatic, a touch Hollywood. But on other occasions, there was a tender luminosity about her, a vulnerable woman hoping to please while struggling to keep her family together. She was the only performer who broke loose from the director's somber, serious approach.

Alex Haley's middle name (also his mother's maiden name) is Palmer; hence the series' title.

"Paris" (9/29/79 to 1/15/80)

CBS. *Ex. P./creator:* Steve Bochco. Cast includes: Michael Warren (as Willie Miller); Hank Garrett (as Deputy Chief Jerome Bench); Cecilia Hart; and Frank Ramirez.

Short-lived, weekly hour-long series that starred James Earl Jones as Woodrow (Woody) Paris, a Los Angeles police captain who also moonlighted as a criminology professor at a local university. This proved to be another of TV's dubious firsts: the first time a black actor starred in a dramatic weekly series. Previously in "I Spy," Bill Cosby had been *merely* the first black actor to *co-star* in a weekly dramatic series. "The Lazarus Syndrome," starring Lou Gossett, also appeared the same season as "Paris." So Gossett and Jones shared this first honor. Neither series was a ratings success though.

Although not graced with the top-notch scripts that might have kept it going a bit longer, "Paris" has a rather agreeable tone, situation, and protagonist. Usually described as a big friendly bear of an actor (a description James Earl Jones unfortunately seems to like), Jones, here toned down, manages to invest his character with a shrewd intelli-

Lee Chamberlain and James Earl Jones are a model middle-class black couple in "Paris," a rather likable detective series, which unfortunately did not last long.

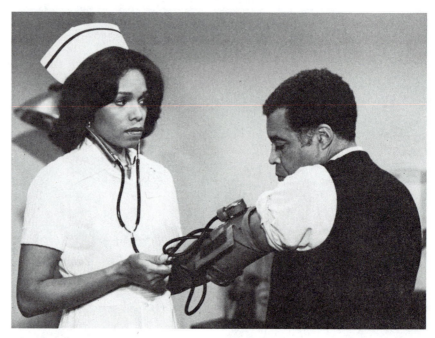

gence. This is more of a detective series than the typical cop action show. Oddly enough, although no one can ever forget Jones is black, he seems the perfect, middle-class, tough-minded but fair and folksy kind of hero audiences should have felt comfortable with. Playing his wife, Barbara, a nurse, is Lee Chamberlain, who complements him perfectly. Their middle-class home and point of view (antiseptic but with a touch of spice) was new to television, a bit fake but a bit real, too.

In reviewing the show, *Variety* expressed optimism:

> "Paris" is slotted in what has to be this season's most competitive timeslot of Saturday at 10, where three separate new hour series of varied promise will vie for audience attention. It may be the recipient of the least effective lead-in of the three, but its adult content and personal appeal of Jones . . . strongly suggest that "Paris" will prevail and develop into a long-running show of solid appeal.

The series barely lasted five months, proving perhaps that audiences still were not ready for a black man in a weekly dramatic leading role.

"The Powers of Matthew Star" (9/17/82 to 9/11/83)

NBC.

Louis Gossett, Jr., turned up in a supporting role in this simp TV series. He plays Walt Shephard, guardian angel of sorts to young Matthew Star (Peter Barton), an adolescent prince from another planet, Quadris, who settles on earth after his father has been overturned by Quadrian tyrants. Blessed with supernatural powers of telekinesis and telepathy, he wants mainly to go to a nice high school and live the life of any ordinary American kid. But he must always be on the look-out for those Quadrian enemies. Only faithful Walt/Lou knows the kid's identity.

The whole affair is still and lifeless. And it's hard to believe that Gossett is actually in this thing, which appeared around the time his movie *An Officer and a Gentleman* had become a surprise box-office hit. Once he was nominated for and then won the Oscar as Best Supporting Actor for his work in that film, it was said he struggled to get a release from the series. Embarrassing as it was to see such a skilled actor cast in such a nothing role, one respects Gossett anyway for carrying himself here with such remarkable composure, looking almost as if he were royalty from another planet himself blessing us with an appearance. Fortunately for him, the show was cancelled.

"The Redd Foxx Show" (1/18/86 to 4/19/86)

ABC. Cast includes: Rosana De Sota as the sexy Hispanic chef at Foxx's coffee shop.

Redd Foxx made yet another return to primetime television in this midseason replacement that starred him as Al Hughes, the owner of a city newsstand and coffee shop. In its opening episode, the show featured a troubled juvenile delinquent in need of a home and some wise counseling. Naturally, a social worker feels crusty Hughes, a widower who in past years had worked with his wife to rehabilitate wayward boys, is a perfect hookup for this kid named Toni. As it turns out, Toni, who looks like a boy, is simply a tomboy: underneath her rough exterior—the leather cap and jacket—is a pretty girl (played by Pamela Segall). As is to be expected, Foxx cracks a lot of jokes, telling Toni, "Me and you got a personality problem. Your personality." But his bluster and tough talk don't mean much. Everyone knows the devilish Foxx and the kid are made for each other.

A weary formula sitcom that never found an audience and soon left the airwaves.

"Roll Out" (10/5/73 to 1/4/74)

CBS.

A year after the arrival of "M*A*S*H," CBS tried out this World War II military sitcom. Set in France in 1944, "Roll Out" recounted the adventures of the 5050th Trucking Company, known as the Red Ball Express, a mostly black unit responsible for getting supplies to the troops at the front. The exploits of the actual Red Ball Express had long been a part of black American legend/folklore. A movie about the unit called simply *The Red Ball Express* had been filmed with Sidney Poitier in 1952. So a number of people were anxious to see how this series was done, also how it fared with viewers. In some respects influenced by "M*A*S*H" and maybe even "Hogan's Heroes," the series is a look at a group of lively comic guys making laughs for themselves while operating under the gun. It's not hard to understand why audiences never warmed to the series. It folded after a year. But a number of talented actors were featured: Stu Gilliam and Hilly Hicks as the central characters, Sweet and Brooks; Mel Stewart as crusty Sgt. Bryant; Darrow Igus as Jersey; Theodore Wilson as High Strung; Rod Gist as Phone Booth; Ed Begley, Jr. as Lt. Chapman; Val Bisoglio as Capt. Calvelli; Penny Santon as Madame Delacort; and in the days before he appeared on "Saturday Night Live," Garrett Morris as Wheels.

"Room 222" (9/17/69 to 1/11/74)

ABC. Cast includes: Michael Constantine as Seymour Kaufman, a very good-natured principal; Karen Valentine as a spunky student teacher; and a group of diverse students played by Ta-Tanisha, Heshimu, Richie Lane, and Ty Henderson (as Cleon). Also: Eric Laneuville, who later appeared as a "St. Elsewhere" regular and also directed the 1986 TV movie "The George McKenna Story."

This low-keyed, low-profile comedy/drama centering on the comings and goings at an integrated high school in Los Angeles may be more important in television history than many of us have thought. It's not that the series is particularly good or clever or even innovative. Its mere existence is what's most important for this was one of TV's earliest attempts to deal with young black and white America coming of age together—and during a very difficult time, the politically restless 1960s. Some may find its portrait of its black leads as hopelessly wholesome, a bit sterile even. True that, like most TV protagonists, theirs are comforting, reassuring characters, but Lloyd Haynes as the young history teacher Pete Dixon and Denise Nicholas as Liz McIntyre, the school's guidance counselor (and Dixon's lady friend), also have a position (and manner) distinct and new for blacks on television at this time: one sees them as the major characters on this series and not simply as background flavor. Moreover in terms of black images, it's such a relief to see black students—and white ones—learning from these two sensible souls rather than going to the traditional Great White Father Figure such as in the later series "The White Shadow." The school itself—called Walt Whitman High—is sheer fantasy, far too relaxed and placid. But for adolescents of this period it must have been great fun to connect to a fantasy about their experiences that did not demean or greatly trivialize them.

Everybody's favorite high school history teacher: Lloyd Haynes as Pete Dixon, here with Elliot Street, in "Room 222."

"Sanford" (3/15/80 to 7/10/81)

NBC. *P.* Sy Rosen, Mel Tolkin, Larry Rhine; *Ex. P.* Mort Lachman. Tandem Productions. Cast includes: Nathaniel Taylor.

Trying to rekindle the old flame, NBC and Redd Foxx reteamed for this series. The network, which had aired the hit "Sanford and Son," hoped to recapture some ratings power. Foxx, after having flopped with his variety show for ABC, hoped for a return to TV stardom. Together they resurrected the character of Fred Sanford.

Here son Lamont has disappeared, having gone off to Alaska to work on, well, naturally, the oil pipeline. Fred meets and marries a wealthy Beverly Hills widow (Marguerite Ray), then has to cope with her daughter (Suzanne Stone), her ne'er-do-well brother Winston (Percy Rodrigues), and her maid, Clara, who (apparently molded after Marla Gibbs' Florence) trades swipes with him. But she's no match for Foxx. "You don't have to use a vacuum cleaner," he tells her. "You could just scare the dirt away." Relying far too much on insult humor (then fashionable), the show wallows in insult dialogue that lacks wit and a distinctive punch. At one point, Fred tells his brother-in-law, "Why don't you stick your hand in your back pocket and massage your brain." Fred also has a new partner in the junk business, an overweight young man named Cal (Dennis Burkley). So there are plenty of fat jokes, too. The whole enterprise falls flat. Missing is a comic foil with whom Fred can not only battle but have fun with. Worse, the Sanford character himself, best when being greedy and crafty, indolent and self-righteous, has been stripped of his idiosyncrasies, mainly because he's out of his element, trying to cope with a new alien world rather than controlling his old familiar one.

"Sanford and Son" (1/14/72 to 9/2/77)

NBC. Developed by Norman Lear and Bud Yorkin. Cast includes: Gregory Sierra (as Julio, 1972–1975); Nathaniel Taylor (as Rollo); Raymond Allen (as Uncle Woody, 1976–1977); Lynn Hamilton (as Donna Harris); Howard Platt (as police officer Hoppy); Hal Williams (as Smitty, 1972–1976); Pat Morita (as Ah Chew, 1974–1975); Marlene Clark (as Janet, 1976–1977) and Beah Richards (as Aunt Ethel, 1972).

Based on the British sitcom "Steptoe and Son," this new-style 1970s black sitcom—brought in as a mid-season replacement—took everyone by surprise. Centering on the adventures of Los Angeles junk dealer Fred Sanford (played by Redd Foxx, whose real name was John Sanford) and his bachelor son Lamont (Demond Wilson), the show won instant popularity. In time, Fred Sanford's littered home and yard became as familiar to audiences as Archie Bunker's living room or Lucy's apartment. Familiar also were so many of Fred's antics. Could he ever resist calling son Lamont "dummy"? Did he ever hesitate to fake a heart attack, calling out to his dead wife Elizabeth that he was ready to join her? Could he ever refrain from surrounding himself with such cohorts as Melvin (Slappy White), Grady (Whitman Mayo), and Bubba (Don Bexley)? And was there ever an occasion when he backed off from pitching battle with his departed wife's sister, the notorious Aunt Esther (LaWanda Page)? Constantly bickering and quarreling, Fred Sanford and Esther went at it like Kingfish and Sapphire or Kingfish and his mother-in-law, Sapphire's Mama. "Watch out, sucker," was a recurring line of Esther's dialogue. The unexpected success of "Sanford and Son," which led the way to such other black sitcoms as "That's My Mama," "Good Times," and "The Jeffersons," changed the face of American television, proving that a black series could pull in audiences black and white.

The series was hailed as a significant departure from standard primetime programming. Yet mixed with the praise was much criticism. In *Life*, Cyclops called it an agreeable show, noting, "If it isn't any sort of triumphant breakthrough into a new honesty and realism about race in this country, at least it escapes the middle-class claustrophobia of 'Julia.'" But the reviewer added, "There is another kind of claustrophobia, however. . . . So far, the plot hasn't really gone out in the streets, where there is material rich enough to float a thousand sitcoms and of course, ten times as many tragedies." At the same time in *The Saturday Review*, Robert Lewis Shayon wrote that it was

America's first TV comedy series featuring a warm sympathetic relationship between black males. . . . Endowing father and son with strong social and political attitudes (as in

Redd Foxx as junk dealer Fred Sanford and Demond Wilson as his son Lamont, the "Dummy," in the hit 1970s' series "Sanford and Son."

"Steptoe and Son") would offer an even better solution; but regrettably American TV is still not ready for full-dimensional black males in its entertainment programs.

But most stinging were the comments of black writer Eugenia Collier who, in a *New York Times* article, denounced the series as "white to the core . . . great example of sick American humor. Fred . . . is a selfish, immature old man who rules his adult son . . . by wheedling, scheming, faking illness, and carrying on like a spoiled child." Collier added that there was nothing in the show that

> has traditionally motivated black humor—no redemptive suffering, no strength, no tragedy behind the humor. There is only the kind of selfishness and immaturity and bigotry that characterizes contemporary American humor. . . . Fred Sanford and his little boy Lamont, conceived by white minds and based on a white value system, are not strong black men capable of achieving—or even understanding—liberation. They are merely two more American child-men.

In response to the Collier article, *The Times* was flooded with letters from irate readers, black and white, in praise of the show.

All the critics had their points. Yes, the harmless, rather naive and childlike protagonists do hark back to the days when comic black characters were to be dismissed with a laugh and never seriously thought about. Because it arrived on the air after the social turmoil of Harlem and Watts, after the rise of cultural nationalism within the black community, many expected more from it, distressed that the black characters were cut off from any serious political statement. Interestingly enough, Cyclops had also raised another issue when he had written, "Why, after all should we expect everything that happens to be black to be automatically redeeming or pregnant with symbolic meanings—unless symbolic manipulations of the idea of blackness are so pathological that we want to be burned?" Of course, he was back at the old question. Can't a black show just be funny? Why all the talk about politics and sociology? And we are right back at the same old answer. For black audiences, things can never be that simple, not when there is only *one* series on television that even remotely touches on the black experience. In its hunger, the black audience may indeed desire too many things from any one particular program.

Yet, ironically, "Sanford and Son" was in tune with a changing national attitude. On the one hand, the series appeared to have a new kind of social realism because its heroes were ghettoites, victims obviously (although the scripts never spelled it out) of a culture that's relegated them to the junkyard. On the other hand, audiences liked the fact that the issue of race was never a pressing matter. This attitude reflected an evolving 1970s flight from the social concerns of the 1960s. "Sanford and Son" *looked* as if it were a series about the oppressed. Yet one was never troubled with having to think about genuine problems of the oppressed. Had the series had more black writers it might still have been funny but also an entirely different kind of product.

Nevertheless where "Sanford and Son" succeeded—the principal reason for its enduring popularity in reruns—was Redd Foxx's performance. There was nothing whitewashed about it. Neither an accommodationist nor a man controlled by any kind of dogmatic ideology, Foxx's Sanford was a black man living as much as possible as he pleased, delighting in his own foolishness, refusing to go by anyone else's books, propelling himself through the inane plotlines and shenanigans with crusty high style. (Foxx and costar Wilson both complained about the scripts and fought to have some say in the series' form.) When teamed with other black performers, Foxx, as was the case with the "Amos 'n' Andy" cast, provided an invigorating example of the old ethnic theater—the all black revues and shows that he was familiar with. The actors delighted in bouncing and playing off one another, caught up in their own professional personas more so than in the scripts.

At the top of the ratings for several seasons, "Sanford and Son" might have lasted longer had there not been internal tensions. Having once left the series for a brief spell, Foxx finally walked out on the production for good. Without him there was no show, although the producers made an attempt to keep the format alive with the "Sanford Arms" series. Later Foxx returned—without Wilson's Lamont—for the shortlived "Sanford." Another spinoff was the series "Grady" (1975–1976), starring Whitman Mayo, Carol Cole, and Joe Morton.

"Sanford Arms" (9/16/77 to 10/14/77)

NBC. Cast includes: Raymond Allen (as Esther's husband); Whitman Mayo (as the lethargic Grady); and Don Bexley (as the bellhop/maintenance man, Bubba).

So successful had "Sanford and Son" been for NBC that when the series lost its two stars—Redd Foxx, as *Variety* said, had gone to "that place from whence few return (another network)" and Demond Wilson had held out for more money—the producers were too determined to salvage their shipwrecked vessel. Thus they took the sets and some of the supporting characters from the old series and created a new show around them. On the first episode of "Sanford Arms," the audience learns that Fred and his son Lamont have moved to Arizona. Widower Phil Wheeler (Theo Wilson) has made a down payment on the Sanford property and turned part of it into a rooming house. Living with Wheeler are his two children (Tina Andrews and John Earl) and making regular appearances is his lady friend (Bebe Drake-Hooks). Weekly we see Wheeler struggling to make ends meet. And weekly who also shows up to collect the mortage payments but Fred Sanford's old nemesis Aunt Esther, played with high-styled downhome gumption by La-Wanda Page. "The vacuum created by the exit of Foxx," wrote *Variety*, "is partially filled by holdover LaWanda Page. . . . She is a genuinely funny lady but she looked considerably better when she had Foxx to work against." In fact, this entire series could have used Foxx's ability to read insights into often trashy scripts. Instead the characters put on a distressingly anemic coon show without verve or vigor. This was one of NBC's first cancellations of the season. Deservedly so.

"Scarecrow and Mrs. King" (10/3/83 to 9/10/87)

CBS.

Veteran actor Mel Stewart appeared as Billy Melrose.

"Shaft" (10/9/73 to 8/20/74)

CBS.

Part of the fun of the *Shaft* movies had been black detective John Shaft's almost defiant sexiness and his ease at handling tricky or violent situations. He'd been one of Hollywood's first cool, baaddd black dudes who could take care of business anywhere, anytime. And who could ever forget his confident boppy strut down the streets of New York? As played by Richard Roundtree, Shaft was black macho incarnate.

But when *Shaft* was turned into a 90-minute TV series (that rotated on various weeks in the same time slot with the series "Hawkins" and "The New CBS Tuesday Movie"), it looked as if Listerine had been poured over him: you could not have asked for a more antiseptic figure without ethnic grit or fervor. His setting too—New York City—appeared surprisingly wholesome and tame without the heated or gaudy look that had made the city seem so menacing in the movies. Shaft seemed out of his element—in more ways than one. He is assisted in solving his crimes not by a black buddy but the requisite *white friend* (Lieutenant Rossi, played by Ed Barth)—who's there, of course, so that the white TV audience has a guy it can *really* identify with. "In the curiously ideal world of TV entertainment," wrote *The New York Times* of hero Shaft, "he is interchangeable with any white detective floating around the dials. His color is incidental, almost non-existent. Nobody seems to notice." Shaft without color or a cultural context is not Shaft at all. The series was cancelled after its first season.

Richard Roundtree was also the star of the TV version.

"Starsky and Hutch" (9/3/75 to 8/21/79)

ABC.

Police action series featuring two talented black actors: Bernie Hamilton (the star of the 1964 movie *One Potato, Two Potato*) as hot-tempered Captain Harold Dobey and Antonio Fargas as Huggy Bear.

"Stir Crazy" (4/18/85 to 12/31/85)

CBS.

Based on the Richard Pryor/Gene Wilder hit movie, this one-hour adventure series followed the exploits of Skip Harrington (Joseph Guzaldo) and Harry Fletcher (Larry Riley), two men falsely accused of murder. Weekly as they run from the law, going to this city or that where they are good Samaritans to those in distress, they are pursued by Captain Betty (Jeannie Wilson; Polly Holiday played the part in the pilot), a tough police officer who had been in love with the man they are accused of killing. Generally, this series—sort of a comic take-off of "The Fugitive"—met with good reviews. Tom Shales of *The Washington Post* felt it had "appealing possibilities."

But this interracially bonded duo was too familiar, their brotherhood theme overworked and contrived. Moreover, Larry Riley, so effective in the film *A Soldier's Story*, was far too much the gentle giant, the good

Lackluster series based on a hit movie and also yet another examination of television's theme of interracial buddy-ism: "Stir Crazy" with Larry Riley (l.) and Joseph Guzaldo as two guys on the run from the law.

old backwoods conciliatory friendly bear, an absolutely perfect sidekick who seems most happy pleasin' his buddy/boss. In the long run, it was hard to warm to him or the notion of the series itself.

"Tenafly" (10/10/73 to 8/6/74)

NBC.

Black private eyes on television were temporarily in vogue in the early 1970s. The very same week that "Shaft" premiered on CBS as part of an alternating series, "Tenafly" showed up as a segment of "NBC Wednesday Mystery Movie," alternating every four weeks with the shows "Banacek," "Faraday and Company," and "The Snoop Sisters." The hero here was Harry Tenafly (James McEachin), seemingly a more realistic, less romanticized detective than Richard Roundtree's John Shaft. McEachin had a gritty look and stance, something of an ordinary hard-working, rather somber man, without the movie-star looks, dash, or sex appeal of Roundtree. While Shaft was a bachelor (and a favorite with the ladies, at least in the movie versions), Harry Tenafly is a solidly grounded family man with a pretty, conventional wife (Lillian Lehman) and a young son (Paul Jackson). David Huddleston appeared as Lieutenant Church. The action took place in Los Angeles. The television audience, however, never gravitated to this show. It was taken off the air after six months—and just two weeks before "Shaft" was also cancelled.

"Tenspeed and Brown Shoe" (1/27/80 to 6/27/80)

ABC.

An adventure-comedy series from Stephen J. Cannell Productions, the illustrious company that later produced that *sterling* TV action series "The A-Team." As two mismatched buddies who run a Los Angeles detective agency, Ben Vereen and Jeff Goldblum weekly pursued the predictable television villains: the mob, American Nazis, petty thieves, and crooks. Because of its casting, the series assumed it was giving audiences a message on interracial brotherhood and harmony. But the old misconceptions are blatantly apparent. As was the case with Stoney Jackson's character in the later ABC series "The Insiders," Vereen, the likable black dude, is a con artist named E. L. Turner (Tenspeed), who is amusing because he knows how to work his way around the law. The goofy but serious (morally upright) character is Goldblum's Lionel Whitney, who's called "Brown Shoe" (street vernacular for a Wall Street banker). The series patronizes both characters but at least bestows on its white hero a certain degree of middle-class respectability while the black hero's jivey, hoody ways are palatable only because he's depicted comically.

"That's My Mama" (9/4/74 to 12/24/75)

ABC.

Mother knows best. That's the premise of this sitcom revolving around a 25-year-old bachelor named Clifton Curtis (Clifton Davis) who runs a barbershop and lives at home in Washington, D.C., with his mother, Eloise (Theresa Merrit). Naturally, meddlesome but good Mom feels sonny boy's reached the age where he should find a nice girl and stop all this running around. Actually, Clifton seems to spend most of his time at the barbershop shooting the breeze with his cronies, played by Ed Barnard and Theo Wilson (both of whom at different times played the mailman friend), Ted Lange, DeForest Covan, and Jester Hairston (as the comic smooth-talkin Wildcat). Also on hand is Clifton's sister (played first, from 1974 to 1975, by Lynne Moody, later, in 1975, by Joan Pringle).

Numerous complaints shot up about the characters on this series. *The New York Daily News* said it was "offensive to blacks and offensive to whites" while *The Washington Star News* commented that Mama and son were nightmares of degrading stereotypes. The critics weren't wrong. Merritt's character, based so she said, on her beloved Aunt Gertie,

A guy's best friend is his mom: "That's My Mama" with (l. to r.) Theresa Merritt and Clifton Davis (as devoted mother and son), also Sam Laws, John Milton Kennedy, and Dennis Robertson.

came across nonetheless as the all-sacrificing, large, dowdy, warm-hearted mammy, and Davis's character Clifton was something of a lively but emasculated black male, living in the standard black-female dominated home that television always seems most comfortable with. The cronies of Clifton were, well, *jive.*

"227" (premiered 9/14/85)

NBC. Cast includes: Hal Williams (as the husband of Gibbs's character); Helen Martin (as the elderly neighbor Pearl); Regin King and Kia Goodwin (as Mary Jenkins's children); and Jackee Harry as the overripe sexpot neighbor Sandra. In time Harry acquired a following and even won an Emmy in 1987 for her performances in the series.

The comings and goings of a group of tenants at a Washington, D.C., apartment house, led by Mary Jenkins (Marla Gibbs) and her friend Rose (Alaina Reed), two gossips who sit on their building's stoop and watch the world go by.

There was only one distinctive factor in this show: Marla Gibbs, formerly Florence of "The Jeffersons." As Tom Shales of *The Washington Post* wrote: "227 . . . perks up whenever star Marla Gibbs . . . bounces an insult off one of the other tenants. This does not happen often enough." In this series, Gibbs fought to go against her old type, to assume a more subdued, possibly more mature characterization (that's open to debate, of course; the old comic Florence was the only real grownup on "The Jeffersons"). No doubt weekly audiences pulled hard for Gibbs, hoping the series would give her more to work with, that indeed it would come up to her high comic standards. Yet it improved in

Life among neighbors in a Washington, D.C., apartment building: (l. to r.) Marla Gibbs, Jackee Harry (who won popularity by playing the sexpot Sandra), and Alaina Reed in the surprise hit "227."

its second season. And perhaps because it followed the hit "Golden Girls" and also because Gibbs, no matter what, retained a great rapport with the television audience, the series did not do badly in the ratings.

"The Waverly Wonders" (9/7/78 to 10/6/78)

NBC.

Tierre Turner appeared as high school basketball player Hasty Parks.

"Webster" (premiered 9/16/83)

ABC.

Another of Hollywood's "Great White Father" fantasies with a plotline similar to that of "Diff'rent Strokes." As the series opened, George and Katherine (Alex Karras and Susan Clark), a recently married couple just learning to cope with one another, suddenly have a third person thrust into their disorganized household. Years before, George had promised his best friends, Travis and Gert, that should anything ever happen to them, he would take care of their son. Sure enough, Travis and Gert have been killed in a car accident, and their tiny 7-year-old tot, Webster Long, played by Emmanuel Lewis, is left on George's and Katherine's doorstep. From then on, the series is fairly typical TV land family stuff: the ins and outs of raising a young 'un.

What nags us though is a simple question: Didn't Webster's parents have black relatives/friends they would have asked to care for their child? Would they not have been concerned about a black child being raised in a white home, cut off from his cultural/ethnic roots? At one point in the series, Ben Vereen shows up as Webster's uncle, who hopes to adopt the boy. But, of course, Webster remains with the good white folks.

Like "Diff'rent Strokes," this series presents the audience with a very special, precocious black child, who, it seems, must have the best kind of upbringing, which in turn can be offered only by financially comfortable white liberal parents. As with "Diff'rent Strokes" the real reason for the white/black situation here is that the producers no doubt felt a black star could be successful on television only if placed in a white setting with white characters with whom the mass white television audience could identify. Even at that, the series minimizes and trivializes the very aspect that might have been of some interest: the cultural differences to be bridged between the white parents and the adopted black child.

Initially the producers no doubt liked the idea of comically contrasting the large hulky frame of former football player Karras with the tiny 40-inch-high Lewis. But too often Lewis looks like Karras's little toy, a deluxe bronze doll baby, who's also often treated condescendingly. Bright, energetic, and, *naturally*, wise beyond his years, Lewis frequently overdoes the little boy bit, widening his eyes in wonderment too often and often lapsing into a baby-talk-whine. As critic John O'Connor pointed out in his *New York Times* review, "'Webster,' in the grand style of Gary Coleman, turns out to be adorable in that odd way peculiar to television kids." Throughout the series he also calls his adopted mother *Mam*, striking us as the little pickaninny from the slave quarters who's finally gotten into the Big House but is ever mindful of his manners and his place. Couldn't the writers have come up with some better way for him to address his new mother?

Joel Swick, who usually directed the episodes, is able to keep the whole thing moving at a sprightly pace, pausing at the right times for the obligatory tender, endearing moments. But because the series repeatedly glosses over racial distinctions and steadfastly ignores the real tensions that might develop for Webster as a black child isolated from the black world, the series is frequently *unpleasantly* fake. And many black parents of the early 1980s found it insulting as well.

"Welcome Back, Kotter" (9/9/75 to 8/10/79)

ABC.

This situation comedy focused on a Brooklyn-born teacher returning to his old high school to teach a group of remedial students. Among Kotter's "sweathogs" (a true ethnic mix if ever there were one) were: Lawrence Hilton-Jacobs (as Freddie "Boom Boom" Washington), John Travolta (as Vinnie Barbarino), Robert Hegyes (as Juan Luis Pedro Phillipo de Huevos Epstein), Ron Palillo (as Arnold Horshack), and (from 1975 to 1977) Vernee Watson (as Verna Jean).

"What's Happening!!" (8/5/76 to 8/26/76; later regular run, 11/13/76 to 4/28/79)

ABC. *Ex. P.* Bud Yorkin, Saul Turtletaub, and Bernie Orenstein. Cast includes: Bryan O'Dell (as Marvin); and during 1978–79, John Welsh (as Big Earl Babcock, later called Barnett), David Hollander (as Little Earl), and Leland Smith (as Snake).

Introduced during the 1976 summer season for a four-week trial run, "What's Happening!!" was loosely based on the hit movie *Cooley High*. It centered on the highjinks of three black high school students in Los Angeles. Ernest Thomas played Roger "Rag" Thomas, the serious

Preteen dreams: Fred Berry (as Rerun), Ernest Thomas (as Raj), and Hayward Nelson (back to camera, as Dwayne) play urban high school students enduring the ups and downs of adolescence; seen here at their favorite hangout with Shirley Hemphill (as the waitress Shirley) in "What's Happening!!"

member of the trio who hopes to be a writer. Haywood Nelson, Jr., portrayed the likable, rather naive Dwayne. And Fred Berry was cast as the maddeningly overweight Rerun, who usually provided the wise-cracks.

During this period when ABC had shot to the top of the ratings with a lineup of such shows as "Happy Days" and "Laverne and Shirley," which appealed mainly to schoolchildren and few adults, "What's Happening!" also had a substantial young following. Within the black community, complaints shot up, however, that this was but another mother-dominated sitcom. Hefty Mabel King played Rag's mother, who worked as a maid in order to support her children. From 1976 to 1977, Thalmus Rasulala was carted in for appearances as King's estranged shifty husband. (It was hard to believe that Rasulala had ever even looked at King, let alone been married to her.) Also on hand was Danielle Spencer as the tart-tongued kid sister, Dee, who was rather popular for a spell. So, too, was Shirley Hemphill, who played the waitress Shirley at the local high school hangout. Changes came about later in the series. During the 1978–79 season, Mabel King left the show. The characters Roger and Dwayne then became college students, moving into their own apartment.

A mishmash of a series, "What's Happening!" proved successful all over again when run in syndication, as a new generation of young viewers watched it devotedly. In 1985 there was also a syndicated new version of the series called "What's Happening Now!," which traced the exploits of the group as young adults.

"The White Shadow" (11/27/78 to 8/21/81)

CBS. Created by: Mary Tyler Moore Productions. Cast includes: Ed Bernard (as the black principal of Carver High; Jason Bernard played this character only in the very first episode); Eric Kilpatrick; Timothy Van Patten; Ira Angustain; Robin Rose; Marilyn Coleman; Gerry Black; Ken Michelman; Bethel Leslie. Joining the cast in 1980 as students were Larry "Flash" Jenkins and Stoney Jackson (who later appeared as a star of "The Insiders").

NBC had only recently failed with "The Waverly Wonders," a series starring Joe Namath as a high-school basketball coach. But in 1978, CBS decided to take a chance with this similar series, which focused on Ken Howard as a former professional basketball player who begins a new career (after suffering an injury) as a basketball coach at Carver High School in Los Angeles. Many of his players are black ghetto youths, plagued by problems on and off the court. The series focused on such "issues" as drugs, teenage drinking, teen pregnancies, police brutality, and the plight of handicapped children.

Early in the series when Howard arrives at Carver High, he is informed by the black assistant principal, played by Joan Pringle, "Don't come charging in here like the White Knight. You can't solve all the problems in twenty minutes." Pringle's comments sum up our own feelings about the basic premise of this series: again we see The Great White Father Figure who endows the troubled black schoolkids with some wisdom and affection. Obviously, would it not have been more interesting (also more realistic *and* encouraging) to see a black coach exchange his experiences and insights with this group of young athletes. Bill Cosby had already attempted such an approach when he appeared as high school gym teacher Chet Kincaid in "The Bill Cosby Show." But "The White Shadow" takes an easy route out, providing the large white television audience again with a leading white character it can more readily identify with. Consequently, the idea prevails that white supervision and advice will see us all through our bad days.

Yet despite its premise, "The White Shadow" found a black audience. And the reasons why are apparent. Often it had sequences of emotional bite and substance. Its talented young actors—Kevin Hooks, Byron Stewart, Thomas Carter—were a refreshing new breed: none of the jokester pranks of the "Welcome Back, Kotter" kids, none of the hollow rhetorical attitudinizing and postering of Jimmie Walker's J.J. One encounters the true pangs and frustrations of adolescence, also the underlying cultural connectives that bond these students. When a group is seen harmonizing to a do-wop tune in a locker room shower, we watch students who have lived through a set of shared cultural experiences. More importantly, because the episodes featured actual basketball sequences, also spotlighted was the camaraderie and communal sweat and joy that sports can elicit in athletes (black and white).

When "The White Shadow" first appeared, *The New York Daily News* felt its execution was sloppy and that "Howard is just not believable as a coach in a ghetto school." Actually, the idea of Howard's character may not be believable, but Howard played the role with modesty and an appropriately rugged sincerity, never pushing for unrealistic heroics. Nor did he let himself lapse into sentimentality. Having been a basketball player himself, he seemed at home on the court, too, able to throw the ball and wisecracks with the same agility.

As "The White Shadow" ran longer, it got even better. And despite the sometimes melodramatic formula plots or situations, its individual moments and scenes of depth and conviction have made it remain one of the more interesting series of the 1970s to focus on black characters.

"The Young Lawyers" (9/21/70 to 5/5/71)

ABC.

Judy Pace played the bright, street-wise law student Pat Walters.

TV Movies, Mini-Series, Specials

"The Atlanta Child Murders" (1985)

CBS. *D.* John Erman. Cast includes: Charles Weldon; Gloria Foster; Percy Rodrigues; Paul Benjamin.

When this two-part, five-hour docudrama was about to premiere on network television, political and community leaders in Atlanta were in an uproar, charging that the mini-series was a distorted, inaccurate, and unfair examination of the trial of Wayne Williams for the murder of two young black men and of the events leading up to the trial (a series of killings of young black children in Atlanta). Anxious to avoid any controversy, CBS agreed to insert a statement at the beginning of each of the two telecasts. "The following presentation is not a documentary," the advisory announced, "but a drama based on certain facts surrounding the murder and disappearances of children in Atlanta between 1979 and 1981. Some of the events and characters are fictionalized for dramatic purposes. Certain scenes may be disturbing to young viewers. Parental discretion is advised."

CBS could not hide, however, the fact that "The Atlanta Child Murders" was a rather tawdry, exploitative piece of melodrama that had overstepped its bounds. What's most disturbing is this mini-series's almost self-righteous determination to cast doubts on Williams' conviction and to rig the production so that the viewer is ready to indict the judicial system. This indeed was a goal of the program's writer/co-producer Abby Mann (who had previously written the script for the 1961 movie *Judgment at Nuremburg* and the mini-series "King"), who told the press:

> It goes beyond the guilt or innocence of Wayne Williams himself. What is on trial is our judicial system. In my opinion, this whole case is a national tragedy. . . . What we are witnessing is a judicial breakdown and the failure of our me-

The trial of Wayne Williams (played by Calvin Levels) as depicted in the highly disputed mini-series "The Atlanta Child Murders," with Jason Robards (l.) as defense attorney Alvin Binder.

313

dium. Enormous things were done in this trial that might affect our lives.

One might agree with Mann's point of view. And were this a news program with a special report by an intellectually vigorous investigative reporter, I doubt if anyone would object to a new probe of the Williams case. A solid investigative reporter, after all, has to stick to the facts. Such new probes have, in fact, been done on some news shows. James Baldwin has also written of this case. But "The Atlanta Child Murders" is not a documentary but a drama "based on facts," a mix of actual events and fictions that uses far too many fictional and dramatic elements to make its statement and to stack its deck. Because a television drama like this one spells everything out (whether through a closeup of a tense face or a sweet smile or a trembling hand), there is no such thing here as ambivalence or ambiguity. The viewer is not supposed to make up his own mind. Indeed most television viewers prefer having their minds made up for them. And in this instance it's been done by the writer and director, not by an objective accumulation of facts.

From the start of "The Atlanta Child Murders," we are told, simply by the nature of the casting, where our sympathies are to lie. As Wayne Williams' mother, Ruby Dee gives a tense, vulnerable performance, a portrait of a decent good woman victimized and tormented. So drawn are we to Ruby Dee, the actress, that it's hard for us to believe she could give birth to a really bad apple. Once Williams is on trial, he's defended by a fine old country gentleman, performed with charm by Jason Robards. Playing the almost villainous prosecuting attorney is a smarmy Rip Torn. Cast as the heavy, the black police chief Captain Major Walker (a composite figure) is blustery James Earl Jones, just dripping and oozing with insensitivity. Standing in the wings as a voice of reason, that of an earnest white man, is Martin Sheen who tells us, "This was the case of the black, mad homosexual killer, with elements that appeal to every prejudice, superstition and hangup in our contemporary society." And as a police officer trying to get at the roots of this tragedy is stalwart Morgan Freeman. There is a clearly defined group of heroes and villains here, without very subtle definitions of character. When all these figures are thrown at us, we end up responding to the personalities rather than the people they play.

Perhaps what's worst about this whole production is that it took a situation then still very fresh for the viewers and trivialized it by condensing characters and altering situations in order to come up with meaty drama. By using real names and real murders, it exploits real events for dramatic purposes. Yet the program doesn't value the real enough to simply present facts without embellishment. Had this been done as a television movie based on the case—dramatizing and altering without using real names—then dramatic license would have a place. We'd know "The Atlanta Child Murders" was one man's point of view, not the real thing but an approximation of reality. As an artistic statement, it might have made us think again about the actual events of the Williams case. Then we'd have come to our own conclusion. It must have been hell for the parents of those murdered children to watch themselves presented in an otherwise conventional television murder mystery.

For the most part, this docudrama was critically well received. *The New York Times* critic John Corry called "The Atlanta Child Murders" "an irresponsible piece of work . . . trial by television." Yet like many other critics, Corry did feel as drama the production worked. In *The New York Daily News*, Kay Gardella wrote: "Meticulously constructed melodrama. . . . Five hours of exceptional television."

The critics aside, frankly, this whole production is so studied and strains so ponderously for a grand statement that it becomes tiresome, never delivering intellectually what it promises. The performances are not without interest, particularly Calvin Levels as Williams. Yet often the actors take sides in the case, not letting a truth develop organically and flow from their interpretations of their characters. And the voice-over narration of Morgan Freeman's character seems tacked on (and tacky, too), almost as if the writer felt that mood, tone, and analysis of some type had to be narrated since obviously none had been effectively dramatized.

"The Autobiography of Miss Jane Pittman" (1974)

CBS. *D.* John Korty. *P.* Robert Christiansen and Rick Rosenberg. Based on the novel by Ernest Gaines. Cast includes: Odetta; Thalmus Rasulala; Rod Perry; Josephine Premice; Joel Fluellen; and Valerie O'Dell (giving an excellent performance as the young Jane).

Pauline Kael has called this "quite possibly the finest movie ever made for television." One cannot help but agree. It's an extraordinary piece of work with an extraordinary performance by Cicely Tyson.

This epic, done in a semi-documentary fashion, tells the story of one black woman, Jane Pittman (Cicely Tyson), from her childhood years during slavery (just before the Emancipation) to the beginnings of the civil rights movement in the South. When the story opens, she's an old woman celebrating her 110th birthday in the year 1962. A young white magazine reporter (Michael Murphy) visits her, asking if he can tape her memories because he wants to see history through the eyes of someone who's lived through it. At one point, Miss Jane says, "I been carrying a scar on my back ever since I was a slave." And the film shows that scar and others: escapes from beatings and murder; the dangerous flight (as a child after the war) through swamps and unknown territory to get out of the South; the Ku Klux Klan vigilantes who storm and terrorize; the loss of her husband Joe Pittman, and the loss later of Ned, the man she had reared from the time he was a child, who was killed after he'd tried educating the blacks around him. Miss Jane has been a keen observer, seldom a participant, and as she has observed, we sense her reticence and shyness, her basic fears and insecurities. As the years move on, she develops a stoicism and a folksy brand of wisdom. She also still enjoys life and its simple pleasures: she likes her Dick Tracy comics, her ice cream, her baseball games (she's an umpire for the games held in the sugar cane fields), and her hero, Jackie Robinson. As a woman who endures and ends up a true survivor, Miss Jane, of course, embodies much of the history and strength of her race. She is a transcendent ordinary woman. And because of that, one realizes how extraordinary the ordinary black woman had to be in order to survive. At the climax of the film, Miss Jane makes her first truly decisive act. At the time when the sit-ins and boycotts have sprung up in her home in Louisiana, she's been asked by a young black college student, Jimmy, to help him and others in their civil rights campaign. After an initial hesitancy, she gives them her support. Her act: she walks up the town's

Miss Jane goes to the fountain: Cicely Tyson in her bravura, Emmy-winning performance in "The Autobiography of Miss Jane Pittman," one of the best TV movies ever made.

courthouse steps, supported by her cane, to become the first black person to drink from the "Whites Only" fountain. As the whites in the town watch her, not daring to touch or harm this black woman they've all always known and have come to respect, Miss Jane slowly drinks the water, and we seem to taste it with her. It is her first taste of freedom and the beginning of a movement for a new generation. The sequence is altogether moving and memorable.

Good as this television movie is, there are still some points to quibble with. The most glaring error of the filmmakers was the decision to have a white reporter taping Miss Jane. In the Ernest Gaines novel on which the film was based, it was a black student from a nearby black college who recorded Miss Jane's memories. By using a white reporter, the film makes the familiar concession to the mass white television audience, giving white viewers a good guy they can identify with. It also makes us believe that Miss Jane's story has been documented only because a white man finds it of value. Another complaint: the uneven quality of much of the rest of the cast, few of whom are anywhere near the high level on which Tyson is working.

Tyson, supported brilliantly by director Korty, holds everything together splendidly. As the elderly Jane, her voice—parched, heavy yet light, experienced—moves us from the start. Her walk—slow, methodical, uneasy—captures the essence of a woman accustomed to moving through life without ever taking a false step. She ages perfectly, too, from the Jane who's in her twenties (she looks absolutely stunning here, the face strong and vital yet always guarded) to that of a woman past 100.

"Cicely Tyson," wrote Rex Reed, "makes 'The Autobiography of Miss Jane Pittman' a personal triumph so that it becomes a tribute to a great woman and a great actress as well. . . . It is one of the most brilliant performances I have ever seen by a woman of any color, any age, any season." In *The New York Times*, critic John O'Connor said the film "firmly establishes Cicely Tyson as a major American actress." And Pauline Kael added that Tyson played her role "with supreme integrity."

"The Autobiography of Miss Jane Pittman" won nine Emmys, including Best Actress (Tyson), Best Director (John Korty), Best Screenplay (Tracy Keenan Wynn), and Best Special Program.

"Backstairs at the White House" (1979)

NBC. *D.* Michael O'Herlihy. *S.* Gwen Bagni and Paul Dubov. *P.* An Ed Friendly Production. Cast includes: Louis Gosset, Jr.; Robert Hooks; Paul Winfield; Bill Overton; Hari Rhodes; James B. Watson; and David Downing (part of the lineup of White House servants); Victor Buono (as President Taft); George Kennedy and Celeste Holm (as President and Mrs. Warren Harding); Robert Vaughn and Claire Bloom (as President and Mrs. Woodrow Wilson); John Anderson and Eileen Heckart (as Franklin and Eleanor Roosevelt); Harry Morgan and Estelle Parsons (as Harry and Bess Truman); and Andrew Duggan and Barbara Barrie (as Dwight and Mamie Eisenhower).

In decades past, America's wealthy were often waited on by an elite corps: black men and women graced with poise, the best of manners, a discreet air, an anxious desire to please, and an astonishing display of common sense and discretion. These were people who could not be treated condescendingly. They were too good at what they did. Happy to have work, most took pride in what they did. No doubt many assumed some of the airs of those who employed them. Old photographs reveal that the pullman porters, the ladies' maids, the footmen, and the butlers possessed extraordinarily high standards. Often their smiles indicate that life's options were not great but that one had to play the hand life had dealt. Other times a melancholia in the eyes creeps through, endowing them with a strange sadness and a heroic nobility.

When depicted in films or on radio of the past, however, notably during the 1930s, this elegant corps was turned into giggling, stumbling, shuffling, comic servants whom black audiences eventually came to deplore. The old movies never tried to tell the servants' story from their point of view. The actors themselves frequently used their humor subversively. To give their characters too stoic a posture—the staple of Louise Beavers's and sometimes Clarence Muse's performances—might have indicated an acceptance of place. Consequently, most like Eddie Anderson or Mantan Moreland had a rowdy energy. Later new generations of blacks were critical not only of the movie servants but the real servants, too, seeing them all as no more than toms or mammies, completely overlooking the skill and intelligence the actual servants had displayed in their work—and most shockingly, overlooking the keen awareness of these people that they *had* to please, to not only be a servant but an ideal servant, too, in order to survive. Granted not every black servant was a model of integrity, but those who were have almost never been given their due in films or television.

"Backstairs at the White House" (like parts of "Roots," particularly those sequences involving the servant Fiddler) sought to set some of the record straight. Based on the book *My Thirty Years Backstairs at the White House* by former White House housekeeper Lillian Rogers Parks, this nine-hour, four-part mini-series (aired on four consecutive Monday evenings) looks at a servant's view of domestic employment, at the demands it made and the costs it had on private lives. The series follows the experiences of two black women (a mother and daughter) who between them worked for 52 years at the White House, serving every president from William Howard Taft through Franklin Roosevelt up to Dwight David Eisenhower.

Olivia Cole, fresh from her triumph as Mathilda in "Roots," was cast as the mother Maggie Rogers: straight of back, diligent, conciliatory at work yet unyielding in other ways. She never sells herself cheap. Amid the elegance of the White House, she works as a hairdresser and maid, earning $20 a month, which she uses to support herself and her young daughter. She must contend with the racism of the tough head housekeeper (Cloris Leachman, giving an embarrassing performance) and the eccentricities—and sometimes insensitivities—of various White House families. (Neither President Hoover nor Eisenhower, it is revealed, ever took the time to learn the names of any of their household staff members.) Maggie also enjoys a certain camaraderie with her fellow black workers at the White House. Sometimes the servants seem too caught up in the affairs of their masters, and we often want more criticism from them, the kind of perceptive, sometimes mocking and bitingly satiric remarks real black servants always made when privately discussing those they worked for.

Shrewdly, this series shows Maggie Rogers at home—away from that big White House—where we sometimes feel she's intolerant and too stern a taskmaster on her daughter Lillian, played first by young Tania Johnson, then later as an adult by Leslie Uggams, whose work, unfortunately, is forced and uneven. Yet the mother knows neither the world nor the White House is an easy, fair place in which to function, and she wants her child prepared for some harsh realities. There is a painful family intimacy here, the kind television had glossed over or debased in series like "Good Times" or "What's Happening!!" It doesn't go as far as we want, but it's a beginning.

Throughout the audience is treated to a great gallery of faces and historical events, all seen through the eyes of the servants as they overhear conversations or spot those who think they're going unobserved. The series reminds one a bit of the popular British series "Upstairs, Downstairs." "Backstairs at the White House" is a popularization of history and of the black servant experience; as such it can't be taken as some deep comment on either. Yet it succeeds as television drama and has much to recommend it today: there is still Cole's impressive performance—and the performances of the other black actors who give us arch portraits of men just as elegant and sophisticated—and just as concerned with their own styles—as their employers.

Newsweek called it a "richly textured history and captivating drama. . . . The most refreshing event of this long, dry season."

Added note: Lillian Rogers Parks' book (co-authored with Frances Spatz Leighton) had been published in 1961; it took almost 20 years though for it to reach television; NBC also announced it had expanded on the memoirs with "extensive additional research."

"Beulah Land" (1980)

NBC. *D.* Virgil Vogel and Harry Falk. *S.* Jacque Meunier (apparently a pseudonym for J. P. Miller); based on the novels of Lonnie Coleman. *P.* Christopher Morgan. Cast includes: Dorian Harewood; Lesley Ann Warren; Paul Rudd; Meredith Baxter Birney; James McEachin; Hope Lange; and Don Johnson.

What would an Old South drama be without a heavy dose of rape, pillage, miscegenation, alcoholism, nuttiness, and violence? "Beulah Land," a six-hour, three-part miniseries, brims with all the Old South movie conventions and cliches but ends by being wholly undistinguished, even as a possible piece of camp. Its only point of interest is the controversy that originally surrounded the production. When "Beulah Land" was completed in May 1980, an ad hoc group called "The Coalition Against the Airing of 'Beulah Land,'" sponsored by the NAACP, labeled the series "demeaning to blacks." The series' chief producer David Gerber complained that no one in the coalition had even seen the program. He offered to screen it for the NAACP's executive director Benjamin Hooks. But NBC flatly refused. Consequently, Yale history professor John Blassingame was brought in for a viewing. He gave suggestions, some of which apparently were taken. Still nothing could save this thing that, as John O'Connor said in *The New York Times*, "cannot bear the weight of an even mildly serious controversy."

"Brian's Song" (1971)

D. Buzz Kulik. *S.* William Blinn, who later co-authored Prince's film *Purple Rain*. Cast includes: Judy Pace, Shelley Fabares, and Jack Warden.

Based on the experiences of two real football players, team roommates Brian Piccolo (played by James Caan) and Gayle Sayers (played by Billy Dee Williams) of the Chicago Bears, this is a buddy picture, as much a homage to male friendship as such films of the period as *Butch Cassidy and the Sundance Kid* (1969) and *The Sting* (1973). It's also a *Love Story* kind of film, using Piccolo's fatal illness (he died of cancer at the age of 26) as the basis for exploring the meaning of a relationship. In this case, the relationship has an added punch—and seemingly an added depth of feeling—because it's interracial. We assume (the film seldom states) that the men, particularly the white man, have had to overcome great social barriers to learn that friendship has no color line. Often sentimental and self-conscious, it offers nonetheless a real friendship turned into an ideal television fantasy. On a gut level, it's hard to resist, the notion that the faithful (and unexpected) friend is there to comfort to the very end his good buddy. And there is not a shred of ambiguity to ever make us question the dynamics of this interracial relationship. The two performers are very appealing. And this television movie, which was a huge ratings success, proved important to their careers. Caan went on to do *The Godfather*. Williams appeared in *Lady Sings the Blues*.

Seen today, both here look fresh, open, rather innocent. Williams is something of a teen dream: handsome, athletic yet thoughtful and sensitive. But there's a twist. He's television's first *tan* teen dream.

Based on the book *I Am Third* by Gayle Sayers and Al Silverman.

"Ceremonies in Dark Old Men" (1975)

ABC. *D.* Michael Schultz. Cast includes Godfrey Cambridge.

To a contemporary audience, this adaptation of Lonne Elder III's 1968 play about a Harlem family coming apart at the seams may look old, cranky, intolerably stagey and set-up. But when first broadcast, this production's crazy vitality and its provocative street images were fresh and scary for a TV audience accustomed to family fare in the form of "The Brady Bunch" or *heavy* drama in the manner of a series like "Medical Center" (not that the latter was at all bad).

Heading the cast was Douglas Turner Ward as Russell B. Parker, a one-time vaudeville entertainer, now an unemployed widower with three grown troubled children on his hands: the oldest son Theo (Glynn Turman), a hustler who believes "ain't nobody going to pay attention to no nigger that's not crazy"; the youngest son Bobby (J. Eric Bell), a petty thief bent on going to nowheresville; and Adele (Rosalind Cash), the oldest of the three, now the family's single wage-earner and the only child who seems able to adjust to the demands of an oppressive system. Into the household slips the slick and cooly corrupt Blue (Robert Hooks), a con man set to take the family into the illegal corn whisky business.

The highly textured language, rhythms, and performances build quickly to an explosive and inevitable tragedy. The actors here seem caught up in a familiar black actor mania: perhaps aware that this is a once-in-a-lifetime chance at performing in a vehicle with some meat to it or at least some energy, they give all-out performances, so fixated on their roles that the lines between performer and character or performer and situation are blurred. In *The New York Times*, critic John O'Connor wrote: "The production, impeccably cast, is superb . . . a remarkable achievement." This drama, which marked the network television debut of a major black theater organization, The Negro Ensemble Company, still retains its edge.

"Charleston" (1979)

NBC. *D.* Karen Arthur. *S.* Nancy Lynn Schwartz. *P.* Beryl Vertue. Cast includes: Richard Lawson; Jordan Clarke; Patricia Pearcy; Martha Scott; and Mandy Patinkin.

Insipid and cold-heartedly shallow post-Civil War story, also a blatant pint-sized rip-off of *Gone with the Wind*, without one redeeming performance and certainly without any *grand*, romanticized vision. Here we find a Southern belle Stella (played by Delta Burke) struggling, like Scarlett O'Hara, to find money to pay the tax collector. She's also crazy about a handsome rake. Meanwhile a former slave, Minerva (played by poor, miscast, uncomfortable Lynne Moody), just sits round waitin' for an eternity for the young white massa who had been her lover. Were this highflung camp, it might be excusable. But it's just a badly done

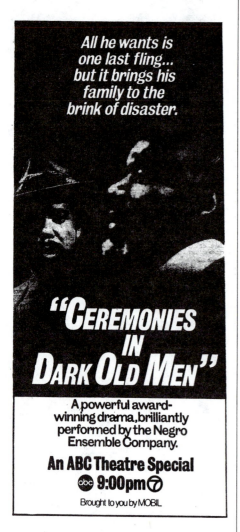

distortion—even in pop's generally simplified terms, it's distorted beyond recognition—of a past history and a series of black/white relationships.

"Cindy" (1978)

ABC. *D.* William A. Graham. *P.* Mary Tyler Moore Production. Cast includes: Cleavant Derricks; John Hancock; Graham Bell; and Helen Martin.

The Cinderella tale done in sepiatone and set in the 1940s during World War II. Cindy (Charlaine Woodard) is a pigtailed Southern lass who ventures to Harlem to be educated and to join her father (Scoey Mitchell). Of course, Cindy's evil stepmom (Mae Mercer) and her two meanie stepsisters (Alaina Reed and Nell Ruth Carter) are out to get her. Dumped on repeatedly, Cindy still manages to get to the big Sugar Hill Ball, thanks to the chauffeur next door, who borrows his boss's limo to drive Cindy to the ball in style. He also supplies Cindy with a gown lifted from the wardrobe of his boss's wife. At the colored ball, Cindy meets Joe Prince (Clifton Davis), a Marine hero. Come midnight, she makes her hasty exit, leaving behind not a magic slipper but one of the sneakers she was wearing. Later all ends happily when Joe Prince, bearing the sneaker in hand, catches up with Cindy.

Patronizing and condescending "Cindy" still might have been some fun had it been directed with some zest. Instead it just totters along while performers like Nell Carter and Alaina Reed, campy and bitchy, struggle to juice things up. The surprise casting of Woodard as the sepia dream girl helps the production out. Had this been made a few years later in the early 1980s, the title role would no doubt have gone to Irene Cara.)

This was the first production of Mary Tyler Moore's production company. Ed Weinstein collaborated with Jim Brooks, David Davis and Stan Daniels (who wrote the music and lyrics).

"Don't Look Back: The Story of Leroy Satchel Paige" (1981)

ABC. *D.* Richard Colla. *S.* Ron Rubin; based on Satchel Paige's autobiography *Maybe I'll Pitch Forever*. *P.* Stanley Rudin and Jimmy Hawkins. Cast includes: Beverly Todd; Cleavon Little; Hal Williams; Ernie Banks; Clifton Davis; Jim Davis; and (as Chuffy Russell) Ossie Davis (none of these Davises is related).

As Leroy Satchel Paige, the legendary pitcher who played in the all-black baseball leagues of the 1930s, then went to the white majors in the 1940s, Louis Gossett, Jr. is a tad too old but seems well cast nonetheless. He has a long, lean athletic look, confident but relaxed movements, and a knowing, somewhat gleeful spark in his eyes, similar to that of Paige himself. But this melodrama is a mishmash, reducing to TV routines Paige's early years in a reformatory, his relationship with his wife, and the tough years on the road playing ball. Disappointing. Added note: Paige, Josh Gibson, and other stars of the black baseball leagues are the subject of the TV documentary "Only the Ball Was White."

"A Fight for Jenny" (1986)

NBC. *D.* Gilbert Moses. *S.* Duffy Bart. *P.* Robert Greenwald.

When a handsome young black man (Philip Michael Thomas) marries a young white woman who has a child (Jaclyn-Rose Lester, above) by a previous marriage, the woman's former husband files suit for custody of his daughter in "A Fight for Jenny."

This TV movie might be viewed as an update of the 1964 film *One Potato, Two Potato.*

A black man (Philip Michael Thomas) and a white woman (Lesley Ann Warren) meet, fall in love, live together, marry, and then are embroiled in a child custody suit with the wife's former (white) husband (Drew Snyder). He does not want his daughter (Jaclyn-Rose Lester) growing up in a home with a black stepfather. The film ends, surprisingly, without a clear, neat resolution (which we very much want), leading one to wonder if the network feared taking a side in the issue. Then why raise it? The network must have had additional concerns/fears about this interracial story, for the movie underwent several title changes, at one point being called "Society's Child," at another "Colors."

Otherwise though not much new happens here, except for the rather frank romantic sexual sequences between Thomas and Warren. In the past a TV drama like "A Killing Affair" (1977) had hedged on explicit romantic scenes between its interracial couple, O. J. Simpson and Elizabeth Montgomery. And in "North and South" (1985), the sometimes steamy scenes between the interracial couple—Georg Sanford Brown and Kirstie Alley—were perhaps acceptable because Brown was killed off (as punishment, we assume, for his having touched that dear white lady). But here under black director Gilbert Moses's sure hand, the romantic scenes are credible, warm, even in TV terms, a little sexy.

What's lacking though is a new point of view. Essentially, this is the story of the white wife. What we long to know more about is what's going on inside Thomas's character David, who, when he takes his future wife home to his family, is eyed cautiously by his mother (Barbara Montgomery) and his sister (Lynn Moody). The latter bluntly informs him of her disapproval of the relationship. But thereafter the tensions or hesitations David faces as a black man in the black community are ignored.

Thomas, however, gives an engaging performance. He's scaled himself down here for the medium; he's not hyper boyish as during his movie star days in *Sparkle.* Nor does he try acting tough as on "Miami Vice." The critics seemed anxious to salute him, too. "Philip Michael Thomas really stands tall," wrote Laurel Gross in *The New York Post.* "It's a pleasure to see this handsome actor display his full stature as a performer." And in *The New York Times,* John J. O'Connor added, "The one person to come out of the movie with reputation enhanced is Mr. Thomas. . . . His performance is nicely restrained and even charming. Mr. Thomas is clearly capable of more than the action-adventure capers of Crockett and Tubbs."

"Freedom Road" (1979)

NBC. *D.* Jan Kadar. Cast includes: Edward Herrmann, Ossie Davis and Alfre Woodard.

Revisionist history and tedious drama.

In this two-part, four-hour, $7.5 million production, Muhammad Ali is cast as Gideon Jackson, an illiterate former slave who, through the help of a free black man (Ron O'Neal), learns to read and write and eventually becomes, during the Reconstruction, the U.S. Senator from

South Carolina. A focal point of this drama is Gideon's friendship and political union with a white man, Abner Lait (Kris Kristofferson). They purchase land and hope to acquire together true political power. This television film wants us to believe in the unity of newly freed Negroes and poor Southern whites. The antagonists are wealthy whites and, of course, the Ku Klux Klan, who are determined to keep all the poor and oppressed in their place. Historically, this is a fabrication that no one in his right mind can or should believe in. Dramatically, things simply plod along, the director assuming that Ali's strong enough to carry the action and keep us interested. Previously in his movie debut, playing himself in *The Greatest*, Ali was resplendently energetic and charismatic, determined that if his acting couldn't win the audience, his personality would. He was right. But "Freedom Road"'s greatest commercial asset is its greatest dramatic liability: Ali is far too subdued, restrained, undramatic, appearing at times as if he's afraid to move. "A glaring distinction of 'Freedom Road,'" wrote John O'Connor in *The New York Times*, "is that it takes Muhammad Ali, certainly one of the more vibrant personalities of this century, makes him dull . . . the performance is a disaster." The show itself was a great disappointment for NBC. The first part, after a major media/advertising buildup, ranked 33rd among the week's 66 primetime programs. Part 2, which aired the next night, ranked 55th. Had this been a great success, Ali might have stuck with acting and not returned to the boxing ring, which, as it turned out, was another mistake. Based on the novel by Howard Fast.

"Goldie and the Boxer" (1979)

NBC. *D.* David Miller. *S.* David Debin and Douglas Schwartz. *Ex. P.* O. J. Simpson. Cast includes: Vincent Gardenia and Phil Silvers.

O. J. Simpson stars as a down-on-his-luck fighter whose life and career undergo a change when an orphaned little white girl named Goldie (Melissa Michaelsen) is left in his care. Her father, also a boxer, has had a fatal stroke. His last words to O. J.: "Take care of Goldie." Set in the 1940s, this television movie seems more like a Depression era drama, the kind of heart-tugging kiddie flick that Shirley Temple and Bill "Bojangles" Robinson might have appeared in together. The name of O. J.'s character—Joe Gallagher—also reminds us of those lower-East-Side tough heroes of a James Cagney or John Garfield, although those men had grit while this hero seems reduced to a series of hollow smiles. It's embarrassing to see O. J. cast in the noble Negro role. As always, he's charming but a trifle vapid, too, and almost asexual (although Annazette Chase slinks around to at least give a hint of heat now and then). For the audience in the late 1970s, this television movie should have been spotted for the fraudulent tale it is, another gooey portrait of black/white harmony but a harmony that means nothing because it isn't grounded in any kind of equality or reality. The boxer's still as much a servant as "Bojangles" was. But "Goldie and the Boxer" proved perfect for the conservative late Carter era. It was a solid ratings hit and even spurred a sequel.

Added note: This was the first product of O. J. Simpson's own production company, Orenthal Productions. Couldn't he have come up with something better?

"Goldie and the Boxer Go to Hollywood" (1981)

NBC. *D.* David Miller. *S.* Ethel Brez, Lew Hunter, and Mel Brez. *Ex. P.* O. J. Simpson. Cast includes: Lynne Moody; Jack Gilford; and Sheila MacRae.

"Lightweight stuff but still winning," wrote *People* of this sequel to "Goldie and the Boxer." I think most, however, will cry out, "Wasn't once enough?" Here again boxer Joe Gallagher (O. J. Simpson) and little blonde Goldie (Melissa Michaelsen), an orphan, go through a series of ups and downs, all performed for the benefit of letting us know how much they—white and black—care for one another. Again like the old Shirley Temple/Bill "Bojangles" Robinson movies, it's another perfect interracial love story because there's obviously no threat of union here. The audience apparently loved the idea that a big strong buck—the powerful Juice man himself—cares most about keeping a little white girl happy and secure. What would this have been like had Goldie been Sandy, a brown-skinned black girl who's been orphaned? Ah, well, anyway, in this episode Goldie and Joe are in Tinseltown now, evading a shifty fight promoter (James Gregory)—and also the adoption board. The two seek their fortunes in showbiz.

Too cute and fake for words.

"Grambling's White Tiger" (1981)

NBC. *D.* Georg Stanford Brown. *S.* Lou Potter, William Attaway, and Zev Cohen; based on Bruce Behrenberg's book *My Little Brother Is Coming Tomorrow*. *P.* Bert Gold and Micheline Keller. Cast includes: LeVar Burton; Deborah Pratt; Bill Overton; Ray Vitte; and Dorsey Richards.

Based on a true story, this is the tale of a white California student—a star quarterback at his high school—who tackles "reverse prejudice" when he becomes the only white player on Grambling State College's black football team. In the black community, Grambling State's football games have been such a part of popular folklore that it's a pity to see the school used in this manner: for yet another family drama about a spunky white kid battling terrible odds to emerge a winner. Why not simply do an action film which uncovers the problems or hassles of the black players (a bit like "The White Shadow" but with a black coach)? Harry Belafonte does have some solid moments as Coach Eddie Robinson. But former Olympic champ Bruce Jenner, in his thirties, hardly makes for a convincing teen hero. Need any more be said?

"The Guardian" (1984)

HBO. *D.* David Greene. *S.* Richard Levinson and William Link, creators of the "Columbo" and "Mannix" series. *P.* Robert Cooper. *R.* HBO Premiere Films. Cast includes: Tandy Cronyn.

A HBO made-for-TV film that looks at first like a vigilante movie in the mold of *Death Wish* or *Black Samson*. Fed up with the muggers, the junkies, and hoods who threaten to take over their neighborhood, a group of New York apartment tenants band together to prevent crime in their building. They hire a black security guard John Mack (Louis Gossett, Jr.), a tall, stern, mysterious man, always immaculately dressed, usually in suit and tie with a proper businessman's hat on top of his head. As Mack institutes tight security regulations—new locks, mirrors, TV monitors—the film undergoes a change in tone and mood. Because it's so darkly lit, somber, and "fraught with tension," we begin wondering what this thing is really all about. When a series of strange beatings, robberies, and the murder of a would-be thief soon follow, the leader of the tenants' group, a TV director named Charles Hyatt (Martin Sheen), suspects the noble Mack of not being all he seems. Is this security guard protecting them or is he a dictatorial megalomaniac who invites or seeks out violence?

That idea is played with but not fully developed. What makes this rather ordinary film all the more puzzling and sometimes fascinating, however, is that, although the filmmakers might not have intended the racial issue to emerge as a major theme, it does and in a rather complex way, partly because of the casting (of white actor Sheen versus black actor Gossett) and partly because of the holes in the script. As we watch Sheen's character's antagonism for the black man steadily mount, we wonder what is its true basis. Is the white man jealous because his young son comes to look up to and even develop a friendship with the black guard? Is the white character resentful because the other tenants also have nothing but respect for this black man whom they view as their powerful, all-knowing protector/leader? Is the white character upset by the flirtatious attentions a white female tenant directs towards the black man? (The white woman is, of course, depicted as something of a "slut," the message being that only a morally loose white woman would have anything to do with a black man.) The subtext of "The Guardian" seems to be telling us something about a white American male's fundamental fears—sexual, physical, psychological—of a black man. In order that he feel again in control, the white character seems to want this nightmarish black security guard expunged from his world.

At "The Guardians'" climax, Sheen's character Hyatt, arriving at Mack's home in Queens to confront him, is unexpectedly assaulted by a group of black teenagers, who threaten him with lead pipes. Their leader announces he'll release Hyatt on one condition: the white man's got to "get it up" within 30 seconds. If he cannot produce an erection, he's going to be pounded into the ground. Scary and not quite as ludicrous as it might sound, the sequence obviously touches on what otherwise remains buried in the script: white male/black male sexual tension, the old familiar ties between sex and racism in America.

Of course, who shows up at the crucial moment and saves the white man from the black thugs but the noble Mack, a powerful black man (he quickly demolishes the leader of the gang with ease and agility) but one determined nonetheless to use his power to defend his white friend/ employer. In this way—as in so many previous movies dealing with white/black male bonding—order is restored. And we know the white man and the black man will now be able to live together in the world because each knows his place. The white man, however, will always feel uneasy about his *protector.*

Although most of the actors give standard, workable TV-quality performances, a few pleasant surprises are on hand. As Hyatt's son, young Simon Reynolds has charm and a pleasant urban good-kid toughness. Often feverish and overwrought, Martin Sheen does manage to work up the right kind of tension in his scenes with Gossett although, frankly, he looks completely bewildered by him throughout the film. Gossett plays John Mack in an almost unfathomable manner, making it impossible to figure the character out. Perhaps because of the direction, he strikes us as part mysterious spiritualist and part movie monster (like something out of the 1977 *Sentinel*). Yet Gossett plays the role in the only intelligent way it could be played. And at this point in his career, he displays such stature, presence, and assurance—he's an actor accustomed to elevating trash through his personal sense of conviction—that we can't take our eyes off him. Moreover, he remains such a likable actor that we immediately identify with him rather than with the white hero, which is yet another reason why this film is so frequently off balance and unsure of itself.

Worth seeing but for none of the reasons the filmmakers originally intended.

"Guyana Tragedy: The Story of Jim Jones" (1980)

CBS. *D.* William Graham. *S.* Ernest Tidyman (who also did the scripts for *Shaft*, "Minstrel Man," and "The Amazing Howard Hughes"); based on the book *Guyana Massacre: The Eyewitness Account* by Charles A. Krause and the staff of *The Washington Post*. *P.* Frank Konigsberg. Cast includes: Ron O'Neal; Ned Beatty; Diana Scarwid; and Colleen Dewhurst.

In the 1930s, Warner Bros. was known for its hot-off-the-presses movies: fast-paced melodramas about gang wars, murders, crime stories, or steamy domestic scandals of the rich and powerful based on the hot tabloid headlines of the day. "Guyana Tragedy" is an update of this type of old-school filmmaking. It dramatizes a shocking headline story of the late 1970s: the mass suicides and multiple murders in Guyana of the followers of religious cult leader Jim Jones. Told in flashbacks, "Guyana Tragedy" works very hard at first at being earnest, serious, fair, slowly showing us the sad and lonely details of Jim Jones's early life: his difficulties with his father (a man who hated "dogs, niggers, and Jews"); his years as a hard-working fundamentalist preacher in Indianapolis where he struggled against racism within the church (and eventually was driven out); his later years in the ghetto where he instituted social programs (hot meals for the poor, a day-care center, counseling for the elderly) and brought hope to an otherwise disenfranchised and alienated group of people. At one point, it looks as if this TV movie wants us to see what Jones's followers saw: the deep convictions and idealism of a charismatic man who became corrupted by his own power.

Surprisingly, this TV movie wants us to believe Jones' real personality transformation—from do-gooder to sex and control-driven egomaniac—comes about after his meeting with the black religious leader Father Divine (played by James Earl Jones), who is portrayed as a con man, preaching denial of earthly pleasures to his followers while living a very heady luxurious lifestyle himself. Not one to hesitate at partaking of the flesh of his parishioners, Father Divine advises the young Jones that it is his duty to bring the desires of followers to the surface in order to eliminate them. This sequence with Father Divine is an abomination, true exploitation and distortion of a complicated black social/religious figure. It uses only one side of Father Divine's personality (the fact that well, yes, he enjoyed his fame and his followers—and his wealth, that he had a pretty good time) without ever giving any glimpse of the other side—the man who coalesced a group of people, working for their good (through social services) and proving to them that in unity there was such a thing as black power and a semblance of black autonomy. "Guyana Tragedy" wants the viewer to believe that a black man (hypocritical, vain, selfish) leads a poor white innocent onto the road of shame and depravity. No matter what happened between the real Jim Jones and Father Divine when and if they met, it could not possibly have been as simplistic and simpleheaded a meeting as this TV movie makes it out to be.

Soon afterwards though the viewer is treated to the lurid saga that became Jones's life. And an entirely different look and rhythm overtake the production. It's almost as if the earlier segments were simply buildups, foreplay perhaps, for a drama that now steadily accelerates its pace, hopping madly to a series of highs and climaxes. While ignoring and mistreating his wife, Jones, the leader, sails off on a rampage of power, drugs, and kinky sex (with his male followers as well as his female ones). As someone in the film says of the Jones/Guyana tragedy, "Blacks, religion, sex, drugs. Got all the elements, doesn't it?"

The New York Daily News critic Ernest Leogrande wrote that it "resembles an exercise in voyeurism," while James Woolcott in *The Village Voice* added that it was "an untidy heap of tabloid clippings."

One tends to agree with both critics. Yet when all is said and done, it has to be admitted that the seamy underside potboiler quality of "Guyana Tragedy" propels it on and keeps us watching. Unlike the overly studious, plodding "Atlanta Child Murders" (where everyone takes himself too seriously and where the proceedings are disturbingly fake), "Guyana Tragedy" holds together because of its galvanizing performances, its tautly controlled excesses and extremes. As Jones, Powers Boothe looks tough but understanding, sort of a friendly older brother with a glint in his eyes that speaks of incest and madness. Then there are the black performers who energize the production. Madge Sinclair, Rosalind Cash, and even Le Var Burton seem so happy to be working on a big-budget project that they believe will be seen by millions that they're at peak energy level. As Sinclair and Cash sashay about and sing the praises of Jones, refusing to hear a single word spoken against him, neither actress is afraid of taking her character to the point of comic absurdity. They make us understand—in gaudy, enjoyably perverse and overblown pop terms—that they're so mesmerized by their leader and their thoughts of a new promised land that they are gladly throwing caution and reality aside, ready to stay on this fast and maddening joyride—this descent into hell—down to the last mile. Neither performance falls into any school or acting tradition I can think of: these are certainly not realistic characterizations. Yet they seem to be on the kind of driven, high, possessed wave-length that no doubt took over many of the actual cult members. We cannot expect a "real" attitude here. Then, too, in terms of the highflung melodrama, the actresses are just right, giving us, for one of the rare times on TV, exciting performances with personal ticks and twitches that make them live on in memory. (The same is true of the work and rhythm of the black actors in "Sister, Sister," "The Sophisticated Gents," and "Roots.") Their white counterparts as well—Brenda Vaccaro, Victoria Cartright, Diane Ladd, Brad Dourif, and Meg Foster—also have the same type of energetic commitment to this material. One could never go to this production for a social or historical comment on the Jones massacre. But the production indicates to us how the popular imagination views such a tragedy.

Added note: the low-budget film *Guyana: Cult of the Damned* (1980) also deals with the Jones tragedy but without focusing on Jones's black followers as does the TV production.

"The Hollow Image" (1979)

ABC. *D.* Marvin Chomsky. *S.* Lee Hunkins (whose script was the second winner of the ABC Theatre Award for new TV playwrights). *P.* Thomas de Wolfe and Stephen A. Rotten; *Ex. P.* Herbert Brodkin. Cast includes: Hattie Winston (as that enigmatic cousin); Robert Hooks; Arthur French—and the lively Anna Maria Horsford and Morgan Freeman (who later emerged as one of 1980s' most powerful actors).

Although it is talky and didactic, this television movie engages attention primarily because of its subject: the educated young black woman, trying to sort out professional and personal problems. The heroine (Saundra Sharp) is a successful buyer at a New York department store. Afraid she's losing touch with herself—her past, her roots—she makes a visit to (where else but) Harlem where she becomes involved with an old flame (Dick Anthony Williams) as she makes an attempt to do something to help "the community."

In many respects, "The Hollow Image" is a bronze version of past standard Hollywood career girl films where strong vibrant women—a Crawford or Davis or Hepburn—were often chastised for their independence, punished for their ambition, and brought back to basics. One isn't sure what to make of the black heroine here. Mainly—from what we see—because she chooses a life of hard work that brings her certain material rewards and comforts, the filmmakers seem to think she's in the wrong; so, too, do most of the other characters who are quick to criticize her for her "white" ways. Yet she has not become successful at the expense of others. And she is the character most anxious to change. The others—poorly defined—seem more adrift than she. Were the protagonist of this film a male, I seriously doubt that the filmmakers would come down so hard on him. Unfortunately, too, the way Saundra Sharpe plays the heroine—she has a finishing-school voice and demeanor and an interesting face that rarely changes expression—we never get close to her. (She strikes us as being as remote as Diahann Carroll in *Hurry Sundown*.) Nor has the writer worked out the character's motivations and dilemma. Had we a real idea of the heroine's past life—her family and connections, some telling incidents of the past—we might see how she's supposed to have sold out. (The real enigma here is the heroine's cousin, a singer, who seems to be straddling both sides of the fence.) Consequently, much of this is reduced to *soap* material, relieved only when Minnie Gentry shows up three-fourths of the way through. As a Harlem resident weary of the heroine's pert suggestions for a community center, Gentry lashes out in haughty, high-minded, proper-lady indignation. "You can't talk to me about nothin'," Gentry cries out, in one of the script's better lines, "cause your mouth don't know what your mind is puttin' down." The same could be said of this production, which remains of interest simply because its subject—the black woman—is so often overlooked.

"I Know Why the Caged Bird Sings" (1979)

CBS. *D.* Fielder Cook. *S.* Maya Angelou and Leonora Thuna. *Ex. P.* Thomas Moore. Cast includes: Esther Rolle (as the grandmother); Diahann Carroll and Roger Mosley (as Maya's parents); John Driver II (as brother Bailey); Paul Benjamin; Sonny Jim Gaines; and Ruby Dee (as Grandmother Baxter).

Maya Angelou's memoir, *I Know Why the Caged Bird Sings*, her account of growing up black and female in the South (Stamps, Arkansas) during the Depression, startled readers in the 1960s. For one of the rare times in American literature, there had emerged on the printed page the voice of a black woman—poetic, dreamy, sensitive, keenly intelligent. Readers saw a black girl coming of age, forced to find herself without the familiar guideposts most Americans could count on. Splendidly written, the book succeeded because of that new voice, that newly expressed sensibility. When dramatized for television though, *I Know Why the Caged Bird Sings* lost its voice.

Young actress Constance Good, cast as the girl Maya, has a wonderful face: you see yearning there and you also see someone, even as a teenager, who will not sell herself short. But the poetry and insights—indeed the reverie—inside the Angelou heroine are never worked out in the script, never dramatized. The big "events" of the book—Maya's relationship with her strong grandmother, her combination of fascination, fear, and admiration for her glamorous mother and father, her childhood adventures with her soulmate brother Bailey, and her trauma when raped by one of her mother's gentleman friends—are treated in such a conventional manner in the television movie (without the all-important connective tissue of the girl's sensibility) that they lose their impact, are mere isolated patches, rather than the slowly woven fabric of the soul of a remarkable woman. It all moves along somberly and slowly without blaze or conviction or the bittersweet heroism that makes the book still a very moving reading experience.

A black girl comes of age in the South: the TV adaptation of Maya Angelou's "I Know Why the Caged Bird Sings," with (l.) Esther Rolle as the grandmother and Constance Goode as the young Maya.

Most of the cast, feeling they're in something special, are nonetheless trapped by the director's TV-ish point of view. All except Madge Sinclair that is. As Maya's schoolteacher, Sinclair stands perfectly erect, enunciates each word with perfect precision, and is such a haughty realist that she's a prototype of the kind of bright, dedicated teacher we'd all have liked to have had: Sinclair's character is a real one, who seems to be properly depicted the way the young Maya must have seen her.

"Just an Old Sweet Song" (1976)

CBS. *D.* Robert Ellis Miller. *P.* Philip Barry. A Mary Tyler Moore Production for "G.E. Theater." Cast includes: Kevin Hooks and Eric Hooks (Robert Hooks' two sons; they had also appeared in *Sounder*); Minnie Gentry; Lincoln Kilpatrick; Edward Binns; Mary Alice; and Sonny Jim Gaines.

Written for television by Melvin Van Peebles (who only five years earlier had outraged audiences with his film *Sweet Sweetback's Baadasssss Song*), this story of a Detroit family that, after a two-week vacation, decides to return to live in the South is fairly tame and subdued stuff. It did touch on the then current trend among some young black families of the Carter Era who were turning their backs on the so-called enlightened northern states to pursue a more relaxed and economically more feasible life in the New South. Some of the dialogue here is pat and predictable. "You know what the South really is?" says Robert Hooks. "It's up North in them ghettos. But the program's the same—ripping off the black man." Most of the dialogue is also unexpected from the pen of former firebrand Van Peebles. "You know," says Hooks on another occasion, "I was taught never to trust a white man as far as I could throw him. Guess I was too hasty." My, how times have changed, Melvin! Hooks and Cicely Tyson play the couple making the move. Beah Richards is Tyson's warm mother. Despite all the homespun wisdom and the general hokum and despite the political evasiveness (it's almost shockingly sweet and wholesome, so much so that it's justifiably been criticized as a kind of black "Waltons"), "Just an Old Sweet Song" may well have been routine TV turned black, but it's not a bad viewing experience at all.

"A Killing Affair" (1977)

D. Richard C. Sarafian. *S.* E. Arthur Kean. *P.* James H. Brown; *Ex. P.* David Gerber. A David Gerber Production in association with Columbia Pictures Television. Cast includes: Todd Bridges; Dolph Sweet; Charlie Robinson.

Because of its interracial love theme, this standard TV cop movie received a lot of press. O. J. Simpson and Elizabeth Montgomery were cast as two investigative police officers who, in the midst of solving a murder, fall in love. The main stumbling block in their romantic path is not so much a set of disturbing interracial dynamics but the simple fact that he is married. (Rosalind Cash plays the wife.) Throughout the dialogue is strictly schlocksville, posing as social realism. The morning after the two have finally locked arms in a supposedly passionate embrace (actually, it's mighty tame), O. J. suffers guilt pangs. "I'll tell you about last night. I loved it. Okay. But this morning I looked at my son. I looked at my wife. And I just can't handle it." Actually, the poor fellow should have looked at a new script. Once the other cops learn of the romance, tensions flare within the department. But a chance at exploring the theme of sex and racism is passed over.

In the long run, the disruptive, socially challenging atmosphere the affair is supposed to have created does not work, mainly because the lovers themselves—an attractive, agreeable enough pair—lack any big emotions. Nor do these two duds have many love scenes. The producers probably did not want to frighten an audience by dealing too explicitly with the very subject we've been led to believe is being explored here. The whole enterprise might have had a truly offbeat ring had white actress Montgomery played the long-suffering wife and the vibrant, quick-tempered Rosalind Cash played the independent girlfriend. Then it might have worked as a tale of an assimilated black man, rejuvenated by returning to his roots.

"King" (1978)

> NBC. *D.* and *S.* Abby Mann. Cast includes: Cicely Tyson (miscast as Coretta Scott King); Ossie Davis (as Daddy King, a role Davis seemed to relish); Kenneth McMillan (as Bull Connor); Dick Anthony Williams (as Malcolm X); and playing themselves—Julian Bond, Ramsey Clark, and Tony Bennett.

Generally, this six-hour, $5 million miniseries on the life of civil rights leader, Dr. Martin Luther King, Jr., was critically well received. A "sprawling, spellbinding biography," wrote *Newsweek*, while *Time's* Frank Rich said the series made "a decent attempt to explain the meaning of a remarkable man's life. Audiences too young to remember the civil rights movement of the 50s and 60s may find 'King' a revelation."

Others, however, were not so kind. The Reverend Ralph Abernathy (King's second-in-command) complained that the series overemphasized the importance of a white adviser in helping to create King's political strategies. Others felt the series overstated the prominence of King's wife, Coretta, in his campaigns. And others believed this series took liberties with history and historical figures. Seeing the series today, we know all the criticism is valid.

When "King" tries showing us something about the man himself, it falls short. The early part, focusing on his student days and his courtship of Coretta, is flat and sometimes simpleheaded. When "King" tries presenting some history, it is adroit and effective enough to make us ask questions. Are we seeing events as they actually unfolded? Can we believe this is the dialogue used in private conversations? There is, for instance, a very effective dramatic sequence wherein we see President Kennedy and his brother, Attorney General Robert Kennedy, in the Oval Office, viewing on television the events in Birmingham. When Bobby asks what they should do, the President answers sardonically, "The same thing we always do. Nothing." A conversation between Robert Kennedy and FBI director J. Edgar Hoover concerning transcripts of some of King's recorded conversations that reveal his various sexual indiscretions, while perhaps true, seems forced and false in tone. And a historic meeting between King and Malcolm X (in which the latter expresses his love and admiration for King while secretly "gloating" over King's decline in power and popularity) is unconvincing and often downright hokey. Perhaps what's really wrong here is that this is

"King": an ambitious but uneven drama about Civil Rights leader Martin Luther King, Jr., with Paul Winfield (white shirt and hat), who gives a stirring performance as King, and Cicely Tyson as his wife Coretta.

sometimes history reduced to standard television drama rather than history, in the hands of a gifted dramatist, elevated to great realistic drama.

Two aspects of this do work though. First: the sequences recounting the events of Montgomery, Selma, Birmingham, and Chicago, as Martin Luther King, Jr., launched his civil rights campaign, capture (thanks to some old newsreel footage) the drama and tension of that time. Second, there is the undeniable power of Paul Winfield's performance as King. He gives the series authority and occasional moments of powerful truth. Having gained weight for the role, Winfield carries that weight well, using it not only to look more like King but to give the character a kind of solidity and form. His face registers the deep humanity and pain of King. Each time Winfield begins one of King's legendary speeches, I think everyone says to himself; "Oh, no, Paul, leave well enough alone." The King sermons and historic speeches are so famous—and still so deeply etched in the mass consciousness because we've seen them frequently rerun on television—that it's almost the kiss of death for any actor to tackle them. Who could bear up to comparison with King, one of the greatest orators of the twentieth century? But Winfield gently eases into each speech, building rhythmically (just as King did), performing a dazzling feat: by refusing to impersonate King (despite the similarities in cadence and inflection), his speeches stand on their own as those of his character. And they're truly stirring. Were Winfield performing this role in a theater, I think audiences would stand and cheer him every night. Had the script and direction been as great as he, "King" might have had true tragic grandeur and beauty.

"King" was a ratings disappointment, drawing only 25% of the audience over its three-night presentation. Because it appeared only a year after "Root"'s, network executives were puzzled by the failure. Television reporter Sally Bedell has written that some network programmers believed the failure was due, in part, to the fact that NBC had not heightened the roles of whites in the production. According to Bedell, former NBC executive Paul Klein felt "'Roots' was nostalgia" but that "King" had lacked "Roots"'s entertainment values and had painted a gloomier picture of the black struggle for equality.

"The Marva Collins Story" (1981)

CBS. *D.* Peter Levin. *S.* Clifford Campion. *P.* Conrad Holzgang and Clifford Campion. Cast includes: Rodrick Wimberly (as Martin Luther Jones); and—as the Collins children—Samuel Muhammad, Jr., Brett Bouldin, and Mashaune Hardy.

Based on a true story first reported on CBS's "60 Minutes," this is the story of Marva Collins, a 14-year teaching veteran of the Chicago school system who, fed up with that system's bureaucracy and its insensitivity to students, decided in 1973 to open her own school (she used part of her house and called her school The Westside Preparatory School) to aid ghetto children sometimes labelled (before being discarded) as "retarded" or "unteachable." At first, she had but five students, three of whom were her own children. The ranks grew, although initially some parents were skeptical of Collins's credentials and even wondered if she were not too strict with their children. But Collins's special brand of teaching worked: she coupled fierce discipline with warmth and commonsense. She emphasized the classics, taught

Based on a "60 Minutes" feature, "The Marva Collins Story" starred Cicely Tyson as a dedicated Chicago educator, who opens her own school and manages to reach students previously labeled as "unteachable."

333

the basics, and personalized her classroom, reaching out for each student individually. Soon her children were reciting Plato and Shakespeare—and scoring higher on standardized tests than most average public school students. Collins herself reminded one of an old-fashioned yet hip schoolmarm whom you could not help but respect—and learn from. On "60 Minutes," Collins's story was a true inspiration and perhaps a better treatment of her experiences than this dramatization because there you had facts and fundamental drama uncluttered by plot devices or dramatic climaxes. Still this dramatization has its moments. At first when we see Cicely Tyson, who plays Collins, I suppose we all think, oh, well, she's back in one of her far-too-earnest and high-and-mighty roles. We really don't want to see a performance that's meant to teach us anything. But Tyson's highmindedness works well. When she tells her charges, "You will never fail again. I won't let you," we're with this actress all the way. There are nice details and other amusing performances. Lending some strength to the basically thankless role of Collins's husband is Morgan Freeman. In this kind of drama about heroic ordinary types, their mates usually just hover around and either say, "I'll stand by you, dear," or "You're crazy, and I'm clearing out"; either way, the actor or actress playing the mate has a tough time of it and just seems in the way of the action.

This is the kind of drama *Bright Road* (1953) might have been had MGM pumped it up some and had there been a different perception about the work of black teachers.

No great shakes but likable.

"Minstrel Man" (1977)

CBS. *D.* William Graham. *S.* Esther and Richard Shapiro, who later created "Dynasty."

A two-hour Mobil Showcase Presentation that never lives up to its fascinating subject matter: Ameica's colored minstrel show performers. During the days of slavery, when only whites had been permitted to perform in minstrel shows, the entertainers had made themselves up in blackface, then cruelly parodied the antics of "comic" plantation darkies. Only after the Civil War were real blacks able to perform in minstrel shows. But they, too, were required to go in blackface. Some believe black entertainers had to make up this way, so that white audiences might not know they were actually seeing real black people onstage; they would assume instead they were watching whites in burnt cork. Sometimes the blacks in blackface were caricatures of white caricatures of black people. At other times they came up with authentic comic achievements and, like it or not, as historian Robert C. Toll has pointed out, the minstrel shows were "the first uniquely American entertainment form."

Opening in the 1880s, "Minstrel Man" is the story of two brothers, sons of a minstrel performer who has died onstage in the middle of his act. The two brothers must decide whether they will continue in show business, living by its rules, or if they will break with its traditions. This television movie earnestly tries telling us what's inside the heads of such men. One look at them performing on stage is enough to make us shiver. They have smeared their faces with burnt cork, have painted white half moons about their mouths and eyes, have dressed in white gloves and top hats and tails, all the while performing outlandishly stereotyped skits and characters. The drama wants us to know that they know they're simply playing a role onstage for the amusement of white America. Obviously, this is complex material ripe for exploration. But "Minstrel Man" takes so long in picking up any speed that we grow bored with it, and instead of real insights, the television film gives us stock ploys and plot situations. One brother (Stanley Clay) is something of a visionary, critical of the blackface tradition, anxious to try his hand at the new "whorehouse music" coming out of New Orleans. The other more conventional brother (Glynn Turman) shrewdly observes the showbiz traditions that will guarantee him the success he craves. There is also a cigar-smoking shifty promoter/hustler (Ted Ross) who determines to turn the brothers into stars with their minstrel antics. And there's a pretty girl around, too, Saundra Sharp.

Nothing ever builds or grows. Everything we're to feel about the brothers is stated for us with all the real complexities wiped away. It's so sensitively and intelligently done that it's devoid of the very things that made the colored minstrels so important: energy—and high style. It almost looks like a primer for the proper uplifting kind of black television movie.

This drama climaxes with a thoroughly unconvincing sequence: following a disastrous performance at which the brothers have eliminated minstrel antics and instead performed ragtime music only to be booed, the Good Serious Brother walks among the insensitive crowd, dramatically made up in whiteface; afterwards, having angered the whites, he's found, still in whiteface, hanging from a tree. "Minstrel Man" then ends with the Bad Brother disgustedly wiping the black makeup from his face; he is soon joined in this act by his fellow black troupe members. This attempt to inject a contemporary "militancy" into a historical drama is sentimental, fake, and ugly, ultimately distancing the audience, black and white, from the true struggle and dilemma of a past tradition and a past era.

Wouldn't it have really been more interesting had this film focused on a character like the early twentieth-century black comedian Bert Williams, a tall, dignified man, forced to wear blackface and perform darky antics, but who, off stage, was a model of poise and refinement, a worldly and well-read sophisticate. To his work, Williams also brought a melancholy air that made audiences aware there was more to him than just a laugh. Bert Williams was a man torn in two; the artist in him had to keep on performing. The professional in him knew that he could perform only within the guideposts of the established American entertainment scene. Yet Williams injected real ethnic folk humor into his work, elevating the whole minstrel syndrome. The two brothers in "Minstrel Man" should really have been one man, who, like Williams, is a split personality. Perhaps then we might have seen the true duality of the black entertainer in America.

Generally, this television film received good reviews. Praised by the critics for his work, Glynn Turman, sad to say, turned in his customary, overly conscientious, stagey performance.

"Motown 25: Yesterday, Today, Forever" (1983)

D. Don Mischer. Music Director: Smokey Robinson. Choreographed by Lester Wilson. Written by Buz Kohan, Ruth Robinson, and Suzanne de Passe. *P.* Suzanne Coston. A Motown Production in Association with Don Mischer Productions. Cast includes: DeBarge; High Energy; Dick Clark; and Linda Ronstadt.

Motown Records, the company that changed the world of American popular music in the 1960s, celebrated its 25th anniversary with this lavish, energetic, incomparably entertaining two-hour special featuring most of its stable of stars: Smokey Robinson and The Miracles, The Temptations, The Four Tops, Stevie Wonder, Marvin Gaye, Martha Reeves (of Martha & The Vandellas), Mary Wells, Junior Walker, Lionel Richie, The Commodores, Michael Jackson and The Jacksons, Diana Ross and The Supremes, Billy Dee Williams, and (the host for this program) Richard Pryor. (Both of the last two appeared in Motown's film *Lady Sings the Blues*; missing from the ranks were Gladys Knight and The Pips, David Ruffin, and Eddie Kendricks.)

The entire evening is a true feast for the eyes and ears. Old film clips showed the stars not so much in their prime as during their *start*. (If anything was apparent during this telecast, it was the simple fact that although these performers had had great hits ten, fifteen, or twenty years earlier, none was past his or her prime; they were all still, in 1983, in top form.) The Temptations and The Four Tops staged a magnificent "duel" of their hit songs, while The Jacksons had a great on-stage reunion, capped by Michael Jackson's solo rendition of "Billie Jean." It was said that Motown chieftain Berry Gordy, Jr., originally had not wanted Jackson to sing "Billie Jean" because Jackson had recorded it for Epic Records, long after he'd left Motown. But Jackson stuck to his guns, saying that he wouldn't appear on the show unless he could include this new hit. As it turned out, TV audiences saw for the first time during the performance of this song Jackson's intricately graceful and fluid *moon-walking* dance steps, and many have felt this program firmly sealed Michael Jackson's ascension to legendary stardom. Here he reached both an older [the middle-aged folks] and a younger audience [pre-teeners] that soon joined the ranks of his fans. Not too long afterward, he and his brothers went on their famous Victory Tour.

The evening climaxed with the appearance of Diana Ross (looking slinkily glamorous and giddy as she glided across stage, dragging her white fur stole) and The Supremes (Mary Wilson and Cindy Birdsong). Word spread that during the taping of this show, Ross had shoved Wilson at one point and snatched the microphone out of her hand. None of this was seen in the televised version, but the story lingers on and has contributed to the image of Ross as an attention-mad superstar. Mary Wilson wrote of the incident in her 1986 book, *Dreamgirl: My Life as a Supreme*.

Today it's also rather poignant to see Marvin Gaye, who was to be killed not too long afterward, performing "What's Going On."

This program, however, has not been spared complaints or criticism. Some have felt that the opening choreography is too Broadwayish and that the integrated troupe of dancers was a concession made to please the large white TV audience. (True.) Of course, the glorious point of Motown's success in the 1960s had been partly that it had proved what great heights black artists could reach when permitted to shape and form their own material, which, in this case, had often grown out of the heat and tension of ghetto life and had pulsated with a new gospel fervor and beat. Black record buyers bought the Motown music and put the company on the map. Eventually, the music proved, like jazz in the 1920s, so distinctively new and invigorating that young white America had no choice but to buy Motown records too. And part of the great shared pop cultural experience of the 1960s of black and white America was this rich new Motown sound. Consequently, there was no need for some of the brief integrated sequences or the appearance of Linda Ronstadt, who seemed totally out of place.

Another complaint: Martha Reeves and Mary Wells were short-changed, not allowed to finish their songs "Love is Like a Heat Wave" and "My Guy." Instead this section focused on a tired disc jockey routine between former "WKRP in Cincinnati" stars Howard Hesseman and Tim Reid.

Yet complaints aside, the opening of the program was so exuberantly performed that one's still dazzled by it, and in the long run, the short-comings of "Motown 25" are pretty negligible. This is a classic music show with songs ("My Girl," "Oooo Baby Baby," "Shop Around," "Can't Help Myself"), routines, and star personalities, that remain enduringly fresh and immediate, a beautiful encapsulation of a period and point of view in American popular culture that will never come again.

In 1985 Motown tried duplicating the success of this program with its all-star "Motown Returns to the Apollo."

"Playing with Fire" (1985)

NBC. *D.* Ivan Nagy. *S.* Lew Hunter. Cast includes: Yaphet Kotto.

In an effort to shed his "child-star" image, Gary Coleman plays a teenage arsonist in "Playing with Fire," with Cicely Tyson and Yaphet Kotto.

One of television's "issue-oriented" movies, centering on the subject of teenage arson. A lonely and frustrated adolescent (Gary Coleman) cannot deal with the separation of his parents (Cicely Tyson and Ron O'Neal) nor with the pangs of growing up. His hunger for attention (*and* love) leads to his pyromania.

Mundane and unconvincing. The fires themselves are almost comically handled: not once does Coleman have a problem getting a fire started. He simply strikes a match or flicks a cigarette lighter and WHAM a room or a field is ablaze.

The denouement in which a reformed Coleman talks things out with his parents, so earnestly and forthrightly that he ends by reuniting them, is wholly implausible and a cheap shot.

Tyson and O'Neal wander through the production looking restless, as if anxious to find more challenging work. In one sequence with a psychiatrist, Tyson does have her moments: tense, angry, baffled, explosive, she's a skilled actress in search of a decent part.

Having outgrown his cuteness stage, Coleman tries valiantly to slip into a more mature role, but his performance is mechanical and self-conscious.

"Roots" (1977)

ABC. *D.* Marvin Chomsky, David Greene, Gilbert Moses, John Erman. Cast includes: Moses Gunn; Hari Rhodes; Ren Woods; Beverly Todd; Ralph Waite; Lorne Greene; Maya Angelou; Thalmus Rasulala; Ji-Tu Cumbuka; William Watson; Lynda Day George; Vic Morrow; Robert Reed; Raymond St. Jacques; Gary Collins; Lawrence Hilton-Jacobs; John Schuck; Macdonald Carey; Lillian Randolph; Carolyn Jones; Lloyd Bridges; Georg Stanford Brown; Lynne Moody; Doug McClure; Burl Ives; Scatman Crothers; Sandy Duncan; and Chuck Connors.

In early 1977, for eight consecutive nights, the sprawling twelve-hour, $6 million miniseries "Roots" took hold of the mass television audience's imagination and refused to let go. Never before in the history of American television had there been anything that even remotely looked like it (its opening African sequence had a visual sweep then new to television): it was a big, elaborate, galvanizing experience of pop mythic dimensions that affected viewers both black and white. Over 130 million people (representing 85% of all television homes in the United States) brooded, cried, cheered, and debated over the agonies and glories of Kunta Kinte and his descendants. And despite the various cliches and concessions, the dramatic inconsistencies, and occasional historical inaccuracies, "Roots" was a genuine once-in-a-lifetime event in the 1970s, a rousing historic mass cult picture that may have altered the popular imagination.

The Alex Haley book on which the television movie was based is also now a legendary piece of work. Perhaps no book written in this country since *Uncle Tom's Cabin* has reached so many people in such a short time or has so affected their view of a social situation. For those who went to Haley's book expecting some experimental, vastly complex, or intellectually revolutionary piece of work, there may have been a disappoint-

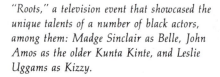

"Roots," a television event that showcased the unique talents of a number of black actors, among them: Madge Sinclair as Belle, John Amos as the older Kunta Kinte, and Leslie Uggams as Kizzy.

ment. Haley was not out to dazzle with language or technique. Instead as the least pretentious of serious popular writers, he wanted to tell a long, epic adventure of heroic proportions. He succeeded surprisingly well. The book was a popularization of the kind of history scholars and college professors had tried drumming into stubborn school-kid heads and ears for decades. Reading *Roots*, one was continually moved (and occasionally astounded) by Haley's adroit interweaving of history and personal experience. Fictionalizing the real lives of his ancestors, putting words and events into their mouths and heads, he came up with a tale that somehow still rings true, so much so that *Roots* strikes us as the story not only of his family but our own as well.

Haley was most adept at telling the story of the slave experience from the slave's point of view. Frederick Douglass's books on his life as well as numerous slave narratives had provided such a view before. But now the big, bold popular novel had come of age with this type of material. Had anyone ever before read an epic that recreated the daily life of an African village (and tried revealing to us at the same time the bearings of African culture on contemporary black American life)? And all those earlier novels and movies about the slave period, everything from *The Birth of a Nation* to *Gone with the Wind* to *So Red the Rose*—had any ever before seriously explained what happened once the slaves left the big house and returned to their quarters? Movies such as *Mandingo* and *Drum* had told of mock slave rebellions and slave atrocities. But had any movie taken us inside the slave's head so that we might understand his peculiar torment over the daily, unsensationalized events of his life? Had any ever recorded the slave's surreptitious maneuvers and curious delights in picking up local gossip or information on historic events while serving at the white master's table? Neither exploiting nor seriously distorting its subject matter, *Roots* was a vastly pleasurable and revealing reading experience. A bit hokey at times. Surely melodramatic at points. Certainly too coy and clever for its own good at moments. And sometimes Haley appeared so quick to point out the unity and sense of camaraderie among the slaves that a basic human experience seemed simplified. But all that seems neither here nor there in the long run because Haley's book arrived at a time when there was a need for a popular historical saga of black unity and brotherhood. Alex Haley had given readers a huge archetypal experience that everyone could share in, and it remains difficult today not to be swept up by its volcanic force and the basic human truth it uncovers.

Newcomer LeVar Burton portrayed the young Kunta Kinte in "Roots."

TV's "Roots" followed the book's straightforward narrative, chronicling about a hundred years in a family's history: it moves from the 1700s when the African child Kunta Kinte is born; on through his youth and eventual capture by slave traders, who ship him to America in chains; through to the story of his daughter Kizzy (raped by a white plantation owner) and her son Chicken George; to Kunta Kinte's great-grandson Tom Harvey, who lives through the Civil War and the eventual emancipation of his people.

Of course, the TV series pinpoints the various joys and disparities of American popular culture. Some intellectuals rightfully rejected the TV version's cliches and compromises. Characters and incidents were inserted that had no real place in the drama. A guilt-ridden slaveship captain (Edward Asner) was introduced as a concession to the mass white audience. No such figure appeared in the book. Here the white viewer is made to feel a bit more comfortable because he can see whites tormented and disturbed by the slave system, too. When the character Good Ole George (who appeared in the book but not as prominently) popped up in the last episode of the series, audiences knew they were in for one of those Waltons, goody-two-shoes happy endings. He was there to reassure white viewers, too. Indeed television observer Sally Bedell has said that a major casting concern at ABC was the injection of white characters into the story. "Our concern," Bedell quotes ABC executive Larry Sullivan as saying, "was to put a lot of white people in the promos. Otherwise we felt the program would be a turnoff." (A turnoff for the white audience, naturally.) Bedell has also quoted another ABC executive, Lou Rudolph, as saying, "I think we fooled the audience. Because the white stories in most cases were irrelevant. It was a matter of having some white faces, particularly in the opening episodes." ABC's Brandon Stoddard added: "We made certain to use whites viewers had seen a hundred times [Edward Asner, Lorne Greene] so they would feel comfortable."

Other viewers may have been disappointed with "Roots'" reliance on the stock television formula of sex plus violence plus more sex plus more violence. The book revealed vividly and graphically (particularly on the slaveship) the horrors and brutalities of the slave period. But the violence had a place in the story. And never was there any gratuitous sex. The TV character Fanta, the dream girl Kunta pursues to another plantation, appeared nowhere in the book. She was simply on television to titillate the viewer. When she loudly argued with Kunta the morning after their night together, her idiotic explosion that led to his entrapment seemed blatantly fake because the very thing other parts of "Roots" pointed out (most notably with the characters Fiddler and Belle) was that the slave population never made a move without a terrifying awareness of the surrounding white world.

The episode that may have been most grating to purists was the opening African segment. The book's Gambia was a paradise of peace and harmony, perhaps too idealized. But at least it seemed like Africa. On television, Africa looked like Savannah, Georgia (where the segment was filmed), and once O. J. Simpson (as an African native) ran across the screen, audiences probably felt as if they'd been immediately transported out of eighteenth-century Africa into twentieth-century Southern California. The African section was far too Americanized; Kunta's manhood rites looked more like a frat initiation.

Generally, movies need not be compared with the books on which they're based. The two are separate entities. But the changes in "Roots" (and in "The Autobiography of Miss Jane Pittman") indicate what happens when the work of a black artist (who has complete control over his material) is put into the hands of others from a different cultural experience. The writers on "Roots" were white as were the producers and the directors, with the exception of Gilbert Moses (who unfortunately did not direct the slaveship segment, which he would have been perfect for). The scripts are nothing sensational. And often the directors, each of whom has a certain skill for melodrama, treat "Roots" as if it were any regular television fare. No doubt many, unaware of "Roots'" future extraordinary impact, assumed that was exactly what they were working with. Consequently, the show was often like a grand soap opera, without the "impeccable taste" of "Masterpiece Theatre" epics. *That* we can be thankful for here. This material called for an all-out punch-and-run impact, and the cast, when the various directors pulled the stops out and just let the emotional experience speak for itself, belted viewers time and again. Some of the stars of "Roots," having drifted through Hollywood's wasteland for years, finally came up with something to challenge their talents. Most seemed to understand and avoid the pitfalls of the scripts. Almost all the leads were able to sink their teeth into each horrifying or triumphant moment. What was rare for TV drama was that neither the black characters nor the actors playing them were standard, comfy, middle-class, reassuring types. Almost all were larger than life with aches, pains, or struggles that filled the viewers with a sense of terror or awe. No one settled for a "little" emotion. None pulled back from a moment that might disturb or upset a viewer.

The hero of "Roots," Kunta Kinte, was played (as a young man) by

LeVar Burton with appropriate intensity and innocence. (Originally, an ABC executive had objected to Burton because he felt the actor's lips were too thick.) Burton's scenes with Louis Gossett, Jr. (as Fiddler, the slave who must teach Kunta work routines and survival techniques in this new country) were all the more affecting because here we witnessed firsthand an older actor showing the ropes (in terms of the movie's plot and perhaps in terms of practical experience in Hollywood itself) to a newcomer. With Gossett, Burton had someone he could play off and connect to. Audiences didn't fully feel the connection between Cicely Tyson and Burton in the earlier African sections because the tension between this African mother and son was never defined. It was also curious that in the African segments, Tyson was one of the few American performers who did indeed seem African.

Actually, Burton should have appeared in at least one more episode because John Amos, who played the older Kunta, seemed much too old when first brought on. The striking chemistry between Gossett and Burton is missing in the first scenes that Gossett and Amos have together. But John Amos is never an actor to be taken lightly. As his Kunta matured, Amos grew in stature. Amos's Kunta endures, copes, fights, holds back and in, and finally, learns to love, only to have his heart broken. His scenes with Madge Sinclair as Belle rocked and swayed with an authentic humor and mutual respect. Unlike the mammy and tom figures of old, Amos's Kunta and Sinclair's Belle directly perceived, even anticipated one another's actions, the way people destined to be lovers always do at first sight. They are an odd pair. Belle, corrupted by her American upbringing, is fiercely anti-African (yet curiously in awe of Kunta's African allegiance). She, as well as Fiddler, works, lives, experiences, not taking time to question. Resolutely refusing to forget anything, Kunta seeks answers to the riddle of the universe. (Where is his Allah?) He broods, ruminates, searches. The two stalk each other carefully, bluffing, inspecting, or behaving formally with an underlying tension that leads us to expect an explosion any minute. Yet, speaking through their postures and their eyes, they seem to comprehend one another's form and essence. Each character realizes that his potentialities (as well as the dimensions of his world) are stunted by the corrupt white society. In the casting of Amos and Madge Sinclair, there was a textured rhythm. It was also there in the casting of Amos and Leslie Uggams.

As Kizzy, Leslie Uggams's strongest moments are those in which her character was consciously aware of how much of her identity and personal pride grew directly out of her father's perspective. In the early sequences, Uggams was far too giggly and assured for a slave girl. One almost feels ready to ship her back to Mitch Miller's singalong troupe. But gradually as her character matured, that cute/ugly imp's smile of hers vanished. In the past, one's often had the impression that Leslie Uggams, when performing, kept one eye on the mirror and the other on the audience. She'd never do anything she felt would not please. But in "Roots," Uggams finally did away with some of her irritating personal traits and let the character take over. When she became involved with Richard Roundtree (also good for a change), Uggams took on a tough, stately sensuality, hitherfore unexhibited. The Roundtree episode did not appear in the book. Instead Kizzy lived an uneventful empty life after the birth of Chicken George, staying mostly in the fields, rejoicing later in her grandchildren. But the Roundtree episode,

"Roots" also showcased Ben Vereen as a triumphant Chicken George.

obviously inserted to keep the audience tuned in by way of sex and romance, was not objectionable.

The sequences when Kizzy returned to her father's grave (and scratched out the slave name Toby) and later when she triumphantly spits into the cup of the old Missy Ann, the former childhood friend who betrayed her, do not appear in the book either. But in these segments, Leslie Uggams is obviously stretching her particular talents, taking on the challenge of her first big serious part, giving something unexpressed before. Watching Uggams get inside her character, audiences may have sensed she might never again have such moments. She may have understood that, too, and so there is a double-edged bitterness and hardness (perhaps a fear, too) that rounds her character splendidly. There is also a poignant sadness here, too. Some may never forgive Leslie Uggams for her wholesome American apple-pie image. She is not Olivia Cole or Cicely Tyson. She doesn't have their power of concentration. But she does have the power of feeling and is able to appropriately use her own raw emotional fiber to create a figure of larger-than-life proportions.

Perhaps the surprise delight for audiences was the fine work of Louis Gossett, who almost stole "Roots" as Fiddler. Gossett accurately conveys the sense of a man forced to operate in two cultures, a man well aware, as most blacks have been, that there is one acceptable code of behavior (and language) for dealing with whites and another totally different manner for dealing with the black community. Fiddler goes through his *yessums* and *nosuhs* with appropriate deference. In the sequence when he rushes to plead that his master prevent the beating of the young Kunta, he is temporarily halted by the white mistress of the house. Fiddler goes through the yessum bit in such a perfectly modulated offhand, matter-of-fact way that we know he could not care less about this white woman standing before him. But if he hopes to save Kunta, he obviously cannot simply pass her by. When he fails to prevent the beating, he washes Kunta's wounds and holds him, telling him not to pay attention to the white man's name Toby. He will always be Kunta Kinte, regardless. It is one of the highpoints of the series and one of Gossett's great moments, etched with controlled anger and confusion and a bitter stoicism. Later when playing the fiddle, he is someone totally changed, all talker, all strutter, all jive-time, joyous extrovert. Had the producers seen fit to include the book's description of Fiddler having saved his money to buy his freedom only to be told by his master that it was not enough, Gossett's character would have taken on yet another dimension. But Gossett's performance, was striking with its unmanageable depths and its clever shifting perspectives from know-it-all loudmouth to Kunta's sensitive mentor.

Basically, audiences responded to "Roots" spirit, the sheer velocity of its images and performances. In order to be enjoyed or appreciated, the series demands nothing intellectually. (Nor does most popular culture.) It's a disturbingly *easy* high. The images swamp you. But the glory of "Roots" was that viewer demands were met nonetheless. In great pop art/entertainment, if the viewer searches, there are always questions or answers to subconscious needs and longings. Something like television's "Minstrel Man" wanted audiences to ask questions but was too studied, with nothing felt or experienced. It was embalmed melodrama. "Roots" wanted its audience to feel. When John Amos's Kunta waved across the field to Leslie Uggams's Kizzy, the audience was moved in an unexpected, unexplained way because of the grace and elegance the two had when together. Sometimes our answers or questions are emotional; other times, intellectual; other times, too personal for anyone to want to discuss. To ask that commercial television *consciously* make demands might be beside the point. Instead, we must ask ourselves why the best of the stuff has indeed affected us. And, more often than not, if our instincts are to be trusted, we can discover on our own the subterranean achievements (or disappointments or cheap manipulations) that may infuse even the most blatantly melodramatic of television fare.

The black experience is far wider, far denser, far more complicated, far more unmanageable than "Roots" implied. But the program, like the book, captured the raw, archetypal, mythic essence of human experience. Seeing on American commercial television slave beatings, slave rapes, family separations, constant daily humiliations, and the basic inhumanity and corruption that have gone into making America the empire it has become and witnessing the victorious spirit of those who survived it all, audiences have been affected in unanticipated ways. "Roots" remains a pop triumph.

"Roots: The Next Generations" (1979)

ABC. *D.* John Erman, Charles S. Dubin, Georg Stanford Brown, and Lloyd Richards. *S.* Ernest Kinoy, Sidney A. Glass, Daniel Wilcox, and Thad Mumford and Daniel Wilcox; based on Alex Haley's books *Roots* and *My Search for Roots*. *P.* Stan Margulies. *Ex. P.* David Wolper. Cast includes: Al Freeman, Jr. (as Malcolm X), Ruby Dee, Ossie Davis, Bernie Casey, John Rubinstein, Fay Hauser, Richard Thomas, Charles Weldon, Rosey Grier, Pam Grier, Dina Merrill, Paul Winfield, Brock Peters, Diahann Carroll, Andy Griffith, Carmen McRae, Damon Evans (who portrays Alex Haley as a young man), Garrett Morris, Hal Williams, Marc Singer, Robert Culp, and as the child Alex Haley, Christoff St. John (who later played the oldest son on the TV series "Charlie & Company").

Two years after the phenomenal success of "Roots," this fourteen-hour, seven-night, $18 million sequel appeared. In a bold and fast-moving fashion, "Roots: The Next Generations" continued the chronicle of Alex Haley's family: from the 1880s when Chicken George (Avon Long) has settled in Henning, Tennessee, to the 1960s when Haley himself has begun his writing career. The family drama is set against the turbulent and sometimes violent history of America from the years of the Reconstruction to the rise of Jim Crowism through the First and Second World Wars up to the rise of the black power movement and Malcolm X. This material had been covered hastily in the last 30 pages of *Roots*, and, afterward, Haley had sat with a tape recorder to provide over a thousand pages of transcript, from which the television writers developed this second miniseries.

Although not the ratings superstar its predecessor was, the sequel nonetheless was successful, with roughly some 110 million viewers watching all or parts of it. Critically, "Roots: The Next Generations," in some respects, scored better than "Roots." Of the two programs, *Newsweek* found the sequel superior, saying, "Richer in physical sweep and psychological shadings, graced with acting seldom seen on the tube." In *The New York Post*, Harriet Van Horne called it "one of the richest experiences in the annals of television. . . . It's a fuller, sweeter, more agonizing story, and its conflicts cut deeper into our twentieth century sensibility." And in *The New York Times*, John J. O'Connor added, "This new production is less obvious, less manipulating, less unsure of itself. In brief, it is more serious."

For the most part, "Roots: The Next Generations" was also more "televisionish" than its predecessor, often conforming to expected tube formulas. Whereas "Roots" had been so startling because its actors pushed for big emotions and big emotional responses from the audience, refusing to pull back and distance themselves, the sequel was frequently a quieter drama focusing partly on class struggle and espousing the American work ethic and a belief in the American Dream. It is more a portrait of people trying to make it within a system rather than seriously questioning or challenging it (as was very much the case with the character Kunta Kinte in the original). Sometimes the sequel also seemed a series of troubled romances, whether it examined the story of Haley's great aunt Liz (Debbi Morgan) who was not permitted by her father Tom Harvey (Georg Stanford Brown) to marry a young black man because he was too light (Brian Mitchell) or the story of Haley himself in conflict with his young wife (Deborah Allen).

Yet the sequel captured aspects of black America's past previously left unexplored on television. Black soldiers of the First World War were seen fighting in Europe, aware that their basic rights and freedom were denied them back home. Young black entrepreneurs struggled for a foothold within an economic system that was almost closed to them because of prevailing racial attitudes and codes.

Here black characters were partly used as social symbols, but they emerged mainly as rather heroic but ordinary people. On the one hand, they wrestled with their own fears or misunderstandings; on the other, they were forced to contend with the everyday forms of discrimination and bigotry that can eat away the spirit and gnaw the soul. Told now that they were free, blacks struggled for equality. The African Kunta Kinte's family has become American now although a strong sense of their cultural heritage informs all their lives.

As it moved through four generations, the sequel also tapped the black audience's nostalgia. The entire series was something of a great archetypal fantasy that captured the stories of family heartache or conflict and the dreams and anecdotes that one generation of black Americans had passed on to its children and grandchildren.

Some might complain that it is not a subtle piece of work. And others might have misgivings because the sequel often employs the tricks and trends that television executives know will succeed. There is some violence here, including an overblown sequence in which an escaped black convict is burned alive by a mob; originally, the character was to have been lynched but producer David Wolper felt lynchings had been overdone.

Yet, because this kind of family story and these middle-class characters have rarely been examined from a black point of view, the drama still has an urgency and poignancy unlike that of most television productions. The narrative of "Roots: The Next Generations" remains compelling.

Most of the performances were top of the line. Curiously, many big-name white stars such as Henry Fonda, Olivia de Havilland, and Marlon Brando played cameo roles and sometimes proved distracting because of their very fame. (We think of Henry Fonda as Henry Fonda, not so much the bigoted character he plays.) That was also the case with a well-known black actor like James Earl Jones (who overacts and is unconvincing). But newer actors like Georg Stanford Brown, Dorian Harewood (as Alex Haley's father), Lynne Moody, Stan Shaw, and Bever-Leigh Banfield brought a freshness and weight to their characters. Sometimes a performer like Irene Cara seemed out of her league, too cute and doll-like. Yet that cute attractiveness was used to advantage, so that when this fragile girl/woman suddenly died, the audience was moved and saddened. Other times when a seasoned pro like Beah Richards showed up—in a sequence in which she spoke to the young Alex Haley of his ancestors and great heritage—her power and conviction lifted the drama completely out of TV land. Here was a rich, varied, moving scene, possibly the most memorable in this series.

"Scott Joplin: King of Ragtime" (1977)

NBC. *D.* Jeremy Paul Kagan. *S.* Christopher Knopf. Cast includes: Art Carney; Margaret Avery; Clifton Davis; Taj Mahal; the legendary Eubie Blake; Godfrey Cambridge; and DeWayne Jessie.

After his music had been successfully adapted by Marvin Hamlisch for the hit film *The Sting,* Scott Joplin, the great turn-of-the-century ragtime composer, was discovered by a whole new audience in the 1970s. Briefly, ragtime—and its era—seemed to be coming into vogue all over again. Joplin's opera *Treemonisha* was performed in New York. And E. L. Doctorow's novel *Ragtime* made the bestseller list in 1975. Thus it was assumed Joplin himself was *commercial* enough to have a television movie based on his life.

That life had been stormy and fiery. Having endured years of struggle and torment, Joplin had died of syphilis in 1917. He had been one of those brilliant, self-destructive monsters that we love to watch from afar but who upclose scare us out of our wits. He was, of course, also a victim of his time, an innovative black musician determined to do things his way yet constantly battling with those who set limits on any kind of black artist.

Unfortunately, this television movie is a tepid piece of filmmaking, slow and misty without enough concrete dramatic episodes that would get us close to the man and his period. One of its greatest failures is that it never captures the flavor of the saloons and rough whorehouses where Joplin served his apprenticeship and eventually began the mastery of his craft. Far too *polite* and *sedate* a production, there's almost no energy here. Cast as Joplin, matinee idol Billy Dee Williams gives a studied, methodical performance in tune with the direction of this television movie. But he's fundamentally all wrong for the role; although he seems a trifle dressed down here almost as if the director felt Williams's looks had to be kept under "control" if the film was to have any credibility, he's still a bit too sleek and handsome and also somewhat too charming for this kind of tragic hero.

"Sister, Sister" (1982)

NBC. *D.* John Berry. *S.* Maya Angelou. *P.* Maya Angelou and John Berry. Cast includes: Lamont Johnson; Christoff St. John (as Cash's son, Danny); Alvin Childress; Albert Popwell; and Gloria Edwards.

Completed in 1979 under the aegis of NBC president Fred Silverman, this Maya-Angelou-scripted TV movie was not aired until three years later, after Silverman had been replaced by Grant Tinker. Stories sprang up that "Sister, Sister" had not been aired earlier because the network had thought it awful, that NBC also feared a black dramatic film would not be able to pull in viewers, and that Tinker had finally broadcast it simply to get rid of the backlog of TV movies (including Melvin Van Peebles's "Sophisticated Gents") that had been sitting on the shelves since Silverman's departure. No doubt there is some truth to all the stories. But thank heaven this program was aired, because it remains a true rarity for American TV: a look at the lives of black women, three sisters, struggling with one another and themselves.

In a North Carolina setting, three sisters are reunited after the death of their father, a demanding and difficult old cuss whom none of the them seems to have really liked. Diahann Carroll, the eldest sister, is an uptight, almost unbearably prissy middle-class spinster who had remained home for years to care for the father after her mother had died mysteriously in a church fire. Irene Cara plays the youngest sister, a teenager reared by Carroll and now in the throes of first love—and emerging adulthood. She wants to be—of all things—a professional ice skater! The middle "wild" sister, who had run away from North Carolina years ago to pursue a life of freedom and abandon in Chicago, is played by Rosalind Cash. She returns to her small town with her young son—and enough rage and hostility about the past for at least one ten-hour miniseries of her own. Also on hand are Dick Anthony Williams as a married shady minister who's been having an affair with Carroll (and who soon slips Cash into his bed), Robert Hooks as Cash's ex-husband, and Paul Winfield as Cash's old flame.

Maya Angelou's script is written with true commitment but it hasn't been worked out. (Angelou here writes more like an observant novelist than a scriptwriter.) It flies off in at least 108 different directions. The plot climaxes and revelations all come far too early in the program, and there are far too many of them. There are also too many characters and incidents. Some of it is ludicrous: for example, the mother's death in the church fire—she just sat there in that church and let herself be burned to death rather than leave and return home to a dull life with a half-crazed husband—might have worked in a Toni Morrison novel but it's almost laughable here. In just about every other scene the characters are letting somebody have it! There is one recrimination after another, one guilt trip after another. Angelou makes the whole enterprise an emotional dynamo: fast moving with peak after peak and tiny valley after tiny valley, sometimes getting completely out of hand *yet* impossible to turn away from because of the sheer unabashed energy and the exuberant style.

All the performers latch onto their roles with a vigor and enthusiasm that's amusingly scary. They all seem to be suffering from a lack of restraint, from proper artistic distancing between themselves and the roles they play. But their enjoyment of the material produces a fervor that keeps this program spinning and turning. And we come to enjoy the great confrontations and some of the silliness because the performers are so committed and understand their black characters so well that they fill in the gaps of the script. They create people many of us in the black community have seen, either at a distance or much too close.

At the *final* climax, there is a knock-down-drag-out fight between

Carroll and Cash that has a comic subtext. Throughout Carroll, who for one of the rare times in her career uses her glacial cool and aloofness as a statement about her character rather than as a form of protection for herself as a performer, has been so bloody proper and middle-class phony that we want to see somebody somewhere knock some sense into her. Rosalind Cash, an actress ready to break loose and get *cullid* on us and not afraid to reveal something that audiences might find unattractive about her or her character, comes on so strong that she seems not only to be straightening out Carroll's character but to be telling Carroll, the actress as well, that it's about time she dropped her poses and became real in a piece of dramatic work. The casting here works splendidly.

This is one of Cash's best roles. The way she moves, the "loose" manner in which she speaks, the manner also in which she eyes and sizes up her men, the total abandon she uses to upset the church folks of her town are all done in high diva, bravura fashion. She brings out the trashiness and the warmth of her character. And she's so sexy that she keeps a pulsating sexual current running throughout the production. She's at the center of this storm, infusing it with her talent and her great sense of her character's mad desire to be truly liberated.

Part soap opera perhaps and often enough uneven and unsatisfying, "Sister, Sister" is still—particularly for the black audience—far more involving than most TV movies. It's fascinating.

"Sophisticated Gents" (1981)

NBC. *D.* Harry Falk. *P.* Fran Sears. *Ex. P.* Daniel Wilson. Cast includes: Beah Richards; Ja'net DuBois; Joanna Miles; Marlene Warfield; Harry Guardino; Alfre Woodard; Robert Earl Jones; Stymie Beard; Sonny Jim Gaines; Charles Blackwell; and Mario Van Peebles.

Completed in 1979, this three-part, four-hour miniseries about the reunion of nine members of a black athletic/social club sat on NBC's shelf for two years before being aired. Having been initiated not long after the success of "Roots" (when television executives still had some interest in black dramas), "Sophisticated Gents"'s unusual rhythms, characterizations, language, and its basic point of view no doubt unsettled the network officials who lost confidence in the production. (The same was true for Maya Angelou's "Sister, Sister.") Once the drama aired, though, *New York Times* critic John J. O'Connor called it "one of the more fascinating television movies of the year." It's hard not to agree with him.

This is material almost never examined on television and certainly not from an insider's perspective. Based on black writer John A. Williams's novel *The Junior Bachelor Society*, the story concerns a group of black men who had come together as adolescents under the wise guidance of a coach. He'd spotted the talent within the boys, and, seeing themselves through his eyes, they became star athletes, realizing their individual potential for the first time in their young lives. Through the years their friendships and loyalty continued. Now as the coach approaches his seventieth birthday, the former athletes—now middle-aged men burdened with demanding jobs, unhappy marriages, or unresolved personal tensions—meet again to honor the man who first believed in them.

The ambitions and inner conflicts of black males in transition: Melvin Van Peebles's gaudily enjoyable "The Sophisticated Gents" with (front row, l. to r.) Roosevelt Grier, Paul Winfield, Melvin Van Peebles, (back row, l. to r.) Ron O'Neal, Thalmus Rasulala, Bernie Casey, Dick Anthony Williams, Raymond St. Jacques, and Robert Hooks.

The men themselves are almost like a bomber crew out of a Hollywood war movie of the 1940s. Each represents some different aspect of the black community; all have worked hard to enter the sanctified ranks of the black bourgeoisie. Chops (Robert Hooks) is an editor of a black magazine; Ralph (Dick Anthony Williams), a playwright; Clarie (Ron O'Neal), a college professor; Dart (Raymond St. Jacques), a concert singer who masks his homosexuality behind a marriage to a white woman; Snake (Thalmus Rasulala), a successful government employee who now has not only a chauffeured limousine at his disposal but also a white wife, seemingly part of the deal, too. Then there is the sensitive president of the group, Bobby (Paul Winfield) and the relaxed Cudjo (Rosey Grier) and Shurley (Bernie Casey).

Into this stolidly respectable group is injected Melvin Van Peebles as Moon, a pimp wanted for murder. (For some reason, Van Peebles, who also wrote the script, views Moon as a distinctive heroic presence. We're to think he's held true to something within himself. But all we really think—and *enjoy*—is the fact that here's black America's beloved Melvin, again playing the fantasy figure that pleases him most, the pimp, a man of the streets who refuses to be respectable.) Finally, there is a corrupt black policeman (played with proper menace by Albert Hall), who has always been resentful of not having been a part of The Sophisticated Gents.

The entire drama is like an adolescent reverie. Van Peebles's script is often windy, rambling, indulgent, overdone. Yet this is an almost rapturously awkward piece of work. The language, which with its use of 'nigga' and 'yessuh massa,' is often playfully *street*, striking a cord with black audiences who've never heard this kind of familiar talk on television. The subject matter itself—of black men struggling to understand the social structure in which they are trapped as well as their relationships with their wives and with one another, their ambitions and dreams, their disappointments and unfulfillment—remains new to television's view of black America.

In some respects, this is a sophisticated race movie: fiercely determined to tell a story to a *black* audience, the drama operates at its own speed, unconcerned with the fact that whites might not understand what's going on or might be scared by it. What makes it all work, of course, are the actors, who are comfortable with their dialogue and their attitudes and are invigorated by the jazzy, sexy style of the script. Like Warhol stars, they seem anxious to announce themselves. Yet the script's structure is tight enough to keep them within the bounds of the story. Although this is really a male drama, the women—Denise Nicholas, Janet MacLachlan, Bibi Besch, and especially that long underrated marvel, Rosalind Cash—*carry on*, sometimes at fever pitch, refusing to back off even if they might appear unattractive or mildly absurd. *To hell with what you may think*, the actresses seem to be saying, *this is what I want you to know.* These are not the formula performances of formula TV. Even when overdrawn, the performers never fail to excite.

While it does not have the high larger-than-life style of "Roots" or the sturdy dignity of "Backstairs at the White House" or stately power of "The Autobiography of Miss Jane Pittman," along with these dramas and that other lopsidedly delirious tale, Maya Angelou's "Sister, Sister," "Sophisticated Gents" remains among television's most absorbing black productions.

"The Toughest Man in the World" (1984)

CBS. *D.* Dick Lowry.

After Mr. T.'s unexpected success (with kids mostly) on "The A-Team," it was decided to cash in on his popularity with this TV movie. He plays himself really (has he ever played anything else?), this time around though he's a Chicago nightclub bouncer who also works, without pay, at a Southside youth center that is in dire need of money. A note of reality pops up here: because of government funding cutbacks, the center may close. T. does all he can to rectify the situation, even going to City Hall, where he's given such a runaround that, with no other recourse, he simply breaks down the door of the deputy mayor. "I've been social, now I'm going to get some service," he announces. He's almost thrown into jail until a pretty city employee (Lynne Moody) comes to the rescue. Eventually, T. enters a Toughest Man in the World contest to win some money for the center. Thus we're treated to tedious segments of T. training, Rocky-style, and during the event T.

undergoes the endurance tests that confront any champ. Naturally, he's victorious. There is also a subplot: T. becomes a father figure to a troubled white youth (John Navin) whose mother is a prostitute.

A very ordinary TV movie in which Mr. T. parades his cartoonish brawn and also his I'se-really-a-good-guy-Huck-honey smile. The fact that he's in a white arena, defending mostly white kids, naturally neutralizes—for the large white audience—any threat he might have once had. In *The New York Times*, critic John J. O'Connor commented on the violent aspect of Mr. T.'s personality in this TV film, pointing out that the might-makes-right message "is devastatingly clear, but, his defenders claim, the sheer exaggeration underlines the fantasy aspects of the situation. No one, presumably is likely to take Mr. T. seriously. Let's hope not." Almost as distressing though as the violence inherent in the T. image is the asexuality. T. supposedly has a lady friend here—Lynne Moody—but they are never shown in a big romantic sequence. *She* kisses him at one point, a peck really. But that's it. Do the moviemakers feel that in order to appeal to kids, T., like Western heroes of the past, must remain chaste? Or do they fear a combination of black brawn and sex?

The buck stops here: the muscle-bound Mr. T., during his 1980s' heyday, as the mighty powerful, no-nonsense hero of "The Toughest Man in the World."

"Wilma" (1977)

NBC. D. Bud Greenspan. Cast includes: Joe Seneca (as Wilma's father; a few years later, Seneca turned in top-notch performances in *The Verdict* and *Cross Roads*); Jason Bernard (as Wilma's coach); and then newcomer Denzel Washington (who later did impressive work in *A Soldier's Story*).

Far too solemn and studious a dramatization of the life of Olympic track star Wilma Rudolph. As a child, Rudolph had suffered from scarlet fever and pneumonia, which left her crippled until the age of twelve. Afterward, against all odds, she trained strenuously and made it to the 1956 Olympics, where she won a bronze medal. Then she went into training all over again for the 1960s Olympics in Rome. Her dreams almost looked shattered though when she became pregnant and, against her family's objections, refused to marry the father of her child. After giving birth, Rudolph went back into training and triumphed in Rome where she won four gold medals. The Rudolph life is dramatic, and she herself a complex woman, hardly your run-of-the-mill, sweet-as-apple-pie kind of Olympic champ. Here we're given the details—the facts of her struggles—but it's all too conventional and folksy. Television seems incapable of dealing with a true individualist, a woman living by her own code; instead it wants to make her like everyone else, a humdrum ordinary heroine. Cast in the title role, Shirley Jo Finney has a good look but not the right power or drive. As Wilma's adoring mother, Cicely Tyson seems almost indifferent to her material; had she been younger though, she might have made a splendid Wilma.

"A Woman Called Moses" (1978)

NBC. *D.* Paul Wendkos. *S.* Lonne Elder III (who also wrote the screenplay for *Sounder*). *Ex. P.* Cicely Tyson. Cast includes: Robert Hooks; Will Geer; James Wainwright; Hari Rhodes; and Jason Bernard.

This two-part, four-hour drama focuses on the life of Harriet Ross Tubman, the Maryland-born slave who in the period just prior to the Civil War led more than 300 slaves to freedom in the North through her Underground Railroad. To those she helped get to the Promised Land, she became known as "Moses."

This drama opens during Harriet's early years as a slave. She sees her sister sold to another plantation. She herself is struck on the head by an overseer. For the duration of her life, she will suffer from that blow, having repeated fainting spells. At another point, an angry landowner has her harness herself to a mule and pull a wagon while a group of whites stand by amused. Having endured such humiliations, Harriet slowly saves $200 to buy her freedom. That $200, however, is stolen from her by her mulatto husband. She has to begin all over again. But, of course, she does. Once she's fled to the North, she starts her rescue missions. And we see her grow in stature.

Newsweek called this "one of the most moving evocations of the black experience ever to grace the small screen." And it praised Cicely Tyson's performance as Tubman: "It would be hard to imagine a life better tailored to Cicely Tyson's own remarkable talents. . . . Tyson is that rarest of video wonders—a great actress tapping a great part." Other reviewers, though, felt differently. *Variety* wrote that Tyson "has pretty much been repeating herself since *Sounder* . . . sometimes with a by-the-numbers indifference." The paper also criticized this production's "lack of direction." Actually, one is tempted to agree with both reviewers.

Parts of "A Woman Called Moses" are indeed stirring. Perhaps that's because we're seeing a heroic black woman (an actual historical figure) presented on television. Consequently, we're a bit grateful for whatever we can get. And Tyson herself, although she appears too caught up in the "importance" of her role, brings some nice shading to the part and some grit and force.

What's hard to take, however, is Dick Anthony Williams's misinterpretation of Tubman's husband, who is depicted too much like a contemporary hustler (we cannot abide the way the script treats this no-count black man). Some of the plot mechanics are downright feeble. On the very day we see Harriet set out to buy her freedom with the $200, she's stopped by the landowner and made (for no clearly discernible reason) to harness herself to that mule. The way it's done is pure Hollywood. We feel we're to respond not to the daily "trivial" humiliations slaves endured but to a big dramatic event wherein the character's heroism is spelled out for us in bold letters and brush strokes much too broad. The scene looks like a set-up for an Emmy nomination for Tyson.

The series also ends too soon—with Tubman in the middle part of her life. Nothing is said about the later years when she became a Union reconnaisance agent, who mobilized 300 black troops and liberated hundreds of slaves. When she staged raids on riverside plantations, was she not the first woman in U.S. history to lead a military maneuver? After the war, Tubman, who lived into her 90s, became a suffragette and also knew many of the nation's great political leaders.

"A Woman Called Moses" holds up only as uneven melodrama. As should be expected though, its events are open to questions and should lead us all back to the history books.

Profiles

Debbie Allen

B. c. 1950. Actress/Dancer/Choreographer.

Two of the best-known sisters working in television in the mid-1980s were Debbie Allen and Phylicia (Ayers-Allen) Rashad. At first, Debbie was the more famous, as a dancer/singer in such Broadway musicals as *Purlie* (1972), *Raisin* (1973), *Ain't Misbehavin'* (1979), and the 1980 revival of *West Side Story*.

It took Allen longer to establish herself in films and television. In 1977, she won excellent notices for the 13-week NBC series "3 Girls 3," a variety show in which she and two other actresses (both white) played show business unknowns hoping to make it big. Later she landed dramatic roles in "Roots: The Next Generations" (1979, as Alex Haley's restless young wife) and *Ragtime* (1981). Oddly in the latter, she seemed tenuous and undefined on the large screen, lacking the self-assurance and strong sense of character/personality that distinguished her as a musical star. But her television/film career snapped into motion with the movie *Fame* and the television series based on it. As the dance teacher Lydia, she had a harsh, abrasive tone that meshed well with the

Dancer/choreographer Debbie Allen in a dramatic role in Jo Jo Dancer, Your Life Is Calling *with Richard Pryor.*

353

series' tough urban point of view. Eventually, she directed, choreographed, and produced episodes of the series, twice winning Emmys for her choreography.

Later Allen appeared as Richard Pryor's embittered wife in *Jo Jo Dancer, Your Life Is Calling* (1986). Her TV credits include "Good Times" (1976). She also appeared in the film *The Fish That Saved Pittsburgh* (1979).

John Amos

B. 1939. Actor.

Skilled and often underrated, this New Jersey-born actor came to national prominence in 1974 as the father James Evans on the TV series "Good Times." Sometimes stern, sometimes unyielding, but always sensitive and understanding, Amos's character was considered by many to be the strongest black male figure appearing on weekly TV during the 1970s. But because of differences with the producers over the delineation of his character and the general direction of the series, Amos left "Good Times" in 1976. Later Amos gave one of his best performances as the older Kunta Kinte in the miniseries "Roots."

Other TV credits include: "The Mary Tyler Moore Show" (1970–1973, he played Gordy Howard, the weatherman); "The Bill Cosby Show" (1970); "Love, American Style" (1972); "The New Dick Van Dyke Show" (1972); "Sanford and Son" (1973); "Maude" (1973–1974); "Police Story" (1976); "Future Cop" (a 1977 series in which he co-starred); "Love Boat" (1983); "The A-Team" (1984); "Trapper John, M.D." (1984); "Hunter" (1984, 1985); "Murder She Wrote" (1987); and "You Are the Jury" (1987).

His film appearances include: *Sweet Sweetback's Baadasssss Song* (1971, a very brief appearance); *Let's Do It Again* (1975); *American Flyers* (1985).

Eddie "Rochester" Anderson

B. 1906; D. 1977. Actor.

The son of two vaudevillians (his father, Big Ed, was a minstrel; his mother, Ella Mae, a circus tightrope walker), Eddie Anderson started performing at age fourteen in all-colored revues, later teamed with his older brother Cornelius in a song-and-dance act that toured for years, and finally by the 1930s settled in Los Angeles. There Anderson began movie work. In such films as *What Price Hollywood* (1932) and *Show Boat* (1936), he had bits. But as Noah in the 1936 *Green Pastures*, he had an important character part which he played with a comic straight-forwardness that made audiences take notice. The next year, he signed for an appearance as a pullman car porter on Jack Benny's radio show. So great was the audience response that Anderson was brought back to the series, then signed as a regular, and later made movies with Benny and also appeared on his television series in the 50s, becoming the most famous of Jack Benny's ensemble players. For years he was known by the name of the valet he played on the Benny show: Rochester.

Working with Benny in such movies as *Man About Town* (1939), *Buck Benny Rides Again* (1940), and *Love Thy Neighbor* (1940), Anderson was always the clever, resourceful, witty, manipulative servant, out to do more for himself than the boss. Because of his association and friendship with Benny, Anderson had roles tailor made for him. Rarely was he forced to go through some of the excruciatingly demeaning types of

Eddie "Rochester" Anderson: witty, clever, confident, resourceful, and skillfully manipulative in his comedies with Jack Benny.

Between scenes: Eddie "Rochester" Anderson and Jack Benny (r.) on a movie set with the directors Mervyn LeRoy and Vincente Minnelli.

antics that a Stepin Fechit had to perform. (The creators of *Topper Returns*, 1941, tried turning Rochester into the typical coon who is scared of ghosts, but the miscast Anderson seemed too sensible for the part to have an adverse effect on his image.)

Unlike later black screen comic stars such as Richard Pryor and Eddie Murphy, Anderson's essential appeal was never an explosive, I'll-go-off-on-you quality; instead he had an almost serene self-control, striking audiences as a man blessed with an awareness that in time everything would work out. Often slyly sardonic, he exuded, like Hattie McDaniel, a carefree, indestructible independence. His gravelly voice reverberated with self-confidence. And Anderson's short stature added to his appeal, making him seem in such films as *Green Pastures* and *Cabin in the Sky* (1943) as the likable Universal Common Little Man, who's just trying to wade his way through life's predicaments.

Had opportunities been different, Anderson might have developed into a major comic star. As it was though, he was, for a spell, Hollywood's highest paid black performer. And he was one of the few black actors to have some semblance of a romantic life in his films. In *You Can't Take It with You* (1938), he was the boyfriend of Lillian Yarbo. And in a couple of the Benny movies, Theresa Harris played Anderson's girlfriend Josephine. He even managed to pull off a comically hot and sexy jitterbug number with Katherine Dunham in the 1942 *Star-Spangled Rhythm*.

Appearing in films through the 1940s, Anderson worked almost exclusively on television in the 1950s, turning up in two new versions, in 1957 and 1959, of "Green Pastures," repeating his role as Noah.

Among his movie credits: *Three Men on a Horse* (1936); *Melody for Two* (1937); *One Mile from Heaven* (1937); *Over the Goal* (1937); *Jezebel* (1938); *Gold Diggers in Paris* (1938); *Exposed* (1938); *Kentucky* (1939); *Birth of the Blues* (1941); *Kiss the Boys Goodbye* (1941); *Tales of Manhattan* (1942); *The Meanest Man in the World* (1943); *What's Buzzin Cousin* (1943); *Broadway Rhythm* (1944); *Brewster's Millions* (1945); *The Sailor Takes a Wife* (1946); *The Show-Off* (1947); *It's A Mad, Mad, Mad, Mad World* (1963). Buried under layers of makeup, Anderson also played Uncle Peter in *Gone with the Wind* (1939).

Anderson's TV credits include: "Bachelor Father," (1962); "Dick Powell Theatre" (1963); and "Love American Style" (1969); and, of course, "The Jack Benny Show" (1950–1964 on CBS; 1964–1965, NBC).

Margaret Avery

Actress.

After some 14 years in the movie capital, Oklahoma-born actress Margaret Avery finally landed a meaty, challenging role as Shug Avery in *The Color Purple*, for which she won an Academy Award Nomination as Best Supporting Actress of 1985. Lovely to look at in such early films as *Cool Breeze* (1972), *Hell up in Harlem* (1973), and *Which Way Is Up?* (1977), Avery cut an enticing figure. But perhaps because she lacked the rather obvious sexuality of a Pam Grier and the more "acceptable" beauty of a Vonetta McGee (Avery was a soothing shade of brown, not yellow), she never commanded important leads or much attention. She ended up doing mostly television work such as "Kojak" (1974) and "Harry O" (1974). Her list of credits, however, was never long. And no one would have guessed the kind of actress she could be. (She reminds us of another intelligent, pretty brown actress of the past, who was encumbered with thankless roles that never tapped her full potential: Theresa Harris.) Somehow—be it luck or timing or whatever—director Steven Spielberg decided to cast her as the weathered Shug. Her performance won her some time in the national spotlight. But, ironically, after all *The Color Purple* hoopla—the television and print interviews—Margaret Avery soon informed the press that again she was having problems finding work.

Among her TV credits: "Sanford and Son" (1975); "Night Stalker" (1975); "The Rookies" (1975); "Louis Armstrong Chicago Style" (1976); "Scott Joplin" (1977); "Murder She Wrote" (1986); and "Spenser: For Hire" (1986).

Her movie credits include: *Magnum Force* (1973) and *The Fish That Saved Pittsburgh* (1979).

Pearl Bailey

B. 1918. Singer, actress.

The cheery, pious Pearl Bailey of 1980s talk shows was such a far cry from the young, vibrant, Pearl Bailey of nightclubs, films, records, and television that a later generation probably has not quite understood what this star had once been all about and why she was once so fresh and exciting for audiences black and white.

Born in Newport News, Virginia, the sister of the famous tap-dancing star Bill Bailey, Pearl had started performing while still a child. Later she appeared at some of the nation's top all-black theaters: The Howard, The Apollo, and The Pearl, all of which provided her with first-hand knowledge of what it meant to touch base with a demanding all-black audience. Here Bailey no doubt perfected her extraordinary pacing, also her comic persona of the tired (and often lovelorn) black girl, who didn't seem to want to do anything but sit around and relax until some good-looking fella came along. A mistress of timing, she developed as the years went on a remarkable comic technique: she was faster with a doubletake or a funny retort than almost all her peers yet she performed in the most offhand manner, as if flicking dust from her shoulder. Shrewdly, Bailey also learned how to market her rather limited but appealing singing voice: she halfway sang her way through a song, then halfway talked her way through the rest, adding funny asides to the standard, sometimes pedestrian lyrics.

By 1946, this marvel of cantankerous wit debuted on Broadway in *St. Louis Woman.* A year later Bailey sang a number in the movie *Variety Girl* (1947), then appeared in *Isn't It Romantic* (1948). Her best movie work though came about in the 1950s in *Carmen Jones* (1954), *Porgy and Bess* (1959), and surprisingly, that stale brew of ale *That Certain Feeling* (1956). Exuding basic commonsense (mother wit's more like it), looking as if she's ever ready to have a good time, too, Bailey may have found herself stuck with chatty-Kathy quasi-Aunt Jemima parts in these films but her energy and her perpetual air—that of a woman moving to her own rhythm and not at all fazed by the shenanigans or silliness of the other characters—saved, even elevated, her work.

In *All the Fine Young Cannibals* (1960), Bailey attempted going against type, portraying a burnt-out, hard-drinking Bessie Smith-type singer hooked on helping a young white jazz musician (Robert Wagner). It's a deliriously cockeyed, highly romanticized, heavy-handed performance that remains rather amusing, even if for all the wrong reasons. And Bailey has such personal warmth that we can accept her and reject the character.

Other Bailey films were *St. Louis Blues* (1958), *The Landlord* (1970), and *Norman . . . Is That You?* (1976). Bailey's theater work includes: *Arms and the Man* (1950), *Bless You All* (1950), *House of Flowers* (1954)—and the title role in the smash all-black version of *Hello Dolly* (1967). Bailey's voice was also used for the owl, Big Mama, in the animated movie, *The Fox and the Hound* (1981).

Her TV credits include: "The Ed Sullivan Show," which broadened her audience in the 1950s, turning her into one of America's first black TV stars; "The Milton Berle Show"; "The Flip Wilson Show"; a special, "An Evening with Pearl" (1974); "Bing Crosby and His Friends" (1974); the sitcom "Silver Spoons"; the 1982 remake of *The Member of the Wedding* (in which Bailey played Berenice); and "Cindy Eller: A Modern Fairy Tale" (1985). Bailey also hosted her own variety series "The Pearl Bailey Show" (1971).

Bailey also had a series of successful record albums: *Tired, For Adult Listening,* and *Takes Two to Tango.* She was also the author of several books, including the autobiographical volumes, *The Raw Pearl* (1968) and *Talking to Myself* (1971).

Matt "Stymie" Beard, Jr.

B. 1925; D. 1981. Actor.

In 1930 at the age of five, Matt Beard, Jr., appeared in the first of his 36 *Our Gang* comedies, playing Stymie, the wide-eyed kid who often wore a derby and sometimes spoke as if his mouth were full of food. Decades later when the old "Our Gang/Little Rascals" series turned up on television in the afterschool hours, some black parents eyed Stymie and his cohorts suspiciously. What kind of role models were these black kids who rolled their eyes and spoke in an *I is* or *you was* dialect? Black schoolchildren, though, gravitated to the series, often selecting Stymie as a favorite, in large part because he seemed smarter and more resourceful than poor frazzled Buckwheat and far more mature and sturdier than the sweetly dazed and placid Farina. Blessed with spunk, Stymie seemed in charge of himself. He stayed in the series for five years, then, having outgrown his role, he left at age ten.

During adolescence, Stymie Beard continued working, playing bits in such features as *Captain Blood* (1935), *Kid Millions* (1934), *Rainbow on the River* (1936), *Jezebel* (1938), *Beloved Brat* (1938), *Way Down South* (1939), *The Return of Frank James* (1940), and (as the bratty snob) in the all-black independent production *Broken Strings* (1940).

Later, times were difficult for Beard, who was arrested and imprisoned for six and a half years for heroin possession. In the 1970s, he returned to his career, appearing on television in "Hawkins" (1973), "Good Times" (1976), "The First Woman President," "Sanford and Son," (1973), "Starsky and Hutch" (1976), "Backstairs at the White House" (1979), "Palmerstown, USA" (1980), and "Sophisticated Gents" (1981). At age 56, Matthew "Stymie" Beard died after suffering a stroke in Los Angeles.

Added note: Stymie's brother Bobbie "Cotton" Beard also appeared in the "Our Gang" series in a non-speaking role. Briefly, Stymie's sister Carlena Beard also was in *Our Gang*.

Louise Beavers

B. 1902; D. 1962. Actress.

During the 1930s and 1940s, Louise Beavers was one of Hollywood's most employed black actresses. In a career that eventually spanned over three decades, Beavers—big-boned, heavyset, brown-skinned—personified the ever-enduring, resourceful mammy-goddess. While Hattie McDaniel's outspoken and irascible characters could raise the rooftops with their tempers, Beavers's cheerful, naive maids and companions were always there to soothe, never to rock the boat. Perhaps it is the unyielding gentleness and submissiveness of her heroines that make them seem less complex and invigorating than the characters of McDaniel or Ethel Waters (who also never thought twice about flying off the handle). Yet today although contemporary audiences may feel patronizing towards the malleable Beavers characters, she is still, when her work has a chance to be seen and evaluated, almost consistently liked. There remains something starkly genuine about her sweetness that stands in marked contrast to the fake, candy-coated attitudes of some of the TV mammy-types of the 1970s and 1980s.

Born in Cleveland and raised in Los Angeles, Louise Beavers's slow showbiz rise began in such movies as the 1927 *Uncle Tom's Cabin*, *Coquette* (1929), and *Nix on Dames* (1929). By the early 1930s, she earned attention with bits in *Ladies of the Big House* (1932), *Bombshell* (1933, as Jean Harlow's trusty maid), *She Done Him Wrong* (1933, as Mae West's faithful maid), and *What Price Hollywood* (1932, in which director George Cukor had her unceremoniously dumped into a swimming pool in a sequence that once broke up audiences but that now makes us wince). In so many of her early films, Beavers was used simply as a comic fixture by directors without much awareness of who she was or what she could do.

Her breakthrough film was the 1934 *Imitation of Life*, in which as the pancake lady, Aunt Delilah, she was a perfect Depression-era fantasy: the perpetually sturdy, all-nurturing, hard-working, God-fearing mammy, ready for self-sacrifice and self-denial. Beavers played her role with a conviction and distilled sweetness that won her praise from both the white *and* black press. Her performance demanded that audiences take her character seriously. Today it is not hard to understand why some critics thought Beavers should win an Oscar nomination. (She did not.)

Unfortunately, for Beavers few roles of significance followed. One day she had been touted as an Oscar contender; the next she was back to giggles and gingham. *Rainbow on the River* (1936) did provide her with another role with some meat to it. And in *Bullets or Ballots* (1936), as a Harlem numbers rackets queen, she had a chance to dress up and delight in her finery while exhibiting a sweet rush of energy. Then in *Made for Each Other* (1939), she took a few scenes and made them add up to a lovely portrait. Here as housekeeper Lily, Beavers gives her distressed white employer (Carole Lombard) some valuable lessons on life, informing her that enduring hardships is like eating watermelon. You just have to learn to spit out the seeds and enjoy the melon. No matter that the dialogue was corny, Beavers delivered her lines with a tender commitment, playing well opposite Lombard, leading audiences to believe that, well, perhaps she *had* found a secret for getting through life. Even now, it's easy to see why Depression audiences fell for her dreamy hokum.

By the early 1940s, Beavers's freshness seemed to be evaporating. In a movie like *Belle Starr* (1941), she sometimes looked as if she could not bear to utter another set of fake lines. Yet trouper that she was, she managed to get through the film with her warmth intact. By 1948, she came back to the forefront of moviegoers' consciousness in *Mr. Blandings Builds His Dream House*. Here advertising executive Cary Grant cannot come up with a slogan for an important ham product called Wham—not until, well, one morning when, while serving breakfast, maid Beavers says to one of Grant's children (who has just asked for some ham), "Not *ham*! WHAM! If you ain't eating WHAM, you ain't eating *ham*!" "Darling," Grant cries out to wife Myrna Loy, "give Gussie a ten-dollar raise."

In the early 1950s, Beavers appeared as America's favorite friendly domestic, Beulah, on the TV series of the same name. Although she continued working (albeit sporadically) through the 1950s and into the early 1960s, she often looked weighed down in such films as *All the Fine Young Cannibals* (1960) and *Facts of Life* (1961), tired no doubt from the years of wasted roles and missed opportunities. Occasionally, when she lucked up with something new or special, such as her role as Jackie Robinson's mother in *The Jackie Robinson Story* (1950), she was aglow and so warmly giving that the heart goes out to her. Here her self-sacrifice was put into another context, not the black woman coming to the aid and service of some white employer but a sensitive mother concerned about her son.

Beavers's movie credits include: *Up for Murder* (1931); *Annabelle's Affairs* (1931); *Girls About Town* (1931); *Good Sport* (1931); *The Expert* (1932); *It's Tough To Be Famous* (1932); *Young America* (1932); *Night World* (1932); *Street of Women* (1932); *Unashamed* (1932); *Her Bodyguard* (1933); *West of the Pecos* (1934); *Wives Never Know* (1936); *Make Way for Tomorrow* (1937); *Scandal Street* (1938); *Brother Rat* (1938); *Women Without Names* (1940); *Virginia* (1941); *Shadow of the Thin Man* (1941); *Reap the Wild Wind* (1942);

Holiday Inn (1942); *The Big Street* (1942, as Lucille Ball's faithful servant); *Du Barry Was a Lady* (1943, again with Lucille Ball); *All by Myself* (1943); *Barbary Coast Gent* (1944); *Teenage Rebel* (1956); and *The Goddess* (1958).

Her TV credits include: "Star Stage" (1956); "Playhouse 90" (1957); and "The World of Disney" (1959).

Harry Belafonte

B. 1927. Actor, singer.

In few other actors' careers have the ties between sex and racism been more apparent than in that of Harry Belafonte. In the 1950s, his romantic good looks made him an ideal candidate for Hollywood's first black romantic leading man. Yet he never seemed at ease with romantic roles; nor did the film industry seem at ease in casting him in such. In retrospect Belafonte's debut film *Bright Road* (1953) marks his most sexual performance. Although he doesn't sweep leading lady Dorothy Dandridge up into his arms, his eyes register heat and romantic yearning. A year later in *Carmen Jones* (1954) though, Belafonte, as a wholesome hunk whose sexuality has been neutralized, was no match for the high-strung Dandridge. Later features *Island in the Sun* (1957) and *The World, the Flesh, and the Devil* (1959) titillated audiences into thinking they were about to see some sexy interracial fireworks between Belafonte and his respective white leading ladies Joan Fontaine and Inger Stevens. But the scripts kept everything clean and boringly above board. Both features lacked passion, be it sexual or political. And Belafonte was left stranded as a sexually attractive black man who was simply not permitted to be sexually aggressive.

Yet sex and romance were usually on the minds of women when they saw him. In concert when he performed his Caribbean ballads, Belafonte, with his tight pants, his shirts opened to the navel, and his smoky voice, sent females into a panting tizzy. In a 1968 TV special his arm casually brushed against that of white British pop star Petula Clark, with whom he was performing a duet, and network officials fell into a dither. So attractive a man was Belafonte that the television executives felt white audiences would have no choice but to think that Clark was attracted to him and that, in turn, the network was promoting an interracial relationship! Ludicrous? Yes. But this was part of the racial dynamics of another era.

Belafonte himself seemed anxious to escape his non-sexual pretty boy roles and to move into character parts, which he did early as the troubled hero in *Odds Against Tomorrow* (1959). Having turned down the lead in *Porgy and Bess*, Belafonte, in the 1960s, seemed to expend most of his energies on the civil rights movement, working closely with Dr. Martin Luther King, Jr. During this period, he made no films. More and more, too, he no doubt realized the importance of controlling a film from behind the scenes as well as in front of the camera. Once he returned to films in the 1970s, he did so as the star and producer of *Angel Levine* (1970) and as co-producer and co-star of *Buck and the Preacher* (1972). In the latter, for one of the rare times in his career, he seemed resplendently confident. His rousing portrayal of a feisty, cantankerous preacher enabled him to reach deep inside himself and to unleash a previous unexplored talent for comic eccentricity. He turned in his most likable screen creation if not his best.

One of Hollywood's few black leading men in the 1950s, Harry Belafonte with Olga James in Carmen Jones.

Two years later in *Uptown Saturday Night* (1974), Belafonte played another eccentric, giving a spirited parody of Marlon Brando's *Godfather* hero. In the 1980s, he appeared as a tough coach in the TV movie "Grambling's White Tiger" (1981), was also the executive producer of the film *Beat Street* (1984), and one of the prime movers of the USA For Africa organization, which sought to raise money for food and supplies for Ethiopia's starving masses. No doubt it is important to remember that Belafonte had come of age during the 1940s, the period of transition of black entertainment images. Influenced by Paul Robeson, he believed strongly in social commitment in the arts, which led him to be quite selective about his roles. Consequently, film audiences never saw him as much as they might have wanted. And he himself seemed most relaxed and charismatic when he didn't have to worry about the industry's or the white audience's concerns about his sexuality, when he instead could lose/discover himself in the wild idiosyncrasies of a character.

Belafonte's TV credits include: appearances on such shows of the 1950s as "What's My Line?" and "The Ed Sullivan Show"; also "Winner By Decision" (1955 on G.E. Theatre); "Three for Tonight" (1955); "Tonight with Belafonte" (1959); "The Strollin' Twenties" (1966); "Harry and Lena" (1970); "America Salutes the Queen" (1977); and "Trapper John M.D." (1982). He also produced and appeared in the 1967 ABC comedy special "A Time for Laughter: A Look at Negro Humor," which starred a host of personalities: Jackie "Moms" Mabley, Pigmeat Markham, George Kirby, Redd Foxx, Diana Sands, Richard Pryor, Godfrey Cambridge, Diahann Carroll, and Sidney Poitier.

Willie Best

B. 1915; D. 1962. Actor.

Lanky, string-bean-thin Willie Best came to American films in the early 1930s. Following in the footsteps of his contemporary, Stepin Fetchit, Best also played the coon stereotype. At first in such films as *Up Pops the Devil* (1931), *West of the Pecos* (1934), *Kentucky Kernals* (1935), and *Murder on a Honeymoon* (1935), he was billed as "Sleep 'n' Eat," the idea being, of course, that a black man was content as long as he had a place to sleep and enough to eat. By 1934 with *Little Miss Marker*, he was using his real name.

Best's dimwitted, head-scratching, tongue-tied, perpetually half-awake, half-asleep characters have often been criticized—and rightly so. Frequently, they are an embarrassment. Yet compared with the work of later black performers in the sitcoms of the 1970s, Best sometimes now seems a marvel, and one has to respect the fact that he often played his parts well and with a certain degree of lopsided commitment. Working in features for some twenty years, his coon figures almost completely disappeared from films after the Second World War. Best did keep working into the 1950s and even turned up on two television series: as Willie, the handyman, on "The Stu Ervin Show" (1950–1955) (called "The Trouble with Father," in syndication) and as Charlie, the elevator man, on "My Little Margie" (1952–1955).

Among his many films: *The Arizonian* (1935); *Make Way for a Lady* (1936); *Thank You Jeeves* (1936); *Blondie* (1938); *Vivacious Lady* (1938); *Youth*

Takes a Fling (1938); *Nancy Drew* (1939); *The Smiling Ghost* (1941); *Whispering Ghosts* (1942); *A-Haunting We Will Go* (1942); *The Hidden Hand* (1942); *Juke Girl* (1942); *The Body Disappears* (1942); *Busses Roar* (1942); *The Bride Wore Boots* (1946); *Suddenly It's Spring* (1947); and *Red Stallion* (1947).

Among his most famous films are *Cabin in the Sky* (1943, in which he played one of the devil's henchmen; he's the evil aide who spends most of his time sleeping on the couch), *The Littlest Rebel* (1935, a Shirley Temple feature in which Best's lazybone-good-for-nothin' coon antics are contrasted with the sobriety of the noble tom figure played by Bill "Bojangles" Robinson; of the two, Best is far funnier and more believable), and *Ghost Breakers* (the 1940 Bob Hope hit in which Best plays the classic black servant petrified by the very idea of ghosts; Best just about walks away with much of the picture).

In his famous poem "Poem for Willie Best," poet/playwright Leroi Jones touches on Mississippi-born Best's tragic Hollywood career.

Jim Brown

B. 1935. Actor.

When football player Jim Brown set off in pursuit of movie stardom, he was considered something of a joke, not thought to be much of an actor (true, he wasn't) nor much of a personality either (true again). But Jim Brown had the last laugh on all his critics, for a while anyway. In the late 1960s/1970s, he emerged as one of Hollywood's busiest actors, a box-office star with a very definite following.

Much of Brown's popularity grew out of his legendary status as a sports star. As a running back for the Cleveland Browns, Brown had been an extraordinary athlete, a man with seemingly superhuman physical skills and a new kind of figure on the cultural landscape, too. In 1971, writer (later film director) James Toback, convinced that Brown's presence (and the reactions to it) was a comment on America's myths/attitudes about sex and race, wrote a book about Brown titled *Jim* in which he stated:

> It was Jim Brown who, during the decade from 1957 to 1965, had done more than any other man to originate what became a national obsession with the game [football]. He was a consistent and spectacular warrior, the embodiment of his team, a crystallization of physical potency. More, he introduced a new dimension to the sport, as its first black hero.
> . . . He had invaded the American imagination, black and white. . . . When he shifted gears and became, in less than a year, a movie star, the potential of his influence erased limitations. If there were a black boy anywhere in America whose vision of manhood excluded both sports and entertainment, he was a freak, a mutation of consciousness. Apart from serving as channels of style for stored rage, such endeavors provided the clean entrance into the American dream of independence, power, wealth, fame, the promise almost exclusively of whites before the sixties. What that dream became in the life of Jim Brown would hold large interest for young blacks.

Inflated as Toback's Nietzschean view of Brown was, his comments nonetheless pinpointed accurately some reasons for a past era's intense preoccupation with Brown. Curiously enough, a series of explosive

tabloid stories also contributed to the Brown image; these reported how Brown had allegedly roughed up this person or that. Thus Brown arrived in films with an image just about carved out for him: this famous athlete automatically seemed to suggest power, strength, violence, and brutality.

Such early action films as *Rio Conchos* (1964), *Ice Station Zebra* (1968), *Dark of the Sun* (1968), and *El Condor* (1970) featured Brown as a flamboyantly assertive man's man, capable of taking care of himself. In *100 Rifles* (1969) when he had the dubious distinction of taking the screen's then reigning white love goddess Raquel Welch to bed, his black constituency (primarily male) cheered him openly in theaters. A comic book creation—the master of movie machismo—Brown was a phenomenon simply because films had rarely featured black men of action—and almost never a black man with the audacity to sleep with a white woman.

But while audiences might have believed they were seeing a pop symbol of political rebellion, actually in his films Brown often was incorporated into the system itself. In one of the early movies to propel him to stardom, *The Dirty Dozen* (1967), in a cast of such other he-man types as Lee Marvin, Charles Bronson, and George Kennedy, Brown was among a group of World War II soldier/prisoners given a chance to redeem themselves by going off on a special dangerous guerrilla mission. In essence, he was used as part of an old-style hymn to American patriotic bravery, a hero fighting for his homeland, and in so doing, abandoning any past resentments or feelings of rebellion. Brown is surprisingly effective in this movie, giving one of his most natural performances. In the prison revolt film *Riot* (1968), fundamentally he represented a prisoner voice of reason. In *tick . . . tick . . . tick* (1970), he was cast as an almost Poitieresque noble black sheriff who tries to quell conflicts within the white town he governs. In one respect, the *tick . . . tick . . . tick* sheriff role might be viewed as important imagewise merely because a black character could be depicted as a figure of authority. Here obviously Brown's strength and power were used to support the status quo.

White audiences no doubt relaxed when seeing how this potent black force was used in films, feeling perhaps as it was said Lyndon Johnson felt about J. Edgar Hoover. Refusing to fire Hoover as head of the FBI, apparently fearful of trouble which a vindictive Hoover might start, Johnson reportedly said he'd rather have Hoover inside the tent pissing out than outside pissing in. Thus, better to have Brown within the folds of the establishment in his films than as a truly menacing physical force threatening to tear the system down.

Throughout his Hollywood heyday, Brown had a magnetic presence: he didn't have to open his mouth; he just looked terrific, a rock of Gibraltar who could not be budged or, as Pauline Kael said, "so blankly beautiful he almost passes for enigmatic." Yet when Brown did open his mouth, he seemed too wooden and stolid to be a daredevil, too lacking in likable rowdy roguishness to be a defiant hero. As time went on, Brown loosened up. The political outlook of his later films—the idea of a brother aware of exploitation—was more in tune with the late 1960s/early 1970s idea of political rebellion or assertion. But the films themselves were shoddy affairs. Because Brown himself was never a real actor, he remained simply an image whose time came and went. Unlike John Wayne or Clint Eastwood who were able to work with perceptive important directors and then later to have real clout within the industry so that they could control their own images and survive as stars, Brown, having wasted himself in too many shoddy films, discovered as the 1970s drew to a close that much of his appeal had faded. Ironically, two of his most intriguing performances were in *Grasshopper* (1970, in which he played a former athlete used as a token figure at a Las Vegas hotel), and James Toback's *Fingers* (1978, in which an older Brown was still a Nietzschean superman but also a terrifying figure of true menace).

In the 1980s, Brown returned to action films in *One Down, Two To Go* (1983) under the direction of Fred Williamson. He also appeared on such TV shows as "T. J. Hooker" (1984), "Chips" (1983), and "The A-Team" (1986). In 1964, Brown had also done an "I Spy."

Among Brown's movie credits: *The Split* (1968); *Kenner* (1969); *Black Gunn* (1972); *Slaughter* (1972); *Slaughter's Big Rip-off* (1973); *I Escaped from Devil's Island* (1973); *The Slams* (1973); and *Take a Hard Ride* (1975).

Adolph Caesar

B. 1934; D. 1986. Actor.

Born and raised in Harlem, Adolph Caesar began his acting career late, after having retired from the Navy as a chief petty officer. He then studied and graduated from New York University with a degree in dramatic arts. For years, he worked successfully, albeit anonymously, as a voice-over announcer (mainly for commercials) and was associated with a range of acting companies, including various Shakespeare festivals in Oregon; Stratford, Connecticut; and New York.

But it was in the Negro Ensemble Company's production of Charles Fuller's drama *A Soldier's Play* that Caesar came to prominence, portraying the steely, grizzled Sgt. Waters. Repeating the role in the film version *A Soldier's Story*, he walked off with an Oscar nomination as Best Supporting Actor of 1984. Although his subsequent performance in *The Color Purple* (1985) proved disappointing, Caesar, with his deep resonant voice and his powerful personality, had proven to be a dynamic actor, possibly capable of playing major character roles. But while on the

Adolph Caesar in A Soldier's Story: *popular success came late and was cut short with his sudden, unexpected death.*

brink of his new film career—in fact, two days after beginning work on the movie *Tough Guys*—Caesar suddenly died of a heart attack. His last film *Club Paradise* (1986) was released after his death.

Among his TV credits: The ABC After School Special "Getting Even." He was also the narrator for the documentaries "Men of Bronze" (1977) and "I Remember Harlem" (1981).

Marietta Canty

B. 1906. Actress.

Character actress who usually played maids. Heavy-set and big-boned, sensitive and understanding, Canty turns up as one of the few sympathetic adults in the classic *Rebel Without a Cause* (1955). She's the domestic who cares for the lost Plato (Sal Mineo). I don't think anyone who's seen the film has ever quite forgotten her although some often confuse her with Louise Beavers. Contemporary audiences also have glimpsed Canty as the maid to the Spencer Tracy/Joan Bennett household and their pretty daughter Elizabeth Taylor in another classic, *Father of the Bride* (1950) and its sequel *Father's Little Dividend* (1951). She's also in *The Spoilers* (1942) with Marlene Dietrich and John Wayne.

Canty's career spanned some 30 years, from the movie *Emperor Jones* in 1933 to *A Man Called Peter* in 1955. Other film credits: *The Magnificent Dope* (1942); *Three Hearts for Julia* (1943); *Lady in the Dark* (1944); *The Reaching Wind* (1946); *Mother Is a Freshman* (1943); *My Foolish Heart* (1950); and *Bright Life* (1950).

Diahann Carroll

B. 1935. Singer, actress.

Born Carol Diann Johnson in New York City, the daugher of a subway conductor, she grew up to be Diahann Carroll, the glittery singer/actress who started her career as a model, then made a vivid impression as a performer in the 1954 New York show *House of Flowers*. Later Carroll performed at major nightclubs and returned to Broadway in *No Strings* (1962, Richard Rogers created it expressly for her; she won a Tony Award as Best Actress in a Musical for her performance) and *Agnes of God* (1983, in which she played a dramatic role). But it was Carroll's film and television work that enabled her to reach—and alternately please and alienate—a huge audience.

In her 1950s films *Carmen Jones* (1954) and *Porgy and Bess* (1959), she was something of a plain jane, a likable homebody but hardly a star. By the time of such later films as *Paris Blues* (1961), *Hurry Sundown* (1967), and *The Split* (1968), she had undergone a startling metamorphosis, emerging as something of a glamorous bronze barbie doll: lovely to look at but so studied and stilted that she struck audiences of the restless 1960s as being plastic and (for young militants of the period who attached political labels to black stars) as but one more symbol of a sterile decadent capitalistic culture. (Some label indeed!) Her television series "Julia" (1968–1971), although successful, did not endear her to a politically conscious age either. Carroll's image—heightened by many of her public statements about being a black star acceptable to white audiences—has always been that of the conformist, some might say, conciliatory performer, anxious to be a part of a system.

Stripped of her glamour makeup: Diahann Carroll in her Oscar-nominated performance in Claudine.

But in the 1970s, she forced her critics to do an about face with her sensitive and fervid performance in *Claudine*, surely her finest screen work, which won her an Oscar Nomination as Best Actress of 1974 and also earned her the NAACP Image Award. Afterwards her appearances were of varying quality.

Unlike a Tyson or a Diana Sands who could flip hack-written roles inside out, Carroll proved herself an actress greatly (almost desperately) in need of the right direction and material. On something like a guest shot on "The Love Boat" (1978), she seemed simply along for the ride, perhaps understandably unable to inject any feeling into such vapid material. (Actually, who could?) In "Roots: The Next Generations" (1979) and "I Know Why the Caged Bird Sings" (1979), audiences, however, weren't sure how to respond to her; with a speaking voice that was often inexpressive (sealing emotion in rather than releasing it), she frequently seemed out of character. In these productions she was always Diahann Carroll. Yet she lacked a strong and complex enough star personality to sustain great interest.

Surprisingly, in "Sister, Sister" (1982), Carroll's mannered performance worked to her advantage, seeming appropriate for the uptight, locked-in character she played. Here in a role not necessarily intended to be a sympathetic one, she won the audience over nonetheless.

By the mid-1980s, Carroll underwent yet another—much publicized—image change as the highrolling, elegant Dominique Devereaux on the nighttime television soap "Dynasty." Here her inexpressive, finishing-school-girl voice just about did her in. And her manner remained that of a well-brought-up lass ready to please, not to shake things up.

To her credit, though, Diahann Carroll, for most of her career, was a tough survivor, changing with the times, always in search of the right property. Throughout, too, she remained, as film and TV demand, a vivid visual creation, her beautiful skin tones, great bone structure, and distinct, sensual body lines were used to her advantage, often to upstage or outshine some of her white co-stars.

Carroll's TV credits include appearances on many variety shows of the 1950s and 1960s (she was one of the first blacks to turn up regularly on them): "Dennis James' Chance of a Lifetime"; "Arthur Godfrey's Talent Scout Show"; "The Jack Paar Show" (quite important to her career in the early 1960s); "The David Frost Show"; "The Ed Sullivan Show"; "The Judy Garland Show"; and "The Garry Moore Show." Among her dramatic TV appearances: "Peter Gunn" (1960); "The Naked City" (1962); "The Eleventh Hour" (1963). She also appeared in the all-star black musical special "The Strollin' Twenties" (1966). In 1976, she starred in her own summer series "The Diahann Carroll Show." In 1985, she was a guest on "Webster" and gave a provocative, well-thought-out interview on "The Barbara Walters Special."

Nell Carter

B. c. 1949. Actress/singer.

Leaving her native Birmingham, Alabama, Nell Carter arrived in New York in 1968 and soon used her distinctive mock-coquettish singing style to find work in clubs and cabarets and a number of musicals (many flops), including *Jesus Christ Superstar* (1971), *Soon* (1971), *Dude* (1972), and *Miss Moffat* (1974). In 1978, she hit paydirt in the Broadway hit *Ain't*

Misbehavin'. (Later she repeated her performance in the television version of the show.) Then in 1981, Carter became something of a household fixture when she starred in the series "Gimme a Break."

As a singer, Carter, on occasion, had a wistful quality, but that side rarely showed up in her television comedy performances. Short (4′11″), chunky, bubbly, playful, and campy, too, Carter created a persona that proved popular: basically she represented the lovelorn, agreeably bossy woman with a self-deprecating humor (calling attention to her size whenever possible) and a sentimental streak as well. Occasionally pushing the sentimental too far, there was something almost disturbingly pathetic about Carter. And audiences may well have felt condescending towards her. Yet she could always flip the pathos and turn playfully bitchy. Although she showed signs of a more "serious" dramatic talent, her appearances away from "Gimme a Break" were mainly in big clubs or guest spots at big musical affairs. She also hosted her own special "Never Too Old To Dream" (1986).

Other TV credits include: "Cindy" (1978) and the series "The Misadventures of Sheriff Lobo," in which she had a regular role (from 1980 to 1981) as the sharp-tongued Sgt. Hildy Jones.

Carter appeared in the film *Modern Problems* (1981).

Rosalind Cash

B. 1938. Actress.

Oddly enough, the actress Rosalind Cash might best be compared to, in temperament and style, is Susan Hayward: each of these talented beauties has been adept at portraying highly charged, restless, aggressive, romantic (but frequently enough, cynical) females. Their voices convey their impatience (with men or a system), their determination to do things their way. And when necessary, they flaunt their smoky

Rosalind Cash: often underrated, sometimes misused, but always a fascinating actress to watch.

sexiness and their independence. Both Cash and Hayward also frequently elevated trashy material, outshining their films and co-stars. Unlike Hayward, Cash, however, did not have nearly enough chances to showcase her rich talents and star persona. But when an opportunity emerged—as in *Melinda* (1972) and the TV movies "Sister, Sister" (1982) and "Sophisticated Gents" (1981)—she grasped it with a sure, firm grip.

Born in Atlantic City, New Jersey, Cash hit the New York stage in such early 1960s productions as *Dark of the Moon* (1960) and *No Strings* (which opened in 1962; Cash worked later as an understudy for Barbara McNair). Her performances in such Negro Ensemble Company productions as *Song of the Lusitanian Bogey* (1968) and *Ceremonies in Dark Old Men* (1968) brought her to the forefront of a new generation of young black stage actresses. Then Hollywood called.

When cast opposite Charlton Heston in *The Omega Man* (1971), Rosalind Cash won a role almost every other black actress in Hollywood was fighting for. Although the script diluted the power of her character, Cash herself was a sexy, independent heroine. With her brooding, intense eyes, her high cheekbones, and her sensuous mouth, she was an actress capable of projecting intelligence and a contemporary aggressiveness. Yet she maintained a traditional brand of femininity. For black males, she was a dream woman to be fought for but never conquered.

Cash had a significant following of black women, too, which was apparent with the release of *Melinda* (1972). Here in her best role of this period as a woman on the edge, holding on for dear life, struggling to keep a relationship with a man who hardly seemed her equal, Cash's tenacity and endurance, despite personal pain, made her a heroine for many black coeds of that era. Capturing the inner conflicts of a woman trapped in a relationship that did not seem to do her any good, Cash's character won respect for plowing through life nonetheless and for displaying, when pushed, a resilient don't-mess-or-play-with-me toughness. Her bank sequence in *Melinda*—when she defiantly demands her money—remains a classic.

As the 1970s moved on, Cash directed energies toward television, performing guest shots in such series as "The Mary Tyler Moore Show," "Starsky and Hutch," "Kojak," and "Police Woman." She was frequently *very* good. But still Cash aficionados longed to see her in more challenging or offbeat roles.

Then just when least expected, Rosalind Cash turned up in "The Guyana Tragedy: The Story of Jim Jones" (1980), "Sophisticated Gents," and "Sister, Sister." The passing years seemed to have toughened her more but also unleashed a new quality. She could be brazenly sexy, also brazenly outspoken, sometimes appearing to delight in upsetting or shocking the other characters on screen. To her everlasting credit, Cash never feared revealing various qualities in her characters that might have made them unappealing to audiences: in "Sister, Sister," she went all the way with her character's sluttiness and anger. And in her scenes in that drama with Diahann Carroll (as her sister), Cash was in high gear as she laid down the law to a woman who had been avoiding reality for years. In a medium that prefers the small and the comfortable, not the grand or aggressive, Cash proved herself capable of giving bravura performances. Significantly, for the black audience, Cash, in her best work, never struck one as a black woman who had lost touch with her roots. The rhythms of her voice and walk, indeed her attitude itself, were rare for television. Often when watching her, audiences no doubt felt that Rosalind Cash, deep inside, remained a high-flung diva from Atlantic City, proud as all get-out of who she was, sweet-tempered when pleased, and gloriously foul when ticked off.

A greatly underrated screen performer.

Rosalind Cash's movie credits include: *The New Centurions* (1972); *Hickey and Boggs* (1972); *The All American Boy* (1973); *Amazing Grace* (1974); *Uptown Saturday Night* (1974); *Cornbread, Earl and Me* (1975); *Dr. Black, Mr. Hyde* (1976); *The Monkey Hustle* (1977); *The Class of Miss MacMichael* (1979); and *Wrong Is Right* (1982, as the first black woman Vice President).

Cash's TV credits include: "What's Happening!!" (1976); "Good Times" (1976); "A Killing Affair" (1976); "Ceremonies in Dark Old Men" (1975); "King Lear" (1975); "Up and Coming" (1980); "Special Bulletin" (1983); "Go Tell It On the Mountain" (1985); and "The Cosby Show" (1986).

Alvin Childress

B. 1908; D. 1986. Actor.

Mississippi-born Alvin Childress played the easy-going, philosophical Amos on television's "Amos 'n' Andy" (1951–53). His career had begun in such stage productions as *Sweet Land* (1931) and *Savage Rhythm* (1931). Early on, he also worked in such films as *Crimson Fog* (1932), *Harlem Is Heaven* (1932), and *Dixie Love* (1934). Once "Amos 'n' Andy" left the airwaves, Childress, unable to find steady acting work, took a job parking cars and later was an employee of the Los Angeles County Civil Service Commission. In the 1970s, he returned to acting with appearances on "Sanford and Son" (1974), "Good Times" (1974), "The Jeffersons" (1975) and such films as *Thunderbolt and Lightfoot* (1974), *The Day of the Locust* (1975), and *The Bingo Long Traveling All-Stars and Motor Kings* (1976).

His other films include: *Keep Punching* (1939); *Anna Lucasta* (1958); and *Man in the Net* (1959).

Olivia Cole

B. c. 1942. Actress.

When Olivia Cole won an Emmy as Best Supporting Actress (Single Performance) in a Drama Series 1976/1977 for her performance as Chicken George's wife Matilda in "Roots," she seemed to have surfaced out of nowhere, so unfamiliar was she to primetime television audiences. Actually, Cole had spent a long apprenticeship in study at London's Royal Academy of Dramatic Arts and the University of Minnesota's Drama Department (which awarded her a master's degree) and in such classic theater productions as *Romeo and Juliet*, *The Rivals*, and *As You Like It*. Daytime TV viewers also had been introduced to her in the 1970s when she played the role of Deborah for four and a half years on the soap opera "The Guiding Light." She also appeared in episodes of such 1970s series as "Police Woman" and "Family."

"Roots" uncovered Cole's distinctive powers and presence. Her great success, however, was followed with small roles in the films *Heroes* (1977) and *Coming Home* (1978) and then, thankfully, a solid star part in "Backstairs at the White House" (1979). Yet Cole's career had dry spells when not much of anything seemed to be happening or when she was cast in projects of, shall we say, rather dubious distinction such as the

TV series "Szysznyk" (1977–1978), the TV movie "Children of Divorce" (1980), and the deliriously cornball, hack miniseries "North and South (Book 1)" (1985). In the latter, Cole played the most loyal of mammy servants, that ever-enduring pillar of strength for her charge, a lovely Southern aristocrat, Madeline, who, it turns out in this Old South drama, has Negro blood! Having known the young woman's secret for years and having vowed never to reveal it, Cole dies valiantly while trying to come to the rescue of her good but not-so-white mistress. Here, in the dopiest of roles, Olivia Cole strutted about like a noble Egyptian queen: her back rigidly straight, her head held high, her eyes looking directly ahead, unafraid and forceful. Part of the pleasure in watching her was that she was so unbending, even in this enjoyably two-bit miniseries. She refuses not to take acting seriously.

In most of her work, Cole has played highly disciplined, meticulously controlled women of quiet power, who cannot be stripped of their dignity or innate self-respect. Occasionally she looks—in parts of "Backstairs at the White House"—as if she's coming precariously close to tipping the scales and overdoing the great lady bit. Even when youngish in "Backstairs," Cole appeared and acted matronly. And audiences were probably screaming for her to loosen up a bit. We wondered if her speech always had to be *that* clipped and precise? But Cole managed consistently to keep her persona splendidly intact. As with the young Cicely Tyson, she earned audience respect not only because she would not budge from her convictions but also because of an underlying warmth and sweetness. She strikes us as a special breed of woman—and actress, really a major dramatic presence who rarely has had the major dramatic roles.

Movie credits include *The Onion Field* (1979).

Cole's TV credits include "Mistress of Paradise" (1981); "Fly Away Home" (1981); "Report to Murphy" (1982); "Something About Amelia" (1984); "Murder She Wrote" (1985); and "Go Tell It On the Mountain" (1985).

Gary Coleman

B. 1968. Actor.

"What is slightly larger than a fire hydrant, uses giant-size words and draws sky-high ratings each week?" *Newsweek* asked in its May 7, 1979, issue. "The answer," the magazine continued, "is 3-foot, 7½ inch, 50-pound Gary Coleman, the 11-year-old star of NBC's 'Diff'rent Strokes'—and possibly the most original vid-kid since Howdy Doody." That week Coleman, along with Robin Williams and Stockard Channing, was *Newsweek*'s cover subject. By then, Coleman was fast on the rise, about to emerge as America's most famous child star of the late 1970s–early 1980s and perhaps, for a spell, the most popular child personality since Shirley Temple. Like Temple, Coleman was celebrated for his exuberant precocity and his brash insights into the way the adult world worked—or failed to work. Usually with adults, Coleman set himself up as an authority figure, never masking his feelings of superiority or condescension toward those who did not meet his standards.

Clearly, Coleman was a national phenomenon, an exceptionally intelligent and articulate child who not only overcame career obstacles but also successfully dealt with serious health problems. He was born in Zion, Illinois, the son of a nurse and a pharmaceutical employee. Suffering from nephritis (a sometimes fatal kidney defect), he underwent, by age five, three operations, the last of which was a kidney transplant. His ailment slowed his growth. But nothing seemed to dampen his indefatigable ambition. By age three and a half, he could read. By age five, he not only had written to the department store Montgomery Ward inquiring about work as a model but had also been hired by the store, becoming a successful child model. After that, he appeared in commercials for McDonald's, Hallmark cards, and a bank in Chicago. Audiences immediately responded to his spunky audacity. Norman Lear spotted Coleman and cast him in a pilot for a remake of "The Little Rascals"—as the new Stymie. The pilot did not sell. But Coleman remained on the West Coast and did guest spots on other Lear programs such as "Good Times" and "The Jeffersons." When television executive Fred Silverman caught a glimpse of Coleman, he knew he had seen a distinctive new comic personality and he informed Lear (who by then had signed Coleman to an exclusive contract) to develop a series around the child. That led to "Diff'rent Strokes."

Once "Diff'rent Strokes" took off, the media promptly focused on Coleman, dazzled as much as the audiences by his wit, his sassiness, and his cool mastery of the put-down. When he appeared on "The Tonight Show," host Johnny Carson, having asked Coleman if he would like to take over the program for the evening, was caught completely off guard by the answer. "With all the laughing and cheering out there—quite possibly," said Coleman. Publications as diverse as *People, TV Guide,* and *The National Enquirer* reported on his activities and ongoing health problems.

Within the black community, reactions were mixed. His gutsy, irreverent style struck some as a being a tad *too* mature for a kid his age. (A few years earlier, there had been similar responses to the wise-cracking kid sister Dee, played by Danielle Spencer, on "What's Happening!!") Yet Coleman commanded respect because of his adroit professionalism. Nor was he the typical eye-popping, scared-of-ghosts black child star of the past. Like most skilled satirists, he delighted in smashing to smithereens many of the pretensions and follies of the adult world.

During the peak years of his popularity, Coleman starred in the movies *On the Right Track* (1981) and *Jimmy the Kid* (1982) and in the TV movies "The Kid from Left Field" (1979), "Scout's Honor" (1980), "The Kid with the Broken Halo" (1982), and "The Kid with the 200 I.Q." (1983). In these productions, Coleman, again like Shirley Temple, was a clear-eyed tot, completely in control of himself and never at a loss for words. He could rattle off his one-liners with the assurance and aplomb of a veteran. At one point, he was even called the pee-wee Don Rickles.

By the mid-1980s, as Coleman grew older but no taller, the image showed its age and its cracks. No longer the cute, chipmunk-cheeked darling that audiences had fawned over, he frequently looked weary and not well at all. (He had had a second kidney transplant.) And, of course, as he moved into his teen years, there were problems in dealing with his budding romantic life. He simply looked too small to be credible as a teen heartthrob. By the time of his appearance in "The Fantastic World of D.C. Collins" (1984), he was playing a less idealized kind of hero; he was a boy lost in his fantasies and alienated from his parents. In "Playing with Fire" (1985), he portrayed another lonely, isolated teenager, who turns to arson in a mad plea for attention. A more serious Coleman hero, however, was not what the audience wanted; it preferred the lively little imp, who could toss his troubles aside without letting anything bother him. The audience simply would not relinquish its fantasy view of him. In all truthfulness, the very nature of Coleman's appeal demanded that he, like Peter Pan, never grow up, that he remain young forever.

Later years found Gary Coleman still struggling with health problems and career shifts. Generations, old and new, may not take much to the older Coleman (just as audiences never took to an older Shirley Temple) but his early work, mainly as Arnold on "Diff'rent Strokes," remains a sparkling portrait of a cocky little Lord Fauntleroy who breezes through life with elan and a lot of common sense.

Coleman's TV credits include: "The Big Show" (1980); "Lucy's Back and NBC's Got Her" (1980); and "Tom Snyder's Celebrity Spotlight" (1980).

Bill Cosby

B. 1937. Comedian, actor.

In the 1980s, Bill Cosby emerged as one of the most successful stars in the history of television. Years before in "I Spy" (1965–68) and in guest appearances on such programs as "The Jack Paar Show" and "The Jonathan Winters Show," Cosby had mastered the minimalist demands of the medium, proving himself a consummate reassuring cool television personality. Over the years he had become so acceptable a tube fixture that by the 1980s the TVQ index—the television industry's annual nationwide survey of a performer's popularity with viewers—gave Cosby the highest rating it had recorded for any personality in over a decade (higher than Clint Eastwood's or Eddie Murphy's rating). Yet as a performer who never offended his large middle-class viewing audience, Cosby had also somehow miraculously maintained his integrity and inner sense of self. He always came across as a man living by his own rules. In the mid-1980s, with the extraordinary success of his sitcom "The Cosby Show" (1984), his career reached a new high point; he not only became one of the best-known and most admired men in America, but he also emerged as an ideal father figure for much of his country's young, both black and white.

All of this could hardly have been predicted for a guy who had grown up in Philadelphia (his father was a Navy mess steward; his mother, a housemaid) and had quit school after the 10th grade to join the Navy for two years. (He acquired his high-school equivalency diploma through a correspondence course.) In 1961, Cosby left the Navy to attend Temple University in Philadelphia. Two years later, at age 26, he was looking for work as a comedian in clubs. His rise in show business was relatively swift. Two years after he started, he was on national television.

Like Dick Gregory, Cosby in the early 1960s was a new kind of black comedian: in suit and tie, he looked like a well-brought-up, serious college student, a smart fellow geared to make it. Unlike Redd Foxx or Slappy White, who for decades had performed material directly pitched towards black audiences, Cosby was crossover from the start. He experimented with racial humor but soon dumped it in favor of tales and skits spun from his experiences with the neighborhood kids he had grown up with: Fat Albert, Weird Harold, Mush Mouth. Never raunchy or explosive as Pryor became, Cosby, even during his early years, was something of a family man who extolled basic American values and a thoroughly American point of view. Yet although there was always a

Bill Cosby: the ideal TV star who never offended his audience yet maintained his integrity and inner sense of self.

politeness about him, audiences sensed that if Cosby were ever crossed, this man would let you have it.

1965 was the year Cosby reached mass America as the co-star of "I Spy." With his guarded but upfront sexuality and with none of the shuffling/jiving antics of "Amos 'n' Andy," he set a new standard for black men on television.

Once the series ended, Cosby continued to appear on television but went for years without another primetime hit. In 1969, he did "The Bill Cosby Show," which lasted only two years. "The New Bill Cosby Show"—a variety series that premiered in September 1972—made it through only one season. Then "Cos," a Sunday evening variety hour aimed at children, folded after a little more than a month in 1976. Only his children's cartoon series, "Fat Albert and the Cosby Kids" (which began its run in 1972), was successful.

But Cosby remained before the public eye. Immensely popular on the nightclub circuit, he also turned out comedy albums (winning four Grammys) and appeared consistently on television commercials, pitching products as diverse as Jell-O Pudding, The Ford Motor Company, Coca-Cola, and Texas Instruments. In these commercials, he was, quite frankly, quite good: in some, he was almost something of a gleeful, giddy kid, and in others, an intelligent ironic, overgrown impish figure. Rarely simply coasting on his charm, he dipped into his imagination to come up with clever intonations. He also appeared in films: *Hickey and Boggs* (1972, in which he co-starred again with Robert Culp, the two playing detectives in pursuit of some stolen bank money); *Man and Boy* (1972); *Uptown Saturday Night* (1974); *Let's Do It Again* (1975); *California Suite* (1978); *Mother, Jugs, and Speed* (1976); *A Piece of the Action* (1977); *The Devil and Max Devlin* (1981); and a concert film *Bill Cosby Himself* (1983). For the most part, his breezy movie performances were effective yet scaled more for the small screen than the big one. Like so many successful TV stars, perfect at playing ordinary everyman figures, he was never oddball or threatening enough to be a major film personality.

Then came the spots as guest host on "The Tonight Show" during the early 1980s. Here with his big cigar and his swanky, tailored suits, Cosby, upon close observation, came across as rather arrogant and occasionally insensitive, looking a little like a Vegas burnout case: the typical self-absorbed and indulgent star. For the first time in his television career, there was something faintly vulgar about him (not so much in what he said or did as in his attitude). Yet audiences loved this particular Cosby, too. In fact, NBC's program chief Brandon Tartikoff said he'd first come up with the idea of having Cosby do a new series after watching him hosting "The Tonight Show."

"The Cosby Show" rejuvenated Cosby, got his juices pumping again. Shaping the program to reflect his sensibility and perspective about child rearing and family life in general, he came up with a new tone for the family sitcom: gentle but bracing. His was an easygoing father who also knew when to put his foot down. The series was graced not only with Cosby's reassuring presence but also with his newfound maturity and parental wisdom. For millions who had followed Cosby's career for years, it was like seeing "I Spy"'s Alexander Scott now off the road, all grown up, and settled down. The element of familiarity essential to any television star had carried over from the past series to the present one. Most importantly though for the first time in television history, a black performer had complete control of his own series. And he had come up with an astounding winner, proving that black creative talents, if given a chance, could invigorate old television forms and formulas.

During this period, Cosby also wrote a number-one bestselling book called *Fatherhood* (1986). As might be expected, stories also circulated at this time of Cosby's arrogance and aloofness. The press seemed anxious to let the public know how Cosby's irritations or anger might surface during the course of an interview. Sometimes Cosby spoke out about his critics. Other times, he simply ignored them, aware no doubt that they were but another piece of a star's territory, to be enjoyed or overlooked.

Cosby's television appearances include: "The Electric Company" (the 1971–1976 PBS series on which he appeared frequently); "Black History: Lost, Strayed, or Forgotten" (1969); "The Bill Cosby Comedy Hour" (a 1975 special), "The Second Bill Cosby Special" (1976).

In 1987, Cosby wrote another best-seller, *Time Flies*, and appeared in the film *Leonard, Part 6*.

Rupert Crosse

B. 1927; D. 1973. Actor.

Oscar-nominated as Best Supporting Actor of 1970 for his performance in *The Reivers*, Rupert Crosse's career finally seemed to be shifting into high gear. He had been working in films since 1961 when he appeared in *Shadows*. Other film credits include: *Too Late Blues* (1961), *To Trap a Spy* (1966), and *Waterhole #3* (1967). Crosse's promising career was cut short, however, when he died at age 46 in 1973. TV credits include appearances on such 1960s series as "Bracken's World"; "The Monkees"; "The Bill Cosby Show"; and later the television series "Partners" (1971–1972), a short-lived, half-hour sitcom in which he played a leading role, as one of two nutty detectives solving unusual crimes.

Dorothy Dandridge

B. 1922; D. 1965. Actress.

In the 1950s, the era of Ike and Korea, of Elvis and the hula-hoop, a time when America seemed to celebrate only the ordinary and looked as if it were politically and socially asleep, Dorothy Dandridge unexpectedly appeared on the national landscape, enlivening the age with her razor-sharp intensity, her haughty glamour, and her breathtaking beauty. She was a complex set of magnetic dualities: bold and dramatic yet soft and vulnerable, shy and lost, too.

Dandridge's career spanned some 30 years. Born in Cleveland in 1922, the second daughter of an aspiring actress, Ruby, and her husband, Cyril, Dorothy worked professionally with her older sister Vivian when they were both children. Under the tutelage of their mother and a family friend, the girls were called The Wonder Kids and toured parts of the South, singing, dancing, and performing acrobatics at churches, schools, and social gatherings.

By the 1930s, mother Ruby—having left her husband and Cleveland—settled with her pretty daughters in Los Angeles, the land of sunshine and dreams, the place where America's mass fantasies were cleverly packaged and merchandised. Ruby struggled for a career in Hollywood. Slim as opportunities were for black entertainers during the Depression, the girls found work. They turned up in a sequence with Ivie Anderson in the Marx Brothers film *A Day at the Races* (1937). As teenagers, Dorothy and Vivian teamed up with a friend, Etta Jones, to form the Dandridge Sisters. They performed with Jimmie Lunceford's Orchestra and Cab Calloway, played the Cotton Club, and also appeared with Louis Armstrong and Maxine Sullivan in the movie *Going Places* (1939).

By the early 1940s, Dandridge started performing on her own in such soundies (musical shorts) made between 1941 and 1942 as *Yes, Indeed, Sing for My Supper, Jungle Jig, Easy Street, Cow Cow Boogie,* and *Paper Doll* (with the Mills Brothers). She also appeared in the features *Lady from Louisiana* (1941), *Sundown* (1941), *Bahama Passage* (1942), and *Sun Valley Serenade*. In the last, she performed a giddy version of "Chattanooga Choo Choo" with the dancing Nicholas Brothers, one of whom, Harold, became Dandridge's first husband.

Once she had settled with Nicholas, Dandridge seemed to temporarily put her career on hold: she appeared content as a wife and mother, caring for her young daughter, Harolyn. But at this time, the first of a series of personal tragedies struck when she learned her daughter had been born severely brain damaged. According to her sister Vivian, Dandridge frantically went from one doctor to another in hopes of some new prognosis on her child's condition. Finally, she was advised to have her daughter institutionalized because she herself was in too frail an emotional state to care for the child. Later her marriage to Nicholas ended in divorce. It was then that she channeled most of her energies and frustrations into her career.

Despite an innate shyness and her surprising insecurities (as the years moved on, she apparently had less and less confidence in her talents), Dandridge soon made her mark in nightclubs on the West Coast and later in the East. Well-covered by the press, she eventually integrated some of the top clubs around the world.

But her great ambition was to be a dramatic film actress. Before her

A cultural icon for Black America and one of the screen's great legendary beauties, Dorothy Dandridge's film career peaked with Carmen Jones, *then slipped into a tragic decline because of an indifferent film industry not yet ready, as Sidney Poitier has said, for the unique gifts she had to offer.*

such black leading lady types as Nina Mae McKinney, Fredi Washington, and Lena Horne had met with limited success. Determined to alter that history, Dandridge first caught the eyes of moviegoers with her sexy appearance as an African princess in *Tarzan's Peril* (1951), then as the young wife in *The Harlem Globetrotters* (1951). 1953 saw her as the young schoolteacher in MGM's *Bright Road.* A year later she had her greatest triumph as Otto Preminger's *Carmen Jones,* which won her an Academy Award nomination as Best Actress of the Year, the first time a black woman had been nominated in the leading actress category. Successful as the film was, three years passed before Dandridge worked again in a movie—in *Island in the Sun* (1957), in which she became the first black actress cast romantically opposite a white actor in a major American film. Although considered provocative for its time, the film was flawed and compromised, unable to go all the way with the interracial situation it had set up. The picture did little to advance Dandridge's career.

Later in Preminger's *Porgy and Bess* (1959), although not blessed with an exciting script or energetic direction, Dandridge's star qualities were on display: her vulnerability and nervous tension provided an illuminat-

Dorothy Dandridge, in one of her first important starring roles, as the young African princess in Tarzan's Peril.

ing subtext, which makes her a compellingly watchable star. Although she won the Golden Globe Award as Best Actress of 1959 in a Musical, here one sees a black actress ill at ease with her character and the very film itself.

The same was true of other Dandridge films such as *The Decks Ran Red* (1958), *Tamango* (1959), and *Malaga* (1962, which, curiously, has her moodiest and perhaps most touching performance), all of which again cast her opposite white actors; none of which used her properly. One look at Dandridge and an audience knew she had been born to play leading roles, either restless mildly manic beauties or soft romantic dream girls. But the film industry failed to construct star vehicles, fearful that audiences would not pay to see a black leading lady.

Eventually finding it difficult to get movie work, Dandridge returned to nightclubs, which she hated. And her private life took a disastrous turn. A new marriage—to white restaurateur Jack Dennison—drained her emotionally and financially. Filing for bankruptcy, she seemed lost and adrift.

In 1965, things briefly looked brighter. With her manager Earl Mills, she traveled to Mexico, where she signed a new movie contract. But a short time later, back in Los Angeles, she was found dead, her death attributed to an overdose of an anti-depressant.

For much of black America, Dorothy Dandridge remains an unsung heroine. American movies have always thrived on troubled mythic star gods and goddesses, be it a Valentino, a Monroe, a Harlow, a Dean, those figures whose personal and professional dilemmas and conflicts —their star lives—command attention. Like Stepin Fetchit and also Richard Pryor, Dandridge has emerged as one of the few such legendary black screen personalities. Her life had a mythic structure, that strikes us as being romantically and tragically larger than life. In retrospect, her life and career are comments on a movie industry—a film colony—and an American way of life that were not, as Sidney Poitier once said, ready for the unique gifts Dandridge had to offer.

Dandridge's film credits include: *Drums of the Congo* (1942), *Hit Parade of 1943*, *Atlantic City* (1944), *Pillow to Post* (1945), and *Remains To Be Seen* (1953). She also appeared in the independent productions *Four Shall Die* (1946), *Flamingo* (1947), and the compilation film *Ebony Parade* (1947).

TV credits include appearances in the 1950s on "The Ed Sullivan Show"; later "Cain's Hundred" (1962); and "Light's Diamond Jubilee" (1964).

A sultry, mature Dandridge in Island in the Sun.

Ruby Dandridge

B. 1904. Actress.

From the 1930s to the late 1950s, this Memphis-born actress appeared, mostly in minor parts, in such films as *Midnight Shadow* (1939), *Tish* (1942), *Cabin in the Sky* (1943), *Gallant Lady* (1943), *Melody Parade* (1943), *Junior Miss* (1945), *Three Little Girls in Blue* (1946), *My Wild Irish Rose* (1947), *The Arnelo Affair* (1947), and *A Hole in the Head* (1959). Her most successful work, however, was on radio and then TV: she played Geranium on "The Judy Canova Show" (1943); Raindrop on "The Gene Autry Show" (1944); and Oriole on "Beulah," a role she recreated in 1952 when this series went to television. She also played Delilah on TV's "Father of the Bride" (1961–1962) series. Her most distinguishing characteristic was her high-pitched voice. Heavy and dowdy, she usually was made to go through the then requisite mammy/Aunt Jemima antics. Ironically, she is now best remembered as the mother of performers Vivian and Dorothy Dandridge, the latter of whom became in the 1950s one of black America's most treasured cultural icons.

Ossie Davis

B. 1917. Actor, director, writer.

Ossie Davis was among the new breed of Negro actors who, in the years following the Second World War, earnestly endeavored to present a modern image of intelligent, articulate black characters. A native of Cogdell, Georgia, Davis attended Howard and Columbia universities, and studied acting with the Rose McClendon Players in Harlem. During the war years, he spent 32 months in the army where he managed to write and produce shows for the troops. In 1946, upon his return to acting, he made his Broadway debut in *Jeb Turner*. The play lasted only nine performances. But an actress named Ruby Dee was also in the cast. The two married two years later.

In the late 1940s and 1950s, this tall, full-faced, sturdily built man (Davis was robust and spirited enough to build a house with his bare hands—by himself, no less) scurried about in search of roles. He performed in some theater, worked with Sidney Poitier and Ruby Dee in *No Way Out* (1950), appeared on Showtime USA's 1951 production of "Green Pastures," and won the title role in Kraft Theatre's TV version of "The Emperor Jones" (1955). But little looked promising for him. Of this period in American entertainment, he once said, "I knew I was going to be rejected so I had very low expectations. But rejection did sting. In the theater it took a peculiar form—of having to compete with your peers, like I did for *Green Pastures* on Broadway, to fight to say words you were ashamed of. Ruby and I came along at a time when being black was not yet fashionable. There was little in the theatre for us except to carry silver trays."

In the 1960s as television opened up to black actors, he fared better, appearing in episodes of "The Defenders" (several times in 1961, 1963, 1965), "The Doctors" (1964), "Slattery's People" (1965), "The Fugitive" (the 1966 "Death Is the Door Prize" episode), "Run for Your Life" (1966), "NYPD" (1968), "Bonanza" (1969), "Name of the Game" (1969), and "Night Gallery" (1969). In all these productions as well as in such movies as *The Cardinal* (1963), *Shock Treatment* (1964), *The Hill* (1965), and *A Man Called Adam* (1966), he could be counted on for solid, workmanlike performances. Yet often he appeared detached from his parts. There was something engaging about him, but there was also something missing. "I'm not a great actor," Davis once said, "I've never devoted myself to my craft with the intensity Ruby has. I've always felt I'd rather be a writer. But we had to make a living." Still on some oddball occasions, as in *The Scalphunters* (1968), he pulled off rather magically inspired performances. Pauline Kael once wrote that Davis "in such movies as *The Hill* and *The Scalphunters* brought a stronger presence to his roles than white actors did, and a deeper joy. What a face for the camera. He was a natural king."

When Davis, who long yearned to be a writer, finally turned his attentions to writing, he came up with the successful play *Purlie Victorious*, which has had a long life in various guises. In 1963, it became the movie *Gone Are the Days*. Later it was revamped and became a smash

Broadway musical called *Purlie*, which still later was taped for television with Robert Guillaume and Melba Moore.

Purlie Victorious may well be the vehicle Ossie Davis will be remembered for, but his career took a very pleasant turn in 1970 when he directed the feature *Cotton Comes to Harlem*. A joyousness ran through the film that lured audiences around the country into the theaters.

Afterward he directed other films with varying degrees of success: *Kongi's Harvest* (a 1971 dramatization of the play by African writer Wole Soyinka); *Black Girl* (a 1972 dramatization of the play by black female writer J.E. Franklin); *Gordon's War* (a 1973 action film); and *Countdown at Kusini* (a 1976 tale of the struggle for liberation in an African nation). Although not always successful with his films; in a strange way, Davis could be called one of the more serious black directors of his era; political undercurrents run throughout much of his work. He has never settled for simply making a standard action movie. Of course, we all know that "seriousness" can sometimes wreck a film. But Davis hoped to take black American cinema into a new, more politically oriented direction and, no matter what the results, for that he has to be commended.

Ossie Davis's other movie credits (as an actor) include: *Harry and Son* (1984).

Davis's TV credits include: "John Brown's Raid" (1960); "Great Adventure" (the 1963 "Go Down, Moses" episode); "Look Up and Live" (1966); "The Outsider" (1967); "Teacher, Teacher" (1969); "Today Is Ours" (1974); "Hawaii Five-O" (1974); "The 10th Level" (1976); "King" (1978); and "Don't Look Back" (1981). With his wife Ruby Dee he also co-hosted the PBS series "With Ossie and Ruby." He co-wrote "For Us the Living," a drama based on the life of civil rights leader Medgar Evers.

Sammy Davis, Jr.

B. 1925. Actor, singer, dancer.

By age five, Sammy Davis, Jr., joined the ranks of professional entertainers, working with his father and his uncle, Will Mastin, in an act called The Will Mastin Trio. As early as 1933 in the short *Rufus Jones for President*, Davis, age seven, turned up in films, giving his most endearing performance. He's a dazzling little dynamo who dances up a storm and drifts off to sleep on the lap of Ethel Waters. Throughout the 1930s and 1940s, Davis remained on the road, working in clubs and theaters with his father and uncle.

In the 1950s, Davis, on his own, emerged as a favorite in nightclubs and television, now a seasoned young old-timer singer/dancer/impressionist, seemingly so ferociously skilled and versatile that many considered him the world's greatest living entertainer. Laurence Olivier, when about to film *Othello* (1965), reportedly studied Davis's routines to have an idea how best to approach the movements and rhythms of his character. Davis himself sought to stretch, playing a dramatic leading role in the 1958 movie *Anna Lucasta*. Afterward he played a glitzy Sportin' Life in Otto Preminger's film of *Porgy and Bess* (1959).

But Davis became best known for the movies made with members of Hollywood's Rat Pack, such men as Frank Sinatra, Dean Martin, Peter Lawford, Joey Bishop, all of whom socialized and worked together in such films as *Ocean's Eleven* (1960), *Sergeants 3* (1962) and *Robin and the 7 Hoods* (1964). At first the Rat Pack movies were saluted as being egalitarian affairs: in this age of integration, everybody was happy seeing Sammy up there on the screen with the white guys. It didn't seem to matter that Davis frequently was used as a token figure. Always game for action, Davis did his best, despite the fact that at times his performances appeared like old routines calculatedly being warmed over for a new audience. The movies themselves portrayed him mainly as a comic sidekick, with racial jokes sometimes at Davis's expense. Because the films were not constructed to showcase any aggressive response he might have had to such jokes, he couldn't come back strong with a putdown retort as Eddie Murphy or Richard Pryor were to do in the 1980s. In some cases, notably *Salt and Pepper* (1968), he lapsed into syrupy sentimentality. And during a period of cries of cultural separatism, younger black audiences found it distressing, not to say politically embarrassing, to find Davis cast in this film as the loyal trusty black friend of Peter Lawford. As if this were not bad enough, *Salt and Pepper* (1968) had a sequel, *One More Time* (1970). During this time, Davis's films, as well perhaps as his much-publicized marriage to white actress Mai Britt, so alienated him from the black community that by the 1970s when he appeared in the 1973 musical documentary *Save the Children*, he was captured on film being booed by a black audience.

Interracial male bonding: Sammy Davis, Jr., and Peter Lawford in One More Time.

During the 1980s, the audience response to Davis had not so much mellowed as turned apathetic. Frequently looking worn and rather burnt-out, Davis's later work in a film like *Cannonball Run II* (1984) lacked the energetic spark and creative free-for-all of his very early appearances. In the eyes of some, he remained a great American performer never imaginatively or intelligently used in films or television.

Significantly, Davis was considered a big enough draw to host two television (variety/talk) series: "The Sammy Davis Jr. Show" (NBC, 1966) and the syndicated "Sammy and Company" (1975–77).

Other movie credits include: *Pepe* (1960), *A Man Called Adam* (a 1966 dramatic role), *Sweet Charity* (1969), *Johnny Cool* (1963), and the German remake of *The Threepenny Opera* (1964), in which as the Ballad Singer he performed "Mac the Knife."

Davis's innumerable TV appearances include: "G.E. Theatre" (1958); "Zane Grey Theatre" (1959); "Lawman" (1961); "Rifleman" (1961); "Hennessey" (1962); "Dick Powell Theatre" (1962); "Ben Casey" (1963); "The Patty Duke Show" (1965); "Wild, Wild West" (1966); "I Dream of Jeannie" (1967); "The Danny Thomas Show" (1967); "Mod Squad" (three episodes during 1969 to 1970); "The Pigeon" (1969); "The Beverly Hillbillies" (1969); "The Name of the Game" (1970); "The Trackers" (1971); "All in the Family" (1972); "The Courtship of Eddie's Father" (1972); "Love of Life" (1975); "Chico and the Man" (1975); "Archie Bunker's Place" (1980); "Fantasy Island" (1983, 1984); "The Jeffersons" (1984); and "Bob Hope's High Flying Birthday" (1986).

The young Sammy Davis, Jr., in an early television appearance with Eddie Cantor.

Ruby Dee

B. 1923. Actress.

An actress with a long career and a solid list of credits, Ruby Dee (born Ruby Ann Wallace in Cleveland, Ohio) turned to acting in New York City in the 1940s, studying first at Harlem's American Negro Theatre along with such other young hopefuls of the period as Sidney Poitier and Ossie Davis (whom Dee later married). Her theater debut was in 1943 in *South Pacific*.

In the 1950s she slowly won movie roles at a time when blacks were rarely employed in Hollywood. Sometimes called "the Negro June Allyson," she was known for her portrayals of pert, helpful, understanding wives. Small, delicate, almost birdlike in her early years, Dee often looked as if the slightest wind would knock her over—for good. But her looks were deceiving for she proved herself a dramatic actress quite adept at playing strong women who wouldn't give in to either domestic distress or personal heartache.

Edge of the City in 1957, in which she was cast as Sidney Poitier's wife, revealed the first flowering of her dramatic powers. She has an unforgettable sequence: upon learning that her husband has been killed, she tells a cowardly John Cassavetes to get out of her house—and to take his white man's money with him.

Four years later she repeated her stage role—of the wife Ruth Younger—in the movie *A Raisin in the Sun* (1961). Hers was a glowing, radiant piece of work, all the more remarkable perhaps because in a cast that ravenously clutches at its high-powered emotional dialogue, Dee's quiet restraint and her tender intensity are direct and almost heartbreakingly real.

Some of Dee's later performances were not as delicately etched. On

Early in her career, Ruby Dee played the pert, near-perfect wife of baseball star Jackie Robinson in The Jackie Robinson Story.

occasion she seemed to lack concentration, looking a bit as if acting had lost some of its charm for her. But when she's been good (as in *The Incident* in 1967, *Buck and the Preacher* in 1972, and the 1974 television movie "Wedding Band," in which she recreated a role she had first performed on stage), Ruby Dee's been *quite good*, in work that holds up amazingly well, moving and touching us in ways that performances of other, more flamboyantly dramatic actresses do not.

Her stage performances include: *Purlie Victorious* (1961) and *Boesman and Lena* (1970).

Among her movie credits: *The Jackie Robinson Story* (1950); *No Way Out* (1950); *The Tall Target* (1951); *Go Man Go* (1954); *St. Louis Blues* (1958, in which she's a very prim good girl); *Take A Giant Step* (1961); *The Balcony* (1963, in which she's cast against type, as a prostitute); *Gone Are the Days* (1963); *Virgin Island* (1960); *Up Tight* (1968, which she also co-wrote); *Countdown at Kusini* (1976); and *Cat People* (1982, one of her few campy roles, as a mysterious New Orleans landlady).

Her TV credits include: guest shots on such series as "The Nurses" (the 1963 episode "Express Stop From Lenox Avenue"); "The Fugitive" (the 1963, "Decision in the Ring" episode with James Edwards); "East Side, West Side" (1963); and "The Great Adventure" (the 1963 episode "Go Down Moses," in which she plays a stirring tough-minded Harriet Tubman); "Peyton Place" (a continuing role in this series, 1968–1969); "Tenafly" (1973); "It's Good To Be Alive" (1974); "Wedding Band" (1974); "Police Woman" (1978); "I Know Why the Caged Bird Sings" (1979); "Roots: The Next Generations" (1979); the black version of "Long Day's Journey into Night" (1982); "The Atlanta Child Murders" (1985). With her husband Ossie Davis, she also hosted the series "With Ossie and Ruby" (1981).

Ivan Dixon

B. 1931. Actor, director.

There are certain black actors who, with the right roles, we connect to in the most personal way. On screen, it is not so much what they do, but who they are. They express something special about the black experience or simply plain human experience that reaches deep inside and moves us. We know we're getting a glimpse at a kind of truth that films generally have no time for. Sometimes the actors who affect us in this way are not the big stars. Perhaps they do not become the darlings of commercial cinema because their work (the individual screen persona each develops) is too personalized. Such performers as Paul Winfield, Juano Hernandez, James Edwards, Madge Sinclair, and Rosalind Cash are among those who have struggled, within the confines of a tough, debilitating entertainment industry, to hold onto and express a personal (as opposed to professional) sense of identity. Included in this group is Ivan Dixon.

This New York born actor, who made his Broadway debut in 1957 in William Saroyan's *The Cave Dwellers* and later broke into movies by stunt doubling for Sidney Poitier in *The Defiant Ones* (1958), has rarely had roles that have matched his talents. But he can be counted on to give sensitive, solid performances, presenting us with men who seem decent to the core, untainted and uncompromised.

Dixon's best role remains that of Duff in *Nothing but a Man* (1964). Watching this film at revivals today, black audiences continue to be impressed by his work, which is so unlike the type of performance we usually see in American films. In his scenes with his wife, played by Abbey Lincoln, he accurately conveys the sense of a black man so eaten up by the hostilities and pressures of the outside racist society that he cannot reveal even to his wife his great hurt, his great love or his great need. It is only after a solitary emotional odyssey that he can come to terms with himself and some of the wrong he has done her. Here Dixon gave audiences an archetypal image of the sensitive black hero of the 1960s, the black man aware that something stinks in the culture around him and conscious that he can choose between life and death, between the existential light and the disastrous leap into despair and self-destructiveness. In the picture, the self-destructiveness and despair are represented in the brilliant portraits drawn by Julius Harris as Dixon's alcoholic father and Gloria Foster, as the father's brooding, spiritually disoriented mistress. Dixon in *Nothing but a Man* is a kind of metaphysical rebel, a man as much the stranger in contemporary society as a Camus hero, but one for whom detachment and withdrawal are not the ultimate weapons of survival. He learns what personal human contact means. And he is even more aware that a man's actions are determined by what he believes to be true about himself.

Dixon's work in *Nothing but a Man* as well as *Car Wash* (1976) reveals he was an actor born for films. Yet we wonder why he did not become a big star in American motion pictures as did Sidney Poitier. Poitier, also born for films, came to master the medium because, I suppose, he understood the peculiar demands of the film industry—what it means to be a movie star. When Poitier is seen today in *The Defiant Ones*, no one can fail to respond to the technical surety of his work. But what adds to the excitement and cumulative effects is the charisma of this great star. Never though did Poitier coast by on charisma alone (as did Jim Brown). He coupled the force of his talents with his compelling screen persona

Ivan Dixon, a sensitive actor best known for his movie performance in Nothing but a Man *and for his role in the TV series "Hogan's Heroes."*

and was able, through magnetic star acting, to hold the audience spellbound—and to provide movie history with archetypal black characters who are fascinating and sometimes infuriating, too.

For anyone to become an important figure in American motion pictures, the charisma—that added dimension—has got to be there for everyone to see. It is one of the great thrills and limitations of movie stardom in this country. (The situation is different for European film actors.) Yet there are times when American audiences do not want the traditional kind of movie star, when we prefer to see someone who is more real to us, who strips himself or herself of dazzling externals to get to basics. Ivan Dixon has been this type of basic actor for years. And that's the quality that makes him undeniably a fine screen presence.

After his critical success in *Nothing but a Man*, Dixon appeared in *A Patch of Blue* (1965) and worked a great deal on television, including a role in the series "Hogan's Heroes" (1965 to 1969). Then he sought to express himself artistically by directing films: *Trouble Man* (1972) and *The Spook Who Sat by the Door* (1973). Because of the latter's strong anti-CIA theme, Dixon once said he had been told not to do the film. But he managed to raise $60,000 from black investors to get the movie off the ground. After three and a half weeks, it looked as if the production might have to shut down. United Artists put up money for the completion of the film and eventually had control over it. Dixon was none too pleased with the way the company distributed his film.

One wonders about Ivan Dixon's other experiences in Hollywood. He has made very few films. How does such a talented man hold onto his convictions? Does he become hardened or embittered? Do we see in his work his disillusionment, cynicism, or anger? When set to watch Dixon in something like the 1987 miniseries "Amerika," one might expect him to be a bit of a worn-out wreck as Rex Ingram was, after all his problems, in *Anna Lucasta* (1958). But Ivan Dixon maintains even here the fundamental decency and solidity that he expressed in his previous films.

Dixon's movie credits include: *Porgy and Bess* (1959); *A Raisin in the Sun* (1961); *To Trap a Spy* (1966); and *Clay Pigeon* (1971).

Dixon's television credits include: "The Bob Hope Chrysler Theatre" (a 1964 episode, "Murder in the First"); "I Spy" (1965); "The Fugitive" (1967); "Ironside" (1967); "The Final War of Olly Winter" (1967, considered one of Dixon's better roles; he plays an army sergeant in Vietnam); "It Takes a Thief" (1968); and "The Name of the Game" (1969). Dixon also directed in the 1970s and 1980s episodes of "The Waltons," "Starsky and Hutch," "McCloud," "Little House on the Prairie," and "Magnum, P.I."

Tamara Dobson

B. 1947. Actress.

Tall, statuesque actress Tamara Dobson came to prominence in the mid-1970s as the tough and assertive narcotics agent in *Cleopatra Jones* (1973) and *Cleopatra Jones and the Casino of Gold* (1975). For a brief spell, as action film stars she and Pam Grier were rivals, each a glorious male fantasy come true with a large male following and quite a bit of attention from the press. Born in Baltimore, Dobson had begun her career as a fashion model. That showed in her films. Her remarkable bearing, her sleek good looks, and her satiny, alluring voice were all important ingredients of her stardom. While Grier was a queen of

raunch, Dobson's characters were classy, ladylike sex symbols. But her giddy heyday in films was brief. By the late 1970s, her starring roles had vanished. She turned up in a supporting part as a good-natured hooker in *Norman? Is That You?* (1976). Not much was heard from her after that until she appeared in the 1983 exploitation film *Chained Heat* (about a woman's prison) and the TV movie "Amazons" (1984). Earlier, Dobson appeared in *Fuzz* (1972).

Katherine Dunham

B. 1919. Dancer, choreographer.

Ebony once wrote that Katherine Dunham's greatest contribution had been her introduction to the world of "authentic African and Caribbean dance forms in concert settings." That may well be her importance in films, too, although her movie work was not extensive and not always firmly under her control.

Dunham's career had first taken off during the Depression when she worked with the WPA. Forming her own dance company, she performed through the years in New York or on tour (in the States and abroad) in her productions *Tropics and Le Jazz Hot* (1940), *Tropical Revue* (1943), *Carib Song* (1945), *Bal Negre* (1946), *New Tropical Revue* (1948), and *Bamboche* (1962). In the 1940s and 1950s, she appeared in (mostly musical sequences) or choreographed such films as *Pardon My Sarong* (1942), *Carnival of Rhythm* (1942), *Stormy Weather* (1943), *Casbah* (1948), *Mambo* (1955), and *Green Mansions* (1959). One of Dunham's best Hollywood dance sequences—and the one most frequently ignored—was her sexy jitterbug number with, of all people, Eddie "Rochester" Anderson in

Star Spangled Rhythm (1942). Here in a highly stylized form, black American popular dance had finally made it to the movies. As with Lena Horne and Hazel Scott, Dunham's sequences were sometimes cut when her movies were shown in the South; it was thought white audiences might be upset at seeing a black woman (not playing a maid) in a "white" film.

By the late 1960s, Dunham left show business, establishing her own museum and dance school in East St. Louis. In 1983, she was among five distinguished American artists honored at a White House reception by President and Mrs. Ronald Reagan. She is the author of *Journey to Accompong* (1946), *A Touch of Innocence* (1959), and *Dances of Haiti* (1949).

James Edwards

B. c. 1918; D. 1970. Actor.

Not well remembered today, James Edwards came to prominence at a time—right after the Second World War—when both Hollywood and black America were in desperate need of him. In this period of transition for American films, the old comic black servants were about to give way to dramatically troubled black movie heroes and heroines. For many Edwards came to personify the restless, anxious black man who cannot shut his eyes to American racism. In some respects, his career itself, with its crazed ups and downs and its disappointments and frustrations, reflected not only a basic change in the outlook of American society but a resistance to and an uneasiness with that change as well. With Edwards we have a portrait of a man who, for one very brief moment, was the right actor at the right time in the right place, only later to discover himself an outsider, a discard, in a film industry not quite as ready for him as everyone had thought.

Having grown up in Muncie, Indiana, Edwards, athletic and bright, had graduated from Knoxville College in Tennessee where he had majored in psychology. Years later he said he'd become interested in acting after he had been injured in a car accident while serving in the army (during World War II). His face badly scarred and having to undergo plastic surgery, he was confined to a hospital bed for months. During the rehabilitation period, his doctors—concerned that he had become withdrawn and hoping to help him boost his confidence and resocialize himself—suggested he take courses in public speaking at nearby Northwestern University. There Edwards studied drama and participated in student productions. Later in Chicago, he appeared with the Skyloft Players.

Longing to make his mark on the New York stage, he managed in the mid-1940s to get an audition for the Broadway-bound play *Deep Are the Roots*. In an interview in *Negro Digest* in 1949, Edwards said he'd arrived in New York from Chicago (thanks to a collection taken up by members of a singing group of which he was then a part) for his audition, hoping to look his best. Wearing a purple zoot suit, a yellow coat, a yellow feather in his hat, a long watch-chain dangling from his pants pocket, and a flashy necktie, he waltzed into the audition room where the director Elia Kazan quietly looked him over, then said little other than to request that before he read for the part he first remove the yellow coat. "But even that didn't do any good," Edwards said.

Although he lost the part, he did win a position as an understudy in *Deep Are the Roots*. Later he assumed the role of the war hero, and toured

James Edwards: a career of early promise and later great professional frustrations and disappointments.

in the play, winding up on the West Coast. There he decided to pursue film work. In 1949 he appeared as the young prizefighter in *The Set Up*. Seeing him today in this film, he remains a startling, almost thoroughly modern figure.

Afterward, working in another play on the West Coast, Edwards was visited in his dressing room on the closing night by a young producer who asked him to stop by his office the next Monday morning. Not taking the appointment too seriously, Edwards arrived at the office two hours late.

The young man—fledgling producer Stanley Kramer—told Edwards of a new film he planned to do if he could find the right actor for the lead. The film was *Home of the Brave* (1949). Edwards won the leading role of the soldier Moss, who, a victim of racial bigotry during the War, suffers an emotional breakdown, then has to undergo psychiatric treatment to recover his equilibrium. In this first postwar film to focus on American racism, Edwards was a new presence: handsome, brooding, bruised, governed by a code of fundamental decency and courage. He was the precursor for the kind of hero Sidney Poitier would popularize in the 1950s. Highly praised for his performance, he emerged as a hero within the black community (he was well liked and well covered by the black press), which saw him, much as it was later to view Dorothy Dandridge, as a beacon of hope for full integration in Hollywood dramatic films.

But Edwards's early promise was not fulfilled. Following *Home of the Brave* he did not appear in another film until two years later in the Korean Conflict drama *The Steel Helmet* (1951). Here and in such other movies as *Bright Victory* (1951), *Battle Hymn* (1957), *Men in War* (1957), *Pork Chop Hill* (1959), *The Manchurian Candidate* (1962), he was cast as a military man, off in combat. Because of his looks and his personal intensity, he was an actor born for leading roles and for movie romance. But romantic black leading men were then taboo. American films still shied away from explorations of black male/female relationships. Consequently, by removing Edwards from the everyday world and from the black community—by keeping him in war movies—his pictures evaded the problem of casting him opposite leading ladies.

Edwards's offscreen outspokenness may have caused him problems within the movie industry. In 1951 newspapers carried an item in which Edwards had announced that three FBI agents had approached him about testifying before The House Un-American Activities Commitee against actor Paul Robeson. Edwards said he had flatly refused. Sidney Poitier, in his autobiography, also said he had been asked to publicly denounce both Robeson and black actor Canada Lee. He, too, had refused. But Edwards's refusal became part of the public record of the 1950s. And it no doubt influenced the way the movie executives viewed him. Fifties America was not a good time for *political* entertainers. In 1953, in an article in the black publication *Our World*, Edwards spoke of the rumors which labeled him a heavy drinker, a womanizer, and an arrogant and difficult man to work with. He was aware of the industry backlash against him.

As the Eisenhower Era moved on, Edwards's career slipped into a decline. By 1958, he was a supporting player in *Anna Lucasta* (the male lead went to Sammy Davis, Jr.), also in the 1959 low-budget *Night of the Quarter Moon* (in which his brief appearance gave this transparent exploitation film a gleam of reality), and then as one of Elizabeth Taylor's bohemian friends in *The Sandpiper* (1965). Seeing Edwards in this later film, in which he looked thin, strained, lifeless, is not a very pleasant experience; the same is true of his last movie appearance, a bit role in the George C. Scott film *Patton* (1970). Ironically, in his final film, he was again cast as a military man, removed from the black community.

Edwards's very early work, though, still has the spark and glow of a new kind of black actor ready to announce himself to the world. He sums up the postwar optimism, fears, and concerns of the black community, then anxious to leave aside its days of "patience" as it launched itself into the civil rights movement.

Edwards's movie credits include: *The Member of the Wedding* (1952); *The Joe Louis Story* (1953); *Innocents in Paris* (1955); *Seven Angry Men* (1955); *Phenix City Story* (1955); *The Killing* (1956); *African Manhunt* (1957); *Alligator Named Daisy* (1957); *Fraulein* (1958); *Tarzan's Fight for Life* (1958); *3 Men in a Boat* (1959); and *Nearly a Nasty Account* (1962).

His TV credits include: "Cavalcade Theatre" (1955); "20th Century Fox Hour" (1956); "Meet McGraw" (1957); "Climax" (1958); "Desilu Playhouse" (1958); "Peter Gunn" (1960); "Lloyd Bridges Show" (1962); "Fugitive" (the 1963 episode "Decision in the Ring"); "East Side/West Side" (the 1963 episode "Where's Harry?"); "Eleventh Hour" (1964); "The Nurses" (1964); "The Outsider" (1968); "The Virginian" (1968); *The Outcasts* (1968); and "Mannix" (1969).

Stepin Fetchit

B. c. 1902; D. 1985. Actor.

For decades after his Hollywood heyday, comedian Stepin Fetchit remained the most controversial black actor to have worked in American motion pictures. Because he was indeed the first black to open doors within the film capital (as he was quick to inform the press in the sad later years), he was also the most burdened. He came to stardom in an age in which almost no one thought twice about stereotypes. Today the fact that he personified the lazy, dimwitted Negro servant (a walking windup toy for the amusement of whites) is well known. The fact that he was also immensely talented has been forgotten.

The son of a cigarmaker, Fetchit was born Lincoln Theodore Monroe Andrew Perry in Key West, Florida, around 1902 (some historians date his birth as early as 1892). He left home by 1914 to pursue a show business career, joining the Royal American Shows plantation revues. Years later he said he took his stage name from a Baltimore racehorse that had inspired him to write a routine for himself and his stage partner of the time, Ed Lee. They billed themselve as "Step 'n' Fetchit: Two Dancing Fools from Dixie." After splitting with his partner, Fetchit kept the name for himself as he spent long, arduous years on the vaudeville circuit.

By 1927, having arrived in Hollywood, he had an almost immediate impact. In a review of his film *In Old Kentucky* (1927), *Variety* noted, "Much mush stuff, but the MGM finish, and a colored comedian hold up the picture. He's just a lazy, no good roustabout, wheedling money out of colored help but he's no mean pantomimist." Later *Variety* singled him out again for his work in the 1929 *Salute*, "Picture has good comic values, through the presence of the priceless Stepin Fetchit, most amusing of Negro character clowns." For a black supporting performer in films, this kind of attention was unprecedented. But the picture that proved his breakthrough was *Hearts in Dixie* (1929), the early all-black talkie. As Gummy, a lazy clod, Fetchit, working with other black actors, frequently strikes even contemporary black audiences as clever, inventive, and very funny. Of Fetchit's performance, Robert Benchley wrote:

> Of course, entirely outside the main story (what there is of it) is the amazing personality of Stepin Fetchit. I see no reason for even hesitating in saying that he is the best actor that the talking movies have produced. His voice, his manner, his timing, everything that he does, is as near to perfection as one could hope to get. . . . When Stepin Fetchit speaks, you are there beside him, one of the great comedians of the screen.

Operating at his own rhythm and perhaps more sexually suggestive here than in any other film, Fetchit was merely one figure in all-black landscape.

But, of course, that was not the case in most of the films that followed during the Depression years, when Fetchit, now fully emerging as American cinema's first colored movie star, provided comic relief—in a now shocking manner—in such films as *Swing High* (1930), *The Big Fight* (1930), *The Prodigal* (1931), *Carolina* (1934), *Stand Up and Cheer* (1934, with Shirley Temple), *Helldorado* (1935), *One More Spring* (1935), and *Zenobia* (1939). The roles are almost always the same. So, too, is Fetchit. Tall, lanky, gawky, bald, he can barely talk, so it seems. Given this order or that, he slowly goes about his chores, scratching his head or mumbling. Curiously enough, he seems withdrawn from the action, often slipping into a self-protective shell that isolates him from the fierce cruelty of the system around him. While audiences have viewed Fetchit simply as a colored dolt too dumb to speak up for himself or to

Lanky, bald, shifty, and whiney, Stepin Fetchit emerged as Hollywood's first black star and remains the most controversial black performer ever to work in American films.

understand (and rebel against) his plight of servitude, the Fetchit character seems instead to have an intuitive grasp of the means of survival amid the restrictive social codes of his culture. Whenever possible, he seems to psychologically retreat, thus denying the culture's existence—and his own pain. What also cannot be overlooked about Fetchit is his legendary sense of timing: he never permits any other actor (or director) to rush him through a sequence. He's also such a strong visual presence that one cannot watch any other actor when he's on screen.

For a spell, Fetchit was a favorite of director John Ford who used him in five films: *Salute* (1929); *The World Moves On* (1934); *The Sun Shines Bright* (1954); *Steamboat Round the Bend* (1935); and *Judge Priest* (1934). In the latter two, he was teamed with Will Rogers (with whom he also appeared in the 1934 *David Harum* and the 1935 *County Chairman*). One always spots the clear rapport between the two. Interestingly, in *Judge Priest*, it's ironic that this colored no-account is the most congenial companion for the town's most honorable man, the white Judge Priest (played by Rogers). The subtext reads that both men stand outside the scheme of things and are therefore buddies. Rogers, in a sense the perpetual American adolescent, is most relaxed when with his trusty colored comrade, Fetchit, who represents freedom from the constraints of polite society. (Of course, it's a bit like Nigger Jim and Huck on the raft.)

In so many of his other films though, such as *Charlie Chan in Egypt* (1935), Fetchit stumbles about, stammers, and is so much the fool that it becomes painful for some black audiences to watch him. Fetchit's work in this *Chan* movie is a far cry from the *Chan* films with Mantan Moreland, who takes his work less seriously and consequently causes the audience to be less disturbed by some of his antics.

Fetchit also had highly publicized exploits offscreen. In this respect, he broke new ground: he was the first black screen actor to have a legend, a life away from films that was known to the public. Newspaper headlines of the 1930s kept readers abreast of Fetchit's car accidents, his alleged fights and brawls, his brushes with the law, his spending sprees. Reported to have made millions, he lost it all and filed for bankruptcy. His studio, Fox Pictures, at first undisturbed by his publicity (it could not hurt his pictures), later grew weary of his highjinks. By 1934, Fox had already informed him to clean up his act. Under the headline "Stepin Fetchit Resumes Screen Career with Fox," *The New York Post* reported:

> Stepin Fetchit has grown up. The Negro comedian, recently brought back to Fox Films, has played roles in three recent pictures without making a single miscue. . . . Fetchit hit the peak of his career four years ago when he "went Hollywood," owning three automobiles, employing as many liveried chauffeurs with epaulets topping off a sandy uniform, boasting fifty suits of clothes, living in the finest home in the "colored" colony and entertaining like a prince. Prosperity went to his head and it interfered with his work. Beside this, he insisted on directing any scene in which he played. Soon he found himself on the outside looking in, and now, after four years of repentence and reflection, he is back in the fold and watching his step. He drives his own flivver, lives in a modest room, is saving his money, or, rather, the studio is saving it for him.

Frequently, the press delighted in depicting him as Peck's Bad Boy. His exploits, much like those of white stars, no doubt enhanced his rather dubious allure. Ironically, though, reading some of the past newspaper accounts today, particularly those in which he's accused of physically striking this person or that, Fetchit comes across as a star asserting himself, his star prerogatives, his star ego. He was something of an intractable Crazy Nigger, as ready to flip out on people as Richard Pryor appeared to be in the 1970s.

Criticized by civil rights groups and perhaps undone by his own recklessness, Fetchit's star-trip came to an end by the late 1930s. Afterward he drifted into obscurity, working sporadically in the independent all-black *Miracle in Harlem* (1949), later in *Bend of the River* (1952), and in the mid-70s in *Amazing Grace* (1974) and *Won Ton Ton The Wonder Dog Who Saved Hollywood* (1976), none of which did him any justice, all of which simply showed a man who appeared drained of his creative resources.

In the late 1960s, Fetchit also resurfaced in the public eye as a member of the entourage of Muhammad Ali and also as the litigant in a lawsuit against CBS for what he felt was a negative portrayal of himself in the TV documentary "Black History: Lost, Stolen, or Strayed" (1968). Sadly, in the later years, he seemed like the prototype of the star whose day had passed him by, a man on the defensive, aware of his own talents but not of what Hollywood's system had done with them.

Fetchit's screen credits include: *The Ghost Talks* (1929); *Thru Different Eyes* (1929); *Show Boat* (1929); *William Fox Movietone Follies of 1929*; *Big Time* (1929); *Cameo Kirby* (1930); *Marie Galante* (1934); *36 Hours to Live* (1934); *Dimples* (1936); *On the Avenue* (1937); *Love Is News* (1937); and *Fifty Roads to Town* (1937).

Redd Foxx

B. 1922. Actor, comedian.

Before TV stardom beckoned in the early 1970s, comedian Redd Foxx (born John Sanford in St. Louis) had been in show business for 37 years, playing nightclubs and theatres around the country, at one point, from 1951 to 1955, teaming in an act with Slappy White, and also spinning out some 54 "party records" (comedy albums with plenty of four-letter words and much blue humor, which were known primarily in the black community). Emerging as the dean of blue comedy in an era before Pryor and Murphy launched their attacks on social taboos on race and sex, Foxx became a master of wicked standup satires on sex and other topics. Even when young, he was often a bit of a dirty old man, using the vulgar and the profane to shatter middle-class pretenses. The old-guard black bourgeoisie was never a part of his constituency although its children were. During the political flux of the 1960s, Foxx, much like Moms Mabley, gradually acquired a new audience, much of which was a young black college-educated crowd anxious for pure "ethnic humor" removed from the taint of the white cultural establishment. Ironically, once this new following had latched onto him, Foxx himself would soon be courted by the mainstream entertainment industry. In the mid-1960s, he came aboveground for appearances on television's "Here's Lucy" (1965), "Mister Ed" (1965), and "Green Acres" (1966), later in the 1970s on "The Flip Wilson Show." Then he won a juicy role in Ossie Davis's unexpected hit movie *Cotton*

The young Redd Foxx: after years of raunchy nightclub appearances and a series of funky comedy albums, he turned top TV star in the 1970s.

Comes to Harlem (1970). Two years later Foxx turned up weekly in the most unlikely of places—some 37 million American homes—as the star of the TV series "Sanford and Son" (1972–77).

Here the seasoned veteran portrayed a crafty junkdealer who didn't seem to want to do much of anything. Talk about triflin! Foxx himself once told a *New York Times* reporter: "No one expected me to be on television because I had a reputation from the party records as X-rated. That's the humor I heard in the ghettoes. They didn't pull no punches, and they didn't want to hear about Little Boy Blue and Cinderella. So I gave them what they wanted. I busted loose." On television, he was restrained, in terms of language and situation, but he kept his raunchy, skeptical point of view. Foxx's critics, however, complained that his character was part of the 1970s new minstrelsy: the standard stereotyped good-for-nothing black roustabout. True he sometimes did a slow quasi-shuffle. But because he had been around so long, he was an expert of timing and knew how to *work* a line. He was a tough old coot suspicious of all institutions and concerned most with his own amusement and welfare. Much of his appeal was based on the fact that his Fred Sanford was rarely bothered by anything. In a state of grace, he seemed inherently above it all.

Although "Sanford and Son" was a hit (with Foxx reportedly earning $25,000 an episode), Foxx never seems to have been at ease with the series or Hollywood, which he once said had a racial prejudice as "strong as the stench of a skunk's armpit." By 1974, the "Sanford and Son" set had become a hotbed of dissension as Foxx publicly let it be known he wanted more script control and better working conditions.

Refusing to even speak to the series producer Bud Yorkin, Foxx threatened to "go back to Chicago and become a clothing salesman." He stayed with the series until 1977, then left to star in a variety show, "The Redd Foxx Comedy Hour" (1977–1978), at another network. In 1980 he returned to the Sanford character in a revamping of the show, now called "Sanford" (1980–1981). It failed. But Foxx continued working in Las Vegas and returned to television again in 1986 with the sitcom "The Redd Foxx Show."

His TV credits include: "The Addams Family" (1965); "Green Acres" (1966); "A Time for Laughter" (1967); "Soul Salute to Redd Foxx" (1974); "Grady" (1975); "The Captain and Tenille Show" (1976); "Diff'rent Strokes" (1979); and the 1987 TV movie "Ghost of a Chance."

Al Freeman, Jr.

B. 1934. Actor.

In his best roles such as Clay in the movie *Dutchman* (1966) and as Charley in the TV movie "My Sweet Charley" (1970), Al Freeman, Jr., portrayed, with telling detail, earnest young men who had mastered the art of understanding themselves and the culture around them. Self-knowledge, self-discipline, and emotional control (until the moment when he feels compelled to explode with rage) were the hallmarks of Freeman's screen persona. Few actors have been able to project the kind of high intelligence Freeman so effortlessly exuded. Few, too, have had his edgy vitality. So why then did he not become in films a figure like Poitier or later like Howard Rollins, Jr. in *Ragtime*?

Perhaps some audiences felt uneasy with Freeman's cunning cool or his sense of detachment—or the rather resigned melancholic streak that ran through some of his best work. Whatever the reasons, Freeman's TV work of the 1960s on such shows as "The Defenders" (1965), "Slattery's People" (1965), or "The FBI" (1968) as well as his appearances in such films as *Black Like Me* (1964) and *The Lost Man* (1969) retains much of its original appeal. In the midst of so much studio artificiality, there is the excitement of seeing a new kind of black actor on screen, one who pares his work down to bare essentials, who refuses to give star performances, and who often looks as if he's going to bore us until an almost magical moment when he flips himself about to emerge as both moving and invigorating. Like some of Cicely Tyson's TV work of the 1960s, Freeman's performances well capture the mood and perspective of the 1960s activists and students: he's bright, committed, straightforward (although, as with Tyson, there is a part of himself always held back), a tad idealistic, but also almost sadly realistic.

In some of his later work of the mid and late 1970s, such as the character of Lt. Ed Hall on the daytime soap "One Life to Live" (his appearances began in 1968), he sometimes seemed so unchallenged (how could he be otherwise with such parts as these?) that he looked as if he were sleepwalking through the performances. But his cool intensity remained undiminished.

Film credits include: *The Rebel Breed* (1960); *Ensign Pulver* (1964); *Troublemaker* (1964); *The Detective* (1968); *Finian's Rainbow* (1968); *Castle Keep* (1969); *A Fable* (1971, which he directed and acted in, based on Amiri Baraka's *Slave*); and *Countdown at Kusini* (1976, which he co-wrote but did not appear in).

Al Freeman, Jr. (top) in the New York stage production The Living Premise *with Diana Sands, Calvin Ander, Jo Ann le Compte, and Godfrey Cambridge.*

TV credits include: "Mr. Novak" (1965); "Judd for the Defense" (1969); "Mod Squad" (1972); "To Be Young, Gifted, and Black" (NET Playhouse, 1972); "Maude" (1976); "Kojak" (1976); and "Hot L Baltimore" (a 1975 series in which he played Bingham).

Minnie Gentry

Actress.

Offbeat and idiosyncratic actress (born Minnie Lee Watson), whose highly controlled and rather mannered performances have been blessed with a mad spark that makes Gentry one of the most perversely enjoyable and interesting character actresses around. An alumna of Cleveland's Karamu Playhouse, Gentry has a long list of theater credits including: *The Blacks* (1961); *Black Quartet* (1969); *Black Girl* (1971); *Who's Got His Own* (1970, at Baltimore's Center Stage); Melvin Van Peebles' *Ain't Supposed To Die a Natural Death* (1971); and *Sunshine Boys* (1972). Coming to television and films later in her career, she turned up in commercials for Shell Oil and Frito Lay's Potato Chips and also on dramatic specials: "Salty" (1974); Van Peebles' "Just an Old Sweet Song" (1976); and "The Hollow Image" (1979). Her film credits include: *Georgia, Georgia* (1972); *Come Back Charleston Blue* (1972); *Black Caesar* (1973); *Claudine* (1974); and *The Brother from Another Planet* (1984).

Often as one watches Gentry in *Georgia, Georgia* or *The Hollow Image*, the actress seems to be stretching and meticulously enunciating her every line as if wringing each word for some elemental truth. She may not always succeed. But like Beah Richards, she consistently engages our attention. Gentry also brings to her work a clear character actress persona (indeed, it's a star persona although no one's ever seemed to note that): she always strikes us as a fundamentally proper woman living by high personal standards—of dress, demeanor, use of language. Yet she often comes across as streetwise. She's a strange, crazed personality who stands apart from the productions she's in.

Marla Gibbs

Actress.

The erstwhile Florence of "The Jeffersons" (1975–1985), Marla Gibbs has remained one of television's underrated comediennes. Her brash, quick-witted delivery as well as her confident above-it-all-I-couldn't-care-less attitude transformed Florence into the classic clever, forceful servant, sure to outmaneuver the boss. Her relationship with George Jefferson might be compared with that of Rochester with Jack Benny, except that while Rochester had to be slyly manipulative (because of racial codes), much of the pleasure of watching Gibbs was that she kept her attitudes, values, opinions right upfront, brazenly on display for all to see but for none to dare question.

The fact that Gibbs ever got to work in television at all still seems surprising. She had been born Margaret Bradley in Chicago; her father was an auto mechanic, her mother a radio evangelist. Once she had married Jordan Gibbs, a postal worker, she had worked in 1963 as a reservations clerk for an airline company, transferring from the company's Chicago office to Los Angeles in 1969. Something of a late bloomer, she divorced her husband in 1973 and studied acting, mainly as a hobby. During the first season of "The Jeffersons," she made a few appearances. Later she signed on as a regular, staying with the series for 11 seasons.

Very briefly, she starred in her own short-lived series "Checking In" (1981). In 1985 she had more success with the series "227," in which she starred and also had casting approvals and some say in the scripts. Although the series failed to fully utilize her verbal skills or her highly extroverted, gregarious personality, Gibbs had an immense rapport with her audience, a woman respected for her comedic skills and also warmly appreciated because of an essential ingredient of her screen persona: she seemed graced with an inordinant dose of commonsense. Always able to see through sham or pretense, Gibbs's characters rarely hesitated to speak up. And they relished the give and take of verbal interplay.

Among her film credits: *Black Belt Jones* (1974) and *Sweet Jesus, Preacher Man* (1973).

Among her TV credits: "The Moneychangers" (1976); "Tell Me Where It Hurts"; and "You Can't Take It with You."

Whoopi Goldberg

B. c. 1950. Actress, comedienne.

Born Caryn Johnson, Whoopi Goldberg grew up in a New York City project, started acting at age eight in a children's theater group, and later in the 1970s played small roles in the Broadway shows *Pippin*, *Hair*, and *Jesus Christ Superstar*. In the mid-1970s, she moved to California where she appeared with The San Diego Repertory Company (eventually playing the lead in *Mother Courage*). After a failed marriage and a bad bout with drugs, she was, for a time, a welfare mother without a very promising future. But Goldberg held herself together, made her mark in improvisational theater in Berkeley, and mounted a production called *The Spook Show* (1984) that evolved, under Mike Nichols's adroit direction in late 1984, into the critically praised, one-woman Broadway show *Whoopi Goldberg*.

Here she introduced a large new audience to a cluster of characters: a talkative dippy Valley Girl; a young black girl who yearns to be white; a bummed-out former vaudevillian; a crippled young woman; a Jamaican immigrant; and a jivey, black male junkie. "Each of these characters," *Variety* wrote, "is deftly limned by the actress with precise characterization, and the cumulative effect elicits admiration for Goldberg's versatility, even virtuosity." *New York Times* critic Frank Rich, however, felt differently. "What is in question is whether she yet has the range of material and talent to sustain a night of theatre," he wrote, adding that "her moments of pathos are often too mechanically ironic and maudlin to provoke. . . . Whoopi Goldberg's liberating spirit fills up the theatre, even as her considerable comic promise is left waiting to be fully unlocked." Rich had touched on what some saw as Goldberg's real flaw: too often her routines seemed like watered-down Pryor and Murphy; so, too, did her comic persona. Regardless, Goldberg had significantly invaded a male-dominated domain: she was the first black woman since Moms Mabley to succeed as a standup comic. After her Broadway success, her show was filmed as an HBO television special called "Whoopi Goldberg Direct from Broadway" (1985).

During this period, Goldberg's great success came with her appearance as Celie in *The Color Purple* for which she was nominated for an Academy Award as Best Actress of 1985. Well-covered by the press and

Whoopi Goldberg: from performances in small theaters and clubs to full-fledged movie stardom in the 1980s.

outspoken about the controversy surrounding her film, Goldberg emerged not only as star but as instant celebrity, too, turning up on the covers of such diverse publications as *Ms., American Film, Us, People,* and *Rolling Stone.* It might not mean much to some, but the point must be made that she arrived as one of the few dark black female performers (Cicely Tyson is another such example) to receive such "glamorous" press attention. The public, however, might well have viewed her more as an oddity than an important dramatic actress. Goldberg also experienced a certain public/press backlash. In fact, within a year after her *Color Purple* triumph, *Rolling Stone* reported, "It's a perfectly familiar irony of the times that the press that tried so hard to make Whoopi Goldberg a star now complains that she acts like one."

Still Goldberg plowed ahead. She appeared in a guest spot in 1986 on the popular TV series "Moonlighting" (cast distressingly as a con artist, no less, named Camille), in the 1986 HBO special "Comic Relief" (a benefit performed with Robin Williams, Billy Crystal, and others to raise money for America's homeless), and in the leading roles in the movies *Jumpin' Jack Flash* (1986), and *Burglar* (1987). With some of her later films, she encountered problems. She argued with director Rip Torn over the way her feature *Telephone* (1987) was edited. In September 1987 the *New York Daily News* reported: "A sizzling love scene between Whoopi Goldberg and Sam Elliot in *Fatal Beauty* has been left on the cutting room floor after preview audiences out West turned thumbs down on the two-minute romp between the sheets." As was the case with *Jumpin' Jack Flash,* studio executives still believed American audiences did not want to see Goldberg romantically paired with a white actor.

Louis Gossett, Jr.

B. 1936. Actor.

By the time he won an Oscar as Best Supporting Actor of 1982 for his performance in *An Officer and a Gentleman,* Louis Gossett, Jr.'s 28-year haul in show business had been flush with peaks and valleys, cycles and phases, periods of drift and regeneration. A graduate of New York University, he had acted in theater, had studied with Lloyd Richards and Frank Silvera, and in the 1950s emerged as a dedicated actor who worked diligently at his craft, honing, refining, and perfecting it. He appeared in such stage productions as *Take a Giant Step* (1956), *Lost in the Stars* (1957), *The Blacks* (1961), *Carry Me Back to Morningside Heights* (1968), and *A Raisin in the Sun* (in both the 1959 stage and 1961 film versions, he played the unbearably proper college student in pursuit of Diana Sands). In 1960s television he worked with authority and discretion within very restricted roles on numerous series: "The Nurses" (1962); "The Defenders" (1964); "Mod Squad" (1968); "Daktari" (1968); "The Bill Cosby Show" (1970); and "The Young Rebels" (1970–1972, in which he was a regular, playing Izak Poole).

What looked like a turning point was his startling performance in *The Landlord* in 1970. As the militant hero breaking down, he had the kind of role his career had been leading up to, and it should have been a springboard for the type of stardom he deserved.

Not much came out of *The Landlord,* though, for this was the early 1970s, that period of the blaxploitation films, and Lou Gossett was out of place, too precise, too thought out, too much an artist for an era that

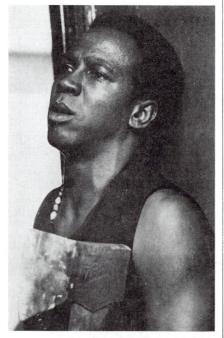

Louis Gossett, Jr., in one of his best roles, as the axe-wielding husband in The Landlord.

wanted simple macho flash and dash, cartoon versions of black manhood. And so while the Jim Browns and Fred Williamsons had one starring role after another, Gossett appeared now and then in such movies as *The Skin Game* (1971), *Travels with My Aunt* (1972), *White Dawn* (1974), and *The Laughing Policeman* (1974). He continued working in episodic television, in everything from "The Rookies" (1972); "Owen Marshall" (1973); "Good Times" (1974), to "Lucas Tanner" (1975) to "The Jeffersons" (1975) to "The Six Million Dollar Man" (1975) and "The Rookies" (1972). Yes, he was employed. But artistically, this was a long, dry period.

Then almost seven years after *The Landlord*, Gossett finally landed another plum role in the miniseries "Roots" (1977).

Cast as Fiddler, a slave who tries teaching the young African Kunta Kinte the ins and outs of life on a southern plantation, Gossett performed a number of amazing feats. Foremost, he showcased something we'd all known but never seen so tellingly drawn on television (or in films, for that matter): he revealed a man with a great innate sense of his own worth who realizes, that in order to survive in this particular social/political environment, he must often play a role at odds with his true nature. Gossett's shrewd Fiddler—the perceptive observer—grins, bows, scrapes, cajoles, flatters, toms, does the whole works whenever around whites. Away from them, he's another man altogether, who sees their petty, cruel games and is not often fooled by them. He has a quiet strong control of himself.

In this role Gossett created a complex hero, a man who was in one manner as much a loner as Kunta Kinte yet a man who still enjoyed the company of other people in a way Kunta never does. Moreover, for black America, Gossett's voice (the intonations and inflections), his body stance (loose, limber), his movements (expressive), and the internal rhythm of the man himself were all things seen in the black community for years. Gossett did not cover up his ethnic roots with Hollywood gloss or excessive attitudinizing. Often a black actor who desires to show he is indeed black, turns an ethnic character into a street figure, as if street affectations represented the only authentic type of black behavior. A skilled actor like Dick Anthony Williams has a tendency to perform in such a way. Or sometimes a black actor will get as far away from the ethnic as possible as Poitier did in *Guess Who's Coming to Dinner* (1967).

Gossett, however (like Poitier in the 1958 *The Defiant Ones* and Paul Winfield in almost everything he's done), struck the perfect balance. He used the character Fiddler to unleash something within himself that he had observed about black males. Certain black men, whether day laborers or porters or engineers, were able in all situations to stride through life with a gallant air and the gift of humor and an uncanny savoir-faire that always inspired our confidence in them. They were heroes partly because they could not be touched. This was precisely the kind of figure Gossett created with Fiddler. He came to full maturity as an actor with this role. The performance earned him an Emmy.

Now Gossett seemed firmly established. Yet it was almost like watching the aftermath of *The Landlord* all over again. Gossett did emerge as a Hollywood oddity: a steadily working black actor. Yet instead of going from one dazzling performance to another, he was saddled with roles that did not match his talents and sometimes he seemed adrift, trying to elevate one shallow part after another. In something like "Backstairs at the White House" (1979), he had a supporting role that he played splendidly. But he wasn't required to do much that was new. That was also the case in *The Deep* (1977), an island drama in which he, like the other black characters, was turned into the familiar dark, forbidding exotic villain. Gossett also got what was considered a big career break when he starred in the 1979 TV series "The Lazarus Syndrome." But the series did not last a full season.

The Lou Gossett story added a new chapter when he learned of a role, that of tough Sgt. Foley, in *An Officer and a Gentleman*. Gossett worked hard just to get a chance to audition for *An Officer and a Gentleman*. Once he had won the part, he walked away with the picture. Aside from his Oscar, Gossett also won a Golden Globe Award and The NAACP Image Award for his performance.

This was not the end of the Gossett story either. Afterward he went from fair-to-decent-to-dreadful roles: on television in "Benny's Place" (1982); "Sadat" (1983); and "The Guardian" (1984); in films in *Jaws 3-D* (1983, the worst!); *Finders Keepers* (1984); and "The Principal" (1987). Surprisingly, Gossett turned up in three starring roles in big-budgeted movies: *Iron Eagle* (a 1986 right-wing fantasy in which he did a reprise of his Sgt. Foley role); *Enemy Mine* (1985); and *Firewalker* (1986) with Chuck Norris. Through it all though Gossett performed with grace and precision.

His TV credits include: "Bonanza" (1971); "Longstreet" (1971); "Love American Style" (1972); "Sidekicks" (1974); "Harry O" (1975); "McCloud" (1974); "Petrocelli" (1974); "It's Good to Be Alive" (1974); "Caribe" (1975); "Police Story" (1975); "The Rockford Files" (1976); "Little House on the Prairie" (1976); and "This Man Stands Alone" (1979).

Pam Grier

B. c. 1950. Actress.

It's doubtful if anyone could have predicted that Pam Grier would emerge in the 1970s as a sex symbol and the queen of B-movies. The daughter of a military man, she grew up on European air force bases until her family finally settled in Denver. At a young age, Grier left Colorado for Hollywood (where she stayed for a time at the home of her cousin football-player-turned-actor Roosevelt Grier). She worked as a switchboard operator at American International Pictures and gradually won supporting roles in low-budget action and exploitation films. Finally, she starred in her own movies, almost all of which were rowdy, gaudy cheapos that made big money at the box office. In such films as *The Big Bird Cage* (1972), *Black Mama, White Mama* (1973), *Coffy* (1973), and *Foxy Brown* (1974), Grier was cast as a sexy, foul-mouthed, gun-totin' woman of action, who, if necessary, could bomb, burn, beat, shoot, or even castrate her way through any trying situation.

At the height of the blaxploitation era, Grier discovered herself enjoying a lopsided type of stardom. Unlike a Diana Ross or a Cicely Tyson, she was not a "respectable" dramatic star. But audiences (mostly black) knew her and paid to see her. Anxious to promote herself as a sexy commodity, she posed nude in the black magazine *Players* and disrobed in her films, almost at the drop of a guy's zipper. A large percentage of her constituency was a group of horny college boys who drooled over her pinups. Other groups, however, came to view her image as being socially significant. When *Ms.* ran Grier's picture on its cover, some white feminists saw her as a liberated movie heroine. In

Grier's action films, men were always the enemy, upholders of a tight, corrupt system in which women were abused or exploited. When *New York* ran her on its cover, she was hailed as one of the few new sex goddesses of the 1970s. Underneath the attention though, Grier must have realized her characters were often cartoonish. Rarely was she permitted a warm, mature relationship with a man in her films. Moreover because the films never placed her in a realistic, everyday type of situation, black women found it hard to identify with her, especially with her physical feats of power and daring—and also with the way in which the films exploited Grier's body.

Pam Grier tried cleaning up her image in the film *Greased Lightning* (1977) and her somewhat slicker star vehicles *Friday Foster* (1975) and *Sheba Baby* (1975). But unfortunately Pam Grier without raunch and an overt sexuality was not the Pam Grier her fans wanted. Once black action films stopped making money, Hollywood looked as if it had abandoned Grier. She had to struggle to get bit parts in productions like "Roots: The Next Generations" (1979). But Grier did a surprising turnaround in the 80s, giving a strong performance in *Fort Apache: The Bronx* (1981). She also appeared in, of all things, the Disney film *Something Wicked This Way Comes* (1983). And she proved a striking, more realistically defined actress in even a bland film like *Stand Alone* (1986) and also in episodes of the TV series "Miami Vice" (1985), "Crime Story" (1986), and "The Cosby Show" (1987). There was indeed more to Pam Grier than had originally met many a male's eyes.

Today although her 1970s films are seldom shown, they remain an interesting point in black movie history. Grier's directors and scriptwriters may have done her a great disservice, only pointing up even more vividly to us that Hollywood rarely knows what to do with its black female characters. But Grier herself has such energy and drive and such a batty sense of humor that she's a definite and distinct screen personality, who can still be watched and enjoyed.

Grier's film credits also include: *Bucktown* (1975); *Beyond the Valley of the Dolls* (1970); *The Big Doll House* (1971); *Hit Man* (1972); *Cool Breeze* (1972); *Scream, Blacula, Scream* (1973); *The Arena* (1974); *Drum* (1976); and *Tough Dreams* (1981).

Robert Guillaume

B. 1927. Actor.

Robert Guillaume came to television as Benson after years of theater work: he appeared with Cleveland's Karamu Playhouse in 1958, later had roles in *Finian's Rainbow* (1960), *Tambourines to Glory* (1963), *Golden Boy* (1964), *Jacques Brel Is Alive and Well and Living in Paris* (1971), and a string of others. Enduring his share of flops, he had become known in theater circles but, considered a second banana, he missed the big roles. A nice turn came in his career in 1971 when he replaced Cleavon Little as the star of the musical *Purlie*. In 1976, he appeared in the black version of *Guys and Dolls*. A year later, he signed to play a supporting role in a new "controversial" sitcom "Soap" (1977–1979). The character was, of course, Benson, which brought Guillaume national fame.

On stage, Guillaume had, in all truthfulness, been a diligent hard worker, smooth and skilled but without that imaginative spark that can ignite a role, making it and the actor memorable. Television, however, or perhaps time itself (Guillaume was no kid when he got his Benson break) unleashed an exuberant, amusingly untamed quality in him. Part of the pleasure of watching Guillaume as Benson was that he looked as if he were going for broke, unmindful of how his outspokenness or comic arrogance might upset some viewers. In the long run, like Hattie McDaniel and Eddie "Rochester" Anderson, he invested a tired old servant turn with spunk, intelligence, and *attitude*, energetically spinning around and outdistancing his co-stars through his vigor and high style. Two years after "Soap," Guillaume starred in the hit spinoff "Benson."

His other TV credits include: "Marcus Welby, MD" (1974); "All in the Family" (1975); "Sanford and Son" (1975); "The Jeffersons" (1975); "The Kid with the Broken Halo" (1982); "The Kid with the 200 I.Q." (1983), and "The Wonderful World of D.C. Collins" (1984), all of which co-starred Gary Coleman; "Love Boat" (1984); "North and South" (1985); a black version of Dickens's *A Christmas Carol* called "John Grin's Christmas" (1986), which Guillaume directed and starred in; and "Purlie" (1981).

Movie credits include: *Super Fly T.N.T.* (1973); *Seems Like Old Times* (1980); and *Wanted Dead or Alive* (1987).

Sherman Hemsley

B. 1938. Actor.

Sherman Hemsley came to acting late but his career accelerated relatively rapidly. Having worked as a postal employee in his native Philadelphia, he moved to New York in the late 1960s in hopes of finding theatre work. Winning the plum role of Gitlow in the Broadway musical *Purlie* (1970), Hemsley's performance made a lasting impression on television producer Norman Lear. Three years later when casting for an actor to play Archie Bunker's neighbor George Jefferson on "All in the Family," Lear originally signed Avon Long, then felt he was all wrong for the role, and remembering Hemsley, set out to find him. Located in San Francisco where he was performing in *Don't Bother Me, I Can't Cope* (1973), Hemsley was tested and signed for the Jefferson role (which he played from 1973 to 1975), proving so strong a personality that eventually he was starred in the spinoff series "The Jeffersons"

(1975–1985), which for years was a top-rated CBS show. At one point, Hemsley earned $60,000 per episode of the show.

Short, slender, quick-witted, fiendishly aggressive, Hemsley became one of America's best-known (by character, not name) but least publicized performers. Seldom venturing into other roles, his occasional other TV appearances were guest spots on variety programs such as "Joey and Dad" (1975), "Dean's Place" (1975), and "The Rich Little Show" (1976). In 1986, he starred in another popular series "Amen."

Hemsley also appeared in the movie *Love at First Bite* (1979) as well as the cable-TV production of "Purlie" (1981, in which he recreated his Gitlow character).

Juano Hernandez

B. 1896; D. 1970. Actor.

Like James Edwards, Juano Hernandez was one of the first of the post-World War II new-style black screen actors: in films he neither sang nor danced but played strong, dramatic, often fiercely independent characters.

Hernandez had been born in Puerto Rico, had grown up in Rio de Janeiro, and in 1922 had made his first stage appearance in an acrobatic act. Later using the name Kid Curly, he was a professional boxer in the Caribbean. He returned to the stage in a minstrel show, also worked as a circus performer, and then performed in vaudeville. On Broadway, he appeared in *Show Boat* (1927), *Strange Fruit* (1945), and *Set My People Free* (1948).

Hernandez's early film performances were bits in the Oscar Micheaux films *The Girl from Chicago* (1932), *Lying Lips* (1939), and *The Notorious Elinor Lee*. But the movie that won him acclaim was MGM's *Intruder in the Dust* (1949), in which he played Lucas Beauchamp, the proud black man wrongly accused of having killed a white Southerner. Unlike Edwards and the young Poitier, each of whom had a bruised boyishness, Hernandez projected maturity and a toughened wisdom. Mahogany-skinned, granite-jawed, and solidly built, he played characters of towering masculinity and surprising sensitivity. In movies such as *Intruder in the Dust* and *Stars In My Crown* (1950, which cast him as a noble old man surrounded by a lynch mob), Hernandez emerged as the screen's first black separatist hero: his characters are self-sufficient, highly individualized men, not concerned about proving themselves or

Juano Hernandez, as Lucas Beauchamp, the screen's first black separatist hero, in the film version of William Faulkner's Intruder in the Dust.

their worth to anybody. Hernandez also represented the Negro as a metaphor for social injustice. And movies such as *The Breaking Point* (1950) and *Young Man with a Horn* (1950) cast him as wise, experienced men offering friendship and advice to the restless, troubled young heroes, played by John Garfield and Kirk Douglas, respectively.

One of Hernandez's most important roles was in Mark Robson's *Trial* (1955), the story of a Mexican youth accused of murder. The judge who tries the case is a black man. (Hernandez played the part.) The movie itself was something of a mixed bag, sometimes provocative for its time, other times lapsing into melodrama and becoming a dogmatic anticommunist tract for the Cold War age. But Hernandez's work was highly praised. *Variety* wrote:

> Perhaps the most offbeat angle in *Trial* . . . is having the presiding judge a Negro. This role will almost certainly go into the books as the highlight of Juano Hernandez's acting career. In the careful, temperate judicious rulings which he is constantly making, Hernandez proves himself one of the great rhetoricians among current character players. But his performance is deeper yet. It has heart, dignity, and the actor has thought through and felt through the implications to achieve an "integration" (to use actor language) seldom encountered. While the picture has many firstrate performances, . . . this is peculiarly Hernandez's own private *coup de theatre*.

Ironically, following his fine work in *Trial*, Hernandez rarely had important roles. In such movies as *Something of Value* (1957) and *St. Louis Blues* (1958), he was pushed into the background, playing unchallenging characters. Sometimes it was painful to see so fine an actor so misused. (One felt the same way seeing Paul Winfield in his supporting roles in the 1980s.) When he appeared in *The Pawnbroker* (1965), Pauline Kael was one of the few critics to point out the beauty of his work. She wrote: "The great old Juano Hernandez, as the man who wants to talk, gives the single, most moving performance I saw in 1965."

Hernandez continued working until the time of his death. He remains a greatly underrated actor.

Among his film credits: *Ransom* (1956); *Mark of the Hawk* (1958); *Sergeant Rutledge* (1960); *The Sins of Rachel Cade* (1961); *Hemingway's Adventures of a Young Man* (1962); *The Reivers* (1969); *The Extraordinary Seaman* (1969); and *They Call Me MISTER Tibbs* (1970).

Among his TV credits: "The Dispossessed" (1961, as the Indian leader Chief Standing Bear); "Studio 57" (1957); "Studio One" (1957); "Adventures in Paradise" (1961); "Route 66" (1961); "Dick Powell Theater" (1962); "The Defenders" (1962); and "The Naked City" (1963).

Gregory Hines

B. 1946. Actor, dancer.

An entertainer since age four, New York-born Gregory Hines first tap-danced with his older brother Maurice in an act called The Hines Kids. Later the two studied with tap master Henry LeTang, renamed themselves The Hines Brothers in 1962, and by 1964 teamed with their father, Maurice Hines, Sr., in an act called Hines, Hines, and Dad. The trio made splashy appearances on "The Tonight Show" and were the opening act for big-name performers at various important clubs. In

Movie stardom came at last to Gregory Hines (with Mikhail Baryshnikov) in White Nights.

need of some time to himself, Gregory Hines left the trio after a 1973 Las Vegas performance. The next five years were spent in Venice, California, where Hines said he lived as a "hippie," experimenting with drugs and taking time to discover what life away from show business was like.

His career might have stopped right there. But in 1978, Hines returned to New York. With the help of his brother, he auditioned for new shows and landed plum parts in three musicals: *Eubie* (1979), *Comin' Uptown* (1980), and *Sophisticated Ladies* (1981), each of which won him a Tony nomination.

In the 1980s, Hollywood called. Hines won supporting roles in major films: he was the young coroner with Albert Finney in the supernatural thriller *Wolfen* (1981); he was Josephus (a part originally written for Richard Pryor), who claims to be Jewish in Mel Brooks's *History of the World, Part 1* (1981); he was a wacko religious nut in *Deal of the Century* (1983); and he also made a cameo appearance in *The Muppets Take Manhattan* (1984).

His career took a sharp surprising upturn with *The Cotton Club* in 1984. Originally producer Robert Evans had wanted Richard Pryor (almost every important black male role of the early 1980s was developed with Pryor in mind), confident that Pryor's box-office clout could insure an additional $4 million in financing *The Cotton Club*. With Hines, as the actor himself has jokingly said, Evans might have scrambled up about $1500. But when Pryor turned the part down, Hines found himself cast in a major role in one of the year's biggest movies. Soft-spoken, offbeat, and disarming as the romantic hero Sandman Williams, Hines proved most effective in his dance numbers. In his dramatic scenes, he was neither dashing nor forceful enough. (The script did not help him out any.) The same was true of his next role—as an angry, rather weepy American performer who has defected to the Soviet Union—in *White Nights* (1985). As a screen personality, Gregory Hines appeared too unformed without much of an inner life. When required to speak or act, he looked as if the camera had robbed him of his energy and creative spark.

Interestingly, Hines fared better as the undercover cop in the action/comedy film *Running Scared* (1986). Working opposite comedian Billy Crystal helped bring out a looseness and playfulness in Hines that rarely (except in *History of the World*) had blossomed on screen. Yet the movie itself wasted the performances of the two stars, failing to develop a strong enough story or characters. It should be noted though that here and in *White Nights*, Hines was granted leading ladies. Generally, he was not sexually neutralized in the way most black male stars were. Perhaps filmmakers found Hines's fundamental easy-going persona comforting, so much so that they did not feel threatened by his sexuality. Women, however, generally responded to his work and playful sex appeal.

Hines also appeared on television on "Saturday Night Live," "Steve Martin's Best Show Ever" (1981), the special "Shirley MacLaine: Illusions" (1982), and Steven Spielberg's "Amazing Stories" (1985).

Lena Horne

B. 1917. Singer, actress.

This legendary performer's career started when she was a sixteen-year-old chorus girl at the Cotton Club. Later she was the girl singer with the orchestras of Noble Sissle and Charlie Barnet and also appeared in Lew Leslie's *Blackbirds of 1939*. For a spell, she billed herself as Helena Horne. In the early 1940s, she turned up at nightclubs on the West Coast, was spotted by a MGM talent scout, and soon signed to the studio (then the most powerful in the country), becoming the first black woman in American films to be fully glamorized, publicized, and promoted by her studio. The NAACP's Executive Secretary Walter White felt Horne could do much to alter the image of black women (then consigned to comic maid roles) in American films. But while Hollywood did not cast her as a domestic, it did not make her a black Harlow either.

In most of her films, Horne appeared only in a musical sequence. Beautifully dressed and made-up, she performed a song or two, then disappeared, her sequences having nothing to do with the picture's plotline or characters. Later, when the studio felt her sequences might offend southern audiences, Lena Horne's scenes were cut. The same was true of Hazel Scott's movie appearances during this same period.

The two exceptions were *Cabin in the Sky* and *Stormy Weather*, all-black musicals released in 1943 in which she played leading roles. Haughty, bourgeois, a bit withdrawn, and a mulatto type (she had the straight hair, keen features, and light skin the studios sometimes fawned over), she displayed neither the fire nor the tender vulnerability of a Dorothy Dandridge (who came later), but she was indeed so astonishingly beautiful (and in *Cabin in the Sky* so seductively playful) that audiences could not take their eyes off her. For black GIs of World War II, she became a sepia pinup girl, her glossy studio photographs gracing their lockers just as those of Rita Hayworth and Betty Grable were stuck to the lockers of their white counterparts. In later years, Horne said her Hollywood period was a rough one in which she never felt entirely comfortable or free. That feeling of constraint shows in many of her films. Yet, ironically enough, today her tight control and the filmmakers' attempts at isolating her from the rest of the action simply enhance her above-it-all goddessy appeal.

In the late 1940s, Horne had more serious career problems. Her marriage to white arranger/composer Lennie Hayton (which she kept secret for three years) did not sit well with many people. Then, too, after she was listed in *Red Channels*, she said she was often blacklisted from television appearances. Horne did hold on though, continuing to perform at major nightclubs here and abroad and then coming back strong in the 1957 Broadway show *Jamaica*. In 1969, she played a dramatic film role opposite Richard Widmark in *Death of a Gunfighter*. In 1978, she made a magnificent Glinda, the Good Witch, in *The Wiz*. And in 1981, she was in top form in her hugely successful Broadway show *Lena Horne: The Lady and Her Music* (in which she discussed some of the tensions of her Hollywood heyday; she does the same in her autobiography *Lena*). The show was taped in 1984 for cable-TV. It also ran on PBS.

Her films include: *The Duke Is Tops* (sometimes called *Bronze Venus*; a movie made outside Hollywood in 1938); *Panama Hattie* (1942); *I Dood It* (in which she teams up with Hazel Scott for a musical segment, 1943); *Swing Fever* (1943); *Thousands Cheer* (1943); *Broadway Rhythm* (1944); *Two Girls and A Sailor* (1944); *Ziegfeld Follies* (1946); *Till the Clouds Roll By* (1946); *Words and Music* (1948); *Duchess of Idaho* (1950); *Meet Me in Las Vegas* (1956); and *That's Entertainment* (1976).

Horne's television credits include: "Ed Sullivan's Toast of the Town" (1950); "The Perry Como Show"; "Lena" (a 1964 special); "Harry and Lena" (a 1969 special with Harry Belafonte); "Tony and Lena" (a 1972 special with Tony Bennett); "The Flip Wilson Show"; "Sanford and Son"; "The Dick Cavett Show"; and "60 Minutes."

Allen "Farina" Hoskins

B. 1920; D. 1980. Actor.

By the age of one, Allen Hoskins had begun film work, playing baby Farina in the 1922 "Fire Fighters" episode of the *Our Gang* series. He continued playing Farina (105 episodes) for the next nine years.

In the beginning, there was a sexual ambiguity about Farina. Was anyone ever sure if he was a little boy or girl? Usually, he was dressed in ginghams with a head of curls/pigtails tied with ribbons (or sometimes it looked as if it were tied with toilet paper). Those curls shot straight up if Farina was frightened or excited. So popular was the character that Hoskins created that at one point, according to film historians Leonard Maltin and Richard Bann, he earned $350 a week as

A new image for black women in films in the 1940s: Lena Horne, the first black actress to be fully glamorized and publicized by her studio MGM.

compared to the $40 weekly salary most of the other *Our Gang* kids received.

But by age 19, Farina was a has-been, too old for the series and unable to find other movie work. During the Second World War, he served in the armed forces and later worked with the handicapped and mentally disabled. In 1975 when inducted into the Black Filmmakers Hall of Fame, Hoskins resurfaced, announcing, "I stayed buried for a long time." Several new generations, though, having viewed reruns of the series on television, had come to like Hoskins's Farina—despite the criticism against the character—as much as had audiences of the past. Unlike Stymie Beard, however, who, after years of obscurity and personal problems, found television work in the 1970s, Hoskins did not return to performing. He died of cancer at age 59 in Oakland, California.

Hoskins's other movie credits include: *You Said a Mouthful* (1932); *The Life of Jimmy Dolan* (1933); *The Mayor of Hell* (1933); and *Reckless* (1935). He also appeared in the 1950s in an episode of the television show "You Asked for It," which reunited the "Our Gang" kids.

Rex Ingram

B. 1895; D. 1969. Actor

Like Paul Robeson, Rex Ingram was a physically robust, athletic-looking actor, who exuded in his films of the 1930s and 1940s an air of unbridled confidence and heroic vigor. Blessed with a resonant baritone voice, Ingram always spoke like a man in charge, and never in his career did he portray the whining, baffled, asexual kind of black male character that the movie industry favored during the Depression era. For black audiences of that time, he was clearly an emblem of pride and assertion.

After a career in such stage productions as *Lulu Belle* (1929) and *Stevedore* (1934), Ingram first came to the attention of moviegoers in the 1936 black heaven fantasy *Green Pastures*. Cast as de Lawd, he gave a

Rex Ingram as De Lawd in Green Pastures, *a fantasy about an all-black heaven.*

gentle but stirring performance as a heavenly host who often seemed world-weary and exasperated by the follies of puny man. In the Arabian Nights fantasy *The Thief of Bagdad* (1940), he was a resplendent genie who, when released from a bottle in which he's been trapped for centuries, exultantly proclaims that he is now free. Black audiences identified with his freedom call in a very special way that went beyond the bounds of the movie. And in another fantasy, the 1943 *Cabin in the Sky*, he gave a joyously mischievous performance as Lucifer, Jr., who plots the downfall of Eddie "Rochester" Anderson. That same year in *Sahara*, Ingram played the heroic Sudanese soldier who sacrifices his life for the troops. And a few years later *Moonrise* (1949) provided him an opportunity to reveal a more sensitive and mature side; here he played a wise and weathered outcast, who helps a restless young white man come to maturity. In all these films and so many more, Rex Ingram seems to stand apart from the Hollywood system, repeatedly refusing to let himself be demeaned by a role. Watching him today, audiences still appear ready to cheer him on.

In time, though, Rex Ingram's private life—often restless and stormy—may well have taken a toll on him professionally. In 1937, he filed for bankruptcy (and later divorce). After 1949, when he pleaded guilty to having transported a 15-year-old Kansas girl to New York for "immoral purposes," Ingram's career seemed to suffer. In his later films such as *Anna Lucasta* (1958) and *Hurry Sundown* (1967) and on episodes of a television series like "Daktari" (1967), he looks worn, almost burntout, although in certain moments he can still summon something within himself that yet impresses or moves the viewer.

Rex Ingram's movie credits include: *Huckleberry Finn* (1939); *The Talk of the Town* (1942); *Fired Wife* (1943); *Dark Waters* (1944); *A Thousand and One Nights* (1945); *Congo Crossing* (1956); *God's Little Acre* (1958); *Watusi* (1959); *Elmer Gantry* (1960); and *Desire in the Dust* (1960).

Ingram's TV credits include: "Ramar of the Jungle" (1953); "Captain Midnight" (1954); "The Emperor Jones" (1955); "Black Saddle" (1959); "The Law and Mr. Jones" (1960); "The Rifleman" (1961); "Lloyd Bridges Theatre" (1962); "Sam Benedict" (1962); "Mr. Novak" (1963); "The Breaking Point" (1964); "I Spy" (1964); "Cowboy in Africa" (1968); "Gunsmoke" (1969); and "The Bill Cosby Show" (1969).

In 1957, Ingram also appeared in an all-black stage production of *Waiting for Godot*, in which he co-starred with Mantan Moreland, Earle Hyman, and Geoffrey Holder.

James Earl Jones

B. 1931. Actor.

The son of actor Robert Earl Jones, James Earl Jones was born in Mississippi, grew up with his grandparents in Michigan, and first acted in New York stage productions in the late 1950s. For years, he played a bit of everything: from Genet's *The Blacks* (1961) to Athol Fugard's *Blood Knot* (1964) to Chekhov's *Cherry Orchard* (1968) to such key Shakespearean roles as Oberon, Caliban, the Prince of Morocco, and Othello.

By the early 1960s, Jones had also started working in television. As one of the first black actors cast in a regular role on a soap opera, he played Dr. Jerry Turner on "The Guiding Light" (1967) and also appeared on such primetime shows as "East Side, West Side" (in the famous 1963 episode "Who Do You Kill?"), "Channing" (1964), "The

Defenders" (1965), "Dr. Kildare" (1966), and—ironically soon after having played Othello—as an African chief on "Tarzan" (1968, also 1969).

By 1964, he had also made his film debut in a small role in Stanley Kubrick's *Dr. Strangelove or How I Learned to Stop Worrying and Love the Bomb.* It's rather amusing and refreshing to see him in the celebrated Kubrick film: Jones was a young whippersnapper of an actor, relaxed, a tad corny, and so filled with enthusiasm at having a "movie part" that he never takes himself too seriously, which was not necessarily the case with his later movie work. A few years later when cast in the Burton/ Taylor *Comedians* (1967), he had grown stouter and also become a bit of a heavy-handed actor.

His film/TV career underwent a significant change after his great Broadway success in 1968 as black boxing champ Jack Jefferson in *The Great White Hope.* When he repeated the role on film—giving a bravura performance that was more geared to the stage than cinema—Jones's confidence and passion for the role carried him through. Nominated for an Oscar for *The Great White Hope* as Best Actor of 1970, Jones later played leading roles in such films as *The Man* (1972), *Claudine* (1974), *The River Niger* (1976), and *The Bingo Long Traveling All-Stars and Motor Kings* (1976). Although often praised by the critics, Jones's work—sometimes blustery, boisterous, and bullish—frequently seemed overdone to the point where he occasionally turned himself (as in *Claudine* and later "Roots: The Next Generations," 1979) into a near-grotesque. At times that famous smile of his was *so* big, it may well have made audiences want to run away; he looked as if he might swallow somebody whole. In *Claudine,* so charmless was he that sometimes he seemed wholly inappropriate as Diahann Carroll's leading man. Often this highly respected stage actor failed to master the subtle technique of film acting, where, for better or worse, less is frequently much more.

As the years moved on, Jones slipped into character roles on film while continuing to do star turns on stage, faring well in the Poitier/ Cosby comedy *A Piece of the Action* (1977, where we're rather relieved not to have to see too much of him) and in *Star Wars* (1977), *The Empire Strikes Back* (1980), and *The Return of the Jedi* (1983) in which he did not appear but provided the voice for Darth Vadar, his big oversized sound itself something of a cartoon and appropriate for this comic-strip adventure series. Other times Jones, enduring his share of clinkers, was almost embarrassingly bad in such vehicles as *Swashbuckler* (1976) and *Conan the Barbarian* (1982).

Perhaps surprisingly some of his most enjoyable television work was as the star of the series "Paris" (1979–1980), where he wisely scaled himself down from his usual grand heights.

Jones's movie credits include: *End of the Road* (1970), *The Greatest* (1977), *The Last Remake of Beau Geste* (1977), *Exorcist II: The Heretic* (1977), *The Bushido Blade* (1979), *Soul Man* (1986); *Gardens of Stone* (1987); and *Matewan* (1987).

Among his other TV credits: "Trumpets of the Lord" (1968); "King Lear" (1975, title role); "The Greatest Thing That Almost Happened" (1977); "Jesus of Nazareth" (1979); "Paul Robeson" (1979); "Deadly Hero" (1980); "Amy and the Angel" (1982); "The Vegas Strip War" (1984); and "The Atlanta Child Murders" (1985).

Max Julien

Actor, writer, producer.

In his early films *Psych-Out* (1968), *The Savage Seven* (1968), *Up Tight* (1968), and *Getting Straight* (1970), Max Julien seemed to be going to nowheresville. Then *The Mack* (1973), which starred him as a snappy, high-living pimp, proved a breakthrough for him. Attractive, boyish, with a light voice that was somewhat inappropriate for the macho characters he preferred to play, and relaxed on screen, he emerged as one of the new-style popular black actors of the 1970s, anxious to control his image and to turn out his own type of product. He wrote and co-produced the very successful 1973 *Cleopatra Jones* (conceived originally as a vehicle for his live-in lady friend, Vonetta McGee; eventually, however, the film starred Tamara Dobson). That was followed by *Thomasine and Bushrod* (1974), which he also wrote, co-produced, and starred in (this time, with McGee). Then it almost looked as if his creative energies (or perhaps the hustler instincts it takes to survive as a writer/producer in Hollywood) had deserted him. Afterwards little was heard from him.

TV credits include: "The Mod Squad" (1969); "Deadlock" (1969); "The Name of the Game" (1970); and "Tattletales" (1974).

Max Julien, the hero/pimp star of The Mack, *the creator of* Cleopatra Jones.

Yaphet Kotto

B. 1937. Actor.

Frequently praised by the critics and fortunate enough to have worked consistently in films and television for almost three decades, Yaphet Kotto rarely, however, had the opportunity for the big dramatic roles that might have propelled him to superstardom. One reason may have been that this robust, muscular actor had a character actor's face and body (he looked lived in, experienced), not the soothing pretty-boy looks of, say, a Philip Michael Thomas.

In many of Kotto's performances—in *Nothing but a Man* (1964), *Blue Collar* (1978), *Alien* (1979), *Brubaker* (1980)—there was a formal control and structure (almost a classical approach to acting) that could readily give way to a contemporary looseness. Often representing the kind of sensible working-class man who labored hard at his job and then wanted merely to return home to unwind perhaps with a beer or a laugh or two, Kotto had an unerring solid decency about himself, a fair-

One of the screen's great underrated actors:
Yaphet Kotto (with Pam Grier in Friday
Foster).

minded intelligence that made him heroic. He was an ordinary sort of
guy who could not be brushed aside, who would not accept hypocrisy,
and who would always maintain a clear-eyed perceptiveness about the
do's and dont's of survival; so strong was his projection of these elements that in a movie like *Alien* audiences almost felt betrayed by
director Ridley Scott when Kotto's character died. Logically, this resilient, shrewd man deserved to live. Moreover, Kotto's highly realistic
characters—everything about them seemed thought out, down to the
way they walked, touched, laughed—held several films together. Without his highly polished craftsmanship and his solid presence, *Alien*, for
all its visual detailing and brilliance, would have been far less textured,
and a film like *Blue Collar*, in which the star Richard Pryor seemed
strained and eerily detached from the rest of the cast, might have
collapsed completely.

Curiously in "Playing with Fire" (1985) and *Report to the Commissioner*
(1975) in which his performances have some masterly dramatic embellishments, Kotto rarely wore his blackness as a badge; he seemed to
refuse to represent the Negro as a metaphor for injustice or exploitation. Yet his stance—the rhythms of speech and movement—let us
know that this everyday man is most assuredly a black man.

Only on rare occasions, such as in the TV miniseries "Harem" (1986)
in which improbably cast as a studdish-looking eunuch, was he done in
by the ridiculousness of a role; here he appeared to rush through his
lines as if anxious to make his money and get away from the entire

looney-tune atmosphere. Generally, if cast in junk such as *Monkey Hustle* (1977), he managed to bring some weight and muscle to the project. Or in *Friday Foster* (1975), so relaxed and agreeable was he—almost as if playing a character in an entirely different movie—that he infused the cheap nonsense with flair, a touch of class, and some much needed savoir faire; he even displayed a romantic side, and audiences longed for Pam Grier's Friday to give this brother a break.

Kotto remained an actor who could be counted on for sensitive, individualized work. Mastering the medium in a way an actor like James Earl Jones never did, he was a consummate film actor.

TV credits include: "Losers Weepers" (1967); "The Big Valley" (1967); "High Chaparral" (1968); "Daniel Boone" (1968); "Hawaii Five-O" (1969); "Mannix" (1969); "The Name of the Game" (1970); "Gunsmoke" (1970); "Night Chase" (1970); "Doctors Hospital" (1975); "Raid on Entebbe" (1977; he played Idi Amin); "Death in a Minor Key" (1979); "Women on San Quentin" (1983); "Rage" (1984); and as Platoon Sgt. James 'China' Bell on the series "For Love and Honor" (1983).

Among his movie credits: *Five Card Stud* (1968); *The Thomas Crown Affair* (1968); *The Liberation of L.B. Jones* (1970), *Across 110th Street* (1972), *Man and Boy* (1972); *The Limit* (1972; also directed); *Live and Let Die* (1973); *Sharks Treasure* (1975); *Drum* (1976); *The Shootist* (1976); *Fighting Back* (1981); *Star Chamber* (1983).

Canada Lee

B. 1907; D. 1952. Actor.

Growing up in Harlem where he was a childhood friend of Adam Clayton Powell, Jr., Canada Lee, as a youngster and later a young adult, seemed constantly in search of himself. He once said that all his life he had been "on the verge of becoming something." Having studied music, he almost became a concert violinist at age 14, but then ran away from home and stopped his music studies. Later he had almost been a jockey until he grew too tall and heavy. When he turned to prize-fighting and changed his name from Leonard Lionel Cornelius Canegate to Canada Lee, he might have become a champion but lost an eye and left the ring. The tragic irony of Lee's life is that just when he finally seemed to have found his true calling—as a dramatic actor on stage and screen—his career was cut short because of politics. Except for Paul Robeson, no other black actor has ever had his career so openly affected by the political atmosphere (the blacklisting) of the late 1940s and 1950s than Canada Lee.

Lee's early theater work included roles in Orson Welles's 1936 *Voodoo Macbeth* (as Banquo) and *Mamba's Daughters* (1939). But what won him critical acclaim was his performance as Bigger Thomas in Orson Welles's 1941 Broadway adaptation of Richard Wright's *Native Son*. Afterward he appeared in such stage productions as *Anna Lucasta* (1944) and *The Tempest* (1945, as Caliban). Then came a dazzling appearance— in white-face—as Daniel de Bosola in the 1946 revival of *The Dutchess of Malfi*.

During this time, he was also cast in films: Hitchcock's *Lifeboat* (1944), Robert Rosen's *Body and Soul* (1947), and Alfred L. Werker's *Lost Boundaries* (1949). His was an unusual presence, particularly for the times. There was nothing servile about him. Brown-skinned with a full face, dark, penetrating eyes, and a sturdy, compact body, he seemed a man cut off from other men; a man who could easily see through the fears and pretensions of others; a man who also chose to keep his deep emotional center in check. Aware of life's vicissitudes and cruelties, the prototypical Canada Lee character appears to have no other choice or manner of protecting himself than by living as a stoic outsider. In *Lifeboat*, as the only black on a drifting lifeboat with a group of white survivors during World War II, he quietly projected an image of a guarded, intelligent black man who somberly maintains his dignity. And in *Body and Soul*, he was perfect as the battered prize fighter, who, having been exploited and abused in a corrupt boxing world, makes a valiant, last ditch effort to save the young hero from a similar fate. Few black actors of this period, save for the young James Edwards, seemed to express as fresh and modern a portrait of the American Negro male as did Lee.

But his political problems escalated in the late 1940s when Lee, having often been outspoken on racial matters, was branded a Communist. Having lost roles and becoming nearly penniless, Lee finally called a press conference in 1949 at which he announced: "I am not a Communist or a joiner of any kind." He added: "I believe the constant screech of 'Communism' is only a smoke screen designed to hide very unpleasant facts. . . . I freely admit that my work, my art, my livelihood is very much affected by the irresponsible, nebulous, false insinuations directed at my name." Still the entertainment industry considered him too controversial to be hired. According to writer Stefan Kanfer in his book *A Journal of the Plague Years*, by 1952, Lee had been banned from forty shows. He once asked the editors of *Variety*, "How long, how long can a man take this kind of unfair treatment?" Kanfer has said that Lee, in desperation, delivered an attack on Paul Robeson in the early 1950s. Not long afterward, he found work in the anti-apartheid drama *Cry, the Beloved Country*, which was filmed in Johannesburg and co-starred Lee with the young Sidney Poitier. When he returned to the States, he still could find no work. Having been in failing health for some time, he died shortly after the release of the film. In his autobiography *This Life*, Sidney Poitier has described an incident which occurred a few years after Lee's death. Then up for a role in the television drama "A Man Is Ten Feet Tall," Poitier was asked to sign a loyalty oath of sorts, in which he was required to repudiate such actors as Robeson and Canada Lee. Poitier has said: "How could I repudiate a relationship with Canada Lee, from whom I had learned so much about life? The advice passed on to me, the fatherly way he took care of me in South Africa—how could I? . . . In the last weeks of his life, because he was broke, that man *walked* in his illness from New York City to White Plains in support of some black people who had suffered an injustice. Though his fires were banked and his energies low, he continued to speak out openly against the way that most of our country had been responding to the black community, completely ignoring our rights." Poitier ended by repudiating neither Lee nor Robeson.

Partly because he played so few film roles by which a new generation could become familiar with him, Canada Lee is barely remembered today. But his work holds up. And as Stefan Kanfer has said: "Overlooked by almost every theatrical or film historian, unmentioned by such retentive and bitter victims as Alvah Bessie and Dalton Trumbo, Lee is the Othello of the blacklist, at once its most afflicted and ignored victim."

Lee's son Carl later carried on his father's acting tradition, appearing in such films as *The Connection* (1962), *The Cool World* (1964, which he also co-wrote), *Super Fly* (1972), and *Gordon's War* (1973).

Calvin Lockhart

B. 1934. Actor.

In such early 1970s movies as *Joanna* (1968), *Cotton Comes to Harlem* (1970), *Halls of Anger* (1970), *Leo the Last* (1970), and *Melinda* (1972), Calvin Lockhart had proved himself such an exciting new presence that he was touted as a logical successor to Sidney Poitier's box-office throne. In *The New York Times*, Vincent Canby wrote:

> The question of Poitier's obsolence is prompted by the emergence of major new black actors like . . . Calvin Lockhart who, in three recent films, has been able to play everything from a dedicated school teacher (*Halls of Anger*) to a bogus preacher promoting a back-to-Africa swindle (*Cotton Comes to Harlem*), and a perennially precious acting student (*Myra Breckinridge* [1970]) who dusts his hair with sequins.

For a spell, Lockhart was a darling of the press. Of course, *that* later changed.

This Nassau-born actor, the son of a musician and a mother who sold baskets to tourists, had come to New York at age eighteen to study engineering at Cooper Union, then dropped out to pursue an acting career. After working in such New York theatre productions as *Dark of the Moon* (1960) and *The Cool World* (1960, playing the junkie gang leader), Lockhart went to Europe for eight years. There he appeared in BBC television shows and also in the movie *Joanna* as the brooding streetwise young man who falls in love with a young white woman (Genevieve Waite). Unlike past black screen actors who had often had a conservative streak and were not permitted by their scripts to be romantic or sensual and not permitted by themselves to even suggest inner sexual hungers, Lockhart startled audiences of the period because he threw such cautions aside, coming across as a sensual daredevil with an appealing hurt-boy quality. In his scenes with white actress Waite, he never held back. To him, she was simply a woman, not a *white* woman. Moreover blessed with chiseled-out-of-marble features and a cool chocolate coloring, he had a continental sophistication and confidence and a surprisingly engaging narcissism that made him distinctive. (Perhaps the only other actor whose narcissism has exceeded Lockhart's has been Prince's.) Lockhart's later performances, notably in *Melinda*, may strike us as dazzling poses, little more. But in the era before Billy Dee Williams, Lockhart was an up-and-coming matinee idol.

Then just as his career seemed ready to roll, he appeared to have a fatal setback. Perhaps his career slide was due partly to his own lack of focus and perhaps partly to his well-publicized temper and "arrogance." In *The New York Times*, Judy Klemesrud wrote that during her interview with him "three faces of Calvin emerged: Arrogance, belligerence, and every once in a while when he dropped his shield of armor, innocence." She went on to report of his heated disagreements with director Paul Bogart during the filming of *Halls of Anger*. Such "bad" press rarely helps a career. Once word spreads within the industry that an actor is

Calvin Lockhart: for a brief spell in the 1970s it looked as if he might become Hollywood's most important new black leading man.

difficult, he's destined to encounter problems unless he's a really powerful box-office star. (Lockhart wasn't, and *Halls of Anger* was not a great success.)

Whatever the reasons, Lockhart, by the mid- and late 1970s, remained stealthily seductive but was consigned to supporting parts in such features as the 1974 *Uptown Saturday Night* (supporting, of course, those past leading men idols whose style was so different from his: Sidney Poitier and Harry Belafonte), *Let's Do It Again* (1975), and roles in such B-films as *The Beast Must Die* (1974), and *Baron Wolfgang Von Tripps* (1976). In the 1980s, he resurfaced, for a few episodes, as one of Diahann Carroll's suitors on "Dynasty."

His movie credits include: *Dark of the Sun* (1968); *Only When I Larf* (1968); *Salt and Pepper* (1968); *Honeybaby, Honeybaby* (1974).

William Marshall

B. 1924. Actor.

This impressive actor with a rich booming voice and a heroic posture became in the early 1950s a favorite action hero (along with Woody Strode) for black audiences, particularly black males. At a time when Sidney Poitier was just begining to play his noble Good Negro protagonists, Marshall audaciously strutted through *Demetrius and the Gladiators* (1952) and *Lydia Bailey* (1954) as if he were a gift from the gods to this planet earth.

Confident, polished, sophisticated, he projected an unusual mixture of physical strength and a sharp, discerning intelligence. He was also sexual in a period when the lid was always kept on a black male's sexuality. Moreover, he was a good actor. But the important film roles never came his way. Turning to television early, he made a splendid De Lawd in the 1951 version of "Green Pastures." Later in the 1970s, he reached a new younger black audience as the dapper, courtly lead in *Blacula* (1972) and its sequel *Scream, Blacula, Scream* (1973).

Other films included: *Something of Value* (1957); *Sabu and the Magic Ring* (1958); *The Boston Strangler* (1968); *The Hell with Heroes* (1968); *Skullduggery* (1970); *Honky* (1971); *Abby* (1976); and *Twilight's Last Gleaming* (1977).

Marshall's TV credits include: appearances in the 1950s and 1960s in *Othello* (on the "Omnibus" series); *Oedipus Rex* ("Omnibus"); "Rawhide"; "Ben Casey"; "Tarzan"; "Star Trek"; "Bonanza"; "The Harlem Detective" series; and later "Rosetti and Ryan"; "Police Woman"; and "Beverly Hills Madam" (1986).

Among his many stage credits: *When We Dead Awaken* (1944); *Set My People Free* (1948); and the title role in *Othello* (in 1958 and 1976).

Helen Martin

Actress.

When Helen Martin first worked in New York theater in the early 1940s, she probably had no idea that her career would span some five decades. Nor could she have imagined that she would go almost completely unnoticed until the 1970s when she appeared in bit parts on such television series as "Maude" and "Good Times." At that time because she played comic characters who were often silly and inconsequential, most audiences did not care much about her background and had no idea that here was an actress who had long struggled for roles in "serious" theater.

Born in St. Louis but reared in Nashville, Martin served a theatrical apprenticeship in the late 1930s in Chicago's WPA Theater and later, upon moving to New York, was a member of the Rose McClendon Players. Her Broadway debut was as the sister of Canada Lee's Bigger Thomas in Orson Welles's production of *Native Son* (1941). Four years later she was back in another strong production, *Deep Are the Roots*, considered provocative for its time. Although cast as a maid, she played an important role nonetheless. Martin was also one of the founders of the American Negro Theatre. And for years, she continued working in such stage productions as *Take a Giant Step* (1953), *Purlie Victorious* (1961), and *The Blacks* (1961). She also toured in the 1950s in Tennessee Williams's *A Streetcar Named Desire* and in 1960 appeared as Susie in another Williams drama, *Period of Adjustment*.

Here and there she found film roles: *The Phenix City Story* (1955), *Cotton Comes to Harlem* (1970), *Where's Poppa?* (1970), and *Death Wish* (1974). For the most part, audiences still did not know who she was. Nor was work always steady.

Much of that changed in the 1970s when she found employment in the new flood of black sitcoms. In "Baby, I'm Back," she played a regular role as Luzelle Carter, the mother of Denise Nicholas. Almost ten years later, she found another regular spot as a nosey neighbor on the series "227." By then, audiences, perhaps still unaware of her name, recognized her nonetheless by her trademark bangs and her tough, testy attitude. Repeatedly, she could give (and perhaps overwork) a long, cold, hard, comic drop-dead stare, letting audiences know she was not taken in by the shams of other characters. She was a suspicious realist, not about to let the wool be pulled over her eyes. Because the scripts developed her characters in the most superficial manner and, consequently, because she was required to play her roles broadly, her characters were often viewed as stereotypes or caricatures. The actress herself had a gift for timing and an unshakable ability to steal scenes. Often, too, Helen Martin had a world-weary quality; she looked as if she had seen everything before. She was much better than most of us may have realized.

Therefore it was both an irony and a pleasure to see her cast as the grandmother in Robert Townsend's *Hollywood Shuffle* (1987), a movie that tried to lay waste to the entertainment industry's black stereotypes. Martin's performance is not something to write home about. But her gentle, wise presence and her relaxed warmth endow the film with a little weight. She reveals she knows more about the subject than the picture's director. It's a nice touch for a career that might not have always been satisfying to her but which proved, however, to be durable.

Martin's TV credits include: "Cindy" (1978); "Dummy" (1979); "This Man Stands Alone" (1979); "Better Late than Never" (1979); and "The Jerk, Too" (1984).

Hattie McDaniel

B. 1895; D. 1952. Actress.

The first black performer to win the Academy Award—as Best Supporting Actress of 1939 for her performance as Mammy in *Gone with the Wind*.

Born in Wichita, Kansas, Hattie McDaniel, by age sixteen, started performing as a singer in tent shows in small towns, later sang with George Morrison's Orchestra, and by 1924, was a headline singer on the Pantages and Orpheum circuits. Seven years later she migrated to Los Angeles, working on radio during the 1930s on "The Amos 'n' Andy Show" and "The Eddie Cantor Show." Her brother Sam and her sister Etta also moved to California, where they, too, worked in films.

Anxious to find movie work, McDaniel took whatever jobs she could find, playing minor parts here and there, sometimes working without credit. Her forceful personality, however, was almost always on full display, so much so that for Depression audiences, she eventually personified the all-knowing, all-seeing, all-hearing, sometimes helpful, sometimes haughty mammy figure, who, when the chips were down, could usually be counted on to come to the aid of her white employers although she would often bark and grumble the whole time. In *Blonde Venus* (1932), she turned up as a faithful soul who helped Marlene Dietrich, then on the run with her young son, hiding from the cops and her hostile husband. In *Affectionately Yours* (1941), she repeatedly cast a mean eye at Merle Oberon, who had made the mistake of acquiring a new boyfriend of whom McDaniel did not approve. In films such as *Alice Adams* (1935) and *The Mad Miss Manton* (1935), she was a could-not-care-less-about-these-white-folks maid (and social arbiter) who moved at her own pace with a point of view on behavior all her own. In *China Seas* (1935), she had a spectacular bit as Jean Harlow's indestructibly independent maid, who was quick to let Harlow know what people were saying about her. Often with Harlow as with Clark Gable, McDaniel was a match in temperament, never hesitating to speak her mind and always looking her co-star right in the eye, refusing to back off into a standard servile position as many black movie servants usually did.

With black men, McDaniel could also be unusually demanding, stubborn, loud, bossy. Her commands to Stepin Fetchit in *Judge Priest* (1934) and even to the great Robeson in *Show Boat* (1936) can be startling, so assertive is she, so quick to criticize and keep the man in his place. She played to the hilt the hot-tempered black woman who finds herself saddled with a no-account man.

McDaniel's voice and her size (well over 200 pounds) became great assets, used by her to show she was a woman who had to be reckoned with, who was born to give orders, not to take them. No one, black or white, ever approached her casually. And in such films as *Affectionately Yours* and *The Mad Miss Manton*, it seemed as if she not only ran the homes of the whites she worked for but that she herself was the homeowner. Although her characters generally supported the values and virtues of the dominant white culture, she herself, because of the push of her personality, seemed totally free of any feelings whatsoever of inferiority; she is a rather unexpected, blazing symbol of self-assertion with a peculiarly American brand of aggressiveness and ambition, appearing almost as if she sees no real limits as to what she can do or say.

McDaniel's career highpoint came, of course, with her *Gone with the Wind* character Mammy, played in the grand style: cantankerous, cynical, unyielding, perceptive, outspoken. When she accepted her Oscar, her moving speech (now said to have been written by her studio) announced that she hoped always to be a credit to her industry and her race. At the time of this historic event, Hollywood patted itself on the back. Louella Parsons wrote:

On screen the classic mammy figure, off screen a very composed, dignified woman, Hattie McDaniel with her husband James Crawford.

A Negress, Hattie McDaniel, has won an Academy Award. In all the years the Academy has been handing out the little gold "Oscars," there has never been an award as popular or as much discussed. . . . Only in America, the Land of the Free, could such a thing have happened. . . . The Academy is apparently growing up and so is Hollywood. We are beginning to realize that art has no boundaries and that creed, race, or color must not interfere where credit is due.

Despite such sentiments, according to the 1986 book *Inside Oscar* (by Mason Wiley and Damien Bona), at the Oscar ceremonies at the Coconut Grove in the Ambassador Hotel, McDaniel and her escort were seated at a special table for two at the rear of the room. Even on the night of her greatest triumph, this immensely gifted woman still found America/Hollywood's social/racial lines tightly drawn.

For years it had been said southern audiences had complained because McDaniel had been just too outspoken. Curiously, post-*Gone with the Wind* McDaniel characters in such films as *Maryland* (1940), *Song of the South* (1946), and even parts of Selznick's *Since You Went Away* (1944) were softened, less wired up, less demanding.

417

By the late 1940s, as the servant roles slowly vanished from films, McDaniel turned her sights again to radio where she successfully starred in the series "Beulah." Just before her death, she had been signed to play Beulah on the TV series.

McDaniel's movie credits include: *The Little Colonel* (1935, with Shirley Temple); *Gentle Julia* (1936); *Hearts Divided* (1936); *High Tension* (1936); *Star for a Night* (1936); *Valiant Is the Word for Carrie* (1936); *Show Boat* (1936, here audiences get a chance to hear the great McDaniel sing; she's not bad at all); *The Crime Nobody Saw* (1937); *Saratoga* (1937, with Jean Harlow; McDaniel sings again, a highly enjoyable number about a woman who's been down on her luck but remains high-spirited nonetheless); *Nothing Sacred* (1937); *45 Fathers* (1937); *True Confession* (1937); *Battle of Broadway* (1938); *The Shopworn Angel* (1938); *The Shining Hour* (1939); *Zenobia* (1939, teaming up again with Stepin Fetchit); *The Great Lie* (1941); *The Male Animal* (1942); *In This Our Life* (1942, in a more serious role); *George Washington Slept Here* (1942); *Johnny Come Lately* (1943); *Thank Your Lucky Stars* (1943); *Janie* (1944); *3 Is a Family* (1944); *Margie* (1946); *Never Say Goodbye* (1946); *The Flame* (1948); *Mickey* (1948); and *Family Honeymoon* (1949).

Vonetta McGee

B. c. 1950. Actress.

One of the screen's great natural beauties, Vonetta McGee (sometimes confused with another screen stunner Lonette McKee) worked regularly in the black-oriented films of the 1970s such as *Blacula* (1972), *Hammer* (1972), *Detroit 9000* (1973), and *Shaft in Africa* (1973), frequently employed as little more than a dazzling ornament. Still this light-eyed, seductive goddess exuded old-style glamor, striking audiences as being less glitzy and more natural than a Diana Ross. When McGee's live-in-lover relationship with black actor Max Julien was publicized by the black press, the two came to represent the new black Hollywood of the 1970s: an attractive, hard-working couple determined to break the old movie rules. Cast opposite Julien in *Thomasine and Bushrod* (1974), a film package they had put together, McGee moved out of the conventional leading lady category, exhibiting signs of a livelier energetic personality. Later Clint Eastwood selected her as his female lead in *The Eiger Sanction* (1975). Yet there McGee seemed strangely ill at ease and inhibited, almost as if she preferred to withdraw from the eye of Eastwood's camera. In 1977, she tried a more serious role, that of the Angela-Davis-like professor in *Brothers*. But by the end of the 1970s, her film career had just about evaporated; so, too, had the talk of the new black Hollywood.

In the 1980s, McGee wisely turned to television although her appearances were infrequent.

Among her film credits: *The Lost Man* (1969) and *Melinda* (1972).

Among her TV credits: "The Norliss Tapes" (1973); "Police Woman" (1975); "Diff 'rent Strokes" (1980); "The Wiz Kids" (1983); "The Yellow Rose" (1984); and "Cagney and Lacey" (1986), and as a regular—playing a nun, no less—on Robert Blake's short-lived series "Hell Town" (1985).

Dream Girl of the short-lived New Black Hollywood of the 1970s: Vonetta McGee.

Lonette McKee

B. c. 1956. Actress, singer.

Tall, vibrant, elegant, and sexy, Detroit-born Lonette McKee became a dream girl for a generation of black teenagers when she appeared in the 1976 cult film *Sparkle*. Praised by the critics and blessed with talent and looks, McKee's film career seemed assured. But what happened? Her only other notable films of the 1970s were *Which Way Is Up?* (1977) and *Cuba* (1979). The latter cast her in a supporting role rather than the part she should have played: that of the romantic lead, a beautiful Cuban woman (which went to a white actress Brooke Adams). Afterward McKee's movie career seemed almost nonexistent.

Fortunately, McKee, in the 1980s, appeared in two well-publicized Broadway productions *The First* (1981, a musical biography of baseball star Jackie Robinson, in which she played Robinson's wife Rachel) and *Show Boat* (1983, in which she became the first black woman to play the mulatto Julie on Broadway). Then she returned spectacularly to the stage in 1986 as Billie Holiday in the critically well-received production *Lady Day at Emerson's Bar and Grill.*

McKee also returned to films although, for the most part, she left behind the high-voltage energy that had made her so exciting in *Sparkle*. Her 1980s films included: *The Cotton Club*, in which she performed a haunting rendition of "Ill Wind"; *Brewster's Millions*; French director Bertrand Tavernier's fictionalized movie biography of Lester Young, *'Round Midnight* (1986); and Coppola's *Gardens of Stone* (1987).

Her TV credits include: "Spenser: For Hire" (1986); "Miami Vice" (1986); and "The Equalizer" (1986).

Nina Mae McKinney

B. 1913; D. 1967. Actress.

A footloose, fancy-free kewpie doll of an actress, Nina Mae McKinney, still a teenager, was lifted from the chorus line of Lew Leslie's *Blackbirds of 1928* and transported to Hollywood to star as the ill-fated Chick in King Vidor's 1929 all-black musical *Hallelujah*. With glowing notices, McKinney emerged as Hollywood's first black love goddess. Yet she learned afterward that there were no significant followup roles for her as a black leading lady. Later she appeared with Eubie Blake and the young Nicholas Brothers in the all-black musical short *Pie Pie Blackbird* (1932). Then in Europe, she performed in cabarets and clubs where she was sometimes billed as The Black Greta Garbo. In 1935, while in England, she co-starred opposite Paul Robeson in *Sanders of the River*. As an African princess in this British production, she was a glitzy Hollywoodized creation, her voice—with its sweet suggestion of a southern accent—totally inappropriate, her makeup and costumes overdone. Yet the movie itself was so fake and trumped up (another tribute to British colonialism) that her highly glamorous presence was one of the few amusing offbeat bright spots. (Another bright spot, of course, was the work of the great Robeson.) In the States in the late 1930s and 1940s, she worked in such all-black independent productions as *Gang Smashers* (1938), *The Devil's Daughter* (1939), *Straight to Heaven* (1939), *Mantan Messes*

Publicity still of Nina Mae McKinney in Sanders of the River: *a highly energetic dancer and Hollywood's first black movie goddess.*

Up (1946), *Night Train to Memphis* (1946). In 1949, she returned to Hollywood for a supporting role in *Pinky*. Heavy, blurry-eyed, and hardened, the middle-aged woman on screen was a far cry from the sweet-faced bouncy Chick of *Hallelujah* whom black audiences had once taken to their hearts. Her last important performance was on the stage in Brooklyn in 1951 as Sadie Thompson in *Rain*.

Other McKinney film credits include: *Safe in Hell* (1931); *Reckless* (1935); *Black Network* (1936); *Dark Waters* (1944); and *Without Love* (1945).

Butterfly McQueen

B. 1911. Actress.

Diminutive, delicate, with a distinctive high-pitched voice and the demeanor of a very sweet, well-brought-up, bright but spacey schoolgirl, Butterfly McQueen burst onto the national entertainment scene in 1939 with her performance as Prissy in *Gone with the Wind*. Afterward she almost disappeared.

McQueen had been born Thelma McQueen in Tampa, Florida, had lived for a time in Augusta, Georgia, and then in New York City, where her mother worked as a cook. Later when McQueen joined Venezuela Jones' Negro Youth Group, she appeared in the company's production of *A Midsummer Night's Dream* as part of the Butterfly Ballet. Hence her nickname Butterfly, which stuck for the duration of her career.

In the early 1930s, she auditioned for George Abbott's production of *Brown Sugar* (1937), won a part with a few lines, then worked in Abbott's *Brother Rat* (1937) and *What a Life* (1938). Shortly afterward she won her *Gone with the Wind* role and found herself in Hollywood.

During her Hollywood years, she worked in such features as *The Women* (1939), *Affectionately Yours* (1941), *I Dood It* (1943), *Cabin in the Sky* (1943), *Since You Went Away* (1944, her part ended up on the cutting-room floor), *Mildred Pierce* (1945), *Flame of the Barbary Coast* (1945), *Duel in*

The woman with the most distinctive voice in show business: Butterfly McQueen (r.) as Prissy in Gone with the Wind, *with Vivien Leigh as Miz Scarlett.*

the Sun (1947), and years later *The Phynx* (1970) and *Amazing Grace* (1974). She never worked regularly as did Hattie McDaniel and Louise Beavers, partly perhaps because of her own temperament and also because she was a hard cookie to cast. A unique mixture of the comic and the pathetic, McQueen seldom seemed to be *in* her movies; instead it's almost as if she had distanced herself outside them, as if she simply were making a highly polished entrance—doing her bit—then anxiously running off to some other world or planet. Her unfailing sense of decorum was the secret of much of her screen charm and humor. Even during the siege of Atlanta in *GWTW*, she remained a model of proper good-girl behavior. During the long wagonride journey back to Tara, Scarlett O'Hara, spotting a moving cow in the midst of the war's devastation and her own fears of starvation, tells Prissy to tie the animal up, to which Prissy, in a very ladylike manner, responds that they don't need no cow. In spite of whatever happens in the external real world, McQueen's internal view of herself and life makes her both scatterbrained and rather inspired. Her characters, we feel, will always survive, oblivious to life's vicissitudes and demands. McQueen also always displayed a very fragile quality, which explains why audiences still jump and are a bit uncomfortable when Scarlett O'Hara gives Prissy a seemingly well-deserved slap. McQueen is such an innocent that audiences feel Scarlett's reaction is too harsh. (Black audiences also long for Prissy to slap Scarlett back.)

Unable to fit into the Hollywood system, McQueen's later New York years were bleak ones in which she found employment as a factory worker, a waitress, a dishwasher, and also a companion for a wealthy Long Island white woman. Perhaps fatigued or desperate, she returned to Augusta, Georgia, for some ten years during which she had her own local radio show and also opened a restaurant.

Then resurfacing in 1968 in the off-Broadway production of *Curley McDimple*, McQueen received good reviews and was well covered by the press. In 1969 she did a show titled *McQueen and Friends*. During the 1970s' era of television's black sitcoms, McQueen seemed ideal for one such show or another. But her appearances remained sporadic. In the mid-1970s she appeared briefly in *The Wiz* but dropped out of the musical before its arrival on Broadway. In 1978, she put together a New York nightclub act. But her career seemed to have almost stopped altogether.

Then in 1980, Butterfly McQueen made the news when she sued Greyhound Bus Lines for $300,000 after she said security guards at Greyhound's Washington, D.C., terminal had arrested and roughed her up, accusing her of being a pickpocket. It was reported the guards had thought her a vagrant because of the strange way she was dressed: head scarf and a long, full "old-fashioned" dress. In fact, as *People* reported, McQueen sometimes dressed as if on her way to appear in *GWTW*.

McQueen's career—its ups, downs, disappointments, odd twists and turns—now seems something of an old-style Hollywood tale: a bit zany, a bit zonked out, a bit larger than life, and rather touching, too. She had a rare talent that few seemed to know what to do with. Yet despite her infrequent appearances, her Prissy has assured her of a place in film histories—and also in the annals of camp and the gossip sheets.

McQueen also appeared in the independently produced all-black film *Killer Diller* (1948) and *Mosquito Coast* (1986). Among her TV credits: the role of Oriole on the series "Beulah" (1950–1952); the 1957 version of "Green Pastures"; "The Seven Wishes of Joanna Peabody" (1978); and "Our World" (1987).

Oscar Micheaux

B. 1884; D. 1951. Director, producer, writer.

With the 1970s' rebirth of interest in the old race movies of the past, much attention was lavished on black producer and director Oscar Micheaux. Praised as a pioneer who had defied the odds to turn out his own films for several decades, Micheaux's reputation no doubt peaked in this period. Later though when some of his work was screened at festivals or conferences, many film enthusiasts were openly disappointed: his movies were technically crude (sometimes downright atrocious) and artistically misshapen. Consequently, by the 1980s, some were ready to dismiss Micheaux altogether. Actually, Micheaux was neither a supreme artist nor simply an inept dud. Instead he made movies that were, yes, frankly, sometimes terrible but which captured some of the spirit of his times and also heralded a new idea: that black movies could be entertainment vehicles for the mass black audience, that indeed a black star system could also exist. Micheaux also left behind his own sweeping legend.

A charismatic, indefatigable showman with a dash and flair he no doubt felt befitted a motion picture director, Oscar Micheaux has been remembered by the actors who worked with him as a man dedicated to his own concept of black cinema (a heady mix of subliminal social messages and sheer entertainment). Born in Illinois, he had once been a pullman car porter, then a farmer in South Dakota, and by 1915, a self-published novelist. Within a few years, he had turned to film, his fervid enthusiasm for moviemaking eventually carrying him to Chicago and, later, New York.

Early on, Micheaux realized (and relished) the importance of promotion. He is said to have toured the country to publicize one film and at the same time to seek financing for his next, often stepping out of cars and into meeting halls as if "he were God about to deliver a sermon." "Why, he was so impressive and so charming," said Lorenzo Tucker, an actor who appeared in several Micheaux films, "that he could talk the shirt off your back." On his tours, Micheaux approached white southern theater managers and owners, often persuading them to show his black films at special matinee performances for black audiences or at special late shows for white audiences interested in black camp. Micheaux's shrewd promotional sense kept him in business, enabling him to produce, direct, and write, by some counts, almost 30 films from around 1919 to 1948. He was one of the few black filmmakers to work in both silent and sound pictures.

Micheaux's features were similar to Hollywood's, only technically inferior, resembling B-movies of the period (but technically inferior to those, too). Lighting and editing were usually poor, and the acting could be dreadful—ranging from *winging it* to *grandstanding*. Often a scene was shot in a single take as the camera followed an actor through a door or down a hallway. Since he was forced to shoot scenes so rapidly, he seldom had time (or money) to do retakes. Consequently, an actor might flub a line, then just pick up the pieces of his sentence and keep on going.

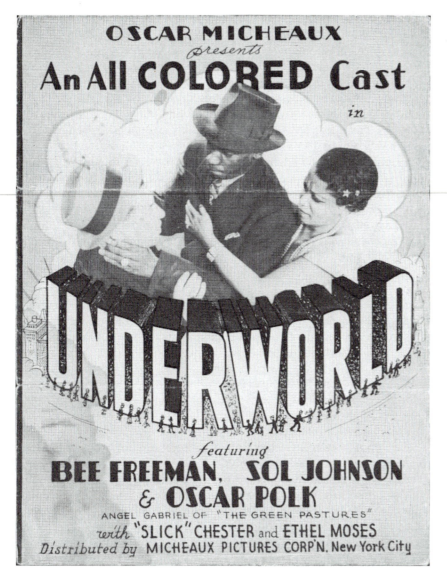

The action in Micheaux's films sometimes centered around one set. In *God's Step Children* (1937), several key scenes occurred in front of a staircase. Filming in the home of a friend, Micheaux discovered that the staircase area offered the best lighting angles, and thus he worked his big scenes around it. Oddly enough, his limitations—the uncontrolled performances and the lived-in tacky look of some sets—endowed his films with a strange realism. One half expects to hear Micheaux call "Cut" and to see the actors walk away from the camera or talk about how they're actually making a movie.

Intertwined in all his films is the consciousness of how race is a force in black life. Just as Negro newspapers and magazines took major news stories and reported them from a black angle, Micheaux took the typical Hollywood script and gave it a black slant. *Underworld* (1937) was a gangster film with a black gangster (he's the recent grad of a good colored college, who's gotten himself mixed up in Chicago's crime world) and a black gun moll. *Daughter of the Congo* (1930) was an African adventure story with a colored cavalry officer bent on rescuing a young Negro girl lost in the savage tropics.

On occasion, Micheaux focused exclusively on the race theme, as in *Birthright* (1924), the story of a young black Harvard graduate who returns to his home town in Tennessee bent upon founding a colored school to "uplift the race." Naturally, he encounters opposition, some of which comes from his fellow blacks, who agree with white Southerners that education ruins a Negro. In its own corny and sly way, *Birthright* made an earnest plea for black unity while satirizing the old-style turncoats and toms. Micheaux liked this material so much that he remade the film in 1939.

On another occasion when focusing on the race theme, Micheaux found himself in the middle of great controversy. His 1920 film *Within Our Gates*, a tale of black southern life (its hardships and racial divisions), caused an uproar because of a lynching sequence. At first the Chicago Board of Movie Censors rejected the film fearful that it might cause race riots. Later after meetings and discussions with various civic leaders and some members of the black press, the board accepted the film for public viewing. But in the South some theaters refused to book it altogether.

For black actresses, Micheaux was something of a dream for he often had vivid, important roles for women in his films. Indeed some of his films might be best described as "women's pictures," his independent, strong-willed heroines often overshadowing the rather pallid males. *God's Step Children* (1937) was part women's film, part race-theme movie, its haughty heroine Naomi punished with death perhaps precisely because of her free-wheeling independence.

Oscar Micheaux's most interesting contribution has often been viewed by some contemporary black audiences as his severest shortcoming. That his films reflected the interests and outlooks, the values and virtues, of the black bourgeoisie has long been held against him. Though his films rarely centered on the ghetto, few race movies did. They seldom dealt with racial misery or decay (although a movie like *Body and Soul*, 1924, tried to). Instead, Micheaux in his later films concentrated on the problems facing black "professional people." Then, too, his leading performers—as was typical of race films—were often close to the white ideal: straight hair, keen features, light skin. (Ironically, *Body and Soul*, stars brown-skinned actor Paul Robeson.) With his light-bright stars, Micheaux also hoped to create a star system like that of Hollywood: thus, Lorenzo Tucker was his Black Valentino; Ethel Moses was considered a Black Harlow; and Bee Freeman, a Black Mae West.

To appreciate Micheaux's films one must understand that he was moving as far as possible from Hollywood's jesters and servants. He wanted to give his audience something "to further the race, not hinder it." Often he sacrificed plausibility to do so. He created on occasion a deluxe, ideal world where blacks were just as affluent, just as educated, just as "cultured" as their white counterparts. Oddly enough, as such, they remain a fascinating comment on black social and political aspirations of the past. And the Micheaux ideal Negro world view popped up in countless other race movies. His films likely set the pattern for race movies in general.

By the late 1940s, the black public had lost interest in race movies. Micheaux, like other independents, held on as long as he could, his last film *The Betrayal* being released in 1948 and opening in downtown New York.

Micheaux's films include: *The Homesteader* (1919); *The Brute* (1920); *Symbol of the Unconquered* (1920: *Gonzales Mystery* and *Deceit* in 1921; *The*

Dungeon, The Virgin of the Seminole, and *Son of Satan* in 1922; *Jasper Landry's Will* (1923); *The Spider's Web* (1926); *The Millionaire* (1927); *When Men Betray* and *Easy Street* in 1928; *Wages of Sin* (1929); *The Exile* and *Darktown Revue* in 1931; *Veiled Aristocrats, Black Magic,* and *Ten Minutes to Live* in 1932; *The Girl from Chicago, Ten Minutes to Kill,* and *The Phantom of Kenwood* in 1933; *Harlem After Midnight* in 1934; *Lem Hawkin's Confession* (1935), *Swing* (1938), *Lying Lips* (1939), and *The Notorious Elinor Lee* (1940). Of these, only a few survive.

Juanita Moore

B. 1922. Actress.

An unusual character actress, best known for her performance as Annie Johnson in the 1959 remake of *Imitation of Life,* Moore's movie career started in the 1950s, a transitional era for black women in American films. Like her predecessors Hattie McDaniel and Louise Beavers, she was cast as a servant, but, partly because of changing racial attitudes and partly because of the movie industry's fear of complaints from civil rights groups, she was never compelled to go through any of the old-style demeaning mammy antics. Yet although Moore always struck the viewer as sympathetic, well-meaning, and loving, her characters were never permitted any of the showy idiosyncrasies and on-screen fun that were the property of her contemporary Pearl Bailey. The most interesting aspect of her character in *Imitation of Life* is, of course, her masochism, which is somewhat neutralized because Moore projects an *intelligent* brand of warmth that the more instinctual Louise Beavers lacked in the original. It's Moore's fundamental intelligence in all her roles that always makes her seem much too good for them. (The same is true of Theresa Harris.)

Imitation of Life won her an Oscar nomination as Best Supporting Actress of 1959. But the best follow-up part the industry could give her was as a housekeeper in *Tammy Tell Me True.*

In retrospect, it's always good to see Juanita Moore in an old film. And she remains the most active black character actress of her period.

Among her many films are: *Lydia Bailey* (1952); *Witness to Murder* (1954); *Woman's Prison* (1955); *A Band of Angels* (1957); *Walk on the Wild Side* (1962); *The Singing Nun* (1966); *Rosie* (1968); *Up Tight* (1968); *The Skin Game* (1971); *Thomasine and Bushrod* (1974); and *Abby* (1974).

Among her TV credits: "Climax" (1955); "Soldiers of Fortune" (1955); "Alfred Hitchcock Theatre" (1963, 1964, 1965); "Wagon Train" (1963); "Mr. Novak" (1964); "The Farmer's Daughter" (1965); "Gentle Ben" (1968); "The Bold Ones" (1969); "The Name of the Game" (1969); "Mannix" (1970); "Ironside" (1971); "Marcus Welby, M.D." (1972); "Adam 12" (1973); "A Dream for Christmas" (1973); "Ellery Queen" (1976); and, dare I add, a well-known laxative commercial.

Tim Moore

B. 1888; D. 1958. Actor.

As Kingfish on television's "Amos 'n' Andy" (1951–1953), Tim Moore was at the center of the action: an impossibly audacious and crafty comic manipulator. Perhaps what's now most striking about this actor's work is his broadness. Without a subtle bone in his body, he spelled out everything for his audience; he was both overdone and perfect at the same time. Significantly, his highflung style succeeded in a medium that we've repeatedly been told demands the laid-back, the comforting, the non-assaulting minimalist approach to acting. But Moore scored in the early years of television when viewers still got happily hepped up in the fiendish energy, the outlandishness, the sheer daring and assault on middle-class values that were the trademarks of larger-than-life performers like Lucille Ball's Lucy and Milton Berle's Uncle Miltie. No doubt audiences of the past, as today, also noted Moore's genuine fondness for his character Kingfish and his unabashed delight in the business of performing. Then, too, because Moore's Kingfish had nothing meek or submissive, shy or retiring, about him, black audiences, which have always responded to black self-assertion on stage and screen, can still enjoy him.

Interestingly enough, by the time Moore took the Kingfish role, he had assumed his days of entertaining were over. He had retired to his native Rock Island, Illinois, "to fish and relax and do both of them real slow." Decades earlier, a 12-year-old Moore had left Rock Island to join a vaudeville troupe, appearing in an act called "Cora Misket and Her Gold Dust Twins." Then at 15, he had been a jockey; at 17, a boxer. In 1925 he had gone back to show business. A big break came with *Blackbirds of 1928*, in which he appeared on Broadway and later toured with through Europe. In 1947, he had appeared in the film *Boy! What a Girl*, in which his star persona beamed out from almost every frame. He also had made some appearances in the late 1940s on Ed Sullivan's "Toast of the Town." But throughout this varied career, he had never emerged as a big name in show business.

"Amos 'n' Andy" changed all that, turning him, yes, overnight into a national celebrity. His late success is similar to that of Redd Foxx, who was also a seasoned veteran long before mainstream America ever knew he existed. Seemingly oblivious to the NAACP's criticism of the show, Tim Moore never backed off from his extravagantly detailed characterization of Kingfish. Accustomed to working in front of black audiences, his rhythm and vocal inflections (the point at which he punched his lines for maximum effect) were really pitched for the type of patron who might show up at the Apollo or any other of America's pre-World War II black theaters. The black intellectual community has been slow or reluctant to appreciate ethnic theater and performers. That may explain why Moore has rarely been discussed.

After "Amos 'n' Andy" went off the air, Moore stayed in Los Angeles, working irregularly. In early 1958, he popped up in the headlines when he was jailed and convicted on a misdemeanor charge and fined $100 for firing a pistol at his wife during a domestic dispute over, of all things, a slab of roast beef that had vanished from Moore's refrigerator. Complaining that his wife's free-loading relatives had eaten the meat, he had hit the ceiling and then gone upstairs for his gun. The press seemed to delight in reporting this story, no doubt assuming Moore was a Kingfish offscreen, too. Shortly afterward Moore shrewdly used the event as material for a nightclub routine that proved relatively successful.

In late 1958, apparently destitute, Moore, after a lengthy illness, died of pulmonary tuberculosis.

Mantan Moreland

B. 1901; D. 1973. Actor.

For black audiences, he was the little guy with the fastest eyes in the West. No one could widen or pop their eyes with quite the abandon of Mantan Moreland. He appeared in over 300 movies and is best remembered for his role as Birmingham Brown, the chauffeur/sidekick in the Charlie Chan mystery series. In his Hollywood features, Moreland usually stood by the hero's side unless, of course, he saw a ghost or criminal coming. Then he might cry out, "Feets, do yo stuff" and take off for the hills. But Moreland also worked in independently produced black films that set him up as something of a comic sporty ladies' man and also launched him as a true star, such movie titles as *Mantan Messes Up* (1946) and *Mantan Runs for Mayor* (1946) standing as testaments to his box-office appeal on the race movie circuit. Repeatedly displaying an arsenal of gestures and grimaces that he used to steal scenes and develop his characters, Moreland executed perfectly timed double-takes and mastered the trick of running in place without ever moving. In a career that spanned more than five decades, he worked in circuses, road companies, carnivals, and tent shows. At one point he teamed with F. E. Miller in a comedy act. At another time, he teamed with Tim Moore. Later in the 1940s and 1950s, he worked with Redd Foxx. He also made comedy albums for the race market. In 1957 his great ambition of doing a "serious" piece of theatre was finally realized when he was cast as Estragon in an all-black New York production of *Waiting for Godot*. Until the time of his death, Moreland continued working in films and television, appearing briefly in Carl Reiner's *The Comic* (1969) and Melvin Van Peebles' *Watermelon Man* (1970). Moreland died in California in 1973.

Among his TV credits: appearances in such 1960s series as "Adam 12" and "Love American Style"; "The Green Pastures" (1959, Hallmark Hall of Fame); and a hilarious episode of "The Bill Cosby Show" (1970) with Moms Mabley as his wife.

Among Mantan Moreland's film credits: *Spirit of Youth* (1938); *Next Time I Marry* (1938); *Harlem on the Prairie* (1939); *One Dark Night* (1939, in which Moreland played a serious role; film also titled *Night Club Girl*); *King of the Zombies* (1941); *Ellery Queen's Penthouse Mystery* (1941); *Treat 'Em Rough* (1942); *Strange Cargo of Dr. Rx* (1942); *Mexican Spitfire Sees a Ghost*

Mantan Moreland as the wide-eyed chauffeur Birmingham Brown in the Charlie Chan mystery series.

Moreland with Maude Russell in the stage production Singin' the Blues.

427

(1942); *Footlight Serenade* (1942); *Eyes in the Night* (1942); *Cabin in the Sky* (1942); *Sarong Girl* (1942); *Tarzan's New York Adventure* (1942); *Bowery to Broadway* (1944); *The Spider* (1946); *Come On, Cowboy* (1948); and *She's Too Mean to Me* (1948).

Greg Morris

B. 1934. Actor.

As Barney Collier on TV's "Mission: Impossible," Greg Morris helped break new ground: one of the first serious black characters to appear regularly on a series. Intelligent, reserved, shrewd, and almost resplendently cool and mildly remote, Morris was also something of a heartthrob, although the scripts usually kept him confined to the nonromantic sidelines of the action. From 1979 to 1981, Morris appeared, with less vitality, in a supporting role in the series "Vegas." On one of the few occasions when cast in a daredevil lead—in a movie, no less, *Countdown at Kusini* (1976)—Morris unfortunately seemed out of his element.

Among his film credits: *New Interns* (1964); *The Lively Set* (1964); and *The Sword of Ali Baba* (1965).

Among his TV credits: "Twilight Zone"; "Dr. Kildare" (1963); "The Dick Van Dyke Show" (1963); "Ben Casey" (1963); "Fugitive" (1965); "Branded" (1965); "I Spy" (1966); "Love American Style" (1970); "Killer by Night" (1972); "Mannix" (1963); "Six Million Dollar Man" (1974); "The Snoop Sisters" (1974); "Lucas Tanner" (1975); "The Streets of San Francisco" (1975); "Sanford and Son" (1976); "Flight to Holocaust" (1977); "Quincy" (1978); "A Night to Raise the Dead" (1979); "Crisis in Midair" (1979); "The Jeffersons" (1983); "The Fall Guy" (1983); "T. J. Hooker" (1984); "The Jesse Owens Story" (1984); and "Murder She Wrote" (1984).

Eddie Murphy

B. 1961. Comedian, actor.

One of the most popular stars of the 1980s, Eddie Murphy first became known on television, later appeared in hit movies, also made comedy albums, and played huge concert dates. He accomplished all this, mind you, by the age of 23. Yet while his fans adored him, his critics, as should be expected, frequently questioned his range and his taste.

Murphy was born in Brooklyn (the son of a New York cop, who died when Eddie was three) and later at age nine moved with his family (his mother had remarried) to the predominantly black Long Island community of Roosevelt. As an energetic fifteen-year-old who had always done impersonations and comic routines for his friends and family, Murphy started performing with a band he'd formed with friends at a local youth center. But when he discovered he had a gift for getting laughs, he turned quickly to standup comedy, working up an act which earned him from $25 to $50 a night as he played Long Island clubs. Not long afterward he appeared at Manhattan's Comic Strip Club (1979, when he was eighteen) and acquired a new manager, then took his act to clubs along the East Coast. Then in 1981 he was signed as a "Saturday Night Live" regular. (He left the show in 1984.)

On television's "Saturday Night Live" he rapidly rose to stardom with his routines and parodies. He created a ghetto version of PBS's gentle "Mr. Rogers," whom Murphy called Mr. Robinson. ("Oh, here's Mr. Landlord with an eviction notice," the character says.) His other characters included: the pimp Velvet Jones (whom Murphy said had just written a book titled *I Wanna Be a Ho*) and the white-hating author Tyrone Green (who announces "I hate white people because they is white. W I T E"; and recites, "Kill my landlord," in which he spells *kill* C I L L.) He also did sendups of *Our Gang*'s Buckwheat and such famous figures as Bill Cosby, James Brown, Stevie Wonder, Bishop Tutu, and Michael Jackson.

Murphy's humor touched base with a young audience that, like him, enjoyed seeing a parody of the clutter of pop culture images it had grown up with. That audience, having come of age in a post-Watergate era of doubt and cynicism, seemed also to expect humor to be used to uncover wicked truths about almost any respectable figure, at almost any cost. In answering those audience needs, Murphy's performances, to a certain extent like those of Don Rickles and Joan Rivers, could border on the cruel. Insult comedy of this period urged laughter at physical attributes or handicaps. To deride someone's appearance seemed par for the course. When Murphy did a Stevie Wonder impersonation, he mocked the singer's lack of co-ordination. When he had a chance to rib Michael Jackson, he did so by parodying the singer's soft-spoken, asexual air.

At the same time in this conservative Reagan age, Murphy seemed content to mock characters who once might have been fit for some type of comic psychological examination. Never was there an attempt to develop a Velvet Jones or a Tyrone Green to the point where we might understand what made those characters tick, what lay beneath the street personality we all took for granted. Watching his satires of those two, one had to ask: why must a black man, in order to be satirized, be turned into an illiterate? Does this not harp on the worst attitudes and beliefs that much of white America has always had about black America?

Murphy rode to the crest of popularity with this type of comedy on television and in concert. But it did not go uncriticized. Nor did other aspects of his humor. Some critics pointed out a hostility that Murphy often seemed to direct towards the women in his audience. During a Murphy concert performance when a woman called out, "Eddie, will you marry me?" *Newsweek* reported Murphy's response. "'No,' he says, pauses a beat—his smile becoming almost gleeful—then suggests in the baldest possible terms that she console herself by favoring him with an oral endearment." Reviewing another Murphy concert performance, New York theater critic Clive Barnes recounted an unfortunate incident: After some young girls had laughingly protested against Murphy's ungracious barbs at Michael Jackson, Murphy had a spotlight thrown on them. Noticing that among the five or six girls, one was black, he singled out the black girl "to suggest that she couldn't get any real friends, and was a traitor to black sisterhood," wrote Barnes. "When he makes fun of Bill Cosby—whom he baits unmercifully—or Leon Spinks or any of those people well able to take care of themselves, that seems okay. But a kid in the audience?"

Others also felt Murphy's comedy had a built-in homophobia. In a "Honeymooners" take-off, he had depicted Ralph and Norton as gay lovers. He also did a routine with a gay Mr. T., which *Newsweek* said "sounds like a funny idea, but isn't." Martin Brest, the director of *Beverly*

80s' superstar Eddie Murphy's movies made a mint and he acquired a huge following. Yet a nagging question remained: were his screen characters free of stereotyping?

Eddie Murphy's career began with TV's "Saturday Night Live." He's shown here with Stevie Wonder.

Hills Cop, has recalled that when he was unsure of how to handle a sequence in which Murphy's Axel Foley bluffs his way into an exclusive men's club, Murphy had quickly come up with the idea of playing "a lisping swish" called Ramon, who sashays his way past the *maitre d'* of the club's restaurant, saying he must deliver a message to a member there about herpes. Sometimes when Murphy seemed lost for an original comment, he fell back into this brand of comedy, which, in all truthfulness, is not too different from early American cinema, which, when in a pinch for a surefire gag, simply carted out a black face, the mere appearance of which guaranteed laughs.

Often critics compared Murphy with Richard Pryor for more than the obvious reason (that both were amazingly successful black comedy stars of the 1980s): Pryor had also created comic street characters, had also let loose against our taboos (and fears) of sex and race with a barrage of profanity. It was apparent that Murphy had been influenced by Pryor. It was apparent also that he had never understood Pryor's work. For Richard Pryor had always gotten inside his winos, junkies, or numbers runners, uncovering their vulnerabilities, their troubled histories, and revealing at times their sadness and touching beauty. Murphy, however, seemed to see his various characters as lowlife figures without any kind of innate dignity. Nor did he ever show the affectionate regard for his characters as a comic like Flip Wilson had done with his Reverend LeRoy and Geraldine. And, obviously missing from Murphy's humor in his television skits were the social/political concerns of a Dick Gregory.

Once Murphy made a career switch from television to films, his superstar status was solidified. His technical skills were, frankly, brilliantly displayed. He was a highly polished, glittering surface. Yet *48 Hrs.* (1982) and *Trading Places* (1983) used him as a sidekick to the white male leads. And in the enormous hit *Beverly Hills Cop* (1984) he wrestled with material that was essentially flat and undeveloped. In the hotel sequence when he could not get a room, Murphy simply *got loud* on the hotel management, unleasing a stream of profanity. Audiences of the 1980s loved the sequence, somehow equating his profanity with a newfound honesty. But there was nothing behind the dirty words. When Richard Pryor had gone off on people, his outbursts brought to the fore years of trouble and discontent with a culture. Profanity was used as a weapon and was integral to his characters. For the huge white audience that supported Murphy, he may well have represented, sad to say, a new stereotyped view of a black man. In that audience's eyes, being black may well have meant being loud and crude. Moreover, in *Beverly Hills Cop* and *Beverly Hills Cop II* (1987), Murphy was sexually neutralized, left stranded without a leading lady. Traditionally, male comedy stars are not thought of as romantic heroes. But whether it was Chaplin or Bob Hope or later Chevy Chase and Woody Allen, the comic star usually had a woman he pined for. In *Golden Child* (1986)—one of the rare occasions when Murphy was paired romantically with a female, he was still not permitted to have explicit love scenes. The question we have to ask is: do white audiences still fear black male sexuality?

Yet interestingly, regardless of his roles, Murphy maintained a large black following too. That audience no doubt responded to his brazen assurance, his cockiness, his rapid-fire delivery, his unpretentious working-class attitudes and outlook, and his immense personal charm. Moreover, unlike a Stepin Fetchit who in films feared or answered to whites, Murphy never backed down from anyone or anything. Throughout *Beverly Hills Cop*, *48 Hrs.* and *Trading Places*, although the scripts treated him as an oddity, a street nigger plopped into a white world, Murphy saw himself as anyone's equal, never a subordinate. He asked nothing from the dominant white culture; he simply demanded he be given what was rightfully his. In the long run—despite the serious misgivings some in the black community had about him and his image—Murphy's self-assertion, like that of so many other black stars, saved him.

Murphy's TV credits include: the 1983 HBO special "Delirious" and "Bob Hope's WHO MAKES THE WORLD LAUGH—Part II" (1984).

His movie credits include: *Best Defense* (1984); and the concert film *Raw* (1987).

Clarence Muse

B. 1889; D. 1979. Actor, writer, composer.

Clarence Muse is best remembered today as an actor who repeatedly sought to invest his servant roles of the 1930s with a semblance of dignity and a degree of seriousness. The fact that he played tom characters in scores of films cannot be denied. The fact that he played those figures with great intelligence and thoughtfulness has often been overlooked. His were never the shamelessly flamboyant figures that someone like the gifted Stepin Fetchit played. Nor were they eye-popping, ingratiatingly dimwitted characters like those of Fred "Snowflake" Toomes or Floyd Shakeford. Something within Muse always compelled him to hold back, to distance himself from his characters and his films, which apparently he felt uneasy with. Consequently, often enough a studied quality underlies his performances. His voice remains theatrical (enjoyably so), and he lacks the fluidity and strange "naturalness" of someone like Fetchit (an actor whom Muse admired and called "the greatest artist in the world"). Yet it is still a pleasure to see Muse, mainly because he is so unlike other black actors of his era. His performances crack the glossy artificiality of his films, injecting them with a healthy dose of unassimilated realism.

Born in Baltimore, Muse was a graduate of Dickinson College's Law School. But by the 1920s he had abandoned a law career to work as an actor in New York with the Lincoln Players and the Lafayette Players (a company he helped found). When offered a role in Hollywood's all-black 1929 musical *Hearts in Dixie*, Muse said years later he wasn't interested at first. When the studio was willing to pay him $1,250 a week, he said he changed his mind.

Afterwards he remained in the movie capital for the next 50 years, working consistently in film after film. Often Muse did bits as in *Cabin in the Cotton* (1932) or *Show Boat* (1936). Other times, he landed real roles. In the 1931 *Huckleberry Finn*, he was a mighty dignified Nigger Jim. In the 1934 *Count of Monte Cristo*, he portrayed the deaf mute. Director Frank Capra, who referred to Muse as his "pet actor," used him in a number of films such as *Dirigible* (1931) and most notably in the highly popular *Broadway Bill* (1934), which was remade as *Riding High* (1950) with Bing Crosby as star and Muse again in a supporting role. Today at revivals of King Vidor's Civil War drama *So Red the Rose* (1935), audiences still are jolted to attention with Muse's performance as the renegade slave Cato, who gives an impassioned speech urging the slaves on the plantation to rebel. Although the way in which the speech is written—and the manner in which Muse plays the part—do not seem quite true enough to the period, one cannot help being swept up in Muse's inflammatory fervor and energy. When the film's heroine Margaret Sullavan, as the plantation's young mistress, marches into the slave quarters to quell the rebels, we long for Muse's Cato to let her have it! But, alas, despite Muse's very "modern" performance, we remember this indeed as a film of the 1930s. The rebellion dies down.

Muse was also a writer and composer. His song "When It's Sleepy

Clarence Muse (with child star Dickie Moore) as the rebellious slave leader in the Civil War drama So Red the Rose.

Time Down South" was performed with great success by Louis Armstrong. He also composed a black symphony called "Harlem Heab'n." And with Langston Hughes, Muse wrote the screenplay for the Hollywood film *Way Down South* (1939), a true oddity in movie history. Directed by Bernard Vorhaus, the film focused on the relationship of a "kindly" young white master (Bobby Breen) and his black charges during the days of slavery. The picture was enlivened by spirituals by The Hall Johnson Choir (which worked in numerous Hollywood films, including the 1936 *Green Pastures* and the 1943 *Cabin in the Sky*). In reviewing the film, *Variety* pointed out that *Way Down South*'s "business possibilities do not appear bright, and there is a question what will happen below the Mason-Dixon Line in view of the slavery background." *Variety* noted that the young white hero might be considered "a little overboard in his sympathies for the colored folks of the plantation." Although *Way Down South* was not a hit, it marks an early attempt by important black artists to work behind the cameras within the established film industry, bringing to American commercial cinema their own unique point of view.

A year later in the independently produced *Broken Strings* (1940), which he co-wrote, Muse, now working outside the Hollywood system, had better luck, giving a highly likable performance as a stodgy classical musician who learns the fun of swing music.

Muse also published a pamphlet (c. 1932) titled "The Dilemma of the Negro Actor," in which he pinpointed problems that were to exist for black film performers for the next fifty years: always the black actor has to struggle with roles that he feels don't explain his experience. Yet if he does not do such parts, he runs the risk of not working at all. Decades later this fundamental dilemma was amusingly explored by black independent filmmaker Robert Townsend in his 1987 satire *Hollywood Shuffle*.

From 1955 to 1956, Muse appeared as Sam on the now forgotten television series "Casablanca." Afterwards he seldom appeared on screen. Among his last performances were roles in *Buck and the Preacher* (1972), *Car Wash* (1976), and *The Black Stallion* (1979).

Clarence Muse's career was examined in a documentary by Thurman White and Woodi Webb, titled *Clarence Muse: Black Star of the Silver Screen*, which was shown in New York City in 1980.

Muse's movie credits include: *Guilty* (1930); *Rain or Shine* (1930); *The Last Parade* (1931); *Safe in Hell* (1931); *The Wet Parade* (1932); *Lena Rivers* (1932); *Attorney for the Defense* (1932); *Night World* (1932); *Is My Face Red* (1932); *Winner Take All* (1932); *White Zombie* (1932); *Hell's Highway* (1932); *Washington Merry-Go-Round* (1932); *Man Against Woman* (1932); *Laughter in Hell* (1933); *From Hell to Heaven* (1933); *The Mind Reader* (1933); *Massacre* (1934); *Black Moon* (1934); *The Personality Kid* (1934); *Alias Mary Dow* (1935); *O'Shaughnessy's Boy* (1935); *Muss 'Em Up* (1936); *Laughing Irish Eyes* (1936); *Follow Your Heart* (1936); *Daniel Boone* (1936); *Mysterious Crossing* (1937); *Spirit of Youth* (1938); *The Toy Wife* (1938); *Secrets of Nurse* (1938); *Zanzibar* (1940); *Maryland* (1940); *Sporting Blood* (1940); *The Flame of New Orleans* (1941); *The Invisible Ghost* (1941); *Tales of Manhattan* (1942); *The Black Swan* (1942); *Shadow of a Doubt* (1943); *Heaven Can Wait* (1943); *Flesh and Fantasy* (1943); *Jam Session* (1944); *Two Smart People* (1947); *Live Today for Tomorrow* (1948); *The Great Dan Patch* (1949); *My Forbidden Past* (1951); *Apache Drums* (1951); and *Porgy and Bess* (1959).

Denise Nicholas

B. c. 1944. Actress.

This Detroit-born, green-eyed beauty worked with The Free Southern Theatre and The Negro Ensemble Company, then won the role of Liz McIntyre, the dreamy high school guidance counselor in the series "Room 222" (1969–1974). Later she returned to series TV as the disgruntled former wife of Demond Wilson in "Baby I'm Back" (1978).

Nicholas also worked, with varying degrees of success, in such films as *The Soul of Nigger Charley* (1973, hers was far too contemporary a sensibility for this pained period piece) and *Blacula*. Later she fared better, displaying her penchant for comic assertiveness, in two of the Poitier/Cosby comedies *Let's Do It Again* (1975) and *A Piece of the Action* (1977).

Often audiences were surprised to find so attractive a woman with so sparkling a gift for funny tough dialogue. More an engaging personality than an ever-changing actress, Nicholas had a hard-edge, resplendently independent, no-nonsense, don't-play-with-me quality. Always the realist, she was quick to let a man know she could only be pushed so far. In the past, an assertive funny black actress was often a desexed actress. But Nicholas retained her femininity and her enduring sexiness.

Ambitious and energetic, Nicholas wrote *The Denise Nicholas Beauty Book* in 1971 and also later formed her own production company, Masai Productions. She also had marriages to two distinctive entertainment personalities, black director Gilbert Moses and singer Bill Withers.

Other film credits include: *Mr. Ricco* (1975).

Her TV credits include: "It Takes a Thief" (1968); "NYPD" (1968); "The F.B.I." (1969); "Five Desperate Women" (1971); "Night Gallery" (1971); "Marcus Welby, M.D." (1975); "Rhoda" (1975); "Police Story" (1975); "Ring of Passion" (1978); "Love Boat" (1980, with Robert Guillaume, Richard Roundtree, and Pam Grier); "Sophisticated Gents" (1981); "Diff'rent Strokes" (1981); "Jacqueline Susann's *Valley of the Dolls*" (1981); "One Day at a Time" (1982); and "Magnum, P.I." (1984).

The Nicholas Brothers

Fayard Nicholas, B. 1917; Harold Nicholas, B. 1924. Dancers.

Among Hollywood dancers, few could match the incomparable Nicholas Brothers, whose sophisticated mastery of an intricate, highly acrobatic, and satiny smooth dance style still makes movie audiences marvel today. The brothers grew up in a show-business atmosphere. Their parents had organized their own band, which appeared at Philadephia's Standard Theater during the era of black vaudeville. By age three, Fayard, having spent most of his time in theaters, was already imitating the dancers he saw on stage. Later when his baby brother Harold was old enough to walk, Fayard began teaching him dance steps and an evolving dance style that the brothers would make distinctly theirs. Harold Nicholas once said, "The only influence I ever had was Fayard. Nobody impressed me except him. Not even Bill Robinson."

In 1931, the pair made their professional debut, surprisingly, on radio's "The Horn and Hardart Kiddie Hour." Fayard was 13; Harold, 7. The next year they appeared at the legendary Cotton Club, where they were regular fixtures on the bill for years to come. The Nicholas Brothers also performed in such Broadway shows as *Ziegfeld Follies of*

1936 and *Babes in Arms* (1937), appeared at other clubs and theaters around the country, and also impressed European audiences in such shows as *Blackbirds of 1936*.

Their movie work started early. In 1932, they were the two children standing by Nina Mae McKinney's side in *Pie Pie Blackbird*. Two years later they worked in the Eddie Cantor film *Kid Millions*, followed the next year by *An All Colored Vaudeville Show* (with Adelaide Hall), and *The Big Broadcast of 1936*. On his own, Harold appeared in *Carolina Blues* (1944) and *Stoopnocracy* (1933). In the early 1940s, the spins, twirls, jumps, and leaps of these sensational young dancers were on dazzling display in such Hollywood films as *Sun Valley Serenade* (1941, in which they performed a memorable version of "Chattanooga Choo Choo" with Dorothy Dandridge, whom Harold later married), *Down Argentine Way* (1940), *Tin Pan Alley* (1940), *Great American Broadcast* (1941), *Orchestra Wives* (1942), and *The Pirate* (1948). In *Orchestra Wives*, they performed a now-famous routine in which Fayard quickly ran up a wall, then landed in a split while Harold ran up another wall, performed a backflip, and then also landed with a split. This kind of routine has never been duplicated and has earned them the respect of such peers as George Ballachine, Gene Kelly, and, later, Michael Jackson. Their most famous performance is in the 1943 *Stormy Weather*, in which their staircase splits still elicit screams of delight and wonder from audiences. Perhaps what adds immeasurably to the pleasure of watching the Nicholas Brothers is that they never seem to be working hard at their numbers; everything flows effortlessly with an uncanny spontaneity and an all-consuming joy.

After the late 1940s, film audiences saw almost nothing of the Nicholas Brothers, although they did appear on such television programs in the 1950s and 1960s as "The Ed Sullivan Show" and "Hollywood Palace" (1964). Harold spent many years living and working in Europe. In 1970, Fayard returned to films for a supporting dramatic role in *The Liberation of L. B. Jones*. Harold also appeared as Little Seymour in *Uptown Saturday Night* (1974) and continued working in such theater productions as *Sophisticated Ladies* (1982–83) and *Tap Dance Kid* (1985–86).

Sequences of the Nicholas Brothers performing also turn up in the compilation films, *Take It or Leave It* (1944), *That's Entertainment* (1974), and *That's Dancing* (1985). They also make a sensational appearance in *Black Network* (1936).

Harold Nicholas (l.), Dorothy Dandridge, and Fayard Nicholas in the famous "Chattanooga Choo Choo" number from Sun Valley Serenade. *Later Harold married Dandridge.*

Two of the screen's greatest dancers, from the time they were children: the Nicholas Brothers. Fayard (l.) and Harold Nicholas with Nina Mae McKinney in Pie Pie Blackbird.

Maidie Norman

B. 1912. Actress.

This Georgia-born character actress's film career started in 1948 in *The Burning Cross*, then continued into the transitional 1950s, a period when black women still played servants. Because the studios feared offending black audiences, the maid characters, unlike movie maids of the past, were developed without tension and were the blandest of bland personalities. Mostly they were just *there*. Norman was often stuck with just such uncommanding parts, some maids, some not, in *Bright Road* (1953), *Torch Song* (1953), *About Mrs. Leslie* (1954), *Susan Slept Here* (1954), *Tarzan's Hidden Jungle* (1955), *The Opposite Sex* (1956), and *Written on the Wind* (1957). Then she lucked up, portraying the housekeeper in the Bette Davis/Joan Crawford modern gothic horror tale *What Ever Happened to Baby Jane?* (1962). In a film full of the bizarre, the grotesque, and the Holly*weird*, Norman's Elvira was the only character wise to some of the shenanigans of the mad Baby Jane, and oddly enough, hers was one of the few characters the audience could identify with and briefly cheer on. Alas, she suffers an unpleasant fate. But audiences still remember the character, if not the name of the actress who played the part.

Other films include: *The Well* (a 1951 controversial and well-known film within the black community); *The Final Comedown* (1972); *Maurie* (1973); *A Star Is Born* (1976); and *Airport 77*, in which she confidently plays a shameless character, the ever-patient maid to Olivia de Havilland; after the plane crash, like many a noble Negro movie character, she dies in her white friend's arms.

TV credits include: "Mannix," "Adam 12," "Ironside," "Name of the Game" (all 1969); "Days of Our Lives" (1971); "Another Part of the Forest" (1972); "Sty of the Blind Pig" (1974); "Streets of San Francisco" (1974); "Lucas Tanner" (1974); "Kung Fu" (1975); "Good Times" (1975); "Harry O" (1975); "The Jeffersons" (1975); "Police Story" (1976); and "Roots: The Next Generation" (1979).

Ron O'Neal

B. 1937. Actor.

Of all the actors to play the buck hero in movies of the early 1970s, Ron O'Neal was probably the most skilled, most interesting, most complex. Unlike Richard Roundtree, O'Neal seemed secure and at ease with the camera. Unlike the Jim Brown kind of hero—a fundamentally dimensionless fellow who we feel shoots neither with forethought nor even much pleasure (instead he does so, we assume, simply because the director's told him to)—O'Neal's Priest in the 1972 *Super Fly* was a complicated man divided in two, torn between his quest for the American Dream at its most materialistic and his baffled hope for something other than what materialism can provide. Moody, withdrawn, restless, his heroes in the two *Super Fly* films are reluctant ones, seemingly trapped by a sense of alienation and dislocation. We sense they might prefer simply walking away from an incident, but they no doubt believe they have no choice but to fight back. Nevertheless, when they rouse themselves to arms, they do so with an intriguing kind of passivity, which indeed has been an important part of O'Neal's appeal, particularly to women. Despite the early sequence in *Super Fly* in which he both

Ron O'Neal in his most famous role as Priest in Super Fly: *good looks and a brooding intensity.*

ignores and lords it over his white girlfriend in an almost shocking way (the woman represents absolutely nothing to him on a personal, human level; she's but one more capitalistic acquisition), he revealed in other sequences a sensitivity to women that actors like Jim Brown lacked. No doubt responding to his good looks and perhaps his moody intensity, female viewers tended to think that O'Neal simply needed the right woman to bring out his natural warmth and sensuality, a sensuality so defined, it should be noted, that even *Playboy* named O'Neal one of the cinema's important sex stars of the 1970s.

Despite his success in *Super Fly*, the sequel *Super Fly T.N.T.* (1973) failed, and O'Neal's movie career faltered. At times he seemed to have forsaken acting altogether. But he intermittently reappeared, playing character roles in *Master Gunfighter* (1975), *Brothers* (1977), *When a Stranger Calls* (1979), and *The Final Countdown* (1980). In 1984, his magnetism was still intact when he played a Cuban officer in the right-wing fantasy *Red Dawn*.

O'Neal's career had begun in the theatre. Born in Utica, New York, he performed with Cleveland's Karamu Playhouse, later in the Negro Ensemble Company's productions of *Ceremonies in Dark Old Men* (1969) and *Dream on Monkey Mountain* (1971) and also in the celebrated production of *No Place To Be Somebody* (1969). Later he returned to the stage in *Macbeth* in 1974, the Broadway farce *All over Town* in 1975, and the New York Shakespeare Festival production of *Agamemnon* in 1977.

Early films include *Move* (1970) and *The Organization* (1971).

O'Neal's television credits include: "Hot L Baltimore" (1975); "Freedom Road" (1979); "Brave New World" (1980); "Guyana Tragedy: The Story of Jim Jones" (1980); "Sophisticated Gents" (1981); "Shannon" (1982); "Bring 'Em Back Alive" (a 1982–1983 adventure series in which he played H.H., the Sultan of Jahore); "The Main Event" (1984); "Playing with Fire" (1985); and "The Equalizer" (1986, a series in which he appeared in some episodes as Isadore Smalls).

Gordon Parks, Jr.

B. 1934; D. 1979. Director.

The son of photographer/filmmaker Gordon Parks, Sr., Gordon Parks, Jr., found himself—with the release of his 1972 first feature *Super Fly*—at the forefront of a new group of black film directors of the 1970s. Exhibiting a good feel for music and a sharp eye for the density of a tough urban setting as well as a fondness for a moody renegade hero, Parks's *Super Fly* touched base with a black audience anxious for some glimpse of black male self-assertion and for some comment on the terrors and tensions of contemporary black urban life.

Afterwards in *Thomasine and Bushrod* (1974), again focusing his camera on a sensitive rebellious black man (Max Julien), who defines himself through a life of crime, as well as a spirited black woman (Vonetta McGee) sometimes forced to call the shots, Parks was less successful. He proved effective at showing male/female conflicts but was unable to invest his southwestern landscapes with any sense of adventure, danger, or affection. When he turned his sights to an action film *Three the Hard Way* (1974), starring a trio of action heroes, Jim Brown, Fred Williamson, and Jim Kelly, he was clearly out of his element, lost in macho maneuvers that he seemed unable to take any real joy in. Later in 1975 he directed a teenage love story, *Aaron Loves Angela*.

Determined in his early years not to cash in on the name of his famous father, Gordon Parks Jr. had worked in New York City's garment district, pushing clothes racks through the streets. He served in the army from 1956 to 1957. In the 1960s, he performed folk songs and played the guitar in Greenwich Village. When he turned to photography, he used the name Gordon Rogers for three years, still adamant about making it on his own. He was a still photographer for the films *Burn* (1969) and *The Godfather* (1972) and a cameraman on his father's film *The Learning Tree* (1969).

In 1979, Gordon Parks, Jr., was killed in a plane crash in Kenya.

Gordon Parks, Sr.

B. 1912. Director.

When his film *The Learning Tree* was released in 1969, *Newsweek* saluted Gordon Parks, Sr., as "the first Negro ever to produce and direct a movie for a major American studio." And so he was.

Parks came to films after a distinguished career, from 1948 to 1968, as a photographer for *Life*. He had grown up in Kansas, the youngest of 15 children. His early years, recorded in his two books *The Learning Tree* in 1963 and *A Choice of Weapons* in 1966, were a rough-and-tumble experience; in Chicago he had worked as busboy; in Minneapolis as a piano player; in Harlem as a dope dealer; and at one time he was also a professional basketball player. In 1933, he had married Sally Alvis, with whom he had three children, one of whom, Gordon Parks, Jr., also became a film director. The couple later divorced. In 1937, Parks, having then decided to become a photographer, walked into a Seattle hock shop and bought his first camera for $12.50. A career was launched.

Parks's films can be divided into two general categories: the more commercial dramas—*Shaft* (1971), *Shaft's Big Score* (1972), *The Super Cops* (1974)—in which he focused on contemporary men of action caught up in the muddle and congestion of modern urban life—and the more personal "romances"—*The Learning Tree*, *Leadbelly* (1976), and to a lesser extent, "Solomon Northrup's Odyssey" (1984)—in which his social/racial concerns were coupled with (and almost consumed by, some would say) his overriding fondness for lush natural settings and his searingly romantic view of life. "I want a continuity of beautiful pictures and beautiful movement," Parks told *Time* in 1969. "I try to start each scene with a beautiful still photo." The pretty look of his romances, especially in *Leadbelly*, frequently undercuts his comments on a brutal, dehumanizing white culture. Almost all his films, however, reveal his determination to deal with assertive, sexual black heroes, who struggle to maintain their manhood amid mounting social/political tensions. *The Super Cops*, which started the white actors David Selby and Ron Liebman, is obviously an exception. Indeed, in some respects, his films, the romances included, can generally be read as heady manhood initiation rituals.

Following the release of the successful *Shaft* features, Parks seemed on solid commercial footing. But a maverick determined to do his own kind of movie, Parks repeatedly found himself in battle with Hollywood, notably with Paramount Pictures over its handling of *Leadbelly*. Parks was outraged by the studio's original advertising campaign, which he believed pitched the movie as simply "another blaxploitation film." Original ads had depicted a bare-chested, muscular man flanked on one side by a scantily dressed vixen and, on the other, by a fight scene. He complained, too, about the film's distribution. *Leadbelly* was not given a big New York city opening, which can be an essential if one hopes to reach the critics.

Later Parks longed to film the story of blues singer Bessie Smith. And he might have been able to do something with *The Color Purple* (1986). Instead, ignored by the major studios, he turned his sights to television, filming for PBS the drama "Solomon Northrup's Odyssey."

Among Parks's other credits: the documentaries "The World of Piri Thomas" and "Diary of a Harlem Family."

Brock Peters

B. 1927. Actor.

Brock Peters is no doubt still best remembered as a heavy in films: the unyielding army officer who berates and hassles poor Harry Belafonte in *Carmen Jones* (1954); the terrifying *and* terrorizing Crown who attacks Dorothy Dandridge in *Porgy and Bess* (1959). In some respects, these were oldstyle buck characterizations, the nightmarish, unrelentingly villainous kind that audiences still seem to love to hate. Peters felt he was locked into such roles and that consequently, his career suffered. "It was almost disastrous," Peters told a reporter for the *New York World-Telegraph and Sun* in 1964. "Producers didn't want to see me. They had liked my performances but couldn't see me as anything but a heavy."

The Brock Peters image underwent a significant change when he was cast in *To Kill a Mockingbird* (1962) as a Southern black man who is accused of having raped a white woman. In *Film Reviews*, Henry Hart wrote: ". . . a remarkable performance by Brock Peters. . . . Single-handed, by his intelligent awareness of how a decent Negro so victimized would behave, and by his skillful ability to project such a Negro's feeling and demeanor, Mr. Peters redeems the plot cliche and makes us remember that the history of the black man in the U.S. *does* include cases like the one on which *To Kill a Mockingbird* is based."

During this period, Peters also found another role that helped stretch his talents: as the jazz musician in the British *L-Shaped Room* (1963). Then came Sidney Lumet's *The Pawnbroker* (1965). In this New York-based drama which starred Rod Steiger as a concentration camp survivor now running a pawnshop in Harlem, Brock Peters gave another strong—scary—performance. Although the film may strike some today as too studied, it remains exciting to see Peters and such other black actors as the great Juano Hernandez, the nearly forgotten Thelma Oliver, and Raymond St. Jacques at work in material they find challenging.

Peters never became a leading man in American films. But he continued working actively for years. In 1973, he co-produced the black screen comedy *Five on the Black Hand Side*.

Peters's movie credits include: *Heavens Above!* (1963); *Major Dundee* (1965); *The Incident* (1967); *P.J.* (1968); and *The McMasters* (1970). At one point, Peters asked that his name be removed from the credits of *The McMasters*, in which he had played a rapist (another heavy). Peters objected to the way the movie had been edited with certain "sensitive" key scenes left on the cutting room floor. "They have totally destroyed a black man's performance," he said at the time, "and taken away the moments that make him a human being." A role that Peters was more pleased with was that of Reverend Stephen Kumalo in the musical *Lost in the Stars* (1974).

Peters's TV credits include: "The Snows of Kilimanjaro" (1960); "Sam Benedict" (1963); "Great Adventure" (the 1963 "Go Down, Moses" episode); "The Eleventh Hour" (1964); "Daniel Boone" (1964); "Rawhide" (1965); "Trials of O'Brien" (1966); "The Girl from U.N.C.L.E." (1966); "Mission: Impossible" (1967); "Outcasts" (1969); "Gunsmoke" (1969); "Mannix" (1970); "Night Gallery" (1970); "The Streets of San Francisco" (1974); "McCloud" (1974); "Baretta" (1975); "Police Story" (1976); "Faerie Tale Theater" (1985); and "Magnum, P.I." (1985).

Sidney Poitier

B. 1927. Actor, director.

Even in the late 1980s, an era when Richard Pryor and Eddie Murphy were celebrated as the first authentic black box-office movie superstars, Sidney Poitier, by then a film fixture for almost 40 years, ironically remained the most important black actor ever to have appeared in American motion pictures. Having worked steadily in films in the 1950s and 1960s, Poitier had almost singlehandedly changed Hollywood's image of black America. And with the possible exceptions of Stepin Fetchit, Dorothy Dandridge, and Richard Pryor, few other black film stars had had as significant an impact on black audiences. Today Poitier's long career, a mixed bag of blessings and disappointments, of highs and lows, still reflects fundamental changes in our nation's political attitudes, values, and tastes.

Looking back at his early childhood years, it's doubtful if anyone would have spotted any telltale signs that Poitier would end up becoming much of anything. Born in Miami in 1927, the youngest of seven children of a poor Bahamian couple, Poitier grew up on Cat Island in great poverty. By age 16, this tall gangly kid, who with very little schooling often seemed adrift and unable to focus on anything, made his way to Miami for a year or so, then went to New York, arriving with but $3 in his pocket and an uncanny hope to do something with his life. He lived a slipshod existence, sometimes sleeping on rooftops because he had no money, other times living in boarding houses and working at an assortment of jobs: dishwasher, chicken plucker, busboy, dockhand, you-name-it.

Alone, without friends, he daily—anxiously—searched the Want Ads of New York's *Amsterdam News*, looking for better work. One day he

Sidney Poitier in an early dramatic performance in the TV drama "The Parole Officer."

read what he thought was an ad: "Actors Wanted by Little Theatre Group." Shortly thereafter when Poitier showed up at The American Negro Theatre on West 135th Street, saying he'd come for the acting job, the Theatre's director, actor Frederick O'Neal, looked at him skeptically, asked was he really an actor, to which Poitier answered, of course. O'Neal then told him to go on stage and read. Terrified, Poitier gave it a try, was just about hooted offstage and told by O'Neal, "Look, boy, don't waste our time. You're no actor. And you can't be one. Go get a job somewhere else." Dejected, Poitier walked away.

Yet strangely enough, he said years later, O'Neal's justified rejection spurred him on. Feeling at ease in the atmosphere of the theatre, he became determined to be a part of it. What held him back most, he knew, was his West Indian accent, so thick that people often laughed when they heard him speak. He studied and struggled tenaciously to rid himself of the accent and to speak like an "American." Having bought a little radio, he listened nightly to its announcers, then repeated every word they uttered. After some six months, Poitier had lost the accent. Returning to the American Negro Theatre, he re-auditioned and became part of a group of post-World War II new-style black actors that included Harry Belafonte, Ossie Davis, Ruby Dee, Earle Hyman, and Lloyd Richards (who years later directed Poitier in the 1959 stage version of *A Raisin in the Sun*).

In a short period of time, Poitier won a small role in the all-black 1946 Broadway production of *Lysistrata* (so nervous was he opening night, so he said, he stumbled through the part, sending the audience into hysterics; the critics, however, ended up praising his hilarious comic bit), was an understudy in the Broadway and touring productions of *Anna Lucasta* (1948), and then—almost miraculously—landed a plum part in the movie *No Way Out*. Few actors in films have had so rapid a rise.

Joseph L. Mankiewicz's *No Way Out* (1950) cast Sidney Poitier in what came to be a typical Poitier role of the 1950s: as an educated, bright, and dedicated young man—a doctor—caught up in a heated racial situation. Unjustly accused by a white hoodlum of having murdered a patient, Poitier's character Luther Brooks must fight to prove his innocence. Of course, by the movie's end Sidney's revealed to be the good guy doctor we knew he was all along. But there's a twist. At the climax, the very hood who had falsely accused Poitier shoots him and is also wounded himself. Poitier's Brooks could easily let the man die but—patient, understanding, all-forgiving—he says, "Don't you think I'd like to put the rest of these bullets through his head? I can't . . . because I've got to live, too. He's sick. . . . He's crazy . . . but I can't kill a man just because he hates me." He then saves the white man's life. Of course, by doing so, he proves himself a *noble* black man.

In this role, Poitier was a striking dramatic force, a wholly new kind of black actor who spoke with conviction, exuded intelligence and strength, and walked, moved, and stood with an innate sense of pride. By his very presence, by his basic sense of self, he was flipping movie history upside down. Moreover, he stood at the film's moral center, represented its conscience and its liberal point of view. In the past, black actors like Stepin Fetchit and Bill "Bojangles" Robinson, always consigned to comic or singing/dancing roles, usually performed a funny antic or two, then disappeared from the picture. Poitier, however, was at the movie's heart or perhaps its soul. His character here (and in later films) was governed by a code of fundamental decency, duty, and moral

Sidney Poitier: he still remains the most important black actor ever to work in American motion pictures, introducing a whole new style and presence for blacks in fims of the 1950s.

intelligence. Yet it is important to note that he was not the screen's first black man of action or intelligence. Previously, Paul Robeson and James Edwards had played important serious characters. But significantly neither had emerged as a leading dramatic actor working *consistently* in American films. Sidney Poitier, however, changed all that.

From *No Way Out*, he went on to work in dramatic parts in such features as *Cry the Beloved Country* (a 1952 drama about South Africa that touched on the theme of apartheid and now seems ahead of its time), *Red Ball Express* (1952), *Go, Man, Go* (1954), *Blackboard Jungle* (1955, one of his most exciting roles as a rebellious high school student), *Goodbye, My Lady* (1956), *Band of Angels* (1957), and *Something of Value* (1957).

For the new Eisenhower era, Poitier answered the needs of both black America and Hollywood. In this period following World War II, black America—increasingly more vocal about its discontents and dissatisfactions with the system's racial inequities and injustices—stood on the brink of the civil rights movement. Anxious to move into the system, black America was also anxious to prove itself *ready* for full integration into American society. And Poitier came to represent the model integrationist hero: a paragon of middleclass values and virtues. No dialect. No shuffling. No singing or dancing. No comic buffoonery. For so many black Americans, he was a fine-looking, composed, refined, articulate young black man who could be reckoned with and pointed to as a sign of hope for the future.

Paradoxically, Poitier represented someting else for the white audience: his characters were liberal conceptions of the manageable Ideal Good Negro. Frequently in his films, Poitier screamed out in rage about the injustices of a racist white society. Black audiences always loved those moments when Sidney looked a white opponent straight in the eye and spoke his mind about black/white issues. But his characters could always be reasoned with and despite their rebelliousness, they usually ended by proving they were on the side of the angels: basically, they supported the dominant white culture.

By the mid-1950s, Poitier was established but still not a star. His performances in *Edge of the City* (1957) and *The Defiant Ones* (1958) turned the tide for him. Sometimes sullen, sometimes angry, sometimes explosive and almost always likable, Poitier proved himself one of the screen's most talented dramatic actors. For his performance in *The Defiant Ones*, he was nominated for the Oscar as Best Actor of 1958. Yet although these films were hailed as breakthroughs in Hollywood's depiction of America's corrosive racial tensions and conflicts, both were also flawed and compromised; so determined were they to promote the notion of the honorable Negro who sacrifices himself in the name of interracial brotherhood that Poitier's characters seemed to be too much symbol and too little reality.

In *Edge of the City*, Poitier, as a railroad worker, befriends a troubled young white drifter, played by John Cassavetes. Taking the fellow under his wing, Poitier's likable and loose character carries Cassavetes home to meet his wife (Ruby Dee) and does all he can to offer good fellowship to an otherwise isolated and lonely young man. At the film's climax when Cassavetes becomes embroiled in a fight with another white man, Poitier comes to Cassavetes's defense. He's fatally wounded by the other white. He dies in Cassavetes's arms but dies content that he's been true to his good white buddy.

A similar situation arises in *The Defiant Ones*. Here Poitier and Tony Curtis were cast as two convicts who escape from prison but are

Poitier: actor turned film director.

chained together as they run from the law. Playing a rabid racist, Curtis taunts Poitier whenever possible and lets it be known that he doesn't cotton to the idea of being tied to a colored boy. No stranger to racism, having lived with it all his life, Poitier's character lashes out. But we know he has a good heart. Gradually, the white character softens. Then at this film's climax, Poitier, having boarded a freight train that insures his freedom, jumps from the train when he sees his white friend in need. Thus the noble black man gives up his very freedom to aid another white buddy.

No doubt Poitier himself had second thoughts about certain aspects of both these popular films. But at this point in his career as he appeared in such other movies as *Mark of the Hawk* (1958), *Virgin Island* (1958), *Porgy and Bess* (1959), and *All the Young Men* (1960), surely the idea was to take a role and invest it with whatever insights he could. One day the right role had to come along. And it did, of course, with the 1961 film version of Lorraine Hansberry's prize-winning play *A Raisin in the Sun*.

Here as the restless, wayward Walter Younger, a chauffeur who struggles with his mother, his wife, his kid sister, and mainly with himself to change the course of his life, Poitier gave his best screen performance, a totally different characterization from his past movie roles. "I open and close car doors all day long. I drive a man around in his limousine and I say, 'Yes, sir,'" he cried. "Mama, that ain't no kind of a job . . . that ain't nothing at all." If Academy Awards mean anything, Poitier should have won his Oscar for this performance as a deeply troubled man operating in a realistically drawn black world, which black audiences could identify with. Yet he went without so much as a nomination.

When Sidney Poitier did become the first black actor in the history of films to carry off an Oscar (Hattie McDaniel had won as Best Supporting Actress of 1939), it was for a film which white audiences may have viewed as being politically more acceptable: *Lilies of the Field* in 1963. Here Poitier played a rather aimless fellow who stumbles across a troupe of white nuns in the Arizona desert. They want him to help them build a chapel. He decides to stick around and do the job. Today *Lilies of the Field* (1963) may strike some as a likable harmless picture. But Poitier's character seems far too accommodating, almost like the old black servants of such films as *Gone with the Wind* (1939) and *Imitation of Life* (1934), who seemed to have no lives outside the homes of the white employers they so dutifully served.

At this point in his career, Poitier, having broken the stereotype mold by introducing the decent, intelligent Negro to films, found himself falling into a trap: by now, his agreeable noble Negro heroes were themselves a new stereotype—or perhaps merely an updating of the old-style friendly, conciliatory tom type. In so many of his 1960s movies, Poitier's code of decency itself seemed corrupted, simply a mask for bourgeois complacency and sterility. Moreover, he appeared sexless in films, so seldom was he permitted to play a realistic romantic role. In movies such as *No Way Out, Edge of the City, All the Young Men,* and later *In the Heat of the Night* (1967), his pivotal relationships were with white males; such films were more interested in the theme of interracial male bonding than in an exploration of a relationship between a black man and a black woman.

Ironically, too, after his Oscar triumph, Poitier's audience changed. Now moving away from a social philosophy of cultural integration and assimilation to one of cultural nationalism and separatism, black America of the 1960s sought movie heroes who showed signs of political consciousness or resistance. When Poitier turned up in the 1965 *A Patch of Blue* as the familiar good-hearted black man who befriends a young white girl, his character's hesitation in revealing his racial identity struck young black audiences (caught up in this new age of evolving black pride) as being a reprehensible act. Nor was that audience thrilled at the prospect of watching Poitier as the do-gooder teacher trying to reach wayward white British students in *To Sir with Love* (1967). Why was he not cast as a teacher in an American ghetto? Even when the audience was excited by Poitier's relatively outspoken character in *In the Heat of the Night,* it felt the movie's theme of interracial brotherhood was out of whack with the spirit of the times. Why was it that Poitier was not shown relating more to other black characters?

But the real turn in Poitier's audience—and his career—came after another triumph, the box-office hit *Guess Who's Coming to Dinner?* (1967). Here cast as a young doctor in love with a young white woman, Poitier's hero seeks permission from the woman's family to marry her. We learn that this Negro doctor is above reproach: he's handsome, articulate, educated, possibly even a candidate for a Nobel Prize. To prove his worth, he has met all of white America's standards—beyond the call of duty!

In his 1980 autobiography *This Life,* Poitier recounted the tough, demanding period following *Guess Who's Coming to Dinner?* Younger militant audiences denounced his characters as being politically obsolete. Articles cited him as white America's favorite Negro actor because he presented an image of a colonized black man who never made waves. Poitier found himself in a position that no white actor has ever had to bear: he had to choose roles not simply with dramatic considerations but political ones, too.

In reaction, he sought more creative input in his projects. But the immediate results were disastrous. The romance *For Love of Ivy* (1968) was dismissed in some circles as simply a paper-thin trifle. In recent years, however, this film has re-emerged as a favorite with black women. Moreover, Poitier's militant hero in *The Lost Man* (1969) was almost laughed off the screen for being so tame and somber—and worst, for falling into the arms of a white woman. Then with such early 1970s box-office clinkers as *They Call Me MISTER Tibbs* (1970), *The Organization* (1971), and *Brother John* (1971), his career seemed in dismal shape. At a time when black audiences went to see *Sweet Sweetback's Baadasssss Song* (1971) or *Shaft* (1971) or *Super Fly* (1972), Poitier appeared to have lost his touch.

Yet determined to bring about an image change in which he could reconnect his roots with the black community, Poitier plowed on, assuming control of a new project *Buck and the Preacher* in 1972, which he directed and co-starred in with Harry Belafonte and Ruby Dee. *Buck and the Preacher*—a look at blacks striking out on their own after the Civil War while in flight from white bounty hunters—proved so rousing an adventure that black audiences openly cheered it. Here was an entertaining black film that cast Poitier again as a noble hero but one now placed firmly in the black community and not isolated in a white liberal fantasy world.

Afterwards he continued directing, turning out in 1973 *A Warm December* (another romance) and a trio of comedies with Bill Cosby: *Uptown Saturday Night* (1974), *Let's Do It Again* (1975), and *A Piece of the Action* (1977). Although the comedies were sometimes criticized as being throwbacks to the shenanigans of a Stepin Fetchit or Willie Best, black audiences of the mid- and late-1970s—now in a more relaxed mood—relished these playful films in which a number of black stars such as Richard Pryor, Flip Wilson, Denise Nicholas, Rosalind Cash, Calvin Lockhart, and Harry Belafonte had a chance to sparkle and shine. For black audiences, Poitier was once again a hero: his career had come full circle.

For much of the 1980s, Poitier abandoned acting in favor of directing such features as *Stir Crazy* (1980), *Hanky Panky* (1982), and the dreadfully misconceived *Fast Forward* (1985). As a director, he was sometimes clumsy and awkward. Frequently, he worked well with actors, drawing from them effective performances. But oddly, these features lacked the dramatic intensity that had distinguished Poitier as an actor. Sadly, too, the 1980s generation seemed unaware of what a great dramatic talent he had been in the past.

In retrospect, despite the different distortions in his Hollywood films and despite the various demands that audiences of different eras placed on him, Sidney Poitier, the actor, remains one of the finest, consistently having given performances of high quality and having approached his work with a singular sense of honesty and conviction. So many of his old films remain worth seeing simply because of his ability to shrewdly outact just about everyone else on screen. Poitier, the actor, also came to realize the importance of controlling an image behind as well as in front of the camera. Having weathered many a difficult storm, he remained a remarkable performer—a constant for several decades—who turned Hollywood film history upside down and over the years, in good times and bad, gave black Americans a significant reason for going to the movies.

His movie credits include: *From Whom Cometh My Help* (a 1949 Army Signal Corps documentary); *Paris Blues* (1961); *Pressure Point* (1962); *The Long Ships* (1964); *The Greatest Story Ever Told* (1965); *The Bedford Incident* (1965); *The Slender Thread* (1966); *Duel at Diablo* (1966); *The Lost Man*

(1969); and *The Wilby Conspiracy* (1975); and after a ten-year absence as an actor on the screen, he appeared in *The King of the Mountain* (1987).

Poitier's TV credits include: "The Parole Officer" (a 1955 "Philco Playhouse" Presentation); "Fascinating Stranger" (1955 "Pond's Theatre" presentation); "A Man Is Ten Feet Tall" (a 1955 "Philco Playhouse" presentation); and the 1966 musical special "The Strollin' Twenties" (with an all-star black cast including Diahann Carroll and Sammy Davis, Jr.).

Oscar Polk

Actor.

Character actor who appeared in three important films: *Gone with the Wind* (1939), *Green Pastures* (1936), and *Cabin in the Sky* (1943). Tall, gangly, and *country*, his performance in *Gone with the Wind* is probably his best: here, as the house-servant Pork, he comes across as a man who, having had to function in a society that denied him his manhood for so long, doesn't know quite how to fend for himself. His is a portrait of true emasculation. As archangel Gabriel in the all-black-heaven fantasy *Green Pastures*, Polk was also at home, just right as a kind of fussy, prissy, protective secretary to a very preoccupied De Lawd.

Polk also worked in the Oscar Micheaux independent feature *Underworld* (1937) as well as other Hollywood films: *Big Town Czar* (1939); *White Cargo* (1942); and *Reap the Wild Wind* (1942).

Richard Pryor

B. 1940. Actor, comedian.

How is it that someone as talented and potent a cultural force in American life as Richard Pryor has appeared in so many bum movies? Actually, Pryor's similar to a number of other significant artistic/cultural figures, be it Garbo, Brando, or Elizabeth Taylor, all of whom frequently came a cropper with poorly conceived films. Yet such stars always proved themselves bigger than their shoddy products, their personal glow and compelling magnetism sailing on undaunted. In the long run, the manner in which Richard Pryor has been mishandled in American motion pictures has now become a part of his intricate, complex legend.

The Pryor legend, of course, traces back to his childhood in Peoria, Illinois, where he grew up in his grandmother's whorehouse. As he himself recounted (and as he attempted to dramatize in the 1986 *Jo Jo Dancer, Your Life Is Calling*), during his formative years he watched the whores with their johns and saw his mother, a prostitute in the family-owned business, as she turned over her earnings to Pryor's father. By no means, was Pryor's a Little Lord Fauntleroy childhood.

Pryor turned to performing early. At age 12, he appeared in a local production of *Rumpelstiltskin*. As a restless teenager, he dropped out of high school and joined the army. After leaving the service, he embarked on his career, playing clubs, bars, joints, dives, anywhere, everywhere, learning his craft in a tough, seedy showbiz atmosphere. While working, Pryor shrewdly observed the strippers, transvestites, dancers, wrestlers, and oldtimers who surrounded him. Perceptive, inquisitive, and ambitious, he also studied his audiences, which could be demanding

Richard Pryor, the director, on the set of Jo Jo Dancer, Your Life Is Calling.

and insensitive and always hungry for fresh and exciting material. These years proved excellent training for him as he developed into a gifted monologist and also showed his talents for mimicking and miming what he saw.

By the early 1960s when he played New York's Greenwich Village clubs to integrated audiences, he was a slim, clean-cut, well-mannered young man, who, so he felt, was patterning himself too much on another popular black comedian of the day, Bill Cosby. Pryor made it to the television shows of Steve Allen, Ed Sullivan, and Merv Griffin. But he grew unhappy with his work, dissatisfied and angered with the direction of his career. He hadn't yet discovered his true artistic voice or his basic professional persona.

A turning point in this first phase of his career erupted in 1970 when, in the middle of his performance at the Aladdin Hotel in Las Vegas, his self-disgust surfaced. "What the f--- am I doing here," he said to his audience, then walked off stage.

For two years, he dropped out of sight, staying in a room in Berkeley where he struggled to find himself. "I read a book," he once told *Newsweek*, "called *Malcolm X Speaks*. And I knew I wasn't crazy. Someone else thought what I thought. And it freed me. I wasn't gonna stand up there and wear a tuxedo anymore. There was something better to do. I got my head out of the white man's dream."

When he returned to performing, a comic metamorphosis took place with his creation of a new collection of characters: numbers runners, junkies, winos, later his macho men, convicts, his classic Mudbone and Oilman, all of whom spoke in earthy metaphors and in the tough, profane language of the streets. Through his street characters, Pryor brought into the clubs the attitudes and expressions, the outlooks and dreams, the disillusionment of an underclass: tales of lives cut short by racism and despair. When working before a black audience, his approach was like that of his predecessors Moms Mabley and Red Foxx: he was no different from the audience. Yet Pryor went farther, making his audience take second notice of its own experiences and of the figures we've all passed on the street without acknowledging the pathos—or the poetry—that we see there. He turned the white man's word *nigger* inside out to become a term of pride and defiance.

During television appearances in this second phase of Pryor's career, as he sat with Johnny or Merv, he kept his language clean. But his Crazy Nigger persona couldn't lie hidden. As Pryor's eyes darted about and his highspeed repartee veered towards the dangerous, for audiences part of the delirious joy of watching him was that no one knew when he might *go off*—on the host or another guest. He seemed capable of saying or doing almost anything. And there was always a political method to his madness. On "The Tonight Show" in 1978, he told the audience, "If you want to do anything, if you're black and still here in America, get a gun and go to South Africa and kill some white people." Black audiences cheered him on.

The white audience that watched Pryor, particularly the young, identified with him on another level, seeing him as an underclass hero speaking out about *their* frustrations and disappointments with a system that also denied them certain rights and demanded that emotion be locked in. Perhaps the most amazing aspect of Pryor's popularity was that once he had crossed over, he remained one of the few such black stars to retain in full force his black following, too.

Of course, Pryor's private life then and in the years to come, also became a part of the public record *and* his public persona. Some stories were reported by the press; others simply hit the rumor mill: of the time Pryor had set a girlfriend's mink coat on fire; of the occasion when he had beaten up a Hollywood motel clerk; of another occasion when he fired a pistol at his wife, then pumped bullets into her car; of the nights when he was bombed out on too much booze and dope. Quick-tempered, explosive, manic, brilliant: all were adjectives used to describe him. Pryor would eventually use some of the incidents from his life in his concerts and films.

Pryor's movie work started in the late 1960s: *Busy Body* (1967); *Wild in the Streets* (1968); *The Green Berets* (1968, with, of all people, John Wayne); later *The Phynx* (1970); *You've Got To Walk It Like You Talk It or You'll Lose the Beat* (1971). Almost all these films have been forgotten by everyone. But *Lady Sings the Blues* in 1972 changed things for him. As the piano man, he proved he could handle a supporting dramatic role and add a vivid texture to a film. What followed were other supporting roles in *The Mack* (1973), *Hit* (1973), *Uptown Saturday Night* (1974), *Car Wash* (1976), and *The Bingo Long Traveling All-Stars and Motor Kings* (1976), each of which, despite the audience's enthusiasm for Pryor, kept him confined to the sidelines, leading to the idea that if he were not the star then he could never get out of hand.

That may have been the attitude of the producers of *Silver Streak* (1976) when they cast Pryor as little more than a symbolic handyman to star Gene Wilder. But with his bebop energy and that skittenish wild child's gleam in his eyes, Pryor saved *and* walked away with the movie, turning it into a major career breakthrough for himself.

In more ways than one *Silver Streak* did the trick, not only leading to Pryor's star roles in *Which Way Is Up?* (1977), *Greased Lightning* (1977), and *Blue Collar* (1978) but also initiating a method for the moviemakers to handle the Pryor persona: at heart these films tried neutralizing Pryor's manic, unmanageable Crazy Nigger, domesticating his untamable presence by incorporating him into a wholesome middle-class system (just as a movie like the 1934 *Judge Priest* had attempted incorporating Stepin

Fetchit's lazy-good-for-nothing nigger into the acceptable cultural mainstream).

In American movies, there had been no historical precedent for Pryor or his persona. In the past, the concept behind the clowns of Stepin Fetchit or the Noble Negroes of Sidney Poitier had sprung from a white consciousness. Pryor's screen personality itself—the suggestion of the uncontrollable and the dangerous—had come from Pryor himself, from a black man's point of view. But while Pryor's personality excited filmmakers, they also sought to keep that personality under wraps. Thus *Which Way Is Up?* and *Blue Collar* turned him sad and serious: here he was stripped frequently of his spunk and his renegade individuality; all his rebellious embers were doused and he was ultimately used (despite the multiple roles he played in *Which Way Is Up?*) as a symbol of the common man, whose aims and ambitions are simply for a good, decent ordinary life. These movies want us to believe that Richard Pryor is really just like anybody else. But the reason he had been so liked was that he was distinctively, uncontrollably *unlike* anyone else. By the time he appeared in *The Muppet Movie* (1979), he was basically a friendly presence alongside America's favorite puppet figures. And in 1980 when reunited with Wilder in *Stir Crazy* (1980), Pryor, much to the dismay of the audience, was back to playing second banana to a white star, not even permitted to have a movie romance or to explode with righteous indignation. All these movies both celebrated and negated Richard Pryor's unique talents and presence.

While making these films Pryor also tried his hand at a television series, "The Richard Pryor Show" (1977). Of course, the one thing TV cannot abide is the weekly presence of an explosive talent. Pryor unsettled the censors at NBC. After only a few weeks, his series left the airwaves. Pryor, however, continued making his record albums, which were dazzlers, his street characters in *That Nigger's Crazy* (1974), *Is It Something I Said* (1975), and *Bicentennial Nigger* (1976) as fierce and comically stunning as ever. And he had his greatest triumph—his first film of true artistic distinction—with his concert movie, *Richard Pryor Live in Concert* (1979), in which, during his skits and impersonations, he came to full life on screen.

Phase three of Pryor's career emerged after the accident that made headlines in 1980: he suffered third-degree burns over half his body while, so it was widely reported, freebasing cocaine in his California home. The networks, newspapers, magazines, and wire services reported the daily hospital bulletins. No black star since Billie Holiday and Dorothy Dandridge had ever received this kind of attention, Pryor looked as if, having pushed his own self-destruct button, he were about to take his place alongside a group of remarkable talents done in by the system and themselves.

Yet Pryor survived, proving himself almost indestructible. In the eyes of the public, Pryor, ironically much like Elizabeth Taylor after she survived a near-fatal bout with pneumonia in the 1960s, almost ceased being a performer: instead he emerged as part-mythic/part-legendary hero who had gone to hell and back and who would eventually tell us his story in two other concert films of varying quality but magnetic appeal: *Richard Pryor Live on Sunset Strip* (1982) and *Richard Pryor . . . Here and Now* (1983). A fusion had come about in private and public personas. When a performer reaches this position in the popular imagination, it can be detrimental because the performer is no longer judged by the quality of his work; instead he becomes entangled and lost in his own fame and myth.

During the post-accident third phase, Pryor's films seemed to soften and sentimentalize him even more. The appealing *Bustin' Loose* (1981, begun before the accident, completed afterward) nonetheless turned him into a Big Daddy to a busload of kids and a schoolmarm. *Some Kind of Hero* (1982) cast him as a disillusioned Vietnam vet. Later *The Toy* (1982) shamefully used him as a literal toy for a spoiled white child. *Superman III* (1983) turned him timid and meek. While *Brewster's Millions* (1985) had some sweetly passable moments, the role demanded nothing special of him. And in *Jo Jo Dancer Your Life Is Calling*, his creative spark and madness seemed to have deserted him at a most crucial point in his life.

In retrospect, most of Pryor's star movies attempted to reduce him, tried cutting him down to size, sought making him more like us, which is the last thing we want from Pryor or any other great star. Instead of casting him as the typical worn-out husband or typical struggling joe-shmo, why couldn't he have been cast as truly rebellious, comically angry and rousing men of action? Or as characters triumphantly overturning things and living successfully on their own terms? If anything, many of Pryor's films indicate that the American movie industry, ill at ease with him, has never really wanted Richard Pryor to be a star. His is a classic case of a star made by the people. And Pryor himself, in so many of his films, summons up some of the best of himself to give us some special moments, some dazzling ones, some scary ones too. The acme of his career—and a true blessing for us, too—are, of course, the three concert films, which still excite and set the skin crawling as audiences sit in the dark and watch a remarkable man in control of his material, his image, and himself, giving us great popular art at its very best.

Pryor's movie credits include: *Dynamite Chicken* (1972); *Wattstax* (1973); *Some Call It Loving* (1973); *Adios Amigo* (1976); *The Wiz* (1978); *California Suite* (1978); *In God We Trust* (1980); *Wholly Moses* (1980); and *Critical Condition* (1987).

Pryor's TV credits include: appearances on such variety shows as "The Midnight Special" and "The Flip Wilson Show"; "Wild, Wild West" (1966); "The Young Lawyers" (1969); "Carter's Army" (1970); "The Partridge Family" (1971); "The Mod Squad" (1972); "Sammy and Company" (1975); "Sesame Street" (1976); as host/guest of "Saturday Night Live"; and "Motown 25: Yesterday, Today, Forever" (1983). Pryor also wrote for "Sanford and Son," "The Flip Wilson Show," and "The Lily Tomlin Special" (for which he won an Emmy in 1974). In 1984 he did the children's series "Pryor's Place."

He also co-wrote the script for *Blazing Saddles* (1974).

Amanda Randolph

B. 1902; D. 1967. Actress.

Deep-voiced, heavyset Amanda Randolph played that enormously funny and enjoyable battle-axe, Mama—Sapphire's Mama, to be exact—on the television series "Amos 'n' Andy." A born belter, Amanda entered show business while still a young girl in Cleveland, singing in nightclubs and musical comedies. Rarely, however, except for the short *The Black Network* (1936), did she have a chance to sing in films. Mainly, because of her look (she was brown-skinned and chunky), she was consigned to comic maid roles. In the 1940s, she worked on the radio series "Amos 'n' Andy" as well as on other programs such as "Kitty Foyle" and "Big Sister." In films, she appeared not only in such Hollywood productions as *No Way Out* (1950) but also in the race movies, *Swing* (1938), *Lying Lips* (1939), and *The Notorious Elinor Lee* (1940).

In the 1950s, she was one of the first black performers to appear consistently on television. After "Amos 'n' Andy," she played the maid Louise on the long-running "The Danny Thomas Show." A whole generation of schoolchildren was introduced to her, seldom aware, however, of Randolph's real name or her long career. Generally, she played tough characters, who could—in a flash—belt out a quip or snap out an order. Few actresses could roll their eyes with as flagrant disdain as Ms. Randolph. And like the later Helen Martin, another actress who played comic realists, Randolph mastered the long, cold stare, which was always used to pierce through the shams or follies of other characters.

Amanda Randolph's sister Lillian was also an actress.

Amanda Randolph's film credits include: *She's Working Her Way Through College* (1952); *Mr. Scoutmaster* (1953); and *A Man Called Peter* (1955).

Lillian Randolph

B. 1915; D. 1980. Actress.

Like her older sister Amanda (with whom she is frequently confused), Lillian Randolph worked on radio, in movies, and on television for several decades, from the 1930s through the 1970s. Also like Amanda, she appeared on the "Amos 'n' Andy" TV series, recreating a role she had first played on the radio version of the series, that of the *bodacious* (vernacular for aggressive) Madame Queen, who was out to snare bachelor Andy Brown as her husband. In the 1940s, Lillian Randolph also replaced Hattie McDaniel as the star of the radio version of the series "Beulah." But she was best known for her role as the maid Birdie on the radio and TV series "The Great Gildersleeve" as well as the Gildersleeve movies: *The Great Gildersleeve* (1942), *Gildersleeve on Broadway*

"The Great Gildersleeve," a syndicated TV series with Mary Lee Robb (l.), Willard Waterman, and in the center, Lillian Randolph as Birdie.

(1943), *Gildersleeve's Bad Day* (1943), and *Gildersleeve's Ghost* (1944). Her character Birdie could be a loudmouth and certainly wasn't one to be pushed around. She also had a fair amount of common sense and did not have to endure the silly routines of other maid characters. Each year when Frank Capra's *It's A Wonderful Life* (1946) is revived in theaters or shown on television, audiences also spot Randolph as the maid Annie, who pitches in with other cast members at the film's memorable conclusion as the hat is being passed around. She also turns up in a few race movies. Later audiences also got to see her in a different light when Bill Cosby cast her as his mother Rose Kincaid on the first season of "The Bill Cosby Show" in 1969.

Lillian Randolph's movie credits include: *Life Goes On* (a 1938 race movie starring Louise Beavers); *Am I Guilty?* (a 1940 race movie starring Ralph Cooper); *Mr. Smith Goes Ghost* (1940); *Little Men* (1940); *West Point Widow* (1941); *Gentleman from Dixie* (1941); *The Mexican Spitfire Sees a Ghost* (1942); *The Bachelor and the Bobby-Soxer* (1947); *Sleep My Love* (1948); *Once More, My Darling* (1949); *Dear Brat* (1951); *That's My Boy* (1951); *Hush, Hush Sweet Charlotte* (1964); *The Great White Hope* (1970); *How to Seduce a Woman* (1974); *Once Is Not Enough* (1975); *Rafferty and the Gold Dust Twins* (1975); and *The Onion Field* (1979).

Randolph's TV credits include: "That's My Mama" (1974); "The Autobiography of Miss Jane Pittman" (1974); "Sanford and Son" (1975); "The Jeffersons" (1976); and "Roots" (1977).

Phylicia (Ayers-Allen) Rashad

B. c. 1948. Actress.

Until her appearance as Claire Huxtable on "The Cosby Show" (1984), Phylicia Ayers-Allen Rashad (who at first was billed without the Rashad; she changed her name after her marriage to sportscaster Ahmad Rashad) had been known best in the early 1980s as Courtney Wright on the daytime soap *One Life To Live* or perhaps better still, mostly as Debbie Allen's older sister.

Texas-born and a 1970 graduate of Howard University, she had come to New York in the 1970s and struggled to find a foothold in show business, working mostly in off-Broadway productions and notably as an understudy in the 1982 musical *Dreamgirls*. But nothing jelled until Cosby had the foresight to cast her as independent, educated, sexy Claire, who's wife, mother, and career woman. At times she delivered her lines in a rather mannered way and even turned on her magnetic smile a bit too often (attempting, it appeared, to engage her audience simply through her great charm) and at first she seemed much too young to be Bill Cosby's wife and the mother of a college-age daughter. But Rashad soon slipped comfortably into her role and worked wonderfully opposite Cosby. Because of the nature of television's demands, she no doubt proved most successful because her sweet warmth and agreeable outspokenness made her the kind of bright woman American audiences did not mind at all having in their homes every week. Of course, her sensational looks did not hurt her either.

Her TV credits include: "Delvecchio" (1976); "The Love Boat" (1985); "Bob Hope's High Flying Birthday Special" (1986); "Hollywood Squares" (1986); "Friday Night Videos" (1987, an episode in which she co-hosted with husband Ahmad Rashad); and "Uncle Tom's Cabin" (1987, in which she played Eliza).

Phylicia Rashad, once billed as Phylicia Allen, then Phylicia Ayers-Allen, now best known as Claire Huxtable on TV's "The Cosby Show."

Beah Richards

Actress.

"Although the critics were divided in the reception they gave to James Baldwin's *The Amen Corner*," wrote Ira Peck in the May 2, 1965, edition of *The New York Times*, "they showed a rare unanimity in acclaiming its leading player, a little-known actress named Bea [sic] Richards. The adjectives they bestowed on her—'superb,' 'astonishing,' 'exquisite,' 'luminous'—might have dazzled a long-established star, a Cornell or Hayes or Margaret Leighton. Miss Richards maintains an impressive calm in the face of praise."

The same calm she displayed off stage might well be the distinguishing characteristic of Beah Richards on stage, too. In role after role, no matter what the emotional dynamics of her heroines, Richards managed to retain a cool clarity and control that added to her unusual power. One always felt Beah Richards was a woman who could never be thrown off balance. Yet we couldn't say her feet were firmly planted on the ground because, frankly, she sometimes seemed to be up in the clouds, operating in some enlightened but unfathomable, highly personal state of grace.

Richards's film and television career did not come about until late. In fact, for too long a time, it looked as if she did not even have much of a stage career. This Vicksburg, Mississippi-born actress attended Dillard College in New Orleans, then served a three-year acting apprenticeship in San Diego. In 1951, she arrived in New York. She made her professional debut in the 1954 Off-Broadway production of *Take a Giant Step*, appeared in *The Miracle Worker* in 1959, in *Purlie Victorious* in 1961, understudied Claudia McNeil in the role of Lena Younger in *A Raisin in the Sun*, and then assumed the role in the national tour of the play. But for the most part in the 1950s and early 1960s her acting assignments were so scarce that she ended up teaching at a charm school. Curiously enough, later in some of her most important roles she often had the air of a well-brought up and mannerly woman, determined to remain polite and ladylike no matter what the situation.

The Amen Corner seemed to break some of the career ice for Richards. When she appeared in the West Coast production of the play, actor Frank Silvera was so impressed that he took out an ad in *The Hollywood Reporter*, hoping to call Richard's reviews to the attention of film companies. But all that came out of the ad was an offer to Richards of two days' work portraying a maid on television. She declined.

Then in 1967, director Otto Preminger cast her in *Hurry Sundown* as Mammy Rose, the faithful but exploited Southern woman who has reared a wayward Jane Fonda. Here Richards threw a new slant on the familiar mammy character, creating a rather sedate (some might say *sedated*), restrained woman, not given to oldstyle hootin' and yellin'. She's almost genteel, so much so that audiences still get itchy to see her break loose from her refined sweetness and to start raising some holy cain. When an outburst finally comes, it cannot be said that her rage is wholly convincing—the script is too much of a hack job for that—but it is impossible to turn away from her unusual, downright bizarre interpretation. Every word is measured and each line is delivered with a fascinating precision. No one may ever be sure what this character is meant to represent, but we accept her on Richards's terms nonetheless.

Some of that same audience confusion occurs when watching Richards in *Guess Who's Coming to Dinner?* It is one of the screen's *oddest* performances. Here, as Sidney Poitier's well-groomed and coiffed mother, she is again so controlled and ladylike that at first audiences find it hard to relate to her. Her lucidity permits us to understand every word she utters, yet she's opaque, too; it's hard to figure out what she's trying to get at. Throughout the movie, most of us probably long for Richards to lash out at son Poitier or even the parents of the white woman he plans to marry. Intuitively, we feel she has too much sense to stand by so idly—and silently—in this hopelessly fake movie. But the script does not allow her an explosion. Ultimately, she's so secure a presence—and there is such a decent simplicity and forcefulness to her work—that we accept her character and do not lose interest. For her performance in *Guess Who's Coming to Dinner?*, Richards received—surprisingly—an Oscar nomination as Best Supporting Actress of 1967. Yet afterward moviegoers rarely saw her.

She continued working, however, in theater on the West Coast and also in such television productions as "I Spy" (1967), "Hawaii Five-O" (1969), "The Bill Cosby Show" (in which she played Cosby's mother during the 1970–1971 season), "A Dream for Christmas" (1973), "Just an Old Sweet Song" (1976), "Ring of Passion" (1978), "Roots: The Next Generations" (1979), "Sophisticated Gents" (1981), and "Hunter" (1987). In almost all these programs, Richards's work is illuminated by a fundamental warmth and tenderness. Like Ethel Waters, she's the type of performer that audiences, for better or worse, could fantasize about: here seemed to be a wise woman who would listen to problems, who would understand and advise, who indeed had acquired wisdom from her own rocky past. Even as a street woman in "Hunter," Richards seemed to entrance the two stars of the series whenever she spoke.

Beah Richards's earlier TV credits include: "Dr. Kildare" (1966); "Big Valley" (1966); "Ironside" (1969); "Room 222" (1969); "It Takes a Thief" (1970); "Sanford and Son" (1972); and "Footsteps" (1972).

Richards's movie credits include: *Take a Giant Step* (1961); *The Miracle Worker* (1962); *Gone Are the Days* (1963); *In the Heat of the Night* (1967); *The Biscuit Eater* (1972); and *Inside Out* (1987).

Paul Robeson

B. 1898; D. 1976. Actor, singer.

Was there ever another figure on the cultural landscape like Paul Robeson? He was the son of a proud minister who had been a slave until he had run away from a North Carolina plantation in 1860. His mother was a schoolteacher who had died when Paul was nine. Winning a scholarship to Rutgers in 1915 (the third black to attend the college), he excelled in the classroom and on the sports field. Although some of his football teammates at first had refused to play with him, Robeson nevertheless became an all-American football star. Called Robeson of Rutgers by sports writers, he was hailed by Walter Camp, who twice helped select him as an all-American as "the greatest defensive end that ever trod the gridiron." Robeson also won letters in baseball, basketball, and track. He spoke several languages and won a Phi Beta Kappa Key in his junior year. The next year he was elected to Cap and Skull. He graduated valedictorian of his class in 1919, then earned a law degree from Columbia. But he never practiced law, instead embarked on a stage and concert hall career, mainly at the prompting, so he later said, of his young bride, Eslanda Cardozo Goode, who had been a brilliant chemistry student at Columbia.

His first performance was in 1920 in *Simon the Cyrenian* at the YMCA in New York. In England in 1922, he played opposite Mrs. Patrick Campbell in *Taboo*, renamed *Voodoo*. (At this time interracial pairings on stage were hardly an everyday occurrence.) Later he joined the Provincetown Players in New York, appearing in 1924 in Eugene O'Neill's shocker of that day *All God's Chillun Got Wings*, the story of a white woman married to a Negro. He also triumphed in a 1924 revival of O'Neill's *Emperor Jones*. In 1928, Robeson appeared in England again in *Show Boat*, and two years later startled London theatregoers in a highly acclaimed production of *Othello*. Thirteen years later, he repeated his Othello role in New York, opposite Uta Hagen. Critic George Jean Nathan once said that Robeson was "one of the most thoroughly eloquent, impressive and convincing actors" he had ever seen on stage. Robeson's magnificent bass-baritone voice was also heard in concert halls around the world.

Robeson could have very easily settled for a comfortable life as a prestigious performer. But repeatedly he chose to speak out on racial and political matters. During the American/Soviet alliance of 1941, his pro-Soviet statements were accepted. But during the post-War years of the Cold War, he fell into disfavor. In 1949, at the World Peace Congress in Paris, Robeson had said, "It is unthinkable that American Negroes will go to war on behalf of those who have oppressed us for generations against a country (The Soviet Union) which in one generation has raised our people to the full dignity of mankind." Afterward in large part because of his pro-Soviet stance Robeson was hounded and haunted by the forces of McCarthyism. Public sentiment—and the press—turned against him although for black and liberal white America he remained a potent political/artistic force. His famous 1949 concert in Peekskill, New York, was met with protests. Concertgoers were pelted with rocks, and cars were overturned and smashed by "patriotic" veteran groups and right wing extremists. The concert was cancelled. A year later the State Department cancelled his passport. Robeson took the Department to court. Although his suit never reached the court, the passport was reinstated in 1958. But the damage had been done. His concert bookings dwindled. His records were taken off the shelves in music stores. His earnings slipped from $104,000 in 1947 to $6,000 in 1952. In 1961, worn, tired, and in poor health, Robeson retired from public view, living the rest of his life in seclusion, first in New York, later at his sister's home in Philadelphia.

Because he became such a legendary/near mythic figure, it is sometimes hard to objectively assess Robeson's film work. Almost always, whenever his films are shown, audiences are rapt with anticipation, hoping to see him leap above the movie's cheap mechanics. (He usually does.) But the truth of the matter is that most of his films were flawed, mangled, misconceived. Robeson's film work did not bring him great pleasure.

Interestingly, his movie career began outside the Hollywood system, first in Oscar Micheaux's 1924 *Body and Soul*, later in the experimental, avant-garde *Borderline* (1928, his wife Eslanda appears with him), then in the independent 1933 production of *Emperor Jones*. In 1936, he went to Hollywood for the role of Joe in *Show Boat*. As melodrama, the movie still works effectively. Robeson himself has to go through servant antics, but his stirring rendition of "Ol' Man River" is memorable.

Much of Robeson's movie work was done in England. Most of those films, too, remain disappointing. Many are rousing adventures that can

Paul Robeson, who won critical raves for The Emperor Jones *(above), left the country at one point, making films abroad where he hoped to escape stereotyping.*

still be enjoyed if one's willing to suspend any knowledge of history or politics. Today audiences may wonder how Robeson could ever have selected certain roles. Usually, he was cast as a helpful, loyal servant figure, standing in support of British colonial powers. In the 1936 *Song of Freedom*, he played a concert-hall performer who sets off for Africa in search of his roots—and also determined to bring the "civilized" manners and ways of the British Empire to the dark continent. In *King Solomon's Mines* (1937), he was the faithful Umbopa helping the dashing white hero in his quest for diamond mines in Africa. In *Sanders of the River* (1935), he portrayed Bosambo (the name is bad enough), so loyal a Congo chieftain that he helps the British crush a revolt of the natives. So angered was Robeson with the way *Sanders of the River* had been edited (a totally different film from what he had envisioned when he had signed to do it) that he fought against its release. Yet the irony of it all was his performance. As Pauline Kael has pointed out, despite the "junkiness of the Edgar Wallace story on which it is based and despite the flagrant racism of the noble-savage concept, Robeson himself has a nobility that transcends the picture's terms. He's magnificently stirring."

Robeson complained about others of his films, too. Sometimes watching them, we think he must have rushed into these movies with blinders on, so transparent are their distortions. The film he is said to have liked best is *The Proud Valley* (1940), in which he played a coal miner in Wales who sacrifices his life to save a group of miners. Of course, he represents the noble black who proves his nobility by sacrificing himself for his white friends. The same kind of procedure was used later in the development of Sidney Poitier's noble screen characters. But here Robeson had some fine moments, in part simply because of his astounding presence. At 6'3", weighing some 240 pounds, he's all confidence, all compassion, all conviction, a commanding larger-than-life hero who seems blessed by the gods with powers and skills far superior to those of mere mortals.

Although often stagey in his movies, without the fluidity of the true film actor, Robeson still stands as one of the least pretentious of the big-name stage stars to have worked in movies. Never viewing his gifts as signs of his own superiority, he maintains a down-to-earth congeniality that shines through. Unlike the later James Earl Jones (who was compared at times to Robeson, let's hope simply because of his size and voice), Robeson refuses to grandstand and he likes the camera; it in turn adores him, revealing him as a humane man filled with the joy of living itself. You can believe his sacrifice in a movie like *The Proud Valley* as the act of a man connected to his fellow man, not as the mechanics of a fake movie hero. In England, Robeson also appeared in *Jericho* (1937, also called *Dark Sands*) and *Big Fella* (1938, with wife Eslanda again).

In 1942, he returned to Hollywood for the disastrous *Tales of Manhattan*, which upon its release he denounced, infuriated by its portrait of blacks as over-religious, singing, naive dolts. He led protests against the film.

Of his film work, Robeson once said,

> I thought I could do something for the Negro race in films—show the truth about them and about other people too. I used to do my part and go away feeling satisfied—thought everything was okay. Well, it wasn't. The industry is not prepared to permit me to portray the life and express the living interests, hopes and aspirations of the struggling peo-

ple from whom I come. . . . They will never let me play a part in a film in which a Negro is on top.

After *Tales of Manhattan* Robeson did the narration for *Native Land* (1942). But he never appeared in another motion picture.

Bill "Bojangles" Robinson

B. 1878; D. 1949. Dancer, actor.

The grandson of a slave, this legendary tap dancer began his career on street corners, performing for nickels and dimes in his native Richmond, Virginia. As a professional entertainer, he acquired a large following (black and white), playing such big theaters as the Roxy and the Palace and appearing in such stage musicals as *Blackbirds of 1928*, *Brown Buddies* (1930), *Hot Rhythm* (1930), and *The Hot Mikado* (1939). But it was when Robinson turned to movies that his fame and legend were firmly sealed.

Little Miss Curlytop and Uncle Billy: Shirley Temple and Bill "Bojangles" Robinson.

He worked first in *Dixiana* (1930), later *Harlem Is Heaven* (1932), then in four films with Shirley Temple: *The Little Colonel* (1935), *The Littlest Rebel* (1935), *Rebecca of Sunnybrook Farm* (1938), and *Just Around the Corner* (1938). Today, seeing TV reruns of Robinson's old films, audiences immediately know his face and fancy footwork (if not his name) when they spot him by little Shirley's side. Together they were a great team, communicating sheer joy in dancing—and also joy in dancing together. In other respects, Robinson was also a perfect movie partner for Temple: he always proved himself trustworthy, good-natured, kindly, just the right sort of asexual man to care for Shirley in the midst of her trials and tribulations. Indeed for movie patrons of the 1930s, the two were something of an ideal interracial couple. They remind us of characters in *Uncle Tom's Cabin*: Tom and Little Eva.

Admittedly, Robinson's characters were blatant stereotypes, Depression versions of the friendly, cheery, self-sacrificing tom hero, the direct antithesis of Stepin Fetchit's outlandish lazybone coons. Black audiences of the period considered Robinson's somber toms a far more acceptable image. As an actor, Robinson was frequently awkward and not always at ease with dialogue, sometimes sounding as if he were reciting his lines from a blackboard. But he exuded a fundamental enthusiasm and optimism that Depression audiences could connect to. The black community also responded to him in a very personal way, viewing him as an important new kind of black star who had been able to go "big time" (or who had "crossed over" in the days before that term was used). Called The Honorary Mayor of Harlem, he coined the word *copacetic*, which was used frequently in black America to mean everything was A-Okay. Offstage, Robinson was known for his foul temper, for carrying a pistol, and for seldom backing away from an argument or fight. The tough early showbiz years had hardened him and taken their toll. But on stage and screen, he remained the quintessentially mellow, sensitive, relaxed black performer, totally in control, unfrazzled, and never failing to please. At his funeral in New York in 1949, thousands lined the streets to pay their respects to the entertainer affectionately known as "Bojangles." He remains a part of popular folklore and legend, that fact no doubt best exemplified by Fred Astaire's "Bojangles" number in the 1936 *Swing Time* and by Sammy Davis, Jr.'s, hit record "Mr. Bojangles."

His film credits include: *Hooray for Love* (1935); *In Old Kentucky* (1935); *One Mile from Heaven* (1937); *Up the River* (1938); and *Stormy Weather* (1943).

Esther Rolle

Actress.

Actress best known for her role as Florida Evans, the wisecracking domestic who first appeared from 1972 to 1974 on the TV series "Maude." Later Florida turned up as the star (and the mother of three) on the hit spinoff series "Good Times" (1974–1979). Because of contractual disputes with the producers of "Good Times," Rolle dropped out of the series for a year, then returned in the fall of 1978. Other TV credits include: "Journey Together" (1978); "I Know Why the Caged Bird Sings" (1979); "Flamingo Road" (1982); "The New Odd Couple" (1982); "The Love Boat" (1983, 1985); "Finder of Lost Lives" (1984); "Mickey Spillane's Mike Hammer" (1985); and "MacGruder and Loud" (1985). For her performance in "The Summer of My German Soldier" (1978), Rolle won an Emmy as Best Supporting Actress in a Limited Series or Special.

Having started her career in theater, Rolle had been one of the original members of The Negro Ensemble Company. Stage work includes: *Blues for Mister Charlie* (1964); *Amen Corner* (1965); *Don't Play Us Cheap* (1972); and as Lady Macbeth in a 1977 production of *Macbeth*.

Howard Rollins, Jr.

B. 1951. Actor.

After his movie debut as Coalhouse Walker in *Ragtime*, Howard Rollins, Jr., was singled out by the critics for his fine performance, walked off with an Oscar nomination as Best Supporting Actor of 1981, was promoted as Hollywood's Great Black Hope, and then had to wait three years before he had a chance to appear in another important film, the critically praised *A Soldier's Story*.

In these, his first two films, Rollins gave untyped portrayals of seemingly mild-mannered black men trapped in hostile environments. Although not the conventional Hollywood notion of the black militant, the characters' fundamental pride and confidence in themselves lead them to what others view as militant (or in *Ragtime*, insurrectionary) acts.

After that second film, Rollins's career unfortunately continued just as before: moving along at a snail's pace. "I'm not turning down any work," he said. "I haven't been approached with anything substantial. I don't like to say it, but it can only be because I am black. Why else wouldn't studios take advantage of an actor who's acknowledged as capable."

Rollins's career setbacks simply pointed up the dilemma confronting most serious black dramatic film actors (Lou Gossett and Yaphet Kotto, for example); the film industry often did not know what to do with them. So the actors either took what they could get or were left vegetating.

Rollins kept working, in television, with mixed results: *The Member of the Wedding* (1982, with Pearl Bailey); in the NBC soap opera "Another World" (1982); "A Doctor's Story" (1984); PBS's "For Us the Living" (1983, in which he portrayed civil rights leader Medgar Evers); "The House of Dies Drear" (1984); "The Wild Side" (1985); "Children of Times Square" (1986); and "Johnnie Mae Gibson: FBI" (1986). Earlier TV appearances include: "King" (1978); "Roots: The Next Generations" (1979); "Eliza: Our Story" "My Old Man" (1979); and "Thornwell" (1981).

Howard E. Rollins, Jr.: early 1980s' leading man who struggled to find leading roles.

Diana Ross

B. 1944. Actress, singer.

Detroit-born Diana Ross came to films after a phenomenally successful career as a pop star. With her childhood friends Mary Wilson and Florence Ballard, she had formed The Supremes, Motown Records' most successful and famous singing group of the 1960s.

In the 1970s, Ross left the trio to pursue a solo singing career. Not long afterwards when word spread that she was to play Billie Holiday in Motown's film *Lady Sings the Blues* (1972), her detractors predicted disaster. But this movie was a personal triumph for Ross, who proved the cynics and skeptics wrong by giving a highflung star performance that won her an Academy Award nomination as Best Actress of 1972.

In *Lady Sings the Blues* and her less successful followup film *Mahogany* (1975), Ross established an intriguing screen persona for herself: she introduced to the movies the modern, hip, independent, aggressive, career-oriented young black woman. Ross's characters were upwardly mobile ghetto girls out to find a place where they fit in and to make something of their lives; in essence to escape the restrictions, traditions, and boundaries of conventional black female life. But these characters also seemed to be punished for their independence and aggressiveness, always reminded not to stray from what the films want us to believe are their black roots. In both *Lady Sings the Blues* and *Mahogany*, the audience is cautioned that these women's roots are represented by the black men in their lives (played each time by Billy Dee Williams); the films stress that the Ross characters are always much better off when they listen to and obey their black man. Fortunately, Ross's co-star Williams himself was so relaxed about his masculinity *and* her independence that audiences tended to ignore the script and concentrate on the appeal of the two stars. Ross's personal push and drive also have provided her movies with a contradictory subtext: she's right to want more out of life; the scriptwriters are crazy to try simply tying her to a man. Curiously enough, in her third film *The Wiz* (1978), Ross went against her established persona, playing a meek and submissive heroine but again a woman off on a quest for identity.

Among Ross's numerous TV credits: appearances with The Supremes on "The Ed Sullivan Show" during the 1960s; "Tarzan" (1968, here The Supremes met the "king" of the jungle!); "An Evening with Diana Ross" (1977); "Barbara Walters Special" (1978); "Motown 25: Yesterday, Today, Forever" (1983); and "Motown Returns to the Apollo" (1985).

Diana Ross: sometimes disliked, frequently criticized, but a distinctive, bona fide American star and in her first two movies, an engaging film personality and a convincing actress.

Richard Roundtree

B. 1942. Actor.

Born in New Rochelle, New York, 6'2" Richard Roundtree attended New Rochelle High School (where he was voted most popular, best dressed, and best looking senior, all attributes that were to play an important part in his convolutedly glamorous image) and later attended Southern Illinois University on a football scholarship. But he soon gave up athletics in favor of an acting career. For a spell, he toured as a fashion model with The Ebony Fashion Fair. In 1967, he enrolled in the Negro Ensemble Company's workshop program. A few years later when he heard of a casting call for a new black detective film to be directed by Gordon Parks, Sr., he auditioned. The rest is pop history.

Richard Roundtree, who went from playing Shaft to a series of starring roles in such 1970s' films as Charley One Eye.

Gordon Parks has said that the studio producing *Shaft* (1971), MGM, balked at the fact that Roundtree had a mustache; MGM wanted it shaved off. But Parks saw the mustache as a symbol of a black man's virility and fought to keep Roundtree from being clean-shaven. Parks was, of course, right, the mustache curiously enough being just as important an ingredient of the *Shaft* look as John Shaft's leather coat and his bold street swagger.

Roundtree himself has admitted that during the filming, "I was scared to death," so inexperienced that he "didn't really . . . begin to feel comfortable with the character until three fourths of the way through the film." His inexperience shows on screen, the performance being part cool, part mechanical, part hip, part novice. But director Parks had wanted Roundtree because of the actor's presence, his ability to hold the screen, which is indeed what carries him through the film and the sequels, *Shaft's Big Score* (1972) and *Shaft in Africa* (1973). Unlike the Jim Brown heroes, Roundtree, on occasion, also projects a boyishness and a covert vulnerability that the scriptwriters don't seem much interested in exploring but which help make him a more engaging movie hero.

After the first *Shaft*, MGM, at one point, was planning to drop Roundtree from the sequel because of money problems. Having been paid $13,000 for the original *Shaft*, which made more than 10 times its $1.2 million cost and which has been credited with helping to save MGM from bankruptcy, Roundtree felt the studio's offer of $25,000 for the second was a mere pittance. The studio finally capitulated. He was offered an additional $25,000.

With the success of the *Shaft* films, Roundtree's newfound national fame won him cover portraits on *Newsweek*, *Ebony*, and *Jet*. He also became a hero for millions of black schoolkids everywhere, who loved the idea of an assertive black man who not only solved the crime but saved the pretty young woman, too. Today it's hard for us to imagine the incredible impact of this film and its lead character.

Other important movie roles followed for Roundtree in *Embassy* (1972), *Charley One Eye* (1973), *Earthquake* (1974), *Diamonds* (1975), and *Man Friday* (1976). But by the late 1970s, the choice roles and national attention had faded. By the 1980s, he was appearing in lowbudget action pictures such as *The Big Score* (1983), *Killpoint* (1984), and *One Down, Two to Go* (1983), all of which took his career nowhere. In a brief role in the Burt Reynolds/Clint Eastwood film *City Heat* (1984), he was far better showcased.

His television appearances include the starring role in the 1973–1974 "Shaft" series, "Roots" (1977, in which he delivers a surprisingly effective performance as a suitor of Leslie Uggams's character Kizzy, a dapper manservant who has attained a certain autonomy but at a terrible price; he's sold his very manhood), "Circus of the Stars" (1978), "Three on Three" (1979), "The Love Boat" (1980), "The Baron and the Kid" (1984), "A.D." (1985), and a role in the 1987 series "Outlaws."

Diana Sands

B. 1934; D. 1973. Actress.

A stage actress of great range and uncommon power, Diana Sands broke down theater racial barriers in the 1960s and performed roles in classic dramas previously considered suitable only for white actresses:

Shaw's *Major Barbara* (1954) and his *St. Joan* (1968) and also *Caesar and Cleopatra* (1967), and Shakespeare's *Antony and Cleopatra* (1968). Her appearance opposite actor Alan Alda in the 1964 Broadway production *The Owl and the Pussycat* was also considered a daring groundbreaker: the first time an interracial couple had been presented on stage without any mention whatsoever of race in the play itself.

The work that first brought Sands to moviegoers' attention was Lorraine Hansberry's *A Raisin in the Sun* (1961). Here she recreated a role she had performed on stage, playing again the kid sister Beneatha, which seemed tailor-made for her. Comic, tough-minded, energetic, independent, she represented the modern Afro-American young woman in search of her cultural/intellectual/emotional roots. Not only did Sands bring out the young woman's restless intelligence but also her poignant desire to fit in. It was a comic and dramatically rousing performance.

Sands's later films were of varying quality. The best is *The Landlord* (1970), in which she was cast as a black woman who bears the child of a wealthy, rather callous young white man. Sands gives a virtuoso performance, breathtakingly intense and astonishingly mature. Admittedly, though, even in a soapy melodrama like *Doctors' Wives* (1971), Diana Sands gave audiences some pleasurably intense trashy moments. And in her 1972 cult film *Georgia, Georgia*, Sands may not give her best acting performance but she is nonetheless a true movie diva: larger-than-life, complex, sexy, temperamental, compelling.

Sands's movie credits include: *Ensign Pulver* (1964), *Willie Dynamite* (1973), and *Honeybaby, Honeybaby* (1974). (The last two were released after her death.)

Sands also did a great deal of television, including: "East Side, West Side" (in the very famous 1963 episode "Who Do You Kill?"); "The Nurses" (1964); "Dr. Kildare" (1966); "I Spy" (1966); "The Fugitive" (1967); "Medical Center" (1971); and various episodes of "Julia" in 1970 and 1971, in which she played Diahann Carroll's rather flighty, actressy cousin from the East.

Diana Sands, who personified the modern Afro-American woman in search of her cultural roots.

Isabel Sanford

B. 1917. Actress.

In the early 1960s, Isabel Sanford, having separated from her husband, picked up her three children, boarded a Greyhound bus, and left New York to head for Los Angeles, hoping to find film and television work. In New York, where she had grown up, she had acted at night with church groups and also in the stage productions *Purlie Victorious* (1959) and *The Blacks* (1961). But her income had come mainly from her job as a keypunch operator. (The same was true during the first years in Los Angeles.) Sanford worked in such television shows as "Bewitched" (1968), "Mod Squad," and "The Interns" (1971) and appeared in such movies as *Young Runaways* (1968), *The Comic* (1969), *The New Centurions* (1972), and *Soul Soldier* (1972). By the early 1970s, it all added up to a thoroughly lackluster career. Her best roles had been in *Guess Who's Coming to Dinner?* (1967) as a feisty maid who did not cotton to Sidney Poitier and in *Lady Sings the Blues* (1972) as a whorehouse madam. Then came a semi-regular spot in the 1970s on "The Carol Burnett Show" and finally from 1971 to 1975 the part of Louise Jefferson (George Jefferson's beloved "Weezy") on "All in the Family." Afterward she continued the role in the spinoff "The Jeffersons" and won an Emmy for her character as Best Actress in a Comedy Series for 1980-1981.

Other film credits include: *Pendulum* (1970); *Hickey and Boggs* (1972); and *Love at First Bite* (1979).

TV credits include: "Love, American Style" (1972); "The Great Man's Whiskers" (1973); "Sanford and Son" (1973); "Temperatures Rising" (1973); "Kojak" (1974); "Dean's Place" (1975); "The Love Boat" (1980); and "The Shape of Things" (1982).

Michael Schultz

B. Director.

Following a successful career as a stage director (*Song of the Lusitanian Bogeyman* and *Kongi's Harvest* both in 1968), Michael Schultz directed the 1975 Hollywood feature *Cooley High*. When it emerged as a cult favorite for young black audiences of the 1970s, Schultz was propelled onto rather hallowed ground. He was hailed as a new kind of commercial black film director, who had drawn a sensitive study of young urban lives in transition. Later with another hit *Car Wash* (1976), Schultz was cheered for the affection he endowed his characters with, for his loose, episodic style, his assured pacing, and his rhythmic use of music and movement. His was *personal* commercial moviemaking. Those who praised Schultz had their points, but so did the Schultz detractors, who complained that his work lacked texture and depth.

Today it's apparent that his most successful portraits have been of adolescent males. A significant shortcoming of his films has been his reluctance (or lack of interest) in examining his female characters, who are either displaced (Sheila E. in the 1985 *Krush Groove*), undeveloped (the intriguing character played by Lauren Jones—Schultz's wife—in *Car Wash*, who ends as a total blank), or misunderstood (Tracy Reed in *Car Wash*; the dreamy light "pretty" girl *and* the darker "homely" girl in *Cooley High*). Oddly enough, the women/girls are among the few Schultz characters with any glimmers of maturity. But the director steadfastly fails to see anything from his heroines' points of view. At the same time, while saluting male camaraderie, Schultz doesn't offer much insight into it.

In the 1970s, Schultz did have the distinction of working well with Richard Pryor in *Greased Lightning* (1977) and *Which Way Is Up?* (1977) (also *Car Wash*). On occasion, he tapped Pryor's softer sentimental side. Yet the movies themselves lacked dramatic coherence, meandering about so much that audiences either sat hoping for some kind of storyline that would pull the diverse sequences together or were lulled almost to sleep by the directorial inertia.

By the late 1970s, Schultz's career momentum slowed down considerably. When he sought to break through to a larger, more general audience with *Sgt. Pepper's Lonely Hearts Club Band* (1979), the results were disastrous. Schultz had no feel for the Beatles' music or the whimsical setting.

By the 1980s, his films grew almost shockingly impersonal. *Carbon Copy* (1981) was so bland and disjointed it could have been directed by almost anyone (it, too, was another treatise on male camaraderie, a white father and his black son). *Berry Gordy's Last Dragon* (1985) was a slowpoke attempt at a "youth" movie that had neither flash nor daring. (The latter film met with some success though.) Schultz did manage to rouse himself with the "rap" movie *Krush Groove* although the results were mixed. For all its supposed hipness, this other youth film was essentially an old-fashioned backstage let's-put-on-a-show musical. He revealed an appreciation—again, his trademark affection—for some of the performers, but was unable to come up with a highly structured or stylized approach that might have complemented or intensified the rap music at the center of the picture.

Schultz's TV credits include "To Be Young, Gifted, and Black" (1971); "Ceremonies in Dark Old Men" (1975); "Benny's Place" (1982); "For Us the Living" (1983); as well as episodes of "The Rockford Files," "Baretta," "Toma," and "Starsky and Hutch." Schultz also directed the movies *Honeybaby, Honeybaby* (1974), *Scavenger Hunt* (1979), and the rather disordered "Disorderlies" (1987) with the Fat Boy.

Hazel Scott

B. 1920. *D.* 1981. Pianist, singer, actress.

As haughty a diva as there has ever been, jazz pianist Hazel Scott, like Lena Horne, did much to alter the image of black women in American films in the early 1940s. Born in Trinidad, she had been a child prodigy who read at three, played the piano at four, and improvised on the piano at five. In 1939, at age 18, she became an overnight sensation on the New York nightclub circuit with her appearances at Cafe Society Downtown (one of the first clubs in New York to have not only an integrated roster of performers but integrated audiences as well). Her specialty was jazzing the classics.

When she went to Hollywood in the early 1940s, a special clause was written into her contract, specifying that she was never to play characters in her films. There would be no dopey maid roles for this young woman. Instead she always came on as herself in movies, immaculately dressed and coiffed, a blazing symbol of black pride and assertiveness. No doubt Scott's most elegant appearance is in a nightclub sequence of *Rhapsody in Blue* (1945) in which she performs, part in English, part in French, Gershwin's "The Man I Love." Sensuous and sophisticated, she

From New York nightclubs to center stage in Hollywood: Hazel Scott (with Lena Horne in the "Jericho" sequence of I Dood It), *who never played maids' roles in films; instead she simply appeared as herself.*

looks magnificent. Of course, the sequence is not without irony. After all Scott, performing for a very hoity-toity white crowd, seems cut off from her own community. There's not one black face in the room. She is indeed a black woman put on display for the perusal and pleasure of a white audience. Still she's so supremely confident you know here's an above-it-all black goddess who cannot be touched. That in itself was something to see in a Hollywood film of the 1940s.

In 1950, Scott starred in her own 15-minute television program "The Hazel Scott Show." But it did not last long. Defiantly outspoken (she was one of the first black performers to refuse to appear before segregated audiences), Scott had political problems during the McCarthy Era of blacklisting. (Her first husband was black politician Adam Clayton Powell, Jr.) Like Lena Horne, she was listed in *Red Channels*, a compilation of the names of entertainers thought to be either Communists or Communist sympathizers. Scott testified before the House Un-American Activities Committee, blasting *Red Channels* as "guilt by listing." Not long afterward Scott's television show was cancelled. Her career slipped into a decline. Later she lived and worked in Europe, then returned to the States, performing in New York clubs in the late 1970s until her death in 1981.

Other Scott films: *Something to Shout About* (1943); *I Dood It* (1943); *The Heat's On* (1943); *Broadway Rhythm* (1944); and *The Night Affair* (1961).

Frank Silvera

B. 1914; D. 1970. Actor, director.

In 1952 when Frank Silvera appeared as the Mexican General Huerta in Elia Kazan's *Viva Zapata*, few moviegoers realized they were watching a black actor. The same was true of this light-skinned black actor's appearances in the films *The Appaloosa* (1966), *Hombre* (1967), and *Che* (1968) and as the wealthy Mexican ranch owner in the TV series "High Chaparral." Writer Arnold Perl has told a story which illustrates the manner in which Silvera handled some of his career difficulties. In 1950 after Silvera had read for a role as a black elevator man in the production "Blind Spot," the show's producer said, "He's great, but he's too light for the part." Silvera responded by saying, "Ask him if I'm light enough for the white lead." The producer then said, "You're right. You've got the part." "Which part?" Silvera asked. He played the black role. But for most of his career, Frank Silvera fortunately managed to ease his way around a problem that has confronted such other light-skinned black performers as Fredi Washington, Ellen Holly, and Lonette McKee; somehow amid the entertainment industry's rigid type casting system (and its adherence to America's tightly drawn color codes), Silvera was able to play an assortment of white, black, and seemingly non-racial roles on Broadway, in films and on television.

Jamaican-born Silvera came to the United States at age eight, later graduated from high school in Boston and attended Northeastern's Law School. His 1945 Broadway debut was in *Anna Lucasta*. Later theater work included *Camino Real* (1953, as Gutman), *Saint Joan* (1954, with Jean Arthur), *The Skin of Our Teeth* (1955, with Helen Hayes and Mary Martin; he was also assistant director on this production), and most notably in the Broadway hit *A Hatful of Rain* (1955). In that production, as the father of Ben Gazzara, Silvera played a "white" character, and oddly enough, no one seemed to make any fuss about it. (He did not play the role in the film version though.) Nor was there any discussion of his "colorless" parts in Stanley Kubrick's films *Fear and Desire* (1953) and *Killer's Kiss* (1955) or any number of other features in which Silvera appeared. His performances were usually well-crafted, committed pieces of work. When Silvera was cast as the Inspector in *Crime and Punishment, U.S.A.* (1959), *Variety* wrote that he gave a "brilliant performance" and displayed "a virtuosity that is compelling." Had Silvera been consigned only to "black" roles, he might never had found significant screen work.

Yet Frank Silvera was fiercely committed to his cultural roots. When he founded the Theatre of Being with Vantile Whitfield, he announced he wanted to show that the Negro "is not trying to assume whitedom but is complete in his own particular reality." Throughout his distinguished career, Silvera was a champion not only for the black playwright but for the black actor, too. And his very career indicated, of course, the great range of roles and opportunities a black performer might have if indeed he could be considered for any part.

In 1970 at the age of 56, Frank Silvera died tragically when he was accidentally electrocuted at his home in Los Angeles. Later The Frank Silvera Workshop was founded in New York in memory of his great contributions.

Silvera's film credits include: *The Fighter* (1952); *The Miracle of Our Lady Fatima* (1952); *Crowded Paradise* (1956); *The Mountain Road* (1960); *Key Witness* (1960); *Mutiny on the Bounty* (1962); *Toys in the Attic* (1963); *The Greatest Story Ever Told* (1965); *The St. Valentine's Day Massacre* (1967); *Up Tight* (1968); *The Stalking Moon* (1969); *The Guns of the Magnificent Seven* (1969); and *Valdez Is Coming* (1971).

Silvera's TV credits include: "The Skin of Our Teeth" (1955); "Studio One" (the 1957 episode "Guitar"); "Wanted, Dead or Alive" (1958); "Ellery Queen" (1958); "Alfred Hitchcock Presents" (the 1969 episode "A Personal Matter"); "Playhouse 90" (1959); "Bonanza" (1961); "Twilight Zone" (1962); "The Defenders" (1963); "Channing" (1964); "Mr. Novak" (1964); "Profiles in Courage" (1965); "Rawhide" (1965); "Gunsmoke" (1966); "I Spy" (1966); "The Wonderful World of Disney" (1968, 1970); "Marcus Welby, M.D." (1969); and "Hawaii Five-O" (1969).

Madge Sinclair

B. 1940. Actress.

This highly skilled Jamaican-born actress first caught the critics' eyes in such 1970s' theater productions as *Iphigenia*, *Kumaliza*, and *T-Jean and His Brothers*. In 1974 she made her first film *Conrack*, snapping audiences to attention with an impressive performance as an intractable elementary school principal. Sinclair soon proved adept at playing highstrung women, determinedly keeping their emotions in check: whether it be as the mother of a young athlete killed by a white policeman in *Cornbread, Earl, and Me* (1975); or as the unyielding madame of a bordello in *Leadbelly* (1976); or, most movingly, as the efficient house slave Belle, wife of Kunta Kinte, whose shield of emotional armor cracks when she sees her only child Kizzy sold off to another plantation owner in "Roots" (1977). Brisk, no-nonsense, and singlemindedly set on doing things her own way, the Sinclair character struggles always to mask her vulnerability, to hide the hurt and fears buried under her hard exterior. In film and on TV, Sinclair has been capable of moments of true power. But her challenging roles have been few and far between.

Although ideal for films, most of her work has been in television: in "I Love You . . . Goodbye" (1974); "Joe Forrester" (1975); "Doctors' Hospital" (1975); "The Waltons" (1976); "Almos' a Man" (1977); "Grandpa Goes to Washington" (1978); "One in a Million: The Ron Le Flore Story" (1978); "The White Shadow" (1979); "I Will, I Will—For Now" (1979); "Guyana Tragedy: The Jim Jones Story" (1980, in which she turns in a floridly dramatic/comic performance that adds greatly to this TV movie's curious potboiler appeal); "Jimmy B. and Andre" (1980); "High Ice" (1980); "Victims" (1982); "An American Portrait" (1984); and "Starman" (1987). In 1980, Sinclair also appeared in a regular role as the unflappable nurse Ernestine Shoop on the series "Trapper John, M.D."

Sinclair also appeared in Sam Peckinpah's *Convoy* (1978) and as the captain of the U.S.S. *Saratoga* in the film *Star Trek IV: The Voyage Home* (1986).

Raymond St. Jacques

B. 1930. Actor, director.

"St. Jacques: Our Next Black Matinee Idol?" So read *The New York Times* headline in December 1968, its article describing actor Raymond St. Jacques as a "6-foot-3-inch tower of elegance, and when he speaks, the tones come rolling out in the mellow Shakespearean baritone of a young Everett Dirksen." Not long afterward *Ebony*'s feature on him carried a headline that simply proclaimed: "Raymond the Magnificent." And so it went for St. Jacques, born James Arthur Johnson (nicknamed Chubby) in Hartford, Connecticut, who looked in the late 1960s as if he were about to enter the hallowed (and precarious) ranks of movie stardom.

He began acting—after his studies at Yale—in such New York stage productions as *High Name Today* (1959), *The Cool World* (1960), and *The Blacks* (1961). He had also worked in various Shakespearean festivals in Stratford (Connecticut), San Diego, and New York. Early on, he wanted a name change, at one time considering "James West," at another "Roy Johnson." "Then I decided I wanted something to fill up the screen," he once explained, "So I picked Raymond St. Jacques. It belonged to a white French boy I knew who is now a milkman in New Haven."

By the mid-1960s, he moved on to such television shows as "Slattery's People" (1965), "The Wackiest Ship in the Army" (1966) and "I Spy" (1966). But his most important credit was as Simon Blake, the Civil War veteran (from 1965–1966) on the series "Rawhide." In many of these early television appearances, St. Jacques's color worked to his advantage. The atmosphere of these shows was often so enjoyably fake and the white actors playing the leads so interchangeable (and so plastic) that St. Jacques, in comparison, had a distinct *brown* freshness and individuality.

In the late 1960s, with good press and the nature of the times on his side (stinging criticism was then being directed at Sidney Poitier; a search was on for a different kind of black movie leading man), St. Jacques won plum supporting roles in *The Green Berets* (1968) and *The Comedians* (1967). In the latter as the sadistic captain of an island's (Haiti) secret police force (the *tonton macoute*), he strutted about in dark glasses with a hard scowl, never mincing words and anxious to grace the white characters with a swift kick or two. It was a performance of manufactured machismo. Yet he jolted audiences nonetheless.

Then came leading roles in *If He Hollers, Let Him Go* (1968), *Up Tight* (1968), *A Change of Mind* (1969), *Cotton Comes to Harlem* (1970), and *Come Back, Charleston Blue* (1972). Here he seemed heavy-handed, not relaxed enough. Perhaps the voice that thrilled *The New York Times* was too theatrical for cinema. Regardless, during the 1970s, once athletes like Jim Brown and Fred Williamson had emerged as stars, St. Jacques's days as a leading man seemed to have passed. Even he appeared to acknowledge such a fact when, while directing *Book of Numbers* (1973), he kept his camera focused on Philip Michael Thomas as the hero and himself as the older worn fatherly figure.

Shrewd enough to endure the vicissitudes of a fickle industry, St. Jacques kept working, even after the leads—and the attendant publicity—had vanished. In the 1980s he appeared as a doctor in several episodes of TV's "Falcon Crest," once again, as in his earlier television days, his presence, his color, and his attitude made him seem a "real" figure in contrast with the otherwise predictable all-white world of the nighttime soaps.

Among his film credits: *Black Like Me* (1964); *Mister Moses* (1965); *Mister Buddwing* (1966); *Madigan* (1968); *Lost in the Stars* (1974); *The Private Files of J. Edgar Hoover* (1978); *Cuba Crossing* (1980); and *The Evil That Men Do* (1984).

Among his TV credits: "Daniel Boone" (1966); "The Girl from U.N.C.L.E." (1966); "Tarzan" (1968); "Invaders" (1968); "The Name of the Game" (1968); "The Monk" (1969); "Police Story" (1974); "Search for the Gods" (1975); "McCloud" (1975); "The Rookies" (1975); "Police Woman" (1975); "Roots" (1977); "The African Connection" (1977); "Little House on the Prairie" (1977); "The Bionic Woman" (1977); "Secrets of Three Hungry Wives" (1978); "Quincy" (1979); "Hizzonner" (1979); "The 416th" (1979); "A Small Circle of Friends" (1980); "House Calls" (1980); "Fantasy Island" (1981); "Hart to Hart" (1981); "Galivan" (1982); "The Powers of Matthew Star" (1983); "Voyagers" (1983); "Love Boat" (1983, 1985); "Matt Houston" (1983); "Trapper John, M.D." (1983); "The Fall Guy" (1984, 1985); "Airwolf" (1984); "Murder, She Wrote" (1984, 1985); "Cagney and Lacey" (1984); and "Hardcastle and McCormick" (1985).

Woody Strode

B. 1914. Actor.

Woody Strode came to attention as a college football star at UCLA in the early 1940s and later as a professional member of the Los Angeles Rams. Once he pursued an acting career, Strode—at 6'4" and 205 pounds—was a commanding presence. Admittedly, sometimes he seemed stiff and ill at ease with his dialogue. Other times his silence added to his appeal. Always, though, his flat-out, rather straight-arrow masculinity and physical strength won him a significant following among black males in the 1950s and early 1960s. During this period when black moviegoers rarely saw an assertive, physical black man of action, Strode was so powerfully built in such films as *Pork Chop Hill* (1959) and *The Last Voyage* (1959) that he looked as if he could overcome almost any opponent or physical adversity. Even in his brief appearance as the King of Ethiopia in Cecil B. DeMille's *The Ten Commandments*

Woody Strode in one of his few starring roles in the European film Black Jesus.

(1956), Woody Strode was a towering, muscular sight to behold as he confidently entered the court of the Egyptian palace. And certainly when he was cast in *Spartacus* (1960) as the gladiator Draba who is locked into physical combat with the film's hero, black audiences yearned for this slave rebellion epic to focus less on its star Kirk Douglas and more on its supporting player Woody Strode.

Strode also appeared in several John Ford films: *Two Rode Together* (1961), *The Man Who Shot Liberty Valance* (1962), *Seven Women* (1966), and most notably *Sergeant Rutledge* (1960). Ironically, Ford, who in the past had shown a disturbing fondness for Stepin Fetchit's coon antics, used his camera to bring out Strode's innate power and nobility, his gallantry and unexpected gracefulness. Woody Strode often looks like a prince from another land, stranded in an alien world that does not see his beauty.

After years of minor and supporting roles in Hollywood features, in 1968 Woody Strode left for Europe to find work. In 1971, his Italian film *Black Jesus* was successfully released in the States, just as the era of the black movie boom was about to be launched. Still, however, Hollywood chose to ignore his very unique star presence and persona.

Woody Strode's movie credits include: *The Lion Hunters* (1951); *The Gambler from Natchez* (1954); *Tarzan's Fight for Life* (1958); *The Sins of Rachel Cade* (1961); *Genghis Kahn* (1965); *The Professionals* (1966); *Shalako* (1968); *Che* (1969); *Boot Hill* (1969); *Once Upon a Time in the West* (1969); *The Last Rebel* (1971); *The Revengers* (1972); and *The Cotton Club* (1984).

Strode's TV credits include: "Soldiers of Fortune" (1955); "The Man from Blackhawk" (1960); "Thriller" (1960); "Rawhide" (the 1961 "Incident of the Buffalo Soldier" episode); "Lieutenant" (1964); "The Farmer's Daughter" (1964); "Daniel Boone" (1966); "Tarzan" (1966, 1967, 1968); "Batman" (1966); "Breakout" (1970); "Key West" (1973); "Manhunter" (1973); "The Quest" (1976); and "A Gathering of Old Men" (1987).

Mr. T.

B. 1952. Actor.

Would anyone in his right mind have believed that this roly-poly muscle-bound creature with his gold chains and modified Mohawk haircut would become a certified star of the 1980s? Well, of course not. But that was clearly the case for the auspicious Mr. T., who, by the middle years of the decade, could boast of quite a number of accomplishments. He made films (*Rocky III* in 1982, *D.C. Cab* in 1983), did videos (such as "Mr. T.'s Be Somebody"), was the subject of a well-publicized Barbara Walters interview, turned up on magazine covers (several times on *People* as well as *US*, *TV Guide*, *California*, and even *The Muppet Magazine*), had a doll designed in his likeness by toy manufacturers (it was appropriately called The Mr. T. Doll—and wasn't a bad seller at all), had a cereal named after him, had a cartoon show done about him, starred in the hit TV series "The A-Team" (for which he earned a salary of close to $1 million a year), wrote his autobiography (*Mr. T.: The Man with the Gold*, published in 1984), and was a hero for school children throughout America. At a White House Christmas party, he even dressed up as Santa Claus (reportedly at First Lady Nancy Reagan's request) and persuaded Mrs. Reagan to sit on his lap and give him a kiss, too! The photo of this *sight* ran around the world, the ultimate symbol of his brazen ascension to stardom.

Mr. T. came to media fame after a checkered past. Born Lawrence Tureaud, the 10th of 12 children, he grew up on Chicago's Southside, wrestled and played football while in high school and won a scholarship to Prairie View A and M College in Texas. After a year, he dropped out. Then he worked as a gym instructor, a bouncer, and a bodyguard, for the likes of Michael Jackson, Leon Spinks, and Muhammad Ali. In 1980, his life changed after an appearance on NBC's "Games People Play," where he was spotted by Sylvester Stallone, who tapped him for *Rocky III*. Cast as boxer Clubber Lang, T. was an aggressive, vicious *outsider*, determined to wreck Rocky—and symbolically to demolish a healthy all-American way of life, too. No one who saw the film could fail to despise his crude and vulgar character. Nor could anyone have imagined him making it on TV where comforting images and characters have long been the call of the day.

But shrewdly in 1983, television's "A-Team" changed the T. image. As part of a team doing good deeds, T. was tamed, his menace and bite dissolved; and he emerged as a palatable, acceptable part of the American system, never battling against the establishment, instead assuring that establishment's endurance.

While adult black America blanched at the spectacle of T. (Could he ever complete a sentence without a grunt or groan? Could he be understood? Did he know anything about grammar?), seeing in him the most shocking of King Kong stereotypes, kids (black and white) loved him because he was so obviously a cartoon, everything about him an exaggeration, every gesture and move a broad stroke without shading or nuance. He was the big burly genie out of the bottle, who talked *baadd* and stomped and roared and was violent with enemies but underneath was no real threat, just mush and an overgrown teddybear to be patronized.

Mr. T. shrewdly played up his appeal to kids, making announcements to the press about his love of children, also visiting ill children in hospitals. Doing all he could to help in the merchandizing of his image, he made "statements" whenever possible. To the kids, he said: "When I be fightin' or whatever on TV, it all just fun. We don't hurt nobody. But I don't want you to be a fighter. Study to be a scientist. Study to be an astronaut. Everyone can't be Mr. T." To Mr. and Mrs. John Q. Public, he said: "I love America. It's the only place where someone can make so much money playing a fool." Not since the days of Joan Crawford (who laboriously answered all her fan letters) had an American star seemed so anxious to court the favor of his constituency.

But as the 1980s moved on, the T. image wore thin. Publicly on the TV program "Entertainment Tonight," "A-Team" co-star George Peppard called Mr. T. "an embarrassment." Rumors spread that T. was dissatisfied with the team on "The A-Team." Then the show's ratings slipped, and it was cancelled. And it looked as if T. might be headed the route of Jimmie Walker's once-famous character J.J.: to oblivion or the TV game shows. Basically, what all the hullabaloo about Mr. T. represented in the 1980s was a shift in the national cultural consciousness: the transformation of the black Macho Holy Terror into a Macho Joke, a cuddly chocolate Cabbage Patch Doll.

Mr. T.'s film credits include *Penitentiary II* (1982).

His TV credits include: "Silver Spoons" (1982); "Twilight Theatre II" (1982); "Diff'rent Strokes" (1983); "SOS: Secret of Surviving" (1984); "A Christmas Dream" (1984); "Bob Hope's Wicki-Wacky Special from Waikiki" (1984); "The Barbara Walters Special" (1984); "AfterMASH" (1984); and "The Toughest Man in the World" (1984).

Billie "Buckwheat" Thomas

B. 1931; D. 1980. Actor.

One of the most popular of the children in Hal Roach's "Our Gang" series, Billie Thomas appeared as Buckwheat in 93 episodes, from 1934 (when he was but three years old) to 1944. He was known for his gingham smocks (that looked like dresses) and later his sporty straw hats. ("Our Gang"'s Stymie Beard wore a derby.) Often he mangled his words and had an air of perpetual confusion and bewilderment. Frankly, dear little Buckwheat was something of an early zonked-out, pint-sized space cadet.

Like his predecessor Farina, should Buckwheat ever be frightened, his pigtails stood on end. And again as with Farina, Buckwheat's sexual identity puzzled everyone. Boy or girl? Interestingly, before Thomas assumed the character, Buckwheat had indeed been played in three episodes by a little girl, Willie Mae Taylor. According to "Our Gang" historians Leonard Maltin and Richard Bann, Stymie Beard's sister Carlena also played Buckwheat in one episode. And when Thomas began playing the part, the character was supposed to be a little girl. No wonder so much confusion. Eventually, of course, Thomas's spunky little manhood came to the fore.

After leaving "Our Gang," Thomas, like so many of the other child actors in the series, had problems adjusting to a new life and dropped out of public view. He worked as a film technician. Years later when a Buckwheat impersonator (named James E. Frazier) claimed he had created the character, Thomas reappeared to assert his rights. He was then backed by his fellow performers as being *the* Buckwheat. And, of course, Thomas's character assumed a whole new type of dubious celebrity once Eddie Murphy spun out his Buckwheat parodies on "Saturday Night Live."

Thomas died at age 49 in 1980.

Billie Thomas as Buckwheat with some of his buddies in the "Our Gang" series.

Prior to his days of stardom in "Miami Vice," Philip Michael Thomas with Irene Cara in the film Sparkle.

Philip Michael Thomas

B. 1949. Actor.

A one-time theology student at the University of California, Philip Michael Thomas worked in theater (*No Place To Be Somebody* in 1971), then in films of the 1970s: *Stigma* (1972), *Come Back, Charleston Blue* (1972), *Book of Numbers* (1973, the lead role), *Coon Skin* (1975), and *Mr. Ricco* (1975). Boyish, low-key, easy-going, and pleasantly narcissistic, Thomas has often seemed more of a teen idol than a typical leading man. That may explain why he became a heartthrob for young black women and adolescents when he appeared as the edgy Stix in *Sparkle* (1976). In 1984 he proved a great success on the TV series "Miami Vice," in which his good looks and cool manner blended perfectly with the overall narcissistic esthetics. A more "realistic" actor would have upset the whole gorgeous unreality of the series.

Thomas's other TV credits include: "Police Woman" (1974); "Caribe" (1975); "Moving On" (1976); "Medical Center" (1976); the pilot "Roosevelt and Truman" (1977); "This Man Stands Alone" (1979); and "A Fight for Jenny" (1986). He also recorded an album of pop tunes.

Lorenzo Tucker

B. 1907; D. 1986. Actor.

At one point in his career, actor Lorenzo Tucker was called "the black John Gilbert." Later he was publicized as "the black Valentino," a tag which stuck to wavy-haired and handsome Tucker for many years.

Born in Philadelphia, Tucker first broke into show business in 1926 as a dancer in Atlantic City. He also worked as a straight man in minstrel shows that starred Bessie Smith, Mammie Smith, and Stepin Fetchit. Then he met up with black director Oscar Micheaux, who cast him in such films as *Wages of Sin* (1927), *Daughter of the Congo* (1931), *Temptation* (1936), and *Underworld* (1947). During the 1930s and 1940s, Tucker also worked in other race movies such as *The Black King* (1932) and *Straight to Heaven* (1939). In 1942, he was drafted into the army where he said he had staged more than a dozen shows in the United States and Europe. Afterward he returned to show business, again working in independently produced all-black movies such as *Boy! What a*

Suave and debonair, Lorenzo Tucker was a leading man in race movies and was called the Black Valentino.

Girl (1947). But the race movie market soon disappeared. From 1953 to 1954, he toured the United Kingdom in the play *Anna Lucasta.* He quit show business in 1963, although he made one last effort to continue his acting career in 1977 when, having then moved to Los Angeles, he sought movie and television work. But nothing came of that. He finally took a job working as a night security guard.

In retrospect, his career was a mixed bag. Sometimes he was a perfectly serviceable matinee idol, just the right type of smoothie for women to take a quick liking to. Other times he was relegated to supporting and minor roles in which he could be easily overlooked. In his later years, Tucker collected and compiled material on black films. He also proved to be a gregarious, thoroughly engaging interviewee for film historians trying to piece together the history of race movies in America.

Tucker's film credits include: *When Men Betray* (1928); *Easy Street* (1930); *Veiled Aristocrats* (1932); *Harlem After Midnight* (1934); *One Round Jones* (1946); *Sepia Cinderella* (1947); and *Reet, Petite, and Gone* (1947).

Cicely Tyson

B. c. 1938. Actress.

After graduating from New York's Charles Evans Hughes High School, Cicely Tyson worked as a secretary for the Red Cross until she decided one day she'd had it. She pushed her desk aside and announced for all to hear, "I'm sure God didn't intend me to sit at a typewriter." Thereafter she worked as a model, studied acting, and appeared in New York theatre productions: *Jolly's Progress* (1959), *Dark of the Moon* (1960), *Cool World* (1960), *The Blacks* (1961, for which she won The Vernon Rice Award for her performance as Virtue), and later *Tiger Tiger Burning Bright* (1962) and *Carry Me Back to Morningside Heights* (1968).

In the 1960s, Tyson was a fresh face (one of the few black ones, too) in guest shots on a number of television series: "Slattery's People" (1965), "I Spy" (1965), "Medical Center" (1969), "The Courtship of Eddie's Father" (1969), and "Here Come the Brides" (1969). But it was her continuing role (from 1963 to 1965) as George C. Scott's secretary on the series "East Side/West Side" that brought her attention. Like Dorothy Dandridge, Tyson had immediate audience rapport. There has not been another black film actress with quite the startling looks and presence of either of these so different stars, each of whom became a true cultural icon. As one of the first black women to wear an Afro on American television, Tyson was a striking figure: slender and intense with near perfect bone structure, magnificent smooth skin, dark penetrating eyes, and a regal air that made her seem a woman of convictions and commitment. At a time when audiences still didn't always know Tyson's name, they sensed nonetheless on "East Side/West Side" her power and range, knowing that this young woman was bigger and better than the roles she had been playing. Watching the young Tyson, one often has the feeling that, through the turn of a line or a look or gesture, at any moment something extraordinary could happen.

The very early 70s—the period of the blaxploitation films—were tough years for Tyson, who has said she flatly refused work she felt demeaning. At one point, she was even ready to forsake her career until friends like Sammy Davis, Jr., and Sidney Poitier prevailed upon her to stick it out. Four years had passed without a major film role until

Sounder (1972) arrived. Her character Rebecca, finely etched and shaded, with attention paid to the most minute details, was a delicate portrait of a strong, enduring black woman, who's also somehow mythically larger than life. Nominated for an Oscar for her performance as Best Actress of 1974, Tyson followed her *Sounder* triumph with another: the lead role in the TV movie "The Autobiography of Miss Jane Pittman" (1974) for which she won an Emmy as Best Actress in a Special in 1974. Afterward Cicely Tyson became a household name, her face gracing the covers of *People, Ms, Encore, Ebony, Jet.* The critics praised her as a major dramatic actress, perhaps the first such black actress of this type since Ethel Waters.

Afterwards Tyson sought challenging roles but with varying degrees of success, turning more to television as a venue to diverse material. Sometimes the standard TV-ish quality of TV films like "Wilma" (1977) and "Playing with Fire" (1985) seemed to strand her. Tyson really cannot play an ordinary woman or at least she cannot play an ordinary woman in an ordinary fashion. So one often felt a tension between the actress and her TV roles. In some cases, too, she appeared either miscast as in "King" (1978) or walking through a part as in "Roots." Other times as in "The Marva Collins Story" (1981), she summoned up her old convictions and injected spirit into what was essentially a formula film. Then as in the feature *Bustin Loose* (1981), opposite Richard Pryor, her endearing and sweetly romantic character (a true departure from previous work) was either overlooked or dismissed by the critics. By the mid-1980s though it became distressing to see her cast in meaningless supporting roles in what was mostly junk: "Acceptable Risks" (1986) and "Intimate Encounters" (1986). Still even here it was interesting and oddly compelling to watch her struggling to invest such material with some intelligence and dramatic flair. She remained a major American dramatic actress for whom the film and then television industries rarely provided the kind of support system (and acting plums) accorded such white stars as Jane Fonda and Meryl Streep.

Tyson's other TV credits include: "Mission: Impossible" (1970); "Gunsmoke" (1970); "Emergency" (1972); "Just an Old Sweet Song" (1976); "A Woman Called Moses" (1978); "Benny's Place" (1982); she also appeared on the daytime soap "The Guiding Light" in 1967.

Among her film credits: *Odds Against Tomorrow* (1959); *The Last Angry Man* (1959); *A Man Called Adam* (1966); *The Comedians* (1967); *The Heart Is a Lonely Hunter* (1968); *The River Niger* (1976); *The Bluebird* (1976); *A Hero Ain't Nothin but a Sandwich* (1978); and *The Concorde: Airport '79.*

Tyson married jazz musician Miles Davis.

A night of triumph for "Jane Pittman" Emmy winner Cicely Tyson, whose career started in the late 1950s on the New York stage.

Leslie Uggams

B. 1943. Singer, actress.

Was singer Leslie Uggams really one of America's early important black television stars? Actually, yes. As a tiny six-year-old, lovingly and sedately dressed, Uggams appeared in the early 1950s episodes of "The Beulah Show." By age nine, she appeared—singing and dancing—on the shows of Milton Berle and Arthur Godfrey. (She also performed on radio.) At age fourteen, after a 1958 appearance on "Name That Tune," she was "discovered" by Mitch Miller, who, in 1961, hired her as a regular performer on his popular musical series "Sing Along with

Mitch" (1961–1966). Weekly, TV audiences watched this young black girl with the impeccable manners and the big toothy smile sing cutesy, innocent, rather bland standards. (One critic described her as "a sepia-toned Shirley Temple.") With much coverage from the press, Uggams emerged as a national celebrity. Then in 1969, at age twenty-six, she hosted her own network variety show "The Leslie Uggams Show," in which she strove for a more mature persona. Running on CBS, the Uggams series lasted but ten weeks. Afterward she disappeared from weekly television.

Years later, explaining her absence from television, Uggams said the public "didn't want to see me grow up. They only wanted to hear the sweet songs. It was tough to shake. Motown was happening. So much was happening." But Uggams in the late 1960s and 1970s couldn't change the good-girl-next-door image that Mitch Miller's show had created for her. "I think it hurt a lot," she said.

It hurt in ways other than simply the public's refusal to accept a new, more womanly image for her. Uggams herself—once she later managed to land important dramatic roles in "Roots" (1977) and "Backstairs at the White House" (1979)—displayed a nagging tendency to come on too girlishly, too cutesy. As is the case with many other performers, her own desire to please and be liked sometimes prevented her from shaping complex characters. The great exception was her later sequences in "Roots." In the early scenes as the girl Kizzy, she overdid the standard Uggams smile and forced spontaneity. But as Kizzy, the young mother of Chicken George, who turns down a chance to marry a handsome black man from a neighboring plantation, she was at her mature best: sexy, troubled, determined to live a part of her life on her own terms. In Ossie Davis's 1972 film *Black Girl*, Uggams also had some effective moments. But, ironically enough, Davis used Uggams's type—the perky, naive middle-class black girl—against her. The character is picked at and gnawed over in a way that neither Uggams nor the other cast members seem to be fully aware of. Here Uggams herself—her professional persona—seems called into question as much as the character she played. It's an intriguing piece of casting.

Uggams's other movie credits include: *Two Weeks in Another Town* (1962); *Skyjacked* (1972); and *Poor Pretty Eddie* (1975).

Uggams's TV credits include: appearances on such variety shows of the 1950s and 1960s as "Johnny Olsen's TV Kids" (her debut), "The Ed Sullivan Show," and "The Garry Moore Show"; also "The Girl from U.N.C.L.E." (1966); "I Spy" (1967); "Mod Squad" (1972); "Marcus Welby, M.D." (1974); "Celebrity Challenge of the Sexes" (1978); "The General Electric All-Star Anniversary" (1978); "Sinatra & Friends" (1978); "The London Palladium Anniversary Special" (1979); "The Love Boat" (1980); and "Magnum, P.I." (1984).

Melvin Van Peebles

B. 1932. Director, writer, actor, composer.

Not since Oscar Micheaux had there been a black director as colorful and controversial as Melvin Van Peebles. Like Micheaux, he was often labeled an amateur by his critics (although if that be true, it must be conceded he was a gifted one), but in the early 1970s he emerged as a folk hero for a new black film community: singlehandedly, Van Peebles proved an independent black filmmaker could survive and most importantly, that with enough hustle, push, and daring, he could reach a large black audience. Both Micheaux and Van Peebles believed in popular black American cinema: making films that touched on the fantasies and desires of the mass black audience. Neither was an art house patron although Van Peebles's early work was geared for art theatres.

Van Peebles came to films in a roundabout way. Born in Chicago during the Depression, he graduated from Ohio Wesleyan University, spent three and a half years as a navigator in the U.S. Air Force, and then, unable to find employment with a commercial airline, became a gripman on the cable cars in San Francisco. A photographer friend sparked Van Peebles's interest in film. On his own, he made shorts. In 1959 after trying his luck in Hollywood and being rebuffed (he once said Hollywood had offered him two spots: elevator operator or parking lot attendant), he took his family to Holland. There he studied at the University of Amsterdam and acted with the Dutch National Theatre. Afterward he went to France where he panhandled to survive. Henri Langlois of the prestigious French Cinematheque liked Van Peebles's early films. Yet Van Peebles could get into the French directors' union no more easily than he could in the American one. When he learned that in France a writer could direct a screen version of his own work, he decided to become a writer, eventually knocking out five novels. With a screen treatment of his novel *Story of a Three Day Pass*, he applied to take the French Film Center's examination for directors. His proposed film was finally declared eligible for underwriting. He was on his way.

A *succès d'estime* that had been shot on a budget of $200,000, *Story of a Three Day Pass* was first shown at the San Francisco International Film Festival in 1967. Promptly—and inaccurately—proclaimed by the critics as America's first Negro film director, Van Peebles soon proved proficient at promoting both his film and himself and in exploiting to the hilt a press eager for a new kind of seemingly renegade black artistic hero. Capitalizing on the momentum he had built up, Van Peebles directed *Watermelon Man* for Columbia Pictures in 1970. The film did so-so business.

Determined to make his kind of film his own way, he shot his next film, the legendary 1971 *Sweet Sweetback's Baadasssss Song*, without major studio financing, using a non-union crew and working on a reported $500,000 budget. The completed *Sweetback* could not find distributors though; only two in the country agreed to back it. The film was distributed through Cinemation, a company that had been known previously for handling exploitation films. At first Van Peebles could not go the normal routes to publicize the picture either. The talk shows declined to book him. The press ignored him. Most were outright offended by *Sweetback*'s graphic violence and its raw sex and, of course, its radical political vision. *Sweetback* might have endured a quick and unheralded demise had not Van Peebles's promotional instincts kept it alive. Doing all he could to hawk the film within the black community, particularly among the "brothers on the street," he bought advertising time on black radio stations and succeeded in getting word of mouth to spread the news that a black movie and hero had arrived that were totally different from the standard Poitier vehicle.

In the fall of 1971, *Sweetback* returned, opening in 60 theaters in the New York area alone, then in another 150 around the country. This time around, the press latched onto the film and its director. Speaking in the vernacular of a dude from the streets and looking trendily scruffy and groungy in his denims with his droopy mustache, the 38-

A rather restrained portrait of iconoclastic director Melvin Van Peebles.

year-old Van Peebles shrewdly used the press again to transform himself into a heroic man of the people. He recounted his problems in making the film and also his rough-and-tumble life as an artist and a former expatriate. On the base of his neck was tattooed a line of dots. Just below it in French and English was tattoed the statement: *Cut on the Dotted Line—If You Can.* "In the last year," Van Peebles told *Life*, "a lot of people have tried." He also wore a sweatshirt that served as an apt comment on the rating given *Sweetback*. Written on the sweatshirt were the words "Rated X by an All-White Jury." The media loved this new bad black dude.

Van Peebles also wisely used the negative reviews of *Sweetback*, taking on the white critical establishment, which he told critic Roger Ebert had not understood the picture. "Like Judith Crist," he said,

> She thought that nice little colored boy that she'd championed had betrayed her. She liked my movie *Story of a Three Day Pass*. She thought it was warm and sweet. But suddenly I'm the most inept, amateurish director she's ever seen . . . because in *Sweetback* I'm telling it straight.

Van Peebles was calling into question the standards and misconceptions of the white critics. And eventually the extraordinary success of *Sweetback*, despite critics within the black community as well, proved he had touched base with a new mood within black America, particularly young blacks. Soon Hollywood sought to reach this new large audience with an array of *Sweetback* imitations.

Riding high, Van Peebles set out to conquer Broadway with two controversial black shows *Ain't Supposed to Die a Natural Death* (1971) and *Don't Play Us Cheap* (1972). He also did a film version of the latter. But it, too, suffered distribution problems, never reaching the mass audience as *Sweetback* had.

Perhaps what's most curious about the rise of Melvin Van Peebles's public persona is its aftermath: following all the attention—in some circles, acclaim—after having become one of the hottest black celebrities on the national circuit, he soon assumed a distinctly low profile. Most had thought he would remain a dominant voice in black films of the late 1970s. But no other films appeared, as Van Peebles almost seemed to vanish from sight.

By the mid-1970s, he shifted his interest to television, writing—not directing—"Just an Old Sweet Song" (1976). Immediately cries went up amid his constituency. Where had the renegade firebrand gone? What had happened to the baadasssss nigger who, at the end of *Sweetback*, had proclaimed he was coming back to collect some dues? For here was a gentle, mild-tempered family drama, suitable for any middle-class, establishment audience.

In 1981, he returned to television with a steamy script for "Sophisticated Gents." Here Van Peebles's old spark as well as both his strengths and excesses were on display. Having to follow television's rules of decorum (conforming to its demands for inoffensive language and antiseptic sex), he had tackled, nonetheless, characters and themes—black men and women trying to figure themselves and the system out—generally avoided by the tiny tube. Moreover Van Peebles proved no matter how fragmented his work might appear and no matter how much he indulged in his own heady excesses, he was able still to come up with highly charged offbeat work with an anti-bourgeois point of view that was distinctly his.

In the early 1980s, Van Peebles also worked off-Broadway, directing *Bodybags* (1981) and directing, writing (the words and the music), and starring in *Waltz of the Stork* (1982). His son, Mario Van Peebles, also appeared in the latter production, then moved on to lively appearances in a string of low-budget movies and then a role on the TV series "LA Law" (1986).

In 1985, the unpredictable Van Peebles surprised everyone when he appeared to have abandoned—at least temporarily—his directing career to become the only black trader on the floor of the American Stock Exchange. From Renegade Buck to Yuppie (or Bumpie: Black Urban Middle-class Professional), Van Peebles—with a twinkle in his eye—seemed to be indicating to his followers that there might be yet more method to his seeming madness.

In 1987, Van Peebles appeared again with son Mario in the film *Jaws: The Revenge*.

Jimmie Walker

B. 1949. Actor, comedian.

In the mid-1970s, Jimmie Walker was one of the most visible and popular stars of television. That bastion of middle-class values, *Family Circle Magazine*, even voted him Most Popular TV Performer of 1975.

A stand-up comic, Walker won national fame for his portrayal of J.J. on the hit series "Good Times" (1974–1979). Schoolkids, black and white, fawned over him as much as a later young audience did over Mr. T. in the 1980s. For pre-adolescents, exaggerated personalities often have the same appeal as cartoons: the kids love the unreality of what they see. Tall, thin, gangly, Walker often played the coon character: fundamentally, a comic dimwitted soul, always in and out of trouble. Physically he reminds one of both the young Stepin Fetchit and the young Willie Best. When complaints flared up from black parents about Walker's J.J., the creators of "Good Times" tried softening and cleaning the character up. Walker himself sought an image change with a serious role in the TV movie "The Greatest Thing That Almost Happened" (1977). But he lacked the range to play another type of character. Once "Good Times" folded, his giddy days of national fame came to an almost abrupt end.

Jimmie Walker, who rose to popularity with his performance as J.J. on the TV series "Good Times."

Movie credits: *Badge 373* (1973); *Let's Do It Again* (released in 1975 during the period of his popularity; Walker again played a coon figure); *Rabbit Test* (1978); *Concorde 79*; and *Water* (1986).

Walker's TV credits include dozens of game shows and specials, including "Tattletales" (1974); "Celebrity Sweepstakes" (1975); "Hollywood Squares" (1975); and "Midnight Special" (1975); "The Dyn-O-Mite Special" (1975); "Donahue" (1975); "Telethon" (1977); "Us Against the World—II" (1978); "Just for Laughs" (1978); "Young and Foolish" (1978); "The Love Boat" (1979); "Murder Can Hurt You" (1980); a role as Rodney Washington on the short-lived 1980 series "B.A.D. Cats"; "The White Shadow" (1980); "Run, America, Run" (1981); and "Cagney & Lacey" (1983).

Fredi Washington

B. 1903. Actress.

Fredi Washington: *light-skinned, green-eyed, straight-haired, and intelligent, an actress whom the film industry of the 1930s did not know how to handle.*

Savannah-born beauty best remembered for her performance as Peola, the lightskinned black girl who passes for white in the original 1934 version of *Imitation of Life*. In the 1920s and 1930s, Fredi Washington (born Fredricka Washington) and her younger sister Isabel were much-talked-about actresses in theater and social circles. Both were the mulatto ideal: lightskinned, with keen features and straight hair. They'd also had an unusual upbringing which may have accounted for their aristocratic air and demeanor.

After the death of their mother, the girls' father had sent them North to a convent for orphaned black and Indian children until they were teen-agers. Isabel returned to the South, briefly married, later divorced, then went to New York where she was a dancer at Connie's Inn and The Cotton Club. She also appeared in the film *St. Louis Blues* (1929) and the stage productions *Singin' the Blues* (1931, with her sister Fredi) and *Harlem* (1929). When she became the first wife of black politician Adam Clayton Powell, Jr., she gave up her career.

Fredi Washington's career was far more extensive. Once she arrived in New York, she lived with her grandmother, worked in a dress company stockroom, later was employed as a bookkeeper for W.C. Handy's Black Swan Records. Then she auditioned—and was hired—as a dancer in *Shuffle Along* in 1922. Later with partner Charles Moore, she toured Europe as a dance team, the two being billed as Moiret and Fredi. In 1926, when she switched from dance to drama in the Broadway show *Black Boy* opposite Paul Robeson, she portrayed what came to be the archetypical Fredi Washington character: the black girl who wants to cross the color line. White theatergoers were said to be openly shocked because the colored actress they'd heard so much about did indeed look so white. For Washington, her public persona and private life looked at one point as if they'd merge. Often urged in the early years of her career to actually pass for white, told that if she did she might enjoy an immensely successful stage career, Washington steadfastly refused.

In 1934, she beat out countless other candidates for the role of Peola, which made Fredi Washington's name something of a household word in part of the black community. The film *Imitation of Life* was greatly written about in the black press and discussed among black intellectuals of the day. But Washington's classic part proved a dead end. Hollywood, unsure how to cast a beautiful black (too beautiful to play the then-conventional black maid parts yet because of Hollywood's/America's strict racial codes, unable as a "real" black woman to play just any part opposite white performers, particularly white leading men), the industry decided not to use her at all. After *Imitation of Life*, Washington did one more Hollywood film, *One Mile from Heaven* (1937), in which she played a young woman who stumbles across a white child, which she wants to keep as her own. Washington returned to New York, acted on the stage in *Mamba's Daughters* (with Ethel Waters in 1939), *A Long Way from Home* (1948); *Lysistrata* (1946); and other plays until the early 1950s when she married a prominent black Connecticut dentist and retired from show business.

Fredi Washington's film credits include: *Black and Tan* (1929, with Duke Ellington); *Mills Blue Rhythm Band* (1933); and *The Emperor Jones* (1933).

Ethel Waters

B. 1896. Actress, singer.

Fortunately, this remarkable singer/actress—surely one of the great talents in American popular entertainment—has been captured on film in most of the various stages of her legendary seven-decade long career.

Ethel Waters arrived at full-fledged stardom after having travelled a long and arduous route. Born out of wedlock in Chester, Pennsylvania, Waters had had a hard childhood (as a girl, she ran errands for the pimps and whores in the red-light district where she lived) with a harrowing set of experiences, all of which are well documented in her 1951 autobiography *His Eye Is on the Sparrow*. By age 13, she was married. Two years later, the marriage was over.

Later she worked as a chambermaid and laundress, then turned to singing professionally, traveling in road shows and playing in tiny theaters around the country. She was billed early as Sweet Mama Stringbean. In this period, as she sang rowdy songs and did sexy bumps and grinds, she was a sex symbol for much of Black America. Often when performing, she appeared to have a chip on her shoulder yet that was one of her ironically enticing attributes for an audience that could take one long look at this willowy girl and know she had not had things easy.

In time, Waters introduced a number of hit songs of the 1920s and 1930s: "Dinah," "Stormy Weather," and "Am I Blue?" Gradually, once she began to appear in the New York clubs in the 1920s, she developed, as Alberta Hunter said, into a very polished, refined singer.

Ambitious, tense, driven, she struggled to make it as a musical comedy star on Broadway, and finally succeeded after a number of setbacks, in the 1933 *As Thousands Cheer* and two years later in *At Home Abroad*. Then in 1939, she turned dramatic—to the surprise of cynics and the critics—with her powerhouse performance in *Mamba's Daughters*. It was a major image change for her—and for black women in theatre, who previously had not been thought capable of playing serious, important dramatic roles. Waters returned to musical comedy in the 1940s but she never abandoned her hopes for other significant dramatic roles. Fortunately, in 1950, she had another dramatic triumph in Carson McCullers's play and film *The Member of the Wedding*.

Waters's movie record stretches back to 1929 when, still slender and retaining some of the spicy raunch she had first become known for, she performed her hit "Am I Blue?" and "Birmingham Bertha" in *On with the*

Ethel Waters in a career that spanned some six decades: as a rowdy singer billed as Sweet Mama Stringbean.

Waters as a slinky radio star.

Show (1929). Dressed to the nines (she now looks a tad campy) as she performed the latter, her energy and attitude (*don't mess with this chile* is what she seems to be telling us) were wholly new to American cinema. Such later films as the shorts *Rufus Jones for President* (1933) and *Bubblin Over* (1934) revealed a slightly more mature Waters, who was beginning to take on the matronly look that audiences now remember. Here she also started testing new territory, although gently, with her heated dialogue and mock-dramatics.

By the time she appeared as a maid in *Cairo* (1942), Waters, having lost her girlishness altogether, looked heavy and dowdy, as if she would slip completely into Hollywood's mammy bag. But in *Stage Door Canteen* (1943)—in which she did not play a role, but simply performed the song "Quicksand"—she's a controlled, sophisticated diva, sure of herself and her talent. With Count Basie playing piano while she sings, Waters is a resplendent symbol of the dignified, thoroughly professional and classy Negro entertainer of the war years.

1943 also marked the appearance of *Cabin in the Sky*, in which, repeating her stage role, she's a gilded Petunia who can turn hot and cold: hottest in her nightclub sequence when she kicks up her heels to do an exuberant jitterbug with John "Bubbles" Sublett. Contemporary audiences still marvel at the sexy energy this very heavy woman exudes.

In later films such as *Pinky* (1950) and *Member of the Wedding* (1952) Waters is no longer entertainer or even legendary star. She's more in the realm of mythic heroine: the embodiment of the strong, ever-resilient black matriarch. In her hands, the mammy stereotype had been transformed into the black mother earth figure. Waters' later TV appearances on episodes of such series as "Daniel Boone" and the 1961 "Good Night, Sweet Blues" episode of "Route 66" lack the vitality of her great performances (she has little to work with in these programs and must rely on her inner resources and sense of self to get by), but they are part of her evolving image: now she's the weathered, ailing-grand old woman of film, whose talents are greater than the projects with which she's involved.

Here is Waters as a rather matronly companion to Jeannette MacDonald in Cairo.

Waters's other movie credits include: *Gift of Gab* (1934); *Hot n Bothered* (1934); *Tales of Manhattan* (1942); *Carib Gold* (1955); and *The Sound and the Fury* (1959).

TV credits include: "Beulah" (1950, played the title role in this series); "Favorite Playhouse" ("Speaking to Hannah," 1955); "Climax" (1955); "G.E. Theatre" (1955, "Winner by Decision" with Harry Belafonte); "Matinee Theatre" (1957); "Great Adventures" (1963); "Owen Marshall" (1972); "The Sound and the Fury" (1955 TV version for Playwrights 56); and the "Billy Graham Crusade" during the early 1970s.

Nominated for an Academy Award as Best Supporting Actress of 1949 for her performance in *Pinky*.

Ethel Waters as a white-haired matriarch in The Sound and the Fury.

Billy Dee Williams

B. 1937. Actor.

During the 1970s, Billy Dee Williams was often called the black Clark Gable. Of course, it didn't seem to matter to anyone that Williams's screen persona was nothing like that of Gable, who was always aggressive, boldly sexual, and a man of action who seldom had to think twice about his moves or motivations. Williams's characters were often hesitant or cautious with women, openly puzzled or baffled by them. His heroes also seemed to enjoy the courtship period as much as (or even more) than the point of consummation. Yet the *black Gable* tag stuck because Billy Dee Williams was the screen's first authentic black romantic leading man, a real lover. Like Gable, when Williams's face was framed in adoring closeups, women in the audience openly fell into a swoon. And he proved best when he had a strong female as a co-star.

By the time of his ascension to romantic stardom, though, Williams had already had a long and varied list of credits. Born William December Williams in New York City, the son of a maintenance man, he had first appeared on stage as a child actor. When his mother, an elevator operator at New York's Lyceum Theatre, had learned of a role for a little page in a new production, she had told the play's producer Max Gordon of her son Billy. The producer looked the kid over. And soon Billy Dee Williams made his stage debut with German actress Lotte Lenya, no less, in *The Firebrand of Florence* (1947). Later he studied acting at New York's High School of Music and Art and The National Academy of Fine Arts and was also taught for a few months by Sidney Poitier at the Actors Workshop in Harlem.

His early work was in theater: *Take a Giant Step* (1956); *A Taste of Honey* (his breakthrough role in 1960); *The Cool World* (1960); *The Blacks* (1962); and later *Hallelujah Baby!* (1967); *Slow Dance on the Killing Ground* (1970); and *Ceremonies in Dark Old Men* (1970). His first film role—as the rebellious ghetto kid in *The Last Angry Man* (1959)—was a good one: he's headstrong, insecure, jittery, a portrait of a bright kid running on empty.

Afterward, throughout the 1960s and 1970s, he appeared on television, in everything from daytime soap operas like "Another World" to guest spots on primetime series: "Hawk" (1966); "The Mod Squad" (1971); "The FBI" (1969, 1971); and "Mission: Impossible" (1971). In this period when a few scattered black performers were just beginning to be cast in serious roles on television, Williams played sensitive troubled young men, who often acted tough to shield their sensitivity. These lukewarm Brandoesque characters were distinguished by Williams's romantic vulnerability, which always lay just beneath the surface.

During this period, black leading men, like Poitier, had been so busy in their films trying to prove themselves worthy of fitting into the system that any suggestion of "soft sensitivity" might have indicated weakness. In *Bright Road* (1953) and *Carmen Jones* (1954), Harry Belafonte's earnest vulnerability had sometimes made him seem like an ineffectual Mr. Goody Two Shoes, hardly a match for his leading lady Dandridge. Usually, Poitier's characters had an explosive edge, which signalled to audiences that despite his sensitivity, Poitier was a tough man who could fight back. In his early work, Williams, too, seemed to have the ability to explode but it was an internal emotional explosion. His battles, unlike Poitier's, always seemed to be with himself as much as with the culture. (The same was true of James Edwards's heroes in the late 1940s and 1950s.) As fresh, handsome, and likable as Williams was though, it didn't look as if his career were headed anywhere. Then came "Brian's Song" in 1970.

Cast as football player Gayle Sayers in this TV movie about the friendship of two athletes during a traumatic period (one is dying), Williams worked opposite actor James Caan and was able to fully display vulnerability and gentleness. "Brian's Song" was very much a male version of *Love Story* (1970).

Not long afterward Williams' stardom was certified with his appearances as Diana Ross's leading man in *Lady Sings the Blues* (1972) and *Mahogany* (1975). Perfect for one another, the romantic chemistry of these two performers kept the movies spinning and twirling. Ross, the more extravagant of the two, highflung, aggressive, energetically determined to do things her way even if her way is the wrong way, was always brought back to earth by Williams's cool calm. She brought out both his paternal and brotherly sides and lifted to the surface his otherwise low-keyed sexuality. With Ross, Williams also proved the most understanding of black men: able to take a backseat to a diva without ever losing his own personality, knowing when to let her

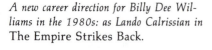

A new career direction for Billy Dee Williams in the 1980s: as Lando Calrissian in The Empire Strikes Back.

sparkle and shine, when to step in and tell her to cut the bull. He softened some of Ross's brittle edges. And her warmth with him was a pleasant balance to her sometimes abrasive assertiveness (which some men have not felt comfortable with at all). Where Williams succeeded best as a screen lover was in his simple *appreciation* of women. Unlike the typical Jim Brown hero who seemed interested simply in tossing a woman in the sack without much tender foreplay or any sensitivity to her needs, Williams appeared to like women and to need them to complete his view of himself, enjoying always the chase, the flirting, cajoling, pampering, sometimes the fighting.

Of course, for women he also always came across as a true rarity: he's a *constant*, always there at the crucial moments for Diana Ross, lending her support. He was as well a man who could be hurt. In the Rome sequence of *Mahogany*, after he has endured Ross's insults, tirades, and simp shenanigans, he finally leaves her and the city, bruised by her brazen insensitivity and her self-destructiveness. Here women saw a strong black male whose feelings went deep enough that he could be injured by a woman. And finally, Williams was a male love object: the early glimpse women have of him in *Lady Sings the Blues* shows him as a handsome dude dressed to the nines, a peacock who likes looking at himself and also likes it when women look him over.

Yet importantly Williams also maintained a male following, primarily because he never collapsed, always enduring on screen as a functioning hero, sometimes keeping his emotions locked in but never denying them. Some might prefer minimizing Williams's importance in American films. But in the world of pop images, his was a new one, filling in a void that had in the past rendered black men asexual or incapable of romance. His was a mature black male, perhaps dreamy and idealized but a clear mark in an evolutionary line of heroic black male images.

Although born to play romantic roles, Williams in too many of his later films was lifted out of a romantic context and thrown into a typical macho arena, which called for standard, rather colorless heroics. Such films as *The Hit* (1973), *The Take* (1974), and to a certain degree even *The Bingo Long Traveling All-Stars and Motor Kings* (1976) never utilized Williams' special gifts or presence. And in some of these, his self-absorption showed through.

For a time, he was under contract to Motown's Berry Gordy. As Motown's interest in films lessened, Williams eventually became a free agent. The changes his career then underwent in the late 1970s and 1980s indicated shifts of focus for black stars in films. By the time he appeared opposite Sylvester Stallone in *Nighthawks*, black America's favorite Don Juan was simply a backup support for an enjoyably ego-crazed white star. As Lando Calrissian in *The Empire Strikes Back* (1980), he was granted a few moments of romantic devilment and some derring-do, but he never seemed completely integrated into the action and epic drive of this *Star Wars* (1977) sequel. The same was true of his appearance in *The Return of the Jedi* (1983), which was rather embarrassing, so poorly (and seldom) was he used.

In the mid-1980s, like other black stars of the 1970s, he turned to television but with a splash, portraying Diahann Carroll's Berry-Gordy-ish husband on "Dynasty" (1984) and also starring with Ken Wahl in the shortlived series "Double Dare" (1985). As an elegant sophisticate in both series, he was outfitted with lavish wardrobes and glitzy settings. But his characters were mostly windowdressing, rarely blessed with dialogue that had some bite or dash. Not given a chance to show some flair or romantic grace, he was a pro, nonetheless, who brought—simply by his presence—the kind of high-style old-time glamor the TV studios hoped for. And eventually Williams acquired a following of white female admirers, too.

TV credits include: "The Defenders" (1964); "Carter's Army" (1970); "The Glass House" (1972); "Scott Joplin; King of Ragtime" (1977); "Christmas Lilies of the Field" (1979 in which he played the character originated by Sidney Poitier in *Lilies of the Field*); "Children of Divorce" (1980); "The Hostage Tower" (1980); "The Jeffersons" (1980); "Chiefs" (1983, one of Williams's better televison roles); "Eubie Blake: A Century of Music" (1983); "Motown 25: Yesterday, Today, Forever" (1983); "Shooting Stars" (1983); "The Imposter" (1984); "Time Bomb" (1984); "Oceans of Fire" (1986); "Courage" (1986); and "Brown Sugar: Eighty Years of America's Black Female Superstars" (1986).

Other films include: *The Out of Towners* (1970); *The Final Comedown* (1972); *Com-Tac* (1977); *Fear City* (1985); and *Marvin and Tige* (1985).

Spencer Williams

B. 1893; D. 1969. Actor, director, writer.

Spencer Williams has come to be remembered best for his performance as Andy Brown on television's "Amos 'n' Andy" (1951–1953). Yet long before his appearance on the sitcom, Williams had worked steadily in motion pictures, surprisingly behind the scenes as a writer/director.

He was born in Vidalia, Louisiana, attended the University of Minnesota, later joined the army, was stationed abroad and travelled widely, and upon his discharge in 1923, turned his eye to a career in show business. Landing a job in Hollywood at the Christie Studios in the late 1920s, Williams eventually worked as a continuity writer and also a writer of Negro dialect for the studio's black comedy shorts. He appeared in such 1929 short films as *Melancholy Dame, The Framing of the Shrew, Oft in the Silly Night, The Lady Fare,* and *Music Hath Charms.* Shrewd, industrious, and tough-minded, Williams, through sheer tenacity and his own dedication to filmmaking, held on in the movie business for the next two decades. In the 1930s, he appeared in the black westerns *Bronze Buckaroo* (1938), *Harlem on the Prairie* (1939), and *Harlem Rides the Range* (1939). The latter was also written by Williams and Flournoy Miller.

During the 1940s, Spencer Williams directed films to which he appeared more committed. Two such features—*The Blood of Jesus* in 1941 and *Go Down Death* in 1944—touch on the black religious experience. Williams's admirers frequently prefer his approach in these "serious" and "dramatic" films. But often overlooked have been some of the lighter 1940s films, especially *Juke Joint* (1947), which, despite its technical crudities and stereotypes, captures the tone of past ethnic entertainment and reverberates with a satiric small-town kind of dopiness that still proves entertaining. In this type of film, Williams also seems more relaxed about himself and his subject and isn't straining for a statement. (As an actor, Williams is also more at ease with his non-serious parts.) Yet he never leaves behind his interest in black religion. Midway in the comedy *Juke Joint*, he pauses for a family dinner prayer sequence that is oddly placed and oddly affecting, too.

By the end of the 1940s, Spencer Williams appeared to have abandoned his career when he moved to Tulsa, Oklahoma, where he taught photography and radio to veterans. Then came word of the role in "Amos 'n' Andy." Ironically, Williams's best performances are in this series. Here he's a gentle, easy-going, rather triflin' guy, a ready-made dupe for Kingfish. Always this heavy-set, big-boned man with his great child's face is a figure the camera cannot help liking. He's so gullible and also so decent and even tempered that audiences still gravitate to him.

Williams's work as a filmmaker came under reassessment in the 1970s. Along with Oscar Micheaux, he remains one of the pioneering black directors, who, no matter what his stylistic and technical flaws and deficiencies, was devoted to personal filmmaking.

Among the movies directed by Williams are *Tenderfeet* (1928), *Of One Blood* (undated), *Dirty Gerty from Harlem USA* (1946), *Beale Street Mama* (1946), and *The Girl in Room 20* (c. 1946). He also acted in those films. Among the movies which he wrote and appeared in are *The Widow's Bite* (1929) and *Son Ingagi* (1940). He also directed *Marching On* (c. 1940s, a tribute to blacks in the military) and produced the undated *Hot Biscuits*.

Fred Williamson

B. 1938. Actor, director, producer, writer.

Former football player turned actor—and a more talented actor than many, including Williamson himself, might be willing to admit. In his earliest films *M*A*S*H* (1970) and *Tell Me That You Love Me Junie Moon* (1970), Williamson projected a cool, relaxed brand of virility: he was something of an easy-going guy, shrewd, secure, fairly perceptive, not greatly troubled by anything and certainly not anxious to prove anything to anybody. The film industry, structured as it was and is, of course, had no place for this kind of black movie hero in the early 1970s. Consequently, once black action movies—with their gritty action heroes—came into vogue, Williamson promptly underwent an image change, emerging as the then-typical buck hero in such movies as *Hammer* (1972), *The Legend of Nigger Charley* (1972) and its sequel *The Soul of Nigger Charley* (1973), *Black Caesar* (1973) and *its* sequel *Hell Up in Harlem* (1973), *Boss Nigger* (1975, Williamson wrote and co-produced), *Bucktown* (1975), *Three Tough Guys* (1974), *Three the Hard Way* (1974), and *Take the Hard Ride* (1975).

During this time when the war in Vietnam as well as the recent explosions in ghetto streets were very much on the minds of Williamson's audience, his macho heroics reflected the violence and fears of the troubled period. Sometimes stiff and unconvincing, he came across as a twelve-year-old's idea of a big tough guy. In many of his films he seemed to be trying a bit too hard to prove he was indeed the baaddest dude on the block.

Yet on other occasions, Williamson also turned in surprisingly effective performances. In an offbeat 1974 B-movie, *Black Eye*, he played a detective enmeshed in a pervasively corrupt system. His girl has even left him—for another girl! Caught in a bind, the Williamson hero handles it with an ironic nonchalance. The same is true of some of his work in a tawdry picture like *That Man Bolt* (1973). And even in that atrocity *Three the Hard Way*, Williamson (unlike his co-stars Jim Brown and Jim Kelly) learned to communicate thought on screen: his physical feats seemed to grow out of the workings of his mind (however large or

Fred Williamson, personable and sleazily likable: inside him there was a decent actor struggling to get out.

small). Unlike the Brown hero, Williamson's figures were not so caught up in (or so insecure about) their masculinity that they couldn't laugh at themselves. When Williamson was serious, he sometimes was awful. But when he relaxed, his swagger and rather loose, decent hip way with a line and a doubletake turned him into a sleazily likable rogue. Part put-on, part clown, Williamson might have developed into a kind of elegant comic sophisticate or at least into the kind of good-ole-boy character that Burt Reynolds popularized.

Inside Williamson there was a decent actor fighting to get out. Had he been more selective and serious about his roles (and had he shown more respect for his audience), he might have emerged as a rare and special black movie hero. But sadly his career was studded with waste. By the late 1970s and 1980s, he had formed his own production company Po' Boy Productions and had turned to producing, directing, sometimes writing, and starring in his own features, such movies as *Adios Amigo* (1975, starring Richard Pryor), *Mean Johnny Barrows* (1976), *Death Journey* (1976, director/star), *No Way Back* (1976, for which he was criticized for his treatment of women), *The Big Score* (1983), *One Down, Two to Go* (1983), and *The Last Fight* (1983), shlock jobs mostly whose main intent seemed only to make a quick buck.

Far more relaxed than some of these heavy-breathing action flicks are Williamson's occasional TV appearances which date back to the early 1970s when, from 1970 to 1971, he appeared as one of Diahann Carroll's boyfriends on "Julia." Other TV credits include: "Police Story" (1973, also 1976), "NFL Monday Night Football" (1974, he was a commentator), "Laugh In" (1970), "The Rookies" (1974), "Wheels" (1979), "Fantasy Island" (1980), and "Chips" (1981).

Other film credits include: *Damnation Alley* (1977); *Mr. Mean* (1978); *Counterfeit Commandos* (1981); *1990: The Bronx Warriors* (1983); *White Fire* (1983); and *Vigilante* (1983).

Demond Wilson

B. 1946. Actor.

Demond Wilson's theater credits date back to 1951 when as an energetic five-year-old, he made his debut in a revival of *Green Pastures*. At fourteen, he played Touchstone in a 1960 production of *As You Like It*. Not long afterward, in 1965, Wilson served in the army in Vietnam. Afterwards returning to the theater, he began in 1969 a two year road tour in *Boys in the Band*, did the films *Dealing* (1972) and *The Organization* (1971), and in the early 1970s worked on episodes of the television shows "Mannix," "Mission: Impossible," and "All in the Family."

His role as Lamont, the son of junk dealer Fred Sanford, on "Sanford and Son" (1972–1977) established him as a national personality. But once the series folded, Wilson struggled to establish another professional identity. He exhibited, however, enough stamina and drive to keep working within a very demanding business in two other short-lived series "Baby, I'm Back" (1978) and "The New Odd Couple" (1982–1983).

Wilson's other TV credits include: "All in the Family" (1971); "Salute to Redd Foxx" (1974); and "Love Boat"(1979, 1981); and "Today's FBI" (1981).

Dooley Wilson

B. 1894; D. 1959. Actor.

Dooley Wilson is best known for his performance in *Casablanca* (1942) as Sam: Bogart's soulmate/buddy, who sits stoically at the piano, performing that great anthem for lovers everywhere "As Time Goes By." Wilson's other films include: *My Favorite Blonde* (1942); *Night in New Orleans* (1942); *Cairo* (1942); *Two Tickets to London* (1943); *Stormy Weather* (1943); *Higher and Higher* (1944); *Seven Days Ashore* (1944); *Come to the Stable* (1949); and *Passage West* (1951). In 1951, he was also one of the actors to play Beulah's beau Bill Jackson on the TV series "Beulah."

Flip Wilson

B. 1933. Comedian, actor.

Although Flip Wilson's days of high-flying popularity might now seem relatively short (about four years), Wilson's extraordinary success in the 1970s cannot be underestimated. He was clearly television's first real black superstar, far more successful than even Bill Cosby had been on "I Spy" (1965–1968). The ratings for his "Flip Wilson Show" (1970–1974) soared to the very top. Over 40 million Americans tuned in to watch him every week. And sponsors paid the then-huge sum of $86,000 a minute for advertising time. For a guy from humble beginnings in Jersey City, New Jersey, none of this was chicken feed.

Flip Wilson: his humor was rooted in the ethnic theater tradition of the past yet was infused with a new consciousness and assurance.

One of 24 children (18 of whom survived), Wilson (born Clerow Wilson) had grown up troubled and, as he once said, "so poor even the poor looked down on me." His father was a carpenter always looking for work. As a child shuttled to various foster homes, Wilson had often run away and ended up in a reform school. Later he quit high school, then at age sixteen lied about his age so he could join the Air Force. Usually assigned to kitchen detail while in the service, he became a jokester, and soon picked up his stage name because he was known for always "flipping out" his military buddies with his funny anecdotes and tall tales.

Leaving the service in 1954, Wilson worked as a bell boy at a San Francisco hotel where he also started performing. Soon he was on the road, playing tiny black clubs and later such major black theaters as the Apollo, the Howard, and the Regal. Slowly, he built up a following within the black community.

His big break came in 1965 when Redd Foxx, appearing on "The Tonight Show," was asked whom he considered the funniest comic around. Foxx named Wilson, who afterward was invited to appear on the program. His "Tonight Show" appearance introduced him to a whole new audience. He also appeared on "The Ed Sullivan Show" (1968), "The Carol Burnett Show" (1970) and "Laugh-In" (1973) and recorded comedy albums. And, of course, when NBC took a chance on Wilson's variety show, he was catapulted to national fame.

Wilson's humor was gentler than Richard Pryor's, warmer and folksier than Dick Gregory's, and more spirited than Cosby's kid monologues. Working-class black America gravitated to him almost as fiercely as it did to Pryor. Wilson's trademark expressions—"The Devil made me do it!" and "What you see is what you get!"—were echoed throughout the country. Yet Wilson was often criticized for playing stereotypes. Wasn't his famous character Geraldine just a ghetto caricature? A transvestite's dream? Didn't his Reverend Leroy of The What's Happening Now Church depict black ministers as money-hungry shysters? Well, of course, yes, and of course, no.

Wilson's humor was very much rooted in the old-style ethnic theater tradition, infused, however, with a new consciousness and assurance. Many of the old ethnic stars had begun their careers assuming they would always appear before all-black audiences. When some did perform before a white crowd, they weren't always sure how to play it. Either they cleaned up their material, thereby neutralizing their comic richness, or they might over-clown (exaggerating themselves even more to be *understood* by the white audience), thereby alienating certain black patrons who felt the entertainers were catering to whites by playing stereotypes. Wilson, however, came of age at a time when he knew he had a chance to go beyond the black clubs into a larger arena. Built into his sketches and characters were an awareness of the white audience and an attempt—through energy, assertiveness, and style—to toss that audience's preconceptions aside. Wilson's characters never tommed with whites or sucked up to a white audience. Instead a Geraldine or a Reverend Leroy was so feistily independent that they'd tell anybody—any color, any size, any sex—where to go or where to get off. They were comic combatants, ethnic types filtered through the consciousness and attitudes of the black power era of the 1960s. Taking no stuff from anybody, his characters could actually say the things that someone like Hattie McDaniel had had to *suggest.*

One of his most famous routines was Columbus's discovery of America. Columbus goes to Queen Isabella—now renamed Isabel Johnson—for capital so he can sail West, informing her that if he doesn't get to discover America, then there will be no Ray Charles. Isabel's eyes just about pop out of her head. "Ray Charles?" she says. "You gonna find Ray Charles? He in America?" "Damn right," Columbus answers. Immediately, Isabel finances his voyages (with a traveler's check), then stands on the dock with the crowd to watch Columbus's ships off, exclaiming, "Chris goin' to America on that boat. Chris goin' to find Ray Charles." Of course, for some Queen Isabel Johnson was merely another simp darky. For others, though, Wilson comically invigorated American history with some incongruous black popular history. (The idea was: forget the rest of America's cultural crap. Are there many national treasures as dazzling as Ray Charles?)

In the past, ersatz black humor in a movie like *Green Pastures* (1936) had striven for this kind of tale: history or religion comically transformed by way of a distinct black perspective. *Green Pastures* had succeeded because its black actors, with the right shrewd intonations and attitudes, made the fake dialogue real. Wilson's intonations *and* his language (the snappy "Damn right" being a prime example) were supremely authentic, the kind of humor and attitudinizing that had turned up in the black community for decades.

Once Flip Wilson left his television series (while it was still popular), his other TV appearances were infrequent. His popularity waned. In 1985, he returned to weekly television with the poorly received sitcom "Charlie & Company," in which he seemed out of place and a shell of his former self. Here he was playing television's conventional middle-class working stiff. What he needed was some outrageous character to dress himself up with.

Wilson also appeared in the movie *Uptown Saturday Night* (1974).

His TV credits include: "Love American Style" (1969); "Here's Lucy" (1971); "Clerow Wilson's Great Escape" (his 1974 special); "Sammy and Company" (1975); "Six Million Dollar Man" (1976); "Celebrity Challenge of the Sexes" (1977); "The Kraft 75th Anniversary Special" (1978); "Roy Clark Special" (1979); and "People Are Funny" (1984).

Paul Winfield

B. 1941. Actor.

A dramatic actor of great skill, Paul Winfield grew up in Watts, attended UCLA, then started his acting career in the 1960s, appearing on various episodes of such TV series as "Room 222," "The Name of the Game," and from 1968 to 1970, as one of Diahann Carroll's boyfriends on "Julia."

It was the 1972 film *Sounder* that brought him national acclaim and an Academy Award nomination as Best Actor of 1972. Winfield also had starring roles in *Gordon's War* (1973) and *A Hero Aint Nothing but a Sandwich* (1978) as well as in the TV movie "Green Eyes" (1976) and the miniseries "King" (1978), in which he gave a rousing, bravura performance as Dr. Martin Luther King, Jr. Winfield proved especially effective at portraying intelligent heroes forced to be men of action while

From the days of Sounder *(l. with Kevin Hooks) Paul Winfield's performances were precise, perceptive, coolly intense. Yet the solid roles came rarely.*

489

Winfield in Star Trek: The Wrath of Kahn.

struggling, all the time, to keep their emotions in check and to resolve internal doubts or conflicts.

Despite his talents, Winfield often found himself relegated to supporting roles. Not too long after his *Sounder* triumph, he played second fiddle to Burt Reynolds in *Hustle* (1975), was cast as a crew member in "Star Trek II: The Wrath of Khan" (1982), and later portrayed a police officer in the Arnold Schwarzenegger actioner *Terminator* (1986). It was disheartening to watch so large a talent used by filmmakers in so ordinary a way. Yet when Winfield had a chance to display his technical assurance and deep commitment to a role—as in the brief television adaptation of Katherine Anne Porter's "The Witness" (1986, seen on PBS's "American Masters" series)—audiences had to take but one look to realize here was one of America's finest dramatic actors.

Winfield's movie credits include: *Brother John* (1972); *Conrack* (1974); *Huckleberry Finn* (1974, as Nigger Jim); *Twilight's Last Gleaming* (1977); *Damnation Alley* (1977); *Carbon Copy* (1981); *Mike's Murder* (1984); Samuel Fuller's controversial *White Dog* (1982) and *Death Before Dishonor* (1987).

His TV credits include: guest appearances on "Mission: Impossible" (1968); "Mannix" (1969); "High Chaparral" (1969, 1972); "The Young Lawyers" (1970); "The Young Rebels" (1970); "It's Good to Be Alive" (1974, portraying baseball star Roy Campanella); "Roots: The Next Generations" (1979); "Backstairs at the White House" (1979); "Angel City" (1980); "Key Tortuga" (1981); "Only the Ball Was White" (1981, narrator); "Sophisticated Gents" (1981); "Sister, Sister" (1982); "Dreams Don't Die" (1984); "Go Tell It on the Mountain" (1985); and "Siege" (1986).

Oprah Winfrey

B. 1954. Actress, talk-show hostess.

Once she walked off with an Oscar Nomination as Best Supporting Actress of 1985 for her performance in her very first movie *The Color Purple*, the media promptly latched onto actress Oprah Winfrey, energetically detailing her climb to fame. Born in Mississippi and raised in Milwaukee by her mother who worked as a maid, Winfrey had endured an impoverished childhood and had briefly become a discipline problem. When she moved to Nashville to live with her father, a barber, she blossomed, her budding interest in journalism and the media rapidly becoming apparent. At seventeen, she was a part-time radio news announcer. Later while a speech/drama student at Tennessee State University, she was crowned Miss Black Tennessee. Afterward she worked as a reporter/anchor for Nashville's CBS affiliate, then in 1976 landed a co-anchor news position on Baltimore's ABC station and also hosted the talk show "People Are Talking" (1977–1983). In 1984 she moved on to Chicago as the star of "A.M. Chicago," which later was redubbed as "The Oprah Winfrey Show."

Having read and loved Alice Walker's novel *The Color Purple*, she longed to work in the film. Fate stepped in when producer Quincy Jones, on a layover in Chicago, spotted Winfrey on television and decided she was perfect for the role of Sofia. The rest became movie history.

Winfrey saw her talk show become syndicated in 1986. During this era of the popularity of the Joan Rivers-type putdown (Rivers not only put down others but herself as well), Winfrey's self-deprecating humor

Oprah Winfrey, in her second screen role, as the mother of Bigger Thomas (Victor Love, r.) in the 1986 remake of Native Son.

became part of her TV appeal. Never hesitating to let her public know of her romantic hassles or weight problems (at 5'6", she once weighed 180 pounds), she once confessed that on a late-night eating binge, she desperately had grabbed the only thing in her house—a package of frozen hot-dog rolls, on which she poured a layer of thick maple syrup. Then she wolfed it all down. For her fans, Winfrey was a woman enlivened by candor. For her critics, she seemed a replay of the lively, chunky black woman good for a laugh. Whatever the reasons for her television success, she emerged in the 1980s as a definite national celebrity.

TV credits include: "The Tonight Show" (1985, hosted by Joan Rivers, who told Winfrey to lose some weight), "Saturday Night Live" (1986), and "Dolly" (1987).

Film credits include *Native Son* (1986).

Alfre Woodard

B. 1953. Actress.

When Alfre Woodard won an Oscar nomination as Best Supporting Actress of 1983 for her performance as Geechee in *Cross Creek*, *The Los Angeles Times* called hers "the biggest surprise in the nominations." Not since the 1967 performance of Beah Richards in *Guess Who's Coming to Dinner?* had a black woman been nominated in the best supporting category. The nomination was all the more remarkable because *Cross Creek* had been seen by few people. And those who had seen it might have enjoyed Woodard's work but been completely turned off by the script's servile conception of her character. Shrewdly, though, Woodard did all she could to capitalize on the media attention her nomination brought, hoping to use it to win other important roles (namely the lead in the 1985 *The Color Purple*, which she was a great contender for—until Whoopi Goldberg showed up on the scene). A year later though Woodard did win an Emmy as Best Supporting Actress in a Dramatic Series (1982–83) for her performance as the mother of a seven-year-old killed by a police officer, in a three-part episode of "Hill Street Blues."

A stage-trained actress born in Tulsa, who had graduated from Boston University and worked in theater at the Arena Stage in Washington and the Mark Taper Forum in Los Angeles, Woodard was respected and admired within the entertainment community. But without the right part in a big film or TV production (she was relegated to supporting roles in such TV series as the 1982–1983 "Tucker's Witch" and "Sara," 1985), she remained unknown to the vast viewing public. Ironically enough when cast in the box-office smash *Extremities* (1986), her character, while certainly noticed by the audience, was too remote to be identified with. In this drama, which starred Farrah Fawcett as a woman who retaliates against a man who has tried raping her, Woodard played Patricia, a mild-mannered (so much so that she seems almost lobotomized) social worker, who spouts textbook pronouncements that seem totally unrelated to the issue at hand. "Let me remind you," she staunchly informs Fawcett after a harrowing attack sequence with the would-be rapist, "he's a human being just like you and me." Audiences howled at the lines, unable to accept such dribble from anyone, let alone a black woman, who could be looked to for some commonsense.

On the occasions when Woodard lucked up with a strong role to play, she gave studied but deeply felt performances as highly controlled women pushed almost to their breaking points. On the television series "LA Law" (1986), she played a rape victim, who, while testifying in court against the man who has attacked her, must undergo a grueling cross-examination. The woman is dying of leukemia. At one point, she screams out in anger, unable to contain her rage, then is made to apologize to the court. *New York Times* critic John J. O'Connor wrote that Woodard "almost singlehandedly brought dramatic clout to the pilot for 'LA Law.'" For this performance, Woodard won an Emmy as Best Guest Performer in a series in the 1986–1987 season. Later in the 1986 TV movie "Unnatural Causes," she played a Veterans Administration counselor, who investigates the links between herbicide sprayings in Vietnam (Agent Orange) and a series of unusual diseases now crippling Vietnam vets. Again her work was praised by television critics.

Her TV credits include: "What Really Happened to the Class of '65" (1977); "Freedom Road" (1975); "Enos" (1981); "The Ambush Murders"; "For Colored Girls Who Have Considered Suicide When the Rainbow Is Not Enuf" (1982); "The Killing Floor" (1984), "Go Tell It on the Mountain" (1985); "Fairie Tale Theater" (1985); "St. Elsewhere" (1987); and "Mandela" (1987).

Index

Index